THE FEROCIOUS ENGINE
OF DEMOCRACY

THE FEROCIOUS ENGINE
OF DEMOCRACY

A History of the
American Presidency

Volume Two
Theodore Roosevelt through George Bush

Foreword by James MacGregor Burns

Michael P. Riccards

Madison Books
Lanham · New York · London

Published by Madison Books
4720 Boston Way, Lanham, Maryland 20706

3 Henrietta Street
London WC2E 8LU, England

Distributed by National Book Network

The paper used in this publication meets the minimum
requirements of American National Standard for
Information Sciences—Permanence of Paper for
Printed Library Materials, ANSI Z39.48–1984. ∞™
Manufactured in the United States of America.

Library of Congress Cataloging-in-Publication Data

The ferocious engine of democracy : a history of the American
presidency / by Michael P. Riccards.
Includes index.
Contents: From Theodore Roosevelt through George Bush.
1. Presidents—United States—History. 2. United States—Politics
and government. I. Title.
E176.1.R48   1994   973'.099   94-15019   CIP

ISBN 1-56833-042-1 (cloth : alk. paper)

To Diana Riccards
with love and appreciation

Contents

Foreword

Today, when major controversies erupt, the media often tell us that we must await the "bar of history" for the full story and the final verdict. But historians know that there is no final bar; rather, there is a series of historical judgments that are revised as perspectives are broadened and deepened, archives are opened, and participants write their self-justifications and journalists their exposés. Revisionism proceeds for decades, even centuries.

But if ever an especially appropriate time arrives for historical judgment and balance, it could be this century's end as Americans review their political successes and failures and consider their implications for the next century, or even for the next millennium. By surveying a whole century, rather than one or two decades or generations, the historian can review and compare a multitude of political forces at work.

In this volume, the author has chosen to look at American political history through the record of all the twentieth-century presidents up to Bill Clinton. This method is one for which presidential historians have long been criticized: for writing history "from the top down," for employing a "great man" approach to history, for ignoring, in political history, the crucial class, interest group, regional, and other fundamental variables that set the stage for presidential and other forms of leadership. The author meets this problem by dealing with the electoral and interest-group factors that emerge from the more fundamental forces and that directly affect political behavior and presidential leadership. He reaches through the White House, in short, to the tens of thousands of national and state leaders and to the millions of voters who empower presidents and at the same time set limits to their leadership. The result is a work that reflects these presidencies in all their richness—the contrasting personalities in the White House, the triumphs and the frustrations, the good luck (FDR, for example) and the bad (Carter?), the policy breakthroughs that have and that have never really occurred (the War on Poverty, for example), and the visions and the failures of vision.

Through the lens of presidential history, this volume, moreover, offers something even more important than vivid details—it traces the institutional and structural forces that run through the whole country and that shape the work of all presidents. This effort is perhaps easier, or at least more rewarding, in the American polity than in some others, because of the remarkable continuities in the American structure of government. In a brilliant feat of political planning the Framers of the Constitution set up a structure of checks and balances among national institutions and a division of powers among national, state, and local governments that confront presidents with an extreme dispersion of powers from the very day they take their inaugural oath.

What is so fascinating is how presidents have dealt with this dispersion—especially presidents with strong agendas—and what the impact of their administrations suggest as to the workability of our constitutional system, especially in the later decades of the twentieth century. The record shows that every president and every Congress have had trouble governing together, just as the Framers anticipated. "Strong" presidents have had as much trouble as "weak" ones, often more. Theodore Roosevelt's opposition entrenched in a conservative Republican Congress, Woodrow Wilson's failed battle with Senate Republicans, FDR's setbacks at the hands of Congress during his second term, and the deadlock, or "gridlock," that has become endemic since, all these give both a sense of continuity in the study of presidential history, and even more important, a perspective on what many political scientists—including this one—consider critical weaknesses in our constitutional system as we approach the inevitable crises of the next century.

This work allows the reader to make other crucial comparisons over the century, especially in the area of real presidential leadership (measured in terms of effectiveness on issues and legislation). Many readers, regardless of their partisan or ideological bias, may conclude that of the last ten presidents, the first five, beginning with

Franklin Roosevelt, were far more effective in realizing their goals and values, than were the next five, beginning with Richard Nixon. If so, this could be a reflection of the general decline of leadership over the past half century (as in so many other fields; who today can compare, for example, with John Dewey in philosophy, Reinhold Niebuhr in theology, Frank Lloyd Wright in architecture, Walter Lippman in journalism?). Or perhaps presidential leadership has been especially weakened by the decline of supportive political parties, the rising dominance of the media and their trivialization of issues, the escalating complexity of both foreign and domestic problems facing the White House and the heightened potency of the "pressure groups" that have bedeviled presidents ever since Madison wrote about factions in *Federalist* Number Ten.

This work is a study in leadership; it is also a study of individual leaders in the White House. Its century-long perspective allows the author to understand the ongoing structures and enables him to offer critical yet balanced judgments on the presidents of this century. I would submit, for example, that the review of the Jimmy Carter presidency is more fair-minded than the verdict of most historians. Opinions will vary widely on all the presidents, but this work will make those opinions more penetrating and judicious.

James MacGregor Burns

Introduction

The first volume of this narrative history of the American presidency covers the origins of the office in British theory and practice and concludes with the end of the McKinley administration. In over a century or so, the nation, the Western world, and the presidency changed beyond any scope imaginable. The expansion of the republic from the Atlantic seaboard states, the persistent conflicts with Great Britain, and the collapse of French and Spanish imperial power in the New World were all hallmark events.

It is not an easy task to create a new system of government. Nothing in life seems permanent, except change itself—or so we are told by our wisest people and our cracker-barrel philosophers. Surely though, this phenomenon is especially so with political systems, states, and regimes that appear so stable at times and then crumble or wither. Civic institutions seem even more prone to the cycles of rise and decline, especially under republican aegis. This brand of doing business, the "res public" or the "people's thing" in our language, rests upon certain assumptions of disinterestedness, altruism, patriotism, personal responsibility, frugality, and above all political education. The true enemies of the republic, according to its advocates, are luxury, sloth, overwhelming ambition, expensive standing armies, and apathy.

In America, the early republic of the Founding Fathers was furnished with a set of balanced institutions: a moderating judiciary, a limited executive magistrate, and a mixed assembly of popularly elected representatives and state-appointed senators.

Republics change and so do the branches of government. The

seedtime is different from the harvest. Governments of reasonable powers must face uncertain futures as well as the turmoils of the present, and change is again the driving force that leads to either adaptation or atrophy. The American presidency became the reflection and then the impetus for widespread democracy, territorial expansion, and the waging of a terrible and fratricidal war in the last century.

Still, all of life is not politics and, especially in a capitalist state, change in the economic and industrial order will have a powerful effect on the nature of the ties that bind people to each other and to the commonwealth. By the end of the nineteenth century, industrialization, persistent agricultural depression, and new and larger waves of foreign immigration challenged the old verities and led to new concentrations of power and influence, and to major upheavals of many sorts in the United States.

Into that age of reform, as some have called it, stepped several major national figures. It was not inevitable that the executive office should have become a focal point for such critical reexamination. It happened by design, by choice, and upon reflection by the political actors and the coalitions that supported them over the years. Thus, it was the presidency at the dawn of the twentieth century that emerged as a reconstructed institution, one that was and is even more of a ferocious engine of democracy.

MODELS OF THE PRESIDENCY—REVISITED

In the first volume of this history of the presidency, I outlined several models that can prove somewhat useful to understanding the office as it developed in the nineteenth century. Those models included the *Federalist* with its emphasis on a nonpartisan magistrate, disengagement from the legislative branch and its domestic policy controversies, preoccupation with the powers and privileges of the executive branch, and a strong assertion of control in foreign policy; the *Jeffersonian* with subtle ties to congressional leadership, a "hidden" executive that works through collegiality and consensus, and a commitment to territorial expansion and popular aspirations; the *Jacksonian* with a powerful executive exercising control over the executive branch and over the agenda of the legislature and even the judiciary at times, strong populist expressions of political issues, and a direct relationship to the citizenry; the *Whig* orientation that focused on a limited executive, a modest expression of U.S. power in the world, deference to the legislative branch, and a domestic agenda emphasizing internal improvements. And then quite out of character, there emerged by necessity the war presidency of Abraham Lincoln with its powerful establishment of executive prerogative, military control over domestic as well as external affairs, and clear role as a national and viable figure of enormous consequences.

Those are the models that appear and reappear in the nineteenth century. They also emerge again in the twentieth century, although often in those more complex presidencies there are differing elements that we can identify. Franklin D. Roosevelt exhibited at various times (and sometimes at the same time) elements of the Jeffersonian, Jacksonian, and Lincoln models. It is clear that in the twentieth century, the preeminent model is one established by FDR himself—a change in the scope of the office and the accessibility to the media, in the range of domestic concerns, and in the responsibilities of foreign policy. FDR, in part, built on the legacies of his cousin Theodore Roosevelt and of Woodrow Wilson in this century. Their definitions of political power, of the dynamics of social reform, and of America's place in the world are very different from anything in the previous century. In a sense, all modern presidents are heirs of FDR.

Still, there are elements of the Whig philosophy in the presidents of the 1920s and in Dwight Eisenhower and George Bush, and elements even of the Federalist and Jacksonian presidents in Ronald Reagan, just to give several examples. If this mixing of models seems confusing, it is not that the models are useless, but that the executive office has become extraordinarily complex in its second century of existence, especially since World War II. It is important to understand the continuities in the American executive and also its critical departures from the past. This volume is to a large extent the story of the decline of the older republican virtues and the ascendancy of a nation-state of impressive and at times frightening power.

1

The President as Steward of the People: Theodore Roosevelt vs. William Howard Taft

There have been more important and more accomplished presidencies than Theodore Roosevelt's, but none as interesting and flamboyant. After the long drought of formal and distant executives, Roosevelt reinvented the presidency in time for, or in league with, the growth of the broad popular media. In part, Roosevelt's astonishing political career was formed not by a string of lasting achievements, but by a chimera of fleeting, but powerfully imposed images. Like John F. Kennedy, another very young president in American history, TR, as he was called, left a legacy of stirring impressions that are still captivating especially when not looked at too closely.

Roosevelt's early years are almost as well known as Lincoln's. TR was a sickly boy who overcame his youthful illnesses by will power, determination, and exercise. He was an author, a learned naturalist, and an aristocrat in a profession dominated by extortionists, ethnic vote peddlers, and mossback politicians. He acquired a reputation as a "good government" reformer in the New York legislature and in the U.S. Civil Service Commission, a cowboy in the South Dakota badlands, an aggressive assistant secretary of the navy, a war hero in the charge up San Juan Hill, and a competent governor of the Empire State. To get the young Roosevelt out of New York, several Republican bosses pushed him on to the McKinley ticket, leaving Senator Mark Hanna of Ohio to exclaim prophetically that they were putting that "damn cowboy" one bullet away from the presidency.

On September 14, 1901, Theodore Roosevelt, at the age of forty-two, became the youngest man ever to assume the presidency. He was, by all accounts, a brilliant, impulsive, and rather calculating politician. And yet he represented a very different view of politics. For the first time in nearly a century, the United States had a president drawn from the patrician eastern class, educated by tutors and at Harvard College, and linked to some of the oldest families in the United States. Despite his occasional opposition to the bosses, by 1898 Roosevelt made a deal with Republican boss Tom Platt and New York railroad interests not to upset the state party machine if he were elected governor. Roosevelt won by only eighteen thousand votes and, as the state's chief executive, compiled a very respectable record, which included measures to tax corporate franchises, promote civil service, and encourage conservation. He was both adored and hated, usually for the same reasons. Roosevelt was harsh, arrogant, the master of a volcano of what seemed uncharted energy. Henry Adams said that he was "pure act," and Henry Demarest Lloyd characterized him as a person with the "same appetite for the spread of ideas by explosion which Napoleon had."[1]

Roosevelt gave the impression of being a man who loved life in its roughest and most concentrated forms, yet his letters to his children are the tender admonitions of a sensitive father. He never fully recovered in some ways from the loss of his first wife and his mother on the same day, and he never revealed his personal anguish to the outside world. Roosevelt's philosophy of life was a gospel of action, which seemed to help him forget the deep pessimism he entertained about human existence. His words reek with obsolete and vulgar nineteenth century concerns about racial purity and ethnic stereotypes. Only TR could seriously define a man's mission in life as to "work, fight, and breed."[2]

He is frequently quoted as advocating that Americans should speak softly but carry a big stick. In fact, TR did just the opposite: he blustered all over the international stage and rarely used force of arms. In an America of unlimited ambitions and vague imperialist dreams, Roosevelt had to face the world with a modest navy and a decentralized military establishment. He generally despised those who got in his way, regarding for example the Latin American nations as "banana republics," headed by "Dagos" and "inferior races." Roosevelt joined his assertiveness with a high sense of moral purpose, which seemed to some Americans the spirited essence of progressivism and to others as sheer hypocrisy.

Roosevelt had great practical confidence in the abilities of a strong government to deal out justice; he supported reforms because he hated revolution and agitation, and saw the presidency as the nerve center of a powerful American nation-state. Roosevelt came out of a tradition that viewed the upper classes and their middle-class allies as the great protectors of the capitalist order. He was labeled the "trust-buster," but in fact he did not wish to break up many of the great concentrations of wealth, but tried instead to force those corporations to acknowledge the regulatory rights of the government. Between those big corporations and organized labor, both of which he was leery, TR positioned the federal government as an honest umpire, dedicated to conservative change and justice.

The world of the early twentieth century saw considerable agitation as the cities and states sought to regulate, if not destroy, the large corporations that led to monopolies in major industries and fields of commerce. Whether it was railroading, oil, banking, or manufacturing, the pattern was the same. A few corporations were controlling wages, prices, and supplies—destroying the free enterprise faith in open markets and honest competition. Some of the populists on the farms followed William Jennings Bryan, and insisted on the breakup of those new combinations of wealth and power. To their strength was added the progressives—middle-class reformers—who sensed a loss of the old America of family farms, established neighborhoods, village stores, and small law firms. In their eyes, the new America was a world run by crude, uneducated men with no old family ties and little respect for the traditional ways of life. Some progressives agreed with the populists—break up the corporations; others, like TR, saw the development of large economic units as inevitable and somewhat advantageous in the long run for society. For the latter group, the government must abandon its laissez faire policy and take its rightful leadership role in this new economy. The personally conservative Roosevelt, though, saw across the land the rise of large number of men and women, on and off the farms and in the middle-class professions, who made their political fortunes advocating reform.[3]

The reform gospel was spread to cities as diverse as Detroit, Toledo, San Francisco, Cleveland, New York City, St. Louis, and many other major urban areas of the nation. In 1902, the journalist Lincoln Steffens wrote a series of articles called "The Shame of the Cities," which rocked the placid elites and spurred on municipal reformers. In the states, a series of reform governors were taking control, the most famous being "Fighting Bob" LaFollette in Wisconsin. Throughout the Midwest and on to the West and the

South, populist-progressive governors were winning elections. In New York and later New Jersey, TR and then Woodrow Wilson were riding the crest of that wave of change and unrest. The progressives, especially in the West, wanted democracy and more democracy. Their tools were the initiative, the referendum, and the recall—each of these devices leaving decision making in the hands of the citizenry. Now the people, over the heads of the legislatures, could initiate legislation, vote on it in elections, and recall public officials by ballot before their terms were up. In the Rocky Mountain area, women were getting the right to vote—a movement that would sweep the nation in the next ten years. Only in the South was the democratic impulse partially thwarted by the disenfranchisement of blacks and the inability of the populists to create a lasting poor white-black alliance.

Several states enacted child welfare legislation and minimum wage laws for women. And five states limited the power of judges to issue injunctions aimed at labor unions and strikers. Thus, by the time Roosevelt assumed the presidency, the republic was in a progressive upheaval, and he was both a participant and a future weather vane in many of its causes. Roosevelt, though, was not a simple opportunist catching which way the wind was blowing; he was in fact a genuine conservative reformer whose national pride and delight in the strengths of the American race led him to counsel justice, demanding what he termed a "Square Deal" for the American people.

THE CONSERVATIVE CONGRESS

Almost immediately the new president was given conservative advice on the need to continue William McKinley's policies—advice that he quickly committed himself to publicly. Roosevelt's brother-in-law, Douglas Robinson, warned him that the financial community was afraid that he might curtail the influence of business, and that he should be closemouthed, conservative, and willing to keep McKinley's cabinet intact. Mark Hanna himself took the young president aside, calling him "Teddy" to Roosevelt's disgust, and asked him to go slow and listen patiently to the right people. Roosevelt's response was instructive: "It would not be possible to get wiser advice and I shall act exactly upon it. I shall go slow."[4]

Even if the president had wanted to quicken the pace and present a strong progressive agenda, he was faced with solidly conservative Republican majorities in both houses of Congress. By 1910, the Senate was in the hands of individuals who saw themselves, and the future of their party, as bound up with the new corporate America. The main leader was Nelson W. Aldrich of Rhode Island, a multimillionaire, who appropriately gave his daughter in marriage to John D. Rockefeller, Jr. Aldrich believed unabashedly that the government should align itself with big business and finance, and he worked quietly behind the scenes and controlled the goings on of the upper house. His major allies, John C. Spooner of Wisconsin, Orville H. Platt of Connecticut, and William B. Allison of Iowa, were important associates in steering the Senate onto conservative paths.

In the House of Representatives, a weak Speaker was succeeded in 1903 by "Uncle Joe" Cannon—a vulgar and effective horse trader who ran that body for seven years with a strong hand. Thus, the conservative alliance in Congress had a powerful braking effect on what Roosevelt could do or even chose to propose. Platt had warned his fellow Republican leaders that they had to watch Roosevelt closely—that he had a tendency to wander. They had to keep in touch or the president might work against their interests. In his first message to Congress in December 1901, the president gave a generally comforting agenda. He denounced assassins and anarchists, pushed for educational and means tests for immigrants, characterized as natural the development of large corporations, supported the tariff, and pushed for expanding foreign markets and upgrading the merchant marine. Yet in the long document, TR also wrote of some of the grave evils of many of these corporations, argued that the laws had not kept up with these economic developments, and asked for a stronger Interstate Commerce Act. He mentioned the idea of a canal connecting the Atlantic and Pacific Oceans and recommended the creation of a new cabinet-level agency, the department of commerce and labor.

While Congress pondered the message, the public was fed a steady diet of Roosevelt's personality. As no president in memory and probably none up to that time, TR became a "personality"—a politician whose every action seemed newsworthy and exciting. His family, his friends, his guests, his large teeth, his thick glasses, his big game hunting, and his horseback riding—all were sources of media attention and delight. In a way that Washington and Lincoln had not done, and even Jackson avoided, TR became a very visible tribune of the people, a popular advocate whose personality seemed immediate, direct, and committed to their personal service. He furthered that impression by getting involved in a variety of interests: from patronage politics to simplified spelling, from stamp designs to foreign policy.

Yet in Congress, his support was much weaker than with the public at large. With his proposal to set up a department of commerce and labor, Roosevelt ran into immediate problems and, even after a compromise with Aldrich, the bill still languished. The president then decided to attack openly John D. Rockefeller, claiming that he was masterminding the secret opposition; eventually, the bill was passed by Congress. Roosevelt then turned his attention to land reclamation and, despite Speaker Cannon's criticisms, he was able to come up with a reasonable proposal that was signed into law. With Elihu Root, his secretary of war, the president tried to gather support for a major reorganization of the armed services, but parts of the proposal went against the American tradition of decentralized control.

The main issue that faced Roosevelt was that perennial tar baby of presidents—the tariff. American corporations wanted to find markets for the products they were turning out in increasingly larger numbers, but the Dingley Tariff, in force then, set rates so high that foreign governments were responding with high rates of their own. Farmers, of course, had historically opposed high tariffs and needed open markets for their foodstuffs as well. The major difficulty, however, was that most manufacturers sold in the domestic market and favored high rates, and those corporations were the backbone of the Republican party.

Roosevelt was not politically committed to lowering the tariff, but focused his attention on getting specific reductions for goods from Cuba and the Philippines in order to cement their allegiances to American foreign policy. But even those limited proposals drew strong opposition from tobacco, cane, and sugar beet farmers in the South and West.[5] Despite the nominal support of the conservative Senate leaders in 1902, a Cuban import bill failed. After a special session of Congress, TR finally won a 20 percent reduction on Cuban products in return for a 20–40 percent reduction on American products entering Cuba. The Philippine bill however was unsuccessful. In general, the president used the threat of tariff reform as a way to force conservative Republican leaders to support his proposals for railroad reform instead—clearly, a more important priority for him in the long run.[6]

A SQUARE DEAL

Roosevelt then started off with a mixed record, and major progressives were concerned about his easy willingness to compromise with the conservative leadership. Characteristically, TR was to make his progressive record not in Congress, but outside of its corridors in two very different and very dramatic exercises of presidential leadership: the Northern Securities Company case and the anthracite coal strike.

On February 19, 1902, Roosevelt had his attorney general, Philander C. Knox, announce after little consultation or advance notice that he would file a suit under the Sherman Anti-Trust Act to dissolve the Northern Securities Company. Stock market prices tumbled, and TR found himself being pilloried for his incredible audacity, although Hanna privately admitted that even McKinley was considering such a step before his death. Northern Securities was a vast holding company that controlled three large railroads in the northeast; the major powers behind the merger were J. P. Morgan, E. H. Harriman, James J. Hill, and the Rockefeller group.

A year later, a federal court, and eventually the Supreme Court, upheld the right of the government to exercise oversight concerning such mergers. It was a striking victory for Roosevelt and for the progressives. What made the decision all the more remarkable was that in 1895 in a similar case, the Court had overruled the Cleveland administration's attempt to dissolve the American Sugar Refining Company. In retrospect, Roosevelt justifiably bragged, "This decision I caused to be annulled by the court that had rendered it." In the next seven years, his administration would file cases against forty-four corporations, many of them large combinations, including the "beef trusts," Standard Oil, American Tobacco Company, New Haven Railroad, and DuPont.

Although, Roosevelt was not in general an advocate of breaking up corporations, his exercise of presidential power in these cases led to a popular, and then historical, image that he was the great "trustbuster." The president probably was motivated by a political need to establish clearly and convincingly his progressive credentials, and this step was one that could be taken quickly and without congressional check. Also, Roosevelt, the eastern patrician, was genuinely disgusted by a parade of examples of new, tasteless demonstrations of wealth exhibited by the Morgans, the Harrimans, and the Rockefellers. He concluded that of all the "forms of tyranny the least attractive and the most vulgar is the tyranny of mere wealth." To Roosevelt and his class, wealth was to be used in unostentatious displays by men and women devoted to community service and good works. Their ideal was a sense of noblesse oblige, a concern of the well born for the less fortunate. The mere accumulation of wealth to the point of extravagance and, more offensively, vulgar display was simply bad taste. Roosevelt would, like most presidents of his time, have to deal with J. P. Morgan during periods of economic crisis. But he detested the feeling that Morgan treated him—the president of the United States—as an equal. As for his own concept of the office, TR later commented, "I did not usurp power, but I did greatly broaden the use of executive power." And so Roosevelt broke up the trusts, even though he would confess that the issue was federal control over all combinations engaged in interstate commerce, and not "the foolish antitrust law." Thus, are legends made.[7]

The second major controversy that solidified his progressive image was the strike in May 1902 of fifty thousand anthracite coal miners in northeastern Pennsylvania. About three-fourths of the anthracite coal fields were owned by six railroads in the region, and the railroad presidents took a tough line on the strike. The strike went on through the summer, and anxious Americans wondered if the winter would see no coal and a danger of freezing in homes, schools, and businesses. A public cry was raised for arbitration, and a Roman Catholic archbishop, John Ireland, offered to mediate the dispute. The answer of the major railroad president, George F. Baer, was succinct and characteristic: "Anthracite mining is a business and not a religious, sentimental, or academic proposition." Later Baer was to credit God himself with having delivered the nation's resources to Christian men who were leading these corporations.[8]

As the situation worsened, the president avoided premature intervention. Finally on October 3, he called the mine owners and the union to the White House, and recommended a joint meeting to try and get them to reach an agreement. The owners led by Baer refused to even talk with the union, and Baer insisted that the president use his power to restore order by sending the army in as Grover

Cleveland had done in the Pullman strike. The owners concluded by refusing TR's request for arbitration of the issues and insisted on a complete capitulation by the union.

Roosevelt was both angered and insulted by this treatment and by what he called privately the owners' "arrogant stupidity." Bluntly, he fumed about Baer, "If it wasn't for the high office I hold, I would have taken him by the seat of the breeches and the nape of the neck and chucked him out of that window." The president decided on several courses of action: first, he asked the governor of Pennsylvania to request federal troops, which Roosevelt intended to use not to crush the union, but to run the mines in place of the owners. Presidents had in the past, of course, used federal troops to preserve peace and order, but not to actually acquire the mines. Then TR had Root meet with J. P. Morgan to get the financier's approval of a compromise for a five-man arbitration commission. Eventually, an expanded commission was set up and came in with a strike settlement favorable to the miners. Consequently, Roosevelt received credit for his statesmanship and assertive leadership.[9]

TR concluded that he had dealt fairly with both the workers and the owners; later he would argue that he was simply guaranteeing all people "a Square Deal"—a slogan that stuck to his administration. Roosevelt, of course, was not an ardent sympathizer of organized labor by any means, but he accepted the need for such combinations in the new corporate economy. In other instances, however, he used troops in Colorado and Nevada in labor disputes and was criticized by union supporters. In cases of industrial violence, TR quickly attacked such transgressions, but at the same time, he was willing to meet at the White House with Samuel Gompers and other labor leaders to solicit their views.

He exhibited the same openness when he invited the black educator Booker T. Washington to the White House. Roosevelt had sought to establish a broader based Republican party in the South, and he was openly consulting Washington about patronage matters— a unique honor for a black leader. However, a firestorm of opposition arose, especially from southerners about entertaining blacks in the executive mansion. TR and Washington both refused comment on the flap, and the president remained ostentatiously warm to Washington, although he did not repeat the invitation during his terms. Personally, Roosevelt was an exponent of racial purity and the destined supremacy of the Anglo-American strain. But beyond the cobwebbed recesses of nineteenth-century thought, he was a good practical politician who liked people and reached out instinctively beyond even the confines of his own prejudices.[10]

THE BIG STICK

As with many presidents, Roosevelt found that foreign policy offered him greater freedom to exercise his initiative than domestic affairs. He believed, quite correctly, that the United States, like Germany and Japan, was moving toward a greater role in the world. A fervent advocate of national assertiveness and imperialism, he shamelessly thrust the United States into new Latin American ventures, into the Pacific region, and even into Morocco. He built up the navy, intrigued in the Panama Canal affair, and moderated the Russo-Japanese War, winning the Nobel Peace Prize for his efforts.

In his imperialist designs, Roosevelt as usual had a righteous justification for his actions—one in common with many progressives in the United States. Like much of the European ruling class, they saw the great powers as the vanguard of enlightened thought with a special civilizing mission to people of color who often not so coincidentally lived in colonies rich in raw resources but poor in organized military and political strength. TR's first diplomatic excursion was in Venezuela, dealing with its president, Cipriano Castro, whom the president found to be "an unspeakably villainous little monkey." Castro had contracted large debts for public works, and by 1901, Germany and England especially were demanding repayment. Roosevelt decided to use the occasion to reinterpret the Monroe Doctrine in a pronouncement that was termed the "Roosevelt Corollary."

In July 1901, he concluded that "if any South American country misbehaves toward any European country let the European country spank it." However, the United States would not permit a European nation to occupy permanently new territory in Central America or South America. In Venezuela, the parties eventually agreed to arbitration. Roosevelt maintained later that he had threatened the Germans with sending Admiral George Dewey and his fleet to Venezuela if the kaiser did not agree to arbitration. It is a colorful story and quite probably the president had made some such subtle threat, but the German government had already agreed to a peaceful settlement before the Roosevelt meeting.[11]

Interestingly, TR, who had so insisted on arbitration in the Venezuela case, refused to embrace it as willingly in a dispute that involved the United States and Canada. For some time, the two nations had been unable to agree on the southern boundary of Alaska, an issue that became important after the discovery of gold in the Klondike in 1896. The U.S. claim was rather strong; Roosevelt not only insisted on asserting that boundary, but actually made secret preparations for war with a historically friendly ally. In March 1902, he instructed Root to send quietly additional troops to southern Alaska. By January 1903, Roosevelt had a change of heart and accepted an arbitration panel of six impartial jurists, three from each side. Violating the spirit of the proposal, he then went on to name Secretary of War Root, Senator Henry Cabot Lodge, and former Senator George Turner. The president informed the three Americans that they should be impartial, but must not compromise on the principle involved—that is, his view of the appropriate boundary line. The final report of the tribunal upheld the United States' position.

Roosevelt continued his enforcement of the Monroe Doctrine in Santo Domingo's disputes with foreign creditors as well. He had already concluded, in the case of Venezuela, that his policy "will show those Dagos that they will have to behave decently." In Santo Domingo, foreign creditors were owed $18 million, and the president grew concerned again about the possibility of foreign intervention. His solution was that the United States would push for an agreement whereby American agents would supervise customs receipts so that 45 percent of the total would go to the Dominicans and the rest to reduce foreign debts. When the Senate refused to approve the protocol with Santo Domingo, Roosevelt insisted that American agents take charge of the customs house until the Senate concurred, which it finally did. Privately, Roosevelt concluded that the Senate was incompetent, filled with yahoos, and indifferent to the nation's honor.

In neighboring Cuba, TR's approach was equally high-handed. The hero of San Juan Hill supported the American demand that the new Cuban constitution should contain provisions that guaranteed to the United States the right to intervene to protect order, and prohibited Cuba from making treaties that granted special privileges to other foreign nations. In addition, Cuba was to lease to the Americans Guantanamo Bay and Bahia Hondo for $2,000 a year.[12]

Across the ocean, the United States still was in conflict with the

Philippines, a nation that been freed of Spanish rule only to find American administration substituted instead. The Filipinos waged a guerrilla war against the United States, which resulted in barbarities on both sides and led TR to conclude that American guilt was somehow balanced against the "far greater atrocity" of the natives.

To deal with the problems, President McKinley had appointed William Howard Taft as civil governor, and Taft was quite successful. At Roosevelt's insistence, he helped settle in 1902 the land claims of the Dominican and Franciscan friars in that country, and, as noted, TR sought to increase the U.S.'s influence by promoting tariff reductions with the Philippines, although he was unsuccessful. In general, these and other initiatives were aimed at building American power in the world, and in the process increased his own visibility at home and abroad. Nowhere was this more apparent than in the Panama Canal dispute.

THE PANAMA CANAL

The dream of building a canal across a narrow strait somewhere in Central America was not a new idea that originated with Theodore Roosevelt. Americans had been talking about a canal for decades, and the French had actually tried unsuccessfully to complete the difficult task. Looking back at his behavior, Roosevelt maintained that the proceedings "were taken with the utmost care," and that his action was "carried out with the highest, finest, and nicest standards of public and governmental ethics." Years later, however, he would boast that he himself "had taken Panama."

Interest in the digging of a canal increased, especially because of the long time it took for U.S. battleships to go around Cape Horn to join the fleet near Cuba during the Spanish-American War. By the summer of 1901, TR, in order to move ahead with the project, was willing to guarantee the right of neutral passage to all ships, but he insisted that the United States had to control the canal. In November, the British agreed with Roosevelt's demand, and a treaty was approved by the Senate. The major question was where would the canal be built. Two routes were being considered, the Panama region of Colombia and the isthmus in Nicaragua. Through the efforts of a French engineer and a New York lawyer, who generally worked separately, the Panama route was favored by the administration, and in the end this decision resulted in endless intrigue and led to Roosevelt's controversial diplomacy.

The main objective of these two agents, Philippe Bunau-Varilla and William Nelson Cromwell, was to garner some $40 million to pay off the claims of the original French investors. Cromwell had been successful in getting the Republican presidential convention in 1900 to avoid endorsing a Nicaraguan canal. Acting on behalf of his New Panama Canal Company clients, he had in fact billed the company for $60,000 which he donated to the Republican National Committee. In 1901, Bunau-Varilla approached Mark Hanna to push for the Panama route and impressed the senator with the merits of his case. In May 1901, however, the McKinley-appointed Isthmian Canal Commission recommended Nicaragua and rejected the high cost of buying out the French stockholders in the Panama venture. The price the French had asked, $109 million, was considered far too high; a $40 million estimate was advanced instead. Bunau-Varilla insisted that the Panama Canal group recognize reality and scale down its demands to the $40 million evaluation. Under Hanna's prodding, Congress passed the Spooner Act, which gave preference to building in the Panama region within a reasonable time. After that period elapsed, the canal would be built instead through Nicaragua if no progress were made in Panama.

To Roosevelt, the building of the canal and sole U.S. possession increased American power and prestige in the world. The negotiations with Colombia, though, added to Roosevelt's problems. The Colombian minister to the United States and Secretary of State John Hay had agreed to a treaty, but the Colombian government argued that some duress and misrepresentation were involved. The treaty draft had provided for $10 million in gold and an annual rent to Colombia of $250,000. In addition, the United States would pay $40 million to the stockholders of the original French company. The treaty also contained serious abridgments of Colombia's sovereignty over its own actions and territorial jurisdiction. To Roosevelt, however, the holdup was simply "those contemptible little creatures in Bogota," those "foolish and homicidal corruptionists," "these cat-rabbits" wanted more U.S. money.

Despite American pressure and the threat of a Nicaraguan canal deal, the Colombian Congress rejected the treaty on August 12, 1903. To the agents of the French company, $40 million was in the balance. As Americans later found out, many of the old stockholders had sold out entirely their interest in the company to people whose names were never made public; what is known is that J. P. Morgan and Company was the middleman in the transactions with the canal company. Roosevelt later wrote that the Colombian government was intransigent because it wanted some of the $40 million earmarked for the French investors. Yet, one of Roosevelt's biographers, Henry F. Pringle, had concluded, "To save the money of the unidentified stockholders, whose names he did not know, Roosevelt made ready to seize Panama. He was not deterred by possible bloodshed or by the fact that the United States would violate the fundamentals of international laws. His program was formulated very quietly."

Three days before the Senate approved the treaty in March 1903, Roosevelt ordered Secretary of War Root to send two or three military officers to reconnoiter the coastal area in South America in case of a confrontation in the Caribbean or Gulf of Mexico. Roosevelt also received an interesting note from Professor John Bassett Moore, an expert in international relations at Columbia University in New York City, which indicated that a treaty signed in 1846 gave the United States the right of way in the isthmus of Panama.

Meanwhile Panamanians, with little love for the Colombian government, planned a secession movement, and Roosevelt, despite his early disclaimers, was aware of the plans for revolution. Both Cromwell and Bunau-Varilla were involved in the upheaval, and the Panamanians finally succeeded in pulling away from Colombian control. The Panamanians, however, were alarmed that the Colombians would send more troops to put down the revolt and urged the Americans to prevent reprisals from occurring. The Roosevelt administration conveniently insisted that the newly remembered treaty of 1846 would provide sufficient justification to assist the Panamanians. On November 2, American naval commanders were instructed to "maintain free and uninterrupted transit" in the area. After some confusion, the Panamanian revolution succeeded, and Roosevelt got the friendly government he wanted and needed.

In his message to Congress on January 4, 1904, the president cited the treaty of 1846 and insisted the United States was acting to preserve free transit. Actually, in the past the United States had sent troops at the request of Colombia (except in one instance) to put down various uprisings. Years later, Roosevelt concluded, "I took Panama without consulting the Cabinet." And in 1911, he told a college audience, "I took the canal zone and let Congress debate, and while the debate goes on the canal does also."

When President Woodrow Wilson later concluded a treaty with Colombia that provided for an apology and $25 million for the canal, Roosevelt was furious and his Republican associates prevented the Senate's approval. By the time of the Harding administration, though, the United States became increasingly interested in Colombia's oil reserves and, with TR dead, even his friend Henry Cabot Lodge supported forwarding the $25 million.

In another development, the *New York World* in the 1908 campaign published a series of articles that indicated that part of the $40 million payment went to Americans, including Roosevelt's brother-in-law and Taft's brother. Roosevelt, still president, was upset at the charges, claiming that all the money went to the liquidators appointed by the French government, just as he had been assured. An angry president pushed for state indictments for libel against several newspapers, including the *World* under an 1898 law based on an earlier 1825 statute. The case rested on absurd grounds, and the government was unsuccessful. In 1908, another footnote appeared in the Panama controversy. Four years before, Cromwell had given $5,000 to the Republican campaign, but in Taft's campaign, he offered $50,000. Taft was markedly uncomfortable with the pledge, but TR admonished him, "If I were in your place, I would accept that contribution of Cromwell's with real gratitude."[13]

THE CAMPAIGN OF 1904

As TR traveled through the Midwest to California on a speech-making swing, he reflected with some melancholy that his popularity was not as high as it seemed to those around him watching the crowds. He argued he would never be reelected on his own. "They don't want it . . . Hanna and that crowd. They've finished me. I have no machine, no faction, no money." Roosevelt maintained that he could not be elected without the support of New York state, which he could not get because of past hostility toward him.

But like so many men in public life, Roosevelt was too removed from what was happening and from the hold he had on the populace. A worried TR decided to trim his sails a bit. The work of his new Bureau of Corporations did not begin until after the election. The president also continued to sidestep the troubling tariff issue.

And after some hesitation, he finally dealt with postal frauds that had been uncovered and that involved the secretary of the Republican National Committee.

His 1903 tour of the country had included some public hunting trips designed to further Roosevelt's image as a great outdoorsman. In the past, the president had expressed concern that he not fail in these manly excursions, and he wanted "sure information" about where the game was. In another letter, he insisted on knowing where the mountain lion region was "in advance." And he wrote later in 1905 to a friend that it was essential that *he* kill the first bear: "This sounds selfish, but you know the kind of talk there will be in the newspapers about such a hunt, and if I go it must be a success, and the success must come to me."

In the campaign, though, Roosevelt noted that people came to "see the President as much as they would have come to see a circus." In Butte, Montana, an enthusiastic mayor ordered the waiter to pull up the shades "and let the people see the President eat." Meanwhile, Hanna had decided not to mobilize any opposition to TR's nomination. Then in February 1904, he died of typhoid fever, and Roosevelt's main opponent, if there really was one, disappeared from his mind. Roosevelt easily won the nomination, and triumphed over the conservative Democratic candidate, Judge Alton B. Parker, carrying all the states except those in the solid South. For reasons that are not clear, Roosevelt decided right after his victory to affirm that under no conditions would he be a candidate for another term, an honest but impulsive remark he would come to regret.

Despite their misgivings, American big business continued to fund the Republican cause. Later investigations showed that the Republican campaign received large corporate contributions from several insurance companies, and that E. H. Harriman collected $200,000 and donated $50,000 himself to the party. J. P. Morgan gave $150,000 in cash, and an associate collected another $165,000. Apparently TR did not know that $125,000 in cash was contributed by Standard Oil. As best can be estimated, over 70 percent of the $2 million plus Republican war chest had come from corporations.

A clearly delighted Roosevelt on the night before his inaugural pledged, "Tomorrow I shall come into my office in my own right. Then watch out for me." In his annual address in December 1904, the president gave the Congress a fairly conservative message filled with his usual pieties. But then the next month at a dinner of the

Union League in Philadelphia, TR lectured the wealthy guests with a warning that no free people would "permanently tolerate the use of the vast power conferred by vast wealth" without some government check. William Jennings Bryan praised the president's speech, and corporate moguls must have wondered why they invested in his campaign in the first place. The Great Commoner urged Democrats to support Roosevelt's new agenda, especially the regulation of the railroads, or lose Bryan's stamp of approval.[14]

THE ROOSEVELT DIPLOMACY

Roosevelt's reelection also gave him the opportunity to proceed more boldly in international affairs. A great nation required a leader who understood the "realpolitik" of the world, and who could position the United States in its proper place in the sun. Before his term was up, the president was involved, to his delight, in the Russo-Japanese War, the Morocco incident, and a series of high-level contacts with the czar, the kaiser, and numerous ambassadors and ministers.

In Roosevelt's world view, the United States was on the verge of being a major nation, and it had to be sensitive toward the balance of power not only in Europe, but in the Far East as well. The great European powers were concerned about commercial opportunities in the China region, and so had the United States in the past. In 1899, the United States had insisted on an Open Door policy in that nation, and now the administration wanted the United States to have the same treatment "as the most favored nation" received in China—that is, parity with the major powers engaged in commerce.

In his analysis of the Far East, Roosevelt vacillated between regarding either Russia or Japan as the greatest competitor to the United States. In 1898, he had leaned toward the Japanese as a counterweight to Russia, and watched as a weak China was being divided up by the major powers, with Russia curtailing U.S. and other nations' interests in Manchuria. As president, TR lamented the general lack of interest by the American public in the fate of China and his inability to press harder American claims. Then on February 8, 1904, the Japanese attacked the Russian fleet near Port Arthur. Roosevelt had, in fact, contemplated war with Russia because of her actions in the Far East, and he now welcomed Japan's attack on the czarist regime. "I was thoroughly well pleased with the Japanese victory," he confessed, "for Japan is playing our game." He even considered the possibility of aiding the Japanese, and told the secretary of state he was inclined to send the Asiatic Squadron northward to bottle up the Vladivostok fleet. But by May 1905, the war was over.[15]

Roosevelt leaned toward some sort of understanding supporting a Japanese sphere of influence, but Secretary of State John Hay warned him that U.S. public opinion would not endorse any action with Britain and Japan against Russia. The president indicated in July 1905 that he had told Germany and France that the United States would side with Japan as far as was necessary to stop an alliance against that nation. Yet, just as quickly, the president wondered if the Japanese would not become "intoxicated by their victory over Russia" and then turn against the United States. He now pushed for a mediated settlement, arguing that the war would end if Japan would abandon her demands for an indemnity from Russia.

Roosevelt served as the mediator of the war, and at the Peace Conference at Portsmouth, New Hampshire, he proposed a set of terms that eventually were accepted. The president was somewhat criticized in Japan, but the international community acknowledged his skill, and he was awarded the Nobel Peace Prize. Thus, it happened that one of the most belligerent of modern presidents, one of the most passionate celebrators of the virtues of war, became the advocate of sweet moderation and reasoned diplomacy.

Roosevelt's sights moved toward another troubled spot—the sands of Morocco, a region that drew the European powers into a strained conflict that prefigured the First World War. In 1880, the European powers had agreed to parity of favored treatment in Morocco and a pledge to protect foreigners there; the United States has been a part of that understanding. France, however, with its claim on Algeria, also wanted to control Morocco, and Britain eventually supported this hegemony if it received French approval of its control of Egypt. Meanwhile, Germany, in an increasingly nationalistic mood, desired also to use Morocco to flex its new muscles. The sultan in Morocco, angered by the Anglo-French agreement, turned toward Germany and even invited the kaiser for a state visit at Tangiers.

The kaiser appealed to TR to join him in affirming the principles of the Open Door doctrine in Morocco, but Roosevelt refused to commit himself to a position opposing the British and French governments. Seeing his prestige buffeted on the matter, the kaiser then advocated an international conference to settle the dispute about European interests in that region. Roosevelt, with no real diplomatic establishment in the areas, was somewhat misinformed about the intentions of the parties, and was especially ignorant of secret Anglo-French understandings. Still, Roosevelt supported French control over Morocco and instructed the U.S. delegate to the Algeciras Conference, Henry White, to "keep friendly with all" and "help France get what she ought to have." In the end, France and Spain were to control Morocco, with Germany having little to show for its humiliating efforts. The results of this disagreement though were far more important than were apparent to the principals at the time, for the circumstances of the dispute led to more tensions among the European powers.[16]

The other foreign policy difficulty Theodore Roosevelt faced was the hostility of Japan due to the treatment of its nationals in California. Added to those feelings, some elements of Japanese society had felt that Roosevelt himself had been unfair in the Portsmouth Conference. In fact, in September 1905, anti-American riots took place in Tokyo and four U.S. churches were burned. Then, in October 1906, the San Francisco school board ruled that Japanese children were to be excluded from its public schools. The president immediately condemned the action and announced he would use federal troops if necessary to force California to honor U.S. policy. Still, the president was convinced that Japan, fresh from its victory over Russia, might become too puffed up to see his line of reasoning on how to handle this matter. So in typical fashion, he sent the U.S. fleet halfway around the world, and when there was some talk about Congress not appropriating funds for this grandstand gesture, Roosevelt observed that current funds would not allow the navy to return! Surely, Congress could not leave it out of port in foreign seas.

Roosevelt in this period was also receiving rumors and diplomatic messages that warned Japan was preparing for war, and had designs on American Pacific territories and even on California. The kaiser indicated that he had evidence that the Japanese intended to come through Mexico. As for the president, he continued to insist on Japanese rights in California, and in a secret agreement, Roosevelt promised that if San Francisco would remove its educational restrictions, he would ask the Japanese leaders to stop immigrants from coming to the United States via Hawaii, Mexico, Canada, and the Canal Zone. But these understandings fell through, and race riots occurred in San Francisco in June 1907.

Arguing that the Japanese were proud and warlike, the president pushed for naval preparedness. Secretary of War Taft reported on the defense of the Philippines, Hawaii, Guam, and the Pacific coast, and the president ruefully judged the Philippines "our heel of Achilles" in case of a Japanese attack. Reviewing his order, Roosevelt wrote of the Japanese, "I am none the less anxious that they should realize that I am not afraid of them." As for the Japanese in California, the issue remained unsettled, and continued to fester as a problem in the Taft and Wilson years and beyond.[17]

Thus Roosevelt devoted his considerable energies to help project American power in a variety of ways on to the world stage. But the willingness of his fellow citizens to support such an aggrandized role was limited. While there was some support for imperialist adventures, many Americans felt uncomfortable in that position. Their tradition was a different one from Europe. Americans fought Indians, annexed land, and created a system of equal states. Empires, colonies, and noncitizenship status were rather alien to most democratic leaders in the United States. Roosevelt was president too soon—he would have relished leading the nation into a war instead of Wilson, whom he despised, or instead of his more pleasant and devious cousin, Franklin.

REFORMING SOCIETY

In the middle of his second term, in 1906, Roosevelt wrote to Taft, "I do not like the social conditions at present." As he had in the past, he found fault with the arrogance and greed of the very rich, and worried that corruption in business and politics had led to an increase in left-wing propaganda and socialist agitation. Roosevelt preached social reform, but stymied by the conservative leaders in his own party, he ended up with very limited achievements in his time in the presidency. An acute observer of American society, Roosevelt feared the rise of socialism and class unrest; being a true conservative, like Otto von Bismarck in Germany and Benjamin Disraeli in Britain, he knew the best antidote to the left is social reforms made by the right.

Roosevelt, however, was aware that business people quickly attributed any downturn in the economy to his antitrust policies, and he warned that party divisions would lead to a Democratic victory. He continued to sidestep the tariff issue, arguing for a revision of the rates, but concluded, "it is not an issue upon which I should have any business to break with my party." Blithely in 1907, he praised the conservative Speaker of the House, Joe Cannon, by saying he had accepted for the last two years the Speaker's views on the tariff, and that his advice was "wiser than the course I had intended to follow."[18]

On the issue of the railroads, Roosevelt was more aggressive. For some time, the railroads had been under attack for their preferential treatment of some customers and for varied rate structures. The 1887 Interstate Commerce Act had been passed in response to these objections, but the law proved to be ineffective. Roosevelt asked Congress to strengthen the act in the area of prohibiting rebating to selected customers, a particularly radical reform, but one that would not be matched by proposals from the president in other major areas that also needed regulation. In an address before the Union League Club in 1905, Roosevelt advocated a tribunal to control railroad rates as well. The railroad magnates counterattacked with a major public relations effort, but TR was helped by a report from the federal government's Bureau of Corporations outlining the business practices of Standard Oil. That study concluded that the company had benefited from secret railroad rates, and popular cries for reform soon mounted. The House of Representatives supported Roosevelt's regulation proposal, but the Senate continued to oppose any changes. After considerable jockeying, the president and the Senate agreed to a law that gave the Interstate Commerce Commission considerable oversight over the railroads. The commission was granted greater rate-making authority, but the conservative federal courts had extensive rights to review its decisions.

Roosevelt's rhetoric was more radical than his actions or than even his basic inclinations would admit. He took on the railroads and the great corporate trusts, but the results were limited. Despite his reputation as the "trustbuster," his administration initiated in eight years about one-half the number of actions to break up these combinations that the conservative Taft did in only one term. One can argue that Taft would have never started his activity if TR had not come before him and shown the way. But still Taft presided over forty-five such actions compared to Roosevelt's twenty-five.

And even though he was a critic of corporate America, Roosevelt was very uncomfortable with the new breed of journalists who were exposing evils in society, labeling them contemptuously as "muckrakers." For example, when he met Upton Sinclair, whose book *The Jungle* exposed the filthy meat packing houses, Roosevelt cautioned, "Really, Mr. Sinclair, you *must* keep your head." Still, the president himself was not above warning the meat packers that he would release a very damaging government study of meat packing conditions unless they told their lobbyists to support his reform proposal. Consequently, on July 1, 1906, an inspection bill passed Congress, following on the heels of the Pure Food Act, which he had signed into law a month before.[19]

Thus, Roosevelt was quite willing to use the forces of dissent in his own crusades, promising moderate reforms but accompanying those initiatives with powerful indictments against whatever miscreants he was taking aim. And, of course, the president established a genuine record of accomplishment in the area of conservation, not only in his handling of public lands and resources, but in extending the sway of the federal government as steward and in building a strong coalition to support his efforts. In his enthusiasm, Roosevelt was not afraid to stretch congressional statutes in this area to their farthest boundaries and to use executive orders to do what those statutes had not covered to his satisfaction.

At times, though, Roosevelt's behavior seems mystifying and contradictory, leading to charges from his critics then, and some historians since, that he was simply a hypocrite who clothed his ambition with high-sounding pieties and hollow morality. One episode that brought considerable censure on him was a deal with J. P. Morgan in 1907. At that time, the nation was faced with serious banking problems, which threatened to upset the speculative base that ran through much of the private enterprise system in the East. When the bank crisis significantly worsened, Roosevelt was busy hunting bear in Louisiana. His secretary of treasury, George B. Cortelyou, put $25 million of government funds in national banks to stabilize the situation, and Roosevelt concurred in that step. Unfortunately, the guarantee had only a temporary calming effect and matters quickly worsened. Especially vulnerable was the Tennessee Coal and Iron Company whose stock had been used as guarantees for loans made by various brokerage houses. Finally, Morgan once again took a hand in the matter and offered to have U.S. Steel Corporation buy up the threatened company for $45 million. However, the wily Morgan wanted a commitment from the president that the Justice Department would not use the antitrust law to challenge the acquisition. His agents insisted on an early meeting with the president, and Roosevelt pledged, "I do not believe that anyone could justly criticize me for saying that I would not feel like objecting to the purchase under the circumstances." Oddly, Roosevelt claimed he never knew nor did he want to know which company was at stake.[20]

Quickly, critics of the deal argued that TR had been duped by the Morgan interests, and that the sale was a giveaway to U.S. Steel, leaving it with another $1 billion in assets, purchased for only $45 million. But the president insisted then and years later that everyone benefited, and that he would have been "a timid and unworthy public officer if . . . I had not acted as I did. I never had any doubt of the wisdom of my action—not a moment." Probably what contributed to the president's decision was the declining economic situation in 1907, and his reluctance to aggravate it, regardless of what benefits may have accrued to the U.S. Steel trust.

The year 1907 also witnessed Roosevelt in a nasty tiff with railroad magnate E. H. Harriman, who was active in New York state Republican party politics. Harriman charged that Roosevelt had asked him to raise $250,000 to save that state from the Democrats and from publisher William Randolph Hearst. When the two had a falling out, mutual recriminations followed, and Harriman and TR published letters supporting their positions. Unfortunately, in one of his letters, Roosevelt had used the gratuitous remark, "You and I are practical men"—a comment that was seen as implying some special arrangements between the two.

Roosevelt's most unfortunate decision, though, came in the Brownsville incident. In early August, three companies of black infantry troops were sent to Texas, and immediately, local white residents objected to their presence. Several weeks later, one civilian was killed and a policeman wounded in an attack presumably begun by some black soldiers. The military authorities were convinced that even if they could not find out who was specifically responsible, it had to be true that some of their soldiers were involved. The inspector general warned the men that the president had authorized that the entire battalion would be dismissed if the guilty men were not found. Roosevelt waited until after the election in 1906 and then ordered about 160 men dishonorably discharged, stripping them of their pensions and ending the careers of some individuals who had been cited for conspicuous bravery and heroism in other engagements. Congressional critics attacked Roosevelt for racism and for making an abrupt decision based on faulty information and evidence. Roosevelt, in typical fashion, continued to defend his decision, but it began to ring less and less true as time passed. Tellingly, he omitted the incident totally from his autobiography of accomplishments.[21]

As has been seen, a part of Roosevelt's appeal was his ability to seem spontaneous—a willingness to express an uncontrollable urge to comment on a variety of topics—from birth control, football, simplified spelling, coinage, pseudo-naturalist writers, to whatever else crossed his attention span. Ruefully he once wrote to a friend in 1907 that a president should probably not go into areas outside those his office were responsible for, but he still did as the spirit moved him.[22]

By the end of his second term, Roosevelt was approaching only fifty years of age and was still filled with enthusiasm and energy. Unlike many of the presidents, he loved the job and commented, "The burdens . . . will be laid aside with a good deal of regret." As a lame duck, he faced increasing resistance in Congress and some vigorous criticism of his views, which ranged from his attacks on the judiciary to his advocacy of simplified phonetic spelling. Almost as if relieved from conventional constraints, Roosevelt turned to the political left and advocated openly a series of reforms that troubled conservative Republican leaders.

In January 1908, the president recommended an employee liability law, workmen's compensation for government employees, limitations on the judiciary's use of injunctions in labor disputes, a strengthened ICC, and restrictions on stock market practices. He attacked the "speculative folly and flagrant dishonesty of a few men of great wealth" who threatened the body politic. Then in late December, Roosevelt unfortunately called into question the integrity of Congress after it moved to restrict the activities of the Secret Service. Rumors in Washington had spread the accusation that the White House was using the agency to collect information about important clients who frequented local brothels. That information would be used allegedly to get recalcitrant congressmen to support the administration's proposals. Whether these fears were well founded or not, Congress decided to make sure that the Secret Service could not be used for any duties except protecting the president and tracking down counterfeiters. Roosevelt angrily reacted that the legislative restrictions would only benefit "the criminal class."

A furious House chastised Roosevelt for what was seen as a slur on Congress, and passed a formal rebuke, which no president since Jackson had experienced.

Undaunted, Roosevelt, in 1907, nearing the end of his term, came up with a novel idea—a House of Governors, and in May 1908, the state chief executives met to consider the president's various proposals on conservation and public land usage. But it was a Roosevelt-led production and the meetings were not well received. Thus having barred himself from a third term, and in the full vigor of middle age, Theodore Roosevelt, surely the most publicly energetic of presidents, faced an early and unwanted retirement. His last legacy was one he would bitterly regret—his handpicked successor, William Howard Taft.

THE BULLY PULPIT

Evaluations of Theodore Roosevelt have wildly varied—from committed progressive to opportunistic conservative, from racist politician to enlightened leader, from ineffectual president to a strikingly great executive. One of Roosevelt's biographers, Henry Pringle, concluded his study with the simple observation that TR's achievements were not substantial. Another authority, John Morton Blum, has argued that some people may find that "much in his career seems in retrospect scarcely worth the strong emotions and heated righteousness with which his speeches and letters are filled. But even when his just causes were narrowly partisan, he felt strongly. Today's insouciant critics, unlike [Stuart] Sherman, censure as quixotic adolescence or dangerous diversion the intensity of act and feeling they no longer share. Even they, however, do not find it dull."[23]

The debate about Theodore Roosevelt, however, has never revolved around the issue of dullness. On that account, he is clearly more fascinating, more varied, more personally colorful than any other man, including Jefferson, who has acquired the office. But what of his judgment, his political skill, the vision he bequeathed of his office and his nation? Those are the true criteria of presidential greatness. When TR is compared with Wilson, his cousin FDR, and Lyndon B. Johnson, he is clearly not in their league as a leader of the legislative process. His accomplishments are far more modest, almost to the point of lending some weight to his critics' charge that he talked a good game, but rarely delivered. What must be remembered, though, is that TR faced a much more conservative, indeed stubbornly mossback, leadership with a cohesive tradition of standpattism. There were powerful currents of reform astir in the cities and the states, but Roosevelt made progressive reform the presidential agenda, like no one before him. None of his predecessors—including Jefferson, Jackson, or Lincoln—so advocated liberal reforms as TR did.

And he was a genuine reformer, one committed to restoring integrity to public life and placing the government in a position as referee between the powerful interests and corporate combinations arising in the new America. Roosevelt was a man guided not by theology, but by moral codes; he thought less of God than of character and good works. He was concerned with stability and public order, and was an advocate of efficiency, scientific method, expert advice, and good government. TR knew the world of rough-and-tumble politics, mastered its nebulous rules, and bested the lower-class bosses and socialist charmers to become one of the fastest rising stars in American politics. Roosevelt knew the ambiguities of power and when he compromised on principles, he still had to convince himself that he was morally justified in some way or another. At one point in his career he observed, "Public men have great temptations. They are always obliged to compromise in order to do anything at all." Yet he disliked the "malicious impracticable visionary" as much as the "vicious and cynical professional politicians," and there were elements of both types in his own personality.[24]

On one level, Roosevelt urged his fellow citizens to "live wise, brave and upright lives," to play one's "part, manfully, as a man among men." On another level, he bluntly extolled them to work, fight, and breed. Roosevelt accepted the nineteenth century's fixation on racial gradations, for him the inferior races were from southern and eastern Europe, and he regretted that their waves of immigration that flooded the cities, debased his version of middle-class democracy, and diluted superior native American life. And yet, he expected that the second and third generations of these immigrants would fit into American society and learn the virtues of self-restraint, courage, and hard work, which he so prized. Roosevelt believed in the building of character, like he believed in the building of one's body, and in the enhancement of national self-determination and the aggrandizing of power to face the harshness of the real world. As America came of age, it was time for her to both seek a proper place in the sun and also assume responsibility for the fate of the family of nations.

In terms of the presidency, Roosevelt had the most articulate theory of the office of any of its incumbents. He observed "there inheres in the Presidency more power than in any other office in any great republic or constitutional monarch of modern times." He advocated, as he said, a strong executive, and he extolled power. Roosevelt, like so many popular leaders, sensed a special bond with average Americans—"people who believed in me and trusted me and followed me." He saw himself as "the man of all others whom they wished to see President," and concluded he "was a steward of the people bound actively and affirmatively to do all he could do for the people." The president could do anything the nation required unless it was specifically forbidden by the Constitution, he insisted. Roosevelt defended his stewardship theory, concluding, "Under this interpretation of executive power I did and caused to be done many things not previously done . . . I did not usurp power, but I did greatly broaden the use of executive power."[25]

He asserted that the new combinations of wealth and labor required giving "adequate power of control to the one sovereignty capable of exercising such power—the National Government." Many of TR's efforts were skillful attempts at building up the expertise and administrative control of that government to regulate trusts, conserve public lands, and fulfill major elements of the progressive agenda. Roosevelt did not become popular just because he identified with progressive reform; he genuinely mobilized public opinion into political channels that made such reforms possible. His record even before his climb to the presidency was dominated by the reform impulse, characteristic of the best sentiments of his class.

It is a mistaken belief in historical inevitability that leads to a simple assumption that progressivism as a movement was so powerful it had to spill over to the presidency. The judiciary and the Congress were controlled by conservative Republicans, and if McKinley had lived, there is no evidence that he would have converted to the reform wing of the party. Why should he? The Democratic party was not a serious threat and the last "liberal" president, if that term can be used at all, was Jackson. Bryan, with his strong western and southern support, was a compelling figure, but one that the Republicans regarded as their best fund-raising asset in that era. Roosevelt, then, was a fateful mistake for the party leadership; as president, he helped to unleash the forces of reform, and using his personality and patronage, he put the presidency behind a generation's reform agenda. Without his presence, it is quite likely that the Republican party would have avoided those sentiments, or so compromised them that they would have had no impact on national life. And most importantly, TR changed the presidency and made it more of a populist, visible, and activist institution. In the end, his unvarnished ambition led Roosevelt to split the Republican party, which he had been loyal to all his life, and resulted in the election of Wilson who picked up the mantle of progressive leadership. As has been seen, before TR, the presidency was a national clerkship, curtailed in part as a reaction to Lincoln's wartime ascendancy and also because of the late nineteenth century bias against using politics as a way of setting priorities in a country of rough and rampant economic development.

When Roosevelt volunteered to step down and told the world he was off to hunt lions, he left an office very different from the one he inherited. Roosevelt created an executive branch that was more visible than Jefferson would have tolerated, more popular than Washington or Cleveland would have wished, more broadly based than Lincoln's term allowed. Roosevelt was not a figurehead, a patriot king, a national clerk, or a prime minister. His model of the presidency was quite different from what had gone before, and with his immense influence on his younger cousin, Franklin D. Roosevelt, TR does indeed merit the label, "the first modern president." His was the beginning of the Rooseveltian presidency, of an assertive executive, advocating a national domestic agenda and a powerfully positioned foreign policy.

Students of history have tried to summarize his views of the office and often become confused in dealing with his complex personality. Yet, TR said it best, the presidency was a "bully pulpit"— and like a secular preacher he proclaimed the gospels of good works, decent character, hard work, and social balance. His compromises may seem too easy and frequent, his rhetoric much too belligerent and often demagogic especially when he was out of office after 1909, but Theodore Roosevelt insisted on using his positions of power to discuss the great issues of his time, as he saw them, and in his own way. After all, what good was a pulpit to him if he had no message to justify his stewardship to himself and to the members of his social class who originally insisted that gentlemen do not enter democratic politics?

WILLIAM HOWARD TAFT AND
THE CONSERVATIVE TRADITION

Roosevelt was successful in naming his heir apparent, Secretary of War William Howard Taft, and predicted that he would be a superb president, only a cut below Washington and Lincoln. But by the end of Taft's term, he characterized him as a "puzzlewit" and a "fathead." Roosevelt from the beginning had misunderstood his friend's political instincts. Taft was, like so many people trained in the law, a deeply conservative man, and while he supported many of Roosevelt's objectives, he chafed at his high-handedness and disregard for procedures and tradition. While Roosevelt proclaimed that the president could do whatever was *not* expressly forbidden in the Constitution, Taft maintained that the executive could only do what was granted to him by statute or the Constitution. In between those parameters lay the immense distance that separates an activist president from a literalist judge. Added to Taft's views were substantial differences of style, personality, and political skill. And above all, Taft suffered from the increasingly large and looming shadow of his predecessor and patron who after a year roaming Europe and Africa returned to the United States to the hue and cries of betrayed Republican progressives.[26]

Taft started his term in office by making a series of miscalculations and misstatements that raised opposition and clouded what ended up being a record better than either history or his contemporaries have usually recognized. He began by naming a cabinet of nine men, seven of whom had studied law and five of whom were corporate counsels. For some, the tone of his administration was already clearly set, while for the president it made sense to recruit men who knew what was going on in the corporate world in order to control it better. In his first major battle, Taft chose to confront the one intractable issue TR had assiduously avoided—the tariff. To the alarm of Republican conservatives, Taft in his inaugural address seemed to accept the Democratic position of a tariff for revenue only. Aldrich in the Senate and Cannon in the House, with their control of the Congress, remained strong high tariff advocates, and Taft immediately risked a split in the party. Cannon in fact had cut short any discussion of tariff reform by observing, "I am goddamned tired of listening to all this babble of reform."[27]

Taft's tariff crusade was affected by the continuing opposition in the House to Cannon's Speakership. The president himself dis-

liked Cannon and what he called "his whole crowd," but he concluded that Cannon would be reelected Speaker, and that he needed
his concurrence for any changes in the tariff. Cannon had pledged
his support for some alterations, or so Taft had thought.

Trying to avoid a major split in the party on the issue, Taft at
first sent up a 324-word message that simply asked that the tariff
question be disposed of quickly so that other business could be taken
up. But the tariff issue was a long-standing national division and
could not be simply dismissed that easily. In the House of Representatives, a mild revision was passed and sent on to the Senate.
To the insurgents, or progressive Republicans led by Robert
LaFollette, the bill was worse than useless. He urged Taft to veto it
if it passed the Senate, and the president seemed to agree. When
the senator asked Taft to intervene more forcefully, Taft argued that
he did not "much believe in a President interfering with the legislative department while it does its work. They have their responsibility and I have mine."[28]

The Senate bill, drafted by Aldrich, included 847 changes in the
tariff rates, 600 of them increases, and LaFollette and his supporters quickly denounced the proposal as "the consummation of privilege more reprehensible than had ever found a place in the statutes
of the country." Added to the controversy was a Democratic amendment to the bill that provided for both an individual and a corporate income tax. The conference committee report recommended
some rate changes that Taft approved of, including those on lum-
ber, and the establishment of a tariff commission. As the debate
progressed, the president refused to budge on parts of the bill he
deemed objectionable, and he and his associates were to claim in
the end a victory for his leadership. Even Henry Cabot Lodge wrote
to TR, "The President refrained from saying anything or doing anything while the bill was passing through the Houses, which I thought
was wise . . . but when the conferees met they went to him and
said they would like to know what his views were and he gave them
his views very freely. He stood very firm for what he demanded
and forced a number of reductions which ought to have been made."
Lodge judged that Taft had strengthened his position in the process
and that of the Republican party in the eyes of the people.

Unfortunately for Taft, he too was satisfied, and in a speaking
tour, he characterized the act as "best tariff bill that the Republican
party ever passed, and therefore the best tariff bill that has been
passed at all." To progressives, the tribute was inaccurate, and they

were equally annoyed by his praise in Utah of protectionist Senator Reed Smoot and by his compliments of Cannon's role.

Progressive suspicions were further aroused by Taft's handling of a nasty dispute between Secretary of Interior Richard Achilles Ballinger of Washington state and Gifford Pinchot, chief of the Bureau of Forestry and a staunch Roosevelt ally on conservation. Under TR's aegis, the Interior Department and Pinchot in particular had stretched the intent of congressional statutes and found every opportunity to extend federal control over natural resources. Taft had generally agreed with Roosevelt's concerns, but he opposed the use of executive orders to circumvent Congress. Taft's approach emphasized much more state control, congressional policy making, and the leasing of public lands for private exploitation. While Roosevelt expected commercial uses of the natural resource areas, he emphasized scientific methods and strong federal—that is executive—control.

In this change of policy, Pinchot was more than a midlevel bureaucrat; he was a national figure in the conservation movement and under his leadership the forest protection program grew from 19 forests covering 20 million acres in 1898 to 149 national forests and 193 million acres. To Western farmers and timbermen, however, Pinchot became the visible target of federal obstructionism; to conservatives, he was as Harold Ickes labeled him later, "Sir Galahad of the woodlands." With TR, Pinchot had worked to obviate Congress's will at times and place the forests and water power sites under federal control. Taft had been critical of such an approach, and concluded that Pinchot was "quite willing to camp outside the law to accomplish his beneficent programs."[29]

Although he supported Ballinger, Taft tried to avoid the controversy and let Pinchot undercut him in public until he was forced to take some action as the situation worsened. Finally the president concurred in Pinchot's dismissal, an event that he feared would bring about an open rupture with Roosevelt who was still out of the country. Privately, Pinchot wrote, "As an executive he [Taft] should have never let the issue reach any such point. Since he was supporting Ballinger, he should have told me long before to shut up or get out." And then Pinchot ran off to Europe to find Roosevelt and tell him first his side of the controversy.

A congressional committee cleared Ballinger of any evidence of wrongdoing, but Taft paid a high price for his victory. Once again, he alienated the progressive forces. Ironically though, Taft's record on conservation was a good one. He withdrew almost as many acres as TR had and regularized by statute much of Roosevelt's executive orders. Still, Taft fractured the conservation alliance, strengthened the power of the Corps of Engineers, and led Roosevelt to wonder if his progressive legacy was safe after all.[30]

When TR returned, he promised his friends to avoid taking sides and even speaking about politics at all—a vow he quickly broke. Roosevelt insisted that he wished to give Taft the "benefit of every doubt," and then cryptically added, "I most emphatically desire that I shall not be put in the position of having to run for the Presidency"—an early indication of his own attitude immediately after his return to the United States. Taft himself seemed bewildered, and pathetically commented to one mutual friend, "If I only knew what the President [TR] wanted. . . ."[31]

By the late spring of 1910, Taft became angered by the progressives' opposition in Congress and decided to attack publicly their major leaders. But the elections, especially in the Midwest, returned insurgent Republicans and introduced a new crop of Democrats including Woodrow Wilson, the reform governor in New Jersey. The Democrats gained control of the House of Representatives with a majority of fifty-nine seats, while the Republican majority in the Senate was slashed from twenty-five to twelve. Despite this shift in fortunes and the partial repudiation of Taft, the president with two more years in office was able to compile a record that surpassed the first Roosevelt term in true achievements.

While each reform increased his conservative enemies, his style of leadership and personal philosophy never led to his being considered a kindred spirit of the progressives. Although Taft traveled around the nation more than any other president in history, he rarely received a warm personal welcome and throughout his term he disliked speech making, campaign trips, and having to deal with newspaper reporters. In many ways, this heir to Roosevelt was his mirror opposite—a political antimatter to TR's field of energy.

As Taft himself admitted, he would have been a better president if he were less lethargic, and one might add, less prone to enjoying the pleasures of fine food and convivial friends. A large man, reaching at times 340 pounds, Taft was agile and good-natured but never epitomized the aggressiveness and activity that Roosevelt did. He was an adjudicator, a conciliator, a man of reason in a world of increasing political passion and commitment. Pushed by his wife and brother, Taft refused TR's offer of a superior court position in order to be what they wanted him to be—the president of the United States. Life rarely gives one a second chance, and even more rarely does it grant a gift without a price. But Taft was to become what he wanted and early enough to enjoy it. In 1921, President Warren Harding offered him the chief justiceship of the Supreme Court, making him the only person honored with the two highest offices in the American political system.[32]

Overall though, his record in the White House was a respectable one for that time, although his leadership included a mixture of setbacks and breakdowns. It is odd that Roosevelt, who seemed so confident in office, so sure of his objectives, so skillful in his use of power, actually accomplished less in terms of legislative achievements than Taft, who was tagged as being inept and weak. In history, as in life, appearance is often a greater reality than experience itself.

What then was Taft's record? He had effected some reforms, however modest, in the tariff and extended the conservation program. In keeping with his interest in efficiency and civil service, the president trimmed back the Treasury Department, cut the military budget, reformed the post office's operations, pushed for a parcel post system, insisted on a centralized federal budget, placed under civil service the assistant postmasters and clerks in major post offices, and extended the merit system to consular officers and lesser diplomats. By the end of his term, the classified service was expanded by covering thirty-five thousand fourth-class postmasters as well. These reforms were good government, businesslike actions— ones befitting a conservative president, but unlikely to fire up the populace.

The president also supported a postal savings bank system in which funds could be deposited with the government, earning a rather modest interest. Obviously, the banking leaders opposed any competition with their operations, but Taft signed a compromise proposal. In early January 1910, the president decided to ask Congress to strengthen the railroad regulations of the Hepburn Act and to establish a U.S. court of commerce to hear cases arising from the Interstate Commerce Act. After numerous amendments from the insurgents, Congress passed the Mann-Elkins Act, which regulated mergers and rates. Taft had in the process abandoned his hands-off attitude and pushed the insurgents and conservatives into supporting the act. He had firmly rejected railroad company demands for raising rates, and when twenty-five western railroads joined together, he had the attorney general obtain an injunction against them. Finally, on June 6 and 7, the railroads rolled backed the increases and abided by the new regulations.[33]

Despite Taft's successes in passing parts of his program and the role of many of the insurgents in aiding him, he continued to be critical of them and decided to work for the defeat of some of them in the election coming up in 1912. As time passed, the president suffered some major setbacks in his term. His alliance with Senator Aldrich to reform the national banking structure failed, and his poorly handled proposal for trade reciprocity with Canada angered leaders of that nation and segments of the American farmers. Once again, the president, wishing to both do well and follow TR's example, undertook a trustbusting crusade of his own. As had been seen, TR picked and chose his fights carefully and his trusts gingerly. He came to deplore not bigness, but abuse of private power—a distinction Taft often ignored. To Taft, the law was the law, and enforcement was unconditional. In actuality, Taft was the real trustbuster—initiating twice as many suits in his one term as TR did in nearly two.

To Roosevelt's embarrassment, Taft went after the United States Steel Corporation—in part for the takeover of the Tennessee Coal and Iron Company, a move TR had approved. The Justice Department's indictment read like a *Who's Who*: J. P. Morgan, John D. Rockefeller, Andrew Carnegie, Charles M. Schwab, George Perkins, and Henry Clay Frick. To Roosevelt's horror, the U.S. government contended that TR was deceived about the transaction, in effect snookered by the capitalist moguls! Roosevelt furiously denied the implication and never forgave Taft for his alleged part in the case.

The administration went after other trusts, including the International Harvester Company, which Roosevelt had also exempted from attack in his time in office. Taft's friends pointed out with glee the support that had been given to Roosevelt by the McCormick family, which had controlled the company. Then the Senate got into the dispute by demanding all the papers the president had on the Harvester trust, a request that Taft refused to honor at first, but that he eventually acceded to during the 1912 presidential primaries. Thus, Taft seemed to be taking Bryan's position: the trusts had to be broken up and not simply regulated as TR was advocating at this period. For businesspeople, the administration's actions and the uncertain policies of the high court left many of them in doubt about what were "reasonable" and "unreasonable" economic combinations.

In terms of foreign policy, Taft entered the presidency with a constructive record of experiences as governor of the Philippines and special emissary of Roosevelt to various nations. His diplomatic activities in office, though, were more mixed. Taft pursued with vigor the advancement of American economic interests in the world ("Dollar Diplomacy" as it was called), pressed unsuccessfully often for economic reciprocity, and became a firm advocate of arbitration of international disputes. In many of these endeavors, he ran into a recalcitrant Senate, and on the last issue incurred Roosevelt's enmity once more.

As has been seen, Roosevelt had approved of the use of arbitration where vital American interests were not involved. Secretary of State John Hay wrote nine "special agreements" that provided for arbitration procedures to be implemented by the president through executive agreements. The Senate rejected that approach and maintained that these "special agreements" were "special treaties" and needed its consent. Roosevelt refused to approve the arrangements, but then his next secretary of state, Elihu Root, did conclude treaties with twenty-four nations concerning many issues except those embracing vital interests, independence, and the "honor" of the countries involved; those treaties contained provisions for Senate approval.

Taft's proposal called for the submission of all "justiciable" disputes to The Hague or a similar international tribunal, with "nonjusticiable" differences going to a commission of inquiry. Roosevelt came out in opposition to the proposal, concluding that it took away powers that rightfully belonged to the president and the Senate. In the Senate, an amendment was added that prohibited arbitration on a host of other issues such as indebtedness, immigration status, unique "American questions" as the Monroe Doctrine, and "purely governmental policy." The amendment in effect gutted the proposal that Taft had hoped would be his proudest accomplishment.

The president also tried to protect U.S. interests in Mexico without upsetting the revolution there, and expressed some mild concern about the harsh treatment of Jews in czarist Russia. But his most extensive foreign policy initiative was his administration's aggressive diplomacy to foster U.S. investments overseas. Taft and

Secretary of State Philander C. Knox saw this step as a rightful extension of American power, one likely to earn profits for the country and further peace and stability in Latin America and the Far East. This economic imperialism would replace the use of troops abroad and establish the United States' destiny as a leader in the world. In Honduras and Nicaragua, especially, the administration joined with American financial interests to establish virtual protectorships over these countries; but in both cases, the Senate refused to approve treaties legitimizing those advances. For Taft, with his concern for constitutional necessities, the Senate's disapproval prevented any sort of initiatives to pursue those investment policies.

Just like Roosevelt, Taft tried to foster U.S. investment in the Far East, especially China, and he pressed for equal access to that carved-up nation. But American investments remained minimal in that country, and instead, Japan and Russia began again to divide up Manchuria. In dealing with the explosive issue of Japanese immigration, Taft followed his predecessor again. A renegotiation of the treaty, signed on February 21, 1911, promised reciprocity of rights for each nation's citizens, but said nothing about landownership, a major point of contention in California. The senate of that state urged Taft to withdraw the treaty, and the issue was still being discussed during the Wilson administration.[34]

Taft, entering the 1912 campaign, felt he had compiled a worthwhile record, but acknowledged that he probably could not win reelection. Instead, he refused to allow Roosevelt's renomination and focused his efforts on denouncing the latter's new radicalism and defending the two-term tradition of presidents. LaFollette had considered running on a third-party Progressive ticket, and Roosevelt was surely maneuvering for the same purpose. Despite his reputation for lethargy, Taft in September and October delivered over two hundred speeches and traveled over thirteen thousand miles to press his case throughout the Midwest, and then added the Southeast to his itinerary. He insisted that he represented "a safer and saner view of our government and its Constitution than does Theodore Roosevelt." Yet, deeply upset by Roosevelt's shift, he admitted "I owe him everything. He is responsible for my being President. I am so disturbed it keeps me awake nights."[35]

Still, Taft controlled the party machinery and, to the howls and protests of Roosevelt admirers, he won renomination. TR had insisted that he did not want the nomination, but he wrote some friendly governors that they should indicate publicly that the people of their states "wish me to run and ask whether I would refuse a nomination." The convention passed him by despite his guile, and an angry Roosevelt accepted the nomination of the National Progressive party with its "Bull Moose" emblem. A collection of social workers, reformers, and progressive idealists put together a platform that included the direct primary, initiative, referendum, recall, women's suffrage, and control over campaign contributions. The party supported a minimum wage, restrictions on child labor, social insurance, agricultural credit programs, and a limited tariff.

While TR promised Armageddon and to do battle for the Lord, as he put it, Taft solemnly concluded that Roosevelt had attracted "the Holy Rollers," and the president found his former friend to be a "freak"—unfitted for popular office and unable to command the people's trust and confidence. Then on October 14 in Milwaukee, Roosevelt was shot in the chest by a deranged man, and campaigning was suspended by all the presidential candidates. Two weeks later, Taft's running mate, James S. Sherman, died, and the national Republican party did not replace him at that late date, seeking to avoid confusion.

It did not much matter—the GOP was clearly divided, and the Democrats ran a good campaign. Woodrow Wilson, in many ways a conservative like Taft, had embraced with newly found fervor the Bryan wing of his party. Taft concluded to his wife that it was, after all, "not the height of my ambition to be popular." He had rejected the publicity and showmanship of the campaign, concluding, "I don't want any forced or manufactured sentiment in my favor. That isn't my method. I must wait for time and the rest of my labors to vindicate me naturally. I have a profound faith in the people. Their judgment will be right." In discussing Roosevelt's view of the presidency, Taft continued to disagree. Taft, the student and lover of the law, found no "undefined residuum of power" to which he could turn if the public interest demanded. He interpreted the grant of power and the office more narrowly, and, as such, restricted the scope of political leadership. Thus, the conflict between Taft and TR was not simply based on ambition and personality; there was a genuine difference of opinion over what the office of the presidency should be and what was permitted and desirable in a constitutional republic that was undergoing massive economic and social changes.[36]

Taft's views remained another formulation of the Whig executive, although surely influenced by the dynamics of progressivism and reform. Roosevelt's conception is clearly a precursor of Wilson and more importantly his cousin Franklin who together changed the nature of the office and of America in ways TR could only have fantasized about. In politics, timing is not all, but it surely is very critical.

2

Prime Minister and World Prophet:
Woodrow Wilson

The election of 1912 saw a split in the Republican party and led the Democrats back to control of the presidency. Freed from the postwar legacy of Reconstruction and willing to accept the mainstream of progressive reform, the Democrats nominated Woodrow Wilson, the governor of New Jersey and former president of Princeton University. In a short eighteen months, Wilson had moved from private life to the White House, and in the process redefined his own understanding about American society and redirected his once conservative political party. The Wilson presidency was to have a profound impact on the domestic life of the American people and an even more dramatic impact on the Western world. His first term was a sparkling triumph of presidential leadership; his second term led the nation to war and left Wilson and a generation of his fellow citizens broken and disillusioned about America's role in foreign affairs. Except for Lincoln's term in office, no presidency up to that date so jarred the settled ways of Americans and so expanded the powers and potentialities of the presidency.

Born in Staunton, Virginia, to a Presbyterian minister's family, Wilson went on to become first a lawyer and then a college professor. At Princeton, he was recognized as a splendid teacher and was in his prime probably the highest paid college professor in the country. A nationally recognized scholar, Wilson criticized in his books the dominance of Congress and its committee system and pressed for a stronger executive. In this period, the late nineteenth century, the presidency was in a state of obvious decline, and Wilson's plea seemed at best novel, and clearly impractical. But in his critiques,

Wilson put forth a very different model of the presidency, one based more on the British prime ministership than on the tradition of either strong presidents or the recent record of weak ones.

Wilson loved Great Britain, its land, its history, its culture, and its institutions. He proposed that the American system emphasize the role of party government and make the president the chief spokesman for his party. In place of the traditional American emphasis on the separation of powers and a limited executive, Wilson advocated a fusion of Congress and the presidency, with the president providing a basic agenda for that party and the nation. The president was obliged, Wilson concluded, to be as big a person as he could be, and the parties had to be more responsible to public opinion and amenable to strong presidential leadership. Looking at the parties of the late nineteenth century, Wilson critically observed that the American system had "no parties, no principles, no principles, no leaders."[1]

But despite his interest in national affairs and his reputation as an original thinker on the problems of government, Wilson's role remained confined to the fiercely myopic disputes and intrigues so characteristic of faculty politics. Leading a group of "young Turks" at Princeton, Wilson was offered the presidency of that institution in 1902. His objective was to take an insular and somewhat mediocre college and place it into the first rank of higher education. During most of his time in office, he was rather successful in expanding Princeton's programs and attracting splendid young faculty. Then, in a bitter controversy, Wilson proposed breaking up the exclusive undergraduate eating clubs and replacing them with college-run residential houses. Opposition mounted to his plans and to his attempt to control the site of the graduate school. Wilson adroitly transformed the campus controversy into a highly touted battle against privilege and for progressive democracy, and he took his position to the alumni nationally, receiving considerable publicity in the process. There on a small college campus, known for its love of elitism, was a president waging a battle for the principles of democracy and the causes of progressive reform everywhere. Wilson in the end lost the battle, but he gained so much visibility that when the Democratic party bosses in New Jersey were searching around for a respectable candidate for governor, they turned to Woodrow Wilson. Wilson accepted their offer, won the election, and ungratefully repudiated the bosses. He quickly compiled a model record of progressive legislation, and in the deadlocked convention of 1912, Wilson received the Democratic nomination for president on the forty-third ballot.[2]

SETTING THE PROGRESSIVE COURSE

In this century, there have been three periods of creative presidential leadership in domestic affairs: Wilson's first term, FDR's first term, and Lyndon Johnson in the 1963–67 years. The Roosevelt reforms were largely due to the frightening consequences of the Great Depression, and Lyndon Johnson's legacy rested on the aftermath of his predecessor's assassination and his own tremendous victory in the election of 1964. What is extraordinary about Wilson's successes is that he had neither a domestic crisis nor a grandiose electoral triumph as a background. He won the presidency during fairly good economic times, in a tranquil period abroad, and by a thin plurality having received no more votes than Bryan did in his races when he lost in a two-man contest. Yet Wilson came into office, as no president did before him, with a sense of having a very specific agenda to fulfill.

No task is more difficult for a president than to provide consistent and ongoing leadership of Congress, with that body's own sense of power and history and its organization of vested interests. But Wilson had written so convincingly about the importance of providing strong executive leadership and, remarkably, he did just that. There were several factors that assisted him in compiling that record. First, Wilson decided that he would work through the Democratic party and not try to build an ad hoc coalition of progressives in Congress. He presented a complete program and worked well with the committee chairmen. Second, the Democrats had a majority of three members in the House in the 1913–15 session, which increased their cohesiveness, and many of the party members were new to that body. Some 114 of the 290 Democrats had been elected for the first time, and they looked to the president of their own party for leadership. Many of the established Democratic leaders agreed with Wilson that the future of the party depended on how well the president performed, and they were anxious to make him in turn look good. And last, the winds of progressive reform had swept through Congress as well, and even among many southern senators there was a general willingness to use the legislative process to achieve some of the reformers' goals.

Wilson focused his attention on the tariff, and he dramatically appeared before Congress with his message. No president since John Adams had personally gone to Capitol Hill, and Wilson's appearance underscored his commitment to work with the legislative branch. The tariff question had been a perennial source of controversy in America from the beginning of the nineteenth century through this period. Lincoln and the Republicans had erected a high protective tariff, which had stayed high despite the persistent efforts of Democrats and even some Republican presidents to alter the duty schedules. Working closely with the chairman of the House Ways and Means Committee, Oscar W. Underwood, Wilson pushed through a tariff bill that cut rates from over 40 percent to 29 percent and eliminated the tariff for a variety of goods. To compensate for the loss of revenue, the administration and Congress approved an income tax.

In his dealings with the Senate, Wilson faced stiff opposition and a massive public lobbying effort directed against the bill. In another dramatic move, the president openly attacked the lobbyists for interfering with the congressional debates, and warned that the people, unlike the powerful interests, have no lobby in Washington and were "voiceless in such matters." When several Republicans attempted to embarrass the president by calling for an investigation of his charges, the tactic backfired. The investigation clearly showed that the sugar lobby, especially, was a well-heeled force willing to use its considerable influence to thwart reform. In any case, the battle for a new tariff bill, which had so stymied presidents before, showed Wilson at his progressive best. He was indeed the prime minister he had envisioned. As he wrote one recalcitrant senator from Louisiana, J. R. Thornton, "No party can ever for any length of time control the Government or serve the people which can not command the allegiance of its own minority." Wilson's principal biographer, Arthur S. Link, has concluded that "by virtue of this victory Wilson's dominance in the Democratic party was firmly established." But the tariff victory was just the beginning.[3]

Wilson's second major triumph came in a cause he himself understood only in the vaguest sense. For some time, the Senate had debated various proposals to reestablish a national banking structure. The panic of 1907 had shown many people some of the problems associated with immobile reserves and an inelastic money supply. The banking interests, through the good offices of Senator Nelson W. Aldrich, pushed for one central bank with fifteen regional branches and a capital reserve of at least $100 million. The branches would be controlled by the member banks, and the branches would elect thirty of the thirty-nine directors of the central board. It was clearly a national bank of the United States, run by and for the banking community.

But different views were emerging on the issue. In 1912, the House Banking Committee, chaired by Carter Glass of Virginia, supported a more decentralized system, and Secretary of State William Jennings Bryan pushed for government control over the whole enterprise, especially over the issuing of currency. The great populist sentiments rose up again to challenge the powerful banking interests, and critics from the western states especially seemed to echo the old Jeffersonian fears about Hamilton's First Bank of the United States. Wilson himself cared little about the proposal and frankly admitted that he was not very knowledgeable about banking in general. But he was concerned about the effect that dispute would have on his party and on his ability to lead the nation. To make matters more difficult, his own secretary of treasury, William McAdoo, proposed another alternative—the establishment of a banking system under his department's control.[4]

Wilson was at first sympathetic to Glass's proposal but, after discussions with progressive spokesman Louis D. Brandeis, he agreed that the government must control in some way the banking system. On June 23, the president once again appeared before Congress and presented his case. He stressed public control as a basic principle, but urged a common approach in working out the details. However, the populist elements in his own party, especially those in the South, demanded a more radical guarantee; they insisted on a prohibition against interlocking arrangements among banks, and strong governmental control over the currency supply.

In response, Wilson pledged himself to the interlocking directorate amendment and the discounting of short-term agriculture paper, while Bryan pushed the agrarian Democrats to support the modified Glass bill. The result was impressive—the Democratic caucus voted to accept the proposal by 116 to 9. After some difficult weeks in the Senate, Wilson's support tipped the scales and the Federal Reserve Act was approved. The bill represented one of the major legislative accomplishments of Wilson's early years, and its central structure is still a part of American life. The final law provided for considerable private control, but also gave the nation some currency elasticity and loosened the concentration of credit reserves centered in New York City. But, as the Great Depression of the 1930s would show, banking and stock exchange practices were dangerously manipulative, overly speculative, and deleterious even to the most ardent free market advocate. Within the perspective of the progressive period, however, Wilson had reasonably protected the public interest and had added another triumph to his increasingly impressive record.

In the early years of the first term, though, Wilson retained many of his conservative views about the limited role of government in American life. He wavered at first on whether to exclude labor unions from the antitrust laws, although he finally agreed to honor the Democratic party's commitment on the issue in its platform. However, farmers were less fortunate: Wilson refused to approve a special measure to grant rural credits to hard-pressed agricultural areas. And as for women's suffrage, an unsympathetic Wilson stood above the fracas, hoping the bill would die in Congress, which it did.

Wilson did support the Seamen's bill, which gave U.S. sailors more contractual rights in dealing with shipping companies and which mandated improved safety regulations. The most glaring violation of Wilson's progressive record, however, came in the field of civil rights for black Americans. Wilson opposed the appointment of a National Race Commission, watched as his postmaster general suggested resegregating federal agencies, and allowed blacks to be fired in that department. Wilson himself wrote that he approved of "the segregation that is being attempted in several of the departments."

Under pressure from Brandeis and his progressive allies, Wilson went on to consider the question of unfair trade practices—a matter of considerable importance within the business community, especially the U.S. Chamber of Commerce. Brandeis and his supporters in Congress, pushed through legislation to establish an independent regulatory agency, and Wilson, for reasons of his own, approved the legislation. His appointees to the agency were rather weak choices, however, and even Brandeis was to observe, "It was a stupid administration."

By late 1913 and into the winter and later the spring of 1914, a major recession swept through Europe and reached the United States as well. Unemployment increased, production dropped, and the president, under attack for his reform policies, began a concerted campaign to court business support. The Justice Department advised corporations on what combining arrangements or mergers would be acceptable, and the president handed over virtual control of the Federal Reserve Bank to the banking interests and business oriented appointees.

By late 1914, Wilson was announcing the end of the New Freedom reform agenda, and the progressives were wondering if he was indeed committed to their long-standing causes. One astute progressive, Herbert Croly of the *New Republic*, bitterly concluded that Wilson had "misconceived the meaning and the task of the American progressive." He found the president a "dangerous and unsound thinker on contemporary political and social problems. He deceives himself with these phrases, but he should not be allowed to deceive progressive popular opinion."[5] Actually Woodrow Wilson was a conservative man who adopted portions of the progressive agenda that aimed at fair play, honest business practices, and fair competition at home and abroad. He did not see his role as a social reformer or a radical activist.

His legislative skills, however, were greater than any president before him; his philosophy of party leadership was well thought out and highly successful. Wilson was above all a persistent and articulate advocate of his positions and a refreshing change in the seemingly leaderless Democratic party. By the end of his first term, he would sharply veer to the left, seeking to capture the advanced wing of the progressive movement in time for reelection and would in the process once again establish an incredible record of leadership. But after the first burst of domestic reform, he turned his attention to foreign affairs—first to Latin America and then to the unfolding of the Great War in Europe.

MARINE DIPLOMACY

Like most of his Republican predecessors, Woodrow Wilson was, at first, not concerned with foreign affairs. During his academic career, he was rather uninterested in international relations and not sympathetic to European preoccupations with a balance of power. With his first secretary of state, William Jennings Bryan, Wilson adopted a moralistic view of foreign policy in which America had a special obligation to foster Christian progress and democratic movements in other countries. Wilson's and Bryan's sense of commitment was so strong that it often led to crude interference in the affairs of other nations, interference that at times was as blatant as the most imperialist nation. Years later, some historians would argue that Wilson and Bryan used the rhetoric of Protestantism and democracy as a smoke screen behind which they promoted American power and safeguarded American corporate interests abroad. While the reforming spirit may have been used by others at that time and surely later in such ways, Wilson and Bryan were Protestant preachers on the world stage, and they seemed to have been especially influenced by the notions of stewardship and public service.

In keeping with his characteristic concerns about international fair play, Bryan was instrumental in 1913 in getting the United States government to withdraw from the Six Power Consortium, which was created to float a $125 million loan to the Chinese regime. Wilson maintained that the United States "ought to help China in some better way." The American government insisted that the loan agreement was a threat to the independence of China, and by the spring had pulled out of the arrangement, thus leaving China more at the mercy of European imperialist powers and the overreaching ambitions of the Japanese.

However, while the president and the secretary of state were sincerely solicitous of Chinese interests, they were less sympathetic to Japanese sensitivities. In California, strong pressure arose to prohibit Japanese ownership of land in that state. The Japanese government felt that such a move was another calculated humiliation of its nationals and of its proud heritage. Instead of insisting that California back off its jingoistic policy, Wilson actually encouraged state leaders to find a solution that would offend that foreign nation "as little as possible," while he explained that he still concurred in their general objectives. As might be expected, the California legislature moved ahead with its discriminatory legislation.

On April 19, 1913, Wilson decided to ask the state's citizens to exclude Japanese from owning land in some way that would not embarrass the federal government, and he sent Bryan off to the state to reformulate its policies and work out some agreement. The secretary was not successful, and the administration then faced an angry Japanese government. Meanwhile, American military leaders became worried about the vulnerability of the Philippines to a possible Japanese attack if matters grew worse, and Wilson belatedly tried to decrease tensions between the two nations. Prolonged negotiations went on, which in the end led to no real settlement. By then, the Japanese had entered the Great War, as the First World War was eventually called, and had pushed the Germans out of Shantung Province in China, moving to consolidate their interests in Manchuria. Bryan insisted again on a reaffirmation of China's rights and stressed the treaty ties between China and the United States, thus seeking successfully to curtail Japanese advances somewhat and helping to foster a history of hostilities that led eventually to Pearl Harbor.[6]

Much more than in European affairs, Wilson gave Bryan a free hand in Latin America, and the secretary of state negotiated in 1913 and 1914 a series of thirty treaties to underscore his approach of formal conciliation processes to solve disputes. Even Britain, Italy, and France signed such documents, and Bryan regarded those agreements as the major achievement of his long public career. Theodore Roosevelt denounced the whole approach as absurd, but Bryan caught the public imagination in his quixotic search for a better world.[7]

Still, the main legacy of the Wilson years in Latin America, especially in the Caribbean, was one of extensive intrusion, involvement, and military control. In 1909, the secretary of state under Taft, Philander C. Knox, had encouraged the establishment of a conservative government in Nicaragua underwritten by American bankers. The new government there pressed on the American administration an option for a canal route through its nation's isthmus for three million dollars. The Senate Democrats defeated the proposed canal treaty, and by the time Wilson came in, the Nicaraguans wanted to renegotiate the failed treaty. American business interests pushed for a draft that would allow for a canal route and also include a provision that allowed the United States to intervene in Nicaragua. Surprisingly, Bryan concurred in the draft, but again Senate Democrats refused to compromise on the intervention principle. It was finally eliminated, although intervention became the U.S. practice in that nation's affair and left a bitter legacy that helped to foster the Sandinista Marxist regime that came to power in the late 1970s. In 1912, a revolt against the conservative government was put down with the aid of 2,700 American marines, and U.S. forces stayed in that country until 1925.[8]

Some of that same philosophy guided the Wilson administration's approach toward the Dominican Republic. Unfortunately, Bryan had sent James M. Sullivan as minister to that country. Sullivan had used his good offices to further the interests of some banking friends, and in the process interfered in that nation's domestic politics. Wilson finally relieved Sullivan and sought to work with the Dominican Republic's leaders to restore stability in the region. After a brief respite, fighting ensued, and Wilson sent in American marines; by 1916, the United States was essentially running that nation also.

Across the border in Haiti, the same set of events seemed to be occurring. Repeated instability in that nation led to the sending of U.S. troops, but unlike the Dominican Republic situation, the Haitian soldiers rose up against the invasion. By September 1915, Haiti became a protectorate of the United States—a step forward in Bryan's drama of putting all of the Central American republics under U.S. aegis.

Historian Arthur S. Link has generously insisted that the United States with all its heavy-handedness was still guided by a general Christian conviction of the need to help the Caribbean countries, whether they wanted to be helped or not. He concluded that Bryan honestly did try to protect the rights and interests of those foreign nations. In Cuba, for example, Bryan told the government there not to sign a loan agreement with Wall Street firms because it was not in that nation's interest. In other instances, Bryan stopped the Nicaraguan government from negotiating a loan that would have given unfair advantages to American bankers. When the Haitian government decided to give unwarranted concessions to American investors to win U.S. favors, Bryan bluntly disagreed and insisted that the American government was willing to protect Haiti from "injustice or exploitation at the hands of Americans." Bryan later went on to try to smooth over bad relations with Colombia, which went back to Theodore Roosevelt's grabbing of the Canal Zone region in 1903. Wilson and his secretary of state negotiated a treaty that constituted an apology for Roosevelt's action, and as has been noted, the former president was furious, and his friends prevented ratification in the Senate. In 1921, the Senate approved a treaty that gave Colombia $25 million, but no apology.[9]

MEXICAN EMBROGLIO

The most serious of Wilson's early foreign policy mishaps was his misguided, but probably sincere, attempt to impose his views of what the Mexican revolution should be on that divided nation. The long history of Mexico has been scarred by foreign conquests, domestic exploitation, and the maldistribution of even the most basic necessities. Wilson and Bryan were in sympathy with the aims of the revolution, but their good intentions took little notice of the uncertain realities of that alien way of life and of the differing ways the Mexicans solved their own problems.

By the time Wilson took office, the reform regime of Francisco Madero had been overthrown, and he was murdered by one of his own generals, Victoriano Huerta. Despite considerable pressure from American financial interests to recognize the new regime, Wilson and Bryan once again had a moral litmus test, which had to be satisfied. They believed that since the constitutional government had been overthrown, they could not proceed to recognize the military coup d'état. Privately, Wilson concluded to a friend, "I will not recognize a government of butchers." Publicly, he maintained that the United States would not accept the legitimacy of Latin American governments established by fraud and force. While he was reaching for justification for his actions, Wilson also became aware of the rise of anti-Huerta forces in the northern states of Coahula and Chihuahua led by Venustiano Carranza, the governor of the latter region.

As the administration watched carefully, major corporate interests in the United States that had a stake in Mexico pushed for a compromise. They urged the State Department to recognize Huerta, and insisted that he was pledged to call an election before late October 1913. Wilson agreed and sought to effect a compromise government in Mexico. But almost from the beginning, Wilson's poorly conceived request went unheeded. Huerta saw Wilson's offer as another example of Yanqui interference, and Wilson's agent, John Lind, gave the impression of trying to bribe the Mexican government. After these unsatisfactory developments, Wilson was assured that Huerta would not be a candidate for president in the upcoming election. Just as that matter was settled, Huerta turned around and arrested 110 members of the Chamber of Deputies, thus breaking off the last connection he had with his nation's constitutional government. To Wilson's chagrin, the new British minister to Mexico, Sir Lionel Carden, backed Huerta's precipitous actions.

Wilson took the developments in Mexico as a personal affront, and he tried to get other governments to withhold recognition of the regime. As Bryan noted, Wilson now came to see that it was "his immediate duty to require Huerta's retirement from the Mexican government and was willing to use any means necessary to do so." From November 1913 to April of the following year, the president made the Mexican question his main preoccupation. Wilson received, at first, support from Germany for his policy, but the British government proved to be the main stumbling block with its concern over Mexican oil imports. For better or worse, Wilson described his own motives—he would "teach the South American republics to elect good men." As the insurgent forces grew stronger against Huerta, Wilson became bolder. He thought about asking Congress to declare war against Mexico and wanted to blockade the ports, shut out European influence, and perhaps even send troops to the northern states in Mexico. Wilson's confidant, Colonel Edward M. House, observed in his diary, that the president realized the problems he would have with some of the European powers if he moved, but "he seems ready to throw our gauntlet into the arena and declare all hands must be kept off excepting our own."

While the anti-Huerta forces were making headway, their leader Carranza warned that he too did not want American troops or advice. Instead, his side needed recognition of its belligerent status and the right to transport arms from the United States. Wilson desperately wanted Huerta out, but he remained reluctant to use American troops in the civil war. As usual, destiny took a hand, and on April, the Mexicans arrested the crew and paymaster of an American ship. The Mexicans quickly apologized, but Wilson used the incident to charge that American honor had been violated. The Huerta government had to salute the American flag as a part of its penance, even though the United States refused to recognize that regime as the legitimate government of that nation.

Wilson went before Congress to stoke the fires of war, and there was talk of occupying Vera Cruz. The president asked for congressional authority to employ the armed forces. While the legislative branch was debating the proposal, the United States learned that a German ship carrying ammunition for the Huerta regime was heading for Vera Cruz. Wilson promptly ordered the navy to occupy the port city, and by April 22, the United States controlled Vera Cruz.

Meanwhile, the Senate refused to approve a resolution giving the executive the power to send troops anywhere in Mexico to protect U.S. lives and property. Protests from left-wing and pacifist groups began to mount, and Wilson's actions seemed out of proportion to his stated objectives. Was the United States really going to war to get an apology from a government it did not recognize—or was it going to war to underscore Wilson's insistence that Huerta was to be removed? Fortunately for the administration, Argentina, Brazil, and Chile offered to mediate the dispute. Wilson agreed with Bryan's decision to accept that offer, but once again he insisted Huerta must leave office.

In Mexico, Carranza refused to accept the mediation offer, and he pushed for a major social revolution in his homeland. In July, Huerta finally stepped down and a month later, Carranza was in power. Soon his forces were split, and a dissident faction, led by Pancho Villa, an admirer of the Americans, fought the new government. From then on, the administration's control over events disintegrated even further. By late 1914, Theodore Roosevelt was charging Wilson with having created the situation in Mexico in the first place, a mess that could only be cleaned up, in his opinion, by the use of American forces. The Catholic Church in the United States, anxious about its counterpart church's interests in Mexico, pushed through the American hierarchy and some groups of influential laypersons expressions of support for American intervention.

The president stalled, trying to get the two sides to stop fighting. At the same time, Wilson was faced with the presence elsewhere of German submarines threatening shipping, and he wanted no war now in Mexico. The administration recognized Carranza's government, bowing to the inevitable. Catholic leaders blasted Wilson's decision, and for a while the president actually thought of publicly attacking the church, but finally abandoned his plan.

Villa, in turn, decided to begin a campaign of terror against U.S. interests in Mexico, hoping to point up the weaknesses of the Carranza regime and to foster a split between that government and the Americans. Wilson responded by getting the Mexican government to approve the U.S. sending the military against Villa, including the right to cross the border in hot pursuit. Led by General John J. Pershing, the Americans pursued Villa's bands some three hundred miles into Mexico. Carranza was soon faced with an uproar about foreign troops being allowed to roam the countryside, and he demanded that the U.S. forces leave. Villa continued his attacks, and Wilson was under pressure to occupy the northern states of Mexico in order to do what the Carranza regime could not do, protect U.S. citizens and the state of Texas.

Events seemed to spin out of the president's control once again. The American military prepared for an invasion of Mexico, and Wilson called up one hundred thousand National Guardsmen and sent more warships toward the Mexican coastlines. Carranza insisted that U.S. troops would only be allowed to go directly north on their exit home, and spontaneous clashes between Mexican and American forces broke out as tensions increased markedly. Wilson prepared an account of the history of these events to be delivered to Congress as a spur to requesting congressional authorization to use armed force. Yet the president insisted on controlling the military's plans, and personally opposed any war efforts, especially with the ominous events in Europe. Carranza, faced with his own internal problems and the shakiness of his regime, was equally wary. Once again, U.S. pacifist groups stirred up the supporters of progressivism against war, and they had a decisive impact on public opinion and on Wilson as well. Finally, the two governments agreed to the creation of a special commission to investigate their problems and outstanding controversies. The commission was unable to secure Carranza's final consent to its recommendations and simply concluded its work in January 1917.

Wilson, faced with a greater challenge in Europe, withdrew U.S. forces from Mexico. Despite his moralistic insistence on supporting the aspirations of the Mexican people and his genuine sympathy for the revolution, Wilson emerged in many eyes as an enemy of Mexico. However, he had courageously resisted pressures to recognize Huerta and remained true to his and Bryan's view of the progress of democratic institutions. But in the process, Wilson gave signs of the inflexibility and ineptitude that would at times characterize his dealings on a larger and more important stage.[10]

TOO PROUD TO FIGHT

Since the Washington administration, the United States had insisted on freedom of the seas, and its presidents had linked national honor and esteem with the ability to trade without condition even at times of war in Europe. The Democratic Republicans, especially Jefferson and Madison, led the nation through a painful embargo and a devastating war to reassert U.S. commitments to free ships and free trade. Now a century later, another president was to come to grips with the same issue, and in the process propel the United States, however reluctantly, into the ranks of the world powers.

The war at first made no sense: an Austrian archduke and his wife assassinated and then a series of ultimata and misjudgments occurred, which led to a terrible stalemated war. To Americans, it seemed like a typical European war—a continuing reminder of the benefits that the Atlantic Ocean brought with its isolation. Wilson responded by affirming American neutrality and avoiding the heavy-handedness that characterized his attempts to implant his kind of democracy in alien lands.

Both the British and the Germans skillfully employed propaganda efforts to woo the American public, but Wilson reminded his fellow patriots that the United States must be neutral in thought as well as in deed. Most Americans, like their president, probably leaned toward the Allies, but few wanted war. On August 9, 1914, the president issued his neutrality proclamation to general praise at home.

But soon the administration was faced with a quandary about the implications of neutrality. In August 1914, the French government sought a $100 million loan from J. P. Morgan and Co. The administration feared that a denial of the loan would lead foreign nations to demand large amounts of gold as payment for obligations already incurred. But Bryan and Wilson held firm—a loan would be a violation of true neutrality. However, in reality, such a policy did work to the practical disadvantage of the Allies, the main borrowers and customers of American goods before the war.

By early 1915, the United States found itself at loggerheads with the British and its great navy over the issue of the traditional freedom of the seas. The British sought to cut off basic supplies to Germany even if those supplies came through neutral ports. Wilson countered with a proposition that, in effect, opposed the British attempt to control goods going through those neutral ports and would have voided the creation of a contraband list. The British ministry refused to give up one of its major weapons in the war, and Wilson did not push them hard on the principle, as the Jeffersonians had a century before. The two governments also disagreed on whether German ships in American ports could be bought by U.S. citizens, since the British feared the establishment of German-controlled front companies.

But during those difficult times, the really important development was the German submarine. In February 1915, the Germans began a counterblockade of the British Isles, with a policy of shooting on sight suspected enemy vessels in that region. To pacify American opinion, the Germans offered to end the blockade of the British if the British would in turn end theirs, and relieve what the German government was insisting was "starvation" in their nation.

For Wilson and his new secretary of state, Robert Lansing, the time was ripe for a special offer to mediate the war. Wilson sent his trusted aide, Colonel House, to Europe to lay the groundwork for a new peace initiative. House seemed to make some progress in England until the sinking of the British liner *Lusitania*, on May 7, 1915. As the Germans proceeded with submarine attacks, Wilson clearly was disturbed. At home, there were demands from Theodore Roosevelt and his allies for a strong response to the German attacks, but the predominant public opinion was still for peace and noninvolvement. The president captured that sentiment in a speech in Philadelphia when he observed, "There is such a thing as a man being too proud to fight."

Wilson found himself buffeted on both sides, however. With support from leaders in the German-American and Irish-American communities, a movement to establish a U.S. embargo was gaining support. But the sinking of the *Lusitania* added to tales of German atrocities and the overall disregard by the barbaric "Hun" of human life and liberty. Then, in a peculiar turn of events, the U.S. Secret Service claimed that it had found a briefcase that contained German propaganda plans targeted at the United States.

After several sinkings and mounting American outrage, the German government gave a written pledge that, in the future, ocean liners would not be attacked without warning. For the president, the German commitment represented a substantial diplomatic victory. On the other side of the conflict, the British, who were aware of growing U.S. opposition to the arms embargo, decided to buy up enough cotton to fix the price at ten cents a pound, so as to prevent southerners from joining with isolationist Midwest representatives in Congress. The secret agreement was officially unknown to Wilson and Lansing, according to Arthur Link. It was a private deal between the British government and several American parties, including W. P. G. Harding of the Federal Reserve Board, to get around the neutrality policy and stabilize cotton prices.

The administration was aware of a public push by the Allies to float a major loan to support the purchase of arms in the United States. In September 1915, the administration reversed itself, abandoned the policy of former Secretary of State William Jennings Bryan, and allowed American lenders to underwrite, in effect, part of the Allied war effort. To the Germans, who lacked the British domination of the seas, the movement of supplies and arms from the United States to Europe clearly benefited the Allies. And the decision to lend the French and British substantial funds turned the United States into a very unneutral neutral.

Faced with the submarine incidents in 1915 and evidence of German diplomatic intrigue, Wilson had to come to grips with calls for more military preparedness. Early in 1914, he had laughed off initial calls for more aggressive responses, and the preparedness campaign was led by major Republican politicians and their associates in influential financial and industrial circles. In July 1915, a wary Wilson asked Secretary of War Lindley Garrison and Secretary of the Navy Josephus Daniels to look at the overall situation and review U.S. military security. As might be expected, the military proposed a major buildup of U.S. naval strength, substantial increases in the regular army, and the introduction of a new Continental army in place of the National Guard. But the president himself had turned toward a more aggressive posture, partially because of the sinking of the *Lusitania* and probably out of a realization that his diplomatic efforts were unlikely to be fruitful. His old progressive coalition, however, bitterly opposed the shift, and major segments of labor and farmer groups in the Midwest joined with traditional left-wing and pacifist organizations to demand a policy of real neutrality and nonintervention. Wilson, preoccupied with his courtship and remarriage at the time, at first simply overlooked the growing opposition.[11]

Sensing finally the battle he was facing, Wilson took the issue to the people, and in early 1916, he traveled across the country, pleading for a stronger defense and citing the explosive situation. But the pacifist spirit was strong, and while Wilson was well received, Congress did not feel any shift of public opinion. Wilson was forced to compromise on the National Guard, dropping the idea of a Continental army and trimming back his recommendations. In the process of capitulation, his secretary of war resigned. In the end, though, Wilson was able to double the regular army to over 11,000 officers and over 200,000 men, set up volunteer summer training camps, integrate the National Guard eventually into the federal establishment, and increase its strength within five years to 17,000 officers and 440,000 men. In the Senate, a bill for a large navy prevailed over the more modest House version, and construction was authorized for a substantial increase in the number of battleships, cruisers, and especially destroyers and new submarines. The long-range objective, in Wilson's mind, was not simply preparedness but eventual parity with the British navy. Congress then approved the establishment of a U.S. shipping board, which could spend up to $50 million on the development of a merchant marine service, which could be attached to the navy.

Wilson accepted preparedness and made it a part of his own program, but his heart in the 1915–16 period still lay in the desire for a diplomatic settlement in which he hoped to play the role of world peacemaker. Colonel House explained to the French that if it appeared the Allies were losing, the United States would intervene on their side, but Wilson and Lansing were in fact working in a very different direction as they dealt with the issue of armed ships. To avoid confrontations between armed ships and German submarines, Wilson and Lansing sought to disarm the ships. The Germans were delighted at first, but Lansing backpedaled and observed that he could not insist on having the Allies accept the proposed change.

In Congress, Wilson's opponents expressed dismay at the president's alleged ineptitude. Even some of his supporters wondered if Wilson was moving the nation inadvertently toward war. The president defensively argued that he had worked for peace more than anyone, but he still had to put down a revolt among his own usual supporters in the Congress on the issue. Now the president found himself the recipient of Republican support as anti-German sentiment mounted.

Would Wilson insist that the Germans rescind their orders authorizing attacks against armed merchantmen? Once again the president refused to take that step. But at the urgings of his advisors, the president demanded an end to German attacks on shipping and threatened to break off diplomatic relations if that did not occur. In April 1916, Wilson went before Congress and repeated his decision. Surprisingly, the German emperor responded by ending submarine activity in the war zone, and announcing that his nation's submarines would stop and search merchant vessels before attacking.

The crisis passed, and American scrutiny focused instead on British violations of freedom of the seas and its brutal treatment of the Irish in the 1916 rebellion. Wilson had grown disgusted with the British opposition to his mediation plan, and when the British published a "blacklist" of American and Latin American companies with which their citizens could not do business, the president bitterly but privately characterized the English leaders as "poor boobs." By the fall of 1916, the United States ambassador to Great Britain, Walter H. Page, recorded with obvious dismay that Wilson "said to me that when the war began he and all the men he met were in hearty sympathy with the Allies; but that now the sentiment toward England had greatly changed. He saw no one who was not vexed and irritated at the arbitrary English course."[12]

THE ELECTION OF 1916

Wilson was a smart enough politician to recognize that the Democratic party was not the majority party going into the 1916 campaign. Theodore Roosevelt had come back to the Republican fold, and major elements of the progressive and pacifist groups had been offended by the president's conversion to preparedness. Bryan was making noises about opposing Wilson's renomination in order, as he put it, to protect the nation at peace.

Then in early 1916, Wilson made a brilliant strategic swing to the left and began to spearhead a new cycle of reforms. In the past, the president had been the major voice of conservative progressivism, of a strategy to restore fair play and honest competition in the marketplace instead of advancing the welfare state. In the process, Wilson had put on a dazzling display of presidential leadership for rather limited objectives.

In January 1916, Wilson nominated Louis D. Brandeis for the Supreme Court—a controversial progressive lawyer and the first Jewish nominee. Senator Robert LaFollette, the symbol of Wisconsin progressivism, praised the nomination, and the president, facing intense opposition, pushed the choice through the Senate after a very tough battle. Meanwhile, Wilson completely reversed himself on extending rural credits to depressed farming areas. For two years, he had held up the proposal, but by 1916, he criticized the bill as too modest and supported a more comprehensive proposal than even the sponsors put forth.

Wilson turned his attention to workmen's compensation and put pressure on Congress to pass the Kern-McGillicuddy bill extending benefits in that area. To that achievement, he added the Keating-Owen child labor law, a proposal that curtailed employment of the young and that had been buried in the Senate. The president went on to reaffirm his anti-imperialist intentions by pushing for autonomy for the Philippines. And for business, he supported a tariff commission and antidumping legislation, and urged American corporations to combine in the export trade. For all practical purposes, the old Democratic coalition of urban machines and southern conservatives had taken over the Progressive party's reform platform of 1912.

As for the Republicans, they were faced with a growing resurgence of Midwest isolationist support and a repudiation of TR's bellicose foreign policy. Roosevelt sought the nomination again and urged his Progressive party followers to disband their third party, which many did. But the GOP wanted victory, and it turned to Associate Justice Charles Evans Hughes, a well-regarded but quite independent former governor of New York with a strong record of progressive reform.

Wilson controlled his party's machinery, and at the St. Louis convention he dictated the theme—"Americanism." Flags draped the gathering, and the platform supported peace, preparedness, progressivism, and a League of Nations. Democratic orators fell all over each other to praise the president's refusal to lead the nation to war. The party's publicity directors coined a simple, but effective, slogan for Wilson, "He kept us out of war." Wilson himself never used that statement, but he did not have to. The party sent its partisans out with the message: the most effective was, of course, William Jennings Bryan who brought his pacifist gospel to great gatherings in the Midwest and the Far West.

Hughes found that he was linked up with TR's bellicose statements, and try as he might, he could not separate his views from the threats of the old Bull Moose warrior. Hughes also offended the important progressive Republican governor Hiram Johnson of California, and was supported too openly by German-American groups and their language press. Also, in the middle of the campaign, Wilson confronted a railroad strike, which he was unable to settle by negotiation. The president then went to Congress asking for new authority to end the strike and, in the process, announcing that he supported the union's demand for an eight-hour day. Hughes at first seemed to have benefited from Wilson's actions, but in the long run, the president's leadership solidified his position with labor and the social work oriented constituencies. Now it was Woodrow Wilson, and not Theodore Roosevelt, who was becoming the great progressive symbol and a proven leader who had refused the path to war in order to concentrate on domestic reforms.

The election was incredibly close; Wilson went to sleep believing that he had lost. But the West surprisingly went Democratic, most importantly, the state of California. Wilson received 9,129,606 votes to Hughes's 8,538,221, and an electoral college victory of 277 to 254. The president had carried the solid South, Maryland, Kentucky, Missouri, Oklahoma, New Hampshire, Ohio, Kansas, Nebraska, North Dakota, Montana, Wyoming, Colorado, New Mexico, Arizona, Utah, Nevada, Idaho, Washington, and California. Even the German-American vote went to Wilson in Maryland, Ohio, and parts of Wisconsin; the Democrats, though, lost their traditional allies, the Catholic Irish-Americans, probably because of Wilson's refusal to endorse the Easter Rebellion in Ireland and his support of the anticlerical Mexican revolution. However, the appeal of peace and reform had swept beyond the expected boundaries. The Socialist party strength dropped by nearly a half—most of those defections probably going to Wilson. The president also did well with women voters, even in certain areas among Republican women, probably because of their fear of war. In Congress, the Democrats still controlled the Senate, although by a margin of eight, and the House was divided with 213 Democrats, 217 Republicans, 2 Progressives, 1 Prohibitionist, 1 Socialist, and 1 Independent. Wilson biographer Arthur Link has concluded that it was a victory of the South and the West, of the farmers, small business people, and labor elements over the large industrial, transportation, and commercial interests. Wilson won on a peace and reform pledge; yet within a year, he would recommend war and then give up the salutary exercises of reform.[13]

A WORLD MADE SAFE FOR DEMOCRACY

In Europe, the terrible slaughter continued, and each side mounted frightening offensives to bring victory, but victory did not come. The British increased their economic blockade on the seas, and earned more animosity from American shipping interests. The winter of 1916–17 saw increasing estrangement of the two English-speaking democracies. At the same time, the German government debated whether to end its self-imposed ban and move toward unrestricted submarine warfare. Wilson maintained that the American people wanted neutrality, regardless of what happened to their rights on the open sea. "I do not believe the American people would wish to go to war no matter how many Americans were lost at sea," he explained to Colonel House and Vance McCormick. And he was undoubtedly correct in his judgment of public opinion.[14]

Wilson had decided after the election to keep faith with his campaign pledge, and he insisted on sending House again to Europe to press for peace. The colonel was concerned: what if the Allies refused the offer and the United States thus moved as a consequence closer to Germany? Would France and Britain declare war on America? Wilson was clear: he would then ask the United States to go to war against them. Then, in brilliant analytical fashion, the president sat down and wrote out his views of the war. He found the causes of the war were confused, and he argued that that confusion left the positions of the neutral nations intolerable.

As the war continued, the president considered halting American bank loans to the Allied nations. Indeed, a majority of the members of the Federal Reserve Board had grown worried that the American economy was becoming too dependent on Allied spending. In the midst of these concerns, the German government announced its willingness to end the war, and Wilson followed that announcement with a public peace message. Unfortunately, it was not clear to the Americans that the German government's terms included keeping or even expanding into the important strategic areas Germany had conquered or had designs on. In addition, the German military had decided to push for a new submarine offensive in the hope of final victory, seeing this as its last chance to win a decisive and favorable end. The Allied position hardened, and the Allies informed Wilson that they intended to destroy German attempts at hegemony in Europe and would then demand reparations from the Central Powers.

At the turn of the year, Wilson moved the United States publicly to a position from which he hoped he could influence the peace. He urged a "Peace without Victory," and a "peace among equals," and stressed self-determination for all nations, disarmament, and freedom of the seas. The president claimed to speak for the "silent mass of mankind" fed up with death and ruination. But events changed his ambitions when the German government finally announced that its submarines would sink without warning any ship in a war zone running from Great Britain down the coastline toward the eastern Mediterranean. The Germans had assumed that they could defeat Great Britain before the United States could mobilize its resources and armies on the Allied side. It was a critical error, one that led the United States into war and tipped the scales against the Central Powers.

Wilson, however, still refused to abandon his role as mediator, fearing that America's entrance into the war would mean the end of "white" civilization as the world knew it. The president broke off relations with Germany, but chose not to advocate war. He did not ask Congress for additional funds or push any more preparedness plans, fearing it would give the Germans cause for more belligerence, and when, on February 23, several members of his own cabinet insisted that the administration protect ocean-bound commerce, the president was sharply critical. Wilson faced two major problems. The Senate Republicans were demanding that he call the new Congress into special session in order to put pressure on the executive for more bellicose action. Then his ambassador to Great Britain, Walter Page, informed him that the German foreign secretary, Arthur Zimmermann, had sent a message to the German minister in Mexico that had been intercepted. The message pledged that if the United States and Germany went to war, the imperial government would be willing to form an alliance with Mexico. If the Mexicans went to war against the Americans, the Germans would guarantee that the "lost" territories of Texas, New Mexico, and Arizona would be returned.

To complicate matters, the Russians in February/March 1917 overthrew the czar and established briefly a Western-style parliamentary government, thus reinforcing the idea that the forces of democracy were grouped on one side opposing the Central Powers' militarism and despotism. By mid-March, Wilson was deeply troubled by the choice before him. He stayed in the White House and listened as the awesome debate mounted. It was clear that the Allies were in bad shape, and that the submarine campaign had severely cut into Allied and neutral shipping.

In late March, the president authorized conversations with the British admiralty about war operations and joint planning, and he called up units of the National Guard. At a critical meeting with his advisors, all of the major cabinet secretaries pressed for war. Wilson prepared to call Congress together for a declaration of war, while he confided to a friend that war would overturn the world as they knew it. One newspaperman recorded that Wilson had solemnly observed that once he led the people into war "they'll forget there even was such a thing as tolerance. To fight you must be brutal and ruthless, and the spirit of ruthless brutality will enter into the very fiber of our national life, infecting Congress, the courts, the policeman on the beat, the man in the street. . . . He thought the Constitution would not survive it; that free speech and the right to assembly would go. He said a nation couldn't put its strength into a war and keep its head level; it had never been done." He seemed to reach out desperately for an alternative.

In the end, Wilson was not, as his critics later charged, carried away by his own rhetoric or moved by blind and passionate idealism. Nor did he fear that U.S. corporate interests were being significantly threatened. To the progressives and the pacifists, the United States went into war to save the $2 billion the bankers had lent the Allied governments. Later after the war, critics would charge that the American economy had been tied to those banks and the munitions makers, and that they and the propaganda agents in foreign governments had led the nation into a war no one wanted. Still others were to say that the American people opposed German power and stayed out of the war only as long as it was clear that Germany would be defeated by the Allies. When it became obvious that that was not going to happen, the United States entered the war to protect the democratic West.

Perhaps all these factors played a role in American intervention. But central to the United States going to war was Woodrow Wilson, his judgment, his sympathies, his sense of history. Despite his pleas for strict neutrality of deed and thought, he personally favored the Allies. He was by training and by inclination an Anglophile, who was deeply concerned about the brutal German invasion of Belgium and the killings at sea. He surely was influenced by evidence of German intrigue against U.S. interests. But he had initially hoped that the combatants would enter into a brokered settlement, and he moved toward an even stricter posture of neutrality. It was the Germans who pushed him over the line—unrestricted submarine warfare confirmed his worst suspicions about their power and intentions, and left the president with the impossible policy of doing nothing while his own citizens were likely to be killed on the seas.

On the evening of April 2, 1917, Woodrow Wilson went before Congress and pronounced that there was no alternative but war. And to explain this step, he reached for a higher moral plane. The German government was a foe of freedom-loving peoples. "The world must be made safe for democracy," he explained in a slogan that would echo throughout the nation and the world. In words that would give clear meaning to an ambiguous cause, the president exclaimed

the right is more precious than peace, and we shall fight for the things which we have always carried nearest our hearts,—for democracy, for the rights of those who submit to authority to have a voice in their own Governments, for the rights and liberties of small nations, for a universal dominion of right by such a concert of free peoples as shall bring peace and safety to all nations and make the world itself at last free. To such a task we can dedicate our lives and our fortunes, everything that we are and everything that we have, with the pride of those who know that the day has come when America is privileged to spend her blood and her might for the principles that gave her birth and happiness and the peace which she has treasured. God helping her, she can do no other.

It was a brilliant statement of American idealism in a world seemingly weary with wars of national interest run by limited politicians who stayed in power by sending other people's sons to war. Now Wilson would join them in their common destiny. But the president remained troubled, troubled even at the moment many of his opponents admitted was his finest hour. Legend has it that as he left the Capitol, he spurned the applause wondering quietly how people could cheer a speech that would send so many boys to their deaths. And when he arrived back at the White House, he sat and stared out at the darkness and deeply cried. Quickly, Congress approved the resolution, and the nation mobilized for war—the war to end all wars, the war to make the world safe for democracy.[15]

ON THE WESTERN FRONT

As the United States Congress voted to enter the conflict, the war on the western front was at a stalemate after several years of carnage. The 1914 Battle of the Marne and the resulting "race to the sea" led to the monumental destruction of armies and men on all sides. And a new type of engagement, trench warfare, entered the popular vocabulary—trenches that were sordid, stinking, filthy hovels that became the horrid destiny of the infantry and artillery forces on both sides. In the East, the Russians, who had suffered great casualties in stopping the German Gorlice-Tarnow offensive in 1915 and gained a costly victory in 1916, finally rose up in desperation after much bloodletting and toppled the czarist government in 1917. A Social Democratic government, headed by Alexander Kerensky, pledged to continue the war, but after its disastrous campaign against the Austro-Hungarian and German forces, a determined Bolshevik regime came to power in October. In the midst of the turmoil and the war, traveling across Europe, partially under German auspices, Vladimir Ilyich Lenin and several associates moved toward their destiny. Communism, the diseased ideology of the liberal West, was to be implanted in precapitalist, peasant-dominated Mother Russia.[16]

Several generations of historians and countless other citizens across the globe have struggled then and now with the question of what caused the First World War. It is as if they sensed that it was too gruesome and far reaching to have come about by accident or as a consequence of the killing of the Austrian Archduke Ferdinand and his wife by a Serbian nationalist on June 20, 1914. Authorities on the war still disagree, but in general there are probably four underlying causes that can be identified.

The most important was the development of a web of entangling alliances in the period following the Franco-Prussian War in 1871. As a result of that war, Germany annexed Alsace-Lorraine, and Otto von Bismarck, the Reich chancellor, created a series of alliances in order to isolate France and prevent retaliation from that humiliating loss. In 1879, Bismarck tied Germany to Austria-Hungary, and in 1882, to both Austria-Hungary and Italy. Then in 1887, Bismarck made an agreement with czarist Russia to guarantee (with some exceptions) each other's neutrality if one of them went to war against a third party. Unfortunately, Bismarck was dismissed from office in 1890, and the kaiser did not choose to renew the so-called Reinsurance Treaty after that year. Thus, Russia and France, both fearful of the newly assertive German empire, came together in their own mutual defense pact, or entente, to guard against a German attack on either one of them. Watching Germany's vigorous naval expansion, Great Britain began to be concerned and entered into a pact with its once hated enemy, France. These pacts then created a sense of mutual concern among the great powers of Europe and forced unaligned nations into one orbit or the other.

A second destabilizing factor was the rapid growth of huge national armies and armaments. The success of the Prussian armies made a profound impression throughout Europe, and those developments led to an increase in standing military forces. By 1914, the five major Continental powers had combined forces of about 3.5 million men under arms plus millions of others on reserve. Those mobilized forces led to growing public suspicions about other nations' aggressive intentions, more forceful diplomatic posturings, and a development of powerful general staffs planning for the next war.

A. J. P. Taylor concluded that "the terrible time-table [for the mobilization] of the European General Staffs had far more to do with the actual outbreak of the World War than the deliberate decision of any man or Government."

A third factor that led to the outbreak of war was the rapid rise of imperialism as a way of thinking and as a way of life. The great powers coveted colonies for their cheap materials and markets for manufactured goods over which they could have a monopoly. Economic competition grew into passionate debates over national honor, civilizing missions, and a nation's rightful "place in the sun." The result was an increase in tensions in areas of the world where conflicts between the great powers and their surrogates might break out.

Added to these dynamics was the spread of nationalism among various groups, especially in the Balkans. Nationalist unrest was not new to Europe, of course, but in this period, Russia and Austria-Hungary sought to use these destabilizing aspirations to further their own designs. Also, despite the attempts by the diplomats to contain these fierce ambitions, periodic crises would break out. The most severe was in 1908 when Austria-Hungary announced that she had unilaterally chosen to annex Bosnia and Herzegovina. Under great pressure from Austria-Hungary's ally, Germany, the Russians were forced to accept the annexation. With that humiliation in mind, Russia with its ally Serbia made preparations for war. Conflicts in Morocco and in the Balkans in 1912 further accentuated tensions among the great powers and the size of standing armies grew.

In December 1912, a secret memo of the German general staff predicted that in the coming war with France, it "would be necessary to violate the neutrality of Belgium." By early 1914, the Russians were meeting secretly to plan for action in the straits near Constantinople and laid out plans for a military offensive in the West. In general, the European chiefs of staff expected a short war, one that would favor the first nation to strike. Their model was the German wars of unification; a more appropriate model would have been the long bloody civil war of attrition in the United States. Grant and Sherman would have been better models for military strategists than the European generals Clausewitz or Moltke.

When Archduke Francis Ferdinand, the heir to the Austro-Hungarian or Hapsburg throne, went to the capital of Bosnia, he was aware of the threat of Serbian assassins in that region. Under the alleged instigation of the head of the intelligence division of the Serbian chief of staff, three Bosnian men volunteered to kill the archduke. To the Hapsburgs, the assassinations of the archduke and his wife lent themselves to a reckoning with Serbia and, with the support of Germany, they prepared for a local war. The Austro-Hungarian regime issued a series of ultimata, to nearly all of which the Serbians surprisingly agreed. But the Austrians wanted war and severed diplomatic relations with Serbia as a prelude to military engagement. Concerned about these happenings and preoccupied with the fate of Constantinople and the straits, Russia supported the Serbians. As tensions increased, the British foreign minister, Sir Edward Grey, proposed a peace conference and a mediation of the dispute. To avoid any such mediation, the Austrians declared war on Serbia on July 28 and bombarded Belgrade the next day. Meanwhile, the Russian military had been preparing for war also, and on July 29, it mobilized against the Austrians. Soon France followed Russia and the war began.

Germany's success in the war depended on rapid action, while Russia because of her vast areas and poor transportation needed more time for mobilization. Now the system of entangling alliances fueled the fires of war. Great Britain insisted that the neutrality of Belgium and Luxembourg must be respected, but the Germans needed to defeat France quickly, and the corridor through those small countries was the fastest way to accomplish that objective. This "brutal" invasion of Belgium was used by British leaders who wanted war to defend their empire's interests. British public opinion was treated to detailed statements on "the rape of Belgium" by the Huns. In fact, British foreign policy had been historically committed to protecting the narrow seas across from the channel and to stopping any one nation from gaining hegemony on the Continent. The British had gone to war in the past, partially for these reasons, against Louis XIV and Napoleon I. The Germans protested that "necessity knows no law," and expressed shock that Great Britain would go to war over "a scrap of paper"—its treaty obligations with Belgium. But by August, even Japan and Turkey were in the war, and it had indeed become a worldwide conflagration. In his own way, British Foreign Minister Grey correctly summarized what was happening when he grimly prophesied, "The lamps are going out all over Europe. We shall not see them lit again in our lifetimes."

Europe had known war before, but never with the mechanized barbarity that this total war brought. The casualties were so high that their count even today numbs the mind. The official statements indicate that Russian casualties reached 1.7 million men—the true total, though, is probably double that; Germany lost 1.8 million, surely another underestimation; France, 1.3 million; the United Kingdom, 744,702 and the British empire, 202,000; Austro-Hungary, 1.2 million; Italy, 460,000; Turkey, 325,000 plus many more unaccounted for; and for the late-arriving United States, the count was 115,660 casualties. Probably not since the black plague of the Middle Ages, which killed one out of every three people, had death visited so many households in Europe.

Even more stark are the casualties of the major battles of the war. A few will suffice to give a frightening sense of the carnage. On the eastern front in September 1914, the Austrian chief of staff Conrad von Hotzendorf lost 350,000 of the 900,000 men in his army near the Galicia region. At Tannenberg, the German generals Paul von Hindenberg and Erich Ludendorff in August 1914 defeated Aleksandr Samsonov's Russian armies and took 120,000 prisoners and decimated that fighting force. In September, they defeated the Russian First Army, inflicting 125,000 casualties alone in the Battle of Masurian Lakes.

In the west, the first Battle of Ypres resulted in the loss of 58,000 British officers and enlisted men—the virtual destruction of its regular volunteer army—and led to conscription to fill the new ranks. On the German side, the battle would be called by some "the slaughter of the children," a lament over the demise of so many young men of promise. In May 1915, at the Battle of Ambers Ridge, the French suffered 100,000 casualties and the British lost 27,000 with the military results negligible. In ten days in September, the French lost another 145,000 men, achieving no military objectives at all. By March 1916, the Germans suffered the loss of 81,000 and the French 89,000 at the Battle of Verdun. After ten months, the total on both sides reached an incredible 700,000 killed and wounded. After four months at the Battle of the Somme even more carnage resulted—415,000 British empire casualties, 195,000 French casualties, and German losses at least equal to the total of the Allied nations they opposed.

In the Balkans, the Serbian army, with thousands of old men, women, and children following, retreated through the mountain snows. Only one-quarter of the 400,000 people survived the march. After eighteen months of war, Serbia had lost over one-sixth of its total population. In June 1916, the Russian general Aleksey Brusilov attacked the Austrians in Galicia, taking 400,000 prisoners. Later in his last desperate offenses, Ludendorff's plans for victory cost the Germans over 350,000 men. And on it continued—staggering casualties for literally yards of disputed territory, incalculable civilian losses, new weapons of frightening efficiency, and the early introduction of gas warfare. It was in the midst of this expensive stalemate, this hopeless vision of death, destruction, and trench warfare, that the Yanks came to save the Old World from itself and guarantee a bright future that promised the triumph of democracy and decency.

Initially, the chiefs of the general staffs of the German and Austro-Hungarian armies had decided to attack France quickly and then turn their forces toward Russia. But in the early weeks of the war, Russian stubbornness and bravery and a series of major miscalculations by the German military leadership prevented a quick triumph and led to an eventual deadlock. After the Russians finally signed a humiliating peace treaty, the Central Powers planned to concentrate their forces and effect a major breakthrough in the west, one that would force the remaining Allies also to sue for an unfavorable peace. When the United States entered the war in April 1917, that last great offensive was not yet in the offing. By 1918, the Americans had somewhat supplemented the Allies' strength and provided supplies and munitions for their desperate war effort. Suddenly when the Ludendorff offensives in 1918 failed, it was the German high command that contemplated surrender. An easy conclusion would be that the American fighting force made the difference. However, American participation was rather slow in coming, especially in terms of experienced warriors in the field. What the American presence did do was to raise markedly the morale of the European leaders and their armed forces as well. After three long years of indecisive fighting against the Central Powers, the Allies now had another major power on their side—one that seemed fresh and free from much of the fatigue of the terrible trench warfare that had undone the sons of the French and British empires. As Churchill showed so ably in a later war, great campaigns are won by spirit, determination, guile, and baffling surprise, as well as by superior manpower and synchronized movements.[17]

When the United States entered the war, it had little to contribute at first but that sense of common participation. In April 1917, the army comprised 5,791 officers and 121,797 enlisted men—a total that would be equal to less than half of the total casualties sustained at the 1916 Battle of the Somme. In addition, there was another semiprepared force of 181,000 men in the National Guard, about 40 percent of whom were called up to federal service.

Wilson had shown little concern initially about the state of the military; as late as 1916, he had abandoned his own secretary of war's proposal to create a Continental army. However, in one brief year, from 1917 to 1918, the American military, buttressed by new civilian agencies, created an incredible war machine of over two million men and laid out a seatrain that carried millions of pounds of food stuffs and munitions to Europe. No one expected the Americans to mobilize so quickly, and few understood the economic and shipping capacity of that nation. As in World War II, the American contribution was not brilliant strategy, or exceptional discipline in the ranks, but rather, the creation of an arsenal of democracy. The Imperial high command misunderstood the United States' capacities, so too would Hitler a generation later.

In a crucially important decision, the president decided to raise an army using the draft rather than volunteers. Thus, Wilson avoided the mistakes of the British government, which had relied on volunteers and their sense of adventure and glory to fill the ranks—until the debacles of 1916 made that approach unworkable. After an acrimonious debate, Congress passed the draft bill and the president signed it into law on May 18, 1917. Men were drafted by a lottery, and the president drew a capsule with a number in it to start the process. In performing his duty, Wilson wore a blindfold made from a strip of cloth from a chair that was used at the signing of the original Declaration of Independence.

The armed forces began a massive building and training program, introducing many young men to a broad range of experiences that they had never seen back home. Optional life insurance made its debut, intelligence or IQ tests were introduced, and GIs were given lectures on moral guidance and personal hygiene. Psychologists declared that a third of the soldiers were illiterate, and half of the white and 90 percent of the blacks were classified as "morons," supposedly having intelligence scores below the mental age of thirteen. The army revised its primitive tests; a new finding emerged as black northerners did better than rural whites in many cases. By January 1919, the army abandoned its testing program after complaints from officers and the general public about its efficacy and accuracy. On a lesser issue, when Wilson was asked his opinion about saluting officers, he seemed to be rather unenthusiastic about the elitist practice; his chief of staff, Peyton March, went on to celebrate its virtues and warned that the Bolsheviks had abandoned the salute just before the collapse of the Russian army.[18]

In day-to-day military matters, Wilson relied on his secretary of war, Newton D. Baker. Baker, a slightly built five-footer, had met Wilson when they were at Johns Hopkins University; he had gone on to become a reform mayor of Cleveland, Ohio. Baker was generally a pacifist by inclination and for nearly two years, from March 1916 to 1918, he allowed the decentralized and inefficient system to continue in the War Department. The department was organized around a collection of virtually independent bureaus with a very weak general staff. But by the winter of 1917–18, it became obvious to Congress, the public, and even the military, especially General John "Black Jack" Pershing then commanding U.S. forces in Europe, that the war effort was going poorly. The mobilization effort was slack and not responsive, production was moving too slowly, and Pershing was unable to build and maintain the type of armed force that he saw as essential.

The president finally moved in and asked the astute financier and Democratic party advisor, Bernard Baruch, to take over the War Industries Board, and Baker decided to call Major General Peyton C. March back from France to be chief of staff. Almost immediately, March had to deal with serious problems of shipping, training, censorship, and relations with Russia. The general staff he inherited was used to normal business hours and rarely worked nights or on Sundays. At the start of the war, the number of general staff officers was limited to 19; by the end of the conflict, the total personnel had jumped to 1,072. Marsh's first order of business was to deal with the need for additional shipping and more efficient coordination of the flow of troops and supplies to European ports.

He clashed with Pershing on the promotion appointment list and with the chief of staff's desire to rotate War Department officers with field officers in the European theater. At home, March was brusquely efficient, firing older and ineffectual bureau chiefs, and pushing for a stronger centralized staff system. One of his colleagues wrote, "He took the War Department like a dog takes a cat by the neck, and he shook it."

March found himself dealing with powerful civilian boards, especially the War Industries Board headed by Baruch. In order to alleviate shipping and supply problems, March had to work directly with these wartime agencies and civilian authorities. Every Wednesday, March would meet with Baruch and the chairmen of the Shipping Board, the Shipping Control Committee, the War Trade Board, and the chief of Naval Operations to coordinate the critical movements of men and matériel.

In terms of strategy, March insisted that the American forces be concentrated on the western front and not be sent to Russian Siberia to divert German forces on the eastern front as some were proposing. To him, Russia was a vast morass, with great problems for any nation that tried to protect and supply its far-flung troops. The best strategy was to focus U.S. efforts in the western theater. March had also previously seen the Japanese army in Manchuria and he did not trust that nation as an ally.

Already in the war a year, the United States had yet to engage the enemy in any significant campaigns. In response to urgent Allied pleadings, March stepped up troop shipments, and the flow of men sent to Europe was double the previous highest monthly crossings. In France, General Pershing insisted on maintaining his control over all American troops, and March pushed for the rapid formation of complete divisions to give him some fighting forces overseas.

Pershing began planning to feed, house, and, most importantly, train farm boys and factory workers as soldiers. He pushed March, Baker, and Wilson for more and more troops, faster supply convoys, and, on his own, committed the United States to a hundred divisions. The War Department was startled; it responded with a plan for eighty divisions, and in 1918 President Wilson agreed with that commitment. By the time of the armistice, the American Expeditionary Force was at forty-two divisions. With Wilson's support from the beginning, Pershing had insisted that the AEF divisions had to stay together and not be amalgamated into British or French units. The Americans were still used to a war effort that relied on individual marksmen and not machine gun saturation, and their officers had no real understanding of gas warfare. Even Pershing himself retained an affection for the horse cavalry. Added to March's burdens and Pershing's difficulties was the chaos in French ports trying to handle the volume of U.S. matériel coming in and the inability of French railroads to move supplies across that nation.

Pershing's problems were compounded by the increase in venereal disease, a situation the general had confronted in the Mexican campaign where he had led U.S. troops against Pancho Villa. About a fourth of the British soldiers had contracted variations of the disease, and Pershing found a similar problem in the American ranks.

French premier Georges Clemenceau, fearing the reputed ardor of American boys present in his nation, offered to set up houses of prostitution with state-inspected prostitutes to prevent the spread of the dreaded disease. Pershing dutifully passed on the suggestion to Secretary Baker, who promptly responded that Wilson should not see the letter "or he'll stop the war."[19]

Despite their occasional disagreements, Pershing was very dependent on March. In advocating more control and professionalism, March resisted political influences in the appointment of officers, even on one occasion refusing a request from the president. His concern for efficiency and personal bluntness incensed some congressional opponents, but March's response was clear, "You can not run a war on tact." March, though, was effective; by the summer months of 1918, the United States was sending about 9,500 soldiers a day abroad. Pershing pushed harder still, insisting that the Americans had to have one hundred divisions by July 1919, and he had the Allied leaders, Vittorio Orlando, David Lloyd George, and Clemenceau, endorse that demand in a letter to President Wilson. To March, Pershing's plan was impossible; by American calculations, one hundred U.S. divisions were equivalent to two hundred European divisions, and when support and replacement troops were added, the American Expeditionary Force would reach five million men. That force would be 25 percent larger than the combined Allied armies then on the western front.

For March, it was an extraordinary request, not only in terms of raising and training soldiers, but in shipping them across the ocean and in providing supplies to French ports that already could not handle the American influx. Despite Pershing's concerns that the home front was lying down on the job, March was indeed pushing ahead. He advocated that the draft age be expanded from the 21–30 age group to 18–45, and he insisted on universal military service. He argued against Pershing's proposal for one hundred divisions, however, and put up strong opposition to any Siberian expedition.

But Wilson and Secretary of State Lansing began to see some military and diplomatic advantages in landing in northern Russia. The Allies apparently felt that a force in the free port of Murmansk could protect that city from the Germans, safeguard Allied war supplies, and guarantee an escape line for Czech troops en route to that region. Baker and March insisted that the United States avoid such a show of force in such a faraway theater of action. At a cabinet meeting, the general continued to oppose the venture until Wilson recited a summary of his opposition: "You are opposed to this because you do not think Japan will limit herself to 7,000 men, and that this decision will further her schemes for territorial aggrandizement." March agreed and added that he opposed the scheme for military reasons as well. But Wilson had made up his mind and responded, "Well, we will have to take that chance."

As expected, March and Pershing were occasionally at loggerheads due to their differing perspectives. While March insisted on establishing preeminence over other segments of the military, Pershing refused to see March as his superior in any way and resented his curt tone in cables sent to his office. The chief of staff position, as originally conceived, was to be a central office and the focal point through which the president and his secretary of war controlled the army. The position was to involve vast supervisory power over line and staff officers. The trans-Atlantic war complicated matters, and Pershing was granted supreme power in France subordinate only to the president's general command responsibilities.

Although Wilson left direct military matters to Baker and the officer staff, he was not removed from making important decisions on critical war matters. On one occasion, for example, he pointed out to March that he was disturbed to find that the current proposals "for the supplying of war needs, either directly, or indirectly, are in some instances far in excess of the productive capacity of the country." On another occasion, it was Wilson who refused to support universal military service, and he also told March he wanted American transports stopped during the influenza epidemic in the fall of 1918. March insisted that such a slack would boost German morale, and Wilson finally backed down.

At the Navy Department, Wilson had appointed a Bryan Democrat from South Carolina, Josephus Daniels, who knew little about the navy, and added to his troubles by appointing an ambitious Franklin Delano Roosevelt as his assistant. The navy still lived in the era of large battleship fleets and ignored the world of the submarine. Its leadership was distinctly anti-British, and its proposed new program was to arm merchantmen, build a 110-foot patrol boat, and use blimps to patrol bases in the Atlantic.[20]

At sea, the Germans placed more emphasis on their U-boats (*Unterseebooten*), and in the 1914–18 period, some 5,700 Allied ships were sunk. In 1914, the Germans had downed about 300,000 tons of shipping; by 1917, it was over 6.2 million tons. To overcome the German assaults, the Allies began to use large convoys to protect shipping and facilitate the movement of men and matériel. The United States Navy with its destroyers provided the protection necessary to send the boys to Europe.

By the spring of 1918, the period of consolidation and training was over, and at last the American troops were ready for combat. And it was none too soon, as the Germans faced with the collapse of Russia could afford to move five hundred thousand troops to the west. Matters had worsened especially in the French army where mutiny had broken out in 1917, and the officers initiated random executions to restore discipline. The new Allied power, Italy, found its army in even worse shape, especially after the costly Battle of Caporetto in October 1917.

The Germans, headed by General Ludendorff, threw dozens of trained divisions in the spring of 1918 against a feeble and weary French force. The end of May seemed to show the tide was turning toward the Germans, and the route to Paris was open to the invaders. Then at the height of the German offenses, the French high council asked for American intervention. As the Germans moved through Chateau-Thierry toward the Marne, the Allies saw a vast throng of young Americans singing, as a huge convoy spit dust down the long, winding roads. Winston Churchill observed how this first blush of Yankee youth and vigor raised French morale along the line, but the Americans were not immune from the terrible toll that had characterized each major battle. At the Battle of Belleau Wood in May–June 1918, a brave Marine Corps of 8,000 was reduced by 5,183 men killed or wounded. Other costly battles at St. Mihiel, Meuse-Argonne, and the taking of Sedall followed as Americans received a true taste of twentieth-century warfare. Then suddenly on November 11, 1918, the war came to an abrupt end.[21]

CONTROLLING THE WAR EFFORT

During this time, Wilson had delegated considerable responsibility to Baker and Daniels and to Chief of Staff March. Because of the distance between the United States and France, the president additionally had granted Pershing great leeway to run the American military abroad as he saw fit. The reconstituted chief of staff system had speeded up the training and supplying of troops to the astonishment of both the Allies and Germany. In the process, though, the United States had entered a total war, one in which the military, economic, social, and propaganda efforts were fused under the national government. Gone forever was the war of part-time soldiers, of summer battles and winter rests, of early armistices and gentlemanly codes of war. War was to be even more a total effort of the nation-state, which led to victory or defeat.

Wilson in the First World War extended the boundaries of presidential power beyond what even Lincoln employed in the Civil War. In addition to the vast powers of commander in chief, Wilson added to them important controls over the economy. One American commentator of the time, Lindsay Rogers, explained to British readers that the president in 1919 had become king, prime minister, commander in chief, party leader, economic dictator, secretary of state, and general supervisor of the administration.[22]

But as political scientist Clinton Rossiter has noted, Wilson acquired his vast power by statute and not by unilateral executive action. He chose to demand from Congress specific authority to meet the crises before him. Indeed, as Rossiter judged, "the basis of Lincoln's power was the Constitution, and he operated in spite of Congress. The basis of Wilson's power was a group of statutes, and he cooperated with Congress."[23]

Wilson, of course, did use his constitutional authority as commander in chief as well as powers delegated by Congress to further American war interests. He armed American merchant shipmen in 1917 after Congress was deadlocked due to a Senate filibuster, he established the Committee on Public Information to further U.S. propaganda efforts and combat unfavorable stories, and he set up a series of emergency agencies, most important of which was the War Industries Board.

But Congress added whole areas to his authority. The president was empowered to take over and operate the railroads and the water systems, to regulate or commandeer all ship-building facilities in the United States, to regulate and prohibit exports, to raise or conscript an army, to control transportation and the telegraph and telephone systems, to deal with resident enemy aliens, to control the foreign language press, and to redistribute functions among the executive agencies. The Lever Act of August 10, 1917, added even more statutory authority. The president could create agencies to regulate importation, manufacturing, storage, mining, and distribution of necessary goods and commodities; could control the distribution of food supplies and fuels; could fix wheat, coal, and coke prices; and run factories, mines, packing-houses, pipelines, and major industrial establishments deemed critical to the war effort.

Given his views about presidential leadership of Congress, Wilson was able to head off attempts to curtail his authority, such as the proposal of Senator George E. Chamberlain of Oregon in 1918 to create a war cabinet to include "three distinguished citizens of demonstrated ability" (a reference aimed at including Theodore Roosevelt), which would be set up by the president and the Senate to conduct the war effort.

To exercise his new responsibilities, the president created a series of boards headed usually by conservative businesspeople to oversee critical industries and food production. The most important were the War Industries Board, chaired by Baruch, the Fuel Administration led by academician Harry A. Garfield, and the Food Administration run by engineer Herbert Hoover. These boards sought through a web of "volunteer" codes and agreements to regulate industry and commerce and resorted to price-fixing, license controls, priority regulations, and if necessary, sanctions. Hard-sell appeals to patriotism, threats of higher taxes, and sometimes strong restrictions were generally successful in persuading individuals and companies to meet the government's goals. These boards acted as extensions of the president, exercising the delegated authority given to the executive by Congress. The Overman Act in 1919 granted complete authority to the president over any administrative agency he chose to create for the successful prosecution of the war. Wilson rarely resorted to such broad power, preferring to use coaxing and softer methods than clear, outright coercion.

Yet, the federal government did not prohibit strikes or restrain the right to change jobs. In April 1918, the National War Labor Board was created and the War Labor Policies Board followed soon after to deal with such difficulties. The president did have the authority to seize companies to get them to cooperate with the government, and he could end draft exemptions for employees who proved to be recalcitrant. Three times during the war, Wilson took over control of industries that violated War Labor Board dictates, but strikes were not curtailed, although critical public opinion led to a reduction in work stoppages.

Unlike Lincoln, Wilson refused to suspend the writ of habeas corpus and opposed military trials for sedition and espionage, arguing that they were unconstitutional. Congress, at the president's request, passed a series of laws aimed at curtailing sedition and espionage, and these statutes made it a crime to aid the enemy, hinder the United States, spread false reports, and incite to disloyalty by obstructing the recruitment of soldiers. They also prohibited people from speaking, printing, writing, or publishing "any disloyal, profane, scurrilous, or abusive language" about the government, the president, the armed forces, the flag, and the Constitution, and curtailed any language that would bring the above "into contempt, scorn, contumely, or disrespect."

Wilson delegated the administration of these laws to his zealous Department of Justice, and over two thousand indictments were made throughout the nation; about one-half of those charged were found guilty. Although Congress refused to approve of prior-restraint censorship, the government did use the Espionage and the Sedition Acts to prosecute individuals, curtail cable traffic and foreign language papers, and close the mails to some printed organs of opinion. In addition, although it was never approved by Congress, the Committee on Public Information, headed by George Creel, worked closely with federal authorities as it directed propaganda efforts and helped to suppress critical information on military activities and what it deemed seditious activities.

By the summer of 1920, however, Congress overwhelmingly repealed sixty wartime measures that had delegated vast authority to the president. Wilson unwisely pocket vetoed the repeal attempt, and the Republicans in the election attacked "the executive dictatorship." The Supreme Court during this period did uphold the vast extension of the war powers of the president; only in 1923 for example did it end rent controls in Washington, D.C., arguing that the emergency was over.[24]

It is interesting to compare Wilson's activities with his two allies: David Lloyd George, the able charismatic British prime minister, and France's Georges Clemenceau. Lloyd George, who took over the flagging war effort from Prime Minister Henry Asquith in December 1916, was an artful manipulator, a brilliant orator, and a person given to high purpose and cheap intrigue—a successful combination for most politicians. In comparison to Asquith with his collegial and lackluster style, Lloyd George was a dynamic and hardworking leader. He was, in the words of one observer, the real British war cabinet himself.

As prime minister, Lloyd George used the war cabinet made up of five people to coordinate and centralize the whole war effort. He met almost daily with the new cabinet, and that group in turn was informed by a collection of ad hoc and standing committees served by a variety of ministers and specialists. Only the Foreign Office, under Lloyd George's close personal supervision, seemed outside this orbit. The war cabinet reported directly to the prime minister who set the agenda of cabinet business and who was assisted by a cabinet secretariat. He was also aided by a personal circle of associates (which was seen as the equivalent of American presidents' "Kitchen Cabinet") called the "Garden Suburb," originally housed in huts in the garden of Number 10 Downing Street, the prime minister's residence. In addition, Lloyd George created in March 1917 an imperial war cabinet under his chairmanship, which was used mostly in preparing for the postwar peace conference in autumn 1918.

Lloyd George accumulated vast personal and political power through these interlocking agencies and even sought to impose his control over land and naval war strategy. In 1917, he forced and won a confrontation with the First Sea Lord John Jellicoe to establish convoys to deter U-boats. He was even willing to use the French to conspire against British military leaders on the issue of a unified military command. By early 1918, he challenged his own chief of staff and finally extended his control over military policy as well. Although he lacked a true parliamentary majority in the House of Commons, as Churchill had during World War II, Lloyd George ruled by the sheer sway of his personality. He was also involved in the details of domestic policy from the fixing of wheat prices to the duty placed on gloves. His ascendancy continued throughout the war, the peace negotiations, and beyond until October 1922. The London *Times* was to call it "the greatest experiment in political improvisation which Great Britain had ever known."

In France, the seventy-six-year-old Georges Clemenceau, a former radical journalist and longtime parliamentarian, took over in November 1917 amid increasing disillusionment in the Allied ranks over the stalemate. Like Lloyd George, Clemenceau was a master of intrigue and was committed to action and victory over the Central Powers. He recast the cabinet with six departments: navy, foreign affairs, armament, blockade, finance, and war, and he emphasized greater civilian and military cooperation. Clemenceau kept the critical war minister post for himself. As he said of his predecessors, "Nice fellas. They had only one fault. They were too decent. They weren't meant for war." In addition to his cabinet, he too had a group of more intimate associates, a "cabinet of reference," as it was called. Clemenceau purged the army of old and inept officers, opened up the military promotion lists to new men, and spread his influence over the départements and prefects. He skillfully used U.S. aid and intervention at the end of 1917 to revive French morale and pushed for a joint Allied command under the direction of the French general staff. Clemenceau was a strong advocate of a Supreme War Council of the Allied Powers, although deep down he trusted neither his allies nor his own generals. The public at first called him affectionately "père-la-victoire"; the infantry, however, respectfully labeled him "The Tiger."

By 1917–18, as Wilson assumed responsibility for the United States' entrance into the war, the Allies were weary and disillusioned by the carnage and stalemate on the western front. They turned to political radicals and veteran parliamentarians who were pledged to the aggressive pursuit of victory and to new strategies; later some were to say that European leaders acted like American wartime presidents. But in the United States with its shorter war effort, Wilson approved a network of national planning agencies to wage that war and redirect domestic life in ways unprecedented in American history.

The same phenomenon was taking place under the German industrialist Walther Rathenau who created for the Wilhemine Empire a system for the distribution and manufacturing of war materials. Rathenau was supposed to have said that all he learned about planned economies he learned from his father, who was managing director of the German Electric Company. In April 1914, Rathenau was granted extensive powers, and the War Raw Materials Department was established to deal with conservation, production of substitute materials, and planned distribution. By the end of the year, his control extended over critical materials such as metals, wool, and timber. The war agencies were tightening the ties between the Reich and business with more emphasis being placed on price controls and manpower distribution. Toward the end of the war, Rathenau exercised vast powers under the military dictatorship that had taken over control of the Reich from the emperor. His position was a forerunner to Albert Speer's similar role in Hitler's regime. Thus, the war had not only changed the nature of the military, but it also deeply affected the home front and taught a new generation of leaders on both sides of the Atlantic how to use the government to control economic and social life.

THE BATTLE FOR A PEACE

Wilson had played a greater role in tipping the scales toward war than any other president in American history. No one at the time realized the consequences of that conflict. At one point, the president had been concerned about the future of "white civilization." Indeed he should have been, for the war ended the naive notions of progress and the inevitable advance of Western civilization. The vast losses from the war created legions of grieving parents, young widows, and men prematurely old. The war and its aftermath upset forever the patterns of deference and class structures that went back even to the Middle Ages in some nations. The war had stripped away the illusions of life, fostered a horrendous mechanization of conflict, and unleased right-wing and left-wing extremist movements.[25]

It is hard to say that the sacrifices of the war were worth it. The world of 1930 was far worse than that of 1910. The way was paved for weak democracies and the rise of Mussolini, Hitler, Lenin, and later Stalin in the West. Without these severe dislocations, rampant fear, and economic disintegration, the twin evils of Fascism and Communism would probably be esoteric ideologies confined to beer hall riffraff and eccentric professors living in shabby flats in Europe. Instead, they became the moving forces that challenged representative governments and gave the world genocidal ventures, gulags, and an even worse Second World War.

But by 1919, the task facing Wilson was a far different one. He was sworn to transform the vague, stirring rhetoric of his speeches into a foreign policy of reconstruction and forgiveness. Like Lincoln, he promised reconciliation, like Lincoln he favored a reconstruction based on new institutions. But unlike Lincoln, he would live to see his ideas fail, rather than bequeath them to a luckless successor.

Presidents, like the people they lead, are given to emotional judgments and are obsessed about the terrible toll that war takes. Men such as Wilson and Lincoln were not Caesars and Napoleons; they were sharply affected by the carnage around them. Lincoln turned a civil war into a quasi-religious referendum about liberty, and in the process raised the moral stakes by ending slavery forever. His actions have been seen as a shrewd calculation aimed at appeasing British public opinion and recognizing the growing number of black troops in the Union army. Perhaps it was a political judgment. Yet in a larger sense he seemed to have consecrated the Union cause, almost as a response to the terrible toll he played a part in exacting.

So Woodrow Wilson, this principled moralistic son of a minister, reacted similarly after the First World War. Before America's entry into France, Wilson had found the war to be confusing, its causes unclear, the hope for a stalemate acceptable. But as he experienced the carnage, as he too led the nation into war and its sons to death and dismemberment, Wilson cast the conflict into a far different light. His plea to make the world safe for democracy was not a slogan meant simply for the masses. He surely believed that he was God's instrument to bring about a different world order. He was not alone in that belief; throughout the West, Wilson was received at first with an awe very different from that reserved for the other victorious Allied leaders. In homes across the ocean, American observers were startled to find over peasant hearths two pictures: Jesus Christ and Woodrow Wilson.[26]

It is too easy to dismiss Wilson as a man who failed; it cannot be denied that he established a hold over large segments of the public imagination. In a mystical way, they seemed to agree with him that young boys should not go to an early death and ancient nations were not ravished of their history and treasure just to reestablish some balance of power among Western imperialistic states. And so, with peace at hand, with famine threatening Europe, Woodrow Wilson sailed from America not as a triumphant victor, but as a prophet in his own time.

THE VERSAILLES SETTLEMENT

For several years, Wilson had thought about the type of peace that must be guaranteed—a peace without victory, he called it. To the European leaders who had been involved in the war for thirty-two months longer, the attractiveness of retribution, territory, and even vengeance was much stronger. They could not go back to their nations with what appeared a status quo ante, and they were less willing than Wilson to speak about the legitimate role that Germany could play in Europe. France was deeply troubled as long as it faced a large and powerful Germany, and Britain opposed German hegemony on the Continent and on the seas since it threatened its own Royal Navy and might compromise the empire. Italy, allied before the war with the Central Powers, had switched sides in May 1915 and was belligerently demanding at the peace conference not only the cities of Trieste and Trentino, but also the port of Fiume and other major concessions from Austria-Hungary.

To many people, these European diplomats schooled in the Old World traditions of balance of power and imperial aggrandizement represented the very reasons why the war broke out in the first place. They had sanctioned unsteady and overreaching alliances, played havoc with nationalities, and used patriotism as the cover for national ambition. This age-old game with its cool air of cynicism and hauteur still dominated the European elites. To these diplomats and politicians, Wilson was naive and unrealistic, a moralistic man who did not understand the basis of world politics as it must be played. It has become commonplace in the United States to accept that judgment and to draw from that bitter lesson that world politics is best devoid of idealism, that it is best rooted in an acceptance of the cynical assumptions of realpolitik. Yet these very practitioners and their colleagues of such a "realistic" world view led Europe into a series of wars and miscalculations that culminated in the devastating conflicts of 1914–19 and the even more horrendous conflagrations of 1939–45.[27]

Wilson's basic peace proposals were in one sense an accumulation of ideas that had been surfacing in different nations over the years, and that reflected the great humanitarian traditions of the West. On both sides of the Atlantic, liberals repudiated the old gospel of the balance of power, of elite secret diplomacy, and of shifting alliances drawn up by bewildered politicians and unsteady monarchies. In their place, they proposed an international organization charged with peacekeeping that would make agreements in public. They saw the large military establishments as one of the causes of tension and not just a consequence of that tension, and they supported the creation of a League of Nations to enforce the peace. These proposals were to be included in the early Wilson platform as he embarked for Europe. The American president came to Versailles not as a victor in search of spoils or as a conqueror ready to inflict retribution, but as the most forward-looking liberal on the world stage. He recognized his unique role, and so did the Allied leaders who suspiciously were to lock horns with him.

Perhaps for this reason, Wilson had kept from the beginning some distance between himself and the others during their common war. He called the United States an "associate" in the struggle to defeat the Central Powers and not an ally. He knew many but not all of the provisions of the secret agreements that the Allied leaders had consummated and refused to acknowledge them as binding on his nation. Even during the early stages of the war effort, Wilson tried to exert pressure on the Austro-Hungarian nation to withdraw from the war by promising that the Allies would not dismember the empire, but would allow it to continue if it were transformed into a federation. Remarkably, he tried the same approach with the Germans in December 1917, saying that the United States did not desire to interfere in their internal politics nor to threaten the existence and independence of the German empire. As for the Allies, they were growing increasingly dependent on the United States, and Wilson judged that they would be "financially in our hands."[28]

In September 1917, he had Colonel House call together a group of experts called "The Inquiry" to look at the war aims of the nations and spell out U.S. objectives. As a consequence, Wilson laid out publicly his famous Fourteen Points, which included general principles and particular dispositions on difficult territorial issues. Overall, the speech promised open covenants, freedom of the seas, general disarmament, removal of trade barriers, impartial settlement of colonial claims, and a League of Nations. Wilson also included the independence of Belgium, self-determination for Russia, the evacuation of French territory and the return to it of Alsace-Lorraine, autonomy for the minority nationalities in the Austro-Hungarian empire, a readjustment of Italy's borders, self-determination in the Balkans, autonomy for subjects of the Ottoman Empire, free access through the Dardanelles, and the guarantee of an independent Poland with access to the sea.

To the Germans, Wilson promised a "place of equality among the peoples of the world." But by March 1918, the Germans had taken advantage of the Bolsheviks' weariness and forced upon them a vindictive peace treaty. Wilson realized that moderate civilians were not in charge in Germany, and that the war was not going to end as he had hoped. His response was clear, "Force, Force to the utmost, Force without stint or limit, the righteous and triumphant Force which shall make Right the law of the world, and cast every selfish dominion down in the dust."[29]

To Clemenceau, Wilson's intentions for a moderate peace were unrealistic from the start. He sarcastically remarked that God had given mankind ten commandments and they were broken; Wilson had given the world fourteen points—"we shall see." The French leader's intention was to prevent the rise of a strong Germany again. Having seen defeat in the Franco-Prussian war in 1870 and the horrendous losses in the First World War, Clemenceau agreed with Marshal Ferdinand Foch that the west bank of the Rhine had to be stripped from Germany, that in its place there would be one or more Rhenish republics under French control, and that his nation would also permanently govern the Rhineland. Under tremendous pressure from Wilson and objections from British Prime Minister Lloyd George, Clemenceau had to back down and accept instead a fifteen-year occupation of that region and a mutual defense treaty with the United States and Great Britain if Germany attacked France again. These concessions, bitterly negotiated, saved the peace conference from total collapse, but also forced Wilson to give in on other points about which he felt strongly.

The second major issue was the question of reparations and indemnities. Lloyd George and Clemenceau pushed for Germany to be liable for the total costs of the war. Wilson recognized the enormous weight of British and French public opinion on the issue and had to give some ground. Germany was thus forced to pay the cost of disability pensions to Allied veterans and their families, to cover Allied war loses incurred by civilians, and also to accept the seizure of $5 billion of German property, French ownership of the coal mines in the Saar Valley, and the occupation of the Saar for twenty years. The French also had the right to occupy the Rhineland beyond the fifteen-year limit if the German government did not pay the reparations on time. The terms seemed harsh even at that time, and Hitler later would use those provisions to inflame German opinion a generation after the treaty was signed. One observer, the British economist John Maynard Keynes, argued that the terms of the treaty were impossible for the Germans to meet. But more recent analysis shows that while the terms were steep, the Germans at the time did have the ability to meet these obligations, and that Hitler himself spent many times more money in rearming Germany in the 1930s.

The third issue Wilson had to face was the future of Germany's colonies. His position was clear: they would be supervised by small nations acting under the League of Nations' stewardship. The British and their allies in the empire and Japan insisted on annexation instead. In the end, Wilson won and a mandate system was created—the first major international blow against Western colonialism, a development accelerated after World War II. In terms of Japan, Wilson had an even more difficult time, especially concerning the Shantung Province in China where the Imperial Japanese Army had defeated the Germans in 1915 and taken control. Wilson argued passionately for self-determination, and although he was forced to compromise on the issue, finally the Japanese granted China full sovereignty in the province.

One of Wilson's bitterest disputes, though, was closer to home with the desire of Italian Prime Minister Vittorio Orlando to take not only Trentino and Trieste, but also the port of Fiume. After a long contest of wills, the Italians gave in on their plans to control the Adriatic Sea. As the conference continued, Wilson and Lloyd George insisted on creating an international port at Danzig and allowing the people of Upper Silesia to determine how their land should be partitioned between Poland and Germany. As for the Austro-Hungarian empire, that old regime broke up into several nation-states, ending the alternative of federation, which Wilson, among others, had proposed.

The great difficulty left was Russia, and here too Wilson insisted on self-determination. He opposed the Allies' plans for intervention to topple the Bolsheviks and was willing to send American troops only for very limited purposes and only for a brief time to Archangel and Vladivostok. He told Churchill that Allied troops had to leave Russia, and while he distrusted the Lenin government, Wilson seemed to remember the difficult lessons he had learned in Mexico about the limitations of using armed forces in civil wars.

Above all, Woodrow Wilson achieved his objective of creating a League of Nations. The League was composed of an international assembly in which all member states were represented and an executive council in which the great powers with some of the other states would sit. There was also an international court and a secretariat and various commissions. The critical article in the League charter was the first one, which guaranteed collective protection against aggression.

Wilson's work was done, and he sailed home to a mounting controversy about the new treaty and the role of the United States in the world. It has become standard historical judgment to say that Wilson failed at Versailles, and in the sense that he could not establish a true peace without making major concessions to the victors, perhaps he did. The Germans called it a "diktat," a dictated peace. But considering their demands at Brest-Litovsk after the

Russian surrender, it is hard to press a sympathetic case. In fact, Wilson had protected German interests even more than they had a right to expect or probably deserved. Historian Arthur Link has concluded that the president fought tenaciously and eloquently, was more prepared for the conference than his counterparts, and was the wisest of the Big Four leaders. He was not outfoxed by the Old World diplomats or overwhelmed by their skill or insight. In fact, the president assumed a task that no one, even a leader of his considerable talents, could totally succeed at. He sought to change the whole character of the nation-state system, to challenge the alliance and balance of power mentality, and to insist on a magnanimous settlement to nations that had exerted themselves for nearly a full three years before America's entrance into the war.[30]

By the time of Versailles, Wilson lacked much leverage over the Allies, for the Germans and the Austrian forces were totally routed, and the war was done. The Allies also knew that Wilson's political base was eroding at home, yet the president did bring back a comprehensive treaty that restored Belgium and Alsace-Lorraine, created an independent Poland, recognized the demands for self-determination in the Balkan and Central European corridors, and established an international League as he promised. In 1926, Germany was admitted to the League of Nations, and in the decade that followed the war, naval disarmament was prominently accepted in the West. Wilson had muted the demands for vengeance more than the Germans had realized. If one looks at their harsh treaty at Brest-Litovsk and compares it with Versailles, one can perhaps get an idea of what a difference a Woodrow Wilson can make.

THE BATTLE FOR THE TREATY

Wilson's return home and his abortive fight for the treaty and the League of Nations is frequently portrayed as the final act in a dramatic classical tragedy. The president, who was facing the hostility of narrow-minded partisans in the Senate, takes his case to the people, suffers a debilitating stroke from the exertion, refuses final compromise, and lives out his remaining years in stoic calm. Historians have looked to his early character and to his battles at Princeton for clues to his final demise. Others have cited his long history of illnesses, illnesses that he overcame, and have postulated that his alleged rigidity in Paris and in the League fight was due to physiological causes.[31]

Yet a closer examination shows that Wilson, while making some serious mistakes, followed a course of behavior that was quite logical. Once again, as in Paris, he took on immense burdens of leadership, burdens that even he could not carry alone. One mistake was the president's appeal on October 25, 1918, for the election of a Democratic Congress—an action perfectly in keeping with his conception of being a sort of prime minister, but one that deprived him of the nonpartisan mantle of chief of state he had assumed so successfully during most of the war. And despite his homilies on constitutional collegiality, Wilson's idea of leadership was to lead with the Senate following.

Returning to the capital, the president was ready to do battle and spurned compromise with his Senate opponents. As he phrased it, how could the United States "dare reject it [the League] and break the heart of the world?" He believed that once more he could appeal to the people and sway them as he had done so often, this time on the major controversies that centered on the League of Nations and its guarantees of collective security to repel aggression. Under the American Constitution, the right to declare war belongs to Congress—a statement of sovereignty that is exercised in varying ways by all nation-states. The Republican strategy was to approve the treaty and enter the League, but insist on amendments and reservations that significantly altered the original charter. Most of these changes were minor, but one clarification mandated that the United States could not guarantee the territorial integrity or political independence of any other nation unless Congress approved such a commitment. In addition, three of the four major Allied powers had to accept these reservations for the treaty to go into effect for the United States.

Wilson tried to gain the support of the Republican moderates, and in late July, he held a series of meetings with eleven senators. In August, he met with the Foreign Relations Committee, headed by his arch foe, Henry Cabot Lodge, for three hours. Wilson was unsuccessful, and even though he was physically under par, he took his case to the people.

In September, Wilson went into the far-reaching Midwest, the isolationist stronghold, and then down the Northwest and Pacific Coast toward the Southwest. In twenty-two days and over eight thousand miles, he delivered forty addresses, an incredible demonstration of presidential leadership. He explained the provisions of the treaty, especially Article X, which he called "the test of the honor and courage and endurance of the world." Wilson pointed out that the Senate's reservation was unnecessary if it was meant to protect the Constitution. Any decision of the executive council to go to war needed unanimous approval, which included the United States. America could not turn away from its new role, "that is the leadership we said we wanted, and now the world offers it to us. It is inconceivable that we should reject it."

Then on September 25, 1919, after his address in Pueblo, Colorado, Wilson began to collapse physically, and on October 2, he suffered a severe stroke, which paralyzed the left side of his face and body. As Wilson struggled to recover, the Senate continued its debate of the treaty. Lodge was successful in stopping the more moderate alternatives and pushed for the Senate to curtail the reaches of Article X. Wilson let it be known that he would not accept the Senate's proposal, and so the Democrats joined with hard-core Republican isolationists to defeat ratification with the Lodge reservations.

For several months, the nation debated the final disposition of the treaty, and pressures mounted for some compromise. Moderate Republicans like former President Taft and Harvard University President A. Lawrence Lowell joined with Democrats like William Jennings Bryan and Colonel House to find common ground for a settlement. As Wilson recovered somewhat in the winter of 1920, he opposed any compromise and began talking of running again for president, promoting his reelection as a solemn referendum on the League. Once again the Senate rejected the treaty with the Lodge reservations.

Wilson's stubborn refusal has been a source of continued controversy, a commentary on his failure to provide that critical element of leadership—compromise—in his own cause. To Wilson, the issue was whether the United States would be willing to assume the world role that was awaiting it. When it appeared that his nation was not so inclined, Wilson judged it best not to accept a treaty that undercut the very principle of collective security. For only under this rubric, with this type of commitment, could the new world replace the balance of power approach that had led to the Great War in the first place. Like an Old Testament prophet, he sat in judgment over the world he had partially formed. Even after his death, his influence on American political figures continued, and his failings and dreams were lessons to Franklin D. Roosevelt, his protégé and assistant secretary of the navy.

Would the League with the United States in it in the 1930s have prevented the rise of Hitler and the development of a conflagration far worse than even the First World War? The shortcomings of the Western democracies were not grounded in the weaknesses of the League, but more basically in the failure of nerve and leadership in Britain, France, Italy, Germany—and yes, the United States. And the record of the United Nations has not led to universal acclaim for collective security organized in international organizations. Wilson was correct in his judgments about the failures of the Old World diplomats, but his solution—the solution of liberals of his age—was not and is not now viable in the age of garrison states and ethnic tribalism.

Wilson's problem then was not that he was repudiated at home. Many of the war leaders were repudiated at home: even Orlando and Clemenceau were all cast out of power after the war, partly as a consequence of its disruptions. The ancient empires of the Ottomans, the Hapsburgs, the Hohenzollerns, and the Romanovs were crushed in this one war. The events unleased by this conflict led to the paralysis of the Western democracies, the rise of the Fascist states, the opportunity for a Communist takeover, and the legacy that fed World War II. No leader controlled these events, none foresaw their advance, and no person could approximate their cataclysmic consequences.

Wilson was not totally successful; who could be under those conditions? But he did prevent German hegemony in Europe, he did insist on a more generous peace than his allies, he did seek to break the cycle of war fed by imperialism and power politics. Yet all of this seems modest within the perspective of what followed Versailles. History had unfairly remembered him for a "lost peace" and for lost opportunities. It has sought to find in his personal character and idiosyncrasies some guides to this unhappy train of events. These examinations have conferred a tragic aura, a sense of failure to Wilson's presidency. In fact, he was one of the most brilliant leaders this nation has produced—a true democratic executive who worked well in his first term with Congress on domestic reform and who inspired his fellow citizens. Then in war, he sought to avoid American involvement, pressed for a mediated compromise, and even after April 1917, positioned America away from reparations, colonial aggrandizement, and a vindictive peace. Wilson asked much of his nation and too much of himself. The student of the presidency can be more understanding of the shortcomings of both.

3

The Republican Ascendancy, 1921–1933:
Harding, Coolidge, and Hoover

The election of 1920 has been usually interpreted as a repudiation of Wilson and the League of Nations. That it was, but more importantly the vote was a mandate, in Warren Harding's words, to go "back to normalcy." The final tally showed Harding with 16,152,200 votes; 9,147,353 for James M. Cox; and 915,490 for the socialist Eugene V. Debs. Harding carried thirty-seven of the forty-eight states and received 404 electoral votes; his popular majority (60.2 percent) was the largest margin up to that date. Especially critical, the GOP gained control of the House of Representatives 301 to 131, and in the Senate, the Republicans took ten more seats and increased their majority by twenty-two.

The reaction to Wilson went far beyond the League of Nations debate. The stresses of the war and the weariness of the progressive social conscience had taken their toll. The administration in early 1919 had no real plan for demobilization, and after $35 billion of war contracts were abruptly terminated, unemployment rose in February to three million people. By November, inflation hit hard, and the cost of living was 82.2 percent above the 1914 level. By July 1920, inflation reached 104.5 percent, with large increases in basic necessities such as food and clothing. Then in 1920, the bottom fell out of the agricultural commodities market, and soon the rest of the economy followed suit. The cost of living fell and by March 1921, prices were only one-third of what they had been the year before. In the industrial sector, unemployment climbed to almost 20 percent.[1]

The Republicans could catch the scent—victory was at hand. At

their convention, they turned to Warren Gamaliel Harding, a senator from Ohio, who originally flirted with the idea of the presidency
only to strengthen his reelection bid for the Senate back home.
Managed by the clever Harry Daugherty and aided by a deadlock
among the front-runners, Harding emerged as the nominee. Despite
his historical reputation as a reactionary, Harding was generally
regarded as a moderate who opposed the League, but really was
not counted among the "irreconcilables." A pleasant person, he ran
a soothing campaign, one that offered relief from the passions of
the Wilson years. In Boston, he promised "not heroics, but healing,
not nostrums but normalcy," and he clearly captured the public
mood. He defined normalcy as not the old order, but as the normal,
natural way of doing things—progress without excess. Overall, he
was successful in pulling together the Old Guard and the
progressives in the same camp and ran a dignified "front porch"
campaign. He avoided personalities, met celebrities at his home in
Ohio, and stayed away from divisive issues. In the end, the voters
agreed with singer Al Jolson who crooned, "Harding, you're the man
for us."

Harding's philosophy and style of government were in a sharp
contrast to Wilson's legacy. The war bureaucracy brought unparalleled regimentation, and Wilson's long and serious illness left a
vacuum at the center of the ad hoc system he had created. Harding,
on the other hand, was a talkative person who seemed to epitomize
the common fellow. He was a joiner, a clubman, a friendly Midwesterner with a deep sense of loyalty to his friends. H. L. Mencken
once snapped that Harding had a "bungalow mind," meaning that
he was a mediocre, parochial man with a limited grasp. Indeed,
Harding worked long hours at the job and lamented that he could
not equal Theodore Roosevelt's energy or Wilson's brilliance. He
concluded, "I cannot hope to be one of the great presidents, but
perhaps I may be remembered as one of the best loved."[2]

Since American history in the twentieth century has generally
been written by liberal scholars, the Republican postwar presidents
have been seen as an unfortunate interregnum between Wilson and
FDR, and the 1920s have been portrayed as a period of mindless
excess, selfish speculation, and extraordinary profit taking, all of
which supposedly led to the Great Depression. Clearly, none of the
presidents of the twenties compiled an extraordinary record of
achievement—perhaps not one even had a successful tenure in office. Harding, Coolidge, and to a lesser extent, Hoover emphasized

the role of the cabinet in decision making and downplayed the type of assertive executive dominance that TR, Wilson, and later FDR epitomized. Within the liberal perspective, these three men are often presented as mossback conservatives who sought to turn back the tides of progressive reform and restore the forces of acquisitive and untamed capitalism to the American temple of democracy.

In fact, none of the three fits this stereotype. Harding was not a man of Wall Street, but of Main Street; he believed in and promoted the more modest and moderate values of cooperation, consensus, and small town America. Coolidge, despite his reputation as a "puritan in Babylon," was really a mild progressive who celebrated business only within a larger framework that stressed how profits were necessary in order to promote a cultured life. He genuinely treasured the New England admonitions of thrift, simplicity, and learning. As for Hoover, one of the saddest ironies of history is that posterity willed to this genuine humanitarian stewardship for the depression and left him scarred by charges of indifference and indecision. Yet, he was a major progressive leader, an associate of Wilson; in fact, in 1920, there was serious mention of a national Democratic ticket of Hoover and young Franklin D. Roosevelt for president and vice president, respectively.

THE GHOST OF WOODROW WILSON

Chronicles of the Wilson administration often tend to end with his tragic illness and the defeat of the League. In fact, from his stroke in September 1919 to Harding's inauguration in March 1921, over a year and a half passed in which the presidency was barely functioning. In this period, especially after his stroke, Wilson's second wife acted as a gatekeeper and advisor to the stricken executive. With the assistance of the president's physician, Admiral Cary Grayson, Edith Bolling Wilson took over informal powers that worried congressional leaders and confused cabinet officials. One senator, Albert Fall, charged, "we have petticoat Government! Mrs. Wilson is president." At first, very few people were allowed to see Wilson, and his cabinet listlessly met without the president, until Wilson fired Secretary of State Robert Lansing for having the audacity to call that group together without his consent.

By December 1919, an old Wilson admirer, Ray Stannard Baker, confided that it seemed "as though our Government has gone out of business." As the summer approached, Wilson called on his immense will power and faith in God's Providence to set right his reputation. In late 1920, he won the Nobel Peace Prize and began talking about running for the presidency again. But it was to no avail, Wilson was a shadow of himself—a man repudiated by his fellow countrymen and resigned to let history justify his actions.

The White House was a quiet and sullen place, and the nation was marred by the Red Scare and then a sharp economic downturn. Throughout 1919, the press played up the horrors of the Bolshevik revolution in Russia and evidence of alleged radical and subversive activities in America. Increasing labor problems and strikes heightened the fears of the middle class; Governor Calvin Coolidge won even Wilson's approval when he belatedly warned the striking Boston police, "there is no right to strike against the public safety by anybody, anywhere, any time." In late 1919 and early 1920, Attorney General A. Mitchell Palmer ordered a series of raids and arrested thousands of leftist leaders—several hundred of whom were deported to Russia. Despite Wilson's warning to Palmer to exercise restraint, the president went along with the general spirit of the times. And in the South, the ugly head of the Ku Klux Klan arose again. One admirer of Wilson's, Colonel Edmund W. Starling, concluded simply, "the country was in a mess."[3]

HARDING'S DOMESTIC POLICY

Harding began his term with a simple pledge to bring together the best minds to solve the nation's problems. What he got was a confused collection of interest groups that impinged on his time, undercut his leadership, and drove him to near despair by the time of his premature death. His cabinet included the stately Charles Evans Hughes, progressive heir Herbert Hoover, multimillionaire Andrew Mellon, farm advocate Henry Wallace, old crony Harry Daugherty, former Senator Albert Fall, and Secretary of Labor James Davis, a leader of the Loyal Order of Moose. Observers were to call it a well-balanced and strong cabinet; a short time after, Daugherty and Fall were embroiled in controversy and court battles.

Symbolic of the new regime, Harding opened up the barred gates of the White House, and later began news conferences with members of the press. In contrast to Wilson, especially the infirmed Wilson, Harding appeared at ease, likeable, friendly, and kind. He

had a profound need for human sympathy and approval, characteristics that led him to trust all too often the shoddier types of people
posing as his friends. Harding once recalled that his father told him
it was good that he had not been born a girl, for he would be preg-
nant all the time since he couldn't say no. He played cards, carried
on discreet affairs, drank in the era of legal prohibition, and smoked.
Inventor Thomas Edison concluded, "Harding is all right. Any man
who chews tobacco is all right." Harding, though, worked long hours
at the presidency and was sincerely concerned about doing the correct thing—if only someone would point it out.

He regarded the presidency as predominantly a ceremonial office and saw himself as a counselor and conciliator. He rejected
the legacy of Wilson, including his strong domination of the legislative branch before the breakdown over the League. As Congress,
especially the Senate, proved to be more and more obstructionist
during his term, Harding began to emphasize the executive's leadership role. Yet he consistently avoided confronting the Senate directly on foreign policy matters, and with Secretary of State Hughes
spent a considerable amount of time devising strategies to promote
U.S. policy without raising old animosities.

Actually, Hughes and the president established close personal ties
and helped cement a working friendship over the years. Consequently, the secretary of state supported by the president held off
patronage demands being made on the State Department and maintained a level of appointments probably above that of Wilson and
Bryan.

Interestingly, the Harding years were marked by the establishment of the Bureau of the Budget and the creation of an executive
budget, two of the most important developments in the establishment of the modern presidency. Proposed during the Taft administration, initiated in the Wilson era, and signed by Harding, the final
law passed by Congress gave the executive complete control over
all budget matters coming from the cabinet bureaus, and required
him to prepare an annual report to the legislative branch that became, in effect, the national agenda.

Another major domestic controversy facing the new president was
the popular clamor to reduce taxes, a cause that Mellon as secretary of treasury vigorously spearheaded. The secretary pushed for a
repeal of the excess profits tax, a reduction of the maximum surtax
rate from 65 percent to 32 percent for the wealthy, and a continuation of the general tax rate at 4 percent for incomes under $4,000

and 8 percent for the remainder. In addition, the president, under Mellon's guidance, stood firm against a veterans' bonus even to the point of going before the Senate personally to oppose it. After intense discussions, Congress passed a more modest reduction than Mellon recommended, still supported the bonus idea, and took up a protectionist tariff.

But the most intensive lobbying came from the "farm bloc"—a group of senators and representatives who were pushing for relief for agricultural interests. The president, however, opposed subsidizing the farmer, although his party was committed to a readjustment of freight rates, better commodity financing, extension of farm credits, broader laws governing corporations, stricter regulations of meat packers, and new amendments to the Farm Loan Act and the Federal Reserve Act. Most important to the bloc was the passage of an emergency tariff aimed at controlling foreign competition and dumping. The president did support the War Finance Corporation's advancing loans to exporters, banks, farmer cooperatives, and foreign purchasers. Harding also encouraged national conferences on farm problems and tried to push the Interstate Commerce Commission and the railroads to lower freight rates. While many of the financial and corporate leaders opposed any special consideration of the plight of farmers, Harding took some modest steps to deal with the suffering and political turmoil in agricultural regions.

Harding's record with organized labor was less salutary. Although he sought to adopt a conciliatory and moderate tone, the controversies resulting from coal and railroad strikes led to intense criticism of his administration. The new president started out well as he laid aside the tensions of the Red Scare and managed to convince the steel industry to abandon the twelve-hour work day and adopt the eight-hour day in its place. But when the coal strike continued into the summer of 1922, the president's efforts to settle the dispute failed. After the United Mine Workers rejected Harding's proposals, the president ordered twenty-eight governors in soft coal-producing states to use law enforcement agencies to maintain security at the mines. A similar outcome took place in Harding's attempt to mediate a railroad dispute. The president sought to get some congressional action, but the legislative branch simply sidestepped the issue. Then Harding unfortunately approved his attorney general's decision to apply for a far-reaching injunction. In September, Judge James Wilkerson of the Northern Illinois District issued an injunction covering the entire territory of the United States and enjoined rail workers from tampering in any way with the railroads. The strikers and their attorneys and colleagues were forbidden to encourage the strike by letters, telegrams, telephones, and personal conversations; picketing and the use of union funds to aid the strikers were also barred. It was an incredibly broad order and even Harding, when he was informed of its implications, told Daugherty to limit his use of the injunction. Still, to labor leaders and progressives, the administration's handling of labor matters was a far cry from its tender loving care of corporations and business leaders.

In addition, the tariff came to symbolize the Republican administration's commitment to big business over other segments of society and its rejection of an intelligent trade policy abroad. Actually, the party itself was seriously split on the issue with the farm bloc and business interests having very different objectives. As for the Democrats, traditionally the party of low rates, their leader in the Senate, Oscar Underwood of Alabama, opposed the president's desire to have some flexibility in administering any tariff law. He warned that such a provision would be "an ignominious surrender to the Executive of one of the great functions of government that belongs to Congress."

Finally, after sixteen months of waiting, the president signed the Fordney-McCumber bill, which gave the chief executive the power to raise and lower rates up to 50 percent within certain guidelines. In order to gather enough support for the bill, the duties on agricultural products were increased substantially supposedly to protect farmers. As for industrial rates, the tariff raised them far above the 1913 tariff, but not as high as some of the previous Republican-sponsored tariff acts. There was very little understanding by the president and Congress that, in the long run, a trading country such as the United States could not rely on protectionism and expect foreign markets to be receptive to what it had to sell.

The president's agenda also included two other items: severe restrictions on immigration, especially from southern and eastern Europe, and a subsidy for a new rebuilt merchant marine. The flood of immigration was severely cut to a little over three hundred thousand people, and no more than 27 percent of the total could come from southern and eastern Europe. In terms of the subsidy, Congress continued to refuse to approve government support despite Harding's insistence that the United States' new role in the world demanded a fitting merchant marine service.

To Harding, looking over his record of two years, the administration had some major accomplishments to show the voters in the congressional elections. But his consensus, probusiness approach also alienated segments of America, especially labor, veterans, low tariff advocates, farm interests, those opposed in general to subsidies, and partisans who generally disliked the tone of the new leadership. In the Senate, the Republicans lost seven seats and in the House, the Republicans lost seventy seats, a higher level of dissatisfaction than is customary in off-year elections. The president concluded, "I confess myself utterly unable to make a satisfactory diagnosis of the outcome." In part, though, the election results may have been more dependent on local issues and candidates, than on Harding's stewardship. Also, the shift possibly reflected a normal readjustment of partisan lines after the president's huge victory in 1920. Harding's attitude toward Congress and toward his own job altered as well as he became tougher and more insistent on providing leadership. But now Harding faced a strong progressive coalition in the Congress and a more cohesive farm bloc group insisting on tangible benefits for its constituencies.[4]

HARDING'S FOREIGN POLICY

The Republican foreign policy of the 1920s was a strange mixture of isolationism and idealism. Nearly all the administration leaders agreed that they had to avoid a confrontation with the Senate, which, having bested Wilson, still attempted to expand its prerogatives. Under the steady guidance of Secretary of State Hughes, Harding compiled a moderately successful record, one that recognized some of the new responsibilities of the United States, and yet avoided Wilson's global outreach, concentrating instead on a more modest calculation of national interests. In the campaign of 1920, Harding had criticized Wilson's "colonialism" and took a potshot at Franklin Roosevelt who claimed to have written personally the Haitian constitution. Harding's reply was to the point, "If I am elected president . . . I will not empower an Assistant Secretary of the Navy to draft a constitution for helpless neighbors in the West Indies and jam it down their throats at the point of bayonets borne by the United States marines."

In the Caribbean and Central American regions, Harding and Hughes attempted to restore normal relations with Mexico, Cuba, Haiti, Puerto Rico, Santo Domingo, and Colombia. By the time of his death, Harding had presided over closer ties with Mexico, removed the marines from Cuba and recognized its claims to the Isle of Pines, phased in a withdrawal of the military from Haiti, reduced tensions with Puerto Rico, evacuated Santo Domingo, and supported passage of a treaty with Colombia that provided for compensation for Theodore Roosevelt's interference in the Panama Canal dispute. The administration also pressed for arbitration of disputes in Latin America, considered recognition of the Soviet Union, and encouraged economic development in the Philippines.

The major foreign policy contribution of the Harding administration was the finalization of peace treaties with former wartime belligerents, since the Wilson treaties had been rejected. With extensive Senate intrusion, the secretary of state won approval of a series of documents that ended the conflict and eliminated any form of U.S. intervention without congressional authorization. For the United States, the Great War was belatedly over officially.

The second important initiative was the United States' leadership in the Washington Disarmament Conference in 1921. Under prodding from Senator William E. Borah, the administration came out for naval disarmament and laid the groundwork for a meeting of the Big Four: the United States, Britain, France, and Japan. The president wisely chose the TR progressive, Elihu Root, Wilson's nemesis Henry Cabot Lodge, and Democratic Senator Oscar Underwood to work with Hughes. Harding also invited China, Italy, Belgium, the Netherlands, and Portugal to the meeting; it opened on Armistice Day, the time set aside for the dedication of the grave of the unknown soldier in Washington, D.C.

The next day, the president gave a moving address on the importance of the conference and left his secretary of state to present a shockingly far-reaching proposal. Instead of waiting for the negotiating sessions, Hughes immediately urged a massive scrapping of the naval fleets of the world's powers and pushed for a ten-year construction moratorium. In its place, he proposed a total maximum tonnage ratio in capital ships of five hundred thousand for the United States and Britain, and three hundred thousand for Japan, France, and Italy. Hughes's open diplomacy annoyed some of the British, but it captivated the public. Here, indeed, were Wilson's open covenants openly arrived at, unlike at Versailles. The conference ended up supporting Hughes's overall approach and abolished poison gas, regulated the use of submarines, and guaranteed the status quo in the Pacific region.

In that region, the United States pushed for an international Open Door policy in China, even though that nation still was having its sovereignty curtailed by outside interests. With Japan, the United States also promised not to add to the fortifications of its bases in the Pacific, a restriction that in light of the later attack on Pearl Harbor in 1941 seems probably unwise in historical retrospection. In the Senate, the usual objections to international cooperation were raised, but once the administration accepted an amendment that certified that the United States was not committed to using its armed forces in any alliance or joint defense arrangement, the treaties were passed overwhelmingly. The contrast with Wilson's failures seemed apparent, and reflected quite favorably on Harding's leadership. Even one of his critics, William Allen White, concluded, "the passage of these treaties is due largely to the good sense and tact of President Harding. . . . Mr. Harding is not an intellectual giant. He may not be a moral heavy weight. That is as it may be. But he is a courteous, sensible American gentleman, and he does bring home the bacon."

As he approached midpoint in his term, the president pushed for U.S. association with the World Court—a red flag to the Republican isolationists. He had already raised some eyebrows by presenting a moderate State of the Union address in 1921, which advocated some federal actions in the fields of social welfare, highway development, aviation, and radio regulation. In early 1923, he informed Secretary Andrew Mellon that he would not support any more cuts in the surtax unless they benefited everyone and not just the wealthy. Responding to farm pressure, he approved the passage of the Agricultural Credits Act of 1923, which extended more credit to cooperatives, rural banks, and livestock associations and expanded overall lending opportunities. Meanwhile, a proposal developed by George M. Peek of the Moline Plow Company was attracting attention. Peek and his associate, Hugh S. Johnson, had advocated control over exports and a subsidy for dumping those commodities at a disposal price abroad. Harding never lived to see the final version, called the McNary-Haugen Act, which Coolidge vetoed, but which made its way in another form into FDR's New Deal.[5]

Harding's appointments and philosophy reflected his overall business sympathies, but as a good politician and a rather sensitive soul, he seemed somewhat more open to people, except organized labor, than Coolidge would be. The tax policies did end up stimulating a period of boom, in some ways like the Kennedy and Reagan tax cuts enacted years later. The expansion was real, the incentives were surely provided to the wealthy and to business for both expansion and for speculation. The rich got richer and the poor and middle classes did somewhat better, although the recovery was uneven as the turmoil on the farms showed to even the most casual observer of that time.

But that personal receptivity had its darker side, too. Before his untimely and suspicious death on a trip to Alaska and the West Coast, the president began to see the tidal waves of corruption that were swirling around him. To a friend he confided, "I am not fit for this office and should never have been here."[6] In early 1923, Harding received evidence that there were questionable activities going on in the Veterans Bureau. The director, Charles Forbes, was selling government supplies to private contractors at minimum prices and engaging in deals on hospital building contracts and site selections. An outraged Harding called Forbes to the White House, shook him physically, and yelled, "You double-crossing bastard." Apparently, the president demanded his resignation and gave him the opportunity to leave the United States, which Forbes did. Then to add to the aura of suspicion, the Veterans Bureau's general counsel committed suicide. Ten weeks later, Jesse Smith, an influence-peddler and friend of Attorney General Daugherty, also took his own life. Working with several Ohio men, Smith had taken money for all sorts of racketeering and government favors. "The Ohio Gang," as it was called, became a nomenclature that rebounded unfavorably on Harding's reputation. An exasperated president remarked, "My God, this is a hell of a job! I have no trouble with my enemies . . . but my darn friends, my God-damn friends . . . they're the ones that keep me walking the floor nights!"

As he moved toward Alaska in the summer of 1923 on his final trip, a worried Harding apparently had evidence of more malfeasance. He pulled Secretary of Commerce Hoover aside, and asked him how to handle the scandal. Hoover's response was succinct and appropriate, "Publish it, and at least get credit for integrity on your side." On August 3, the president died, probably of a cerebral hemorrhage.[7]

In October, Congress investigated the Veterans Bureau, and Forbes's corruption was exposed. When Attorney General Daugherty refused to testify, implying that he was protecting the memory of the late president, Coolidge dismissed him. He was tried twice, but the jury in each case could not agree on a verdict. Then in the winter of 1924, the Senate investigated the conduct of Secretary of Interior Albert Fall, a former United States senator from New Mexico. Fall had leased the great Elk Hills reserve in California to the Pan American Petroleum Company and the Teapot Dome reserves to Continental Trading Company, allegedly receiving $100,000 and $300,000 for each deal. In another transaction, $185,000 was delivered to the Republican National Committee as a loan from Harry Sinclair of Continental Trading Company.

In the end, the agents of these two companies were not convicted of bribery and conspiracy, but Fall was found guilty of accepting a bribe, fined $100,000 and sent to jail for a year. In civil cases arising from the controversy, the Supreme Court found collusion and fraud, cancelled the leases, and required restitution to the government. Harding's reputation was severely scarred by these scandals and by a later series of exposés about his marital infidelities. His administration increasingly became portrayed not for its business orientation, its successful adjustments to postwar realities, or its modest gains in foreign policy. The Harding term became a synonym for corruption, malfeasance, and rapacious capitalism. He never extricated himself from the friends he came to fear.

COOLIDGE'S WAYS

The handsome, backslapping, hearty pose of Harding gave way to a vice president who was quiet, taciturn, and very private. TR's daughter, Alice, once commented that Calvin Coolidge looked like he had been weaned on a pickle. Coolidge, though, seemed to sense immediately the causes of Harding's troubles. He ordered the White House living quarters closed to his predecessor's cronies and drinking buddies; he decided that it was to be the way it was before—a place of dignity and privacy. Coolidge's rise to the presidency was extraordinary because it was so mundane. Born on the Fourth of July, he held a variety of local and state offices in Massachusetts, gained fame with a pithy but relatively late remark on the Boston police strike, and was nominated against the wishes of the Old Guard bosses. He said little, calculated carefully, and established overnight a homey New England image. He took the oath of office from his father in a Vermont farmhouse lit by kerosene lamps. Once in Washington, he tried to sit in front of the White House in a rocking chair, just as he would on the porch of an old Yankee homestead. Coolidge successfully created his homey image in part because he genuinely lived it.

Coolidge's taciturn behavior was, on occasions, carried to extremes, to a point of near rudeness toward those to whom he chose not to talk or to even listen. But his reserve at first served him well. He entered the office without a national power base, close to the opening of the 1924 nomination convention, and surrounded by men whose integrity was being questioned. He pledged not to remove Harding's appointees, unless absolutely necessary, while he completed his predecessor's term. Coolidge waited patiently, too patiently in the case of firing Attorney General Daugherty, sought counsel and advice from a variety of people, and moved only when he saw the clearing up ahead. Even more than Harding, he rejected the activist legacy of TR and Wilson, let Congress go its own way, and showed even more of a deferential attitude toward the great personalities in his cabinet, especially Hughes, Hoover, and Mellon. He fully supported Mellon's policy of cutting taxes for the rich, although in fairness it must be noted that the federal income tax reforms by then exempted mostly all American households earning under $4,000 a year, which meant the lower and middle classes.[8]

Coolidge's philosophy of government is usually summed up by his remark that "the business of the American people is business." But the context was one that stressed how wealth leads to the advance of civilization, money being the means to an end, not the end itself. He opposed placing government under the control of business since it resulted in oligarchy and selfishness; but he also opposed government entering into the realm of business since it would crush competition, lead to extravagance and inefficiency, and close the doors of opportunity. Much of what seems to be an apologia by Coolidge toward big business is really an almost classical American fear of concentrated government power—ideas close to the Founding Fathers whom Coolidge revered all his life. Yet while Coolidge was not the epitome of Babbitry and philistine commercialism, his administration seemed at times so inactive that it gave those forces, already dominant, considerable leeway.[9] There was none of Theodore Roosevelt's commitment to public stewardship, no sense of involvement in the responsibilities of modern social life, which so many great Republican progressive governors and mayors exhibited. Even within his own party, far away from the shadow of Woodrow Wilson's legacy, Coolidge represented a truncated view of the state and a modest perspective on the great office he held. What can be claimed is that after the collapse of Wilson and the scandals of Harding, he restored some common dignity and quiet decorum to the office. Roosevelt's daughter, Alice, once again summed up the contrast by concluding that when she first "went to the White House after the Coolidges arrived, the atmosphere was as different as a New England front parlor is from a back room in a speakeasy."[10]

Coolidge, early in his term, reached out to a variety of people for advice including Samuel Gompers of the American Federation of Labor, Chief Justice Taft, farm advocate Hugh S. Johnson, and progressive dynamo, Senator William Borah. In working with his cabinet members, he gave them considerable discretion in running their areas and rejected any real oversight over their initiatives. His argument was that if he were aware of all those proposals and controversies, he would be dragged into them and face public criticism more than necessary. One biographer, Donald R. McCoy, has called his administration "government by nondirective therapy," and Coolidge would probably have agreed with the definition, and would have pointed out that after years of progressive reform, wartime regulation, and free and easy corruption, such therapy was just what the doctor ordered.[11]

The president once concluded that "If you see ten travelers coming down the road, you can be sure that nine will run into the ditch before they reach you and you have to battle with only one of them." In dealing with Congress, Coolidge seemed a master of delay and indecision. Faced with an increasingly factionalized GOP and a sullen partisan Democratic party, Coolidge would have had an almost impossible task even if he had chosen to apply some energy to the legislative process. But he saw his role as one of recommending items for Congress and judging those bills that ended up coming to him. Coolidge rarely provided strong guidance and, except for the veterans' bonus bill and the McNary-Haugen Act for farm relief, he did not stand forcible against Congress's will.

At brief breakfast meetings, the president entertained congressmen but often left them guessing at his agenda and his intentions. He rarely got involved in the Republican party's internal disputes, concluding at one point,

> Some of our presidents have appeared to lack comprehension of the political mind. Although I have been associated with it for many

years, I always found difficulty in understanding it. It is a strange mixture of vanity and timidity, of an obsequious attitude at one time and a delusion of grandeur at another time, of the most selfish preferment combined with the most sacrificing patriotism. The political mind is the product of men in public life who have been twice spoiled. They have been spoiled with praise and they have been spoiled with abuse. With them nothing is natural, everything is artificial.[12]

Added to Coolidge's own timidity was the general weakness of the Republican leadership in Congress. The president, though, generally tried to remain on good terms even with his opponents, a practice that led to little discipline in the party and also to a lack of personal rancor on Capitol Hill. Part of the president's equanimity was due to the fact that he promoted a rather limited agenda. His single most persistent call was for tax reduction, and in an America run by corporations and business, such a proposal was welcome news. Led by Mellon, the president pushed for the abolition of wartime excess taxes and a decrease in the income tax rates. Coolidge supported the high tariff, some internal improvements, court expansion, and restrictions on immigration. On the last issue, he warned that "those who do not want to be partakers of the American spirit ought not to settle in America . . . America must be kept American."[13]

With 1924 being an election year, Coolidge proceeded even more cautiously. He invited Harry Slattery, a conservationist who had explored the details of the oil-leasing scandals, to talk with him about the story. As the Senate continued its investigations, Coolidge apparently decided to upstage the members by proposing the creation of an important special counsel to investigate the issues. However, he refused to dismiss Secretary of Navy Edwin Denby and Attorney General Daugherty. Denby was innocent of wrongdoing, but probably somewhat naive in his dealings with the leasing operators. Finally, he resigned, leaving Daugherty still under fire but remaining in the cabinet. Coolidge had Senator Borah directly confront the attorney general in front of him on the charges being raised, but still the president did not act, probably seeing Teapot Dome as a partisan plot to discredit the administration and the GOP.

While Hoover and Hughes pushed for the attorney general's resignation and party officials warned that Daugherty's departure would hurt Coolidge's reelection bid, the president said little. When the

Senate uncovered in March a series of questionable deals involving the attorney general and his friends, the investigators demanded that the attorney general open up the Justice Department's files for inspection. Daugherty quickly refused, and Coolidge used the occasion to remove him, arguing that he could not be defending himself and also acting as attorney general. In the end, the evidence against Daugherty was found by the courts to be inconclusive.[14]

In February, the partisan bitterness had spilled over to other individuals, including Mellon, who was attacked for having presided over the treasury while it gave huge tax rebates to corporations, including some with which he was affiliated. Coolidge stood firmly behind the secretary, and also confronted Congress by vetoing a veterans bonus and the McNary-Haugen crop dumping bill. The president's dealings with Congress had gone disastrously downhill, and now in 1924, he faced a renomination battle.

Surprisingly, the Republican party overwhelmingly nominated Coolidge, but in a touch of independence gave the vice-presidency spot on the ticket to Charles Dawes, the former director of the Bureau of the Budget. The campaign saw a divided and lackluster Democratic party, headed by Wall Street lawyer and former Ambassador John W. Davis of West Virginia, and the brother of William Jennings Bryan, Charles, and a Progressive ticket led by Senator Robert LaFollette and running mate Burton K. Wheeler, a senator from Montana. Coolidge, who was emotionally distressed from the death of his son, said little during the campaign. When pressed by newspaper reporters, his response was characteristically simple and somewhat insightful, "I don't recall any candidate for president that ever injured himself very much by not talking." He cultivated photographers though, dressing up as a Vermont farmer, and hosting pilgrimages of politicians and industrialists. Davis was correct when he concluded that the real issue in the election was "tranquility." The slogans of "Keep Cool with Coolidge" and "Coolidge or Chaos" seemed appropriate to the times. The Republicans outspent the Democrats six to one, and the final tally gave the president 15,725,016 votes to Davis's 8,385,586 and LaFollette's 4,822,856. The country concluded that the times were good; as Justice Oliver Wendell Holmes, Jr., remarked, "While I don't expect anything very astonishing from [Coolidge], I don't want anything very astonishing."[15]

Now with his own mandate, Coolidge faced Congress, and he resorted to his past hands-off style. He refused to get involved in the majority leadership's plans for disciplining LaFollette and his followers by expelling them from the GOP caucus and stripping them of their committee seniority as Republicans. He presented his proposals, did little in the way of garnering support, and tried to be amiable and businesslike. Even though the Republicans had picked up twenty-two seats in the House and five seats in the Senate in the 1924 election, the party still lacked cohesion, and regional and economic differences cut through the ranks and continued on into the New Deal period.

As for the president, he was committed to delegating to his cabinet secretaries much of the day-to-day functioning of the executive branch, expecting to hear little from them, even if they disagreed on public policy. With Coolidge still depressed by his son's death, his term seemed even more subdued, and whatever joy he got out of politics was lessened. He had a relatively low energy level, slept about ten hours a day, and was rarely given to bursts of creativity, although he remained a hardworking and conscientious executive within his narrow view of what the office should entail. Every working day, Coolidge greeted the public at 12:30 P.M. and shook hands with an average of four hundred tourists visiting the White House. At one reception, he met more than two thousand people in little over an hour, surely some sort of endurance record for such occasions. Oddly enough, he spent an incredible amount of time dealing with pension claims, government jobs, and personal constituent matters usually left to staff people. His critics charged he was lazy, a captive of business, an uninspiring leader. Wit H. L. Mencken commented that Coolidge's ideal day "is one in which nothing whatever happens."[16]

But to Coolidge, public service was a religiously sanctioned activity, a service in which one should represent the opinions of one's fellow citizens and not one's own views. He insisted that a state should be primarily concerned with the development of character, the moral inclinations that mold the young and give sustenance to the mature. And yet his view of government was not one of intervention and positive action, but of laissez faire and retreat from all intrusion—good or bad. As for himself, he was, he claimed, what he seemed to be. When a biographer, William Allen White, said he wanted to peek behind the mask, the president responded, "Maybe there isn't any."

The high point of Coolidge's leadership was appropriately an issue of his own choosing: the tax cut of 1926. With much of the residue of scandals out of the public mind and pressure building up for some tax relief, Coolidge and Mellon won overwhelming approval in both houses of Congress for a comprehensive reduction package. The gift tax was repealed, estate taxes cut by 50 percent, surtaxes on the wealthy reduced by up to 50 percent, and income taxes lowered across the board. A pleased president canonized the legislative branch as "the most efficient Congress that we have had for a great many years." Still, though, Coolidge had to come to grips once again with the McNary-Haugen bill, the most popular panacea for the farmers' despair. Faced with overproduction, excessive borrowing, foreign competition and tariffs, and often increased local taxation, farmers demanded some relief. The bill would allow subsidized dumping of American surpluses abroad, thus providing incentives for increasing production based on an unrealistic view of international trade markets. Coolidge attacked the proposal as one step away from having the government fix prices, which is exactly where the New Deal's regulatory policies would lead.

By 1926, the partisan alignment in Congress began to change. The Republicans lost ten seats in the House of Representatives and seven in the Senate. In the upper body, insurgent Republicans actually joined with Democrats to block Coolidge's modest agenda. Even as the president celebrated the virtues of untrampled economic development, he saw some worrisome warning signals. Coolidge seemed concerned about reports of pyramiding holding companies, stock market riggings, and unbridled speculation. But he laid aside his doubts, and by his statements fostered confidence in a system increasingly shaky. He continued in 1927–28 to stress economy, battled the friends of McNary-Haugenism, and proposed some money for internal improvements. In May 1928, Congress reduced the corporation tax further, a continuing vindication of Coolidge's philosophy and Mellon's advocacy.

COOLIDGE'S OTHER WORLD

Coolidge's foreign policies generally followed the lines laid down by Harding and Hughes, and Secretary of State Hughes remained in his first cabinet. The administration moved toward normal relations with Mexico and allowed American financiers to help that government buy the arms it needed to subdue rebels in its unstable regions. Also, the administration considered recognizing the Soviet

Union, but nothing came of that proposal. Like Harding, Coolidge also expressed some interest in having the United States join the World Court, thus antagonizing the vociferous League opponents once again. In addition, the president kept some lines of communication open with a group called the "Outlawry of War" movement. That organization sought to bar the use of force in foreign affairs, believing that such a prohibition would promote lasting peace. That concern would eventually lead Coolidge to back into the Kellogg-Briand pact later in his second term.[17]

The major international point of contention was, of course, the payment of the war debt, some $10 billion at 5 percent interest. Faced with economic problems at home and political opposition to repayment, the European allies requested that the United States cancel the loans. Because of high tariff barriers and domestic dislocations, the Western European countries could not easily come up with the surplus payments needed to meet their obligations. The Coolidge administration instead offered to renegotiate interest charges and extend periods of repayment.

The Allies had expected that the reparations from defeated Germany could be used to ameliorate their own economic problems. Ironically, the United States government and banks took over the reparations payments and, in turn, worked out liberal repayment provisions—a development that proved to be unwise in the long run. The so-called Dawes Committee created a schedule of payments for Germany, while the bankers helped Germany finance its reconstruction. American opinion, both Democrat and Republican, from Wilson to FDR, consistently insisted on repayment of the debts; Coolidge's response was characteristically simple, "They hired the money, didn't they?" In terms, though, of encouraging investment, American money flowed into Europe. Total investment rose from $7 billion in 1919 to $17.2 billion by 1930. Whereas Wilson was leery of large investments abroad, Coolidge followed a policy of laissez faire. In the end, some $2.5 billion went to Germany, which supported the whole structure of reparations and debt payments, an exchange that Winston S. Churchill was to call "insane."

By his second term, Coolidge's new secretary of State, Frank B. Kellogg, promoted U.S. foreign policies that included commercial access in China. However, when pressure was building to use U.S. troops in that region, the president moved away from such an abrupt commitment. The major crisis that Coolidge faced was in Latin America, where new turmoil racked Nicaragua, an already unstable nation. Since 1912, U.S. Marines had occupied that nation, and the last of these forces was not scheduled to be withdrawn until 1928. In December 1926, the president directed that additional Marines be sent there to safeguard American citizens and to protect that nation from what he judged to be its own follies. Troops were phased out finally in the 1931–33 period.

The president and Secretary of State Kellogg concluded their tenure with two final efforts, one resulting in failure and the other in a much heralded international agreement. In the first, the administration proposed that the United States join the World Court. The Senate, however, insisted on attaching a series of reservations to the treaty before the United States could accept the court protocol. Coolidge stayed out of the fray, and finally refused to negotiate with foreign governments over the Senate's terms.[18]

Then in fall 1926, the administration indicated its desire to consider extending the Washington Conference ratios to all types of naval vessels. That effort was unsuccessful, but the president decided to accept a proposal to outlaw war. The French government, hoping for some alliance with the United States, supported the policy. Coolidge, after expressing constitutional reservations about the proposal, jumped aboard at Senator Borah's instigation. The idea to outlaw war quickly captured the public imagination in the United States and abroad, and Coolidge became a reluctant convert. He even lent his support during the Senate debate where the treaty was passed 85 to 1. This treaty of good intentions represented the high point of the disarmament and utopian aspirations. After the terrible losses of the Great War, pacifist sentiment and the popular mood made such movements seem a proper postscript. As it turned out, those movements became a blind preface to the next, more horrendous war.[19]

COOLIDGE AS PRESIDENT

On August 2, 1927, Coolidge issued a simple statement, "I do not choose to run for president in nineteen twenty-eight." That was it—no explanation or comment. A single statement from a man who prized his privacy and brevity. Some thought that he did indeed want to be drafted; others mentioned that the president was tired, ill, and still depressed about his young son's death. Coolidge was quoted as saying that if he had won reelection, he could have been president for ten years, longer than any person in American history. "Too long," he concluded. His wife indicated that the president foresaw a major economic depression in the works, and that he had added that his training had been in thrift and in saving money. Now perhaps, "the time has come when we ought to spend money. I do not feel that I am qualified to do that." He is supposed to have argued that "there must be something constructive applied to the affairs of government, and it will not be sufficient to say, 'Let business take care of itself.'" He watched as his would-be successors jockeyed for his job, and sourly judged the front-runner, Herbert Hoover, as a man who had "offered me unsolicited advice for six years, all of it bad."[20] He departed from Washington stressing the successes of his term—tranquility, contentment, prosperity, peace, and friendship among nations. "The country," he observed, "can regard the present with satisfaction and anticipate the future with optimism."

Thus Calvin Coolidge closed out the Harding-Coolidge era, the reaction to Wilson's reforms and global vision, the reaffirmation of the values of achievement, frugality, and business success. For Harding, such values were the logical extension of the upbringing of Midwest Main Street; for Coolidge they were the necessary bases from which civilized, autonomous people ascended. Those sentiments flow throughout American history, in exalted ways from the Founding Fathers through Lincoln and even the progressives. But the postwar Republican presidents were deficient in any real understanding of the complexities of the corporate world and the uneasy practices that were being ignored if not condoned. They lacked an appreciation of the historic role of government in fostering economic development in the United States and of the moral tenet of the great conservative Edmund Burke, that society is more than a holding company.

One casualty of this tunnel vision was the strong presidency; there was a depreciation of executive power that saw Congress, especially the Senate, riding roughshod over the executive in embarrassing ways. But the most telling criticism of any viewpoint comes from within its own set of assumptions. The Harding-Coolidge presidencies aimed at restoring and furthering prosperity and in guaranteeing political stability by avoiding confrontation with the legislative branch. The pent-up demands of the postwar period and the tax cuts furthered a marked upturn in economic activity and wealth, although much of that upswing did not affect the farmers, most blacks, and many of the urban immigrants. But by 1929, the bottom fell out of the stock market, the economy declined, and then surprisingly collapsed for reasons still not totally clear. If the Harding-Coolidge presidencies get credit for the rain, they must be assigned blame for the drought as well.[21] And in the process, the presidency did not restore political stability—it drifted into ceremonial preoccupations and often obsequious gestures to congressional clamorings. This was the legacy bequeathed to Herbert Hoover, and as a consequence of it, the circumstances were created by 1933 for a presidency far more powerful than TR's or even Wilson's. Just as the Republicans replaced a repudiated Democratic regime, so too the wheel of fortune turned full circle.

THE AGONY OF HERBERT HOOVER

In American history, few men have compiled a more distinguished record of civilian public service, both before their presidency and after, as Herbert Hoover. Born of Quaker parents in West Branch, Iowa, Hoover lost his father when he was six and his mother three years later. As a diligent youth, he attended Stanford University and went on to become a bright, hard-driving engineer who accumulated a large, personal fortune and then turned to public life. In 1914, he headed up the American Citizens Relief Committee which aided nearly 120,000 Americans returning from Europe. Hoover then directed the Commission for Relief in Belgium, which aimed to feed and clothe hundreds of thousands of Belgians displaced by the German invasion. When the United States entered the war belatedly, Wilson appointed Hoover as food administrator.[22]

Over those years, Hoover developed a philosophy of philanthropy, volunteerism, and enlightened administration. He insisted on emphasizing the voluntary aspect of food administration, promoting persuasion and public relations to convince the American public and corporations to conserve and readjust their life-styles. After the war, he headed up the Inter-Allied Food Council and a variety of reconstruction agencies. A strong supporter of Wilson, he endorsed the League of Nations, but in 1920, he declared himself a Republican and sought that party's nomination for the presidency. Franklin D. Roosevelt at that time wrote of his future competitor, "He is certainly a wonder and I wish we could make him president. There couldn't be a better one." John Maynard Keynes remarked that Hoover was "the only man who emerged from the ordeal of Paris with an enhanced reputation." Harding, a strong admirer of Hoover, paired his name as secretary of commerce, with Andrew Mellon in treasury in order to guarantee approval from the conservative Senate.[23]

Hoover's record as secretary of commerce was an extraordinary one, considering the dimness of the Harding-Coolidge terms. He fostered a "middle way" between laissez faire capitalism and a centralized planned economy. Hoover's emphasis on volunteerism, rationality, efficiency, and trade associations reflected both the progressive ideals of good government and the inclinations of many corporate leaders who advocated a more coordinated economic life. By 1925, the Supreme Court had approved trade associations as legitimate combinations and exempted them from the antitrust laws. To Hoover, a social balance with government, labor, and corporations working together promoted true individualism and genuine public service.

In 1928, Hoover and his public relations-wise staff promoted the "Great Engineer" into a nearly flawless nomination lead that rolled over so-called experienced politicians. In the general election, riding on the Republican tide of the 1920s and basking in the sunshine of his extraordinary career record, Hoover overwhelmed Governor Alfred Smith of New York. Smith was a Roman Catholic and an opponent of Prohibition, who had a discernible New York City inflection in his voice that was not well received over the airwaves, especially in the South and Midwest. Smith lost 21,392,190 to 15,016,443, carrying only eight states, but the Democrats captured fifty of the largest urban areas and took 122 counties that had been GOP territories. Hoover, however, had cut into the solid South and carried Florida, North Carolina, Tennessee, Texas, and Virginia in the contest.

No president had given so much intelligent thought to the changing economic realities of his time, and none has played a greater role in promoting, on a national scale, laws, practices, and informal agreements to further nonmonopolistic, cooperative economic associations. Corporations, and later farmer groups, were to share general information, technical skill, and planning data in order to promote a more efficient and rational economic order. In that scheme of things, Hoover, more than most any other major public figure, acknowledged a place for organized labor.

History has so linked up Hoover with the Great Depression that posterity is denied a true picture of his first exciting and successful year in office. Hoover was the engineer, the statistician, the planner who appointed topflight study commissions to lay out informed recommendations on a variety of areas including those that affected the poor and minority groups. Hoover was the nonpartisan, progressive expert par excellence, and his presidency was an administratively centered one; he was not a partisan advocate nor a leader of the legislative process. He generally sought to avoid interacting with Congress, not just the opposition Democrats, but also the western insurgent Republicans, called ungraciously by their detractors, "the sons of the wild jackass."[24]

Dealing with the mounting farming problem, Hoover signed the Agriculture Marketing Act of 1929. Although he had some reservations about possible government control, Hoover approved the creation of the Federal Farm Board with a $500 million revolving fund, which could loan money to organize and foster cooperatives that would, in turn, assist farmers to produce and market their crops. The president regarded the Board as the equivalent of the Federal Reserve System with its relationships with the financial community, but he opposed any attempt to stabilize farm policies by having the federal government buy up excess commodities.

Hoover started off his term with several popular nods to the progressive legacy of which he was a part. Despite Mellon's advice, he advocated a more graduated income tax, instructed his attorney general to list publicly those who nominated candidates for the judiciary, curtailed search and seizure efforts in Prohibition cases, ended Red baiting by the Justice Department, and pushed for prison reforms. His administration turned to restructuring Indian education, strongly pushed conservation, and examined the quality of the health and welfare of the nation's children. He showed the traditional Quaker sensitivity to blacks and invited a black congressman's wife, Mrs. Oscar De Priest, to the White House. His commissions on social trends and law enforcement were impressive expert enterprises. In the areas of foreign policy, Hoover began to push for a "good neighbor policy" in South America, approved the withdrawal of U.S. troops in the Caribbean, sought to phase in independence for the Philippines, and advocated a nonbelligerent and straightforward policy in Asia.

By the end of eight months, Hoover emerged as an impressively competent chief executive, a sort of undramatic, noncharismatic Theodore Roosevelt. A chronicler of those times, Mark Sullivan, concluded that Hoover was alienating the "Higher tariff barons, jingoes, brass hats, big Nayitas, Prohibition fanatics, patronage hounds, and in general, those who dread change." Then in October, the bottom fell out of the stock market, and eventually out of the Hoover presidency.[25]

THE HOOVER DEPRESSION

The standard liberal history records how the Hoover administration stood deficient and naked before the depression until Roosevelt's string of New Deal initiatives took its place. In fact, Hoover and FDR confronted not each other, but the Great Depression, and in the end the depression bested both of them. Neither the New Era nor the New Deal ended the economic downturn; the preparation for World War II dealt the death blow to the depression finally in the United States and in Europe. There is some continuity between Hoover's policies and FDR's, just as there is between the TR and Wilson administrations and the New Deal. But it is misleading to imply, as some historians have, that Roosevelt was simply following Hoover's major forays; the New Deal contained elements of government persuasion and coercion that placed the Federal establishment squarely into the lives of the average American in ways that Hoover had opposed all of his adult career. His "middle way," his emphasis on volunteerism, was an attempt to postpone, if not forestall altogether, the type of intrusive and/or supportive welfare state that the New Deal established. In fact, Franklin Roosevelt, in the 1920s and even in the 1932 campaign, opposed a large federal government that would regulate and assume responsibilities over people's lives, but under political pressures mounting from an unsolved depression, he shed his inhibitions in a way Hoover never could.[26]

A second misunderstanding runs in the opposite direction—that Hoover was a do-nothing president, a sharp contrast to the activist FDR. As we will see, Roosevelt was one of the true giants of the presidency, not the amiable lightweight that was assumed before the 1932 election. But because FDR was such an activist executive, that does not mean that Hoover was simply a boring backdrop or a continuation of Harding and Coolidge. In fact, Herbert Hoover during the early depression that plagued his term was a forceful, creative, and knowledgeable executive who tried a variety of thoughtful and intuitive strategies to roll back that depression. But as those strategies failed, public confidence dropped, and he became increasingly morose, intransigent, and prone to substitute homilies on liberty for more opportunistic, populist ventures. Hoover's reputation as a reactionary, unresponsive president is due to his later defensiveness and to his postpresidential years when he insisted on casting himself as Horatio at the gates, warning against the destructive tendencies of FDR and his welfare state. The progressive Hoover became a casualty of the depression that unfairly bore his name.

The stark central facts of Hoover's term were the stock market crash and the depression. Why didn't the Hoover strategies work and what caused this economic paralysis in the first place? Liberal historians and economists writing in the 1950s had a simple response: the abuses of the Republican period, the maldistribution of wealth, and the stock market binges of the 1920s wreaked havoc on the nation and led to the Great Depression. Hoover's answer was that the depression was a worldwide phenomenon, experienced throughout the industrial West. Actually, the economic collapse of the 1930s remains an extraordinary complex topic, one as inconclusively explained as the origins of the American Revolution or the effects of slavery on the coming of the Civil War.

Hoover biographer Martin L. Fausold has summarized what the economic situation looked like before the crash-depression hit. After the war, a surplus of agricultural goods on the world market cut into American exports to Europe by 80 percent for the fifteen years that followed. The agricultural crisis was due to a variety of circumstances: dietary changes, decrease in population growth, overproduction, mechanization of agriculture, additional acreage being farmed, and a drop in prices. It should be remembered that in 1930, about half of the American people were living on farms or in rural communities, so agricultural depressions affected more families than is realized or possible today.[27]

In addition, the United States had set up tariff barriers to cut down on imports from Europe, and consequently hindered the ability of those nations to pay off American loans. The economy of the 1920s also witnessed a severe decline in the percentage of working people in organized labor unions, and thus denied to many employees strong bargaining power regarding wages. A large proportion of profits went into capital formation, and eventually cut into purchasing power at a time when production was increasing and thus saturating the consumer market. Corporations increasingly turned to mergers; in 1922, there were 67 major mergers in manufacturing and mining, by 1928 that number reached 309, and by 1929 that total climbed to 1,245.

The crash saw the stock market averages drop dramatically in October 1929 and throughout the winter. In September 1929, the price of industrial common stocks was at 469.5; by October it was at 247.6; by November, 220.1; by the end of 1930, the level was 196.1; by the end of 1931 it was 116.6; by the end of 1932 an incredible 84.81. Hoover's reactions were prompt and salutary. He tried to instill confidence by preaching that "the fundamental business of the country, that is, production and distribution, is on a sound and prosperous basis"—words that would haunt him and the Republican party for over a generation.[28] But Hoover was not a mindless cheerleader. He called together the leaders of the nation's major industries and warned them not to lay off employees to meet the problem. They were told that they had to absorb the downturn, and remarkably the industrialists agreed. The president also called upon the governors and mayors to expand their public works programs to help alleviate the unemployment problem.

The conservative economist Milton Friedman has argued that the most important hypothesis for explaining the Great Depression was the decline in the money supply, and he blames the Federal Reserve System for that contraction. Hoover at the time seemed to sense clearly that the Federal Reserve might indeed be a contributing factor in the economic downturn, and he pushed and prodded, often not too successfully, the Board of Governors of the system for more credit and fewer restrictions.

A more recent popular explanation of the depression is the work of Russian economist Nikolai Kondratieff who has put forth a cyclical explanation in which in a fifty-year period, there is a decade of depression, thirty years of technical innovation, and ten years of economic uncertainty. The Great Depression is thus explained in terms of macrodynamics that no president or political system, especially at that time, could have controlled or even managed. A major challenge to this sort of determinism is John Maynard Keynes's theories about deficit spending and the need to "prime the pump," policies followed in differing degrees by every president since FDR.[29]

In any case, even without a definite causal explanation of the depression, one can still judge Hoover's record in this period. He seemed to reach out in modest, but determined steps in nearly all of these directions. He urged the Federal Reserve System to loosen

credit; he incurred a deficit budget; he sought to restore some of
the purchasing power of the hardest hit sector, which was agriculture; he counseled optimism and confidence; and he prevented short-
term layoffs at first. Within the context of the presidency up to that
time, it was an extraordinary performance; within the dire context
of his times it was not enough. The Hoover presidency was a failed
presidency—a mistake due to several factors including his inability
to deal with Congress, his uninspiring personal leadership, his increasingly heavy ideological baggage that had served him so well
before. And of course, it failed for reasons beyond his control as is
obvious and paramount.

In 1930, the second year of his term, Hoover seemed consumed
by a need to poke into all areas of government and to establish
special commissions to examine the major problems of the time.
Soon, though, one would be all consuming and most telling, the
disaster of the economy. Walter Lippmann, the influential columnist, concluded that the president had been unwilling to take on the
important Washington power brokers, Congress, the Farm Board, the
Federal Reserve System, and the advocates of high tariff and cozy,
unethical stock market practices. Hoover believed in legislative independence, and he provided little leadership on such important
issues as the tariff. As might be expected, he got back a high duty
hodgepodge called the Smoot-Hawley Act, which even former President Taft concluded seemed to mark Hoover as a conservative.
Democratic leader Cordell Hull of Tennessee summarized his opposition to the measure by observing, "The hog had returned to his
wallow, and the dog to his vomit." Hoover pushed for some presidential flexibility in setting rates, a provision that barely passed.
Of the 3,293 tariff items in the bill, some 1,122 were changes—
887 upward. Overall, the tariff was to offer little protection to
American industries and farmers, and it lessened the ability of the
United States to further foreign trade, so important to a new creditor nation.

By the time of the congressional elections in 1930, Hoover could
rightfully point to an impressive record of effort and some achievement. But the electorate made a quite different judgment, one that
reflected the usual off-year decline for the party in power and that
also gave additional signs of deeper disenchantment. The Republicans lost fifty-two seats in the House, which gave the Democrats
control of that body, and held on to the Senate by only one vote.
Of even more important consequence was the reelection of Frank-

lin Delano Roosevelt by over three-quarters of a million votes in New York State where only two years before he won election by only twenty-nine thousand votes. Ironically Roosevelt was warning at that time about the dangers of federal centralization and the loss of personal liberties. He even expressed reservations about Hoover's public works spending![30]

Then by early 1931, the president faced a divided Congress and worsening economic problems. Added to his woes was the controversial enforcement of the Eighteenth Amendment, the prohibition of alcohol, the last great Protestant moral crusade of the progressive era. Hoover was strongly committed to Prohibition, calling it "noble in motive and far-reaching in purpose," words that would be later juxtaposed almost comically with the outgrowth of speakeasies, gangsters, and illegal activities.

In the first session of 1931, Hoover found it increasingly difficult to sell self-help, voluntary charity, and local governmental responsibility. Senators and representatives, returning to the capital, had heard enough talk about "character building" and self-reliance, and numerous relief bills were introduced into the legislative branch to ameliorate the effects of the depression. Congress passed a cash bonus for veterans, and the president's veto was quickly overridden. Insurgent Republicans and traditional Democrat liberals pushed for direct relief and one of them, Senator Robert Wagner of New York, presented three bills that included a provision for public works, statistical information on the state of the nation, and the creation of government-run employment agencies. In the Senate, George Norris of Nebraska continued his personal campaign to have the federal government operate the Wilson Dam on the Tennessee River and sell cheap electricity. The bill this time passed Congress, only to meet Hoover's veto. Years later it would become the forerunner of the TVA, the Tennessee Valley Authority.

By June 1931, 15 percent of the total workforce (and some 28 percent of the factory labor force) was unemployed, and stock prices, which had risen dramatically in the first quarter, dropped sharply. Personal income and industrial production also tumbled. On June 20, Hoover announced a one-year moratorium on foreign debts—a bold move at the time, and one consistent with the president's views about the worldwide nature of the depression. He issued his declaration following the collapse of the Kredit Anstadt in Austria, the major bank of that nation. Congressmen applauded Hoover's initiative, and European bankers were relieved. But still, it was not enough. When Congress adjourned, Hoover was visibly relieved.

In the summer and fall of 1931, the president pushed hard to get the Federal Reserve and the banking community to stimulate the economy by increasing credit and promoting borrowing. On September 15, he suggested that the bankers create a $500 million credit pool, but the plan went nowhere. Then Hoover, with the consent of Congress, created the Reconstruction Finance Corporation, probably the single most important initiative he or even FDR came up with to combat the depression. Conceived along the lines of the old War Finance Corporation of World War I days, the RFC would be able to both aid troubled financial institutions and underwrite new credit. As Martin Fausold has summarized, the bill provided for a $500 million capital appropriation and $1.5 billion in RFC bonds and debenture notes which would support federal loans to banks, railroads, and various agricultural organizations. Unfortunately, by then the economy needed not only an infusion of credit, but major structural changes to increase demand, ensure employment, and guarantee sound financial practices.

At first, Congress in 1932, even with its backbiting and restiveness, generally supported the president in his major policy initiatives, but it was clear as the economy worsened that his personal popularity was slipping. When Hoover recommended a sales tax to help balance the budget, the legislative branch snapped back angrily. In the end, though, the surtax, corporate tax, estate tax, and limited excise tax were upped and raised over $1 billion in revenue. By spring 1932, general unemployment hit 23 percent, and the RFC in February and March alone had to rescue 160 banks, 60 railroads, and 18 building and loan associations. By July 1932, the president even compromised enough to sign a massive relief bill, the Emergency Relief and Construction Act. One and a half billion dollars for public construction of income producing projects, $300 million for loans to states for direct relief, and $200 million to assist in liquidating closed banks flowed from the federal coffers.[31]

NONINTERVENTION

In the midst of the general economic collapse, Hoover and his secretary of state, Henry Stimson, pursued a foreign policy that built on the moderate noninterventionism of Harding and Coolidge and extended it especially in Latin America. Hoover, of course, had a vast knowledge of the world based on his years as an engineer and then as an international humanitarian. The administration pushed for a new disarmament conference of the Big Five nations (United States, Great Britain, Japan, France, and Italy) to cut down the full naval forces as had been done for capital ships at the Washington meeting in 1921. France and Mussolini's Italy both proved unwilling to approve such constraints for differing reasons, and the agreement that emerged was a modest one. The treaty placed before the Senate extended the Washington Pact shipbuilding "holiday" and its ratios (with some changes) to 1936, allowed the United States to exceed those ratios if the other nations did, and added a list of conditions on replacements and conversions.

The major foreign policy initiative of the Hoover administration, though, was the United States' response to Japanese aggression in Manchuria. Called the Stimson Doctrine, the American policy was probably more the president's idea than his secretary of state's. Briefly, it provided that the United States would not recognize any treaty that was not in accord with existing treaties, especially the Kellogg and Nine Power pacts. The rationale of the policy was that nonrecognition of Japanese aggression in the area would work to that nation's disadvantage and put pressure on the militarists in that government. For a United States committed to nonintervention and a repudiation of collective security, the Stimson statement allowed the nation the opportunity to express outrage at aggression, but avoided having to confront the Japanese, thus refusing to grant tacit support for such actions. It is easy to point out the lessons of such limited diplomacy, but in the 1920s and early 1930s, the Western democracies were both weary of the bloodletting of war and more malleable than the belligerent powers they would soon have to confront.

In Latin America. it was Hoover who introduced the "good neighbor" policy—an expression FDR used and made his own. The president pushed hard for the withdrawal of American troops from Nicaragua and Haiti, and the administration publicized the Clark Memorandum of 1930, which repudiated TR's Corollary to the Monroe Doctrine. Basically, Hoover and Stimson sought to avoid American intervention in Latin American internal affairs and promoted peaceful resolutions of disputes, especially in the Chaco and Leticia disputes.

Hoover's major concern, of course, was still Western Europe.

There the worldwide depression and the large war debts remained his central preoccupation. Like Harding and Coolidge before him, Hoover refused to take the politically impossible step of renouncing the debts. By the end of his term, a peculiar triangle was established: U.S. banks loaned money to the Germans at high interest rates, then the Germans used the money to pay the Versailles reparations to the Allies who in turn used the reparations to pay off their war debts to the United States. Because the American-sponsored Dawes and Young plans reduced the reparations and slowed down the payment schedule, this peculiar arrangement stayed together. By 1931, Germany had borrowed heavily to reconstruct its nation's industries and could not pay off its debts and the reparations too, and it was in that year that the Kredit Anstadt failed. Hoover's moratorium was a prudent recognition of the realities in Europe, and an attempt to forestall the economic and political collapse of Germany. Throughout 1932 matters worsened, and in January 1933, Adolf Hitler came to power.

In 1932, Hoover also sent a U.S. delegation to the World Disarmament Conference in Geneva, and he proposed a 30 percent reduction in armaments, which the French, fearing the Germans, opposed. Gradually, the efforts at the conference dissipated, leading to failure. The next year, the Hoover administration agreed to attend the economic conference in London, one that Franklin D. Roosevelt would help to confuse, and which also concluded in disarray. Overall, Hoover's diplomacy emphasized traditional American concerns and values, but departed somewhat from the interventionism and use of the U.S. military in Latin America. But in the Far East, Japan was establishing its sphere of empire, and in Western Europe, the democracies were laying the groundwork for years of miscalculation, appeasement, and then war. These were all events that Hoover would witness and comment on—out of power.[32]

THE END OF THE NEW ERA

The Republican party, almost as if directed by the compulsions of fate, renominated Herbert Hoover in June in Chicago. He came out for Prohibition, liberty, and national restoration. But the country turned instead to the Democratic candidate, Governor Franklin D. Roosevelt of New York, who dramatically flew to the convention to accept his party's call. Roosevelt, for nearly twenty years a bit player in other men's dramas, now came center stage, promising a "new deal for the American people."

As expected, Hoover faced massive public repudiation, as he fought the proverbial good, but desperate fight. In late July, he was hurt even further when the Bonus Army, seeking early payment of veterans' bonuses, marched on Washington and was violently disbursed by forces led by General Douglas MacArthur. The incredible sight of American veterans being driven off public land by the American army left an indelible imprint on the public psyche. Hoover had given no such order, but he had said in a moment of stupefying weariness, "Thank God, you have a government in Washington that knows how to deal with a mob." It was a sad commentary on the final bankruptcy of the Hoover stewardship.

As for Roosevelt, he hit the president's record from the right and the left—denouncing him for inaction and for deficit spending. Hoover complained that FDR was a "chameleon on plaid"—and Roosevelt probably seemed so even to his advisors. The Democratic candidate wanted not a programmatic mandate, but a smashing victory, and that he got. FDR won 22,821,857 to 15,761,841, and he carried 472 votes to 59 in the electoral vote count. Hoover had won only six eastern states: Connecticut, Delaware, Maine, New Hampshire, Pennsylvania, and Vermont. It was a stunning repudiation of the Hoover term, and Roosevelt had voiced the view privately that Hoover might step down early and let him succeed to the presidency before the March inauguration.[33]

In fact, Hoover regarded the latest economic downturn in late 1932 as a lack of confidence in his successor's stated policies. In the November to March period, the so-called interregnum, the two men and their aides met to try to reach common policies to deal with the grave domestic problems and the European debt situation. Roosevelt seemed charming to Hoover, but unsure of his directions when the president pushed for commitments.

In part, Roosevelt may indeed have been unsure of his policies; 1932 was not a time for certainties. But instinctively, he sought to keep his options open. As Hoover prodded for joint declarations, FDR moved further away, sensing that Hoover was trying to get him to agree to positions after the election that he had differed with in the campaign. FDR watched as the economy hit its lowest depth, as the financial structure became completely immobilized, and the banks shut down. There is some element of truth in Stimson's observation that the president-elect waited "to get the benefit of having matters as bad as they can be." By March 4, the Hoover term was mercifully over.

THE REPUBLICAN STEWARDS

The 1920s are frequently seen as a time of raging abuses and unchecked commercialism, a materialistic era in which the three Republican presidents served neither their country nor themselves well. But as we have seen, there were major accomplishments in toning down the excesses of the last years of the Wilson era, in fostering a more limited view of America's role in the world, and in providing some sense that liberty and economic prosperity are frequently wholesome allies. But the period also saw a presidency too deferential to the legislative branch, and presidents who avoided both leadership and confrontation with Congress. Considering the caliber of congressional debates and Congress's weak leadership, one can be sympathetic. But political officials in the United States must deal with miscreants, fools, self-seeking politicians, and entrenched interests. To ignore the stuff of reality is to forfeit the chance to plant and nourish genuine reform. Harding was too much one of the boys, Coolidge and Hoover too far removed from the boys.

Most of all, the Republican stewardship did not reflect well on the presidency. A constricted vision of politics led to a constricted view of the office. Harding knew he should not have been president; Coolidge seemed to wrap it up and put it away almost for safekeeping; and Hoover had a notion of the presidency that befitted the ambitions of a brilliant manager of tasks not of men and women. It is little wonder that Franklin D. Roosevelt substituted a more visible, immediate, populist, and in the end, political office. More than Lincoln, Wilson, or even his cousin Theodore, FDR seemed at times to elevate the sly and devious to a management style. Perhaps it was his nature, or perhaps it was a reaction to the ceremonial, quietest, and nonpartisan legacy that came out of the failed Republican ascendancy. This era was in one sense a reinstatement of the Whig model and the Whig presidency in terms that seemed so far removed from the conditions and leisure that gave rise to that interpretation of executive authority and responsibility.

The administrations of Wilson and TR were, on the other hand, preludes to the development of a more activist model of the presidency, one that is best epitomized in this century by Franklin Roosevelt. It was to become the highwater mark of executive assertiveness, and unlike Lincoln's term it permanently recast the office, the men who served, and the nation that embraced it.

4

The Advent of the Modern Presidency:
Franklin Delano Roosevelt

The awesome challenges of both the Great Depression and World War II led to the conditions that clearly established Franklin D. Roosevelt as the most important president of this century and probably the most powerful chief executive in American history. Only Lincoln's term can compare in the magnitude of the domestic crisis facing the presidency at that time, but even so Roosevelt's impact on international politics was far more significant. In dealing with the depression and the war, Roosevelt changed the nature of the presidency, the alignment of the political parties, and America's role in the world.

Those three terms, those twelve years, mark a clear watershed, or more accurately a cleavage between what occurred before FDR and after him. Even "weak" presidents who followed FDR appear strong in comparison to most of the powerful pre-1933 executives; even later presidents who distrusted FDR have in many ways lived off his legacy. For two generations, liberals and conservatives, Democrats and Republicans have operated under the model of the Rooseveltian presidency. And yet of all our "great" presidents, FDR remains somewhat suspicious, with a reputation for suppleness that is frequently seen as deviousness. If as one of his biographers, James MacGregor Burns, says, he was both a lion and a fox, Americans are still wary of the fox. On the fiftieth anniversary of his presidency and the one hundredth year of his birth, FDR was not commemorated by the nation for which he labored so long, and even today the capital that he once dominated lacks any memorial to his services. This neglect is partly due to the ambiguity of the man, and partly to our national ambiguity about power, the welfare state, and the outcome of the last terrible world war.

THE SQUIRE OF HYDE PARK

Franklin Roosevelt was born into a well-connected and doting family with an estate and deep roots in the Hudson River region of rural Dutchess County, above New York City and its immediate suburbs. There Roosevelt lived the life of a son of a country squire, acquired the security of a warm if not overly protective family, and grew up free from many of the anxieties of the rest of his generation. At an early age, he modeled himself after his colorful older cousin, Theodore, and consciously imitated his political rise. As part of the Roosevelt clan with loyalties to the Democratic party, Franklin entered politics, ran for the state senate, fought Tammany Hall, and landed a post as assistant secretary of the navy—the path TR used to reach the White House. When World War I came, Franklin Roosevelt sought to join the combat, hoping to emulate further TR's legendary Spanish-American War record. But Wilson insisted that his ambitious assistant secretary stay home, and the war ended more quickly than Franklin anticipated. In 1920, the Democratic party looked around for a vice-presidential candidate to complement the lackluster James M. Cox on the ticket and chose the thirty-seven-year-old bearer of the famed Roosevelt name. After the landslide defeat, Franklin finished up his time in Washington and headed for the Canadian coast to vacation with his family. There suffering from stress due to the controversies resulting from some of his decisions in the navy and exposed earlier to a polio virus, Roosevelt contracted the crippling disease, and its effects were to stay with him for the rest of his life.[1]

For several years, Roosevelt fought to regain some physical mobility while he continued dabbling in national Democratic politics. In 1924, he placed the name of Alfred E. Smith, the governor of New York, in nomination for the presidency in the famous "Happy Warrior" speech, and reestablished himself in the process as a major figure in the party. In 1928, the party leaders in New York, guided by Smith and probably encouraged by Eleanor Roosevelt, insisted that FDR run for governor to bolster Smith's chances of carrying that state in the upcoming presidential election. Preoccupied with his physical therapy in Warm Springs, Georgia, Roosevelt reluctantly accepted. Although Smith lost New York and the nation, Roosevelt squeaked by and became governor of the most important state in the Union. Overnight he was recognized as the leading Democratic politician, and he and his advisors calculated on a 1936 attempt at the presidency, following an expected two terms for Hoover.

But from 1929 to 1932, the economic depression proved to be more acute than anyone imagined, and Roosevelt decided to run in 1932 instead. After a monumental reelection victory as governor in 1930, FDR was clearly the front-runner for the nomination, but knowing that any candidate needed two-thirds of the delegates under the party's rules, he realized he would have a difficult time in the convention. Roosevelt's managers made several compromises to assure his nomination. Most critically, FDR repudiated his old Wilsonian faith in the League of Nations, thus encouraging John Nance Garner of Texas and publisher William Randolph Hearst in California who threw their support to Roosevelt in order to stop Wilson's secretary of war, Newton Baker, from gaining the nomination. Breaking the tradition that candidates waited to be notified by the convention, Roosevelt flew from New York to Chicago and personally accepted the nomination. Thus FDR showed himself as a man not bound by political traditions and as physically equipped for the presidency and able to overcome one of the most debilitating diseases.

Roosevelt's name was known across the nation, for he was in some ways a linear descendant of TR: a progressive, a vigorously handsome and captivating figure, and an official in the previous Democratic administration. But on a personal level, Franklin Delano Roosevelt, even to those who served him over the years, seemed a bit of a charming enigma, an asset he used well and often. Early in his political career, Roosevelt was seen as ambitious, superficial, and sparklingly buoyant—a man who wore lightly both commitments and intellectual achievements. He was a publicity-seeking state senator and a driving and competent assistant secretary, but he remained a cut below his cousin in political skill and personal curiosity about the world around him.

Then in the 1920s while he fought the effects of polio and matured emotionally, Roosevelt seemed to change. Earlier, his relationship with his wife, Eleanor, had become chilly due partly to his marital infidelities, but now she went on to nurse him and also chart out her own life. They became allies however in a common political career, but were no longer husband and wife in an intimate sense. Both looked for affection elsewhere and devised networks of other supportive relationships. FDR became more guarded and manipulative than in the past. He had been throughout his life a charming fellow, a person so confident and ebullient that it was assumed he was somehow hiding his real frustrations and disappointments behind a mask. In fact, young Roosevelt was simply what he seemed— a pleasant Boy Scout, blessed with good looks, important connections, and a bright future. But after his battle with polio, FDR experienced, as he never did before, anger, fear, and deep frustration. Out of that dark night of the soul, his biographers often say, he emerged more sensitive to the problems of the vulnerable.

Actually, Roosevelt's afflictions may have increased his personal complexity. In order to be a strong candidate for public office, he and his associates erected a facade that denied the effects of his disease, and the media helped by never showing him in a wheelchair or as handicapped. His disability led him to be more manipulative and devious, tendencies he exhibited often, but usually filtered through layers of calculated charm. The Roosevelt of the 1930s was a public figure with a carefully concealed private world, and this may have contributed to the reputation for shiftiness that has clouded his record and real achievements to this day.[2] That Franklin Roosevelt was a great president there is no doubt, but why he remains less revered than Lincoln or Washington is a mystery. Perhaps the reason is that FDR's personal characteristics seem less noble than those other two individuals. There is surely evidence that FDR seemed to enjoy the game a bit too much, that he relished using and confusing people unnecessarily, that his idea of leadership was just too Machiavellian for a people in love with the ethos of common sense and straightshooting.

Roosevelt, then in the privileged world of his youth and in the life of an invalid, developed personality traits that served him well at times and yet left a legacy of distrust in how he approached the use of power. Years later, some historians and political scientists would look at Roosevelt's chaotic administration of public affairs and canonize it as true genius. Since FDR could not run the huge bureaucracy he was creating, he had fostered jurisdictional disputes, overlapping responsibilities, and organizational competition in order to create a situation where he alone held real power. While there is some truth to that observation, a better explanation was that

Roosevelt was simply overwhelmed in his first two terms with the miasma he had created, and confusion was the result. Both as assistant secretary of the navy and as governor, FDR was a rather traditional administrator; during the war, the president delegated many of the day-to-day military responsibilities to General George Catlett Marshall and to aides who accepted the importance of coordination and decision making. However, in terms of domestic mobilization, confusion and disorganization seemed to be often the order of the day. Overall, Roosevelt was neither a brilliant administrator who saw order in chaos, nor an initiator who pioneered a novel way to use presidential power by creating competing advisors. Franklin Roosevelt was a skilled politician who was preoccupied with public opinion, who rarely shared his true emotions with even his closest associates, and who was uncertain about which domestic policies would work and which would not.[3]

Justice Oliver Wendell Holmes, Jr., once concluded that Roosevelt had a second-class intellect, but a first-class temperament—an observation that FDR's biographers have obediently followed. But in fact, Roosevelt had a quick mind, a retentive memory, and an ability to understand the complexities of popular opinion and public policy. He was not extremely knowledgeable about economics, but the conventional wisdom of that discipline had little to offer politicians at that time. Liberal economists lament the president's ignorance of the theories of John Maynard Keynes, feeling that Keynes's theories of "priming the pump" in the depression economy by incurring more deficits would lead to the golden road to recovery. Conservative economists equally deplore that Roosevelt went off the sacred gold standard and never appreciated the need to restore business confidence in America, which in that vocabulary meant business dominance. But in the early 1930s, Roosevelt like most everyone else in politics did not understand what had happened, only that the economic downturn had destroyed the Republicans' lock on the national government and opened up the way for the Democrats once again.[4]

THE FIRST NEW DEAL

In his first inaugural, FDR captivated the American people with his admonition that the only thing they had to fear was fear itself. It was a brilliant and reassuring expression of confidence—just what the people needed, but, of course, it was quite incorrect. With over one-quarter of the wage-earning population unemployed, with hundreds of banks closed, with mortgages unpaid, and foreclosures on farms dramatically up, desperation was quite in order. But Roosevelt perceived that the country needed to first believe again in itself, and to do that, he assumed, it had to believe in him. What has been less commented on was FDR's startling determination that he wanted speedy action from Congress on his recovery recommendations, and that if "Congress shall fail to take one of these two courses, and in the event that the national emergency is still critical, I shall not evade the clear course of duty that will then confront me. I shall ask the Congress for the one remaining instrument to meet the crisis— broad executive power to wage a war against the emergency, as great as the power that would be given to me if we were in fact invaded by a foreign foe."

Clearly he was the linear descendant of Theodore Roosevelt. And as the crowds cheered, the New Deal advisors dealt with the most apparent crisis—the collapse of the nation's banking structures. Many states had already closed banks, and Roosevelt's declaration of a "bank holiday" was a defensive move to buy some time. He called a special session of Congress on Thursday, March 9, 1933, and asked the legislative branch to confirm his initial proclamation and grant him new powers over banking and commerce. The reaction was spontaneous—without much debate and concern for its usual procedures, Congress approved the bill, and FDR signed it that evening.

Sensing the mood of Congress, the president on the next day requested powers to cut government spending, but strong opposition from veterans organizations led to an open revolt among Democrats in the House of Representatives. With the support of sixty-nine Republicans, the House, however, backed the chief executive. Meanwhile, Roosevelt began his fireside chats, the homey talks that added immensely to his personal popularity and imprinted the office on the needs of his fellow citizens whom he addressed simply as "my friends." Humorist Will Rogers was to remark that FDR explained the banking crisis so clearly that even the bankers understood it.

Within the next several weeks, called "The Hundred Days," the president asked Congress for additional powers to deal with the depression. In the process FDR put his prestige behind a cornucopia of measures that flooded the legislative branch and revamped forever the role of the federal government. The president urged a new agriculture bill to raise farmers' purchasing power, ease farm mortgage terms, and deal with the problems of farm loans. The Agricultural Adjustment Act passed the Congress in mid-May by a three to one majority; several weeks later, Congress approved the Civilian Conservation Corps, which was to employ a quarter of a million young men engaged in reforestation, fighting forest fires, and building dams. The president also pushed for direct federal grants to the states for unemployment relief and for a major overhaul of the securities markets. He followed up with a proposal for the Tennessee Valley Authority, legislation to save home mortgages from foreclosure, reform of the railroads, and a far-reaching cooperative effort for industry. Called the National Industrial Recovery bill, it provided for codes limiting competition and some recognition of the rights of workers to unionize.

"The Hundred Days" became an impressive legislative feat closely identified with FDR's dazzling leadership. Obviously it was, but in another sense, the president acted as a brake on Congress, which was willing to go even further in authorizing public expenditures to fight the depression. FDR did believe in a balanced budget, and while he recognized the obvious state of the emergency, he periodically went on binges of parsimony and cost cutting. Roosevelt's style, though, was broad and eclectic; he was the honest broker among power blocs, the leader whose greatest gift was an incredible sense of confidence. Confined to a wheelchair, he reminded a paralyzed nation of the curative powers of laughter, optimism, and American common sense. It was a prescription any doctor could profitably prescribe. Even usually critical commentators suspended judgment; Kansas editor William Allen White wondered what had happened to Franklin Roosevelt. Before, he seemed like the typical progressive governor who had fallen under the influence of TR and LaFollette, but was not really presidential timber. Now Roosevelt seemed to have "developed magnitude and poise, more than all, power!"[5]

In those early years, FDR insisted on being a nonpartisan leader of the nation, even to the extent of avoiding Jefferson Day dinners so beloved by the Democratic faithful. He had the support of right-wing agitators and left-wing crackpots, of labor leaders and businesspeople afraid of the very system they had left prostrate. Even Adolf Hitler wrote, "I have sympathy with President Roosevelt because he marches straight to his objective over Congress, over lobbies, over stubborn bureaucracies."

Taking a lesson from his old mentor, Woodrow Wilson, the new president delivered his messages in person to Congress. He sent up detailed proposals often drafted jointly by selected congressmen and bureaucrats working together, a practice Lyndon Johnson would revive in the 1960s. He was willing to veto legislation he disagreed with and used the full patronage resources of the office to push his proposals. On one occasion, he approved the appointment to the post of U.S. marshal of a man who was an ally of Senator "Cotton Ed" Smith but also had been found guilty of homicide. In return, Smith concurred in the nomination of leftist academician Rexford Guy Tugwell as under secretary of agriculture. Roosevelt gleefully confronted Tugwell saying, "Today I traded you for a couple of murderers!"[6]

Congress continued to be receptive to other presidential initiatives: a reciprocal tariff, a gold reserve act, and the ending of Prohibition. In addition, Roosevelt decided to recognize the Soviet Union and unsuccessfully pushed for a waterway between the United States and Canada. The most controversial act passed during this period created the National Recovery Administration—the government's major attempt to get businesses to draw up codes of fair competition in each area of industry and commerce. Headed by the blustery General Hugh Johnson, and symbolized by the Blue Eagle emblem, the NRA represented the corporate state grafted onto the American voluntary marketplace. It led to some stabilization in the economy, an increase in the power of the organized special interests, and a mass of red tape and endless codes for subcategories and tiny shares of industry. As early as 1934, FDR felt the heat of complaints, and he finally appointed radical lawyer Clarence Darrow to investigate the problems. Darrow's conclusion was that powerful economic interests controlled the code process. FDR cut back on the NRA's powers, fired Johnson, and tried to recoup his losses. Finally, the Supreme Court put the NRA out of business.

The rural counterpart of the NRA, the Agricultural Adjustment Administration, realized a better fate, but not without controversy. The AAA was meant to restore farm prices to parity, which was defined as the relationship they had to nonagricultural prices in the 1909–14 period. Processing taxes, passed on to the consumers, financed the subsidy, and farmers were urged to curtail production and keep lands out of use. Stories appeared of crops being allowed deliberately to rot in the fields and warehouses, and of baby pigs being slaughtered to stabilize prices—the destruction of surplus crops and animals in a nation facing urban famine and general distress. As with the NRA, organized farm groups and wealthier farmers controlled the AAA, and the new restrictions on the use of their land forced many tenant farmers and sharecroppers out of agriculture altogether.

By the fall of 1933, FDR concluded that enough people were still not employed, and he pushed for a rapid increase in public works spending and an end to the rigid gold standard. Under the aegis of Harry Hopkins, the New Deal's Civil Works Administration spent a billion dollars on quick relief programs, aimed at putting money in the pockets of poor people. Some of those jobs were make-work, leaf raking, and lawn cutting, but they provided funds in the worst part of 1933–34. Hopkins acted quickly to meet the obvious emergency; when told about the virtues of long-run projects, he snapped, people "don't eat in the long run—they eat every day."

As for Roosevelt, he presided over a host of reforms without much of a cohesive philosophy or overall public policy. His view was simply experimental—to try a variety of programs and keep what worked. As expected, he relied on divergent experts, resurrected old collectivist notions of governmental regulations from World War I, experimented with new approaches of cooperation, moderated disputes and personality conflicts, and restrained an inflation-oriented Congress. He avoided partisanship and insisted on staying above the numerous frays that dotted the landscape.[7]

In the 1934 congressional elections, the Democrats won even more seats than they had two years before. The usual pattern then and now is for the majority party to lose some seats, often 40 or so. Instead the Democrats picked up 9 seats in the House, running up their total to 319 and added 9 seats in the Senate, bringing their total there to 69. They gained some additional state governorships as well. It was an incredible vote of support for FDR, even as he donned his nonpartisan mantle. Yet just as this popular vote was being counted, strong right-wing opposition was gathering among the business classes and a group called the American Liberty League. Wealthy industrialists and manufacturers such as the Duponts, William S. Knudsen, J. Howard Pew, and Sewell L. Avery joined with conservative Democrats, such as Al Smith, John Davis, and Bainbridge Colby, to oppose Roosevelt and further the League's philosophy of safeguarding the uses of private property and free enterprise as they defined them. More subtly and more pointedly for Roosevelt, the wealthier classes—from which he came and where he had spent his life socializing—began to question his personal motives and his commitment to their interests and values. By the end of his first term, FDR was seen by many of the rich and well-born as "a traitor to his class," and was attacked with a ferocity that was stronger than even that directed toward TR during his Bull Moose days.[8]

Roosevelt was first bemused and then baffled by right-wing criticism, seeing himself quite rightfully as a champion of capitalism rather than the enemy. But the heavy weight of opposition on the scales fell out not on the right, but on the left. The misery in the land was very real, and in that land new leaders arose promising redistribution of the wealth and greater security for the common people. While FDR talked vaguely of the "forgotten man," these radical leaders promised a better future.

Some important reformers and agitators who had large popular followings were at the height of their appeal in the early 1930s. For FDR, the most accomplished and therefore the most dangerous to him was Senator Huey P. Long of Louisiana. Long was one of the most fascinating political leaders of his generation—a southerner who generally avoided race baiting, attacked the powerful economic oligarchy in his state, and accomplished genuine populist reforms for the poor. He was also an autocrat, a person who ripped asunder normal political processes, and a true demagogue. Long's career was partially the basis for the novel by Robert Penn Warren, *All the King's Men*, and the popular film by the same name, which chronicled the times of the fictional dictatorial governor Willie Stark. To break Long's hold on Louisiana, FDR actually considered sending federal troops into that state at the time, but decided against it. By the mid-1930s, Long had won national attention with his "Share the Wealth" program, which promised a $2,000 annual income, free education and homesteads, cheap food, veterans' bonuses, and a limit on private fortunes. He would make "every man a king," and consequently Long was titled "the Kingfish," after the character in the popular radio show "Amos 'n Andy."

Equally prominent was the Roman Catholic priest from Royal Oak, Michigan, Father Charles E. Coughlin, an eloquent orator who had originally supported Roosevelt. But after a personal falling out, Coughlin charged that Roosevelt was in league with "godless capitalists, the Jews, Communists, international bankers, and plutocrats." Added to Long's and Coughlin's following was a movement in California named after Dr. Francis E. Townsend, who devoted his efforts to aiding the old and destitute, and who advocated guaranteed pensions.

Roosevelt's allies in 1934–35 were concerned that this attack from the left, especially from Long, might lead to a third major political party and deprive him of enough votes to win reelection. An opinion poll done by Postmaster General James Farley's agents for the National Democratic Committee indicated that Long had remarkable appeal across the United States and not just in the Gulf region as had been thought. If the Republicans in 1936 nominated a progressive candidate for president and if Long also ran, FDR might be in serious trouble.

Roosevelt, with his superb sense of timing, decided to let the protest leaders play out their hand in 1935, observing that the public's attention "cannot, because of human weakness, be attuned for long periods of time to a constant repetition of the highest note in the scale." He concluded that people grow tired of seeing the same name in front of them, and that he could not keep up the pace of 1933 and 1934 without losing his audience. Yet behind the scenes, he moved to counter the protest leaders' appeals. First, he cut off all patronage to Long and his allies. Then, he used the services of Catholic businessman Joseph P. Kennedy to deal gingerly with Coughlin; finally, by 1942 the Vatican silenced the priest after his anti-Semitic rhetoric and pro-Fascist leanings became too much of an embarrassment. As for Townsend, FDR suddenly attached himself to the movement for a social security act, which would cut into the physician's major appeal.

Also, by 1935, FDR embraced the collective bargaining movement, adding an important component to the Democratic party, the unions. The president supported in a nonchalant way the incorporation into the NRA of Section 7a, which recognized the right of collective bargaining, but he was not particularly an ally of organized labor, especially in his earlier role as a national broker among groups. Then, in 1935, he enthusiastically embraced the proposal of Senator Robert Wagner of New York, which encouraged employee representation instead of company unions. Originally, FDR opposed the Wagner bill, but after the Supreme Court ruled the NRA unconstitutional and Section 7a was declared void, the president embraced the new bill.[9]

Clearly, by 1935, Roosevelt had decided to abandon his posture as mediator among diverse interests and to throw the full weight of his office into a partisan and aggressive defense of his administration. Some historians have seen his shift as a simple calculation that the population wanted a more radical approach to complex problems, and FDR as usual followed the crowd. In addition, Roosevelt was being severely attacked by conservatives, especially by big business and by the Supreme Court, which was declaring major New Deal initiatives unconstitutional. Unlike Lincoln, FDR was not a person given to absorbing abuse; he struck back and in the process effected a split from the business and financial communities that lasted until the onset of the war.

In the Seventy-fourth Congress, the legislators limped along approving several additional New Deal acts, but then in the summer of 1935, that body and the president came forth with a second burst of energy—one so exuberant it was labeled "The Second One Hundred Days."[10] It is this session and not the earlier two years that set in law many of the true historical achievements of the Roosevelt years. However, in the beginning of 1935, FDR was not clearly in charge. The president told Congress that he wanted stronger laws concerning unemployment insurance, old age benefits, work relief, conservation, and other areas. Yet he criticized the federal government's role in providing "relief" jobs and asked for $4.8 billion for related programs, a lower estimate than many proponents in the Senate wanted to aid the poor and unemployed. Thus, for all his conversion to the left, FDR in 1935 still shared Hoover's concerns that federal relief or welfare would destroy personal initiative, even in an economy where such enterprise would find no access to employment. However, when the bill ran into opposition in the Senate from conservatives and progressives alike, FDR was out fishing, and it was left to his capable aides and legislators to work out a compromise. In April, he asked the Senate to approve the United States' participation in the World Court and ran into tremendous opposition. In addition, his Social Security bill was stalled in Congress and an unwanted veterans' bonus bill was making its way though the legislative mill. In May, the Chamber of Commerce attacked FDR publicly, and a group of progressive senators demanded more assertive leadership. On top of those pressures, the Court in the same month declared invalid the NRA.[11]

Now as summer approached, Roosevelt roared back. Applying enormous pressure and the full powers of patronage, he demanded action from a recalcitrant Congress. The Wagner Labor Relations Act was approved, the Social Security Act passed, a stronger TVA bill was accepted, and a holding company bill to curb utility company prices was enacted into law. The president asked Congress for new taxes on gifts, inheritances, and corporations, and preached the beginnings of a "soak the rich" philosophy. Then, like God after six days of creation, the president rested, leaving on a trip across the country in late 1935.

THE MANDATE OF 1936

As Roosevelt pushed for domestic reforms and recalibrated his political stance to the left, the world situation in Europe was rapidly deteriorating. While Americans clamored over the increased role of government in their lives, the Fascist and Nazi regimes came to power and began their descent into the hell of war. The history of that period is the chronicle of the failure of nerve on the part of the democratic governments, old settled aristocracies, and flaccid socialist parties. In Russia, an even more brutal Joseph Stalin was consolidating his power, putting to an end the myth that Communism was democracy by another name.

Roosevelt was genuinely disturbed about the turn of events in Europe, but even though he expressed public concern, his primary focus was on domestic recovery and on his own reelection. FDR did not look any the poorer for his term in office. He still responded to life with a sense of zest and cheerfulness that was contagious to those around him. By his own account, he was an actor, a gifted master of poses, gestures, and expressions. The alphabet agencies of the New Deal went off in all sorts of directions, some of them novel and untried, some cynical, a few naive, many idealistic, and in the process they attracted all sorts of people. In a few instances, even Communists found their way into the New Deal bureaucracy— though far fewer than Republican orators liked to imagine or feared.

Roosevelt was less the chief executive than a sort of sensitive nerve center, which judged public opinion, matched strategy to tactics, left open options while pressing the vague goals of recovery and reform. To many of his subordinates, he was increasingly an enigma, and they grew dismayed by his guile and unreliability when pressure came. But in 1936, the popular impression of the man had been set in the first gruesome months of 1933 and then in the achievements of the following legislative session. FDR was the individual who saved the banks and small passbook savings accounts, the leader who stayed mortgage foreclosures, pushed for work relief, cared deeply about conservation and the Dust Bowl, furthered labor's organizing efforts, and created Social Security. The New Deal was seen as a cornucopia of benefits and Roosevelt the funnel of hope. Glumly, Al Smith concluded that FDR would be reelected; the reason—nobody shoots Santa Claus, he observed.

Smith was right; the New Deal pumped $5 billion of work projects and relief programs into the limp American economy, over six million new jobs were created, and the unemployment rolls dropped by four million people. Boys left the street corners and went to reseeding forests and wrote home proudly about it. FDR knew that reelection was in the wind, especially after the assassination of Huey Long in Louisiana. But now the president wanted to make the election "a crusade." The depression was not over, unemployment was hovering at eight to nine million people, and conditions in 1936 were not back to the inflated times and expectations of pre-1929 levels.

For Roosevelt, there was only one issue: "It's myself and people must be either for me or against me." At the Democratic national convention in Philadelphia, FDR accepted renomination, this time having also ended the two-thirds rule once and for all. He attacked "the royalists of the economic order" and "dictatorship by mob rule." Roosevelt went on philosophically, "Governments can err, presidents do make mistakes, but the immortal Dante tells us that divine justice weighs the sins of the cold-blooded and the sins of the warm-hearted in different scales. Better the occasional faults of a Government that lives in a spirit of charity than the consistent omissions of a Government frozen in the ice of its own indifference." Then he pronounced that his generation of Americans has a "rendezvous with destiny."

As for the Republicans, they nominated Governor Alf Landon, a moderate from Kansas, who turned to the right as he joined the main chorus of opposition to FDR. But the issue clearly was Roosevelt as a leader, as a president, as a friend to those who knew fear and desperation four years before. As the campaign progressed, the president relieved some of his pent-up resentment about the attacks that had been unleashed against him: a traitor to his class, a destroyer of American free enterprise, and even a sick cripple given to bouts of madness. At the end of October, he baited those forces in bitter rhetoric rarely matched by any president before or since: "Never before in all our history have these forces been so united against one candidate as they stand today. They are unanimous in their *hate for me—and I welcome their hatred.* I should like to have it said of my first administration that in it the forces of selfishness and lust for power met their *match.*"

In the raw meat of democratic politics, Roosevelt had few equals, and the populace loved it and loved him. He carried every state but Maine and Vermont, won the electoral vote 523 to 8, and beat Landon 27,751,597 to 16,679,583 in the popular tally. His proportion of the vote, 60.7 percent, was the highest margin in modern American presidential history up to that time. In addition, the Democratic majorities in Congress swelled to an even higher number: 331 seats to 89 in the House and 76 to 16 seats in the Senate. The GOP seemed on its way to becoming an extinct species.[12]

The election sealed the popular impression that Roosevelt was a flawless politician and invincible in national politics. But like a great classical tragedy, pride cometh before the fall. The large increase in the size of the Democratic forces in Congress led to a decline of party cohesiveness and more factionalism. The fruits of overwhelming victory in electoral politics are frequently disappointing, especially in a nation without a strongly disciplined parliamentary party system as in Britain. Roosevelt felt that he had received a personal mandate to continue his programs, a vote of confidence in himself, and that his party must follow.

One of his most astute biographers and a student of leadership in general, James MacGregor Burns, has attributed FDR's early success to several factors. First, the president had a fine grasp of public opinion and its moods and was one of the first politicians to use opinion polls systematically. He also had a good sense of timing, of when to move and when to stand still until an issue matured. As he himself said, "I am like a cat. I make a quick stroke and then I relax." Roosevelt, for example, would wait until the ferocity of an opposition's attack toned down before he responded. He also paid attention to political detail, to the minutiae that separates good politicians from memorable ones. In the same tone, he kept himself abreast of the internal operations of various groups and could split the rank and file from opposition leaders. He picked his fights and carefully staged when they would take place. Above all, Roosevelt was personally charming and adept at reading the minds, intentions, and agendas of the ambitious.

SETBACKS FOR THE CHIEF

The American political system places a premium on controlling power, checking leadership, and curtailing popular passions. The system has prevented classical types of tyranny and modern versions of totalitarian states, inclinations the United States is probably not fertile territory for anyway. In 1937, Franklin Roosevelt took aim at two major checks in that system: the Supreme Court and the loose party allegiances of elected officials. By the end of the year, the president suffered a major defeat in the Court-packing battle and, after the election of 1938, he hit a brick wall in his attempted purge of Democratic conservatives. By that time, the New Deal's legislative agenda ran into increasing difficulties, and by the end of the 1940 campaign, FDR talked foreign policy instead.

Did Roosevelt by these major miscalculations destroy his political base and thus end prematurely the cycle of recovery and reform? And why did an unusually astute judge of the popular mood and legislative folkways stumble so badly after such a monumental victory only months before? The Supreme Court seemed to many observers to be the last bastion of conservative political strength, the nemesis of New Deal liberals, and the salvation of the business classes. When on May 6, 1935, the high court in the Schechter poultry case struck down unanimously the NRA, its decision was welcome in more than conservative quarters. The act, drawn up in the period of the bank crisis in 1933, was poorly drafted and terribly administered by Hugh Johnson and his staff. Roosevelt himself called it "an awful headache." But the Court's rationale was somewhat disturbing—it found that the NRA was an unconstitutional delegation of legislative power and an unwarranted effort to control interstate commerce. Roosevelt's response was to argue, somewhat justifiably, that the nation had been "relegated to the horse and buggy definition of interstate commerce."

In 1935, the Court voided the AAA on the grounds that the processing tax, which financed the subsidies, was an expropriation of money from one group to another. The majority in the six to three decision ruled that agriculture should be a state rather than a federal responsibility. The intent of the decision was clearly to undercut the ability of the national government to use its powers to effect social regulation since any effective agricultural policy had to transcend state boundaries. The minority on the Court, led by Justice Harlan Stone, warned that the courts "are not the only agency of government that must be assumed to have the capacity to govern." The Court then upheld the TVA—to Roosevelt's regret as he had planned to campaign for a constitutional amendment to change the Court after the election in 1936.

In May, the Court also turned around and ruled against an attempt by Congress to regulate the bituminous coal industry, finding that the federal government could not justify its contention of a substantial impact on interstate commerce. Having zealously defended the province of the states in previous cases, the high court struck down New York State's minimum wage law for women saying that it violated the employer's and employee's right to bargain conditions—a right not particularly strong for women in the middle of massive unemployment. One-third of the states had similar protections, and the Court's philosophy seemed based less on law than on a laissez faire, uncaring caprice. Even some Republican leaders shuddered at the decisions, and their party platform supported state laws guaranteeing a minimum wage. The Court itself was badly split, five to four, with even Chief Justice Charles Evans Hughes voting at times with the liberal bloc. Critics noted that three members of the conservative wing had been corporate lawyers and the average age of the Court was 71, rather advanced for the population at that time.

The Court also voted five to four against the Municipal Bankruptcy Act saying it infringed on the rights of states to control their own municipalities, a position more rooted in legal imagination than contemporary realities. The opposition to the New Deal seemed more philosophical than strictly legal—it was a matter of power and privilege in the eyes of some liberals and conservatives alike. And Roosevelt's response was interesting. Harold Ickes reported that "the president said today and has said on other occasions, that he is not at all adverse to the Supreme Court declaring one New Deal statute after another unconstitutional. I think he believes that the Court will find itself pretty far out on a limb before it is through with it and a real issue will be joined."[13]

Roosevelt, though, did not make the Court an issue in the campaign; instead he sought a broad victory—a personal mandate, but not a programmatic one. Elections in America, unlike in parliamentary systems, are personal triumphs or retrospective judgments. They are not seen as mandates for more change, or a carte blanche for leaders. Yet after his reelection, the president seemed to judge that the people, and the Congress that was elected with him, would concur in his future moves. And high on his agenda was bringing the judiciary to heel.

After weeks of quiet planning, the president decided to present a plan aimed at changing the composition of the Court. However, rather than confronting the issue directly, once again he relied on a back door approach—seeming sly and wily rather than open. He argued that the issue was judicial efficiency and the congestion of cases in the court system. His reform was to ask for the power to appoint a new justice to the Supreme Court for every justice over seventy who did not retire. Under this scheme, FDR could name six new justices. The number of justices is not set by the Constitution, and in fact it fluctuated in the early and middle years of the republic. Jefferson, Jackson, and even Grant have been critical of the Court, but no president directly confronted it as FDR proposed. With no discussion with his cabinet and little more with his own Democratic leaders in Congress, the president dropped his bombshell. Oddly enough, a similar proposal had been put forth back in 1913 by Wilson's attorney general, James C. McReynolds, who was one of the conservative justices being criticized.

It was a typical Roosevelt ploy: dramatic, secretive, shrewd, and clever. The results, though, were almost uniformly negative. Among the Senate progressives, Burton Wheeler and Hiram Johnson refused support as did the prestigious George Norris. Conservatives this time lay back and watched the Democratic party divide and the progressive leaders struggle with Roosevelt's stratagem. FDR clearly misjudged the opposition, writing to a friend, "What a grand fight it is going to be! We need everything we have got to put in it!" And he concluded to visitors, "the people are with me." But Congress found itself inundated by mail, newspapers warned of dictatorship, law associations recalled the sanctity of law and the hallowed place of the Court's history, and New England town meetings passed resolutions criticizing the plan. In addition, in early 1937, industrial labor unions fostered an epidemic of sit-down strikes, events that represented to many a challenge to property rights. Elements of the middle class began to see the Court as a safeguard against the more radical segments of society that the president seemed to dally with in the election. And abroad, the presence of legal safeguards had been starkly wiped away in Soviet Russia, Fascist Italy, and Nazi Germany.

Concerned about the opposition, FDR dropped the efficiency argument and directly attacked the Court's philosophical underpinnings. Once again the party whips were cracked and patronage flowed, but still Congress appeared recalcitrant. Then in the midst of the battle, Chief Justice Hughes wrote a letter to the Senate explaining that an increase in the size of the Court would lower its efficiency, and that the "old men" were actually keeping up with the pace of work. Shrewdly, he took FDR's weakest point and rammed it home tellingly.

In April 1937, the Supreme Court found the Wagner Act constitutional and later upheld the Social Security Act. Pro–New Dealers remarked that a switch in time saved nine. The chief justice, working with his fellow conservative Owen J. Roberts, added two swing votes to the liberal bloc, and consequently FDR lost his main issue. As the Court changed suddenly and the reform bill languished in Congress, FDR claimed a moral victory. Then on May 18, conservative Justice Willis Van Devanter formally submitted his resignation. Eventually, Roosevelt's measure was mercifully buried.[14]

Liberals have argued that FDR achieved his objectives—to curtail the Court and break the laissez faire bloc that had so dominated it for generations. To conservatives, the battle was another example of the insatiable desire for power by "that man in the White House." Having mastered Congress and wooed the public, he tried to take on the judiciary. Most historians have seen the battle, though, as a serious miscalculation that proved the president was vulnerable and led to an abrupt end to New Deal reform. The Court fight showed all the shortcomings of what FDR had earlier created: he lost in part because he never built a new Democratic party, one bound by philosophy and not based on his personality. He continued to be evasive, almost for the fun of it, and paid a terrible long-term price—the destruction of the fruits of his election victory only months after his triumph.

Clearly, a great deal of New Deal legislation, drawn up quickly, was poorly drafted and devoid of any constitutional base that would appear familiar in the vocabulary of the 1930s. Not just the Supreme Court, but lower court judges raised valid points of concern. But the record of the Supreme Court up to that period was not the chronicle of independent philosopher-kings devoted to promoting rights and liberties. Historically, the high court has been interested in expanding the authority of the federal government over the states under John Marshall, of protecting slavery and slave interests, and of fostering nearly unbridled power for new industries in corporate America. In the process, the Court took the Fourteenth Amendment, aimed at protecting the rights of freed black slaves, and suddenly covered these new corporate aggregates with what were guarantees of personal rights. The Court did this at the same time it upheld segregation and Jim Crow laws. To see the Supreme Court as a guardian of individual liberties over these years is a misreading of history. As Oliver Wendell Holmes, Jr., observed, it is the elected representatives who have been the most responsible branch of government in that regard.

Those opposing Roosevelt in the Senate were motivated by many objectives: some philosophical, some political, some stirrings of conscience. But a crucial element among the Borahs and the Wheelers in the Senate was a desire to beat the president, to restore a sense that the executive is only one baron dealing with others in the disjointed, almost feudal landscape of American politics. When FDR misjudged public opinion, they saw this opportunity and exploited it to the fullest. Despite the view that American politics is a debate of philosophies and ideologies, it is more often about the balance of power, deference, and egotism. The Supreme Court was indeed attacking the reforms put together and passed by popularly elected congressmen and the president. Many of the same men who so loudly tagged on to FDR during election time were willing to allow that unraveling to continue.[15]

FDR had personalized politics and to many of his enemies the time had come to cut him back down to size. Those liberal opponents, those Democrats who ran below him on the ticket in 1932 and 1936, became the point men in the court battle and were joined by progressive Borah and even Norris. Wheeler, for example, encouraged Hughes's letter and its timely release, and urged Van Devanter to announce his resignation earlier than expected. Politics is less the allocation of values, than posturing, handbills, and blood on the floor—to paraphrase David Lloyd George.

FROM MASTERY TO DRIFT

Publicly FDR remained jovial, but in private he erupted against the press and "the fat cats" who had taken him on. In addition to the difficult world situation, Roosevelt now had problems with the pace of recovery at home. By October 1937, the nation began to slip back into a deep depression. His secretary of the treasury, Henry Morgenthau, warned, "We are headed right into another depression.

The question is Mr. President—what are we going to do about it?" As matters worsened, a sense of paralysis set in. The cabinet was deeply divided on whether to expand the New Deal or to quiet things down and court business in order to restore confidence.

Roosevelt seemed genuinely unable to make sense out of what was happening. He reached out for more and more advice and could not get any consensus. In exasperation, he uncharacteristically said of the presidency, "God, what a job!" When Congress convened in November, the president expressed concern about the downturn, but was unable to get anything of note through that body. The magic had worn off. By the beginning of the year, the president was still bewildered, and still seeking some solutions. Business leaders blamed the New Deal for failing to restore confidence in the economy, and the president for his attacks on their morality and achievements. Many New Dealers desperately fought to protect and expand their bureaucratic turf. FDR in 1936 and in 1937 swore up and down that fiscal year 1938 would bring a balanced budget. Meanwhile, groups of big spenders were meeting in 1937 and promulgating the economic theories of John Maynard Keynes, who had suggested the seemingly absurd idea that a government in a depression should not cut expenditures, but deficit spend its way to recovery. It was a prescription that made little sense in terms of traditional economy doctrine and conventional American wisdom, but such ideas were to be used successfully later in the United States and abroad.[16]

As for Roosevelt, the eclectic style that seemed so appropriate in the experimental gropings of this first New Deal, now led to disorganization and drift. The president organized meetings with businesspeople, attacked monopolies and profiteering, and gave his approval to a symbolic crusade against trusts. An exasperated ally, Henry Wallace, pleaded with him that he "must furnish that firm and confident leadership which made you such a joy to the nation in March of 1933." Finally, Roosevelt moved—this time to push for more government assistance, and he prepared a $3 billion spending program. Congress passed the bill overwhelmingly; the legislators too knew little about what to do. Then going back to the comfortable certainties of the past, the administration and Congress began a full-scale campaign against the trusts and concentrations of wealth. Somehow Theodore Roosevelt's earlier tactics seemed more reassuring than Keynes's unproven theories.

In this period, it has generally been assumed that FDR must have lost considerable popularity in order to explain Congress's recalcitrance. Actually, the polls showed very little slippage from his 1936 ratings. Instead, the Democratic party—with its bloated majorities in the legislative branch—and its cohesive conservative wing became undone as a governing coalition. There seemed to be no viable alternative to Roosevelt. Even in drift, he commanded the heights. But Congress stalemated over his agenda, and FDR's allies asked for an end to controversial legislation. Congress approved a reformulation of the Agricultural Adjustment Act and a modest reorganization of the bureaucracy, but a more extensive proposal for overall reform led to charges of executive dictatorship and the threat of an end to constitutional government.

Disgusted with disloyalty in his own party, including many who used his name and prestige in their campaigns, FDR decided to purge some of his opponents in the 1938 election. It was another major miscalculation, this one firming up the conservative wing of his own party. He argued that as head of the Democratic party he had a right to speak about contests where "there may be a clear issue between candidates for a Democratic nomination involving these principles, or involving a clear misuse of my name." Yet once again, he moved circuitously in identifying and attacking those apostates. In the end, except in one instance, FDR's opponents were reelected. The purge failed and so did this seeming last gasp of Roosevelt's domestic leadership. The Republican ranks in the House increased from 89 seats to 164 and they picked up 7 seats in the Senate. The GOP also carried the governorships of Ohio, Massachusetts, and Minnesota. The new Republican-conservative Democratic coalition would prove congenial to stopping any New Deal initiatives. But by then, Roosevelt's attention was shifting from domestic concerns to the worsening international situation.[17]

THE DOMESTIC RECORD

It is commonplace to state that the New Deal did not end the Great Depression, the war did. In one narrow sense, the conditions of depression persisted especially in the 1938 downturn until the expenditures for defense rapidly expanded. Keynes had been correct: government deficits—whether for domestic programs or military preparedness—would liven up a prostrate patient. But the New Deal did provide for both relief for the needy and some substantial reform. What major elements of the welfare state America has—

elements the conservative Junker Chancellor Otto von Bismarck instituted in Germany in the nineteenth century—came mainly from New Deal initiatives and, to a lesser extent, subsequent Great Society legislation. The Social Security Act, TVA, stock market controls, federal insurance of bank deposits, aid to dependent individuals, farm subsidies, and a host of other reforms stayed with the American people. Work relief, welfare, employment opportunities, handouts, all of them prevented even more misery, and some of the make-work efforts left the nation with forests, dams, post offices, libraries, and public works that built up the country's infrastructure.

The New Deal did not destroy capitalism; it propped it up, smoothed some of its rougher features, and made it more hospitable to the America of the 1930s. Roosevelt was no socialist, nor was he a closet conservative as the left believed. Roosevelt identified with planned change and progressive reforms. In the convention and election of 1932, FDR was the most liberal candidate who had a chance of winning the presidency. If at times he covered up confusion with a generally buoyant confidence, Roosevelt viewed leadership more as an emotional than an intellectual activity.

Still, the New Deal was not a short-run success; it did not end the Great Depression. When Roosevelt took office, he tried a host of experimental programs, many of them ideologically at variance with one another. Liberals have praised this eclectic approach seeing it as a welcome contrast to Hoover's narrow-gauged responses. But FDR allowed those initiatives to proliferate because he simply did not know what would work, and rather than go down to defeat with one concerted and systematic program, he hoped that a collection and then a succession of activities would allow him to ferret out the worthwhile ones. Yet he remained committed to a balanced budget, disliked federal bureaucracy, and generally disavowed relief and make-work efforts.

In the first New Deal of 1933–34, this very openness seemed to bring benefits and allowed FDR to be chief broker and friend to all people and all interests. But the criticism of the administration from the very circles that had benefited the most from his dramatic actions, the business interests and upper classes, confused and then angered Roosevelt. To him it was simple avarice, and with a strong challenge from the left both in Congress and in the country, he responded with a "second New Deal," featuring rhetoric and proposals clearly antibusiness and hostile to inherited money.

Thus, by 1937–38, the New Deal was in a quandary. To bring

full recovery, the administration had to restore business confidence, resort to government ownership of selected businesses, or engage in massive spending. FDR's personalized campaign of 1936 and the ferocious and often mindless attacks by the rich on him prevented the first course of action; the American people would probably not have approved of government ownership beyond a TVA type of innovation except perhaps in 1933 for the collapsed banking community; and as for the third alternative, the president was unwilling to buy wholeheartedly a Keynesian approach to recovery—a blind spot shared by most educated Americans, including many economists. So, the New Deal, which was a product of the "middle way," may have been undone in the end by that very confusion that compromise and moderation bring.

Watching FDR operate in this domestic context has led some observers to see persistent patterns in his leadership: a tactical skill, an unwillingness to commit himself wholeheartedly to anyone or any program, a style of dealing with conflict that depended on personal charm, a superficial attention to detail, a sense of timing that often followed public opinion rather than forming it, and a guarded view about the efficacy of being able to educate the populace and the elites. FDR could stir the masses, charm the malcontents, and cajole and bargain with the professional politicians. But in some ways, he lacked Lincoln's ability to link up tactics and purpose, to take the hurt and pursue some overall sense of direction. To Roosevelt, the issue often was himself—all else seemed secondary.

That style served him well at first. By 1940, FDR had been elected president twice overwhelmingly and could have the nomination again if he so indicated. His domestic record was more impressive than any president before him, and his very name remained magic in the air. His enemies were well heeled and well established, but "that man in the White House" retained a hold on the public imagination. And even though he was privately an unhappily married man who craved attention and approval, FDR seemed buoyant and immensely successful to the public.

The greatest failure in public policy, the persistent depression, remained as the bad times of 1939 continued, but that too gave way—not to the charm of FDR or to the concerted efforts of ardent New Deal activities, but to the harsh realities of the war in Europe. Making America an arsenal of democracy, Roosevelt was able to end the Great Depression quicker and more permanently than anyone could have imagined.

EARLY INTERNATIONAL CONCERNS

By background and experience, Franklin D. Roosevelt was an internationalist. His family had made its fortune in part from the Asian trade, and many of the Hyde Park mementos were partially bought from the profits of its exotic fare. FDR knew world history and geography, spent summers abroad, and watched as Cousin Theodore positioned the United States to be a world power. During World War I, FDR absorbed the Wilsonian internationalist doctrine and went down to defeat in 1920 on a ticket committed to the League.

But Roosevelt was not one to wear his ideology heavily; he soon argued that the League of Nations was not Wilson's original dream and, in 1932, he shocked his old Wilsonian friends by caving in to Hearst's demand that he repudiate the international organization. He did so and probably got the nomination in part because of that betrayal. In the early 1930s, FDR learned quickly that anti-international feeling was strong, as the Senate rebelled and refused to approve his modest proposal to join the International Court of Justice in The Hague. During those years, he initially encouraged the London Economic Conference in 1933 and tried to play a leadership role in dealing with the international depression, high tariffs, and the debts owed to the United States by the European democracies. But faced with the choice to make real commitments on these issues or his desire to adjust the American dollar to help recovery at home, FDR chose the latter course, dashed the hopes he had raised, and incurred severe criticism abroad.[18]

During the early 1930s, FDR tried to interject himself repeatedly in the affairs of Europe and Asia, but was unwilling to extend any efforts to garner domestic support for his proposals. These abrupt stops and starts have given the mistaken impression that he was either a true isolationist or a weak-kneed Wilsonian who waited for the war in order to resurrect his predecessor's dream of a true family of nations. FDR was neither; he understood rather well what was happening in Europe, was unwilling at first to expend his political capital generally to explain those events to the American people, waged an undeclared war to aid Britain months before Pearl Harbor, and placed his hopes on a postwar alliance of the great powers rather than in his own United Nations. The last misconception about Roosevelt is that having led the nation brilliantly during the military effort, he then "sold out" Eastern Europe to the Soviet

Union, leaving a legacy that became the Cold War. A more correct appraisal is that FDR did little in the day-to-day operations of the war, delegating those to gifted subordinates, most especially General George Marshall, but that he still probably made a half-dozen key strategic decisions that set the framework for the Allies' marches. As for his wartime diplomacy, much of the criticism is misdirected and historically unfounded even though legions of Americans and Europeans have linked up FDR, Yalta, and appeasement as if they were modern synonyms.[19]

In March 1933, while Roosevelt sought to restore to Americans faith in themselves, he also encouraged the World Disarmament Conference taking place in Geneva. He pushed for a nonaggression pact, the end of offensive weapons, and a curb on arms and armed forces. But with Hitler's rise to power, Germany withdrew from the conference and from the League of Nations. The newly inaugurated American president was also concerned with naval disarmament and with Japan's demand for parity. Consequently, Roosevelt sought to get the British to stand firm against parity, but the British were more concerned with a newly aggressive Germany than with the Japanese.

Roosevelt's secretary of state, Cordell Hull, at the same time, had pushed hard for trade agreements and for an end to interference in the affairs of Latin America. Roosevelt and Hull laid aside the Platt Amendment, which allowed the United States to intervene in Cuba, and FDR also pulled the marines out of Haiti and made friendly overtures to Panama. The administration called its new sensitivity the "Good Neighbor Policy," and presented it as a more fruitful direction than the mixture of marines and economic imperialism that had so marked administrations before Roosevelt.[20]

THE ISOLATIONIST FERVOR

From his first inaugural to Pearl Harbor, FDR had to face the consequences of widespread American disillusionment with World War I. That sentiment was fed by the hearings of Senator Gerald P. Nye and his committee, which investigated the munitions industry. Amid charges of bribery, collusion, gross profiteering, and tax evasion, the committee laid the groundwork for linking up munitions makers and the advent of the war. These "merchants of death" had been responsible for encouraging America's entry into the conflagration, and throughout the country, peace societies and isolationists pledged to prevent a repetition of those mistakes.

Oddly enough, FDR also denounced the arms trade and granted Nye access to documents that were to assist his committee with its allegations. As isolationist feeling grew, Congress was pressed to enact legislation that would require the president to embargo the export of arms to all belligerents in the case of war abroad. The president pushed for some provision to discriminate between aggressor and victim, but the tide in Congress overwhelmed him, and FDR signed a bill that would in the future severely tie his hands.

As the president approved the Neutrality Act, Benito Mussolini's Italian forces invaded Ethiopia. A U.S. arms embargo under the law would work against Italy, which had the ability, more than the Ethiopians, to buy and ship significant amounts of arms. But neither France nor Britain seemed willing to stop Mussolini, and the League of Nations proved to be ineffectual after the attack. The president retreated even further behind the isolationist curtain.[21]

Thus, the early pattern of FDR's behavior seems clear. He was genuinely concerned about the deteriorating state of affairs in the world, and he tried to use suasion, moral appeals, and goodwill to foster disarmament, peaceful settlement of conflicts, and economic prosperity. But behind these mild and well-meaning intentions, there was strong public isolationist sentiment, which Roosevelt was unwilling to confront. Thus, despite his personal reservations, FDR approved the initial neutrality law, and watched as Italy invaded Ethiopia, Japan gobbled up China, and Hitler took over the Sudetenland, Austria, and Czechoslovakia. The foremost study of Roosevelt's foreign policy, done by Robert Dallek, has shown that the president was very well informed and quite involved in a detailed way with the full international picture. Yet, again and again his modest advances were followed by retreat in the face of congressional opposition or the suggestions of public disapproval. At times, it appears that FDR bent not with the wind, but with the zephyr, that he did not inspire, but responded on a calibrated range so fine that the possibilities of leadership were too easily forfeited. James MacGregor Burns has concluded that, "as a foreign policy maker, Roosevelt during his first term was more a pussy-footing politician than political leader."[22]

During that term, FDR was obviously more concerned with domestic politics and was unwilling to offend the isolationist bloc—many of whose members were supporters of the New Deal. But it is also probable that he, too, shared many of the assumptions of the isolationists. In his speeches and in his personal correspondence, Roosevelt insisted that the United States should stay out of future conflicts. He counseled the American ambassador to Germany, William Dodd, "I do not know that the United States can save civilization but at least by our example we can make people think and give them the opportunity of saving themselves."[23] In August 1936 in a Chautauqua address, FDR took up the merchants of death theme and warned about the "fool's gold" of trading with belligerents. Then, in one of his most powerful appeals, Roosevelt remarked,

> I have seen war. I have seen war on land and sea. I have seen blood running from the wounded. I have seen men coughing out their gassed lungs. I have seen the dead in the mud. I have seen cities destroyed. I have seen two hundred limping, exhausted men come out of line—the survivors of a regiment of one thousand that went forward forty-eight hours before. I have seen children starving. I have seen the agony of mothers and wives. I hate war.

Perhaps it was just a 1936 campaign speech finely tuned to a pacifist audience. But more likely it was a genuine expression of Roosevelt's horror of war, the consequences of which he had seen only late on his trip to Europe as assistant secretary of the navy. But by 1935, the president clearly comprehended the rising threat of the totalitarian states. He allowed Hull to promote a coordinated and publicly indignant policy, which was aimed at supporting the League of Nations' sanctions against Italy for its invasion of Ethiopia. But when the League failed to act, and the British and the French agreed to the dismemberment of a large portion of Ethiopia, the issue became moot. Whether Roosevelt would have persevered if it mattered is not clear, but he definitely did try to prevent American citizens from profiting from such conflicts.

A similar dilemma faced FDR with regard to Japan's invasion of China in the summer of 1937. An arms embargo in that case would have worked against the Chinese, and the president decided to withhold a neutrality proclamation unless a formal declaration of war came. Despite his sympathies for China, and strong U.S. sentiment against the Japanese, Roosevelt feared a conflict on the high seas with the Japanese navy. He ended up announcing new restrictions on American trade with China.[24]

Then on October 5, 1937, FDR decided to make a major address on aggression and "the reign of terror and international lawlessness" that was taking place. With the Japanese attacks on China obviously in mind, he deplored the bombing of civilians, the sinking of ships on the high seas, and the brutality of conquest. Then he warned that the New World would not ultimately be spared the horrors of war. He called war a contagion, and argued, "when an epidemic of physical disease starts to spread, the community approves and joins in a quarantine of the patients in order to protect the health of the community against the spread of the disease." He went on to request vaguely that there should be "positive endeavors to preserve peace." The speech seemed a clarion call to action, but what did Roosevelt have in mind? It is difficult to say, for no sooner had FDR staked out a position than he equivocated and backpedaled. Privately, he wrote his old headmaster at Groton, "As you know, I am fighting against a public psychology of long standing—a psychology which comes very close to saying, 'Peace at any price.'"[25]

Indecisiveness characterized Roosevelt's behavior toward Nazi Germany as well. As Hitler rearmed Germany in 1935 and later marched into the Rhineland, the administration said nothing. When Neville Chamberlain reached an agreement with Hitler at Munich, Roosevelt seemed to be of two minds. He was relieved that war was temporarily averted, and yet he was privately skeptical that peace was at hand. War would mean the loss of millions of lives "under circumstances of unspeakable horror," and yet negotiations would postpone "what looks to me like an inevitable conflict within the next five years." The president retained the same standoffish attitude concerning the Spanish Civil War. In 1936, during the presidential campaign, FDR insisted on the United States being neutral and placed an embargo on the export of arms to either side. As time passed, though, the president recognized that noninterference would really end up assisting the pro-Fascist regime of General Francisco Franco. At one point in the spring of 1938, he proposed to lift the embargo on arms, but then he decided against a change of policy. The president understood that the munitions would not go across the Spanish frontier anyhow, but his real concern was alienating the Catholic vote. Even Ickes was disgusted that these foreign policy determinations were being dictated, in his opinion, in the United States and Great Britain by Catholic minorities. Thus, by the end of 1938, FDR had made his own transition as he came to view the world as a more hostile and threatening place than before. But his own leadership remained vague and almost shadowy.[26]

In July 1939, the president warned Congress that "philosophies of force" were threatening the American way of life, and that no nation would be safe where aggression went unchecked. He counseled, "There are many methods short of war, but stronger and more effective than mere words, of bringing home to aggressor governments the aggregate sentiments of our own people." The president asked for a revision of the neutrality laws, which "may operate unevenly and unfairly—may actually give aid to an aggressor and deny it to the victim."

After Hitler's conquest of the rest of Czechoslovakia in March 1939, an attempt was made in the Senate to repeal the arms embargo and permit U.S. citizens to trade with nations at war on a cash and carry basis—terms that would favor the British and French. The president, though, remained silent on the debate, and only when it was too late did he strongly push for revision of the arms embargo. Then on September 1, 1939, the Germans invaded Poland and FDR proclaimed U.S. neutrality and enacted an arms embargo. Again the president pressed for a revision of the Neutrality Act and insisted that his purpose was to keep the United States out of the war, not to help the British or the French. He concluded that "my problem is to get the American people to think of conceivable consequences without scaring the American people into thinking they are going to be dragged into this war."[27]

THE NAZI ONSLAUGHT

The American people were indeed to do more than ponder the conceivable consequences of war: they were to see the Nazi forces sweep through Norway, Denmark, the Low Countries, and France. The "phony" war gave way to the war of lightning movement, the "blitzkrieg." As the British scrambled from France and imprinted their retreat on Dunkirk, Americans of many persuasions realized that German advances were indeed a threat to U.S. interests. Roosevelt knew what he could not probably admit: that his nation's security was dependent on the ability of the British and the French to stop the Nazi armies. But he was unwilling to confront directly the isolationist and pacifist elements in America. Indeed, the best summary of American public opinion was that it supported the British and the French against the Germans, but wished that the United States would stay out of the war.

On June 14, 1940, the French premier, Paul Reynaud, asked for American troops and supplies to save his nation. Roosevelt's response was to praise French valor and resistance and to increase arms and munitions. But he would make no military commitments because of Congress. Two days later, the French surrendered to the Nazis, leaving the British to fight alone.[28]

By May 1940, the new British prime minister, Winston S. Churchill, pleaded for American destroyers to protect the Atlantic supply lines from German submarines. Roosevelt hesitated, unsure what to do. He insisted that he needed an act of Congress to transfer destroyers to Great Britain. His own cabinet pressured the president to meet Churchill's demands, while Congress insisted that the executive could not transfer any warships until the chief of naval operations certified they were "not essential" to the defense of the United States. Roosevelt's response was again inaction. Churchill pleaded, "Mr. President, with great respect I must tell you that in the long history of the world this is a thing to do NOW." But the president seemed undecided as to how to proceed.[29]

By August, several people had proposed a trade—American destroyers for British bases. Roosevelt, though, still believed that the agreement needed congressional approval, and he was concerned the Republicans would use the deal as a campaign issue. Thus, some four months after Churchill's desperate appeal, Roosevelt acted but only after public support had swung over to strongly favor the British, after Wendell Willkie privately promised not to raise the matter in the campaign, and after FDR's advisors found a way to avoid having to go to Congress over the deal.

Roosevelt was especially sensitive to criticism in 1940. After some real hesitation and deliberate coyness, he had decided to challenge the two-term tradition and run for a third term. To his surprise and that of many political observers, the Republican party did not turn to established politicians such as Thomas Dewey, Robert Taft, or Arthur Vandenberg. Instead the Grand Old Party nominated Willkie, an activist and an energetic, rumpled utilities executive. Roosevelt had shrewdly reached out to the traditional Republican elites before the election by bringing two well-known Republicans into his cabinet: Henry L. Stimson as secretary of war and Frank

Knox as secretary of navy. Knox had been a Rough Rider and the running mate of Landon's in 1936, and Stimson was a cabinet member under Taft and Hoover.

Willkie ran a strong challenge against the president and openly charged that FDR was preparing to lead the nation into the European war. FDR had already hesitated on the destroyer deal until Republican cabinet members Stimson and Knox pressed him on the bases swap. Then he faced an even touchier subject: compulsory military service. Throughout the summer until August 2, FDR simply avoided providing any leadership on the bill that Secretary Stimson pressed for. He instead visited defense installations, stressed the importance of preparedness, and warned about the gravity of the European situation.

Still, FDR knew that Willkie's charges were making some headway. People had reservations about a third term, strong executive power in a world of totalitarian states, and the abuses of some New Deal programs. But the most explosive issue was the advance of war. Roosevelt faced not only the powerful forces of isolationism and pacifism, but the reservations of Italian, German, and Irish-American voters in the United States. The polls in October showed that Willkie was cutting into FDR's large early lead.

Roosevelt, who played a waiting game all summer, swung into action and launched a powerful offensive against the Republican party. He recalled once again the world of the Great Depression, the economy before the New Deal, and its cornucopia of benefits. He attacked the party of "Martin, Barton, and Fish"—three conservative Republican leaders in Congress who went rhythmically together in his ridicule. But most importantly, the president went into Irish-dominated Boston and pledged, "Your boys are not going to be sent into foreign wars." In the past, he usually added "except in case of attack." Now, facing Willkie's sharp attacks, he deleted the commonsense guarantee and simply told advisors, "If we're attacked, it's no longer a foreign war."

The final results gave FDR a popular vote of 27,243,466 to 22,304,755 and an electoral vote of 449 to 82. The president lost only ten states, although Willkie had picked up five million more votes than Landon in 1936. The Democrats lost three seats in the Senate and gained seven seats in the House. Roosevelt's victory, then, was a personal vote of confidence and a rare opportunity for him to exercise leadership in the explosive events unfolding.[30]

HESITATIONS IN 1941

With the election behind him, Roosevelt seemed to be somewhat detached from the terrible fate that was about to fall on Britain in late 1940. The president made no shifts in the cabinet, indicated that he would not ask for any changes in the Neutrality Act, and did not respond to Churchill's frantic calls for still more assistance. But then in December, Roosevelt began to lay out the general outlines of what became know as "Lend Lease." The United States would send the British government munitions without requiring payment, and when the war was over, the British would repay in kind, not in dollars. He presented his plan in a homey analogy—lending your garden hose to your neighbor whose home was on fire. To the American people, he insisted, "Our national policy is not directed toward war. Its sole purpose is to keep war away from our country and our people." The president summarized the United States' role in the struggle, "We must be the great arsenal of democracy. For us this is an emergency as serious as war itself."

In the early weeks of 1941, the polls showed that the American people favored Lend Lease by margins of two to one, with opposition strongest in the isolationist areas of the Midwest and the Great Plains states. That opposition was most pronounced in the Senate where some major leaders such as Hiram Johnson of California, Burt Wheeler of Montana, the younger Robert LaFollette of Wisconsin, Arthur Vandenberg of Michigan, Bennett Clark of Missouri, Gerald P. Nye of North Dakota, and the newly emerging senator from Ohio, Robert Taft, son of the former president, spearheaded the opposition. Against the combined forces of isolationism, the president proceeded cautiously, even avoiding responding to personal attacks on his motives.[31]

In addition, FDR established an advisory commission to the Council of National Defense, a collection of advisors that included William S. Knudsen of General Motors, Edward R. Stettinius, a wealthy financier, labor leader Sidney Hillman, and Leon Henderson, a dedicated New Dealer. Later, Roosevelt set up the Office of Production Management, with Knudsen, Hillman, Stimson, and Knox, to deal with production problems and national mobilization of resources. Bernard Baruch, who had served Woodrow Wilson in a similar capacity in the last war, advocated a centralized agency to oversee allocations, priorities, and price-fixing. Roosevelt opposed any czar, arguing that only the president had such authority, and he opposed delegating it.

It was this decentralized style, the overlapping jurisdiction of many layered agencies, and above all, Roosevelt's fear of political competition that was to plague the American war effort. The techniques that seemed so creative in the early ferment of the first New Deal had led to immobilization and near domestic deadlock in the late 1930s. Those same techniques applied to preparedness worsened critical production delays and led even Stimson to conclude that Roosevelt was the worst administrator he had ever worked for.[32]

Some of his closest advisors in early 1941 added to the informal criticism of their beloved leader. Felix Frankfurter wondered why the president did not seize the initiative, and Stimson told Roosevelt directly in April that his leadership was clearly lacking. But the president was carefully weighing public opinion before the next guarded and tentative step. Even Frances Perkins and Frank Walker were amazed at the ignorance and public apathy they saw as they crisscrossed the nation over this most basic issue of war and peace.[33]

Halfway around the world, Hitler continued his record of awful successes and pondered his boldest move, an attack in the east on the Soviet Union, a nation that he characterized as "the scum of humanity" led by "common blood-starved criminals." At the end of April, five weeks before his planned attack, Hitler was sure: "We have only to kick in the door and the whole rotten structure will come crashing down."[34]

The British, thrown back on their own reliance and courage, worried about Nazi threats to their traditional ally Greece, endured the rapid successes of General Erwin Rommel's attacks in North Africa, and experienced the loss of Crete. Churchill openly faced his critics in the House of Commons; he was stoically to conclude only that "defeat is bitter." In his darkest hour to date, the prime minister implored Roosevelt for more support. Then on May 10-11, the Nazis attacked London and damaged much of the Houses of Parliament.

In Asia, the flow of events was equally ominous. Japan seemed committed to an expansion of its "Greater East Asia Co-Prosperity Sphere," but the exact direction of the advance was unclear. The most obvious objective was to take control of the rest of China, a nation furthered split by the rise of the Communist Chinese rivals to Chiang Kai-shek's regime. Engaged in fighting in other theaters of action, the Soviets and Japanese agreed to a nonaggression pact, one consequence of which was to increase anxiety in China. In mid-April, FDR quietly approved an executive order that allowed U.S. airmen to resign from the military service in order to form volunteer civilian groups to go to China. This move led to the formation of the Flying Tigers under Colonel Claire L. Chennault, which was pledged to assist Chiang's forces.

In the crucial months of late 1940 and early 1941, FDR still refused to commit himself to long-term action. He warned Secretary of Navy Knox to avoid making authorizations that extended beyond July 1, 1941, and he refused to allow his military chiefs to engage in military planning with the British. American military leaders had insisted on the need to coordinate intelligence and planning with the British. After the presidential election, the chief of naval operations, Harold Stark, put forth four basic scenarios for the United States: (1) emphasize hemispheric defense; (2) concentrate on stopping Japan; (3) commit equal forces to the Atlantic and Pacific theaters; or (4) give the Atlantic operations priority over the Pacific war.

The president did not approve any of Stark's options, but he did permit some conversations with the British. By 1941, the army and the navy chiefs had apparently come to favor the last of Stark's options—an "Atlantic First" strategy if war came. But as for the president, he seemed at times eclectic if not confused in his approach to the complex crisis; he did recognize the need to choose a strong army chief of staff, and his choice was career officer George Marshall. Marshall provided a sense of cool efficiency, organizational comprehensiveness, and genuine strength of character that later earned him the title "architect of Allied victory." In this period, he too was struggling with Roosevelt's facile charm, disorganized ways, and seemingly short-term commitments to plans and people.[35]

As the American and British military leaders prepared some joint agreements, Roosevelt stayed somewhat away from the plans. Inevitably the Atlantic First strategy became firmed up, without any serious strategic discussion at the presidential level about the feasibility of other options. The United States was committed to providing Britain with all aid short of going to war itself. But Hitler's forces were brutally impressive, and by April, there was serious doubt that Britain could survive. A worried Roosevelt authorized the repair of British ships in American docks, allowed their pilots to be trained in U.S. airfields, widened the American neutrality patrol zone, transferred ten Coast Guard cutters to the Royal Navy, and put Greenland and the coast of West Africa under navy surveillance. With the Danish government's agreement, FDR first placed Greenland under the aegis of the United States and then started the construction of military bases there.

As the Nazis continued to sink British convoys in the Atlantic, the president faced intense pressure from his own cabinet to provide some protection for shipping. But FDR again hesitated, waiting, it seemed, for some provocation from Hitler. He confided to Morgenthau in May, "I am waiting to be pushed into the situation." Stimson also thought that the president was waiting for some incident to move the nation closer to war, but Ickes wrote FDR that Hitler was not going to allow that to happen.[36]

Roosevelt carefully watched the May Gallup poll that indicated that about one-quarter of the respondents thought the president had not gone far enough to help Britain, the same number thought he had gone too far, and half pretty much approved of his actions. As Roosevelt struggled with a public statement on the convoy question, the German battleship *Bismarck* swept across the North Sea threatening Britain. The president wondered if the *Bismarck* would show up in the Caribbean and if U.S. submarines should attempt to sink it. He speculated that he then might be impeached for such an action. Two days later, the British sank the great invader, and the president rested more comfortably not having to make a decision. The president's speech resulted in a proclamation of unilateral national emergency, but he neither made plans for American convoys nor advocated revising the Neutrality Act. Once again, FDR backtracked, waiting for an event to bring about the opening his leadership skills could not provide. Then in June 1941, Hitler invaded Russia.

FDR's attitudes toward Russia were more guarded than has generally been portrayed. Although he recognized the Soviet Union diplomatically early in his first term, he retained a basic antipathy toward Bolshevism. When Russia suddenly became Britain's necessary ally, FDR indicated in general terms that he would be willing to extend aid to Russia as well. He wrote one editor, Fulton Oursler, that he "would write an editorial condemning the Russian form of dictatorship equally with the German form of dictatorship—but at the same time, I would make it clear that the immediate menace at this time to the security of the United States lies in the threat of Hitler's armies."

His cabinet pushed for an immediate and major commitment to Russia before Hitler could effectively sweep through the western part of that vast nation. Then the cautious FDR approved navy escorts for American shipping and that of other countries that were joining the U.S. convoys west of Ireland. That decision represented some movement on Roosevelt's part, but still he refused to protect all friendly shipping in the west Atlantic, a step Secretary of Navy Knox had insisted on. The president desperately sought not to raise the level of opposition in Congress by bolder actions; he waited for an incident in the Atlantic, but Hitler, in turn, had commanded his admirals not to rise to the bait.

In the Pacific, FDR was even more cautious. He argued that since trouble was coming in the Atlantic, it was important to avoid conflict in the Far East. When Ickes told him to cut off oil to Japan, FDR warned, "It is terribly important for the control of the Atlantic for us to help to keep peace in the Pacific. I simply have not got enough Navy to go around—and every little episode in the Pacific means fewer ships in the Atlantic."[37]

In Japan, various factions were vying for control of the government and the emperor's favor, until finally the militarists seized power. As their armies swept through Indochina and ripped deeper into decaying China, Roosevelt made some modest moves. He froze all Japanese assets in the United States, closed the Panama Canal "for repairs," and placed Lieutenant General Douglas MacArthur in command over the Filipino military.

Faced with British demands for more war supplies and the new list of Russian needs, Roosevelt had to deal with the consequences of the disorganized production mechanisms he had insisted on. In March 1941, he created the National Defense Mediation Board to deal with the increase in industrial strikes. A month later, the president added the Office of Price Administration and Civilian Supply, and then in May, he had the energetic and flamboyant mayor of New York City, Fiorello LaGuardia, head up the Office of Civilian Defense. The problems he faced were by no means minor ones. In April, John L. Lewis took four hundred thousand coal miners out on strike, and the president had to intervene in getting a settlement in that crucial industry. Then in the summer, a wildcat strike hit North American Aviation Company, and Roosevelt eventually ordered the secretary of war to take over the plant. Thus, while the Nazis were at Britain's throat, and the Russians were forced into their frozen positions, it was business as usual in the United States, and the president did not seem to be too far in front of popular sentiment.

The British economist Keynes warned that the mobilization efforts were deficient and that a stronger conversion program had to be pushed through. In Congress, the Senate Special Committee to Investigate the Defense Program pointed out a host of delays and production problems. One committee member, Tom Connally of Texas, concluded, "We are just advertising to the world . . . that we are in a mess." To increasing charges that he had not exhibited forethought, FDR seemed oblivious. On one hand, the president may have had a better sense of the divisions on Capitol Hill than anyone recognized. For in the summer of 1941 the Selective Service Act renewal passed the House by only one vote. The supposedly stronger consensus on preparedness was just as Roosevelt had assumed—much more fragile and tentative than other people had asserted. Amidst all those pressures, FDR received increasing complaints about racial discrimination in defense industries. Black leaders, led by A. Philip Randolph, insisted on an executive order barring discrimination, but FDR resisted. Randolph threatened a march on Washington to press the case, and the president capitulated with a high-sounding and rather vague document that finally created the Committee on Fair Employment Practices.

In August, FDR agreed to a surprise meeting with Churchill off the coast of Newfoundland. While the military staffs on each side presented their differing perspectives on the war, the president and the prime minister agreed to a statement of principles, later called the "Atlantic Charter." Roosevelt assiduously avoided making any commitments that could be interpreted at home as "secret agreements." Churchill, not surprisingly, pressed for some evidence of greater support, some hope for a struggling ally.

Back in the United States, Roosevelt was indeed faced with charges of planning a secret invasion of Europe and of leading the nation into another foreign war. Every move the president made resulted in bitter scrutiny and isolationist charges. Yet his own cabinet, led by Stimson, insisted the nation needed more leadership to meet production schedules, and that military strategists needed more of a sense of FDR's views. And despite his assurances to Churchill that he would act more forcefully in his dealings with Tokyo, FDR was still cautious about his moves in the Pacific. The Japanese government responded with vague assurances of goodwill and a pledge to withdraw from Indochina. As the two governments parlayed, the imperial armed forces prepared for war. Initially, the emperor insisted that he would not approve of going to war unless all possibilities for peace had ended. Finally, the Japanese Empire was geared up to go to war by the end of October 1941 unless its demands were met. Basically, its leaders wanted an end to American and British interference in China, support for the Chungking regime there, and cooperation in Japanese economic development.[38]

WAR IN THE ATLANTIC

As Roosevelt and Hull were pondering the reality of Japan's expressed objectives, an American destroyer, the *Greer*, began trailing a German U-boat and reported the latter's position to a British plane. The U-boat fired on the *Greer*, and FDR took this incident as the occasion for a major change of policy. He announced to the American people a policy of "shoot on sight"—in effect, a declaration of naval war against Germany. The U.S. Navy was ordered to protect all shipping of any nation in convoys going to Ireland. It was a clear challenge to Hitler, but the Fuhrer again refused to respond.

The polls showed a two to one approval rating for the shoot on sight policy, and FDR moved to modify the Neutrality Act emphasizing the need to arm American merchant ships. Then on October 16, 1941, a convoy of forty ships escorted by four corvettes was attacked by a group of U-boats; one of the American destroyers rushing to give assistance, the *Kearney*, was hit by a torpedo. As the House of Representatives debated a revision of the Neutrality Act, the report of the attack tipped the scales and the act was changed after a vote of 259 to 138. The bill moved to the Senate, and FDR helped to lay the groundwork there by disclosing he had two important documents in hand. One was a Nazi map of South and Central America that divided those regions into states; the other was a Nazi plan to abolish all religions if Hitler were successful in his conquests. The Senate supported some revision of the Neutrality Act by a vote of 50 to 37. Several days later an American destroyer, *Reuben James*, was torpedoed and went down with 115 members of its crew.[39]

DECISION IN THE PACIFIC

Roosevelt thus was able to get some moderate changes in congressional policy with these inflammatory incidents, but still he lacked any consensus on going to war or facing Hitler directly. By November 1941, the "Old Master" had no more options to play out; he was stalemated in his policies and he refused to be too far in front. His admirer and speech writer, Robert Sherwood, concluded, "He had no more tricks left. The bag from which he had pulled so many rabbits was empty." FDR systematically avoided a showdown with Japan, expecting the need to move fast in the Atlantic theater. But there Hitler refused to be Roosevelt's foil and give him the clear attack necessary to the mobilize American people. So in late 1941, the Americans waged an undeclared war in the North Sea and watched uneasily as the Japanese Navy seemed to be on the move in the Pacific. The administration had decided in November 1941 to augment the defense of the Philippines and had planned in two or three months to make it viable in case of attack.

The president also waited until Congress passed the Lend Lease bill before he notified the Russians that they could expect aid totaling one billion dollars. To circumvent Catholic opposition to aiding a Communist regime, the president quietly appealed to Pope Pius XII for some understanding. The Vatican was not impressed by his plea, but indicated that there was a distinction between aiding the Russians in war and aiding the Communist regime.

In any case, by November the Japanese government had its own timetable for the completion of talks with the Roosevelt administration. Some bitter Roosevelt haters have charged that FDR knew about Japanese designs on Pearl Harbor before the attack and allowed American forces to be left vulnerable there, realizing that such aggression would end the debate over American foreign policy once and for all. The general weight of the evidence, though, favors the view that FDR did not know about the specific targeting of Pearl Harbor. Still, in early December, the president seemed to sense that war was in the immediate vicinity. On December 1 he told Morgenthau, "it is all in the laps of the gods." And five days later he told another associate, "we might be at war with Japan, although no one knew." However, he expected that the Japanese would move in the Dutch East Indies or Thailand, rather than in the Philippines or Hawaii. He miscalculated that the Japanese would first attack the smaller nations before encircling the larger ones in the region. Then on December 6, the president received reports of a large Japanese convoy and ship movements in the southwest Pacific. He observed, "this means war." But when Hopkins lamented that the Japanese would pick the target and the U.S. couldn't strike the first blow, FDR replied, "No, we can't do that. We are a democracy and a peaceful people. . . . But we have a good record." A little after 7:30 A.M., on December 7, 1941, the Japanese attacked with a fury at Pearl Harbor.[40]

Roosevelt at first seemed calm, in fact relieved that the long debate had ended; only later was he sobered by the terrible list of losses, especially to his beloved navy. Stimson pressed for a declaration of war against Germany as well as Japan, but the president again cautiously refused. When he approached Congress on December 8, he called the surprise attack "a date which will live in infamy," and pledged the nation to the inevitable triumph with the help of God. Only one member of Congress, Jeannette Rankin, who had opposed going to war in 1917, voted against the war declaration. Still, it was only half a war until Hitler and Mussolini decided to honor their loose alliance with Japan and declare a formal state of war with the United States also.

As for Roosevelt, he acknowledged the serious setbacks in the Hawaiian Islands and in the Philippines. He expected heavy casualties and concluded, "It will not only be a long war, but a hard war." Events were to prove him correct. But with the brutal sneak attack on Pearl Harbor, isolationist and peace sentiment ended almost totally. After years of hesitation, false starts, and lethargic leadership at times, Franklin Roosevelt got the dramatic event he needed to unite the nation, an event more final and more traumatic than even the banking crisis that greeted him in 1933. More than Wilson or Lincoln, FDR entered the war with little domestic carping and fifth column activity. And because of the Nazi attack on Soviet Russia, the organized left, traditionally opposed to the American military and defense preparedness, now welcomed U.S. participation in the war. As the record of atrocities of the Nazis became more visible, this conflict between and among great powers for position, empire, living room, and colonial expansion took on a different tone. The Second World War became a great moral crusade in which the simplicities of good and evil seemed to be a truthful relief on which the ambiguous battles became memorialized. Because Hitler, Mussolini, and the Japanese warlords seemed so truly evil, the Allied leaders stood out in heroic terms. The buoyant FDR, the gallant Churchill, the prickly Charles DeGaulle became international figures to freedom-loving peoples. Even the tyrannical Stalin became in World War II metamorphosed for a time into a father figure, although a suspicious one. Only later was he more appropriately measured beside Hitler in his deeds of butchery. Together, they became the nightmare of the twentieth century—the demons of the left and the right. But in the depths of the war, Stalin was a critical, if not indispensable, ally. When asked to explain why he was willing to make common cause with the Russian dictator, Churchill told the House of Commons that he would make an alliance with the devil to defeat the Nazis. He did, and so did FDR.

A YEAR OF DEFEATS: 1942

The year 1942 would prove to be a very bad start for the formal Anglo-American alliance. The Japanese swept across the Pacific basin and beyond, taking the Philippines, Guam, Midway, Singapore, Thailand, Hong Kong, and other strategic points. The Americans had to pay the piper for their slow mobilization, the transfer of Lend Lease to Europe, and the neglect of the armed forces for a generation. The president and his advisors faced not one front, but two, and Roosevelt made the first critically important decision of his wartime stewardship. Despite the outrage of Pearl Harbor, the United States would concentrate on an Atlantic First strategy so as to join the British in defeating the Nazis and Fascists before turning full force on the Japanese. "Plan Dog," as it was called, was an important commitment to the British, and Churchill was unashamedly delighted.

At a Christmastime meeting, the prime minister, and his major associates Lord Beaverbrook and Lord Halifax, were better prepared than the American staff for a discussion of strategy. The British expected the Germans to move down the Iberian Peninsula into North Africa, and they were ready to check the advance by having the Americans invade near Casablanca and drive toward their forces in the east in the direction of Tunisia. Roosevelt at first seemed amenable to the idea, but then downplayed the initiative.

The Americans and British joined in a spirit of common defense, while insisting on important differences in strategy. The American military chiefs, true heirs of the tradition of Grant and Sherman, believed in the need to build up their force strength and then begin

a massive thrust toward the heart of Germany. The British, still remembering the terrible stalemate of trench warfare in the previous
war, insisted on a strategy of moving at soft spots of opportunity
and enemy imbalance. The Americans regarded that approach as a
wasteful expenditure of resources, a "peripheralism," as it was called,
that had led to the type of disaster in the Dardanelles with which
Churchill had been associated in the previous war.

Actually, both staffs were correct in some ways. The Allies in
1942 were not ready for the type of concentrated invasion the
Americans were contemplating; and yet the war could only be won
by a bloodletting across the European continent. Meanwhile in the
Pacific, the Japanese advance continued as the Christmas strategy
session took place. General Marshall insisted on a unified Pacific
command, and the Allies agreed, thus placing the troops of the
Americans, British, Dutch, and Australians under the command of
British General Archibald Wavell. The Allies accepted a combined
British-American chief of staff command, which in the long run
would give the United States increasing ascendancy in the direction
of the war. Since FDR still had no real joint chiefs structure as the
British had, he created such a component made up of Marshall,
Admiral Ernest J. King, the chief of naval operations, and General
Henry Arnold. As a result of their deliberations, the Allies agreed
on the North African campaign, "Operation Gymnast"—more as a
recognition that victory had to be garnered somewhere, and that
Europe was not the place. It is sometimes forgotten that while the
Americans were mobilizing for action, and the British held to a
defensive strategy by the skin of their teeth, the real battle against
the Nazi war machine was being waged in 1942 in the eastern theater. There the Russian soldiers, fighting for the survival of their
nation and not any particular ideology, waged a terrible struggle
against the advancing Germans. Stalin's demand to the Allies was
brutally simple and easily explainable: a second front, a major assault on the Nazis in the west to divert troops away from his theater. The Anglo-American strategy, its mobilization problems, its
frequent postponements on that front in 1942, 1943, and 1944 led
him to suspect that the real strategy was to let the Nazis and the
Soviets bleed each other dry.

Wisely Stalin had decided to avoid declaring war on Japan, and
the Japanese likewise wanted to avoid fighting on a second front.
The combined Allied command under General Wavell did not stop
the Japanese as they moved effectively across the Pacific and

threatened even Australia. Roosevelt desperately tried early in the war and insistently throughout it to prop up the Chinese regime, headed by Chiang Kai-shek. Churchill, while expressing his respect for the Chinese "as a race," thought the president greatly overestimated their importance in the world. In this disastrous theater of the Pacific, the United States was to find a hero: General Douglas MacArthur. MacArthur was vain, difficult, disobedient, and a publicity hound of the first order; but he was also a brilliant and creative American military strategist. In 1942, he insisted on staying in the Philippines as it fell to the Japanese forces. Roosevelt had other plans—he ordered Filipino President Manuel Quezon and MacArthur out of the country to Corregidor. MacArthur was to prepare for the defense of vital Australia, but not before he dramatically pledged to the Filipino people, "I shall return." Thus by springtime, the Japanese were approaching the Australian perimeters and moving on India.

To Churchill, India was the very center of his vision of an extended British domain, and its possession still fired up his Victorian imagination. But to Roosevelt, the true future was clear: the war would sound the death knell for British and French imperialist aspirations. When FDR raised the issue right after Pearl Harbor, Churchill was passionately opposed to any independence; although the president later intended to suggest various compromises, including an Indian Union modeled on the U.S. Articles of Confederation, he made no real headway.

As his navy regrouped and began its defensive operations in the Pacific, the president offered no advice, followed the train of events carefully, but stayed out of tactical matters. Admiral King in the capital and Admiral Chester W. Nimitz in the Pacific laid out in 1942 the basic strategy for the war in that region. In the equally disheartening Atlantic theater, the president watched as Hitler ordered his troops to wipe out the Soviets. Stalin insisted on more aid and a cross-Channel invasion. The Communist chief would have been surprised to find that the American high command was agreeing with him. Secretary of War Stimson, Marshall, and his aide, Lieutenant General Dwight D. Eisenhower, were all pushing for an end to the waste of resources and valuable time. German victories in Libya had led to the postponement of the Allied invasion of North Africa, and the American staff was pressing FDR for a major assault in April 1943 across the English Channel. Marshall and Stimson expected from Roosevelt a vague dismissal or a continued capitulation to British thinking, but the president in fact supported their decision and sent Marshall and Hopkins to convince Churchill. The president wrote the prime minister that the people were demanding action and that "these people are wise enough to see that the Russians are today killing more Germans and destroying more equipment than you and I put together. Even if full success is not attained, the big objective will be. . . ." As Marshall was to learn later, for democratic politicians in a war, there is nothing worse than the impression of no military engagements being fought. To the surprise of the Americans, the unusually skeptical Churchill did not dismiss the plan, probably because he feared FDR might concentrate then on the Pacific, or that Stalin would negotiate a separate treaty with the Nazis.

Stalin agreed to send Vyacheslav Molotov to Washington to confer on the matter, and the president blithely observed that he could handle Stalin better than the British Foreign Office or the State Department since he "thinks he likes me better and I hope he will continue to do so." To a later generation of Americans, such remarks provided convincing proof that FDR was naive in dealing with the Soviet leader, a naivete that led to a miscalculation of Russian intentions and trustworthiness. Yet the truth is that Stalin, who was highly suspicious if not a classic paranoid, probably did prefer FDR to Churchill, although his decisions were not likely to be influenced by the president's considerable charm. Stalin had grown up in a world of brutal party intrigue, lived by peasant cunning, and survived in a world of grim shadows and dark experiences. He did not choose the name Stalin—steel—for nothing. Roosevelt, and Harry S Truman for a while after him, tended to deal with Stalin as if they were dealing with difficult urban party bosses or obnoxious labor leaders like John L. Lewis. Stalin was a different type of animal.

Molotov's instructions seemed clear—to get a second front going as soon as possible. The Russians wanted to have the Allies in the west drain off forty German divisions in 1942; if that occurred the war would be over in the late months of that year or its outcome assured by then. In their planning for such a front, the Americans focused on the shipping problems, the difficult landings, and the need to provide adequate air cover. But FDR promised, at least in Molotov's eyes, a cross-Channel landing in August or September. Churchill, when he was informed, was clearly upset—1942 was not reasonable. The prime minister decided to visit Washington to press for more time, and he volunteered to break the news to Stalin, arguing that a North African invasion was the best plan of attack. Stalin was bitterly disappointed and criticized the valor of the Royal Air Force. As his English visitor was counseling delay on starting the second front, the Soviet leader was receiving grim news of the Nazi movement toward Stalingrad.

In October 1942, the Russians were to hold out in that critical battle, and in the Pacific, the Americans stopped the Japanese at a tiny island called Guadalcanal. The president had the Joint Chiefs transfer weapons in short supply elsewhere to turn the tide in what would be the first of a string of costly American victories in that region. And in late 1942, the Allies launched "Operation Torch"— the attack on North Africa. Just before the congressional elections and against the advice of most of his inner military circle, Roosevelt approved the operations. The public demanded action, and this was the theater the commander in chief had chosen. At one point, FDR playfully implored the Almighty in front of others, "Please make it before Election Day." But instead it came five days after the election, and the Americans were successful beyond their hopes.

FDR himself appealed to the French (in their own language) over the BBC, asking them in North Africa to oppose the crushing yoke of Nazism and to end the degradation of France. In North Africa, though, the quicksand of political factionalism in Vichy France with its Nazi agents clouded up the great cause. American military personnel began dealing with pro-Nazi sympathizers, headed by General Jean-François Darlan, a move that bitterly offended Free French leader General DeGaulle and that caused liberal criticism for FDR at home. In late December 1942, Darlan was assassinated, some said by the Free French leadership, and the Allies were relieved of what had become an acute embarrassment.

Thus, by the end of 1942, the wearying string of defeats seemed to have come to a merciful end. The Allies had diverted some Nazi strength away from the eastern front, although surely the laurels for heroism and determination rightfully belonged to the Soviet warriors. The Americans had waged quite successfully their first major engagement by landing and moving into North Africa. And in the Pacific, the Japanese Empire was reaching what would be its farthest boundaries; the tenacity of the navy and the leapfrogging strategy of MacArthur's armies and the marines would begin to turn the tide in the Pacific.

In all of this, Roosevelt remained consciously, almost self-consciously, calm and self-assured. He had his press secretary, Stephen Early, stress right after Pearl Harbor that the president had been through this before in World War I, had visited many defense establishments at home and abroad, and had seen more of the previous war in Europe than most other Americans. For Roosevelt, who was always defensive about not serving in that conflict, this was the chance to leave his mark on the great successor conflagration. In 1942, the president had begun to work out the command structure for the war, although in typical Rooseveltian fashion it was overlapping, frustrating to subordinates, and designed to leave ultimate power in his hands alone. But war has an impetus all its own, and as it ground slowly, more of the decisions flowed to the military, especially to General Marshall.[41]

Still, the important objectives set early in the war were clearly the president's, made sometimes in the face of opposition from his own military chieftains. Roosevelt was responsible for sending scarce supplies to the British and later the Russians before Pearl Harbor; although Americans may have regretted the loss of these supplies, it was surely a correct judgment. It was FDR who, for better or worse, insisted on proclaiming unconditional surrender as Allied policy, FDR who accepted an Atlantic First strategy, and FDR who, against his counselors' advice, approved the North Africa invasion. And by the end of 1942, Roosevelt was clearly an international figure, eclipsing even Churchill in the role as democracy's premier spokesman. Faced with those accomplishments as a backdrop, the president still suffered from the vices of his virtues. He had an unparalleled grasp of world politics, yet seemed superficial at times in his judgments of events as if he were a bright boy who skimmed across the surface of life, learning enough for the tests but doing poorly on the final exam. He managed to stay in touch with a variety of administrative military matters, and yet confused his major advisors about his initiatives and how they could help him. Last, he inspired the nation's mobilization efforts, but his management style helped at times to stymie the very process he so exhorted.

MANAGING THE WAR AT HOME

One of America's greatest roles, perhaps its most essential contribution, was being the arsenal of the Allied effort. The British fully admitted, the Russians grudgingly so, that the United States provided a veritable seatrain of supplies, food, and war armaments to buttress the war effort against the Nazi and Fascist forces. Unlike the previous war, the conflict was not for Americans an eighteen-month affair characterized by deadlocks, stalemates, and pauses. The war in 1942 was going poorly for the British and Russians, and Lend Lease and related programs were the major American contributions through most of that year as it had been before.

Roosevelt recognized that stark fact, and he tried wholeheart-edly to gear up the nation quickly for war production, and more extensively, for national mobilization. It is quite possible that a free people do not respond well to total war on the home front—even when united by direct attack and motivated by a clear need for sur-vival. On one hand, the American mobilization was often character-ized by greed, selfishness, and short-term concern for profit and salary increases in specific areas. On the other hand, however, those American efforts represented a powerful mobilization through in-fluence, pressure, and government coercion to fight a long and costly war.

Like most leaders of his generation, FDR had one major experi-ence in the domestic politics of war mobilization, and that was af-ter the U.S. entrance into World War I. As assistant secretary of the navy, he had, on one occasion at least, advocated a unified struc-ture to deal with domestic priorities. It was a commonsense posi-tion, one that he rejected again and again in the 1940s conflict in order to keep that power in his own hands. But pressed with mili-tary command decisions, diplomatic conferences, and his own fail-ing health, even Franklin Roosevelt could not make sense at times out of the ad hoc structures he erected. He changed staff, combined agencies, redesignated them, and exhorted their efforts. In one sense, his management style contributed to his difficulties, but in another sense, his wartime predecessors—Lincoln and Wilson—were no more successful in mobilization in the long run; indeed, consider-ing the magnitude of the task, probably less so.

The major advocate of centralizing the war mobilization effort was Bernard Baruch, the head of Wilson's War Industries Board during that earlier war. Not unexpectedly, Baruch pushed FDR pub-licly and had in mind resurrecting old WIB alumni to run it. Un-fortunately for Baruch, his two senior aides—Hugh Johnson and George Deck—had opposed FDR's reelection, a fact the president was not prone to overlook. Baruch's message was remarkably simi-lar over the years—conversion demanded the five M's: mobilization (the draft), minds (propaganda), money (taxation), materials, and manufacturing. Throughout the 1930s, Baruch pushed for more planning and foresight in mobilization and gathered about him many military men as well as politicians who were beneficiaries of his considerable campaign largesse. Roosevelt, who liked to be the only king on the hill, listened to Baruch, courted him, gave him seeming access, and went his own way.[42]

In one sense, FDR had used these emergency agencies during the New Deal, with Johnson and Peck heading up two such establishments, and he was not pleased with their inability to work with the cabinet departments. Then, too, Roosevelt was leery of creating agencies filled with businesspeople, many of them unsympathetic with the domestic goals of reform. During the war, New Dealers remained alert to short-term policies that would lead to eventual rollbacks of domestic legislation. Because of Baruch's power base in Congress, FDR avoided putting him in a position of authority that could challenge his own prerogatives.

When the army came in with a proposal for a Baruch-style "war cabinet," the president's antennae went up. He saw it as an attempt to cut him out of the direct control of industrial mobilization, and bluntly warned associates: "What do they think they are doing, setting up a second Government?" Aware of Wilson's need to go back to Congress for many administrative changes, FDR insisted on keeping the war management free of legislative interference. He refused to delegate powers to a committee or a czar and insisted that mobilization agencies report to the president. On May 25, 1940, the president had quietly signed an executive order creating the Office of Emergency Mobilization; invoking the Defense Act of 1916, he established an advisory commission that reported to him. When one of the members asked Roosevelt, "Who is the boss?" the president characteristically responded, "I am."[43]

In December, the president created the Office of Production Management, under the joint leadership of William Knudsen of General Motors and Sidney Hillman, a high-ranking labor leader. But soon even Roosevelt's Bureau of the Budget chief was complaining that OPM lacked the ability to pressure business into recognizing the need to meet national rather than market demands or profit expectations. In late August, FDR placed into OPM a Supply Priorities and Allocation Board with OPM's purchasing director, Donald M. Nelson, as its executive director. Still, the mobilization effort lacked what Baruch and others insisted on—one final authority. FDR wanted to make sure he was that authority. Thus by Pearl Harbor, the United States still lacked a system to coordinate priorities and a price controls policy.

By early 1942, FDR created the War Production Board (WPB) with Donald Nelson as chairman. Nelson, however, left the procurement of supplies to the military, and the armed services found a strong advocate in the Army-Navy Munitions Board headed by an energetic Wall Street lawyer, Ferdinand Eberstadt, who supported their proposals before the WPB. Still, the president's role was critical. When the war brought forth a quick shortage of rubber, FDR was compelled to deal with the issue himself. Congress, concerned about the critical shortages, had passed a bill to create a rubber supply agency to be run by a czar appointed by the president and approved by the Senate. Roosevelt vetoed the bill and appointed a committee headed this time by Baruch. When the report recommended rationing, the president used the findings as an excuse to move ahead.

The war, of course, involved not just problems of supply and priority, but also price control as well. The Office of Price Administration (OPA) created a general maximum price policy that aimed at freezing all retail prices at the highest levels of March 1942. FDR had been warned by his Bureau of the Budget people that in 1915–16, before the United States entered World War I, the cost of living shot up 15 percent and that that rate of increase could be repeated in 1942. A concerned president undertook a fireside chat to warn the public, and he pushed for an anti-inflation policy.

Workers feared that price controls were simply wage freezes by another name, and some liberals saw this step as a smoke screen for repealing the New Deal and were urging in its place trust-busting. Then Roosevelt, who had generally avoided becoming associated with rationing and who carefully sidestepped talk about taxation, decided to announce publicly that nobody during the war should have an income in excess of $25,000 per year. The remark created an uproar in Congress, and the president was forced to back down.

By the fall of 1942, production had fallen far short of the goals Roosevelt established. As the civilian and military sectors locked in conflict over appropriate spending levels and production for each area of need, the controversy again landed on Roosevelt's desk. Since he had created a system or nonsystem which resulted in overlapping levels of jurisdiction and no final authority but "Papa," as he phrased it, it was obvious that the president would have to deal with these problems. But FDR hated conflict, and so he urged both sides to work out the problem amiably.

Concerned again about the lack of coordination in the production crisis, Congress pushed for a single czar, a proposal FDR opposed. As intrigue mounted, Roosevelt created still another agency, the Office of War Mobilization, headed by former Supreme Court Justice James Byrnes. The deficiencies of the mobilization effort were becoming clearer in the areas of manpower. The administration had no real policy, and by 1943, the West Coast aircraft factories were in competition with the armed forces for men. The problem led to a proposal from Baruch that there be local commissions in each community to deal with deferments for men in critical industries. That recommendation in the West Coast controversy became the policy followed across the nation. But throughout late 1943, strikes sprung up and hampered the war effort.

These problems were confounded by plans for peacetime conversion being drawn up already in various parts of the executive bureaucracy. The issue once again turned New Deal liberals and businesspeople into enemies, and in October, FDR authorized Byrnes to deal formally with the prospective issues. Some liberals wanted to return to the familiar public works projects, while businesspeople instead placed their faith in private enterprise. The president facing a reelection campaign in 1944 was reluctant to began any reconversion or incur unemployment, and warned that the war was still going on. After the German counterattack at the Battle of the Bulge, talk of reconversion quieted down.

Roosevelt then insisted throughout most of the war on avoiding creating a czar, fearing it would undercut his own power, lead to congressional control over mobilization as in World War I, and encourage end runs around the established departments. But at times, even the president grew weary of the system he had partially wrought; on one occasion he complained, "I get so many conflicting recommendations my head is splitting." But the constant reshuffling of agencies, inconclusive directions, and loose priorities did not prove, as has been noted, his style to have been any more or less successful than Lincoln's or Wilson's. Perhaps the difficulties of mobilization are a telling commentary on FDR's loose management, or perhaps a free people just do not lend themselves too well to protracted total war.[44]

The war took a toll on the democratic fabric of America, just as it had under Wilson. Despite his reputation as the archliberal of modern America, FDR in fact incurred serious blemishes on that record, especially in dealing with some ethnic minorities before and during World War II. Although blacks were an important part of his political coalition, Roosevelt shied away from civil rights. His New Deal, of course, did provide some economic relief to blacks, especially in the urban areas, less so in the poorest farm regions. But he needed the cooperation of southern congressmen, and FDR avoided any overtures on civil rights, antilynching legislation, or fair employment practices until black leaders forced action on the last demand. His neglect was partially a political calculation, but FDR knew few blacks in his personal life and cultivated a public image as an honorary Georgian due to his Warm Springs attachment. Still, blacks proved to be the most loyal and grateful of the New Deal Democratic constituencies from 1936 down to the present.

Roosevelt's record in dealing with Japanese-Americans is less ambiguous and more stark. After Pearl Harbor, waves of hysteria swept across the Pacific Coast, and political leaders in California pressed for their removal. Anti-Japanese and anti-Japanese-American sentiment had been historically intense in that state, often encouraged by national leaders over the years and pushed by various economic interests.

Ironically, FBI Director J. Edgar Hoover, who had interred 942 Japanese aliens right after Pearl Harbor, informed Attorney General Francis Biddle that the push for mass evacuation was based on hysteria and political pressure rather than the facts. The federal authorities met with Governor Culbert L. Olson of California and agreed that all Japanese, including those born in the United States, had to be removed from the state. Even before the president received their report, he had approved of the evacuation adding only that the government officials should be "as reasonable as you can" in implementing the order.

As a result of the executive order of the president, and against the advice of the Justice Department and the FBI, some 120,000 Japanese on the West Coast were forcibly relocated. In addition, the president pushed for the evacuation of 140,000 Japanese from Oahu, where some espionage had occurred, and wrote that he was not worried about the constitutional questions.[45]

The internment, which was upheld by the Supreme Court in 1944, lasted until the end of that year, although Secretary of War Stimson and others argued for a quicker end. Only in the 1980s did lower federal courts begin to question critically the executive order and did Congress consider giving compensation to the evacuees. The record shows that there was not one single hostile act by Japanese-Americans against the United States during the war period; in retrospect, it appears that J. Edgar Hoover's early judgment in 1942 was correct. The removal of these people, many of them native-born U.S. citizens, is the single gravest example of presidential abuse of civil liberties in American history. The president's decision showed the thinness of traditional liberalism in the United States, especially during crisis, and it also is a sad example of the superficiality, racism, and crude political calculations that sometimes warped FDR's usually decent inclinations.

On a vaster scale, Roosevelt's moral blindness is even more apparent in the genocide of the Jews and other ethnic groups targeted by the Nazis for extermination. There were very few Western leaders who showed much concern about the reports of mass murder taking place in the concentration camps sprawled across central Europe. However, at times, FDR did express some interest in resettling Jews in sparsely settled areas, and he spoke to King Abdul ibn Saud about admitting Jews to Palestine. Yet the president declined to support the modest Wayne-Rogers bill to admit twenty thousand refugee children in 1939–40 on top of the quota system. At first in September 1942, Roosevelt refused to believe that a "final solution" was occurring. On several occasions the State Department seemed to stymie various proposals for rescue, including a Treasury Department's plan in June 1943 to evacuate seventy thousand Jews from Rumania at a cost of $170,000. Secretary Morgenthau was shocked to find out that the State Department had created a commission to rescue European art and museums, but not to save the Jews. By February 1944, the War Refugee Board, created by the administration, began work to help deal with the calamity of obvious genocide.

Roosevelt's inaction is usually attributed to his preoccupation with the war and a reluctance to divert resources away from that vital struggle. But in fact, FDR was rather remarkable in his ability to both direct the war effort and retain a staggering command of detail about the complexities of borders, strategic advances, and internecine political battles across the globe. In fairness, he did try at times to raise the Jewish refugee question, but when he found domestic resistance to quota changes or international resistance to Jewish settlements, he simply refused to overcome the lethargy, if not hostility, of his own State Department and others. The United

States, and the Allies in general, had refused to bomb the death camps and upset their normal extermination processes. Assistant Secretary of War John McCloy called such a step a diversion in the effort to win the war. But in fact, the Allies had in other instances diverted substantial war resources to aid other Hitler victims, especially the heroic Polish resistance in Warsaw in July 1944. In the end, Roosevelt was a bystander, as were so many other Western political and religious leaders, on the question of genocide.[46]

There are other less momentous, but somewhat troubling lapses in FDR's liberal record. He received reports from the FBI director on his political opponents and on potential troublemakers. There is also some evidence, although it is not conclusive, that Roosevelt allegedly had men who he thought were close to his wife, Eleanor, placed under surveillance during the war period. Taken together, the Roosevelt record then has its troubling episodes, its genuine blind spots, and a certain dark side that only the most partisan observer can ignore. Just as FDR laid the groundwork for the contemporary presidency, so too he exhibited in many ways the objectionable abuses of power that mark that great and at times frightening office.[47]

THE STRATEGY OF 1943

Franklin Roosevelt saw 1943 as the major year of change in the difficult defensive strategy of the Allies. He was correct: 1943 proved to be the turning point—if one can be so defined—in the war. At the end of the previous year, Nazi Germany suffered reverses in North Africa and at Stalingrad. The Fascist Spanish forces stayed neutral, the Turks began to listen to Churchill's warnings against the Nazis, and the Allies were regaining the offensive in the Atlantic. The crucial question was when would there be an invasion of France.

In November 1942, FDR asked for a conference of the three Allied leaders to deal with future military strategy. Stalin refused to attend, citing pressing military matters. Churchill and Roosevelt did meet together at Casablanca in North Africa, and there laid out the major differences between the two sides. The British insisted on an attack on Italy and a postponement of the cross-Channel invasion until August or September. The Americans pushed for such an invasion as their primary objective, and reminded their ally of the Pacific war as well. FDR seemed unclear about the feasibility of a July invasion, and thus left for Casablanca not totally committed to the advice of Marshall and other advocates of the invasion.

The president, denied some quick victories for home consumption and facing a division among his own advisors, supported Churchill's plan to move into the Mediterranean. But in typical fashion, he also reasserted his firm support for the invasion of France. At the conference, FDR insisted on bringing DeGaulle and his rival, General Henri Giraud, together for a joint meeting. And the president, surprising Churchill, cited Ulysses S. Grant in pronouncing a policy of "unconditional surrender." Later, critics of the president were to characterize his remarks as ill-advised, leading to a declaration that complicated surrender at the end of war. But the Casablanca meeting was a meeting of minds at least on the highest levels. A pleased Churchill concluded, "I love those Americans. They have behaved so generously."[48]

Churchill notified Stalin of the Casablanca decision. The Soviet leader was not happy with a further delay of the much promised second front. He bitterly wired back that since December the Germans had transferred twenty-seven divisions from the western front to the Soviet battle line. Then in March 1943, Stalin received notice that shipping losses in the Atlantic had caused his two allies to postpone convoys to Europe. Understandably, Stalin felt betrayed and bitter. Meanwhile in their chosen battlefield, North Africa, events were not going well. In February, German General Rommel had proved a difficult competitor, and the expected final victory in that theater was slow in coming. In April, American General George Patton's armies pushed eastward hoping to rout the Nazi forces. Finally, Allied forces won a major victory at Tunisia and took a quarter of a million prisoners. Stalin wired his congratulations.

In March, Churchill sent his foreign secretary, Anthony Eden, to confer with FDR on major territorial issues arising out of the war. Both sides were concerned about Russian intentions in the Baltic states, East Prussia, and above all, Poland. FDR was especially sensitive to the effect Russian domination would have on Americans, especially those with relatives in Poland and the Baltic nations. The president seemed to hope that Stalin would arrange a plebiscite, even a phony one, to offset some of the criticism. U.S. Ambassador to the Soviet Union W. Averell Harriman recorded that in May 1944 FDR indicated that he did not care if the countries bordering Russia became Communist, and the president was supposed to have told Francis Cardinal Spellman of New York that Eastern Europe would simply have to get used to Russian domination The Allied leaders explored the idea of dividing Germany up and establishing a worldwide international organization after the war. Roosevelt, however, was not committed to a new Wilsonian League; to him, the Big Four (which included divided China) would police the world.[49]

When in May Churchill visited FDR, the president insisted on a cross-Channel invasion in spring 1944, and avoided putting troops into Italy after the landing in Sicily. Again, Churchill, representing his own fears and those of the British staff over a war of attrition in France, pushed for knocking Italy out of the conflict and encouraged Turkey into the Allied camp. Marshall, though, insisted on the Channel landing. Finally, the British agreed to an invasion in May 1944 and an increase in bombing missions over Germany, while the Americans supported an attack on Italy with some additional troop commitments going to that front.

For Stalin, it was another postponement—on top of all the others. In addition, FDR expressed his concern once again about the future of Poland. He wanted some sort of rapprochement between the London Poles and the Soviet-backed partisans. The president clearly let Stalin know that he was concerned about the impact on domestic Polish-American public opinion as well. But Stalin distrusted the London Poles, seeing many of them as Nazi sympathizers, and knowing the history of Poland as a corridor to Russia, he insisted on imposing a friendly regime there. No wartime decisions have been as criticized as FDR's "sell-out" of Poland at this time and later at Yalta. In fact, Roosevelt did try to mediate between Communist and non-Communist forces as best he could. The determining factor in the future of Poland was not to be FDR's naivete or inattentiveness, but the presence of the Red Army in that region. FDR never sold out Poland, because it was never his to give. In 1941, 1942, and 1943, the Russian armies had carried the brunt of the war against the Nazis, and as they moved west, many chaotic lands and regions freed from the Germans fell under the Russian sphere of influence.

In July, Patton and General Bernard Montgomery, with a sense of professional rivalry only conquerors know, successfully stormed the island of Sicily; two weeks later, the king of Italy, Victor Emmanuel II, dismissed Mussolini from power. Now, Roosevelt had to confront the problem of how to implement his "unconditional surrender" edict. Did it apply to deposing the king of Italy? Did it apply to all of Mussolini's senior aides? The president pleaded for "common sense," and said that he didn't care with whom he dealt, including the king, as long as it wasn't a "definite member of the Fascist government."[50]

The president tried to finesse the question by allowing Churchill to negotiate with the caretaker Pietro Badoglio in Rome, while the British prime minister worried that the end of Fascism would lead to a very strong Communist presence which could take over parts of Italy, especially the industrial northern cities. A pragmatic Roosevelt wanted Eisenhower to honor the meaning of unconditional surrender, but gave clear indications that the Allies would be lenient, especially if Italy gave aid to the cause against the Nazis. Under pressure, mainly from Marshall and Stimson, the president pushed now for a cross-Channel invasion while the British temporized. The British argued for a larger offensive in Italy as a way to prepare for the French cross-Channel invasion. But the Italian campaign was much more difficult than the Allies had imagined as they moved slowly up the peninsula and finally captured Naples on October 1, 1943.

Then in November, FDR decided to visit Churchill and then Stalin to discuss strategy and postwar security. At Cairo, he joined the prime minister and Generalissimo Chiang Kai-shek. The president reiterated his pledge of a major role for China in the postwar world, extensive reparations, the return of Formosa and the Pescadores, and joint occupation of the Ryukyus with the United States. Chiang, though, needed more immediate American support, troops, and supplies—commodities already stretched thin in the twin theaters. When the president and Churchill finally met with Stalin, his immediate salutation was "Let us get down to business." Stalin's demand was a second front moving across the continent toward Germany. In the face of Stalin's logic and Roosevelt's agreement, even Churchill had to approve a 1944 landing. In their conversations, FDR curiously proposed an Allied offensive near the Adriatic to join with the Yugoslavs and push east toward the Soviet armies. Churchill still advocated a Mediterranean operation; Stalin proposed a swift advance into the heart of Germany; and Roosevelt seemed to vacillate, probably trying to mold some consensus.

Stalin later expressed some reservations about FDR's Big Four arrangement, arguing that the smaller nations would oppose their domination, and indicating that he was skeptical about the future of

China as a major power at the end of the war. He wondered if the U.S. Congress would approve American forces being a part of a European alliance that could insist on U.S. troops. Stalin had already pledged to come to the aid of the Allies in the Pacific against Japan once the Nazis were defeated. Now he agreed to help get the Turks into the war and demanded the division of Germany and reparations from Finland. As expected, Stalin and Roosevelt could not agree on the future of Poland. FDR insisted on the need for some agreement that did not alienate the six to seven million Polish Americans, and he discussed with Stalin the new borders that would expand Russia in the west at Poland's expense, and shift Poland in the west into Germany. Such were the spoils of war. The Allies finally accepted Stalin's borders, but did not agree on the government. In terms of the Baltic states, FDR tried again, stressing the sensitivities of American-Lithuanian, Latvian, and Estonian voters. But Stalin's argument was that these states were part of Russia under the last czar, and no one had complained.

The Tehran conference ended then with a commitment to the cross-Channel invasion, with Stalin's pledge to enter eventually the Pacific war against Japan, and with a clear division of opinion on the fate of Poland. Roosevelt had to make a major decision concerning the command of the invasion, "Overlord," as it was called. He passed over General Marshall and named Dwight D. Eisenhower to lead it. And in the Pacific, the military chiefs prepared for a massive attack along two lines: the New Guinea-East Indies-Philippine region and a thrust into the Mandated Islands.[51]

THE LAST ELECTION

In January 1944, the Russians bested the Nazis and broke the Leningrad blockade; in April they captured Odessa. As the president returned from Tehran, he was experiencing some of the symptoms that would prove to be telltale signs of declining physical health. By early 1944, he seemed to be weary, but politically still a colossus. Yet FDR had clearly lost his great ascendancy in the legislative process, even in the firestorm of the war. Inflation was worsening in late 1942, and still Congress was unwilling to enact his policy of taxes and food and price controls. In the area of wage policies, the president seemed reluctant to take the lead, and his War Labor Board reacted on a case-by-case basis. Disgusted with Congress and its delays in passing his tax and farm mobilization policies, the president bluntly warned in words rarely heard in a democratic society, "I ask the Congress to take this action by the first of October. Inaction on your part by that date will leave me with an inescapable responsibility to the people of this country to see to it that the war effort is no longer imperiled by threat of economic chaos. In the event that the Congress should fail to act, and act adequately, I shall accept the responsibility, and I will act." Clearly, he was expanding the definition of the commander in chief's war powers. Congress obediently passed a modest bill in early October.

FDR visited defense establishments, insisted on nonpartisanship, and became increasingly the voice of the democratic alliance. At home, he avoided Wilson's mistake in 1918 and refused to counsel the public to vote for the Democratic party's candidates. The 1942 election, however, had led to the Republicans picking up forty-six seats in the House and nine seats in the Senate or about double Wilson's losses in 1918. The New Deal was surely dead as a domestic reform movement, but its legacy had become institutionalized, and so it seemed had Roosevelt in the American mind.

In early 1943, an embattled president felt compelled to defend the emergency management of the mobilization effort. The major problem, manpower, was still apparent, and yet Roosevelt shied away from the issue. The American economy was plagued by strikes in civilian industries, especially coal mining, by absenteeism, and by high turnover. The influx of blacks to industrial jobs and women into the workforce would be expedients that later ended up changing the nature of American society.

Both the legislative and executive branches tried to deal with the difficult problem of labor-management unrest at home. Congress overrode FDR's veto and passed a law restricting the right to strike. Faced with continuing problems in the coal mines, the president had considering seizing the mines and drafting striking miners between the ages of thirty-eight and forty-five. The railroads presented an equally troubling situation. In late 1943, FDR ordered Stimson to seize and operate the railroads; three weeks later, the president himself arbitrated the dispute. When he turned over to Byrnes considerable authority to run the mobilization effort, the press promptly dubbed him "assistant president" and "chief of staff"—concepts inimical to FDR's temperament.

Still the president had little choice. The public outcry and congressional pressure required more coordination if not centralization of policy than he had implemented. His own head of the Bureau of the Budget had warned him of the breakdown of his earlier approach. In February 1943, Bureau Director Harold Smith enumerated the duplication, confusion, disorganization, and fragmentation. One of Roosevelt's most acute observers quoted his attitude at the time, "A little rivalry is stimulating. . . . It keeps everybody going to prove he is a better fellow than the next man. It keeps them honest too." On another occasion, he demanded teamwork, remarking, "I am the boss. . . . I am the one who gets the rap if we get licked in Congress. . . . I am the boss. I am giving the orders." By the end of the year though, FDR had moved toward a greater emphasis on a larger White House staff—the beginnings of the contemporary presidency. Earlier in 1937, a presidential commission headed by Louis Brownlow proposed a stronger executive office, arguing that the president needed help in performing his augmented responsibilities, and the war showed the wisdom of those prescriptions for the new American presidency.

FDR's span of attention swung also to military procurement. He created the Office of Scientific Research and Development and also set up an American-British committee on scientific exchanges. Unlike in previous wars, civilian businesspeople and scientists increasingly became a regular part of the military's weapons development programs—not just tanks, rockets, planes, and radar, but the initiation of the first atomic bomb, originally suggested to FDR in a letter from physicist Albert Einstein.

Amidst all of this, Roosevelt had promised that "Dr. New Deal" had given way to "Dr. Win-the-War." But in January 1944, FDR lashed out at self-seeking promoters, profiteers, and those who feathered their nests while the young went to war. He asked for new taxes to control high profits, and more authority over the terms of war contracts and food distribution. In addition, he proposed a national service law to prohibit strikes. The president then asked Congress for a "second Bill of Rights"—an economic charter that would out deal the old New Deal, and he clearly confronted the Republicans with a demand for easy registration of servicemen, which the GOP took as a ploy by the commander in chief to win reelection with the soldiers' vote.[52]

Thus in early 1944 Roosevelt was ready to wage his last campaign, adopting Lincoln's slogan that one did not change horses in the middle of the stream. But as much as the "Old Master" tried, it was clear to all who wished to observe that FDR looked tired and sick. His doctors had confidentially diagnosed that he was suffering from hypertension, and heart disease, and he might have had cancer as well. He seemed more preoccupied, less interested in the job at times, and more annoyed by persistent press criticism. He pressed his attorney general, Francis Biddle, to push for trials for right-wing extremists who had attacked the president and preached anti-Semitism. The trial judge had the indictments dismissed. The most troublesome single opponent for a time proved to be Sewell Avery, the head of Montgomery Ward, who refused to negotiate with the CIO unions. After a strike was called, FDR ordered the Chicago plant seized by the secretary of commerce, and tried persuasion to get Avery's cooperation, but to no avail. The secretary of war eventually took over operations.

But the great event of 1944 was not the recalcitrance of corporations like Montgomery Ward or even the presidential campaign, it was the long awaited invasion across the English Channel. That landing, "Overlord," was to be the greatest amphibious invasion in the long annals of warfare. On "D-Day," June 6, 1944, 4,900 warships and over two and a half million Allied troops started the waves of assault that were to destroy the Nazis in the west and alleviate pressure on Russia. In the evening, the president asked God's good blessings on "our sons, pride of our Nation," and commended faith in God, in the soldiers, in each other, and in the great crusade. Once again, American and British strategy began to divide, as the former wanted to invade southern France and the latter emphasized the importance of moving up the Italian peninsula. Churchill apparently considered promoting again the idea of Western forces in the Balkan region as a counter to the advancing Soviet armies. Roosevelt, with a long Pacific war ahead of him and the need to show Stalin some Allied unity, bluntly refused. The president's decision was clear, and he added to Churchill, "for purely political considerations over here, I should never survive even a slight setback to 'Overlord' if it were known that fairly large forces had been diverted to the Balkans." Years later, Churchill was to judge in retrospect that his counsel would have enabled the Allies to reach Vienna before the Russians and that would have had important consequences for the postwar world.

But in fact, the Americans insistence to join the "Overlord" forces and the "Anvil" armies in southern France was a correct one. The problem with Churchill's penchant for attacking the soft underbelly was that the underbelly in World Wars I and II was not soft after all. The diversion of troops from France to Italy and on into the Balkans might have imperiled the major offensive that meant the beginning of the end of Nazi power. There is little evidence that Allied troops moving toward Vienna, if indeed that march could have occurred as easily as Churchill foresaw, would have changed the postwar world appreciably. It may have cut the Russian postwar empire somewhat, although by 1954 Austria was given its autonomy. Actually, Churchill had already recognized many of Stalin's claims in the Balkans when he made a private deal between the two of them that established British hegemony over Greece and Soviet control over Rumania with Yugoslavia and Hungary being split fifty-fifty. The Polish issue remained, unless the Allies were willing to move toward a possible confrontation with the Russians.

In the Pacific, FDR had divided the military command into several sectors, which once again left him with the final say. Now as the fighting grew more intense, some major strategic decisions had to be made. The navy, under Admiral Nimitz, pushed for bypassing the Philippines while MacArthur insisted on fulfilling his promise to return. Not coincidentally, FDR chose to go to San Diego to inspect the troops while the Democratic party renominated him for a fourth term. Then the president left for Honolulu and a meeting with MacArthur and Nimitz. MacArthur insisted on the liberation of the Philippines and warned that the American people would vote against the president if he deserted their old allies and "wards." Consequently, FDR approved MacArthur's plan and returned home in time for his last campaign.

His own nomination was assured, but pressure had built up in the party for a replacement to the mystical progressive, Henry Wallace. FDR, in typical fashion, assured Wallace of his support and also encouraged others—notably James Byrnes, Senator Harry S Truman, and Justice William O. Douglas among others. As for the president, he insisted before he began that this was his final campaign, stressing also his commander in chief role and his apparent zest and good health to offset rumors to the contrary. With some carefully crafted speeches and after several difficult days of campaign ordeal, FDR refurbished the image that he was still the grand master of American politics. He rebuffed the Republicans by citing their alleged attacks on his dog Fala, and in New York and later in Philadelphia, he endured rain and long hours to show the people that he was indeed fit for the years ahead. Roosevelt carried 432 electoral votes to Thomas E. Dewey's 99 and the Democrats gained twenty-four seats in the House of Representatives, but lost two seats in the Senate. His popular vote was 25.6 million to Dewey's 22 million. The fourth inauguration was a simple, almost perfunctory ceremony. A gaunt president took the oath of office, celebrated American courage and fortitude, and then, in the evening of his life, he nostalgically returned to his boyhood—to the wisdom of "my old schoolmaster, Dr. Peabody"—that life was not always smooth sailing.[53]

THE ORDEALS OF ALLIANCE

The movements of the Allied armies into France led FDR face-to-face with having to deal with General DeGaulle, the inspiring leader of the Free French. Churchill, recognizing DeGaulle's popular appeal and sympathizing with his pride and patriotism, urged Roosevelt to acknowledge the general as the major force in that nation in 1944. But FDR insisted, almost petulantly, that the French should choose their leaders uninfluenced in any way.[54]

Of more critical concern, though, was the continuing problem of Poland, where Stalin refused to give the London-based Poles a role in that government. In conversations with the Russians, the future of the alliance seemed unclear. The Russians insisted on Big Four unanimity in any international organization and demanded that all sixteen Soviet republics be seated with each having a vote. Roosevelt had reservations about the veto power of the Big Four, but the Americans themselves had cited the veto as a guarantee they could present to the Senate when the treaty came up for ratification.[55]

The question of Germany also again presented difficulties. American councils were divided. Stimson wanted to punish Nazi leaders, destroy their army, and partition the nation. But the secretary of treasury, Henry Morgenthau, insisted on reducing Germany to an agricultural society—an approach that Churchill and FDR seemed to agree with at first, but later backed away from.

The Roosevelt aspirations for China also began to fall through. Chiang Kai-shek's forces were no match for the Japanese, and a concerned FDR implored Chiang to put American General Joseph Stilwell in charge. The president also sent a personal emissary, Major General Patrick J. Hurley, to mediate between the Communist Chinese and Chiang's Kuomintang. There is some inconclusive evidence that FDR had grown disgusted with Chiang and ordered at the Cairo Conference a contingency plan drawn for his assassination. Overall, the president hoped to use China as a mainstay of the Allies and as a center from which to attack Japan.[56]

Bone-weary and ailing, Roosevelt tried once again personal diplomacy with Stalin on the question of Poland, the proposed United Nations, and the Pacific war. In early February 1945, the three leaders met at Yalta, near the Russian Crimean Sea. Stalin dropped his request for seating sixteen republics in the United Nations and proposed instead the admission of the Ukraine, White Russia, and Lithuania. The British, with their Commonwealth, supported the general approach and FDR gave in. He later asked for two extra votes for the United States, which was agreed upon but never implemented.

On Poland, though, Stalin stood firm. He regarded the London Poles as pro-Nazi and definitely anti-Russian. Stalin did agree to some minor concessions—a recognized government with broad representation, but it was clear that the Russians saw the issue as central to the security of the USSR. For two generations, FDR would be criticized for appeasing the Soviets and selling out Poland. But then and now, the Soviet army was the telling point. Roosevelt neither sold out Poland, nor was American policy undermined by his poor health or diminished capacities. Most important for the Americans, Stalin reaffirmed his intention to attack Japan, and he insisted that the Kurile Islands and lower Sakhalin be returned to the USSR. Although there was some disagreement over the fate of Manchuria and other areas, the Russians did not push aggressively for more concessions to guarantee their entry into what promised to be a very bloody war against determined Japanese forces.

Tensions between the Big Three continued even as the war was coming to a successful conclusion in the West. Soviet promises on Poland were proving to be meaningless, and Stalin feared that the Americans and British were negotiating a peace behind his back. Then as he was dealing with the conclusion of the Western war, the climax in the Pacific, and the shaky edifice of postwar cooperation, Roosevelt suffered a massive cerebral hemorrhage and died at Warm Springs, Georgia. Stalin was sure he had been poisoned by Churchill and so informed Roosevelt's son. Churchill paid his profoundest regrets, but strangely did not choose to attend the president's funeral. The long eventful presidency of Franklin Delano

Roosevelt ended far from the capital he so dominated and far from the ancestral estate where he grew up and which he so loved.

THE OTHER WARLORDS

Another perspective on Roosevelt's war leadership can be obtained by examining the control exercised by the other major leaders of this period. In Japan, the conduct of the war had shifted to the military, of course, but in Europe, the civilian chiefs of state, in various ways, assumed the role of commander in chief. Their styles were very different, the national systems of military command were diverse, and their subtle uses of power are still not fully apparent. Their prosecution of the war and the resulting domestic mobilizations were complex matters, untidy to historians and participants alike. But still some generalizations can be made. As one moves from Churchill to Stalin to Hitler, the measure of direct control increases as influence changes to unvarnished power. In war, as in science, measures of degree lead to changes in kind.

Of the principal leaders during the Second World War, none had a greater breadth of experience in government than Winston S. Churchill. By the beginning of the war, he had held nearly every major cabinet position in the British government except foreign secretary and had been extensively involved in the conduct of the previous war. One of Churchill's advisors during this period and probably the greatest military strategist of his time, Basil Liddell Hart, has provided a balanced historical assessment of the prime minister's role. Churchill above all exhibited a fighting spirit that inspired the beleaguered democracies during their darkest hour—1940. But in his exuberance, he was involved in some major miscalculations. His public appeals to the Belgians, the Dutch, and the Norwegians probably encouraged the Nazis to move into those areas before they intended in order to forestall the possibility of the British taking over. Churchill clearly overrated the power and fortitude of the French Army (as did Stalin) and, after its surrender, he insisted on attacking the French fleet to prevent it from falling into German hands. His own admirals had judged the move as unnecessary, countering that the French admirals had promised that they would never surrender their ships or allow them to be seized.

Churchill's best move in 1940 was his decisive step to send reinforcements to Africa, but he continued to divert resources to far too many theaters of action. Once again he tried to open up an avenue of advance by attacking the Balkans, and the British drew the Nazis into Greece—an area they probably would not have gone into so soon. And then, the British had to retreat as at Dunkirk. Many historians have argued that it was Hitler's attack on Russia that saved Britain and prevented a crushing and final fate. After that invasion and Pearl Harbor, Churchill's preeminence slipped away. The Russians provided the armies and the United States the matériel in 1942 to begin to turn the tide. Churchill became, in his own words, "President Roosevelt's lieutenant."

And so, Churchill's role as senior partner declined as the war progressed—it was a harbinger of things to come as the world slipped into great power constellations in which Britain was a satellite and not a sun. But what of Churchill in his own land—was he as singularly powerful a military warlord as had been generally assumed? Liddell Hart provided a clear picture, when he called Churchill "the great animator of the war," and he marveled at the prime minister's "fertility, versatility, and vitality." Churchill's mind ranged over vast areas of diplomacy and military strategy, and he was constantly pushing and coaxing his ministers, officials, and generals to greater activity and progress in the war effort. Yet this very approach leads one to conclude that his actual influence was not as great as had been previously assumed. He frequently hesitated to insist on his views prevailing, even when they were well founded. Liddell Hart wondered if Churchill's deference to officialdom was due in part to his firing in World War I when he opposed the weight of such opinion.

Churchill himself recorded in his history of the latter war, "The reader must not forget that I never wielded autocratic powers, and always had to move with and focus political and professional opinion." At one point after the Germans took Crete, he concluded, "This is a sad story, and I feel myself greatly to blame for allowing myself to be overborne by the resistances that were offered [to his original plan for more troops there]." On another occasion, he admitted, "I print these details to show how difficult it is to get things done even with much power, realized need and willing helpers."

Liddell Hart also rejected the view, so prominent among critics of FDR, that Churchill in contrast had a grand strategy that superseded the daily necessities of war. He found that for Churchill the goal was "the defeat, ruin and slaughter of Hitler, to the exclusion of all other purposes." Indeed, Churchill tended to concentrate his energies on one objective often to the neglect of equally important other ones. The contemporary view that he saw more clearly than FDR the likely future is probably not substantiated, and Roosevelt was not as oblivious to the character of Stalin and the historic ambitions of the Soviet Union as has been charged; with regard to the future demise of the colonial empires, the president had far greater foresight than Churchill.

Churchill's overall reluctance in exercising control, then, may be due to many causes: the British coalition government, the cabinet government tradition, and the prime minister's own experiences in World War I. One of his colleagues, Lord Boothby, concluded that Churchill learned two great lessons from Lloyd George's leadership in World War I: first, the loss of political power that arose from the lack of party leadership, and second, the price of continuing and costly clashes between the prime minister and his military advisors. To avoid these problems, Churchill pushed for a close working relationship among his officers, the chiefs of staff, and the departments.

Unlike Lloyd George who inspired and welcomed men of brilliance and talent, Churchill often seemed to surround himself with lesser men as colleagues and assistants—men less threatening and less likely to break with him over disputes. Toward the end of his life, Churchill despondently observed that the political results that came from victories were less clear-cut than the stirring wartime leadership itself. Judged by that standard, he concluded on one occasion, "I am not sure that I shall be held to have done very well." And later he glumly added, "I have achieved a great deal to achieve nothing in the end." It was a melancholy he shared with his great ancestors, the Marlboroughs, and one that would be alien to a Roosevelt.[57]

Churchill as warlord exercised considerable influence especially in the 1940–41 period, but he remembered all too well the lessons of the World War I, and struggled to avoid the acrimony and personality struggles that characterized the brilliant but divisive term of Lloyd George. As a parliamentary leader, he drew his institutional power from the House of Commons and, unlike FDR, did not have to run for reelection during the war; also in contrast to FDR, he did not have a separate source of legitimate power outside the legislature.

In Russia, Stalin maintained, especially in the early years of the war, a fairly tight control over the military. He had been responsible for the purge of the upper echelons of the military, having had over a thousand Soviet generals shot between 1938 and 1940, and had misjudged Hitler and signed a pact with the Nazi regime. When the Germans turned and attacked the Russian frontier, it was Molotov and not Stalin who broke the news to the Russian people. For weeks, from June 22 to July 3, Stalin did not choose to address his people and even later his first address of the war was poorly given and uninspiring. His initial defensive policy was one of "scorch the earth," destroy everything of value before retreat just as Russia had done against Napoleon in 1812. Privately, a shaken Stalin even welcomed American troops on any part of the Russian front under U.S. command—an incredible concession from a Bolshevik who remembered the Allied occupation after World War I.

Stalin's major British biographer, Isaac Deutscher, concluded that he was "his own commander in chief, his own minister of defense, his own quartermaster, his own minister of supply, his own foreign minister, and even his own chef de protocole." Stalin insisted on being in constant and direct communication with his field officers, oversaw the evacuation of 1,360 plants and factories in western Russia and the Ukraine, and was involved in detailed decisions on moving supplies, ammunition, and men.

Stalin initially divided the front into three huge regions and assumed supreme command himself. The State Defense Committee, which included Stalin, Molotov, Kliment Voroshilov, Lavrenti Beria, and Georgi Malenkov, was given the task of running and coordinating the total war effort. As the Nazis advanced toward Moscow, coming within twenty or thirty miles of their target, Stalin rallied the Russians, this time citing the great heroes of imperial days as well as the more familiar Lenin. Most importantly, while the government planned to leave the capital, Stalin stayed, thus becoming a symbol of perseverance and constancy.

He avoided visiting the front, but he had a superb command of the vast operations in which his army was engaged. Stalin oversaw the logistics of the enormous effort, raising armies, rerouting them, massing them at critical junctions, and ensuring that supplies found the troops. Logistics were even more critical in a nation that was having its western industrial sector devastated. At the end of 1941, the occupied section embraced the regions where 40 percent of the population lived and from which came 65 percent of the coal, 68 percent of the pig iron, 58 percent of all steel, 60 percent of the aluminum, 38 percent of the grain, and 41 percent of the railroad lines. All this boded poorly for the Russians and Stalin's war leadership; then the harsh Russian winter and later the mud came, and the Nazis knew what Napoleon had found out—one does not invade and conquer that vast nation easily.

By the end of 1941, Pearl Harbor had occurred, and Stalin began to pull away from supporting international Communist parties and proletariat revolutions against capitalist states that were fighting his enemy. To stiffen resistance in the all-important Stalingrad defense, the Soviet leaders issued a simple order, "Not a step back." Throughout September, October, and November, the two titanic armies clashed in a series of costly battles that led to an important Nazi defeat. As early as 1941, Hitler was supposed to have seen the Moscow campaign as spelling eventual defeat for him; to other observers, the Stalingrad campaign was the turning point. As for Stalin, he refused all attempts to divert resources from the Moscow front even for this climactic campaign. He instructed his chief of staff, "No matter how they cry and complain, don't promise them any reserves. Don't give them a single battalion from the Moscow front."

In the middle of the Stalingrad campaign, he did away with political commissars who previously oversaw the military. Recalling the reforms of Peter the Great, Stalin also abandoned old Bolshevik egalitarianism and reinstituted guard regiments and divisions, formations, saluting, officer messes and clubs, and even epaulets, and took for himself the title of Marshal. He brought in promising young officers and promoted them rapidly after they succeeded, and in one month alone 360 new generals were named while attempts were made to restore military pride and privileges. To prop up the war effort, he even reached out to the Russian Orthodox Church for support.

Unlike Hitler, Stalin did not usually ride roughshod over his generals, and as he had been in his early years in the Communist party, he became the arbitrator once again. He collected opinions, weighed them, relayed viewpoints back and forth, and tried to fit the particular judgments into the general state of conditions. And like his colleagues at the top of the other war machines, he spent hours and days trying to relate diplomacy to the confusions of inconclusive campaigns and the battles of awesome destruction.[58]

Of the four major war leaders in the West, Hitler undoubtedly was even more openly involved in the day-to-day military operations. The others may have periodically interfered or intervened, but Hitler regarded himself as the "greatest military strategist of all times," and he acted accordingly. Some of his intuitive military judgments were bold and brilliant in their effectiveness; his mind was quick, retentive, probing, and often daring. But in the final analysis, within the balance of history, it is clear that his military leadership led to disaster, ruin, genocide, and defeat. In the heady atmosphere of idealizing the war, he moved beyond the grandiose rhetoric of sacrifice used by the others. When told that Germany might lose the war, the Fuhrer's summary observation was that if that happened, it proved that the Germans were unworthy of him. That perverse identification shows much about the Nazi world and its immoral architect.

As a corporal in the First World War became the supreme commander in the Second, he reduced his greatest generals to agents of his will. One of his field marshals, Baron Wolfrom von Richthofen, called the commanders in chief and the commanding generals under Hitler "highly paid noncommissioned officers." One of the fuhrer's closest associates and a historian, Percy Ernst Schramm, has concluded that over the years Hitler consolidated his dictatorship over all elements of society, including the armed forces. In the process, he extended his surveillance over the military, not respecting or trusting most of his senior officers—a suspicion that proved to be well founded in light of the officers plot to kill the Fuhrer in July 1944.

He encouraged the growth of the Waffen-SS, which in time became independent of the military. And for reasons of his own, he permitted conflicts between the General Staff of the army and the Operations Staff of the OKW (High Command of the Armed Forces), a continuation of the World War I antagonism between the Eastern High Command and the Imperial Supreme Headquarters.

Like Roosevelt, he encouraged a divide and conquer approach, but unlike FDR, Hitler directly dictated military movements, often against the advice of the field commanders. Two days before his suicide, an order was issued that major military plans had to be presented to the fuhrer with thirty-six-hours' notice. "Independent decisions are to be justified in detail," the order read. In his hands Hitler held the positions of chancellor, foreign minister, Nazi fuhrer, supreme commander of the armed forces, and commander in chief of the army. As the war effort began to go against the Nazis after 1942, Hitler accepted even less advice than before. He opposed retreats, checked regroupings or realignments, and even punished a general's daughter for her father's misfortunes on the battlefield. As the war worsened, Hitler's directions were replete with "no retreat," "only with permission," "accepting the risks," and "swift mopping up operation." He became more committed, more obstinate, more fanatical as he appropriately phrased it. Early in the war, a general could appeal an order that he disagreed with; soon, though, Hitler ended that practice.

Hitler saw the drift of the war, apparently after his failure to conquer Moscow in the winter of 1941. But he insisted that the Allies would be unable to maintain their coalition. Without realizing it, he had helped to create the cement that held them as one. Despite the deep differences among the British, American, and Russian leaders, they together and singularly had come to hate with a personal vengeance the Nazi regime and the man who controlled it.[59]

FDR AS COMMANDER IN CHIEF

More than Wilson and even Lincoln, Roosevelt enlarged the commander in chief role of the presidency. Wilson interfered little in the detailed work of his secretary of war, his chief of staff, or the generals in the field. Lincoln, of course, did intervene frequently, but he presided over a nineteenth-century military establishment with a weak general staff and a rather unformed command system. Roosevelt, however, as early as 1939 moved to exert his authority over the uniformed services. In July, he signed an executive order transferring the Joint Army-Navy Board, the Joint Army-Navy Munitions Board, and several other military procurement agencies into an executive office of the president. The assistant secretary of war became the president's chief deputy dealing with mobilization, independent of his superior, the secretary of war. Thus, the military chiefs were placed directly under the president, leading Admiral William Leahy to conclude years later that the war was run without any civilian control except for FDR. In fact, the secretaries were not included in the distribution lists for Joint Chiefs of Staff papers, even though these reports dealt with the basic questions the secretaries were legally responsible for.

Once again while these boards and chiefs operated in their separate spheres, the president alone was the coordinating link, sharing power with no one and giving him considerable authority over the military chiefs. In the years before Pearl Harbor, the president was willing to override his military advisors; for example, he disregarded their production goals in 1940, and pushed aside their caution in supporting Britain. When the Pacific Fleet commander, Rear Admiral James O. Richardson, appealed to Washington in autumn 1940 to shift the fleet out of Pearl Harbor to San Diego, he felt the commander in chief's annoyance.

Secretary of War Stimson, observing FDR's lack of coordination, recorded, "He has no system. He is haphazard and scatters responsibility among a lot of uncoordinated men and consequently things are never done." Oddly enough it was Assistant Secretary of the Navy Franklin D. Roosevelt who had called on Wilson in 1919 to create a joint planning agency to lay out American objectives and capabilities in the previous war.

After Pearl Harbor, though, significant changes began to occur. FDR had to allow the major theater commanders considerable discretion over operational commands. And by early 1942, the Americans had come to establish a military high command, in part, to interface with the British system. On some matters, as in war production, however, FDR was remarkably laissez faire, allowing each separate service to set its own requirements. In addition, the president did little to influence strategy in the Pacific, except in 1943, when he refused to accept the Joint Chiefs' recommendations for an offensive in Burma and the Bay of Bengal.

At times, especially at the Quebec and Tehran conferences with Churchill, FDR became a mediator between his own military chiefs and the British strategists, including Churchill. As has been noted, the president overruled his divided military leaders and sided with Churchill in the North African campaign. In 1942, an aggressive FDR made it abundantly clear to his advisors that he had accepted the Atlantic First strategy and intended to reach an agreement with the British on the first great Allied offensive. After the debate, FDR underscored his decision in writing and signing the agreement "Franklin D. Roosevelt, Commander-in-Chief." The point was clearly made. A disappointed General Marshall noted that "in wartime the politicians have to do *something* important every year."

In July 1942, the president appointed Admiral Leahy as his chief of staff, a position that FDR described as "a sort of leg man." After differences of opinion over the North African campaign, however, the Joint Chiefs and the president rarely disagreed on major strategy, but that consensus may have been due to their anticipating his reactions rather than his deference to the professionals.

By 1943, though, the president supported his chiefs often against the British and, as has been seen, he finally ended up pushing for "Overlord" and preventing another diversion of forces. By late 1943 and 1944, the conduct of the war moved along accepted lines agreed to by nearly all major figures in the United States government. The president and the chiefs recognized the need to defeat Germany decisively and quickly and return the troops home in preparation for the final campaigns in the Pacific. FDR did not envision that American public opinion would support the stationing of U.S. troops in Europe, and he wanted to stay away from the morass of postwar Central and Eastern Europe. In the Pacific, however, he did seem to anticipate a more interventionist role after the war.

There was much of the isolationist in the early years of FDR's presidency. He spoke of avoiding the problems of Europe, of its "ancient hatreds, turbulent frontiers, 'the legacy of old forgotten, far-off things and battles long ago'." In 1944, he wrote, "I do not want the United States to have the post-war burden of reconstituting France, Italy and the Balkans. This is not our natural task at a distance of 3500 miles or more . . . our principle object is not to take part in the internal problems of Southern Europe, but is rather to take part in eliminating Germany at a possible and even probable cost of a third World War."[60]

ROOSEVELT IN RETROSPECT

For twelve years, Franklin Delano Roosevelt led the nation through two of its most severe crises. He found a nation with limited federal responsibilities and presided over and fostered actively a patchwork of domestic programs that comprise the welfare state. He inherited a nation committed to isolationism and redirected its massive energies into war and far-flung diplomacy. In the process, he reoriented American partisan allegiances and created the framework that led to the modern executive office of the presidency and the antecedents of the military-industrial complex. No president was so powerful, no president so self-assured in his love of executive authority.

Yet FDR was no revolutionary or radical; he was a conservative patrician who retained a flexible mind—suspicious of ideology and open to ambiguity. His New Deal did not restore the nation to prosperity; mobilization for war and the expansive role of government spending prevented another Great Depression. But his leadership did provide an early sense of inspiration, of faith in the future, and confidence in the viability of the American dream. Leadership is more than process, it is inspiration and energy, and FDR epitomized both. Even acknowledging the limitations of the New Deal and its neglect of the unorganized segments of society, many of its basic initiatives remain institutions in American life. In comparison with the welfare states in Europe, even of Bismarck's Germany in the late nineteenth century, it may seem modest, but within American history, it is the culmination of the progressive impulse and its greatest triumph. Roosevelt moved across the political spectrum in that first term from a nearly nonpartisan executive to a fierce reformer, smiting the evils of selfishness, monopoly, and corporate greed. The liberals remembered him for this latter pose—they loved him for the enemies he made. His open and loose administrative manners may have hindered his leadership at times, but the chaos of the 1930s led many citizens to accept experimentation and uneven management. And such a style, for better or worse, was endemic to FDR, as he showed in his confusing domestic mobilization during the war.

Roosevelt was so concerned with keeping power in his own hands that he tolerated, if not promoted, the types of sloppy, uneven, and competitive morass that hurt the mobilization of resources and manpower and taxed an already overburdened and ill president. But the Roosevelt most criticized is the FDR who conducted personal diplomacy with Stalin at Tehran and Yalta. Some fifty years after these conferences, Roosevelt's name is linked in many circles here and abroad with naivete and appeasement.

Partly, he gave some fuel to these charges by announcing that he knew how to deal with Stalin. Stalin, however, was a brutal, dedicated party functionary who sincerely believed in Communism, who ruthlessly crushed the old Bolsheviks who brought it forth, and who seemed to share in many of the historical memories and ambitions of the czars. When FDR met him, the president confided to Frances Perkins that he just did not understand the Russians. He seemed to believe that by the sheer charm of his personality and by humorous jibes at Churchill and Britain's pretensions, he could win "Joe's" favor. That strain of superficiality was a part of Roosevelt's personality. He could ignore what was disturbing, the same way he ignored the plight of blacks in the United States, the

Japanese-Americans in U.S. detention camps, and the Jews in Hitler's Europe. Behind the mask was a complex personality and also a certain hollowness in his character.

Still, much of the criticism of FDR's diplomacy is misguided. None of the Allied leaders, including Stalin and Churchill, placed diplomatic objectives before the immediate and final defeat of the Nazis. Stalin's great triumph was not any brilliant ploy—he took what the Red Army basically won by its blood and sacrifice. It is possible that the Western Allies might have moved more quickly through Germany and less likely might have gone up the Balkans to cut off the Red Army. But in 1942, 1943, and even 1944, the campaigns in Italy and France and the prospects of a long war in the Pacific gave FDR legitimate reasons for pursuing his strategy of trying to keep the Russians as allies.

Somehow the Second World War is seen as a triumph for Stalin in the eyes of FDR's detractors. But from Stalin's perspective, what had it wrought that so eclipsed FDR's record? After massive sacrifices, the Russians controlled Eastern Europe and consequently brought forth a united Western alliance with a string of nuclear warheads encircling its bloc until the late 1980s. Stalin created in large part the conditions that led to an American presence that even FDR never contemplated—a long commitment of U.S. combat troops in Europe and an economic plan to rebuild the Atlantic nation-states. Historian A. J. P. Taylor has said that Roosevelt was the really astute leader who emerged from the crucible of war. The United States lost comparatively few soldiers and emerged as the most powerful nation on earth. In the world of realpolitik, FDR is an outstandingly successful and shrewd national leader, overshadowing the Bismarcks and the Pitts of different eras.[61]

But FDR was not that sort of practitioner of realpolitik, although Taylor is correct about the outcome of his leadership and the modest price the United States paid. Nor was FDR Stalin's foil or Churchill's lesser light. He did not see the United States as a land power in Europe after the war, and he prepared his nation to be one of the policemen of the world in an alliance with Britain, Russia, and a romanticized version of China. He knew the suspicions of Stalin toward the West and honestly tried to calm them. Today it seems a bit unrealistic, but in the context of waging war in the West and preparing for what was supposed to be a terrible struggle in the Pacific, it was common sense to keep in the war the nation that had tied up 80–90 percent of the Nazi army in 1942—the Soviet

Union. As late as 1945, Eisenhower was asking Stalin for help in order to alleviate the pressure on the Western armies moving into Germany. And Stalin complied.

Roosevelt, in one important sense, did foresee the future course of imperialism and the collapse of colonial empires more clearly than any of the other major statesmen of his time. He not only predicted the end of traditional colonialism, but he also welcomed it, although he did not shrink from the policy of the big powers as trustees policing the world.[62] Still, there is the question of Poland. FDR tried to convince Stalin of the need for an open government, but at times he seemed more concerned that the Soviet marshal give a public show of good faith just to keep Polish-American voters and others pacified. Perhaps he was simply phrasing it so, in order to appeal to Stalin's appreciation of self-interest. FDR's weakness, though, was not one of intention or commitment; as has been noted, Poland went to the Red Army and not Stalin's shrewd diplomacy. And as for Stalin his objectives were clear: they were echoes of the ambitions of the czars—control the flatlands of Poland, the Slavic peoples of the Baltic, and the warm water ports of access on the borders of Russia.

Last, it must be remembered that Roosevelt's leadership was important in the defeat of Fascism, the Nazi war machine, and Japanese militarism in three years' time. That achievement, the negative one of preventing the triumph or at least a deadlock with those forces, was no cheap victory. When FDR demanded unconditional surrender, Churchill and Stalin both had reservations. It would steel the enemies' resolve and determination, they feared, but FDR sensed, perhaps intuitively, that the war demanded a moral crusade that portrayed the enemy as not simply a threatening force, but as a criminal mutation of the human spirit. A simplified credo—a propaganda ploy, perhaps—but one with a powerful ability to inspire captive peoples and sustain the war weary. FDR was a manipulative and, at times, deceitful person, but he sincerely held to a common morality and accepted its pieties. In a world of amoral war barons, genocidal demagogues, paranoid autocrats, FDR was a pleasant rather admirable shaft of light. Roosevelt's diplomacy was more circumscribed by real constraints than the American conservatives have admitted, and he was more skeptical of Soviet intentions than the radical-left historians like to believe.

The Roosevelt presidency represents the high point of executive leadership in the sheer scope of its sweep and in the lasting consequences of its changes. Admire him or not, one must admit that Franklin Delano Roosevelt, like Shakespeare's Caesar, was a colossus that bestrode the American political scene and the Second World War, and his personality and achievements profoundly reshaped the office and influenced his successors of both parties for over two generations. The Age of Roosevelt is still with us and has become the centerpiece of the modern presidency.[63]

5

The Cold War and American Liberalism: Truman, Eisenhower, Kennedy, and Johnson

The half a century that has followed Roosevelt has seen a much changed America and a much changed executive branch of government. From a provincial, isolationist nation, the United States emerged as a superpower, with an expensive standing army, a nuclear arsenal of indescribable power, an activist intelligence service with a capacity for far-reaching covert activities, and a strong alliance of privilege and power encompassing government, business, universities, and the military. The presidency became the center of this very transformation; it became an office sitting on top of the bureaucracy perched above the executive branch of government. While Truman had 13 assistants, Nixon and Ford had over 550 each. Offices dealing with economic projections, culture, ethnic affairs, national security, overseas intelligence, and science and technology were grafted onto the more prosaic traditional presidency.

Yet the post-Rooseveltian presidency revolved around two great issues that FDR was partially responsible for in his eventful tenure, one emerging out of the New Deal and the other from the uneasy wartime alliance with the Soviet Union. First, the political parties continued to redefine themselves from 1945 on partially in terms of the development of the social welfare state. And second, the foreign policy preoccupation of the postwar presidents through George Bush was the power, ambition, and expansion of the Soviet Union.

On a personal level, most of these presidents were either protégés of FDR or were deeply influenced by his personality and politics. Truman was his vice president; Eisenhower was plucked from obscurity by FDR and General George C. Marshall to head the Allied forces; John F. Kennedy knew and admired the president and watched as his father, Joseph P. Kennedy, fell in and out of FDR's favor; Lyndon Johnson was an actual political satellite in the Roosevelt New Deal constellation; Ronald Reagan, while serving to destroy the underpinnings of the welfare state, came from a family that directly benefited from the New Deal administration and was genuinely enamored with the liberal president of his youth; and George Bush remembered fondly serving as a teenager under FDR, commander in chief.[1]

TRUMAN AND THE UNCERTAIN LEGACY

On the eighty-third day of his vice presidency, Harry S Truman received the news of FDR's death. Although Truman was a Roosevelt loyalist, and the president surely had intimations of his own mortality, the usually secretive FDR had not shared any information with Truman about the major decisions made at Yalta and Tehran or the development of the atomic bomb.

In many ways, this unusual team that won the 1944 election seemed to be very different. Truman was the only person in this century to sit in the White House whose education ended in high school; he later enrolled in a few law courses in night school, never completing the program. He had been a farmer in Missouri, a haberdasher who went bankrupt at age thirty-eight, and a local boy who joined the state National Guard, and ended up a captain in World War I. He then entered politics, became an honest acolyte in the corrupt Pendergast machine, was elected judge (commissioner), and went on to the United States Senate. Over the years, Truman compiled a record for personal honesty, doggedness, and a strong allegiance to the New Deal. In 1944, widespread opposition to the erratic Vice President Henry Wallace led the Democratic party leaders to look for a replacement. FDR, devious as usual, encouraged Wallace, let it be known he would accept Truman or Supreme Court Justice William O. Douglas as a running mate, and made very favorable comments about James Byrnes of South Carolina.

Truman represented the values that Americans like to believe are characteristic of themselves: hardworking, honest, simple, free of ostentation and pomp. He was the product of machine politics, of men who attended funerals and loved parades, who drank bourbon and protected each other with a fierce communal bonding. Truman never abandoned those values, and for better or worse continued to exhibit a sense of loyalty that at times impeded his performance as president. He held on to the Democratic party as surely as he held on to his Baptist religion. One was born and died in those faiths.[2]

Because of his poor eyesight, he wore glasses, avoided sports, fought the sissy label, and read extensively history and biography— making him in some ways the most knowledgeable president since Professor Woodrow Wilson. He was a man given to some profanity, except in the company of women, and he was proud of his rather extraordinary rise in station. Then at the age of sixty, this interesting American success story was propelled onto the international stage. The Truman presidency was surely one of the most eventful and consequential in U.S. history. It was a presidency of great policies, petty partisanship, and deep public disillusionment. Speaker of the House Sam Rayburn predicted, "Truman will not make a great, flashy president like Roosevelt. But, by God, he'll make a good president, a sound president. He's got the stuff in him."

Truman, though, added to his critics' early underestimations by declaring that at least a million other people were more qualified than he to be president, and he once commented to Senator George Aiken of Vermont, "I'm not big enough. I'm not big enough for this job." In his first term, he had a portrait of Roosevelt hung up in his office, and when faced with a decision he would ask, "Would he think this is the right thing?"

Looking at Truman in his first cabinet meeting, he seemed to FDR's press secretary, Jonathan Daniels, "a little man." New Deal partisans could not imagine that this parochial and seemingly unlettered individual could replace the political giant who so dominated American politics. But even Truman, looking at the ashen and worn FDR in 1945, realized that the president's days were clearly numbered. Truman was sworn to uphold his predecessor's legacy— but what was that legacy, what did FDR agree to or believe in about the unformed issues that were being crystallized as the war in Europe was coming to an end?

The central confusion was FDR's policy toward the Russians. By late March 1945, FDR himself clearly had become fed up with Stalin. At one point he simply concluded, "Averell [Harriman] is right; we can't do business with Stalin. He has broken every one of the promises he made at Yalta." The Russian Maxim Litvinov placed the blame elsewhere when he said to Edgar Snow in Mos-

cow in 1945, "Why did the Americans wait until now to begin opposing us in the Balkans and Eastern Europe?. . . You should have
done this three years ago. Now it's too late and your complaints
only arouse suspicion here."

Immediately on taking office, Truman was notified that the war
against Germany would last another six months, and the war against
Japan another year and a half. Cooperation with Russia was important in that long struggle, and Truman reaffirmed FDR's controversial objective—unconditional surrender of the Axis powers. He
quickly nominated James Byrnes as secretary of state and set a different tone at press conferences. Where FDR had been jaunty and
cagey, Truman answered questions quickly and straightforwardly. His
Gallup poll rating climbed to a phenomenal 87 percent—three points
higher than FDR ever received at the apex of his popularity. And
although he was loyal to the New Deal and its master, Truman disliked professional liberals or "the lunatic fringe" as he called them.
The new president concluded that "The American people have been
through a lot of experiments and they want a rest from experiments."
Yet Truman did associate himself with the New Deal's programs
for the future—pushing for more public electric power, full employment, expansion of Social Security, and broad unemployment compensation. Soon he would surprise Southerners and blacks alike by
extending liberalism into the realm of civil rights, a move FDR
would never have undertaken.[3]

But Truman soon learned that Congress was not willing to follow a liberal domestic agenda, and that the alliance with Russia was
a fragile marriage, coming undone over the contentious issue of
Poland. As Truman read the diplomatic messages between the Soviets and the United States, he grew angry over Stalin's insults and
accusations concerning American motives. When he first met Soviet Foreign Minister Molotov, Truman bluntly demanded a truly
representative government in Poland as provided for in the Yalta
accords. To Truman this was in keeping with FDR's legacy; in reality it was a hardening of attitudes toward the Soviet Union and
Stalin. The new president also adopted the general State Department line in opposing spheres of influence. For Stalin, though, the
eastern territories were the bounty of the Red Army's costly victories and, equally important, a series of friendly buffer states that
would eventually be linked economically and militarily to the Soviet state.

On May 8, Truman formally announced victory in Europe, "VE

Day"; in terms of the Pacific theater, he gave formal assurances that unconditional surrender would not mean "the extermination or enslavement of the Japanese people." Sticking with what he thought were FDR's promises, Truman honored the agreement on occupation zones and refused to accept Churchill's advice that he keep American troops in the Soviet zone. Seeking to overcome postwar difficulties, Truman, Stalin, and Churchill met in Germany at Potsdam from July 17 to August 2, 1945. Churchill expressed approval with his new American partner, concluding to a friend, "he is a man of immense determination. He takes no notice of delicate ground, he just plants his foot down firmly upon it." As for Truman he too eyed up his colleagues at the conference, comparing the ruthless Stalin to Tom Pendergast and to the New York Tammany Hall boss, William Marcy Tweed. He quickly got a taste of the Russian leader's thinking, however, when he asked what had happened to thousands of Polish Army officers allegedly massacred in the Katyn Forest. Stalin's response was brutally succinct: "They went away."[4]

Truman had initially refused to support the Morgenthau Plan to agrarianize Germany, and he suggested instead a trade link between the food-producing areas of Hungary, Rumania, and the Ukraine with the coal-producing regions in the West. As after the First World War, the reparations issue also came up at Yalta. The reparations figure debated there was $20 billion, half of which would go to the Soviet Union. But since the Russians were proving to be so difficult, the administration now saw no compulsion to expedite reparations. Meanwhile, the Soviets turned over to its client government in Poland a major part of Germany within their zone of occupation. In return, the Soviets insisted on taking a portion of what was eastern Poland, consequently pushing both Russian and Polish borders west at the expense of defeated Germany—a settlement discussed by the Big Three leaders before.

At Potsdam, Truman's style was rather different from what the Allied leaders had seen with FDR. Charles Bohlen concluded, "where Roosevelt improvised, Truman stuck closely to positions worked out in advance. Where Roosevelt, in his argumentations, would work in extraneous ideas, Truman was crisp and to the point." But Truman found, as FDR and Churchill had discovered, that Stalin did not intend to allow any reorganization of the Eastern European states then under his control.

Having received confidential notice about the atomic explosion at Alamogordo, New Mexico, Truman had a stronger position, and he insisted again that the Russians honor their commitments at Yalta concerning Poland. In their discussions, Stalin decided to link up the future of Italy with that of Eastern Europe, and concluded that the latter governments were closer to the people than the Italian regime was. Truman was blunt in his response, "I have made it clear—we will not recognize these governments until they are reorganized." The debate on reparations became intertwined with the future of Poland and the fate of other eastern states, as Secretary of State Byrnes pronounced it, an all or nothing deal. Stalin continued to resist. Thus, Four Power administration (France had joined the Big Three) over a divided Germany began, and eventually the reparation agreements broke down altogether.[5]

As suspicions mounted among the Allies, the war in Asia continued. A major and costly offensive against the Japanese was a critical part of the administration's calculations to end the conflict. The development of the bomb and the decision to drop it in two locations over Japan upended all those calculations. The use of the atomic bomb remains one of the most controversial aspects of the American conduct in the war. Truman did not know of the existence of the bomb until after he took office and, despite his own comments later, the new president was less responsible for the decision than is usually assumed. The ultimate decision to drop the first bomb was surely his. But in fact the bureaucratic process to go ahead and develop and use it had moved along like a juggernaut. The only decision Truman could have made was to stop that process, one that had acquired a momentum of its own. The most important figure in the decision was Secretary of War Henry Stimson, and Truman concurred in order to end the war and avert the frightening prediction of enormous casualties in order to subdue Japan. In addition, the administration came to see the atomic bomb as a bargaining tool with the recalcitrant Soviets and a way of averting their intervention in the Pacific war—an intervention the Americans had vigorously insisted upon previously. And so on August 5, 1945, the first atomic bomb was dropped on Hiroshima.

Stimson was undoubtedly correct when he wrote, "At no time, from 1941 to 1945, did I ever hear it suggested by the president, or by any other responsible member of the government, that atomic energy should not be used in the war." Years later, Truman was to dismiss criticism of the decision with almost facile disdain, but at the time he told an associate, "I'll make the decision, but it is terrifying to think about what I will have to decide." On August 9, he had received a telegram from a religious official asking him not to use the bomb again, and he responded, "Nobody is more disturbed over the use of the atomic bomb than I am but I was greatly disturbed over the unwarranted attack by the Japanese on Pearl Harbor and their murder of our prisoners of war. The only language they seem to understand is the one we have been using to bombard them. When you have to deal with a beast you have to treat him as a beast. It is most regrettable but nevertheless true."

He later concluded, "It occurred to me that a quarter of a million of the flower of our young manhood were worth a couple of Japanese cities, and I still think they were and are." Truman, though, told Stimson at Potsdam he hoped that only one bomb would be dropped, but as biographer Robert Donovan has concluded, "this wish was not translated into policy." And so a second and probably unneeded atomic bomb was unleashed on Nagasaki on August 9.[6]

With the quick end of the war in the Pacific after the use of the atomic bomb, Truman refused to share the occupation of Japan with the Soviets. Stalin's response was curt, "I and my colleagues did not expect such an answer from you." The abrupt end of the war also had an impact on the government's reconversion plans, which were geared to an end of the war sometime in 1946. Roosevelt, who had been less than successful in mobilization, had even less control over demobilization planning. Remembering the dislocations after the previous war and the terrible depression of the 1930s, many feared the worst. And within ten days, 1.8 million people did lose their jobs. It seemed like a repeat of past miseries. On August 18, Truman directed that government agencies move as rapidly as possible to remove wage, price, and production controls. The president and the nation soon faced the prospect of rampant inflation, labor strikes, and enormous pressure to cut back the army and bring the troops back home. In the end, however, the Great Depression did not resume. The balancing effects of the New Deal welfare state, remobilization for the Korean conflict, and continued pressures of a Cold War economy all infused the types of stimuli that Keynes had insisted would bring prosperity.

Lacking a liberal majority in Congress, Truman faced the same intransigence that FDR confronted after 1938. Indeed, a coalition of conservative Democrats and Republicans successfully blocked

major legislation from the end of Roosevelt's second term until the
1960s. As for the president, he generally held high the liberal ban-
ner, but rarely pushed for social welfare legislation once he introduced it.

TO ERR IS TRUMAN

By late 1945 and early 1946, Truman faced a series of problems that seriously undercut his initial public support and left him
battered and besieged. Faced with strikes in some essential industries, the president vigorously opposed some stoppages and alienated segments of labor. On top of that problem, postwar shortages
of food supplies added to the president's woes, a problem complicated by real fears of famine in Europe.[7] In November 1945, U.S.
ambassador to China, Patrick J. Hurley, abruptly resigned and
charged that Chiang Kai-shek did not have the full support of the
State Department because of a "pro-Communist, pro-imperialist"
faction there. It would be the beginning of a bitter and grossly unfair
campaign against the administration leading to the overall judgment
that somehow the United States had "lost China" when Mao Tse-
tung took over.

The president's foreign policy got further muddled when his
secretary of state, James Byrnes, negotiated in Moscow an agreement with the Soviets on atomic energy, military forces in Iran, and
other disputed matters. Byrnes had not kept the president properly
informed on the developments, and Truman resented his show of
independence. The president concluded that Byrnes "had taken it
upon himself to move the foreign policy of the United States in a
direction to which I could not, and would not, agree." Increasingly,
the president believed that the Soviets understood only military
power, and their willingness to negotiate in good faith was being
increasingly called into question. The wartime alliance was quickly
becoming undone once the common foes were vanquished.[8]

On the Soviet side, Stalin increased pressure on Iran, Greece,
and Turkey; on February 9, 1946, he praised the might of the Red
Army and pronounced that peace was not possible because of the
forces of capitalism and imperialism. Nine days later, evidence of
Soviet atomic espionage was made public in Ottawa, Canada. Then
in March, Churchill with Truman sitting on the platform gave his
"Iron Curtain" address. The aging British leader concluded that

"from Stettin in the Baltic to Trieste in the Adriatic an Iron Curtain has descended across the Continent." The speech called for a union of "English-speaking peoples"—an old idea of Churchill's, but one that Stalin surely interpreted as an anti-Soviet alliance in the making. At the same time, the State Department sent a forceful protest to the Soviets about their military forces in Iran. By the end of the month, however, the Russians and Iranians had made major progress in working out an agreement after all.

At home, Truman continued to face an increasing number of strikes and work stoppages from restive labor and toughening corporate management. In 1946, over 4.6 million workers went on strike with the loss of the equivalent 116 million days. The president also had to deal with staff turnover in the government, and the burdens of creating a modern executive branch were taking their toll. His budget director, Harold D. Smith, warned that while the president was "an orderly person, there is disorder all around you, and it is becoming worse. . . . For one thing, you need good, continuous staff work, and you are not getting it." Truman complained of an enormous amount of paperwork—some 30,000 words of memoranda a night. Part of the problem was his inability to put his own brand on the administration he inherited, part of it was a legacy of FDR's freewheeling style, but a good deal of the difficulty came from the transition period Truman was in. He was, in effect, the first "imperial president," the first president as a matter of course and not crisis to sit on top of the expanding bureaucratic executive branch. As the welfare state became institutionalized and as the United States became a global power, the modest federal government grew enormously, and the presidency as the hub also had to change. In his time in office, Truman would expand the executive office of the White House, bring in specialists in economics, resource management, labor, atomic energy, and other areas. He would push for some centralization of the armed forces, a large standing army, an intelligence agency, and a strong military and foreign policy establishment. In many ways, it is Truman more than even FDR who created the modern presidency as we and his heirs have come to know it.[9]

In steering his own course through all of this, Truman was more often a man of tenacity than of subtlety. He quickly welcomed the departure of Harold Ickes in Interior and fired Henry Wallace in Agriculture. Ickes, the crusty New Dealer par excellence, blasted "government by crony" and then left the cabinet. Wallace, farmer, mystic, and make-shift expert in foreign policy, had decided to depart from the administration on the question of how to deal with Stalin. He would later coalesce his group of fervent New Dealers, Communists, and some fellow travelers into a presidential bid in 1948. Parts of the New Deal coalition were spinning off as the president faced the difficulties of 1946. As for labor, Truman refused to allow strikes in critical industries to go unchecked. He threatened to take control of the railroads when a settlement seemed beyond reach, and in one year he seized the coal mines twice, 134 meat packing plants, 91 tugboats, and the facilities of 26 oil producing and refining companies as well as the Great Lakes Towing Company. Fed up with railroad strikes, on May 8, 1946, the president decided to draft the strikers, and then order them back to work on the railroads. Truman dramatically appeared before Congress with a tough message, and as he reached his conclusion, he was handed a note indicating an agreement had been reached. Triumphantly, he announced, "Word has been received that the railroad strike has been settled, on terms proposed by the president!" It was a major victory for Truman, one that he needed desperately to reassert his leadership.[10]

Then the president took on John L. Lewis of the United Mine Workers, a tough negotiator who had challenged Roosevelt's authority even during the war. On November 20, 1946, the mine workers went on strike even after extensive efforts by the administration to work out a fair settlement. The Truman administration's tactics were to take Lewis to court, and the labor leader was fined $10,000 personally and the union $3.5 million. The showdown worked and Lewis called off the strike, citing the Supreme Court's review of the injunction. The high court finally upheld the convictions for contempt of court, but reduced the fine.

By the end of 1946, Truman seemed to go from one crisis to another, some of his own making, but most due to the difficult postwar problems of reconversion and social dislocation. In terms of foreign policy, the president was moving away from what he initially perceived as FDR's legacy of cooperation with the Soviets, to a hardheaded and often belligerent confrontation with Stalin and his imperialist ambitions. To replace Byrnes at State, Truman named retired General Marshall—a person the president was to call the greatest living American of his time. But even Marshall, the organizer of victory in World War II, could not succeed in ending the civil war in China. American foreign policy was contradictory: the administration claimed to be an honest broker between Chiang and Mao, but it opposed the Communists in their bid for power. With a declining military establishment, serious problems in Europe, and a crumbling Chinese Nationalist regime, the Americans could not dictate a settlement in China, try as they might.[11]

Republican critics of Truman's foreign policy were correct on one count: the administration was primarily concerned in 1947 with the fate of Europe, which tottered on the brink of catastrophe, social chaos, and in some cases, Communist takeovers. First, food and later fuel shortages became critical, and only the United States could respond with much-needed supplies. Through 1947, faced with British withdrawal in Greece, Turkey, and the Middle East, the administration moved with unaccustomed brilliance into the gap. First, the president proposed granting aid to Greece and Turkey as a way of curtailing Soviet influence. Republican Senator Arthur Vandenberg, the symbol and carrier of bipartisan foreign policy, was clearly stunned and implored the president to tell the Congress and the country about the crisis in the most threatening terms. Thus, the Truman Doctrine, as it was called, was born. To get congressional support, the president heeded Vandenberg and accentuated his anti-Communist rhetoric. The Cold War heated up.

The administration followed up its requests with a major rehabilitation program for Europe, named after General Marshall. The Marshall Plan included large-scale U.S. assistance for the recovery of Europe and did not initially exclude Eastern Europe. Luckily for the administration, the usually suspicious Soviets saw it as an attempt to isolate the Soviet Union, and so the plan also became a tool in the arsenal of Western democracies. Thus, in a relatively short period of time—about eighteen months—the Truman administration in a fury of activity and with some broad conceptualization changed the very basis of American foreign policy. It put in place the Truman Doctrine, the Marshall Plan, Point Four (expert economic assistance), and later the Western military alliance called the North Atlantic Treaty Organization.

The policy behind these initiatives became known as "containment," the encircling of the Soviet Union with military bases and the establishment of a tougher line drawn in the sand. Considering the isolationist history of the United States and its genuine war weariness, the Truman foreign policy was an incredible political achievement. Its successes were due to the president's persistence, his advisors' care, Republican cooperation, and above all to Stalin. The Russian dictator in the last years of his brutal reign had reached

too far and too fast after the war both to recoup Soviet losses due
to the Nazi onslaughts, and to extend Soviet control over the eastern sectors of Europe and beyond. Russian apologists would later
say that Stalin was simply pursuing the age-old policies of the czars;
in large part, though, his reactions were excessive, those befitting a
man of incredible brutality and true paranoia. Truman's responses
were clear and blunt—no more Hitlers, no more Munichs, no more
appeasement.[12]

To win congressional approval, he was not above overdramatizing
the Soviet threat and using the anti-Communist rhetoric so popular
in Republican and conservative circles. Partly, but not totally, as a
result, Truman later found the Communist issue turned on him and
the Democratic party. Unable to gather public attention with their
laissez faire social philosophy, the Republican leaders used the Red
scare issue to garner support. Truman tried to stop the rush by announcing his own internal security program, which aimed at dis-
missing government employees who were found to be disloyal.
Investigators had access to FBI files, military and naval intelligence,
the information of the House UnAmerican Activities Committee, and
records of local law enforcement agencies. Loyalty boards were set
up, and employees were not guaranteed the right to confront their
accusers. Without realizing it, Truman helped lay the groundwork
for the assaults of Senator Joseph McCarthy and a whole generation of attacks on due process and basic American civil liberties. In
politics, halfway steps are often more dangerous than wrong policies, for the latter are easier to see and to challenge. But in any
case, by April 1947, Truman's approval rating bounced up to 60
percent—nearly double his low point of a year before.[13]

Truman's standing fluctuated wildly in his first term, his popularity being linked up with the difficult concrete problems he faced
and how he dealt with them. He lacked the great resources of public affection that FDR and later Ronald Reagan would have. Like
Lincoln, he was never a beloved figure while in the White House,
and the controversies in which he was embroiled took a toll. At
times, Truman seemed, like all of us, to be his own worst enemy.
He was tolerant of diverse opinions, then resentful when those advocates went public with their differences. He seemed at first to be
deferential to Roosevelt's memory, wondering what the great man
would have done on this matter or that. Then Truman, especially in
his second term, seemed too self-assured, if not cocky. Still, in the
period of 1947–48, Truman became president in his own right, and

in the crucible of events, he laid the groundwork for the strange election before him.

Fortunately for Truman, the Republicans decided to go beyond the president's tough stand against strikers and take on the whole organized labor movement. In April 1947, the GOP-controlled House of Representatives passed the Hartley bill to limit the power of organized labor. The Senate passed a milder bill, and a conference committee compromise was sent to Truman in June. Union halls and closed shops (which required union membership to hold a job) were forbidden, states could pass "right to work" laws, which outlawed union-shop agreements, and various unfair labor practices were prohibited. Injunctions were permitted, and the president could ask for an eighty-day cooling-off period to delay a shutdown. Although the bill does not seem after nearly fifty years of implementation to have been so devastating to organized labor, in 1947 the unions regarded it as a clear attack by their traditional enemies, which indeed it was. The president vetoed the Taft-Hartley bill, sending back a stinging message. Congress quickly overrode his veto, but for Truman, the controversy added to his shaky coalition the powerful labor constituency. The Republicans would help to reelect Truman in 1948 without realizing it. In addition, the AFL and the CIO became more partisan and politically active than ever before, making organized labor one of the most important sources of strength for the Democratic party nationally and often locally well into the 1980s.[14]

In the fall of 1947, Truman was facing another explosive situation that in the end would add to his political problems and then political clout—Palestine. Truman's position on a homeland for displaced Jews was a moderate one: in mid-1946, he encouraged the immigration of one hundred thousand European Jews to the region but reserved judgment on the future of Palestine. While the president seemed sympathetic to the plight of the survivors of the Holocaust, he deeply resented pressure from American Zionist leaders. The British had proposed a Palestine federation with four areas: Arab and Jewish provinces, a district of Jerusalem, and a district of the Negev. Truman seemed to support the idea at first, but the reaction at home was so critical that he backed off. Senator Robert Taft attacked the plan, Jewish groups demanded that it be repudiated, and influential Americans spoke out against the compromise. An angry Truman focused only on Jewish criticism and harshly concluded to an associate, "Jesus Christ couldn't please them when he was here on earth, so how could anyone expect that I would have any luck." But after all was said and done, Truman saw the political realities, and abandoned U.S. support for the compromise.[15]

Yet the president did retain a genuine sympathy for Jewish refugees and began to push, often against State Department advice, for support for a Jewish homeland. When the issue went to the United Nations, administration representatives heavily pressured smaller nations to support such a homeland, although Truman may not have been aware of the threats or heavy-handed methods used by his own delegation. After the General Assembly voted, fighting broke out in the region, and the president grew concerned about having to send U.S. troops there. While Jewish demands in the election campaign mounted, the State Department feared that a separate homeland would alienate the Arabs. Dissension in the administration led to differing views being made public, and the president's own position seemed to be unclear or undercut by his own subordinates. Clark Clifford and others warned Truman of the political ramifications of not recognizing a separate Jewish state, while Secretary of State Marshall insisted that he himself would vote against Truman if he succumbed to the pressure. While the American representatives at the UN were discussing the issue, the president decided to recognize the State of Israel. On May 15, 1948, Arab armies invaded Israel and war began. As for Truman it is easy to cite political considerations in his defense, but probably he was also just weary of the controversy and the alleged confusion on America's position. He correctly judged U.S. sentiment and surely considered the long campaign ahead of him.

Just as FDR had been able to finesse the Jewish homeland-Arab issue, he had also been able to sidestep civil rights. Truman, however, did not have that luxury and he had to deal with the latter controversy as well. At first it seemed to bring him toward political disaster, but once again, controversy rebounded to his credit and to his advantage. Ironically, this small town Missouri politician who was not averse to racial epithets became the most pro-black president since Lincoln. Truman at first simply misjudged the intensity of southern opposition to his civil rights program. He pushed for support of a special government commission's recommendations: a permanent commission on civil rights, a civil rights section in the Justice Department, an antilynching law, and a statute to curb police brutality. The commission also advocated an end to the poll tax, protection of qualified voters, an amendment to give residents of the District of Columbia the right to vote in presidential elections, and home rule for the predominantly black District. The commission attacked segregation in a variety of ways, insisting, for example, on a pledge of nondiscrimination from recipients of any federal program and an end to racially restrictive covenants that were especially prominent in housing deeds at that time.[16]

The president supported the thrust of the report and ran into a buzzsaw of southern political opposition. One minister wrote Truman from Florida, "If that report is carried out you won't be elected dogcatcher in 1948. The South today is the South of 1861 regarding things your committee had under consideration." The president at first remarked that he hadn't really read the report, but in December he instructed his staff to present a civil rights program to go to Congress early in 1948.

Thus, as he faced the nominating convention, Truman had compiled an impressive record and an impressive list of foes. On the left, Henry Wallace had begun his own quixotic campaign, attacking Truman's "global Monroe Doctrine" and his supposed abandonment of FDR's policy of cooperation with the Soviets. He even criticized the Marshall Plan, saying it was a tool of U.S. domination. To much annoyance, Truman watched as some of the hardcore New Dealers, mainly in the liberal Americans for Democratic Action, wooed General Dwight Eisenhower as a Democratic candidate for president. FDR's sons backed the nonpolitical military man as did Hubert Humphrey, Arthur Goldberg of the CIO, Walter Reuther of the UAW, Harold Ickes and other liberals. Eleanor Roosevelt was also supposedly "discussing" whether to grant her support.

But as that intrigue continued, Truman was adding Democratic delegates and state caucuses to his cause and relying on the Democratic national convention's leaders and old congressional friends to put his candidacy over. Then Eisenhower announced that he was not interested, and the opposition to Truman had no viable alternative at that late date. The hard-core liberals had not only misjudged Truman and the American electorate, but almost humorously had misjudged Eisenhower, as his time in office would bear out.

The Democratic convention supported a strong civil rights plank, much to Truman's dismay, and southern delegates left the floor; later some established a states' rights presidential ticket of Strom Thurmond of South Carolina for president and Fielding Lewis Wright of Mississippi for vice president. Truman thus began the so-called Impossible Campaign of 1948—an ordeal for a modest man facing monumental domestic and international problems, lacking a southern base so essential to any Democrat, and hurt by attacks on the left. Truman insisted, though, that he would win, and throughout the long summer, he whistlestopped throughout the great heartland of America, into its unsettling cities and through the mixed landscapes of the South. The underdog suddenly emerged as the prosecutor. He threw away his set speeches, which he fumbled through, and talked as an old stump speaker to his fellow citizens. To cries of "Give 'em hell, Harry," he did. He called the Republican Congress back into session on "Turnip Day," and gloated as they defeated liberal legislation. He branded them the "Do-Nothing 80th Congress," and the title stuck. The Republicans called him the worst president in history; the *Chicago Tribune* insisted he was a "nincompoop." Sixty-five percent of the editorials in the newspapers favored Dewey, and only 15 percent supported the president.

The Republican candidate, Thomas E. Dewey, had been criticized in 1944 for attacking FDR too harshly, so in 1948 he acted boringly "presidential" until it was too late. The public overall seemed genuinely disgusted with Wallace's attacks on his own country's foreign policy, and Stalin's behavior lent more credibility to Truman's view of the world than that of the Progressives and their fellow travelers. Surprisingly, the states' rights ticket did not prove as powerful a draw in the South as some had expected. The issue was still the New Deal, and Truman wrapped the cloak of FDR around himself. Added to that, a misbegotten farm policy hurt the Republican Congress and Republican candidates in the Midwest. When election day came, Dewey was considering cabinet appointments, and Truman sat counting the remaining pieces of the old Roosevelt coalition. Remarkably it held—Truman garnered 303 electoral votes and carried twenty-eight states, including Arkansas, Florida, Georgia, Kentucky, North Carolina, Tennessee (11 of 12 electoral votes), and Texas in the traditional solid South; he also carried, in the Midwest, Iowa, Illinois, Minnesota, and Wisconsin. In addition, the Democrats regained control of both houses of Congress. Enough of the New Deal political alliance stayed together in the end.[17]

THE COLD WAR AND LIMITED WAR

But the pleasure of public vindication gave way to a heightened sense of personal responsibility. Even during the high jinks of the campaign, Truman had to stop and consider the problem of Soviet threats over the future of Berlin, which was also divided into zones. When the Allies moved toward a single German government in their joint sectors, the USSR responded with an attempt to curtail movement into West Berlin, which was within the Soviet sector. Truman supported a massive airlift of supplies to the city and ignored American General Lucius Clay's proposal to give the Russians an ultimatum by announcing that a land convoy would come through their sector to the beleaguered city.

Faced with a distraught secretary of defense, James Forrestal, who could not pull the new unified services command together, and always suspicious of the military mind, the president himself exercised considerable civilian control over the armed forces, and specifically kept custody of the atomic bomb in his hands alone. Then in July, he issued a dramatic executive order to end racial discrimination in the military and to assure equal opportunity in the civil service as well.

At the beginning of his second term, Truman proposed a tax increase, a modest military budget, and new programs in low-cost housing, higher Social Security benefits, and federal aid to education. In his 1949 State of the Union address, he observed, "I expect to try to give every segment of our population a fair deal." But in Congress, the conservative alliance of southern Democrats and Republicans lined up even more, and the GOP, stunned by unexpected defeat, turned ardently to the right.

The new generation of Republican congressional figures concentrated a drumbeat of attack on what was previously a bipartisan foreign policy. The focal point became China, and the charge was that the Democratic administration and the State Department were allowing, if not encouraging, a triumph by Mao and his Communist armies. To add to Truman's woes, in December 1948, Alger Hiss, a high-ranking State Department figure and friend of Secretary of State Dean Acheson, was accused of perjury in denying that he passed on government documents to a Communist agent. To many, it seemed that the reckless charges of people like Senators Joe McCarthy and William Jenner were not without some foundation. The president unwisely agreed in an answer to a reporter's leading question that the Republican subversive hunting campaign was nothing more than "a red herring to divert public attention from inflation." The red herring remark was to haunt him later. Hiss was eventually found guilty of perjury and one of his main accusers,

Congressman Richard M. Nixon of California, was to become a household name.[18]

Meanwhile, Truman's and Acheson's battle against the forces of Communism abroad accelerated. The blockade of Berlin by the Soviets pushed the Allies closer together on the need for a strong Atlantic alliance and encouraged the creation of a West German government. On April 4, 1949, twelve nations signed the North Atlantic Treaty and laid the groundwork for the military and political alliance that became NATO. For Americans it was an extraordinary break with tradition; Truman concluded that if the treaty had existed in 1914 and in 1939, it would have prevented two terrible wars. Stalin seemed almost on cue to buttress the arguments for the alliance as Czechoslovakia went Communist, Finland was pressured by the Russians, and Norway also expressed public concerns about its Communist neighbor's intentions.

The keystone of that Atlantic alliance would be the military strength of the United States; but at that time, the nation was struggling to cut the armed forces, hold down the budget, and reorganize the military services. The United States had slashed its military force strength from nearly 12 million at the end of the war to 1.5 million in the summer of 1947. The budget cap caused a major row within the armed forces hierarchy, especially in the navy, where the public was treated to a steady stream of panicky complaints from what became known as the "revolt of the admirals." In addition, Congress proved again unwilling to enact universal military training, a favorite notion of Truman. Although the president retained by American postwar standards a large standing army, the new role he was leading the nation into required even more conventional military might. The administration seemed to count on the atomic bomb in its defense calculus, while shying away from the use of that terrible instrument ever again. The revolt of the admirals was only the first problem that Truman would face with a strong, assertive military establishment. He would end up firing one of the most accomplished and insubordinate generals in U.S. history at the height of the Korean War that was to come.[19]

In addition, two major events rocked American self-confidence. First was the fall of China, and second, the Soviets' detonation of their own atomic bomb. The president had at first followed FDR's quixotic support of Chiang Kai-shek's government and also attempted to moderate Mao's war aims. With the Soviets in Manchuria, the Communist Chinese received additional support and encouragement from their allies. Truman tried in vain to strengthen the Chiang regime and curtail Soviet influence in the region. As noted, he finally sent George Marshall to mediate the differences between the two Chinese regimes, while at the same time insisting on preserving Chiang's government as the legitimate one. The result was a predictable failure; in addition, Marshall, distressed by what he saw, insisted that the United States should avoid military intervention even as a last resort to rescue the Nationalists. Preoccupied with European problems, troubles at home, and his own reelection, the president spent little time informing the people or Congress about the steady deterioration of Chiang's regime. Mao was clear in his objective in 1948; it was "to drive out aggressive forces of American imperialism . . . and establish a unified democratic people's republic." Soon after Truman's inauguration, all of China north of the Yangtze River had fallen under Mao's control. Republicans howled at the contrast between broad support for Europe and the alleged meagerness of aid to China. Secretary of State Acheson declared that American policy in China was waiting until "the dust settles." Critics concluded that the State Department regarded the Communists as simple "agrarian reformers," and charged that the trail of appeasement starting at Yalta was continuing. By October 1, 1949, the People's Republic of China was established and Chiang fled to Formosa, converting it into the last bastion of his Nationalist government. With a Communist China and a divided Korea, the administration began to support a stronger Japan and reassessed the importance of Formosa in that region.[20]

Then in late August 1949, the Soviets detonated an atomic device—the American monopoly on nuclear weapons ended much earlier than the administration and the public expected. Vandenberg wrote, "This is now a different world." Thus the keystone of the Truman military strategy, the awesomeness of the bomb and the U.S. monopoly of it, lost much of its potency. In a bipolar world, or at least within a bipolar military strategy, the existence of Soviet nuclear capability made that alien nation even more feared and more mysterious. Some Americans insisted that the breakthrough was possible only because of Soviet espionage; a backward country could not by itself compete with U.S. science and technology. But the results were clearly the same. Soon the administration would be debating the creation of a more devastating weapon: the "superbomb," or hydrogen bomb, a development Truman approved only because he feared the Soviets would move ahead on their own.

They did and so did the United States—in the first round of nuclear escalation and supposed deterrents. As Truman was making that decision, reports came in of another high-level espionage case: Dr. Klaus Fuchs in the British atomic energy research establishment was charged with passing on secrets to the Soviet Union.

Faced with an increasingly hostile world, the administration drew up in spring 1950 a major policy statement on national security—NSC 68—which advocated a massive upgrading of the nation's military might. Acheson observed later candidly, "The purpose of NSC 68 was to bludgeon the mass mind of 'top government' that not only could the president make a decision but that the decision could be carried out." The administration was contemplating an increase in the defense budget from $13 billion up to $40 billion and a vast upgrading of U.S. and Allied military strength.[21]

At home, the steady assaults on Truman continued. The opposition and the press found additional evidence of Democrats who had used their influence to win government contracts or garner special treatment for clients. One particularly vulnerable target was Truman's friend and military aide, General Harry Vaughan. The president, loyal to old acquaintances, refused to discharge him and so the controversy continued. In Congress, the majority refused to support the president's major recommendations on social legislation. Federal aid to education got caught up in the church-state issue as Francis Cardinal Spellman of New York and Eleanor Roosevelt became involved in a nasty spat on the issue. The administration's farm program, pressed by Agriculture Secretary Charles F. Brannan, went down to defeat with its attempt to support farm income rather than stabilize or inflate farm prices. Oddly enough, President Richard Nixon in 1973 would approve that same approach in trying to deal with similar problems. And Truman's attempt to promote national health insurance fell victim to a well-organized campaign by the medical profession; a partial initiative was finally enacted by Congress and approved by President Johnson in 1965 and a comprehensive plan was being devised by President Bill Clinton in 1993–94.[22]

Then in late June 1950, as Truman took stock back home in Missouri of the postwar world he faced, he received shocking news—North Korea invaded South Korea—a new war had begun. The president's initial response was to downplay the crisis, hoping that U.S. support and supplies would turn the tide. But it quickly became apparent that the South Koreans were on the way to being routed. To the president and his senior advisors, it was a choice of following the course that had led to appeasement and World War II or of standing firm. Truman saw it as a test of collective security, the first real trial of the UN. Would that body go the way of the League of Nations? Also, the Americans viewed the North Korean invasion as a cat's-paw of Stalin's ambitions. They assumed, probably incorrectly, that the Russians had provoked the invasion rather than having simply accepted their allies' plans.

The administration sought UN support for South Korea and, since the Soviet delegate was fortuitously absent, they received it. The Seventh Fleet was interposed between Formosa and mainland China to protect Chiang; MacArthur in Japan was ordered to send supplies and a survey group to Korea, and the air force was to draw up plans (but not to take action) to destroy Soviet air bases in the Far East. Previously, both Secretary of State Acheson and General MacArthur had excluded South Korea from their calculations of the American sphere of defense interests. But now, the attack on the lower peninsula was seen as a direct challenge to U.S. power and influence. Politically, an administration charged with the loss of China would not stand by and see the loss of Korea, regardless of its real significance to American interests. Support for Truman's actions was nearly unanimous. Even Henry Wallace expressed approval.

The military situation rapidly deteriorated, and the president soon faced fateful decisions to commit first naval and air support and then American ground troops. The president viewed Korea as the Greece of the Far East. "If we are tough enough now, if we stand up to them like we did in Greece three years ago, they won't take any next steps. But if we stand by, they'll move into Iran and they'll take over the whole Middle East." Faced with these problems, the president reversed his direction and committed himself to the military defense of Formosa. Aid was also sent to French Indochina— a decision of monumental importance later. Congress cheered Truman's commitment of naval and air forces in the Korean conflict, as Republicans and Democrats temporarily closed ranks. It would be a brief marriage of true minds.[23]

Truman's initial concern and his continuing preoccupation was that the United States avoid any war with Russia. "We must be damned careful. We must not say that we are anticipating a war with the Soviet Union. We want to take any steps we have to to push the North Koreans behind the line, but I don't want to get us

overcommitted to a whole lot of other things that could mean war."
His goal was to drive the North Koreans back to the 38th parallel
dividing line, and he asked the Soviets to use their influence to get
the victorious North Koreans to withdraw. They refused.[24]

Faced with continuing bad news of South Korean defeats and
General MacArthur's urgent appeals, Truman on June 30 crossed
the political Rubicon and authorized a regimental combat team.
American ground troops entered the war in earnest. In response to
MacArthur's appeal to accept Chiang Kai-shek's offer of Chinese
Nationalist troops, Truman at first agreed. But Acheson insisted that
it would bring the Communist Chinese into the war, and the Joint
Chiefs of Staff cited logistics and supply problems if such a step
took place. Truman backed down and laid the groundwork for one
of the major criticisms that MacArthur would later level at the administration's handling of the war.

The administration though should have noticed the early storm
warnings in Congress over the president's unilateral commitment of
troops in Korea. Early in the Senate deliberations, right after the
commitment of naval and land forces, the question was raised as to
whether the executive could respond without Congress's approval.
The Democratic leader, Scott Lucas noted, "more than a hundred
occasions in the life of this republic the president as commander in
chief has ordered the fleet or the troops to do certain things which
involved the risk of war." Later, Republican Senator Taft charged
"a complete usurpation by the president of authority to use the
armed forces of the country" was taking place. He then made political hay out of Acheson's speech on January 12, which did not
include South Korea and Formosa in the U.S. defense perimeter.
Yet Taft made it clear, he would support the president's policy if it
came to a vote. When Secretary of the Army Frank Pace wondered
why the president did not push for a resolution of support, Truman
responded, "They are all with me." He insisted that the United States
was not at war with North Korea, but was a member of the United
Nations going to the relief of the Korean Republic to "suppress a
bandit raid." Later he was to agree to characterize the war as "a
police action"—a term that would come to haunt him as American
sacrifices increased dramatically in the war.[25]

Truman had considered a message to Congress, but fearing a
wave of panic over economic controls and hoarding, he delayed and
then finally abandoned the move. To buttress the administration's
position, Acheson had the State Department draw up a position paper

listing historical and legal precedents for the commander in chief's use of military forces. Eighty-five instances, many of them rather limited, were cited as providing a basis for Truman's decision not to go to Congress.

The onslaught of the war had laid the basis for the rapid increase in military expenditures projected originally in NSC 68 and led to an institutionalization of the National Security Council. Once again a president asked for authority to allocate resources, control credit, and undergird the war effort at home. Money flowed into upgrading the armed forces and creating tactical nuclear weapons. By 1951, the budget for defense and related matters jumped from $17.7 billion to $53.4 billion.

As American commitments increased, the North Korean forces continued their assault across the peninsula, driving the Republic of Korea and UN forces farther south. The Republicans supported the war, but attacked the administration for its lack of military preparedness. To some extent they were correct. General Omar Bradley was to admit, "It is a bruising and shocking fact that when we Americans were committed in Korea we were left without an adequate margin of military strength with which to face an enemy at any other specific point. Certainly we were left without the strength to meet a general attack . . . except for the atomic bomb." Recent liberal critics have argued that Truman laid out carefully the confrontations of the Cold War in order to assert U.S. strength or imperialist intent, yet his policies of frugality and civilian control over the military seem at variance with such intent.[26]

NO SUBSTITUTE FOR VICTORY

By the fall of 1950, MacArthur had eight U.S. divisions, some regimental combat teams, a modest collection of UN forces, and a beleaguered South Korean Army at his disposal. MacArthur obviously felt the frustrations of such limited support. To him it surely was another example of shortsightedness, similar to the lack of commitment in Washington that he saw in the last war in the Pacific. As for Truman, he had already formed a negative opinion of MacArthur even though he had never met him. He referred to him as "Mr. Prima Donna, Brass Hat," a "bunco man." Concerned about MacArthur's independence, Truman sent Averell Harriman to assure the general of his personal support, and to warn that Chiang must not become the cause of a war with the Communist Chinese. MacArthur promised to abide by his commander in chief's directives. But by late August, the general issued a statement of his views on the strategic importance of Formosa—a challenge that the administration chose not to unfurl at Mao's regime. Truman forced a retraction, but Republicans made political capital charging that the general had been unfairly censured and chastised.

Truman then had to face the question of whether to fight up to the 38th parallel and let the North Koreans retreat to the spot of their initial advance or to push them back toward the Yalu River and the Chinese border. The risks were obvious: such a step would pressure the Communist Chinese to enter the war and, worse still, the Russians to add their support. On the other hand, should the North Koreans be allowed to stay above the line, able at a later date to resume their drive south? Should they not suffer because of their initial aggression? Now the State Department and the American advisors chose to raise the ante by agreeing, "It is U.S. policy to help bring about the complete independence and unity of Korea." The CIA had warned of "grave risks" in crossing the 38th parallel, but as Averell Harriman reflected later, "It would have taken a superhuman effort to say no. Psychologically, it was almost impossible not to go ahead and complete the job."

Then on September 15, MacArthur conducted one of the most brilliant strategic maneuvers in military history. Against incredible odds, he implemented an amphibious assault two hundred miles behind enemy lines at Inchon. Suddenly, the tide of war, and even more importantly, the scales of morale tipped heavily in favor of the United States and the forces of the Republic of Korea. An emboldened Joint Chiefs of Staff sent MacArthur the fateful directive, "Your military objective is the destruction of the North Korean Forces." Marshall on September 30 informed MacArthur, "We want you to feel unhampered tactically and strategically to proceed north of the 38th parallel." The general's response was clearly in line, "Unless and until the enemy capitulates, I regard all of Korea open for our military operations." The Joint Chiefs' order, though, had contained one important caveat: MacArthur was not to move forces above the 38th parallel if there were a threat from Chinese or Soviet forces.

By fall 1950, the president's advisors were counseling a meeting with the victorious MacArthur, a meeting less to clear up ambiguities than to help Truman and the Democrats politically in the upcoming elections in 1950. The president at first refused, but later he agreed to go to Wake Island to see MacArthur personally. Although there has been a variety of accounts about personal bitterness and protocol disputes during the visit, it appears that the two got along fairly well together. MacArthur was supposed to have apologized for the controversy surrounding his statement to the Veterans of Foreign Wars on Formosa and assured Truman that the Chinese Communists would not enter the war. The general hoped to withdraw the Eighth Army by Christmas. The president was clearly relieved by the prediction, and overall the two of them avoided discussing basic U.S. and UN objectives in Korea and what practical limitations were imposed on the field commander. Truman bestowed an additional citation on the general, ironically praising "his vision, his judgment, his indomitable will and unshakable faith." Later, Truman called MacArthur an intellectually honest man and a loyal member of the government. It was a short and eventful honeymoon.[27]

Back home, the elections of 1950 were not affected by the staged Wake Island meeting or by the changes in the fates of the war. McCarthy continued his assaults on the administration and, in several key races, his influence seemed to turn the tide in favor of the Republicans. The reckless senator from Wisconsin became a feared commodity on Capitol Hill, a bully doing what bullies do best, intimidating the timid. In California, Richard Nixon skillfully used the Communist issue to defeat Helen Gahagan Douglas for the Senate; in Illinois the Democratic Senate leader, Scott Lucas, was defeated by Everett McKinley Dirksen; in Maryland, a McCarthy foe, Millard Tydings, went down to defeat; in Utah, liberal Democratic Senator Elbert Thomas lost as well. In Massachusetts, former Ambassador Joseph P. Kennedy and his son John quietly contributed to Nixon's election, and their family members defended McCarthy publicly. McCarthyism seemed to be sweeping across the land. The Democrats lost twenty-eight seats in the House and five in the Senate, not an unusually high number for the majority party in an off-year election, but it left little support for the Fair Deal's domestic reforms. A depressed president surveyed the results grimly.

Truman's real problems though were ahead of him—another and more dismal turn of events in Korea was in the works. MacArthur, high in the saddle, had interpreted his mandate to unite the peninsula and to destroy the North Korean forces as broadly as he could. Without consulting the Joint Chiefs, he ordered a major bombing

attack on all enemy facilities in North Korea and the blowing up
of the bridges over the Yalu River. Truman asked for a review of
the general's intentions, fearing that they would lead to a Chinese
attack. The Joint Chiefs, in part in deference to MacArthur's immense military prestige and unwilling to second-guess the field
commander, wavered. MacArthur appealed to the president and
warned of a "calamity of major proportion" unless he were allowed
to continue. The president approved the bombings, but had the
Chiefs warn MacArthur about possible Soviet involvement.

By early November, MacArthur asked for the right to pursue
North Korean aircraft as they returned to Manchuria, and the administration approved "hot pursuit" engagements—an unclear line
at best. Under heavy pressure from the Allies, however, that approval was withdrawn. The president sought to assure the Communist Chinese that he did not desire to widen the war and threaten
their borders, but they refused to accept such assurances; on November 29, their armies launched a major assault across the Chinese borders and flooded into North Korea. MacArthur's response
was brief and frightening, "We face an entirely new War."

The general's Christmas pledge came back to haunt him, as
Marshall advocated finding a way out without a loss of honor, and
Acheson pushed for an exit as well. Truman added to the panic by
indicating that he might give MacArthur authority to use the atomic
bomb at his discretion. Immediately, British Prime Minister Clem-
ent Attlee flew in to Washington to insist on prior consultation before any such serious actions were undertaken.[28]

MacArthur continued to emphasize his own line of attack. He
told the editors of *U.S. News and World Report* on December 1 that
the inability to pursue enemy pilots into Manchuria was an "enormous handicap, without precedent in military history." Faced with
this new war, the president declared a national emergency and applied selective controls on the economy. Some Republican leaders
pushed for unleashing Chiang to conduct a second front on the
mainland Chinese, and a series of resolutions were introduced in
Congress that opposed sending U.S. troops without legislative approval. The once much-cheered bipartisan police action had become
"Truman's war."

The Joint Chiefs told MacArthur to fight on as long as possible,
inflicting maximum losses but being ready to retreat to Japan if
necessary to protect his armies in Korea. Then in mid-January, the
Joint Chiefs presented MacArthur with a draft document that would

have approved a blockade of China, unleashed Chiang, and allowed naval and air attacks on China if the Communists there attacked U.S. forces outside of Korea. Thus it appears that there is some justification to MacArthur's charge later that the Joint Chiefs had been close to approving an enlarged war. At the same time, Truman wrote MacArthur that if the UN forces were expelled from Korea, "we shall not accept the result politically or militarily until the aggression has been rectified."[29]

Washington's siege resolve may have been lessened by the fortuitous appointment of General Matthew Ridgway who quickly reorganized and upgraded the Eighth Army and the Tenth Corps in Korea. As those forces improved, the extreme choice MacArthur sought to force on the administration was reexamined. Then, while the administration was pressing for a cease-fire, MacArthur issued his own declaration on March 24, offering to meet with the enemy commander in chief and outlining what could be topics of negotiation. The objectives were clearly to upstage the president, issue an ultimatum to the Red Chinese, and lay out again the general's political objectives. In addition, the general had written to Republican Congressman Joseph Martin that the war had to be won for the good of Asia and Europe—"we must win. There is no substitute for victory."

Truman had had enough; he began discussions that would lead to the firing of MacArthur. At first, Marshall and General Omar Bradley favored a reprimand, but in the end, the Joint Chiefs and the major civilian advisors were unanimous in approving MacArthur's removal. After reflecting on Lincoln's agony over McClellan, Truman moved decisively and brought on himself a firestorm, greater than any other that had confronted the president.

Cries of impeachment rang through the halls of Congress, as the general returned home to an admiring and somewhat alien land for him. His speech to Congress—one of the genuine pieces of high drama and great oratory—gave way to an old soldier's goodbye. But public sentiment ran its course, and Truman watched as the fervor and intensity died down. With some sympathetic Senate supporters, a congressional investigation revealed that the Joint Chiefs of Staff unanimously disapproved of MacArthur's course of action. The most telling conclusion was General Bradley's observation, "this strategy would have involved us in the wrong war, at the wrong place, at the wrong time, and with the wrong enemy [China]." The firing stuck, Truman was battered but prevailed, and the war became enmeshed in a deadlock hovering around the 38th parallel again.[30]

There is little debate today that MacArthur was clearly insubordinate and merited firing, and that Truman had both sound reasons and constitutional justification for his actions. But one can also appreciate MacArthur's position a bit more in historical hindsight. The orders of the Joint Chiefs did lend encouragement and support to his strategy and his boldness. The Chiefs individually and collectively were less than a towering source of strength and were unclear and often deferential to the prestigious field commander nominally under their supervision.

At Wake Island, and on numerous other occasions, the president had the opportunity to rein in the general, and he too passed up the opportunities. They all expected MacArthur to win a war they chose to fight and then dangerously enlarged, and when he pushed on, they demanded some assurance that the Communist Chinese would not enter it. And when the Chinese did, the administration seemed to blame MacArthur as if he betrayed them or deliberately misled them.

MacArthur, looking for that last great victory, unnecessarily raised the ante in 1951; the response of the Joint Chiefs and the president seemed clear: no escalation, but they too considered the very steps that they later chastised him for considering when they finally testified before Congress. If, as General Bradley said, it was the wrong war, at the wrong time, with the wrong enemy—it was the president and the Joint Chiefs who injected U.S. troops into that regional theater in the first place and allowed them to go north of the 38th parallel. While MacArthur was excessively pessimistic about the Eighth Army and the UN-ROK effort in 1951, the administration also probably seriously misjudged Stalin's willingness to go to war over Korea. The Soviet leader's preoccupation was the Russian empire, and while he would acknowledge North Korea's intentions and support his Asian allies, he was not going to follow up the destruction of Russia in the West in World War II with a war with the United States in Asia, especially using nuclear arms.

The Truman administration pleaded the wisdom of a "limited war"—one that ended where it began. MacArthur was pictured as reckless and uncompromising, a figure from the distant past. In part, he was a true soldier who loved the cadence, the loyalty, the grandeur of war as a profession, as he had been taught it at this father's knee and his beloved West Point. He warned that there is no substitute for victory—but what is victory in a world of nuclear weapons, biological warfare, and doomsday devices? And how can one ask a generation of young men to give up their lives for a limited war, a war without a cause, a war of political objectives where the battlefields deny one a sense of progress or liberation? Paid mercenaries in the past had fought such wars, but not democratic armies mobilized since the time of the French Revolution to fight for great causes and hopeful ideals. The Truman administration sought to fight the first, but not the last, limited war—and it ended without triumph, without parades, with only a terrible sense of public frustration and private loss.

As that war continued through 1951, the nation also heard of other espionage cases, most tellingly the alleged spying of Julius and Ethel Rosenberg. Pressure built up on Truman to deal with subversion, and on April 28, 1951, he issued an executive order that allowed government employees to be dismissed if "there is reasonable doubt as to the loyalty of the person involved." Ironically, as the president moved farther away from protecting constitutional liberties and due process, he expressed concern to his associates over the looseness of the very loyalty boards he created.[31]

THE CONCLUSION OF
THE NEW DEAL REIGN

By the end of the year, the president had little political capital left to draw on. Congress refused to enact tough price, credit, and rent controls, a rash of scandals broke out in the Bureau of Internal Revenue, and Truman moved to dismiss his attorney general, James McGrath, for firing Newbold Morris, whom the president appointed to investigate government corruption. Then to add to his problems, the president precipitated a major constitutional crisis— and lost. In April 1952, Truman seized the steel industry to avert a strike, which he argued would damage the war effort. Privately encouraged by his friend Chief Justice Fred Vinson, the president refused to use the Taft-Hartley Act and instead relied on his powers as commander in chief to stop the threat. He could have invoked the law and asked for a cooling-off period, or seized the steel industry under the Selective Service Act if defense materials were not delivered as contracted for, or he could have simply gone to an unsympathetic Congress for new legislation.

The district court judge, however, refused to uphold the president's action, calling it "illegal and without authority of law." Truman's response was that if he were wrong, so were Jefferson, Lincoln, Wilson, and FDR in their exercise of prerogatives, and he insisted they were not. The Supreme Court heard the appeal, and by a vote of six to three, the Court also found Truman's action unconstitutional. The decision is normally seen as a rebuff to the notion of executive powers. But the opinions of the majority are in fact confusing, and one can read some of those opinions and those of the minority of the Court as giving a president the authority Truman wanted if emergency conditions were graver than existed in 1952. What seems like a clear precedent on the limitations of executive power is, on reflection, more ambiguous than meets the eye. In any case, Truman obeyed the Court, ended the steel seizure, asked Congress for new legislation—which it in turn refused to pass citing the Taft-Hartley remedy. The strike ended in late July with basically the wage and price terms that were presented four months earlier.[32]

The year 1952 was a time of presidential election politics, and although Truman toyed a bit with another term, he was genuinely tired of the demands of the office. The Republicans looking for a winner finally swayed Dwight Eisenhower who, much to Truman's dismay, criticized elements of the very foreign policy he himself had helped the Democratic presidents put into place. To add to Truman's annoyance, even his own party's candidate, Governor Adlai E. Stevenson of Illinois, promised "to clean up the mess in Washington."[33]

After twenty years of rule, the Democratic party had left a rich legacy of social legislation and had forged a Western alliance that destroyed the Nazis and the Japanese Empire and held in check somewhat Stalin's ambitions. But the public grew weary of sacrifice, of scandals, of war, and of the strange sense that American achievements were traded away by spies, fellow travelers, and naive State Department dupes. Nixon, running with Eisenhower, called the Democrats the party of Communism, corruption, and Korea, and as unfair as it was, the seeds of discontent flowered in many American minds.

Truman remained one of the most vilified and unpopular presidents of his time, but a president whose reputation soared after his retirement. He became the common man made good; the honest, dedicated servant in the cause of democracy around the world. His record is a mixed one to assess. Speaker of the House Sam Rayburn once observed that Truman was wrong on the small things, but was right on the big decisions that often recast America's international responsibilities. Revisionist and left-wing historians have seen him as the cause of the Cold War, as if Stalin were a sensitive soul seeking only secure boundaries for his troubled state.

There is no question that Truman hired many mediocre people, fired too many individuals, and, like Lincoln, was plagued by his poor choices. Perhaps the United States was not ready for the burdens of postwar global leadership any more than it was ready for the protracted Civil War. Yet as noted, in a mere eighteen months, the administration recast American foreign policy in the most creative and lasting period in its history. Like the assumptions or not, Truman and his small band of brothers were effective in mobilizing public support, compromising with Congress, supporting allies in Europe, and laying the groundwork for a rebirth of the Atlantic community, economy, and military might. He had, of course, considerable assistance from Stalin in selling that harsh view of reality.

On the home front, amid all the controversies, half turns and twists, the United States did a fairly good job at reconversion, and some of that credit goes to Truman. Surely, the United States handled its recovery better than after the Civil War, World War I, or Vietnam. Most of his domestic proposals did not see the light of day, and some liberal critics argued then and later that the president proposed but did not press. That is somewhat true, but after 1938, even the skillful FDR had been blocked. The New Deal was over and by recasting it as the Fair Deal, no one was fooled or pacified. Only in 1964–67 did Lyndon Johnson, an uncommonly skilled practitioner of congressional politics, and a president with a solid liberal majority in those two houses, enact the Fair Deal agenda in housing, education, medical care, civil rights, and other areas.

Truman as president went from being excessively modest in 1945 to cantankerous and often cocky by the end of his second term. He was blunt, too opinionated, often loyal to the wrong people, and continually contentious, almost like a bantam rooster out to show the political barnyard his stuff. But he was also an ardent patriot, an honest commoner sworn to the public interest. It was noted he put his own two-cent stamps on his personal letters, never profited from public office in any way even after he retired, and was deeply committed to the dignity of the position he inherited.[34] Truman also put in place the institutions of the new executive office—the National Security Council, the Council of Economic Advisors, the Joint Chiefs of Staff, the CIA, and other bodies that surround the contemporary office. It may be said that FDR was the first modern president in what he did and the office he created. But it was Harry S Truman who institutionalized the modern presidency, transforming it by crisis and practice into the nerve center of the national government and of the Western alliance. He was later asked what was the first thing he did after giving up the immense burdens and powers of the office and arriving home. Characteristically, he responded that he carried the "grips [suitcases] up to the attic."[35]

IKE: FROM COMMANDING TO MANAGING

The election of General Dwight David Eisenhower was a long awaited victory for the Republican party, but it did not bring the conservative wing any real comfort in the end. Eisenhower had spent his prime years under the command of Democratic presidents, and many of his attitudes about the office and about American commitments in the world were part of the Roosevelt-Truman view. And like many military men, who had seen young soldiers fight and die, Eisenhower was reluctant to embark on the type of adventuresome foreign policy that marked the Kennedy-Johnson period. Of all the presidents of the postwar period, he was ironically the least willing to use direct force or to give a blank check to the Pentagon.

Eisenhower was not a fighting soldier or a great strategist. He was a consummate soldier-diplomat who as leader of the Allied forces during World War II in Europe helped forge a successful military alliance against almost insurmountable odds. Historians have debated at length how effective Ike was as supreme Allied commander in Europe, examining his critical decisions, his frequent deference to the British, and his management of prima donnas on and off the battlefield. But there is no question that he developed a unique theory of management, delegation of authority, and teamwork that he brought to the White House. His critics claimed that Eisenhower avoided acrimony almost to the point of weakness, engaged in obscuration as a style, and used consensus building often, as a substitute for decision making. His wartime leadership and his presidency were to some extent a continuum of that style and those concerns. Beneath it all, Eisenhower remained unpretentious, deeply patriotic and personally incorruptible. He was all his life the farm boy from Abilene, Kansas.[36]

One of his associates, General Bernard Montgomery, observed that Eisenhower had "the power of drawing the hearts of men toward him as a magnet attracts the bits of metal. He merely has to smile at you, and you trust him at once." Truman though had a different view, especially after the campaign. He remarked that his successor would "sit here, and he'll say, 'Do this! Do that!' And nothing will happen. Poor Ike—it won't be a bit like the Army. He'll find it very frustrating." They were both right about Eisenhower.[37]

Eisenhower chose a cabinet filled with wealthy men, the type of people he enjoyed dealing with, and added a union leader to head up the Department of Labor. Columnists quickly labeled it a cabinet of eight millionaires and a plumber. The new president also created a network of interdepartmental committees, and he upgraded the National Security Council into a sort of British war cabinet to lay out policy options for him. His first major problem was to end the Korean War, and he paid an obligatory call on MacArthur, his old boss in the Philippines, who had once branded Ike his clerk. The old generals conferred, and MacArthur confided his secret solution to the end the war—use the atomic bomb if a proposed summit conference failed. Eisenhower listened noncommittally, and left unconvinced that he wanted to use that awesome weapon once again. Later, MacArthur bitterly observed, "The trouble with Eisenhower is that he doesn't have the guts to make a policy decision. He never did have the guts and he never will." In the end though, Eisenhower did indeed "go to Korea" as he promised in the campaign, and through unofficial channels he also informed the Communist Chinese and the North Koreans that he would consider using nuclear weapons if the war did not end promptly.[38]

Once elected, Eisenhower—a true heir and part of the Democratic-designed foreign policy—carefully sidestepped the issue of attacking FDR's Yalta agreements or continuing to criticize Truman. As he noted to one columnist, "I have no interest in going back and raking up the ashes of the dead past." And while he pledged to cooperate with Congress, he refused to support the proposed Bricker amendment to the Constitution, which would have curtailed the executive's prerogatives to make agreements with foreign governments and which promulgated that "a treaty shall become effective as internal law in the United States only through legislation which would be valid in the absence of a treaty." Again and again

Eisenhower was to insist on protecting the powers of the post-Rooseveltian presidency in the areas of foreign policy and national security. The right-wing Republicans had expected that from Truman, but not from Ike.[39]

Eventually, he found himself at odds with Senator Joseph McCarthy who insisted on expanding his Communist hunt and attacked, of all institutions—the U.S. Army, Eisenhower's true love and home since his adolescence. To the chagrin of many right-thinking moderates, however, the president refused to deal directly with McCarthy, blithely remarking, "I won't get into a pissing contest with a skunk." He did encourage Secretary of State John Foster Dulles to purge the State Department of many of its top bureaucrats, charging that they were selected "through a process of selection *based upon their devotion to the socialistic doctrine and bureaucratic controls practiced over the past two decades.*" And he did refuse to pardon Julius and Ethel Rosenberg, the couple convicted of giving atomic secrets to the Soviet Union and sentenced to die.

Throughout his term in office, Eisenhower would rely on his superior experience and proven judgment to hold back military expenses and press for economy. As happened before, the Pentagon was projecting a year—this time, 1954—as the time of "maximum danger." Ike called the whole approach "pure rot" and particularly targeted the air force for its scare tactics. "I'm damn tired of Air Force sales programs. In 1946 they argued that if we can have seventy groups, we'll guarantee security for ever and ever and ever." By 1954, the air force insisted on 141 groups instead, much to Eisenhower's opposition.[40]

In contrast to his aides' simplistic attacks on the Soviet Union, the president demanded to know what the United States in turn had "to offer the world." When critics pressed for a military solution in Korea, Eisenhower insisted on a serious bid for peace. Throughout his presidency, Eisenhower would be plagued by two conflicting attitudes: he genuinely wanted peace and a detente with the Soviets, but he distrusted them to carry out their part of the bargain if it were ever struck. By the time he nearly reached an agreement with them in his second term, a U-2 spy plane was shot down over the USSR and all hopes of amity vanished.[41]

Yet within six months after his inaugural, against the advice of his own secretary of state, the Republican Old Guard, and an angry Syngman Rhee, Eisenhower concluded an armistice. Quietly he also decided that the United States should reexamine its policy toward China. While he was unwilling to lead publicly, he supported recognition of Red China and allowing it into the United Nations—cardinal sins in the eyes of conservative Republican faithful. As he promised, he ended the vexatious war in Korea. One of his biographers, Stephen E. Ambrose, has concluded, "The man who had ordered the Allied troops back onto the Continent and into the hell of the Bulge could not bear the thought of American boys dying for a stalemate. He wanted the killing ended, and he ended it."

COVERT WARS AND UNEASY PEACE

The new president's major focus of concern shifted to Iran; indeed British Prime Minister Anthony Eden confided that Eisenhower "seemed obsessed by the fear of a Communist Iran." Because of its border with Russia, its critical geopolitical location in that region, and its rich oil reserves, Iran took on a pivotal role in the Cold War calculations of both great powers. Eisenhower was left with a dilemma. As Ambrose has concluded, the president believed "that nuclear war was unimaginable, limited conventional war unwinnable, and stalemate unacceptable. That left the CIA's covert action capability."[42]

Unlike Truman, Eisenhower used the agency as a surrogate army, one able to wage war quietly with minimum domestic oversight and yet effective in promoting the administration's objectives abroad. By the end of June, the U.S. government decided to instigate a coup against the Iranian prime minister, Mohammed Mossadegh, who had pushed for the nationalization of British oil fields and accepted the support of his nation's Communist party. The president received only oral reports on the coup planning, did not discuss the matter with his cabinet or the NSC, and ordered intervention only behind closed doors.

Because in that period there was little oversight of the CIA, the president could also use funds from the agency to support the activities he wanted accomplished. The administration provided 90 percent of the Radio Free Europe budget, for example, from CIA accounts. Later the administration held a private dinner for major donors and raised $10 million to undergird the RFE operations, a similar technique to what Ronald Reagan used a generation later to encourage aid to the Contras in Nicaragua.[43]

The coup in Iran succeeded and on August 22, the young shah, Reza Pahlavi, assumed power, and Mossadegh was arrested. Soon the shah entered into a new oil arrangement with the West, and consequently American firms got 40 percent of the deal. At the same time as Eisenhower countenanced the coup, he rejected Dulles's insistence on raising U.S. troop levels in Asia and Europe and increasing the production of nuclear weapons. The president maintained that leaders had to educate the people and tell them the truth about the horrors of nuclear war. He feared the consequences of those instruments of death, concluding that "the cost would either drive us to war—or into some form of dictatorial government."

It was with those misgivings in mind that Eisenhower in late 1953 proposed "Atoms for Peace," an overture motivated by genuine concern over nuclear weapons and an equally powerful urge to seize the propaganda initiative from the Soviet Union. After overcoming opposition in his own administration, the president advocated that the three nuclear powers make contributions from their nuclear stockpile to an International Atomic Energy Agency under the control of the United Nations. Clearly swords were to be beaten into plowshares. Even the Russian delegates cheered the speech at first, but the Soviet government waited for three years before sending a positive sign, and the arms race by then had entered a new phase of acceleration and mutual suspicion.[44]

Meanwhile, despite the president's efforts at statesmanship, he was faced with the continuing annoyance of McCarthyism at home. With his moderate inclinations, Eisenhower told Attorney General Herbert Brownell to "search out some positive ways to put ourselves on the side of individual right and liberty as well as on the side of fighting Communism to the death." The attorney general reported that the administration had fired a host of persons considered security risks since coming into office and later cited the number as 1,456. To McCarthy, these alleged firings were due to obvious Communist leanings, a sure proof that the Truman administration was packed with Reds just as he wildly charged.

Then in a rare departure from political etiquette, Eisenhower approved Brownell's attack on retired President Truman by allowing the attorney general to assert that the former chief executive had protected aide Harry Dexter White who had been accused of being a Soviet spy. The House of Representatives UnAmerican Activities Committee served a subpoena on Truman, and an angry Truman refused to appear, citing the constitutional separation of powers and denying that he had ever seen any FBI report on White's activities in 1946. Eisenhower both supported Truman's refusal to appear before the committee and upheld Brownell. A livid Truman then attacked the administration's embrace of McCarthyism, admitted he had read the FBI report after all, and claimed that he kept White on the job because firing him would tip off other individuals in the spy group. It was an absurd ending to a nasty dispute.

Through all of this, Eisenhower still refused to confront McCarthy, exhibiting even to his closest aides the type of personal weakness and public vacillation that so frequently characterized the president. His response was the same: "I will not get in the gutter with that guy." When pressure built up on the question of the security status of noted physicist Robert Oppenheimer, a troubled Eisenhower dealt gingerly with the issue.

Try as he might though in 1954, Eisenhower could not bob and weave fast enough to avoid the controversies surrounding Senator McCarthy and his investigation of alleged subversion. The senator would not be ignored, nor was he denied the headlines he so eagerly pursued. In one sensational case, McCarthy had charged that the U.S. Army had promoted a dentist, Dr. Irving Peress, who had refused to take the loyalty oath. In a brutal hearing in February, the senator berated the commanding officer at Camp Kilmer, and a frightened secretary of war agreed to a compromise with McCarthy. While the president gave some vague positive sentiments of support to the army leadership, he was more troubled that McCarthy's fishing expeditions into the records of the executive branch might prove embarassing to the administration. Eisenhower's real concern was that McCarthy would find out about his personal decision to withhold Oppenheimer's top secret clearance until an investigation was completed. McCarthy had already charged that there had been an eighteen-month delay in developing the H-bomb "because of Reds in government." Later the committee reviewing the scientist's record found that he was not disloyal but had certain "fundamental defects of character" that justified having his security clearance lifted. Oppenheimer had opposed the development of the hydrogen bomb, fearing that it would lead to even more terrible instruments of destruction than the one he had helped to create at Alamogordo. Eisenhower accepted the conclusion that Oppenheimer was loyal, but he still barred him from having access to further government secrets.[45]

The specific controversy over the Peress case started when

McCarthy demanded the names of all army personnel connected with the matter. General Matthew Ridgway vigorously protested the inquiry, and McCarthy threatened to subpoena the White House staff. Eisenhower finally responded with a strong assertion of executive privilege. He insisted that Congress had no right to ask them to testify and warned he would take this test of principle to the country. Publicly he maintained that it was "essential to efficient and effective administration that employees of the Executive Branch be in a position to be completely candid in advising each other on official matters." Occasional claims of privilege had been considered since George Washington, but no president ever asserted it so definitely and so broadly before. A furious McCarthy reissued his threats but, in the army hearings, he appeared shrill and unconvincing. The eye of the television camera had begun to undercut the man who so loved publicity. As time passed, McCarthy rambled on, was eventually censured by the Senate, and became increasingly prone to bouts of alcoholism. McCarthyism passed away; its living monument however was a new doctrine of broad executive privilege.[46]

As the president wrestled with charges of weakness in dealing with the senator, he tried to refashion American military policy around the very weapons he deplored. Calling his defense plans the "New Look," Eisenhower moved to cut conventional forces, trim costs, and rely even more on atomic weapons. The key would be the air force, much to the chagrin of Ike's old army friends. Even Army Chief of Staff Ridgway protested at the imbalance; it was an "all or nothing" strategy he warned.

Eisenhower seemed to abdicate responsibility in another critical area at that time as well. Faced with the monumental decision from the Supreme Court in *Brown v. the Board of Education of Topeka, Kansas*, which ended legal segregation, the president clearly distanced himself from the controversy. He urged people to obey the decision, ended up reluctantly enforcing it, but never embraced it. He privately warned Chief Justice Earl Warren that he understood why white parents would insist that their "sweet little girls are not required to sit in school along side some big overgrown Negroes." Later he was quoted as having allegedly said that his greatest mistake in office was "the appointment of that dumb son of bitch Earl Warren" to the Court.[47]

In that first term, the most important decision that Eisenhower confronted was one he deliberately did not make. Some historians have come to see his refusal to have the United States go it alone into Vietnam as a brilliant example of his wisdom and foresight. Yet the president's own actions were more tentative and somewhat confusing. With the French imperial system collapsing, that nation was seeing Vietnam slip from its orbit into the hands of the most organized indigenous force, the Communist-led cadres of Ho Chi Minh. In 1952 Dulles warned the president-elect that while Korea was important, Indochina was the key to south Asia. After having attacked the Democrats for losing China, how could the Republicans allow Vietnam to go Communist?

The president proposed a British-U.S. shipment of military hardware and joint air support of the French. Eisenhower appealed to Churchill to seize this "priceless opportunity," and later reminded him of the mistakes of not standing up to Hitler, Mussolini, and Hirohito. But the aging prime minister, who had sounded those themes before, refused to rise to the challenge or to the bait. Churchill simply expressed his confidence in the ability of the English-speaking peoples to stick together.

The cautious side of Eisenhower emerged as he realized that the United States, if it aided the French, would do so alone and on the side of a deteriorating imperialism. He candidly admitted that he was "frightened about getting ground forces tied up in Indochina." Still he introduced American military personnel there for the first time, although he probably saw that as a temporary expedient rather than a telling precedent. Years later in 1963, he wrote that the jungles of Indochina could have "swallowed up division after division of United States troops, who unaccustomed to this kind of warfare, would have sustained heavy casualties." Faced, though, with tremendous pressure, especially in his own party and in conservative circles, Eisenhower allowed talk about U.S. involvement to build. But the conditions he set for such an intervention were so stringent that he must have known the plan would die. The president carefully insisted that the French must grant independence to the region, the British must join the Americans, some of the Southeast Asian nations had to be involved, Congress must give its clear approval ahead of time, and the French must turn the direction of the war over to the United States but guarantee they were not withdrawing themselves.

Eisenhower talked of the loss of Indochina as a "falling domino"—a powerful image that gripped policy makers throughout the Vietnam War. But he himself refused to enter unilaterally, and he showed a deep sensitivity to charges that the United States would be replacing its rule for French imperial control. The United States with its tradition of anticolonialism had to avoid such a mistake, he argued. When the NSC circulated a draft considering the use of atomic weapons in Vietnam, the president bluntly responded, "You boys must be crazy. We can't use those awful things against Asians for the second time in less than ten years. My God." Later when the Vietnamese and the French agreed to a peace conference in Geneva, Eisenhower continued his high stakes game. When Dulles feared Chinese intervention and asked the president to get a resolution from Congress approving an American response, Eisenhower said he would not ask for halfway measures. There would have to be consideration of a possible strike at Russia too! Thus, in the end, the United States stayed out of the Indochina conflict during Eisenhower's terms in office.[48]

Elsewhere, the president proved to be more adventuresome. When he was faced with a challenge in the Western Hemisphere, he applied not the overwhelming force his defense policy was based on, but relied instead again on the CIA's covert operations. The scene was Guatemala, and the president became convinced that a Communist takeover was imminent because of the misguided activities of Jacobo Arbenz Guzmán, the elected president there. While some advisors around Eisenhower were influenced by Arbenz's nationalization of the plantations of the United Fruit Company, the president, sitting in Washington, D.C., was more preoccupied with the threat of international Communism than protecting U.S. economic interests.

Using the lessons of the coup in Iran, the agency planned to have the Army turn against Arbenz thus forcing him to leave the country. The president insisted that there be no direct U.S. intervention, but when arms arrived from Czechoslovakia for dispersal to Arbenz partisans, Eisenhower changed tactics. He ordered a naval blockade of Guatemala, called for a meeting of the Organization of American States, and sent in an airlift of arms to neighboring Nicaragua and Honduras. When the Soviets sent ships with ammunition into the region, the United States interrupted the freighter. The president sent airplanes to opposition leaders, and CIA pilots secretly joined in the air offensive. Even the British and French supported Arbenz, and for the first time, the United States used its veto in the UN to keep the matter off the agenda. As the bombing raids continued, Arbenz resigned and a military dictatorship was established. Unlike Kennedy at the Bay of Pigs later, once Eisenhower made his decision to upset a foreign government, he carried through even when the cover of the CIA was exposed. Overall, the president saw the falling dominoes again—citing Panama, the Canal, and eventually Mexico as being threatened by Communism.[49]

That same confusing mixture of caution and decisiveness can be seen in Eisenhower's handling of Communist China's threats against the remnants of the Chiang regime stationed in Formosa, the Pescadores, and the tiny islands two miles directly off the mainland, Quemoy and Matsu. When Chiang in 1949 was forced out of China, he stationed his Nationalist troops on those two islands and took control of Formosa and the Pescadores. The Joint Chiefs of Staff had assured the president that those two islands were not necessary to the defense of Chiang's regime. The Communists regularly shelled Quemoy and Matsu and appeared ready to invade them. The president insisted that the United States had no treaty with Chiang, and he was unwilling to assert that the nation would go to war with Communist China and probably Russia without congressional authorization. Eisenhower would use the Seventh Fleet defensively if the Chinese attacked Chiang's regime, but he was not going to retaliate against the Communist mainland without congressional approval.[50]

As Communist threats increased, the president signed in December 1954 a mutual defense treaty with the Nationalists, but Chiang had to agree not to attack unilaterally the Communists. The treaty deliberately left out clauses guaranteeing any protection of Quemoy and Matsu. When the Communists attacked the Tachen Islands, two hundred miles from Formosa, the president refused to intervene. Instead he turned to Congress and asked for a resolution that would allow the chief executive to protect Formosa, the nearby Pescadores Islands, and "such other territories as may be determined." As historian Stephen Ambrose has written, "The resolution Eisenhower wanted was something new in American history. Never before had Congress given the president a blank check to act as he saw fit in a foreign crisis." The Democrats supported the president, and it passed the House 410 to 3 and the Senate 83 to 3. The Formosa Doctrine, as it was called, turned the constitutional war-making process on its head; for the president it was meant "to serve notice on the Communists that they're not going to be able to get away with it."[51]

Yet the president's attitude on Quemoy and Matsu was confus-

ing to the Communists and to the nation—perhaps, artfully confusing or just reflecting the mixture of caution and steadfastness
Eisenhower had in mind. He insisted that Quemoy and Matsu were
important to the Nationalists' morale, yet he privately told his press
secretary, Jim Hagerty, that he wished the "damned islands" would
just sink. He reasserted his notion of the domino theory, and
Quemoy and Matsu took on added importance to the future of a
free Asia. Yet he truly did not want to go to war to save them.
Eisenhower and Dulles rattled the nuclear sabers as in Korea and
threatened to use nuclear weapons if war came into the Formosa
straits. But when he was warned about answering questions on the
controversy, the president blithely responded to his press secretary,
"Don't worry, Jim, if that question comes up, I'll just confuse
them."[52] The question did come up and his response was so confusing syntactically that it is incomprehensible in English; years later
Eisenhower would wonder how those remarks were translated into
Russian or Chinese! Privately, the president thought that the best
solution would be for Chiang to withdraw voluntarily from those
islands, and he offered some inducements toward that end. Chiang
was obstinate, but across the straits the Communist Chinese regime
declared that it did not wish to go to war with the United States
and pledged to negotiate. Eisenhower had basically rejected all the
advice offered him on all sides, and carefully navigated to a settlement, though not a conclusion, that he alone worked through. It was
a dangerous, but most impressive performance.

When the Chinese challenge abated, the president took a sharp
turn and proposed one of the most remarkable peace initiatives to
mark the Cold War era—"Open Skies." Although the president distrusted the Russian leadership and was opposed to disarmament, he
was sincerely concerned about the possibility of war. Again, almost
totally on his own, Eisenhower held forth the idea that each side
open up its airspace to the other and allow continuous reconnaissance missions. Like many military people of his era, he vividly
remembered the surprise attack at Pearl Harbor. Access to Soviet
airspace would calm those fears of another sneak attack and, since
American society was open anyhow, it was in his nation's interests
to push such an idea. He realized that technology would enable both
sides to roam the skies at high altitudes sooner or later; the notion
was a decisive symbolic attempt to lessen mutual distrust and the
possibilities of hostilities.[53]

Then dramatically at a summit conference in Geneva, the president presented his proposal for the approval of the British, the French, and even Soviet leader Nikolai Bulganin. But by then it was Nikita Khrushchev who was the master of the Kremlin, and he immediately rejected the overture. Two weeks later, the Russians began a series of hydrogen bomb tests. Soon Eisenhower was to consent to U-2 spy flights over the Communist state, a decision that led to invaluable information about Soviet defenses and was the cause of the final breakup of a later summit conference of such promise in 1959.

The end of Eisenhower's first term showed a record of moderation, cautious foreign policy, bold clandestine intervention, and broad popular approval. After a mild heart attack in September 1955, the president considered not running again. But the call to duty and his own personal pride led him to continue on and seek reelection. The president remained concerned about the right wing of his own party, feeling quite correctly that he was the only viable option to a return to conservative social policy and a rigid foreign policy. Because of his age and questions of health, concern arose about the vice presidency. Eisenhower offered Richard Nixon a choice of cabinet positions, arguing rather disingenuously that he could compile a better record for the 1960 campaign from there. The president, however, seemed to offer encouragement to moderate Republicans to drop Nixon, but in the end Eisenhower waffled, and the vice president's strong hold on the rank and file party leadership prevailed.[54]

Once again the Democrats turned to Adlai E. Stevenson, who alternated his high-sounding rhetoric and prophetic calls for peace with shrill observations about Ike's health and the horrors of Richard Nixon. The greatest challenge that Eisenhower faced during the campaign, though, came not from the Democratic party, but from the crisis building up in the Middle East. The main flashpoint was Egypt with its belligerent nationalist and pro-Soviet adherent, Gamal Nasser. The U.S. government after some commitments to Nasser had promised to fund the Aswan Dam on the Nile River, but domestic opposition in Congress and the Egyptian leader's haughty attitude led to a reconsideration. Meanwhile, the British and the French conspired secretly with the Israeli government in a bizarre scheme to halt any Egyptian takeover of the Suez Canal.

On July 26, Nasser seized the canal and British Prime Minister Anthony Eden saw it as a replay of standing up to the dictators of the 1930s. Eisenhower, however, refused to accept that logic or to

be swayed by old ties from World War II toward Eden and his senior ministers. The president recognized the winds of anticolonialism
in the area, and urged the Western nations to appreciate that they
may be at times "victims of the tyrannies of the weak." Disregarding
advice from hardliners in the Joint Chiefs, his own cabinet, and even
Democratic leaders, Eisenhower insisted on negotiations over the
canal dispute. Then in October, the Soviet empire was rocked by
an uprising in Hungary against its occupying regime. Soviet troops
eventually marched into Budapest, and the American administration's
rhetoric about "liberation" of that region rang hollow. Eisenhower
would not commit U.S. troops to going into Russia's backyard—
saying that Hungary was as "inaccessible to us as Tibet." The Hungarian rebels were called "Freedom Fighters" in America, but at
home the Russian grip tightened. Myths of liberation and fictions
of Communist solidarity both took a beating in the fall of 1956.

At nearly the same time, the Israelis mobilized their armed
forces, and confused administration officials finally realized that the
British, French, and Israelis were involved in a veiled joint effort
to topple Nasser. The British and the French had announced that
unless both the Egyptians and the Israelis withdrew ten miles from
the canal, they would move in to guard the facility. The Israelis
promptly agreed as if on cue, leaving the Egyptians as the aggres-
sors in many people's eyes. An angry and betrayed Eisenhower refused to go along with the fiction of his old allies. Faced with an
election at home and the telling revolt against Communist imperialism in Hungary, the president rejected the old colonialist powers'
overresponse. With a surety of purpose and a remarkable clarity of
decision making, Eisenhower once again steered his own course.
To the horror of the British and the French governments, the administration condemned the whole plot and brought the matter to
the United Nations. The president went on television and in a calm,
determined mood insisted on a negotiated way out of war. Once
again, Eisenhower prevailed and, in the election, he was
overwhelmingly reelected, doubling his popular margin of 1952. This
time, though, the Democrats held on to both houses of Congress;
the people had clearly differentiated between the president and the
legislative branch. The Middle East crisis, however, showed Ike in
full command.[55]

It would be a mistake not to appreciate the importance of the
Middle East and Southern Hemispheric relations on Eisenhower's
geopolitical thinking. In his second term, the president stepped up

his support for a broad-reaching foreign aid plan aimed at winning the sentiment of Third World nonindustrial nations. The keynote words became "trade *and* aid," as the president asked for a three-year, $2 billion long-term loan fund. But Eisenhower found that Congress was unwilling to match its tough words about stopping Communism with a more subtle sense of enticing Third World nations, and it substantially cut the president's request. A frustrated Eisenhower observed, "I am repeatedly astonished, even astounded, by the apparent ignorance of members of Congress on the general subject of our foreign affairs."[56]

The legislative branch proved almost as difficult in giving Eisenhower another blank check to intervene in the Middle East. Focusing on that region, the president wanted prior approval if he had to move. But this time, opposition grew to aiding friendly Arab states, and the Democratic party leaders in Congress indicated that they would not go along with the proposed resolution. Finally in early March, Congress passed the so-called Eisenhower Doctrine, which gave legislative authorization to the president to send U.S. troops into the Middle East to support any nation facing aggression from "International Communism," if that nation so desired.

Anxious to underscore U.S. interest in the Middle East, Eisenhower in the summer of 1957 decided on a show of strength in moderate Lebanon. With the approval of pro-Western President Camille Chamoun, Eisenhower committed sending the marines into Lebanon to protect American life and property, although it was never clear that either was in danger. Eisenhower cited U.S. commitments to Lebanon, despite the fact there were no treaties with that nation; even the doctrine that was aimed at foreign invasions did not apply. The president insisted that he acted "to stop the trend toward chaos"; Anthony Eden bitterly observed however that the Americans now were "doing a Suez on me." Rather than fearing some vague elements of chaos, it is more likely that Ike's initiatives were meant to impress Nasser and friendly Arab states who, according to the president, later changed their attitude toward the United States.[57]

While Eisenhower moved with some sense of surety in foreign affairs, whether one agreed with him or not, in domestic matters he seemed distant and at times utterly confused. His leadership in the McCarthy affair left much to be desired, his hope of rebuilding a moderate Republican party lacked any real commitment, and he avoided giving his imprimatur to black stirrings for civil rights.

Unlike Kennedy and especially Johnson, he seemed blind to the moral responsibilities before him, and unlike Truman, he never put the weight of his great office behind desegregation.

The real leadership on civil rights in the administration came from Attorney General Herbert Brownell, who called for a strong bipartisan commission to investigate civil rights violations, an augmented Justice Department effort, new laws on voting rights, and citizenship protections for blacks. Soon the president put some distance between himself and his own attorney general, and later concluded that legislation could not lead to changes in morality. But events forced the president into the heart of the controversy when the governor of Arkansas, Orville Faubus, called out the National Guard to stop the desegregation of Central High School in Little Rock. Reluctant as he was to get involved, Eisenhower could not permit the orders of a federal court to be openly defied. The president was at first unwilling to use troops to enforce those orders, but as racial animosity heated up and Faubus proved unreliable in negotiations, Eisenhower had few options. Trusting in the army, he called up airborne troops to maintain law and order, and cited examples going back to the Whiskey Rebellion to deny that he was seeking to set some precedent by using federal forces. The president's attempt to rally moderate southerners went down to defeat; Little Rock was not the end of controversy, but merely an early firebell in the night.[58]

Eisenhower's domestic troubles increased in his second term; the effort to balance the budget and his insistence on controlling military expenditures were especially difficult battles that he continued to wage. His own party leaders often refused to support the president's budget, and in some cases the Democratic majority leader in the Senate, Lyndon Johnson, and the Speaker of the House, Sam Rayburn, provided crucial support for Eisenhower instead of his own party. The nadir of presidential leadership in the period came in discussions over the 1958 budget when the president, his own cabinet officers, and Republican leaders released a confusing set of statements and contradictions.[59]

THE POLITICS OF DEFENSE

But the issue on which he felt the strongest and on which he was the most knowledgeable proved to be the most contentious—

defense spending. It is ironic and telling that the highest ranking military officer ever to hold the presidency would become the most articulate on the need to disarm. Throughout his terms in office, Eisenhower warned of the dire consequences that excessive military spending would bring, and he opened himself to attacks from the Democrats that he had left the nation at peril. At the end of his second term, he told Secretary of State Dulles that he was "desperate with the inability of the men there [in the Defense Department] to understand what can be spent on military weapons and what must be spent to wage the peace." He was disturbed by the high cost of defense, the size of the armed forces, the costs and quality of the CIA, and above all the ties between the military and the economic leadership of the nation.

The old soldier opposed the escalating costs of ballistic missiles and had a low opinion of their efficacy in war. But pressure from the scientific and military communities grew, and opposition carping from the Democrats continued. Senator Stuart Symington, Truman's secretary of the air force, led the charge, claiming "the United States has never been more vulnerable to Soviet attack than now." In language soon to be heard in the 1960 campaign, leaders in Congress discovered "a missile gap"—an issue exploited skillfully by Senator John F. Kennedy in his presidential race.[60]

Partly though, Eisenhower's polices did present a major contradiction—he believed that nuclear weapons gave a nation a psychological advantage over its prospective foes, but as a military man he thought they were too horrible to use. Yet he built his cheaper military strategy on the doctrine of "massive retaliation"; thus, he like Truman could call for a more modest conventional armed force because of the abundance of nuclear weapons. To some strategists— both in the Pentagon and outside—this all or nothing choice was inflexibility approaching irresponsibility. They pushed for a graduated response—from large armed forces, to more varied and expensive weapons systems, to a capacity to wage guerrilla warfare. They became the fathers of the American decision to enter the war in Vietnam.[61] As for Eisenhower, he used the CIA for many clandestine activities, thus avoiding the controversy of public debate and providing himself with some deniability for actions done. When he did not want to use force, he simply reminded his critics, as in the Indochina or the Formosa controversies, that he needed congressional approval to move. It was a shrewd approach that left the president with more options than anyone realized at the time.

The president flirted with total disarmament, and even supported a complete ban on testing of atomic weapons if it were coupled with general disarmament. Like all presidents of the postwar period, he distrusted the Soviet government and insisted on guarantees concerning inspection. In June 1957, the president even spoke of a temporary suspension of testing, a proposal made by the Russians and attacked in U.S. military and scientific armament circles. Then in October 1957, the American people were shocked, angered, and confused by the Soviet Union's successful launching of a small satellite called Sputnik. To a generation of Americans brought up to believe in the superiority of U.S. technology and the American way of life, Sputnik struck a nerve. Cries to reform the schools, win the space race, cast off the sense of moral complacency—all fueled the newspapers and the airwaves.

Eisenhower calmly sought to put a rather minor achievement in perspective, but the Democrats gleefully and patriotically picked up the issue. The Joint Chiefs of Staff divided, each blaming the other services, and the press corps, in rare departures from etiquette, went after the beloved president. A new impetus for scientific research and military expansion gathered steam, and Congress began a series of investigations to find out what went wrong. One committee headed by H. Rowan Gaither of the Ford Foundation found Soviet GNP growing at a faster rate than the United States' and demanded an immense increase in defense appropriations of $38–40 billion with most of it going into resources to protect the population in case of war from nuclear arms fallout. Eisenhower dismissed the doomsday report and its whole tone.[62]

Then in late November, Eisenhower suffered a minor stroke that left him unable at first to talk clearly. For a time, there was speculation that he would resign and let Vice President Nixon assume his responsibilities. On February 5, 1958, Eisenhower sent the vice president a formal letter outlining conditions under which he would surrender the office in case of disability. If the president were incapable of recognizing his own condition, Nixon would alone decide when to take over. Eisenhower would determine later "if and when it is proper for me to resume."

Fortunately, the stroke proved to be more of an inconvenience than a major impediment, and Eisenhower moved on, again focusing his efforts on foreign policy. He seemed disturbed at the steady attacks on Secretary Dulles and complained about his secretary's frequent travels and preoccupation with details. Eisenhower implored

Dulles for some "new ideas," and in February the president proposed himself that ten thousand Russian students visit the United States at the government's expense to see the American way of life first hand. By that year, even Dulles was concerned over the increase in military spending and pushed for a test ban agreement.

In 1958, Eisenhower complained increasingly about military end runs around the civilian authorities to Congress and the media, and bluntly observed that "people in the service either ought to obey orders or get the hell out of the service." He moved to reorganize the Pentagon, giving more power to the secretary of defense and to keep the Chiefs away from congressional committees, an idea not well received in that branch of government. In another development, his chief of staff, Sherman Adams, was forced to resign. Adams had accepted gifts from a New England industrialist, Bernard Goldfine. In the highly charged atmosphere of 1958, Adams left the government despite the president's genuine pleas that he needed him. On top of mounting conflicts in his own administration, the aftermath of his stroke, criticism over his alleged lack of leadership, the trauma of Sputnik, the loss of Adams, and the severe setbacks for the Republican party in the 1958 congressional elections, the president lost the strongest man in his cabinet, Secretary of State Dulles, who died of cancer. Eisenhower moved into the lameduck period of his last two years in office on what looked like a sure decline.[63]

Then in a rather remarkable show of resilience, Eisenhower seemed to come alive again, reasserting his prerogatives and taking charge of his own administration. He came close to a major postwar rapprochement with the Soviet Union—only to see it destroyed by the downing of the U-2 spy plane. Throughout late 1958 and early 1959, the president pressed for greater attention to a moratorium on nuclear testing. He candidly admitted that continuing testing and the arms race "frightened him." Still he did not trust the Russians and, while they conducted two tests in the first week of the Geneva talks, the U.S. secretly tested later as well.

He was dismayed at the Defense Department's plan for increased bomb production and was angered at the pressure to build still more missiles. "How many times do we have to destroy Russia?" he wondered, looking at the proposed arsenal estimates. When Khrushchev blustered that he would sign a peace treaty with East Germany and cut off Allied rights in West Berlin, Eisenhower rejected the Joint Chiefs' advice that he send a U.S. division down the Autobahn as a show of force. To the president such a step was the wrong way to go, and he refused to accept that proposal or the opposite extreme from some European leaders to give in on the issue totally. In the end, Khrushchev postponed any confrontation and instead invited the hero of World War II to visit the Soviet Union, promising "heartfelt hospitality."[64]

But a new challenge was to arise in early 1959—one that would not go away so easily, the triumph of Fidel Castro in Cuba. Although there was then considerable controversy about whether Castro was a Communist or whether the administration's reactions to him moved him in that direction, it is now fairly clear that Castro was, even before the revolution and in the early days of his rule, a dedicated Communist and an anti-American in both rhetoric and by personal conviction. Faced with this hostile leader, Eisenhower once again turned to the CIA.

In 1955, the president had created a special oversight group, called the 5412 Committee—named after an NSC working paper. The group was supposedly to approve all covert operations; in fact, it was a cover to protect the president and reported only to him. In 1959, the National Security advisor, Gordon Gray, complained that his group never approved many of the activities the CIA was undertaking. The president in response insisted that no records of the 5412 meetings be kept except by the director and demanded that he be kept informed of all activities.

The CIA conducted a careful watch on Castro, and admitted they found him to be "an enigma," but concluded also that it was possible to establish "a constructive relationship with him and his government." However, as Castro continued on his revolutionary ways, Eisenhower began to see a different pattern emerging. Efforts to use the OAS to restrain the regime failed to gather support, and the president turned to the agency. Their leaders began a series of assassination attempts against Castro over the years, some of them bizarre such as attempting to poison the Cuban's cigars. Whether Eisenhower approved the assassination order is not clear from the evidence. What is indisputable is that the president agreed to create a Cuban government in exile, step up propaganda attacks on the regime, support a covert intelligence and action organization on the island, and fund a paramilitary force for future use. Eisenhower thus set the stage for a covert operation that was never completed in his administration; Kennedy would inherit it, and consequently in the 1962 Missile Crisis would become involved in one of the most frightening episodes of the postwar presidency.[65]

But that was in the future. By early 1959, Eisenhower moved decisively to work out some accommodation with the Soviets. In his first term, the president had very reluctantly approved U-2 flights over the air space of the Soviet Union. He held that such flights were "undue provocation," and observed that nothing would move him toward war more than Soviet violations of U.S. air space. The Russian leaders knew about such flights, and the president was probably aware that they were alerted on the matter. He worried about "the terrible propaganda" value of such a downing and was assured that the airplane would be destroyed rather than be forced down, and the pilot presumably killed in the process. Under pressure to build more weapons to keep up with the Soviets and having failed to sell the Kremlin on "Open Skies," Eisenhower overrode his own early objections. With valuable information in hand, the president had superior knowledge about the state of Soviet defenses, but could not tell his critics the source of his estimates of their strength. The president again and again sought to contain defense spending, arguing on one occasion that cries for more military appropriations provided only more money for those "obviously fat cats." But the Democrats and members of the military encouraged talk of fears about a missile gap, "a space gap," a weak defense posture, and the like.[66]

But by mid-1959, Eisenhower began, largely on his own, a major peace initiative. In June he criticized the Defense Department's policy of placing IRBMs so close to the Soviet Union in Greece, and he questioned the establishment of U.S. bases in places like Morocco or Libya, seeing them as a drain on the American economy. In July the administration continued discussions about inviting Khrushchev to the United States in September, and in late August Eisenhower undertook a series of visits to Germany, France, and England. Everywhere the man who symbolized the great Allied victory over the hated forces of Nazism was greeted with tremendous crowds of cheering admirers. Even Khrushchev, awaiting his own trip, must have felt some residual ties to the old common alliance that once toppled Hitler.

The Russian premier, visiting the United States in the fall, gave a feisty defense of Soviet material progress and proposed finally a total end to all nuclear and conventional weapons within four years. Despite being hesitant and suspicious, the two sides seemed to move toward each other, and Khrushchev went home talking about the "spirit of Camp David" and of the extraordinary American he had met. In November Eisenhower began to consider reducing U.S. contributions to NATO and returning some army ground units home. Then in late December 1959, the president embarked on a goodwill tour that included India, Greece, Spain, Afghanistan, Pakistan, Turkey, Italy, Iran, and other stops. Millions of people saw the famous American leader; the last year of Eisenhower's administration seemed bright indeed.

But then events dashed that optimism. Eisenhower biographer Stephen Ambrose has written that 1960 was a bad year for the president, full of mistakes brought on by "his fetish for secrecy and his misplaced trust in the CIA." Whatever the causes, the president's determination for peace suffered a sharp setback, and he lost the last political initiative he started. Most importantly, the most profound chance for a major rapprochement with the Soviet Union ruptured. To supporters of such an accommodation, that setback was a tragically missed opportunity; to critics of any accommodation, it was a welcome flight back to an understanding of the harsh reality of Soviet expansionism. In either case, Eisenhower's blunders spelled the end of his presidency in any effective sense.[67]

Throughout the winter, Eisenhower wrestled with his own administration as he worked out proposals to present before the Soviets on controlling nuclear weapons. On February 11, 1960, he unveiled a test ban treaty that would end all tests in the atmosphere, in the oceans, and in outer space, as well as underground tests "which can be monitored." When his own advisors warned the president that the Soviets would cheat, Eisenhower bluntly informed them that the United States was already "doing some experimenting" as well—that is, cheating itself. The president was considering a one-year moratorium, and as he prepared for another meeting with Khrushchev, this time in Paris, he seemed genuinely close to working out an agreement.[68]

Then just before the summit meeting, Eisenhower against his better judgment approved additional U-2 flights. On May 1, a U.S. plane was shot down, and the pilot, Francis Gary Powers, was captured alive. The president at first said little, believing that the plane and the pilot would "self-destruct," as the CIA had assured him. Khrushchev, probably embarrassed and under pressure from his Politburo for this violation of Soviet air space and honor, insisted on parading the incident across the summit conference. Eisenhower refused to deny responsibility as he was urged to do. There was in the end no saving face, and at the Paris summit the Soviet premier insisted on berating Eisenhower. The president's trip to Russia was canceled; bitterly the president privately wrote his own political obituary and noted how he had wanted to conclude the Cold War and felt he was making great strides, and how the U-2 ended it all.[69]

In the summer of 1960, as the two political parties nominated their prospective successor to Eisenhower, the president was forced to cancel abruptly his trip to Japan due to organized protests over the mutual security pact between the two nations. Back home, the president in July stepped up his opposition to the Castro regime by ending the Cuban sugar quota, although Eisenhower rejected any military action. But once again, he turned to the CIA for a covert operation aimed at toppling Castro.

In another corner of the world, the former Belgian Congo was inflamed in a civil war, and American intelligence feared the strength of Patrice Lumumba, the new prime minister. Lumumba had at first asked the Eisenhower administration for help, but when he was rebuffed, he went to Khrushchev who obliged. His fate in the eyes of Eisenhower and his advisors was sealed—he was surely a Soviet agent. The president and his closest advisors gave the orders to the CIA to "remove" Lumumba; years later in 1975, a Senate committee investigating the CIA argued that it was reasonable to infer that Eisenhower approved an assassination attempt. Whether that accusation is true or not is not clear, but it surely represents one of the low points of American postwar behavior. Before that "removal" in any form was accomplished, Lumumba was kidnapped and murdered by his main opponent's forces.[70]

Thus Eisenhower ended his last year not in triumph, but listening to two junior-grade officers from World War II, Nixon and Kennedy, stepping all over each other trying to show the American people how they would restore vigor and decisiveness to the executive office. Eisenhower's presidency lends itself at times to a judgment of lethargy, moral insensitivity, and political secrecy. But the general also faced monumental challenges with a sense of command and strategic balance that prevented the United States from blundering into crisis after crisis. Many times Eisenhower shrewdly steered the nation between the rocks of the Republican hard-line doctrines and the uninformed expressions of weakness and weariness at being a new great power. He was no Republican interlude, but a man educated in the arts of war, trained in the crucible of grinding Allied diplomacy, and truly committed to maintaining older and more moderate American values. He was both a period piece and perhaps, in some ways, a guide.

KENNEDY AND THE PERILS OF CAMELOT

Kennedy's inauguration presented a sharp contrast as the youngest president ever elected sat next to the oldest president ever to retire from office up to that time. Kennedy throughout the campaign and in his brief term in office would trumpet calls for reform, self-sacrifice, and national renewal. Few presidents have so captivated the imagination of the American people, and his quick shocking death left him forever young in their memories. He was a man who experienced pain and a tragic death, but was never to know decline, decay, and old age. After his passing, friends and spinners of modern yarns called his brief reign a modern Camelot, evoking mythical themes of King Arthur and his charmed, but doomed knights of the round table.

The death of the young is always a poignant experience and, for a nation in grief, the Kennedy promise seemed cut off and betrayed by an irrational fate. The Camelot myth caught the popular imagination very soon after the president's assassination in Dallas. But the political divisions of the 1960s and the disillusions of the 1970s led to a sharp reassessment of Kennedy and a discovery of the darker side of Camelot. Kennedy was transformed from being the golden prince to a compulsive womanizer, a user of drugs, a man who shared a mistress with a Mafia chieftain, and an obsessed chief executive who may have countenanced political assassination himself. It seemed that the man who lived the faint life of glamour had stepped over the line into dark realms and recesses that lesser but wiser men know better to avoid.[71]

That Kennedy was and remains an attractive figure there can be no doubt. He was a man of immense charm, dashing good looks, and engaging style and wit. Men enjoyed his company and women competed for his brief flirtations. But those characteristics are not necessarily central to the core of what constitutes a great president—and Kennedy strove to be, as he said, a truly great president. But when his life was tragically over, when a tentative but informed judgment was made, the Kennedy years are troubling ones. There are too many instances of lapses in judgment, overblown rhetoric, and gross miscalculations. The Kennedy legacy is a dangerous one, not heroic but perilous and at times irresponsible.[72]

It is odd that such a conclusion should be drawn from the works of a rather cautious and conservative politician. Kennedy was in his career neither a great social reformer, as FDR or even Lyndon Johnson, nor was he a particularly passionate man in his personal relationships. He was the scion of a wealthy Boston Irish family headed by former Ambassador to Great Britain Joseph P. Kennedy, a Harvard man from a traditional Catholic background, a true war hero, and a proud professional in the art of politics.[73] He loved history, wrote history, and intended to live it. Like many members of his generation, he was fascinated by the epic appeal of Churchill during World War II and converted the challenges of postwar Soviet Communism into another test of wills between the Western democracies and the forces of totalitarianism. Kennedy seemed to realize that greatness could only be garnered in battle with a great enemy, and he turned his times into a period more perilous than the facts should have accounted for.[74]

Eisenhower had matched the challenges of the Soviets with a mixture of caution, moderation, and secret violence. He avoided much of the high-blown rhetoric of the Kennedys; in part, he had already made his historical reputation in a conflict of true global significance. Most telling is the story of Kennedy and Eisenhower riding to the 1960 inauguration. The new president asked his predecessor what he thought of a particular history of the landing on D-Day. Eisenhower blandly responded he had not read the book. He didn't have to, he had lived it.[75]

The president was immediately faced with certain realities: his election was only by the smallest margin, and he recognized Jefferson's axiom that one could not undertake great reforms upon a slim mandate. Kennedy had won the office by only 120,000 votes out of the 68 million cast, and there was substantial evidence of vote fraud in Illinois and Texas, both states that JFK had carried in the official tally. He generally ran behind congressional candidates in their own districts and, unlike Franklin Roosevelt, he could not claim much of a coattail effect to win their gratitude. Nixon had run a surprisingly strong campaign, considering the fact that the Democratic party was then the majority party, and the GOP under Eisenhower had been stymied, especially in the 1957–60 period.

Kennedy was helped by his first television debate with Vice President Nixon, but his Catholicism hurt him, losing him a net of 1.5 million votes.

The new president's brief inaugural address was a clarion call to greatness and to self-sacrifice for the common good. Years later to an America weary from Vietnam and angered by Watergate, Kennedy's admonitions seemed hollow, self-serving, and bellicose. His words epitomized the hard line toward Communism, the high-level mark of Cold War rhetoric. Friendly historians have tried to reinterpret Kennedy in a more moderate light, but his basic views are fairly clear: he believed that the two superpowers were locked in a fierce rivalry, and that his role, like Churchill's a generation before, was to awaken the complacent to accept the awesome challenges and achieve once again superiority. The keynote word of the Kennedy years was "vigor," and the test of a man's mettle was his "toughness." Yet when faced with the consequences of his pose, Kennedy would fall back on more pragmatic and prudent behavior, preaching the need for a world of diverse political systems and an accommodation with the Soviet bloc. It is difficult to be Churchill in a period of nuclear weapons and limited war.[76]

Kennedy's initial conservative inclinations could be seen in his early appointments: he named Eisenhower's assistant secretary of state, wealthy banker C. Douglas Dillon, to head Treasury, Ford auto executive Robert McNamara to Defense, and he kept on J. Edgar Hoover in the FBI, and Allen Dulles at the CIA. The new president passed over the darling of the liberals in his party, Adlai E. Stevenson, and named a little known Acheson protégé, Dean Rusk, to be secretary of state. His cabinet was substantially younger than Eisenhower's by an average of ten years, more academic in background, and infused with his own sense of activism. Later as the Kennedy and Johnson administrations moved into the morass of Vietnam, more critical judgments were passed on the men who liked to think of themselves as "the best and the brightest."[77]

Kennedy named his younger brother Robert, or Bobby as he was called, attorney general at the insistence of his father. The new president quickly abandoned Eisenhower's formal advisory committees and abolished the chief of staff position altogether. Kennedy saw himself as the nerve center of his personal staff, at the hub of a wheel of spokes leading out to the various arms of government. However, instead of encouraging creativity and innovation, his administration often seemed amateurish and confused, especially in making policy in foreign affairs and defense matters. The president called his administration the "New Frontier," and the New Frontiersmen seemed filled with style, ambition, and invincible self-confidence about their ability to reawaken the weary world and the somnolent American republic. Action, ideas, options were the new president's agenda, but the problems he faced often seemed distressingly intractable.

THE POLITICS OF CONFRONTATION

In the transition, Eisenhower had warned his successor about instability in Laos and urged a tough stand, and the new president quickly learned that those predictions were correct. Both Eisenhower and Kennedy shared a belief in the domino theory—that the loss of that once quiet kingdom would lead to vast repercussions for the Western world in its battle against the forces of expansionist Communism. Kennedy, like Eisenhower, shied away from placing U.S. forces into such an uncertain theater, and so once again an American president approved of the CIA's covert actions to keep a nation in the U.S. camp. Under Eisenhower and under Kennedy, Laos became a major recipient of millions of dollars of military assistance in order to keep Prince Souvanna Phouma and his neutralist government out of power. The better organized pro-Soviet Pathet Lao became more aggressive and Kennedy considered what steps to take. Preoccupied with Cuba, as will be seen, and bitter at the Bay of Pigs fiasco, the new president hesitated in intervening so far away. He moved toward a diplomatic settlement and applied pressure on the Soviets to help reach an accommodation.[78]

The situation in the region became more complicated by Communist threats in Vietnam. The United States under Eisenhower had refused to accept the treaty settlement there, although it had in fact recognized the bankruptcy of French rule. The Communist nationalists, led by Ho Chi Minh, had consolidated their control in the north and were moving to undermine the South Vietnamese regime of Ngo Dinh Diem. The Eisenhower administration had initiated plans to combat guerrilla warfare and was pressing for social reforms to win the minds and hearts of the people. In mid-February 1961, Kennedy's advisors began to negotiate with Diem and offered him U.S. troops, which he proudly rejected. Concerned about the strength of Communism in the underdeveloped world, Kennedy overruled the U.S. military and created a separate antiguerrilla military unit, called the Special Forces, or the "Green Berets," and he established a new National Security Council committee on counterinsurgency.

Early in Kennedy's administration, American policy makers began flying back and forth to Vietnam, becoming more aware of the bizarre politics and complex hostilities that characterized Diem and the world in which he functioned. In March, Kennedy pushed for a guarantee of neutrality in neighboring Laos. The president's military advisors were sharply divided over Laos, and Kennedy walked away from their councils discouraged and dismayed. The debate over Laos showed early warning signs of a split between political and military leaders—a split that was to plague Kennedy later in his responses to Castro's Cuba. The Joint Chiefs recommended committing sixty thousand U.S. troops to the area, with a warning that they must be supported even if nuclear weapons had to be used. Observing American movements in Southeast Asia, Soviet Premier Khrushchev philosophically concluded that Laos was like a ripe apple that would fall into Communist laps without going to war. In the end, he proved to be correct.

Kennedy found that U.S. allies in the Southeast Asia Treaty Organization (SEATO) would not concur in unified action, and having raised up the conflict into a test of wills, he now had to figure out how to back down. In a peculiar development, the president urged British Prime Minister Harold Macmillan to contact his old friend Eisenhower and explain his dilemma. Kennedy especially feared Republican cries of appeasement after the loss of another Asian country to Communism. The Kennedy brothers also decided not to bring charges against Ike's former chief of staff, Sherman Adams, who had resigned in 1958 after allegations of receiving gifts and favors while in public office. That move was probably designed to assure the former president's gratitude at a particularly difficult moment for the administration. Deeply committed to a bipartisan foreign policy, but privately suspicious of Kennedy's judgment, Eisenhower, like the good soldier he was, publicly supported his successor on Laos and on so many other matters as well.[79]

By late April substantial support was building in the government for committing troops in Laos. The CIA was already using the Meo and Montagnards in Vietnam to undercut Communist support in those areas. Kennedy's civilian advisors opposed the use of U.S. troops, and the president approved of covert activities but shied away from committing conventional forces at the time. The British and Russians supported a cease-fire, and a peaceful settlement began to gather support just as Kennedy was faced with rising intransigence by his own military.

The administration finally accepted a coalition government headed up by Souvanna Phouma, although U.S. leaders knew that the chances of that country becoming Communist were rather high. Kennedy's advisors were clearly looking for a temporary respite in order to distance themselves from the "fall of Laos." Despite the tough talk, the New Frontiersmen did not choose the tiny kingdom to be the wall of freedom they wanted to stand watch on. In this sense, they were no different from Eisenhower and Dulles.

In South Vietnam, however, the administration drew the line, and its implications were far reaching for the nation and the Democratic party. Soon after the Laotian cease-fire, the president decided to send Vice President Johnson to South Vietnam, and the United States added four hundred Green Berets to the advisors already there training the Diem army. Kennedy approved an expansion of intelligence and covert and political/psychological activities to support the regime. Back home, the major Republican leaders, except Eisenhower, stepped up their attacks on Kennedy for an ineffectual foreign policy, and Vice President Johnson warned that the Laos settlement had shaken Diem's confidence in the United States.[80]

Kennedy's troubles in Southeast Asia were mounting, but nowhere would he encounter more problems than in dealing with Cuba. In the campaign of 1960, JFK had hit hard at the ineptness of the Republican administration in letting Communism be transplanted in Cuba. His position on Cuba allowed Kennedy to appear tough on Communism and to deflect the GOP charges of how Truman lost China and FDR had betrayed the West at Yalta. Now the Democrats turned the issue around and used it with the same zest and vigor as Nixon and McCarthy had exploited the fall of the Chiang Kai-shek regime on mainland China.

Following the pattern of the CIA's moves in Iran and Guatemala, Eisenhower had begun planning, as has been noted, a covert operation to topple Castro. Kennedy apparently was informed of the plans in a general sense during the 1960 campaign, and later allowed the agency to move along on its initiatives with the proviso that the United States would not be demonstrably involved. Kennedy apologists later argued that the new president was reluctant to cancel plans drawn up by his predecessor, and that he was not fully briefed on the proposed invasion at the Bay of Pigs. However, the record surely indicates that Kennedy and his brother were determined to remove Castro, and that that determination at times bordered on obsession.

Even Theodore Sorensen, John Kennedy's closest professional associate, observed that the president "should never have permitted his own deep feelings against Castro (unusual for him) and considerations of public opinion . . . to override his innate suspicions." The president pointedly realized the possibility of failure and went ahead; as he explained to Sorensen in the macho vocabulary of the New Frontier, "I know everybody is grabbing their nuts on this." The president's national security advisor, McGeorge Bundy, concluded later, "I never realized until after he made the decision what I now believe, that he wanted it to work, and allowed himself to be persuaded it would work and the risks were acceptable."[81]

President Kennedy, however, continued to insist that the invasion be accomplished without visible U.S. involvement. The CIA planners and the Cuban exiles doubted that would be possible, but they apparently let the president believe otherwise, figuring that if circumstances warranted a change in policy, Kennedy would be forced to do so. As has been seen, Eisenhower had tried a similar guise in Guatemala, but when faced with a choice of defeat or naked intervention, he realized that the United States had gone too far to back down. Also, Eisenhower, the strategist of the greatest amphibious invasions in the history of warfare, was able to ask detailed and informed questions on this type of assault. As it turned out, the CIA misjudged Castro's ability to move quickly, his knowledge of the terrain and the people of the region, and the weakness of the resistance to him on the island.

But central to the disaster was Kennedy's decision not to use U.S. air cover to protect the landing of anti-Castro forces. The president did try to make clear again and again his position that the invasion must be a Cuban response to Castro, and the CIA fostered that illusion by creating a revolutionary council or government-in-exile under the former Castro premier, Jose Miro Cardona.

As rumors spread about the invasion, Kennedy publicly disassociated himself from it, indicating that "there will not be, under any circumstances, an intervention in Cuba by the United States Armed Forces." Reports came in that three Cuban air bases were being bombed by B-26 bombers, and Castro moved decisively to thwart the invasion he had predicted and that the administration was still denying. At the United Nations, Ambassador Adlai Stevenson denied the charge that it was a United States-sponsored invasion only to find out he was misinformed by his own government.

Now Kennedy was faced with a critical decision: would he approve the second strike at Castro's air bases as a prelude to establishing a beachhead for the landing? The president refused. By miscalculation, secrecy, and poor planning, the insurgents stood naked before Castro's command of the air and his superior forces on land. Some rebels were killed and many others were captured while Kennedy belatedly ordered six unmarked jets to provide cover for a B-21 raid from Nicaraguan bases. The entire plan turned into a major fiasco and intense criticism fell on the administration. Kennedy resolutely faced the consequences, taking full blame and remarking later that while victory had a thousand fathers, defeat was an orphan. Privately his advisors laid the blame at the door of the CIA, and the Kennedy brothers' resentment turned toward the military and, oddly enough, Castro.[82]

Kennedy moved to offset some criticism by visiting with major Republican leaders, most importantly Eisenhower, again. Once more Ike publicly supported his successor, while he sharply criticized him to his face, and he wrote down his impression that "if the whole story ever becomes known to the American people," it would cause an uproar. The old general concluded it was a "profile in timidity and indecision." Later Kennedy paid a courtesy call on another aging military man, Douglas MacArthur, who told Kennedy to avoid intervening in Cuba since it did not represent a military danger at that time, and warned him against committing American troops in Asia.[83]

As the postmortem reports came in, the Cuban invasion plans drew more intense criticism, as did the CIA's role in it. It was never clear what a successful invasion was meant to accomplish. Despite the bravado talk of a possible uprising against Castro by the people, such an eventuality was obviously remote. Castro was not Arbenz; he was a professional revolutionary, a dedicated guerrilla warrior, and a fighter who never would quit. What was the purpose of the invasion and of the terrible sacrifice of brave men? Kennedy, who treasured bravery, felt especially troubled by their capture and loss, and he struggled to get them ransomed and sent back home. Ironically his hold on the American people continued, and his popularity hit an incredible 83 percent approval rating after the fiasco.

To add to Kennedy's woes, he decided to meet with Russian Premier Khrushchev, who continued to threaten the West about the status of West Berlin. The new president was anxious to see his adversary face-to-face and to reason with him on the great controversies that divided the superpowers. With little preparation for the summit in Vienna, Kennedy, in considerable back pain, left for the meeting in June. To deal with the pain, he was under care of Dr. Max Jacobsen, a physician catering to the rich and famous, who earned the name "Dr. Feelgood" for his easy prescription of amphetamines. One Kennedy biographer, Thomas Reeves, has concluded that for the rest of his term, the president was under Jacobsen's care, and that Kennedy even wanted to put him up in the White House. Whether Kennedy was affected at Vienna by potent drugs or whether he simply misjudged Khrushchev at first, the results of the meetings with the volatile Russian were disappointing.[84] The young president seemed to have emerged from those conversations "shaken and angry" in the words of one newspaper columnist who saw him. Bobby Kennedy later agreed with the conclusion that the president seemed "a tongue-tied young man" on the first day, but insisted that at the second meeting with Khrushchev he was more forceful. Khrushchev, however, later wrote in what are believed to be his memoirs that Kennedy was well prepared and seemed more in control than Eisenhower, but that he was committed to protecting the forces of the status quo in the world.[85]

While the Russian premier reiterated the need for a separate East German peace treaty, Kennedy repeatedly warned about miscalculations and the possibility of war between the two great nuclear powers. After the summit, Soviet attitudes began to harden and Khrushchev pushed the German issue, seeking a treaty recognizing the postwar division of that nation. Bobby Kennedy later concluded that Khrushchev thought his brother was "not going to be a strong figure based, in my judgment, on the fact we didn't use American forces to crush Cuba . . . and thought he was a young, inexperienced figure."

After the summit, the president himself felt that the probability of war was close, and he began to speak of a preemptive first strike—a reversal of U.S. doctrine of striking only in self-defense. Then on July 25, 1961, he addressed the nation in a frightening speech in which he doubled the number of draftees, called up reserve units, added two hundred thousand men to the armed forces, and increased the defense budget by $3.25 billion. In addition to those steps, he proposed an upgraded civil defense program and supported the construction of bomb shelters on an unheard-of scale.

The public once again agreed with the president, and 71 percent of the respondents in public opinion polls supported using armed forces to protect Berlin. Harry Truman lost his qualms about Kennedy and praised his "great speech."[86]

Whereas Eisenhower tended to downplay crises, Kennedy had done the opposite. His meeting with Khrushchev was ill thought out and weakly conducted; his response to the premier's blusterings (probably due in part to Red Army pressure) was overblown and a clear overreaction. Khrushchev's next step was novel and harsh: he constructed a wall through the heart of Berlin, keeping in prospective refugees and creating a new symbol of the Cold War. Kennedy refused to heed calls to rip it down and may have even secretly viewed it as a solution to the Berlin crisis. Then, at the end of August, Khrushchev resumed nuclear testing and Kennedy ordered a U.S. resumption of testing also. Kennedy's first year on the foreign policy stage had left much to be desired.

UNSTEADY REFORMS

Domestically, the president's record was equally unimpressive as the conservative coalition of southern Democrats and Republicans provided him with little in the way of major victories. Liberals yearned for a return to FDR's One Hundred Days of legislative reform, but Kennedy was no Roosevelt, and 1961 was not 1933. Supporters of the president began to lament the "deadlock of democracy," that is the inability of the executive to assert ascendancy over the Congress as Wilson had done in his first term and FDR in his first six years.[87]

But in fairness to Kennedy, he had no preparatory period of reform the way Wilson had, or the sense of urgency that greeted FDR. Education in the American system must precede activity, and it was Kennedy more than any other political figure who was creating the modest reform agenda of the early 1960s. Unlike Theodore Roosevelt and especially Woodrow Wilson, Kennedy was not the beneficiary of the progressive impulses. The 1950s were not a stagnant period, but the currents of reform were not paramount in either political or social life. Slowly were they gathering, especially in civil rights, and civil rights was not a consensus-building issue for a Democratic president dependent on southern committee chairs in Congress.

The conventional wisdom about Kennedy's legislative record is that he was not successful. But actually, he did make some real advances in domestic affairs. In part, he did not accomplish more because of the brevity of his term in office and the margin of the 1960 election. And to some extent, he just lacked the patience and legislative skills to flatter, cajole, and threaten members of Congress. His successor, Lyndon Johnson, would both reap Kennedy's bounty and harness it to his own considerable skills as a legislative strategist. The age of reform would come as the Great Society and not as the New Frontier.[88]

The president, however, was outstandingly successful in using live television at his news conferences and quickly became a star in his own right. He was successful in pushing through the Alliance for Progress as an antidote to Castroism and a reaffirmation of the possibilities of democratic reform in Latin America. Kennedy also sought out a moderate policy in the emerging nations of black Africa. At home, he increased food distribution to the needy, pushed for labor-management harmony, extolled the values of production, and finally agreed to a modest tax cut that stimulated the economy even with a deficit budget. Congress approved his Area Redevelopment Act to aid depressed areas, raised the minimum wage, and agreed to a comprehensive housing bill. But carefully and cautiously, he stayed away from any real initiatives on civil rights. Fearing he would antagonize southern Democrats, he even avoided signing an executive order that he promised would abolish, with the stroke of a pen, discrimination in public housing.

But controversial proposals for medical care for the elderly and aid to public schools got immersed in hostile lobbying. Most exciting but probably in the long run less consequential, Congress passed a bill establishing the Peace Corps, an idealistic proposal to send young Americans and also older ones to foreign countries to help them upgrade levels of education, public health, and social services. In a short period of time, the president's Gallup approval rating was at 72 percent and even increased, as has been seen, after the Bay of Pigs. Thus, it seemed that, despite problems in Congress and a string of difficulties abroad, the president had charmed his way into the hearts of many of the American people.

Kennedy's popularity, though, was soon affected by two issues, the first being his decision to force big steel to roll back price increases, and the second, civil rights. The administration had thought that by using its influence on the unions, the steel companies would gratefully not raise prices. In fact, U.S. Steel did exactly that by $6 a ton, and the president and his administration responded a bit heavy-handedly to what they saw as a personal betrayal. As with Castro and Khrushchev, the Kennedy brothers tended to view differences of opinion as personal challenges to their leadership and to their sense of toughness. Finally, U.S. Steel rolled back its increases, in part because segments of the industry refused to raise prices due to demand problems. The president incurred more criticism when he was quoted as agreeing with his father that businessmen were "sons of bitches."[89]

But the steel controversy was less significant than the increasing conflict over civil rights. Kennedy had never been a flaming liberal on many issues, least of all race relations. His upbringing was one of wealth and privilege, and his contacts with blacks were few and far between. To him, discrimination was the way Yankee Boston treated the Irish, rich and poor. But he opposed racial discrimination and assumed a position of true moral leadership on an issue that excited the types of passions that he could never feel. At first, the president was hesitant and did the minimally correct things. He deplored violence, pointed to the irrationality of racism, and reminded Americans of how badly such behavior reflected on the great United States' democracy all over the world. But racism does not lend itself to a reasoning away, nor could it be compromised out of existence.

The civil rights movement born in the 1950s to a new generation of leaders had moved from the courts into the streets. Nonviolent civil disobedience, led by Dr. Martin Luther King, Jr., and his associates, was aimed at disrupting the status quo and forcing a reevaluation of segregated ways of living. Gradually and irrevocably, the Justice Department, the attorney general, and the president were drawn into the vortex—to protect black and white bus riders, to ensure the rights of blacks to go to public universities in the South, and to guarantee them the right to vote.

Kennedy pleaded for law and order, and reached back into the American democratic heritage for an antidote against its older sister, racism. Finally, he signed an executive order quietly barring discrimination in public housing. Still he refused to tie up Congress by submitting a civil rights bill to be filibustered to death. Civil rights was not his issue yet.

Meanwhile in Birmingham, Alabama, Dr. King pushed hard to recoup his losses elsewhere, as he aimed at destroying discrimination in that tough, recalcitrant city. There King and later the administration faced increasing difficulties, which yielded to no easy settlement. In addition, the governor of that state, George Wallace, stopped black students from being admitted to the University of Alabama at Tuscaloosa. The National Guard had to be federalized, and administration officials were sent to the city to force the issue. Faced with increasing unrest, the president decided to forward a civil rights bill to Congress that included the right for all to use public accommodations, attacked segregation in public education, and guaranteed voting rights. A proposal to end discrimination in employment was not added originally, but the president later endorsed it.

As President Kennedy stepped forward beyond the violence and the recriminations, he assumed that much vaunted position of moral leadership he so often spoke of . . . and his popularity began to tumble. Gallup polls showed that 36 percent of Americans thought he was pushing integration too fast, and by September his approval rating had dropped from a high of 81 percent to 53 percent. And as he feared, the legislative process came to a halt as a divided Congress considered civil rights. The animosity spilled over to other bills being considered, as border states and southern Democrats proved more reluctant to go along with New Frontier legislation in social and economic areas. Kennedy never saw the successes of the civil rights legislation he advocated. By the time it passed, it was Lyndon Johnson's responsibility, and he made it his issue and his cause in a way Kennedy never did.[90]

THE CUBAN MISSILE CRISIS

With all of this activity in the brief three years of his tenure, Kennedy will still be mainly remembered for his actions during the Cuban Missile Crisis. In the Cold War period, the two great superpowers had come close to conflict but almost always through surrogates. As has been noted, the United States avoided getting involved in the Hungarian Revolution or in the Polish uprisings just as the Soviets refused to confront the United States in Latin America or even in Korea. Prudence on both sides staved off direct confrontation.

The Cuban Missile Crisis was a major and dangerous exception. Kennedy's own role in the crisis has been misunderstood, for he was more responsible both for the initiation of the crisis and also for the ending of it. In the process, he and Khrushchev brought the world dangerously close to nuclear war, not by design but by possible miscalculation. The Missile Crisis is usually portrayed as a fine example of flexible response and determined presidential leadership. Instead Kennedy's behavior was oftentimes directed more by crass domestic political calculations than by a rational sense of American security interests. Twenty years later, the survivors of the Kennedy inner circle celebrated that great triumph and even praised reckless Khrushchev for his statesmanlike behavior. Such is the way revisionist history is rewritten, and heroes created in a secular world.

The first confusing question is why did the Russians, usually a fairly conservative power, allow missile bases to be built so far away from their borders. Unlike the United States, Britain, and even China, Russian regimes have been wary of losing control over their military might. In 1992, after the demise of the USSR, it was alleged that the Soviet troop commander in Cuba had the authority, if circumstances warranted it, to unleash nine Soviet short-range atomic weapons against invading U.S. troops. Khrushchev in his memoirs, however, never indicated such a delegation of power. He did explain that he decided to build missile bases to protect the Castro government from U.S. aggression, to equalize the balance of power, and to teach the Americans what it was like to have enemy missiles pointed at their land. For years after the crises, Kennedy historians and friends ignored the first rationale, but more recent evidence shows that there is considerable credibility to Khrushchev's and Castro's claims.

It is obvious that the Kennedy brothers had a nearly consuming obsession with Castro, viewing his regime not only as a problem to American security interests in the region, but also as a personal affront. Despite traditional views that President Kennedy's failure at the Bay of Pigs led to a more moderate or at least a more restrained policy toward Cuba, it is clear that the administration actually stepped up its covert operations to topple the Castro regime and eliminate, that is, assassinate the Cuban dictator.

Just before the Missile Crisis, Robert Kennedy told the Special Augmented Group (SAG) that the president was concerned about the slow progress of "Operation Mongoose," and "that more priority should be given to sabotage operations." Years later, Secretary of Defense Robert McNamara told a Senate committee, "We were hysterical about Castro at the time of the Bay of Pigs and thereafter." Those same hearings revealed that the CIA had undertaken a variety of schemes—some zany and harebrained—to discredit and/ or eliminate Castro. The CIA director at the time, Richard Helms, pointedly testified that the pressure from the Kennedys over Castro was very intense, and that if killing Castro were one of the things to be done, then that was within what was expected. The Senate committee concluded that it had evidence of at least eight American government-directed murder plots against Castro over the years, although the Cuban dictator said the number was closer to twenty-four.

At that time, President Kennedy was having an affair with a woman who was also involved with a major leader of the Mafia. Kennedy biographer Thomas Reeves has concluded that the Kennedys had used him and other organized crime gangsters to help carry Illinois in the closely fought election in 1960. That underworld figure and an associate had also been allegedly hired by the CIA in the Eisenhower years to kill Castro for $150,000. When Attorney General Kennedy heard of the arrangement, he apparently warned his brother (who ended his relationship with the woman), expressed his outrage at the use of alleged gangsters, and demanded to be informed if the CIA ever became involved with underworld types again. Interestingly, there is no record of Robert Kennedy having been upset about the assassination plot against a foreign leader.

President Kennedy admitted that assassination schemes aimed at Castro were brought to his attention, but he insisted that he rejected them. Yet it is a matter of record that Secretary McNamara openly raised the possibility of assassination, and in 1971, Lyndon Johnson observed that on taking office he found that "we had been operating a damned Murder Inc. in the Caribbean." Kennedy's special assistant, Harris Wofford, has speculated that Robert Kennedy's long and deep melancholy after his brother's death was due to the fact that the attorney general had tolerated, if not encouraged, assassination plots against foreign leaders, and thus made his own brother more vulnerable to reprisals. After President Kennedy's death, endless and often unsubstantiated rumors circulated about the roles of Lee Harvey Oswald, Castro, the Mafia, and other named and unnamed characters in the assassination.

Despite Kennedy's warnings about a "missile gap" in the 1960 election, the United States was far ahead of the Russians, and Khrushchev, for all his blusterings over Berlin, recognized that fact. In October 1961, the administration decided to let the Russians know that U.S. intelligence sources had comprehensive knowledge of those force levels, and in early 1962, the president spoke of a first-strike use of U.S. missiles—a sharp reversal of America's more restrained policy. All of these steps surely added to the anxieties of the Russian leadership and probably encouraged Khrushchev to try to even the balance of power. Based on Kennedy's handling of the Bay of Pigs and his weakness at Vienna, Khrushchev may have judged that there was little chance that the new president would press the issue once presented with a fait accompli. Kennedy's assessment of the Russian premier was blunt, "That son of a bitch won't pay attention to words. He has to see you move."

At first the administration saw a buildup taking place in 1962 in Cuba, and warned about the placement of "offensive" (but not "defensive") weapons—a qualification difficult to delineate. Later the president spoke forcefully about the balance of power in the region, but his secretary of defense, the head of the Marine Corps, and advisor and former Secretary of State Acheson all agreed that missiles in Cuba presented no military threat.

Kennedy was worried about more than the strategic balance; he was also concerned about personally appearing to look weak and ineffectual once again. That political fear was so profound that he was willing in the end to risk nuclear war rather than face that threat to his image and self-concept. All his adult life, Kennedy had cultivated a pose of courage and toughness, and yet in two years in office he had taken responsibility for the Bay of Pigs fiasco, proposed an unsteady neutralization of Laos, committed American troops to the worsening situation in Vietnam, supported some less than viable moderate leaders in Latin America, been bested by Khrushchev in Vienna, watched helplessly as the Berlin Wall went up, and failed to win greater unanimity among the NATO nations. At home, his ability to lead Congress was frequently criticized and his legislative track record was denigrated, especially in comparison to FDR's first brilliant term. Armed with U.S. intelligence showing Soviet military levels much lower than he had assumed, Kennedy was prepared to draw the line on this issue. Khrushchev's recklessness and clandestine behavior left the burden on him, a burden he could not extricate himself from in a theater of action thousands of miles away from the Soviet Union.

Kennedy associate Roger Hilsman concluded, "The United States might not be in danger, but the Administration most certainly was." John Kenneth Galbraith went further and added, "once they [the missiles] were there, the political needs of the Kennedy Administration urged it to take almost any risk to get them out." The president had confided that if he did not act, he thought he would have been impeached.

And so the president informed the American people, and the world, of his institution of a naval blockade around Cuba and warned, "The greatest danger of all would be to do nothing." With dissension from some of the military and congressional leaders who wanted an air strike or invasion, the president held to the blockade, hoping that it would give Khrushchev time to rethink his position before a confrontation occurred on the high seas. When the premier's intentions were unclear, Kennedy apparently considered a deadline after which he would launch an air strike that surely would end up killing Russian technicians and military men. Khrushchev sent two responses—one conciliatory, a later one more bellicose. Kennedy admirers like to tell how Bobby urged them to respond to the first and ignore the second, a brilliant ploy that was supposed to have ended the crisis.

In fact, the president ended the crisis, fearing always that miscalculation would bring nuclear war. When a U.S. reconnaissance plane entered Russian air space during this tense period and the Cubans shot down a U-2 plane over their island, the president on both occasions urged restraint and pulled back. He knew he had most of the cards in the game, but was too much a student of World War I not to remember the missteps that supposedly led to that conflagration. Finally, the president let it be known that he would guarantee that there would be no further invasion attempts of Cuba, and also that he would dismantle Jupiter missiles in Turkey after Russian missile sites were dismantled on the island. The allies and the American people were not to know about the latter deal until years after the crisis when JFK's major aides confirmed the conditions of the understanding, which they had previously denied vigorously. Thus Kennedy learned all too well that it was the president's decision alone. He had helped to force the confrontation, and he took seriously the possibilities of human error in such tense times.[91]

Khrushchev's withdrawal was celebrated in the United States and in Western Europe as a defeat for the premier, and Kennedy had his greatest triumph. Even his bitterest critics were silenced and the president became in his own time an almost mythical figure. He had "gone eyeball to eyeball," in Secretary Rusk's words, and the Soviets had blinked. JFK had his big victory, and yet he characteristically refused to gloat. In part, Kennedy recognized the terrible lengths he had gone to in reasserting his leadership, the ambivalences of the situation, and his own role in precipitating the crisis. As for Khrushchev, he began to lose his control over the Communist party. For important elements of the Russian leadership, his behavior confirmed that he was just too erratic to stay in power. Added to those resentments was opposition to his post-Stalinist liberalization; later in October 1964, he was forced to retire. His successors began a massive buildup of the military—in part, probably to avoid such a humiliation ever again.

Kennedy in late 1962 and early 1963 had seen the nuclear precipice and drew back from its horrors. After Khrushchev's initiative in December to end nuclear testing, the president pushed for a nuclear arms control treaty and abandoned much of his Churchillian rhetoric. With a concerted and skillful campaign to get bipartisan support, Kennedy obtained Senate approval for the treaty. Now he began to talk about making the world safe for diversity—for different ideological systems and not about an endless twilight struggle in which one side must vanquish the other. The only exception was his impassioned speech on June 26 in East Germany when he emotionally attacked the Berlin Wall and declared that he, like all people who loved freedom, was a true citizen of Berlin.

With all of these preoccupations in foreign affairs, the president still had to deal with the deadlock on civil rights. The civil rights controversy continued to garner attention and forced him to spend precious political capital. American intervention in Latin America and the Mideast showed the limits of U.S. power, and Congress proved even more reluctant to follow his lead in general. The president was learning the complexities of the postwar presidency—how easy it is to bring the world to the brink of destruction, how difficult to reform its habits either at home or abroad.

GOING INTO VIETNAM

Before his assassination in Dallas on November 22, 1963, the president helped to plunge the nation into the quagmire that would become American foreign policy in South Vietnam. Those initial commitments of U.S. forces and money would lead to full-scale war, civil disturbance, disillusionment, and the eventual division of the Democratic party's ruling coalition. When he avoided sending troops

to Laos, the president noted that the Bay of Pigs fiasco was ironically fortunate, for it kept him from moving into Southeast Asia.
DeGaulle and MacArthur had both warned him about making military commitments there—both men experienced in the complexities
of ruling and waging war.

In 1962, however, Kennedy had increased U.S. involvement,
pushed Diem unsuccessfully to make reforms, and made the decisions that led to a greater American presence and American casualties in that faraway nation. The Viet Cong forces supported by the
North Vietnamese began to control more and more villages in the
south, and military and civilian authorities were plotting to overthrow Diem. In September, Kennedy publicly supported the "domino
theory" and argued that South Vietnam was essential to the future
of a free Southeast Asia. A Communist victory would give impetus
to Red China and its allies. As Buddhist opposition to Diem grew,
the regime there was imperiled. Partially to co-opt the Republicans,
Kennedy made a decision to send Republican Henry Cabot Lodge
to be U.S. ambassador to Vietnam.

There is some evidence that Lodge was sent to aid in Diem's
overthrow, although the president concluded, "the Vietnamese are
doing that for themselves and don't need any outside help." As for
his part, the South Vietnamese president was both attacking Buddhist pagodas and quietly trying to work out a deal with the North
Vietnamese. Lodge supported the generals opposed to Diem, and
some of the major leaders of the U.S. government agreed with his
stance. That decision however split the administration, and a reti-
cent president seemed confused as to what to do. Lodge informed
him that it was too late to turn back, and Kennedy gave his full
support to the ambassador.[92]

Concerned about persistent rumors and reports that Diem was
dealing with Hanoi, the president sent his secretary of defense and
General Maxwell Taylor to South Vietnam. Diem reassured them
that the war was being won by his forces, and he refused to adhere
to U.S. demands for some outward signs of reform. McNamara and
Taylor reported their findings and warned against the United States'
trying to change the government there, while they both advocated
contacts with "alternative leadership if and when it appears."

On October 2, the administration indicated that one thousand U.S.
military personnel would be withdrawn from Vietnam by the end
of the year, a sign of the president's deep disillusionment about

America's growing role in the war. Later Kennedy, however, approved an increase of U.S. forces to seventeen thousand, but expressed reservations about any further commitment. In a critical decision, the administration pushed for an end of the Diem regime, leaving to the plotting Vietnamese generals what would happen to their president. When Diem was murdered, Kennedy expressed horror and shock to his aides, but confided to Francis Cardinal Spellman of New York that he knew the Vietnamese president would be murdered, but could not control the situation himself. When Kennedy was later killed in Dallas, Diem's widow let it be known that she did not share in the public grief. Kennedy's most balanced biographer, Herbert Parmet, has concluded that Kennedy sent his friend Torbert MacDonald to Diem three times supposedly to warn him that his life was in danger. Diem stubbornly refused to leave his nation and abdicate his position. The president was quoted as having blamed "the bastards" in the CIA and vowed to do something about them later.[93]

After the public disillusionment with the war, some Kennedy aides would insist that the president was ready to withdraw American troops once the 1964 election was over. Such a discovery seems less a statement of wisdom on JFK's part than a damning commentary on his stewardship. Bobby Kennedy, however, insisted that his brother felt that South Vietnam was worth defending more for psychological and political reasons than because of any other consideration, and Dean Rusk insisted that the president never suggested withdrawal. As for the suggestion that Kennedy was waiting for the end of the 1964 election, the secretary of state observed that such a proposal "would have been a decision to have Americans in uniform in combat for domestic political reasons. No president can do that and live with it." The president himself had planned to declare on November 22 that while U.S. assistance in Southeast Asia could be painful, risky, and costly, "we dare not weary of the test." He had in September insisted that while the Vietnamese had to win the war, "I don't agree with those who say we should withdraw. That would be a great mistake."[94]

Kennedy's public position on Vietnam seemed clear despite his deep personal reservations, and it is understandable that Johnson could argue that he was carrying out those policies as he plunged deeper and deeper into the morass of Vietnam. That decision to remain in South Vietnam and move toward a more supportive role in the land war, however, helped to destroy the most significant period of domestic reform since FDR and severely maimed the Democratic party.

On November 22, on a political fence-mending trip through Texas, President Kennedy was assassinated and his alleged murderer, Lee Harvey Oswald, was subsequently slain in front of television cameras by a nightclub operator, Jack Ruby. The nation and most of the world reeled from shock to horror to far-reaching expressions of grief and sadness. The troubled presidency of John F. Kennedy became transposed into a mythical episode of youth, light, and brilliance.

In response to Kennedy critics who cited the paucity of his achievements, Arthur M. Schlesinger, Jr., reminded them that in a thousand days, the time Kennedy spent in office, none of the truly great presidents—Lincoln, Wilson, Franklin D. Roosevelt—had completed their most important accomplishments. Schlesinger is correct that three years is a very brief moment in the life of a nation or the conduct of institutions. Still, one can only judge Kennedy in the end by his record, and it is a chronicle of inspiration, ineptness, overreaction, and genuine achievement in certain areas. On balance, the Kennedy years were ones in which the young president, by either overdramatization or inexperience, added to the peril and uncertainty of those times. Surely as long as people prize wit and grace, the Kennedy circle will have a certain charm because of the images it created and the élan it manufactured. But it is equally certain that as long as sober reflection follows the initial glow, there will be serious questions raised about maturity, wisdom, and personal character. Kennedy will be forever youthful and forever suspended between those two criteria of judgment—earnest popular fascination and responsible public stewardship.

JOHNSON: THE POLITICS
OF PEACE AND REFORM

The sudden and accidental presidency of Lyndon Johnson turned into one of the most creative and controversial in American history. Like the man himself, the Johnson administration seemed at times bigger than life, larger than the vast continent it rested on, more explosive than the sticking fabric that holds a heterogeneous people at rest. If the American political system were a parliamentary system, then Lyndon Baines Johnson would have been America's greatest prime minister, the equal or the superior of William Pitt the Younger, Robert Peel, and William Gladstone. No president, including his patron, Franklin Roosevelt, ever exerted a greater command over Congress; no executive ever mastered the arts of compromise, timing, and consensus better than Johnson. The Eighty-ninth and Ninetieth Congresses unleashed a torrent of domestic legislation, some of it magnificent and humane, some of it undercooked and misguided, but all of it dedicated to the vague axiom that government could make people's lives better and more decent. It is odd and cruelly ironic that a man who so practiced consensus and who was so skilled at it ended up ripping the nation apart and nearly destroying his own party after five short years. By 1968, fearful of his poor health and weary from the controversies of war, Lyndon Johnson bowed out of national politics and the exercise of power he so loved.

He was born into a respectable and well-regarded family in the hill country outside of Austin, Texas, became a legislative assistant in Washington, and finally ran for the House of Representatives and then the Senate as a staunch follower of FDR and the New Deal. In the 1950s, he emerged as an astute master of the Senate's Democrats and a committed supporter of Eisenhower's foreign policy.[95]

The assassination of Kennedy in Johnson's home state presented him with special problems. By all accounts, most importantly Jacqueline Kennedy's personal statements, Johnson handled the transition with sensitivity and strength. He immediately reached out to all segments of American life and touched easily the power centers with care and finesse. Johnson quickly exerted his mastery over a balky Congress, pushing hard for tax reform, foreign aid, and most importantly civil rights. Wearing heavily Kennedy's legacy, he moved to complete the slain president's agenda. He was later to observe, "I took the oath. I became president. But for millions of Americans I was still illegitimate, a naked man with no presidential covering, a pretender to the throne, an illegal usurper. And then there was Texas, my home, the home of the murderer and the murderer of the murderer [Oswald's assailant was Jack Ruby of Dallas]. And then there were the bigots and the dividers and the Eastern intellectuals, who were waiting to knock me down before I could ever begin to stand up. The whole thing was almost unbearable."[96]

If one excludes Virginia-born Woodrow Wilson, Johnson was the first "southern" president since Zachary Taylor, and he knew the importance of ridding himself of the suspicions that he would be weak on civil rights. He insisted on and got a far more comprehensive civil rights bill than Kennedy would probably have signed. Johnson concluded, "I knew that if I didn't get out in front on this issue, they [the liberals] would get me. They'd throw up my background against me, they'd use it to prove that I was incapable of bringing unity to the land I loved so much. . . . I couldn't let that happen. I had to produce a civil rights bill that was even stronger than the one they'd have gotten if Kennedy had lived. Without this, I'd be dead before I could even begin."[97]

And when his term was up, no one could say that Johnson had not proven to be a good and dedicated friend to racial minorities. His record was better than FDR's, more sustained than Kennedy's, more deeply felt than Lincoln's. With a simple sentence he could sum up his concern: he supported civil rights, he said once, because a man had a right not to be embarrassed in front of his children. His philosophy of government was direct and personal. His civil rights efforts rested not on base opportunism or on reckless drama— it ran deep and true, reflecting an optimism that the American dream must reach people of all races. The Great Society represents the high-water mark of political liberalism in this country, and at no time before or since has the income gap between the races closed as rapidly as in the 1960s.

Johnson, a briefly employed teacher of poor Hispanic children, had a dreamer's recourse to education. For him it was the instrument of progress, the mother of social mobility, the destroyer of prejudice and stereotypes. He was called, and he called himself, "the education president," and his administration unleashed the pent-up energies of reformers in preschool education, bilingual and remedial education, aid to the handicapped, assistance to poorer local school districts, financial assistance to college students, and on and on. Johnson skillfully passed a package of federal programs in health, most importantly Medicare and Medicaid. The federal government of LBJ outdid the Roosevelts, both Theodore and Franklin, and extended its sway over conservation, land use, highway beautification, and the whole panoply of what became known as environmentalism.

Many of the ideas and concerns of the Great Society were retreads of the New Deal, in the same way that the New Deal partially recapitulated the progressive movement. And just as with the New Deal, its least successful reforms or innovations were those aimed at helping the very poor rise up the social ladder or achieve a measure of power and dignity. Much of the criticism of the Great Society focused on its attempt to end poverty and give the disadvantaged a greater say in their lives and the operations of government programs affecting them.

The American welfare state is most successful and least politically vulnerable when it provides a cornucopia of benefits to the middle class, such as Social Security, Medicare, GI benefits, low-cost mortgages. But the great discrepancy in wealth is between the very rich and the very poor. The New Deal prevented starvation by nationalizing concern, creating real and make-work government jobs, and providing subsistence wages for millions. Johnson's Great Society focused more energies on these varied groups in the lower class, proclaiming a war on poverty, and promising to abolish economic distress in the land.

The administration set up a new agency, the Office of Economic Opportunity (OEO), headed by a Kennedy brother-in-law, Sargent Shriver, to spearhead those new programs. The enabling legislation, poorly drawn up and loosely planned, called for "maximum feasible participation" of the poor. This gratuitous remark became the charter for the establishment of community action organizations, often manned by local activists and perceived as threats to local Democratic urban machines.[98]

Later those community organizations would be attacked as preserves of black radicals, of opportunistic poverty merchants who really wanted to line their own pockets and create their own political machines. Surely some abuses grew up (just as in old-line urban machines), but the community action groups in many cities became the nurseries for a new generation of leaders, often dedicated to opening up the system to broader representation, which is after all the purpose of democracy. Johnson's subordinates reported to him the tensions between the old and new leadership groups, but apparently the president never publicly broke with the newer grassroots urban populism. Later liberals and conservatives alike attacked the community action initiatives, seeing them as symptomatic of what went wrong with big government and its interventionism. But the community action part of the Great Society was really very small in terms of resources and the government's overall attention. In politics though, one seeks out an opponent's weakest spot and hammers away at it. Empowerment of the powerless was the Achilles heel of the war on poverty, yet in many ways it was as

American as the New England town meeting and a lot more rel-
evant to modern times.[99]

Johnson started out his presidency by striking the proper theme:
"let us continue." He remained faithful to the Kennedy legacy, publicly dedicated to the Kennedy memory, and generous in keeping
his predecessor's team in place. In the month following the
assassination, the new president saw 673 people individually or in
small groups and 3,062 in large gatherings. He confronted Congress
on the issue of foreign aid, and in a powerful display of leadership
just before Christmas, he prevailed in an important vote on the issue. By early 1964, Johnson presented a full agenda of social legislation and carefully exploited the groundwork that Kennedy had
laid for the Civil Rights Act. He took a latent idea on dealing with
poverty and developed it into a full program that he identified with
and that became one of his major domestic legacies.

In his first State of the Union address on January 8, 1964, Johnson called for an offensive against the conditions of poverty, asking that opportunity replace despair. The OEO never had a budget
over $2 billion, but the major departments and agencies adminis-
tered large segments of the Great Society in education, health, and
other areas. Later, critics were to attack the war on poverty as being "underfunded and oversold." Surely the conflict in Vietnam cut
into projected revenues, and the attention directed to that war and
the opposition it generated turned the public's attention away from
domestic reform and good works. Johnson has also been attacked
for his hyperbolic rhetoric, for overpromising, and for raising
expectations especially in the ghettos, which led to black disillusionment and eventually urban rioting. The later criticisms are a bit
out of perspective though. American politicians—right and left, cen-
trist and extremist—overpromise, oversell, and place our meager
temporal existence into the context of various historical destinies
to win support. And to argue that Johnson controlled the tempo of
black discontent is to ignore the dynamics of race relations and rage
that began to permeate both urban ghettos and rural churches in the
1960s.

Johnson at first seized the civil rights initiative with one of the
finest speeches ever given by an American president. On March 31,
1965, he addressed Congress, criticized white resistance to integration in Selma, Alabama, and concluded that the time had come for
full equality for the blacks. "Their cause must be our cause. Because it is not just Negroes, but really it is all of us who must

overcome the crippling legacy of bigotry and injustice." Then he electrified the audience by adopting in his southern cadences the language of the black activists, "And we shall overcome!"[100]

The president recognized that the only hope to break a determined filibuster in the Senate against the civil rights bill was to let the Republican minority leader play the center role in the debate. Skillfully prodded and stroked along, Everett McKinley Dirksen of Illinois eventually provided the GOP votes needed to break the deadlock and get the bill to the floor. The final law mandated open public accommodations, a tougher civil rights commission, more supervision over voter registration and literacy tests, and a greater overall role for the federal government in race relations.[101]

Johnson had begun preaching the benefits of a new burst of liberalism, a Great Society more comprehensive and decent than the fondest dreams of the New Deal. Laying aside the growing problems in Southeast Asia, the president straddled the political system from left to moderate business conservatism. Then he cautiously but delightfully eliminated Robert Kennedy as a vice-presidential possibility, both paying him back for past humiliations and also hoping that he would not be a mere pause between the Kennedy brothers in the White House. The Republicans responded by nominating Senator Barry Goldwater of Arizona, the first real ideological right-wing leader to run on the national ticket since Coolidge. The GOP convention was a bruising and divisive one, and the Democrats simply repeated the charges of Goldwater's foes—that he was trigger-happy in the dangerous nuclear age and willing to destroy Social Security.

When Goldwater paraphrased the Roman orator Cicero and asserted that "Extremism in the defense of liberty is no vice and . . . moderation in the pursuit of justice is no virtue," the worst expectations were confirmed. America in 1964 wanted what Johnson seemingly offered—peace abroad and consensus at home. What they got very soon after the election was war and internal dissension. Oddly enough, civil rights faded from sight in the campaign. The major exception was an extraordinary address in New Orleans where the president courageously spoke about the rising tide for equality, and showed his disdain for politicians in the South who talked at election time only of "nigra, nigra, nigra."[102]

The final result was overwhelming—Johnson carried forty-four states with 61.05 percent of the vote, exceeding even FDR's popular victory in 1936 and Harding's in 1920. Most importantly, the

Democratic party gained over five hundred seats in state legislatures, twelve state governorships from the Republicans, and the
Senate was to be Democratic controlled by a 68 to 32 margin and
the House by a margin of 295 to 140. Johnson had the type of
popular approval that he translated into love; he concluded, "I have
spent my whole life getting ready for this moment." But he also
understood the fleeting nature of victory. He rushed and pushed hard,
remarking on one occasion to congressional liaison staff people, "I
was just elected president by the biggest margin in the history of
the country—16 million votes. Just by the way people naturally think
and because Barry Goldwater had simply scared hell out of them,
I've already lost about three of those sixteen. After a fight with
Congress or something else, I'll lose another couple of million. I
could be down to 8 million in a couple of months."[103]

The president moved skillfully to fuse his personal popularity
and a legislative agenda into a common program. He pulled together
task forces in different areas, which worked on a confidential basis
and courted key congressmen. As the president explained it,

> The trick was to crack the wall of separation enough to give the
> Congress a feeling of participation in creating my bills without ex-
> posing my plans at the same time to advance congressional
> opposition before they even saw the light of day. It meant taking
> risks, but the risks were worth it. Legislative drafting is a political
> act. The president is continually faced with a number of tough
> choices: how to strike a balance between the bill he really wants
> and the bill he's got a good chance of getting; how to choose be-
> tween a single-purpose or omnibus bill; how to package the bill for
> the Hill, when to send it up. In all the choices the president needs
> congressional judgment, and if he's wise, he seeks it.

Johnson later remarked that people tend to associate legislative
success with crises or assassinations, but he emphasized how he laid
the groundwork for his successes. "I'd do it like the British system," he observed, advocating close working relationships with
Congress, advance notice, and rewards and visibility for instrumental legislators to bask in. "There is but one way for a president to
deal with the Congress, and that is continuously, incessantly, and
without interruption. If it's going to work, the relationship between
the president and Congress has got to be almost incestuous."

The astute tactician counseled, "A measure must be sent to the

Hill at exactly the right moment and that moment depends on three things: first, on momentum; second, on the availability of sponsors in the right place at the right time; and third, on the opportunities for neutralizing the opposition. Timing is essential. Momentum is *not* a mysterious mistress. It is a controllable fact of political life that depends on nothing more exotic than preparation." Still, a master of the process like Johnson warned about pushing Congress too much, observing that the legislative branch "is like a dangerous animal" that is likely to "turn around and go wild" if your timing is off.[104]

Even John Kenneth Galbraith had to admit, "He was far better than Kennedy (and I think than Roosevelt) in winning the requisite response from the Congress." Carl Albert, later Speaker of the House, concluded also that Johnson's legislative performance was "far greater than Roosevelt's." LBJ concentrated his efforts usually on swing legislators, read carefully each morning the *Congressional Record*, dealt with legislators one on one or in small groups for maximum effect, analyzed what they wanted and needed, and masterly controlled the pace of his immense stream of recommendations. He warned, "Without constant attention from the administration, most legislation passes through the congressional process with the speed of a glacier."[105]

Despite popular belief, Johnson did not seal support with patronage or direct deals. He cultivated legislators, letting them know he needed their help, and that they could count on his assistance later for matters of concern to them. After thirty-four years in the legislative branch, he knew its idiosyncrasies and oddities better than anyone in his time or maybe of any period in American history.

Johnson worked closely with his congressional liaison people and controlled his staff in a way alien to Nixon and Reagan. Like FDR, he avoided firm staff assignments and played advisors off against one another in often childish ways to keep power in his own hands. Yet the bureaucracy was more complex and rigid than in FDR's time, and Johnson often talked only to the top echelons of government. Unlike Kennedy, Johnson maintained a personal and intimate relationship with his staff—eating with them, socializing, swimming naked, even inviting some of them into the bathroom as he discussed issues.

He moved to control information and publicity in the White House, cut the Democratic National Committee budget in half, and reduced the power of his cabinet secretaries substantially. He regarded the press as another power center to be mastered and moved decisively to extend his sway. Johnson observed that "reporters are puppets. They simply respond to the pull of the most powerful strings. . . . There is no such thing as an objective news story. There is always a private story behind the public story." He tried to control the news, the plans and details, so as to control the media. By 1965, he seemed to be successful in bringing to heel Congress, the party, the staff, and even the press by an extraordinary display of skill, prowess, bullying, and energy. Then the world changed.

Democratic statesman Averell Harriman passed judgment on Johnson's record by concluding, "LBJ was great in domestic affairs. Harry Truman had programs, but none got through. Kennedy had no technique. FDR talked simply during the crisis, but didn't act enough later. Johnson went back past the New Frontier all the way to the New Deal. He loved FDR, and it was fantastic what he did. If it hadn't been for . . . Vietnam, he'd have been the greatest president ever. Even so he'll be remembered as great."[106]

WAR: THE NEMESIS OF REFORM

Early in his presidency, Johnson also found himself involved in other foreign policy issues besides Vietnam. He soon discovered that Kennedy's Alliance for Progress was not working well at all. The president moved a fellow Texan, Thomas C. Mann, the ambassador to Mexico, to the State Department to guide his Latin American policy. They emphasized more the role of private investment in the region, and Mann seemed to be less committed to the New Frontier gospel emphasizing the primacy of social democratic reforms south of the border.[107]

Observing an unstable and vacillating Panamanian government and hostile crowds in the Canal Zone, Johnson refused at first to negotiate a new treaty. Elsewhere, faced with unrest in the Dominican Republic, Johnson insisted on sending troops there, arguing that Communist forces were threatening American citizens living in that small nation. Dictator Rafael Trujillo had been assassinated, and liberal Juan Bosch was elected president on December 20, 1962. Bosch was, in turn, overthrown by the military less than a year later. When civil war broke out, Johnson sent in the marines to protect U.S. lives, and later he insisted that there was a danger of a Communist takeover, an accusation that was roundly criticized, but which some historians had asserted later was a possibility in that chaotic situation. On the defensive, the president though did overemphasize the scale of the Communist threat, and major segments of the liberal establishment attacked Johnson as he responded with an orgy of rhetorical justification and round-the-clock consultation. The Organization of American States finally sent in a peacekeeping force, and on June 1, 1966, a free election led to a moderate rightist being elected, Joaquin Bolaquer. As for Johnson, he began to show some of the characteristics that marked his conduct in Vietnam: hyperbolic rhetoric, a compulsive need for consensus, a deep sensitivity to criticism, and a preoccupation with tactical detail.[108]

Of all the foreign policy problems he faced early on, none was more important than Vietnam. Indeed, Vietnam became the undoing of Johnson, the shackles on the Great Society, the immediate cause of the election of Richard Nixon, and the downturn in the fortunes of the Democratic party. When he was vice president, Johnson was sent by President Kennedy to South Vietnam, and he promoted the basic assumptions that led to increasing support for the Diem regime. Johnson, as most of his generation, accepted the Munich analogy and opposed compromise in Vietnam as appeasement. The Communists would only increase their demands just as Hitler had done in the 1930s.

After his 1961 visit, Johnson warned that the battle against Communism in Southeast Asia had to be joined and waged successfully, or the United States would "surrender the Pacific and take up our defenses on our own shores." He did have problems with the Kennedy-sanctioned removal of Diem by South Vietnamese generals and his eventual assassination. Increasingly in the early 1960s, Western support grew for "neutralizing Vietnam," a formula that Johnson insisted "would have meant the swift communization of all Vietnam, and probably of Laos and Cambodia as well." Faced immediately with a rapidly deteriorating situation after taking over the presidency, Johnson in the winter of 1963–64 decided to increase U.S. support rather than withdraw or seek a diplomatic solution.[109]

As noted, some Kennedy apologists would later indicate that JFK was planning to withdraw, but his public statements and the early remembrances of the major advisors Johnson inherited underscore the conclusion that there was a strong consensus to stick with South Vietnam. Later some of those advisors would assert specifically that Kennedy was ready to withdraw from South Vietnam as soon as he was reelected in 1964. But at the ill-fated summit meeting in Vienna,

Kennedy had insisted, "Now we have a problem of making our power credible, and Vietnam looks like the place." Just before his death, JFK bluntly concluded, "We are not there to see a war lost." Johnson believed that the United States had a commitment under the SEATO treaty, and from Rusk, McNamara, Bundy, and even Bobby Kennedy, he heard repeatedly about his late predecessor's determination to stay the course. Indeed, Johnson probably feared that Robert Kennedy would attack him as cowardly and unmanly if he retreated in Vietnam.

It is clear that in December 1963, Johnson knew full well that the situation was rapidly deteriorating and could not be rectified easily or early in the struggle. CIA Director John McCone reported, "There are more reasons to doubt the future of the effort . . . than there are reasons to be optimistic about the future of our cause in South Vietnam." Thus within a month's time in office, Johnson had cast the die that would undermine his most memorable achievements and wound fatally his consensus presidency.[110]

In March 1964, a report from General Maxwell Taylor and Secretary McNamara informed the president about the poor state of the South Vietnam war effort. They urged new steps against the North Vietnam regime and a broadening of U.S. commitments. In early August of 1964, U.S. destroyers, including the USS *Maddox*, were attacked in the Tonkin Gulf off North Vietnam, and Congress supported the president's call to protect American military forces. The Tonkin Resolution, which authorized the executive to do what was necessary to afford such protection to U.S. forces and its Asian allies, would later be cited as a functional equivalent of a declaration of a war. But critics of Johnson would also charge that he misled Congress and the people, not telling them about the covert raids being conducted by South Vietnamese gunboats and electronic espionage being done by the USS *Maddox*. But the House of Representatives passed the resolution by a voice vote and the Senate concurred eighty-eight to two, giving the president the support he wanted. Johnson had pressed for a resolution because he felt that Truman had mistakenly not gotten congressional approval of his defense of South Korea. Later congressional critics would maintain that the legislative branch did not mean to give the president a blank check, but only limited and specific approval in this one incident. But the sponsor of the resolution and later an opponent of the war, Senator William Fulbright of Arkansas, was clear that the resolution gave the executive the authority to use force that could lead to war.[111]

After the resolution passed, the president unleashed a series of air attacks that destroyed 10 percent of Hanoi's oil-production facilities, and his approval rating jumped from 42 percent to 72 percent as the presidential campaign heated up. Denouncing Goldwater as a war monger and speaking the language of peace, LBJ overwhelmed his opponent in the election; then as the new year came, U.S. policy changed substantially. Like FDR before him, LBJ chose to lead the nation into war while covering over the course. After the election, Johnson informed Taylor in Vietnam that he had reservations that large-scale bombing could win the war. Instead he was considering introducing more ground forces as the new year came. On February 7, 1965, the Communists attacked a U.S. military installation at Pleiku leaving eight Americans dead and 109 wounded. With the strong support of his advisors, Johnson ordered retaliatory bombing ("Rolling Thunder") against North Vietnam. Still Johnson insisted that changes in policy had not taken place. However, to protect air bases, U.S. ground forces were introduced, and by March 20, the Joint Chiefs of Staff approved American units being sent for combat—a major escalation in the war. On June 16, McNamara announced a planned deployment of 70,000–75,000 men; on July 2, the Joint Chiefs asked for 179,000.[112]

The central assumption of the policy makers was that increased pressure on Hanoi would force them to cease their support of the Communists in South Vietnam. Surely the greatest military power in the world would not be defeated by a guerrilla force even in Asia. The administration also hoped to push the Soviet Union into a position where it would help control Hanoi's strategic objectives. Yet a steady steam of ships carried munitions from the Soviet Union and Poland to the North Vietnamese, and the Chinese Communists sent three hundred thousand troops into Vietnam. The Chinese also provided 2 million guns, 270 million rounds of ammunition, 37,000 artillery pieces, 18.8 million artillery shells, 179 aircraft, and 145 naval vessels.

Then on July 28, 1965, the president informed an afternoon television audience and press conference that U.S. troop strength would jump from 75,000 to 125,000, and that draft calls would be doubled. Also U.S. strategy was changed from holding particular enclaves to more aggressive "search and destroy" tactics that would lead to great havoc in the villages and towns. A flood of refugees engulfed the cities, causing rampant unemployment, extensive prostitution, and increased drug trafficking. Johnson in the summer of 1965 talked wistfully of peace and of a Mekong River development project, patterned after the electrification schemes of the TVA and FDR's New Deal. Johnson naively insisted, "Uncle Ho can't turn that down." By early 1966, General Taylor defined victory as simply allowing the South Vietnamese to chose their own government, and leaving observers to conclude that Hanoi would suffer little because of its activities. Johnson claimed to have been deeply concerned at that time that a wide open war might bring in Russia or China or both, an unlikely possibly, but a view surely influenced by Chinese Communist intervention in Korea.[113]

Later Johnson admitted that both he and Kennedy had made mistakes in their response—Kennedy by not putting more than eighteen thousand [actually sixteen thousand] military advisors in the early 1960s, and he by waiting eighteen months before putting more men in. Yet he denied that during the 1964 campaign he had secretly planned to bomb the north once he was reelected. He claimed that at least five times he rejected that option, and only after the attack at Pleiku in February 1965 did he feel he had no choice but to retaliate.

As the war heated up and the draft began to affect the white middle class, Vietnam started to be more of an issue, and the college campuses became the centers of opposition to the war. In 1968 alone there were 221 college riots. Not only did opposition to the war grow, some elements of the American liberal community began to openly support the North Vietnamese regime. Ho Chi Minh became the Vietnamese George Washington in their eyes; novelist and literary critic Susan Sontag described North Vietnam as "a place which, in many respects, *deserves* to be idealized"; Frances Fitzgerald downplayed Communist assassination tactics in her scathing study of American involvement in the war; and historian Staughton Lynd and political activist Tom Hayden compared U.S. anticommunism to rape. Actress Jane Fonda openly embraced the North Vietnamese regime, and campus teach-ins increased the intellectual level of opposition to the war. To Johnson, who so loved the accolade of "education president," the centers of dissent seemed incomprehensible and ungrateful.[114]

Johnson's strategy of keeping the war at a low profile was crumbling, and his desire both to feed the military effort and keep the

Great Society afloat was becoming undone by the sheer economic costs. As the American people saw more of the war in their living rooms, a revulsion slowly began to take place against the destruction and wanton brutality that conflict brings. Unlike the carnage of World War I, the mass destruction of World War II, Vietnam was now experienced directly by the noncombatant Americans at home, and it added fuel to the fires of pacifism and resistance. Johnson, with his alternating between tough anti-Communist rhetoric and his fervent desire to contain the war, appeared brutal to the left and vacillating to the military.

General Earle G. Wheeler, chairman of the Joint Chiefs of Staff during most of the Johnson years, later argued that the war should have been brought into the north, and the Joint Chiefs pushed for a call-up of the reserves, which the president refused. The military also wanted to bomb Hanoi extensively, but Johnson again demurred. In addition, the president avoided bombing North Vietnamese sanctuaries in Cambodia or closing down Haiphong port. Johnson kept tight control over tactical military decisions and even target selections. He plotted strategy with the "Tuesday luncheon" group, which included the secretaries of state and defense, the chairman of the Joint Chiefs, the director of the CIA, the special assistant to the president for national security affairs, the White House press secretary, and a staff person who took notes.[115]

In Washington, the war became an obsession with the president, Congress, and the national bureaucracy. The chief executive spent endless nights planning and controlling the bombing targets in order to limit civilian casualties and avoid a confrontation with China or the Soviet Union. The Great Society was becoming paralyzed and inflation was setting in. To the military, Johnson's policy of gradualism and escalated responses did not force the enemy to pay a heavy price for its aggression. To the left, the war was a Vietnamese civil war and the Vietcong in the south were really independent from Ho Chi Minh. In fact, the Vietcong were exactly what the military and the anti-Communist American policy makers said they were—a resistance force that was nearly totally controlled and supplied by the North Vietnamese, especially as the years wore on.

To limit U.S. casualties, Johnson tried to avoid an extensive land war—another Korea—and employed air strikes aimed at crippling North Vietnam. But the generals in South Vietnam could not engage in hot pursuit into Laos or Cambodia, invade the north, or bomb the dikes. When the war was enlarged under Nixon, those initiatives did not bring victory either. Later studies of the bombing effort done by U.S. government agencies showed that bombing was not really effective and had helped the north mobilize in some ways.[116]

As the war dragged on into 1967, dissent began to creep into the highest echelons of government, even while a majority of Americans still approved of the president's policy of staying the course. Secretary McNamara commissioned a secret study, called later the *Pentagon Papers*, tracing the origins of American involvement in Vietnam. That report implied that the Kennedy administration knew more about the plot to kill Diem than was generally assumed at the time, that contingency plans for massive intervention were secretly developed during the election campaign in 1964, and that Congress and the public had been systematically misled from 1964 to 1966.[117]

On March 18, 1967, General William Westmoreland asked for 200,000 new troops on top of the 470,000 he commanded. His request would mean a massive call-up of reserves, and Johnson refused. By then McNamara had parted company with the Joint Chiefs, advocated a coalition government in Saigon and a limiting of American military operations, and urged curtailing air attacks to infiltration routes below the 20th parallel. To add to Johnson problems, a subcommittee of the Senate Armed Services Committee scheduled testimony that was clearly meant to present the hawks' views against gradual escalation. Caught between those sentiments and increased disillusionment with the war, the president struggled to stay the course. By late November, McNamara was nominated to head the World Bank, and Johnson brought in an old Truman aide and establishment figure, Clark Clifford, as secretary of defense.[118]

In early 1968, Harris opinion polls showed that the public was taking a tougher line on the war and favored invading North Vietnam and mining the Haiphong harbor. The major blow to the Johnson policy came when the Communists attacked in a variety of places across the south during the Tet holiday. Throughout South Vietnam, nearly seventy thousand enemy soldiers assaulted more than one hundred cities and towns including Hue. Rumors spread that even the U.S. embassy had been penetrated, which was incorrect. The Communists actually suffered a major military defeat, but politically the mere fact that they could launch such a bold, massive assault seemed to provide support to the opponents of Johnson. Influential American journalists and the television networks, especially CBS, pictured the campaign as a defeat for the allies and not as a setback for the North Vietnamese. Ronald Reagan was later to conclude that CBS should have been charged with treason for its unsympathetic coverage of the war.

Regardless of their motives, there is no question that many of the main instruments of public opinion misled the American people and further encouraged a decline of morale even among those in charge of the war in Washington. Years later, General Vo Nguyen Giap who planned the Tet offensive disclosed that one of the purposes of the drive was to inflict casualties that would help to increase dissent in the United States. Another North Vietnamese officer admitted after the war that the Communists had never defeated U.S. troops in a major battle. Yet he went on to claim that that fact was irrelevant.[119]

Johnson never sought to communicate the opposite impression either. He refused to go to Congress for additional authorization and approval for the war. Bitterly Westmoreland was to conclude, "Johnson hoped the war would go away, so he could concentrate his energies on building a 'Great Society' at home, but his key Vietnam decisions were destined to drag out the war indefinitely." Later research was to show that public support for the war in Vietnam actually remained at a higher level than during the Korean War. Increasing casualties did begin to turn around public opinion in the United States, although until mid-1967, television coverage was rather positive, despite Johnson's feelings to the contrary. By early 1968, however, Tet had played a role in that disillusionment, and Johnson lost substantial newspaper editorial support as well.

The brutality of the war, any war, the discovery of a massacre by American troops at a village called My Lai, and endless debate about the morality and the effectiveness of the military efforts undercut the president's policies even further. When one officer remarked at Ben Tri that it was "necessary to destroy the town to save it," he seemed to summarize the cruel and self-defeating strategy in Vietnam. The lines between civilians and soldiers, combatants and women and children were blurred. War in all its horror was front page news and living room evening entertainment. Unlike World War I and II, censorship was not imposed, and important elements in the media became persistent critics of Johnson and his policies.

The president refused to arouse the energies and animosities of the American people, and his constrained leadership was seen as a sign not of restraint but of dishonesty. His foes demanded a wider war or no war at all, proving to some that the American nation cannot wage a limited war for long. He would not withdraw, feared major escalation, discounted invasion, opposed neutralization as a front for eventual Communist domination. Why Johnson continued his war policies within those constraints seemed unclear. The best explanation may have been given by Secretary of State Dean Rusk, "We thought we could win." How could "a raggedy ass little fourth-rate country," as Johnson called North Vietnam, hold out under the pressure he applied? Deep down Johnson searched for the right button to push, the appropriate compromise to bring Ho to the bargaining table. As he had done for over thirty years, he eyeballed his opponents to see what leverage he could use to get them to bend to his will. Bargaining, compromise, deals were his way of life. Johnson had never dealt with a revolutionary zealot, a true ideologue, a leader whose life was devoted to a cause, and who took defeat as a temporary occasion to regroup. Ho did not want a TVA on the Mekong, nor was he the Vietnamese George Washington. He was a ruthless, brutal, dedicated Communist revolutionary whose mind-set was too removed from Johnson's world to negotiate a peace. Ho either had to be destroyed or Vietnam had to be abandoned by the United States as not worth the costs. Johnson chose to do neither; later in the 1970s under Nixon and Kissinger the United States tried the first option and settled for the second.[120]

By early 1968, Johnson, weary of the war and worried about his health, quietly resolved not to run again. His administration had split the Democratic party, and opposition to the war was most intense among traditional liberal constituencies. The media, many of the young, and racial minorities walked away from the president. How could those segments of society he had so cared for in his Great Society abandon him, Johnson wondered? To add to his hurt, Johnson watched as the antiwar elements coalesced around Senator Eugene McCarthy of Minnesota, a traditional liberal who had desired to be Johnson's running mate in 1964, and later around Robert Kennedy who had so vigorously supported the war and urged the president to make him ambassador to South Vietnam.

In a primary election in New Hampshire, Johnson defeated McCarthy only 49 percent to 42 percent, but lost twenty of the twenty-four delegates to the senator. Kennedy quickly decided to enter the contest for the Democratic nomination. At first he insisted that he would not run against the president, but now seeing Johnson vulnerable and joining with the turning of public opinion, Kennedy moved. Since his election to the Senate from New York in the 1964 election, Kennedy had moderated his abrasive style and become the darling of the New Left, which was to be affected by his sudden death in a way they had not been even after his brother John's assassination.[121]

On February 28, the military requested another 206,000 men, which would mean $10–15 billion in additional revenues and would result in a call-up of the reserves and the National Guard. Westmoreland probably did not need or really seek that many more forces, but the Joint Chiefs were using the Tet atmosphere to push for higher military strength levels. Instead of having the effect they expected, Johnson began a major review of the whole Vietnam situation. His new secretary of defense, Clark Clifford, and some of the establishment foreign policy leaders Johnson leaned on clearly urged the president to stop the escalation and seek a negotiated settlement.

A weary Johnson in April 1968 announced another bombing pause and then his own end. He would not run again for president, eliminating himself as an issue and as a target. The Johnson era was over, but the war was to continue into the Ford administration. The year 1968 saw the murder of Dr. Martin Luther King, Jr., and then Robert F. Kennedy. The Democratic party ripped itself apart in Chicago at the convention, and Hubert Humphrey received the presidential nomination covered with bitterness. The nation was treated to still another "new Nixon," and this one squeezed by and won the presidency. Johnson warned his party and its presidential candidate not to do anything that might look like they were abandoning his failed war policies, and that delay probably cost Humphrey the White House. Not until September 30 did the vice president speak out forcefully in favor of negotiations and an end to bombing. Johnson himself finally ordered a halt, an action Nixon denounced as a political move—even as Republican intermediaries were secretly trying to persuade the South Vietnamese government to hold firmly against the administration's change in policy.[122]

As has been seen, the Johnson presidency, like the man himself, seemed bigger than life. His definition of the welfare state and the possibilities of ameliorative government far exceeded FDR's, and his concerns for the poor and the dispossessed were genuine. Underneath his crude calculus of life, the cynical displays of power and privilege, his personal style of bullying and bravado, Johnson remained a man genuinely given to sentiment and sympathy. Power did not corrupt him as much as it liberated him, and his liberation gave way to excessive behavior and egotism. At parliamentary maneuvering and domestic law giving, he had no peer. Robert Donovan has summarized, "Johnson was a tragic genius of bottomless pettiness, volcanic energy, brilliant intellect, disgusting manners, wild emotions, voracious appetites, habitual mendacity, restless cunning, nagging insecurity, great achievements, and sometimes near lunacy."[123]

Critics of the Great Society—left and right—argued that his domestic programs were a failure, and they launched a broad-reaching assault on the efficacy of government concern. Surely some of the programs were poorly drafted and badly administered, but the Great Society did alleviate much suffering, close the income gap somewhat between the races, guarantee legal but not economic equality for blacks, moderate medical costs for the elderly, subsidize a generation of the young in college, and open up the avenues of ideas in ecology, conservation, and a score of other areas. The Great Society, underfunded and overshadowed by the war, went from idea to implementation in five short years. It is hard for one to image a weapons system or a farm subsidy program that would be deemed a failure after such a short trial. The Great Society proved that federal intervention can work in many areas, and that the Johnson strategy of getting the laws passed first when one has a legislative majority is not an ideal plan of action, but the most realistic path in a political system such as the United States.[124]

With Vietnam, Johnson's supporters and foes saw the breakdown and failure of his consensus politics. One of his most astute biographers, Doris Kearns, viewed the Vietnam debacle as not atypical but as symptomatic of Johnson's deceitful, misguided, overly personalized style of politics. What worked so well in the cloakrooms of the Senate, she argued, failed on the world stage. The inference is that a different political style would have led to a more successful war, greater public support, or a more mature judgment to stay out of the quagmire.[125] Any or all of these would have been preferable to what we got, so the morality tale goes.

Yet that popular line of thought cannot be valid. Harry Truman was fairly forthright in his analysis of Korea, finally turned to mobilization, and was not a believer in bringing the North Koreans to the bargaining table by charm or by hydroelectric projects. Still he was attacked for many of the same reasons, discrediting himself and his party as Johnson did. There are some similarities—both did not get a formal declaration of war, but can one doubt that the Congress strongly supported Truman after the immediate invasion? Truman, too, lost the nation's support, and no one can say that he deceived the legislative branch, the public, and the media. And like Johnson, much of the strongest opposition came not from the pacifists, the liberals or the intellectuals, but from the military and the hawks in the electorate.

Johnson has been criticized for overvaluing Vietnam as a deciding point in the Cold War. Yet every American president from Truman to George Bush has made a similar judgment. And Johnson was correct—the war was not a civil war, it was a conquest of the south finally by the North Vietnamese Communists, and the South Vietnamese government of Diem and Nguyen Van Thieu was not any more corrupt that some of the European allies and the liberation movements the United States and Britain associated with in World War II.

Johnson's failure was grounded in the fact that the American people do not wish to be involved in long limited wars of attrition. They want wars of clear goals, visible battle lines, and realizable objectives in which their actions are not only identified with good, but can be achieved quickly. The wars in Asia—in Korea and Vietnam—were for limited objectives, circumscribed by their presidents in order to prevent what they feared would be a more terrible World War III. Before Johnson and after him, American presidents waged war secretly by using the CIA and related agencies in order to avoid many of the problems of declared or quasi-declared conflict.

One should say that the people and their representatives have a right to know and to concur in or not concur in those decisions. The Cold War did more than change attitudes; it changed the balance of representative government in its most critical task, providing for the common defense.

Johnson's war in Vietnam, and Nixon's escalated and more hidden strategies, did not bring victory. The Communists now control much of the whole region, except Thailand, spilling over as the American presidents feared into Cambodia and Laos. The social dislocations of the war and the brutal pacification policies of the combatants and later the victorious Communists sunk those areas into repression and later genocide. The "thought reformers" of the Vietnamese, the holocaust in Cambodia under Pol Pot and others, the snuffing out of civility in once gentle Laos have turned the

Southeast Asian area into a long human nightmare. Many of those who opposed American intervention and fell under the charm of Communist revolutionaries have to admit now that totalitarian regimes soon followed the romance and the wooing. And those who saw U.S. power as a stabilizing force in the region must surely have qualms about the consequences of this nation's involvement for those lost peoples.

A major nuclear and conventional power such as the United States can wage war in theaters where indigenous populations are supportive or held captive as in Europe, or where military objectives can be won and firmly held. But wars in far-off lands, in nations without stable allies and with permeable borders, are very difficult to bring to victory or resolution. Wars of attrition, wars of guerrilla action waged in Third World environs, are inevitably exercises in punishment, resolve, and morale. When the American military forces swept through, defoliating and destroying enemy or suspect hamlets, the war was not won, but merely shifted to other locales. All that was left was death and disillusionment. The classical historian Tacitus could have warned Lyndon Johnson of the perils of such a strategy. Observing the ancient Romans as they marched through Africa, he caustically concluded, "they made a desert and called it a peace." Johnson did not even have that solace in the end.

6

The Cold War and American Conservatism: Nixon, Ford, Carter, Reagan, and Bush

No president, including Franklin Roosevelt, has stayed in the public eye longer than Richard M. Nixon. From the late 1940s with his leadership in the Alger Hiss case through his presidency, near-impeachment, and retirement, Nixon remained a controversial, highly visible political figure. Few modern Americans have been so vilified, so frequently made a target of hostility, and so willing and able to remember and pay back slights and insults. Nixon's rise to power is a remarkable story. He was born to a modest Quaker family in Southern California, proved to be a hardworking and bright student, and entered politics with the backing of traditional conservative Republicans. The nation then was deeply concerned by the growing power of the Soviet Union, and young Congressman Nixon serving on the House UnAmerican Activities Committee supported the accusations of former *Time* magazine editor Whittaker Chambers against prominent Truman official Alger Hiss. In the end, Hiss was found guilty of perjury and Nixon's career skyrocketed.

Intensely ambitious, a quiet and shy Nixon proved willing to use the Communist issue in unscrupulous ways to win elections to the House of Representatives, and later to the Senate. Supported by some prominent Republican leaders and many rank-and-file party people, Nixon was nominated for vice president on the Eisenhower ticket in 1952. During the campaign, a major controversy developed over Nixon's use of a private fund to supplement his office expenses. In one of the early uses in politics of television, he defended the ethics of his behavior, concluding that the only gift he had ever taken was a puppy named "Checkers" given to his two daughters. Nixon stayed on the Republican ticket, and in eight years as vice president compiled the best record of achievement in that office up to that time. Eisenhower's illnesses and heart attack put Nixon closer to the throne than any vice president, and he performed discreetly and well. During Ike's two terms, he emerged as a forceful spokesman for the GOP, bringing on himself increasing Democratic hostility and Republican loyalty.[1]

NIXON AND HIS ENEMIES

In 1960, Richard Nixon lost the presidency to Kennedy by 120,000 votes in an election that was probably stolen from the Republicans. Nixon refused to contest the election, ran for governor of California in 1962, and after losing there promised the press they "wouldn't have Nixon to kick around anymore." He left public life even more bitter and cynical toward the press and more haunted by the unfairness of a bare knuckles political process, a style at which he himself had been a master. One of his most perceptive supporters, Raymond Price, noted that Nixon felt "we were babes in the woods in 1960, and that over the years he learned that the only way to survive in politics is to do unto others before they do unto you."[2]

From 1962 to 1968, Nixon made a considerable amount of money as an attorney in New York City, spoke frequently to the Republican faithful, and pondered foreign policy issues. The demise of the conservative right after Senator Barry Goldwater's defeat in 1964, and the controversial divorce and remarriage of liberal Republican Governor Nelson Rockefeller made Nixon a viable candidate again for the presidential nomination. He easily won the GOP nod, and then barely carried the election against Senator Hubert Humphrey. Johnson's war and the loss of southern white voters helped to defeat his vice president and split the Democratic party for years to come.

Starting with Nixon's election, the political landscape slowly changed, especially in the setting of a new conservative national agenda. The emergence of that conservative movement from 1968 to 1988 was due to several causes: the polarization of the racial conflict beyond the South; the persistence of inflation; the rising strength of tax revolts; general discontent with federal welfare policies; and the increasing globalization of the American economy. Out of this complex domestic vortex would emerge Richard Nixon, a man whose interest was purely in foreign policy.

Nixon came into office committed to ending the Vietnam War and restoring a sense of quiet and decorum back into American politics. He liked to recall the poster he saw carried by a teenage girl in Ohio—"Bring us together once again." But faced with the lessons of a media that had helped to destroy his predecessor, and resurrecting his own past hurts, Nixon opted for a strategy of deception and secrecy in foreign policy. In that strategy, he found an able partner, Henry Kissinger, a brilliant Harvard University professor, an expert on international affairs, and a Rockefeller protégé. Acting as special assistant for national security affairs, Kissinger used his position to coordinate and then manage foreign policy at Nixon's bequest, and often behind the backs of the State Department and its secretary, William Rogers, the Defense Department including the Joint Chiefs and its secretary, Melvin Laird, and even the CIA.

Nixon's primary interest and his major achievements are usually seen as being in the area of foreign policy, but his term in office did embrace some little-noticed, but rather important domestic initiatives as well. Every modern president has lamented the independence of his cabinet and the power of the federal bureaucracy. Some exceptions such as FDR and Johnson set up parallel bureaucracies to do their bidding. Nixon, however, wanted not to build new programs, but to dismantle the Great Society, to shift the focus of action and domestic controversy away from Washington and back to the states and localities.[3]

The Nixon agenda in terms of revenue sharing, welfare reform, and civil rights was part of a new strategy to foster conservative objectives. Its main purpose was to cut the power of the federal bureaucracy—which Nixon identified as a critical component of the enemy liberal establishment. His approach was a sharp reaction to the Great Society with its open-ended national agenda and controversial interventionist programs. Still, Nixon's domestic advisors sought support for substantial reforms in areas that had long troubled even the most impartial observers. Nixon's first domestic advisor, Daniel Patrick Moynihan, also from Harvard, tried to convince himself, Nixon, and the press that the president was really Benjamin Disraeli, the conservative prime minister who instituted broad social reforms in Victorian England. But Nixon had none of Disraeli's sense of perspective and irony. For him the concentration of power was an initial step to sticking it to his old enemies, rectifying old hurts, and outflanking the liberal establishment he so envied and hated.[4]

Early in his first term, Nixon gave up on his own cabinet, avoided direct contact with many of the secretaries, and sought to create a mechanism to concentrate power in the White House for domestic affairs as he had done with Kissinger in foreign affairs. By mid-1970, Nixon created a Domestic Council patterned after Kissinger's redefinition of the powerful National Security Council.[5] The president's initial objective, however, was to devolve domestic programs to the states through revenue sharing and decentralized administration. The White House called the approach the "New Federalism," and later renamed it the "New American Revolution." On August 8, 1969, Nixon focused on four specific proposals: welfare reform, revenue sharing, a new Manpower Retraining Act, and a reorganization of the Office of Economic Opportunity. Early in the 1968 transition, presidential counselor Arthur Burns had set up dozens of task forces to make recommendations to the new president in those and other areas.

One of the most interesting and controversial initiatives, however, came from Secretary of Labor George Shultz who supported the "Philadelphia Plan," a quota system for putting blacks into the building trades unions that had been historically closed to minorities. As for the president, at least since the election of 1968 and probably before, he generally had abandoned his Quaker sense of racial toleration, expressing several times to his advisor, John Ehrlichman, that federal programs could only marginally help blacks because of their alleged genetic inferiority to whites.[6]

A second major innovation was Nixon's welfare reform policy, which focused on an "income strategy" advocated by Moynihan. That initiative was meant to move the government from providing social services to giving the poor cash assistance. A combination of traditional conservative and New Deal-oriented liberals combined to defeat the bill in Congress. However, the Nixon administration did put into effect Supplemental Security Income (SSI), an important national benefits program to augment Social Security payments for the very poor.

The initiative for a guaranteed national family income is a good example of how ideas germinate, grow, and come to fruition under the most unexplainable circumstances. A proposal for a "negative income tax" or a guaranteed income came out of the Democratic-oriented federal bureaucracy under the impetus of Sargent Shriver, a Kennedy brother-in-law, Johnson's associate in the war on poverty, and later vice-presidential candidate under Senator George McGovern in 1972. Pushed by Moynihan and others, the proposal ended up on Nixon's desk and after some modifications by domestic aide John Ehrlichman, it became the administration's major domestic reform proposal. The program would have tripled the income of the poor in the South, replaced inadequate state welfare systems, and made welfare finally a federal responsibility—a shift even FDR and Lyndon Johnson could not have accomplished. In the words of two authorities on welfare reform, it was "Nixon's good deed," even though in many ways he could not have cared less.

But the conservatives were frightened by opening up the welfare rolls to millions more children and blacks, and the liberals were cowed by the militant National Welfare Rights organization, which skillfully used charges of racism to block any reform they considered too moderate. Black congressmen, Democratic liberals, and the social work bureaucracy all opposed the proposal for different reasons. Nixon's plan would have offered little to northern blacks on welfare, since it was aimed at the South where the poverty levels were higher and the benefits rather low. Also an added provision requiring that able-bodied people on welfare must work drew the criticism of liberals, even though the provision was rather weak. Nixon finally abandoned welfare reform altogether after months of intense criticism. The conservatives had struck a meaningless blow for the status quo welfare system, which they claimed to hate. The left, once again, linked up ideology and opportunism to kill reform by holding incremental improvements hostage to its vision of the ideal. The Senate also rejected the idea of a guaranteed income for children, but, as noted, Congress approved SSI, which gave an income floor to the most needy who were old, blind, or disabled. Also, the administration proposed a major increase in food stamps, which would help pay part of the grocery bills for many poor. Congress approved a compromise of the administration's initiatives, although the final act passed by the Democratic-controlled Congress was less generous than Nixon's original proposal.[7]

In his first term, there were frequent contacts between Nixon's domestic cabinet people and the Urban Affairs Council, a high-level committee that provided some overall direction. As that term wore on, the White House staff doubled in size above the level of the Johnson years, and the staff took over much of the power of the cabinet secretaries. Nixon appointed Ehrlichman as executive direc- tor of the Domestic Council, and that change led to White House "working groups," which sought to coordinate the White House staff and agency chiefs below the secretary level. Ironically, the work- ing groups looked similar to Johnson's approach under his aide, Joseph Califano.

To avoid treading unnecessarily on the toes of the cabinet sec- retaries, Ehrlichman confined the working groups approach to what he called issues of "a multi-dimensional character." But the Domestic Council and the staff of the Office of Management and Budget began to assume oversight responsibilities for existing programs and routine matters. Nixon and Ehrlichman created, in Robert Nathan's words, "a counterbureaucracy," which undermined the old-line cabi- net officers.[8]

The problem with Nixon's approach was that his White House staff became more preoccupied with detail and less with major policy issues. Also, the counterbureaucracy had the opposite effect that Nixon wanted. The bureaucracy became in some cases stronger as lines of authority were blurred, and career officers with expertise in their specialized areas ran their entrenched programs. Lower-level White House aides began criticizing presidential cabinet officers and increased the confusion. By late 1972, Nixon himself critically reviewed the expansion of the White House staff. The public relations office alone had grown to an operational staff of seventeen communicators. Faced with the rapid increase in the White House staff and the inconclusive drift of power the president's men exercised in domestic affairs, Nixon abruptly changed strategy in 1973.[9]

His associates in the administration probably expected to share in the goodwill and confidence that emerged from Nixon's massive reelection victory over Democratic Senator McGovern of South Dakota. The president's popular vote margin was 47 million to 29 million or 60.7 percent to 37.5 percent of the vote, and he carried every state except Massachusetts. Instead of celebrating, the presi- dent held a cabinet meeting the day after his election, thanked his secretaries, and asked that all political appointees submit their res- ignations. Nixon then vanished to Key Biscayne, Florida, and later to Camp David. Nixon concluded that the second term of presidents

usually lacked vitality, and he was determined to alter "the historical pattern" by a changing of the guard. His proposed budget would
cut the executive office in half and eliminate the symbol of the Great
Society—the Office of Economic Opportunity. The president was
obviously returning to the older model of strong and loyal cabinet
officers rather than relying on his White House staff. Critics noted
later, in the middle of the Watergate controversy, that the president
had readjusted his administration away from the staff system that
led to his downfall. Yet his chief of staff, H. R. Haldeman, has
argued that Watergate occurred because of a breakdown of staff
control. His view was that aide Charles Colson in particular operated outside of channels and reported often directly to Nixon, ap-
pealing to the president's "darker" impulses and unleashing some
of the illegal activities that led to the Watergate scandal.[10]

After his reelection, Nixon named several new secretaries in
HEW, Defense, and Labor, and a new director of OMB; in early
1973, he announced that some of these department heads would be
given the title "Counselor to the President" as well. These three
supersecretaries were to chair Domestic Council committees, including Earl Butz of Agriculture in the area of the natural resources;
Caspar Weinberger of HEW for human resources; and James T. Lynn
of HUD for community development. In addition, George Shultz of
Treasury was made an assistant to the president for economic affairs. Four presidential assistants were to integrate and unify policy
initiatives for Nixon: Haldeman, Ehrlichman, Kissinger, and Roy Ash
of OMB. These supersecretaries were thus given responsibilities over
programmatic areas that before had been the sole province of individual cabinet members. The president wanted not only better management and coordination, but greater direct control. On April 19,
he complained to Ehrlichman, "We have no discipline in this bureaucracy. We never fire anybody. We never reprimand anybody. We
never demote anybody. We always promote the sons-of-bitches that
kick us in the ass."[11]

Regardless of the president's span of control, his administration
did witness a major expansion of the welfare state. It may seem
odd that Richard Nixon the conservative was involved in major
domestic innovations that accelerated such a development. As has
been noted, the president had embraced the notion that the most
durable reforms came under right-wing leaders such as Disraeli in
Britain. Nixon probably took a perverse pleasure in outdoing do-

mestic liberals at their own game. But many of those domestic accomplishments during his time in office were due to other major
factors: the political pressures for reform continued in certain areas
such as environmentalism even after Johnson's demise, some of
Nixon's aides (most notably John Ehrlichman) were somewhat progressive in specific policy areas, and the president believed in delegating authority and supporting his aides even if he disagreed at
times with them.

Despite his use of the "southern strategy" in the 1968 election
when he appealed to segregation supporters in that region, Nixon
was also instrumental in forging alliances quietly with Southern
leaders to end once and for all the dual system of formal segregated education. After some ambivalence, he also pushed for stronger environmental legislation, appointed proenvironmental regulatory
officials, and openly associated himself with the national parks
movement. He was also remarkably sympathetic to the plight and
claims of Native Amerian tribes, in part, Ehrlichman has argued,
because of Nixon's mother's concerns, which were passed down to
her son at any early age.

As noted before, under Nixon's aegis, George Shultz implemented the "Philadelphia Plan," and with the support of New York's
governor, Nelson Rockefeller, the president pushed for revenue sharing to the states and welfare reform. The administration also supported the establishment of the Occupational Safety and Health
Administration (OSHA) and the rapid expansion of the food stamp
program for the needy. To deal with the challenge of inflation this
conservative president took the United States off the international
gold standard and imposed wage and price controls on the nation.
He presided over the overall growth of the welfare state, as the
payments to individuals category went from 6.3 percent of the GNP
in 1969 to 8.9 percent in 1974 while the Pentagon's share of spending declined from 9.1 percent of the GNP to 5.8 percent. In part,
this development was the consequence of being at the tail end of
the Kennedy-Johnson period of domestic reform. But Nixon also was
not a laissez faire conservative during his career. He had himself
suffered as a youngster from an economic system that was callous
even to the hardworking, and deep in his marrow he realized that
destiny or fate had resurrected Richard Nixon not to deal with the
squabbles of domestic reallocations, but with the grandeur of historic, foreign policy opportunities.[12]

THE TENETS OF THE NIXON-
KISSINGER FOREIGN POLICY

Historians will be unraveling for generations the fine dividing line between Nixon and his national security advisor and later secretary of state, Henry Kissinger. Kissinger, a German Jewish refugee, was, as noted, a professor of government at Harvard University and an associate of New York's liberal Republican governor, Nelson Rockefeller. His major scholarly work exhibited two themes: a genuine respect for the balance of power statesmen of eighteenth- and nineteenth-century Europe, and an insistence that nuclear weapons could be used in strategic or limited ways, a doctrine abhorrent to most of the civilized world after the destruction of Hiroshima and Nagasaki. Kissinger's academic approach to a global worldview paralleled Nixon's practical experience and his own reflections. To them, the earth was dominated by two superpowers, and they had very little concern with the southern parts of the globe except as they were prospective ideological battlegrounds. At times, during the long and difficult path to a Vietnam settlement, the president and his principal foreign policy advisor seemed to stumble all over each other seeing who could be more hawkish in tone and in policy.

The Nixon-Kissinger foreign policy is usually seen as the apex in American realism, a carefully modulated and professional demonstration of the use of power and diplomacy. In fact, though, it was a more complex mosaic that at times was harsh, reckless, and counterproductive to the interests and ideals of the United States. The best testimony of the success or failure of a government's actions is not contained in the memories of its participants, but in the assessment of whether or not a nation is more secure, its people happier, the world safer, its aspirations more noble than before one's stewardship. If those criteria are truly applied, the Nixon-Kissinger foreign policy is studded with deficiencies.

Immediately on assuming the national security advisor position, Kissinger with Nixon's approval drew up a plan for control of information and for the formulation of policy options that effectively centralized power in the White House staff and downgraded the State Department. Nixon's own secretary of state, William Rogers, allowed that development to occur, believing that his old friendship with the president would compensate for any structural changes. Rogers never realized that Richard Nixon had no real friends, only allies of varying degrees and enemies of great intensity. Later, commentators on the Nixon presidency would lament Rogers's slights. But in politics, one can spend little time on those individuals content to become victims. Rogers limped along into Nixon's second term as the clouds of Watergate darkened, and watched with some satisfaction as the president's two closest advisors, Haldeman and Ehrlichman, were forced to resign.

The National Security Council and the role of its main advisor had changed dramatically from the Truman administration when they were created. Truman relied mainly on the cabinet and the Joint Chiefs during his eventful presidency, and his special assistant for national security affairs actually operated independently of the National Security Council and its executive director. Eisenhower created a host of intra-agency committees and bureaucratized the council with the establishment of a formal planning board that sought consensus before policies reached the president for his review. With a great deal of personal experience in world affairs, Eisenhower and Secretary of State John Foster Dulles were clearly the capstone of any system of policy making. Kennedy distrusted the formal intra-agency committees and bypassed the NSC, often preferring more ad hoc arrangements. His national security advisor, McGeorge Bundy, and Johnson's, Walter Rostow, became important policy makers, and the NSC staff—still separate—provided support when asked. Nixon consolidated the two and approved a new system that gave Kissinger the power to set the NSC agenda and made him chairman of the review groups that would consider the various option papers that filtered up through the bureaucracies to the president. This strategy to tame the foreign policy machinery had as its primary objective not coordination, but control—and control through secrecy. It was to become the hallmark of the Nixon-Kissinger foreign policy.

In making foreign policy in a democratic nation, public opinion and broad approval are essential to success and long-standing commitments. But Nixon and Kissinger conducted much of their work behind closed doors, sealed off at times not just from the American people, but from the leaders of Congress, the State Department, the Joint Chiefs, and even the intelligence agencies. In many cases, the Russians, the great competitor in the administration's bipolar world, knew more than elected officials in the United States about American policies and intentions. Early in his first term, Nixon with

Kissinger's assistance set up a separate system of communication with the Soviet leaders through Ambassador Anatoly Dobrynin, a "backchannel" that was meant to cut out the American State Department and its cabinet secretary.[13]

This penchant for secrecy, for at times even duplicitous diplomacy, for freezing out other essential leaders of the U.S. government from American policy making became patterns of behavior on Nixon's part. He also tried to conduct domestic policy that way, but gave up or got started too late in his doomed second term. However, those basic attitudes carried over to his handling of the Watergate affair. To understand that controversy and its aftermath, one must speculate as to why the normal bureaucratic lag did not restrain Nixon in his handling of the affair. One of the reasons was the alienation of large segments of the government's upper echelon from the administration; fewer and fewer bureaucratic players had a vested interest in Nixon's successes.

In a sense, one can understand the origins of Nixon's preoccupation with secrecy and his wariness about opening up to scrutiny his conduct of the first and greatest foreign policy challenge he faced. He had watched, as more than a disinterested observer, while Lyndon Johnson was destroyed by the Vietnam War. Johnson had overwhelming Democratic majorities in both houses of Congress, while Nixon was a partisan Republican with an equally partisan Democratic Congress. Johnson historically had enjoyed a better press than Nixon in the 1950s, and he was an acknowledged master of the politics of consensus. Nixon, on the other hand, had made a career of exploiting the fault lines of divisiveness. Yet Johnson was forced out of office, and Nixon's pledge to heal the nation's wounds was bound up with settling the war. He publicly promised a peace with honor. Privately, though, Nixon intended to end the war like Ike concluded a Korean settlement—by threatening the enemy with a wave of destruction.

Nixon knew that Eisenhower had informed the Communist Chinese indirectly that he was considering using atomic weapons if the war in Korea continued. Nixon wanted to apply the same strategy in Vietnam. He would pressure the Soviets and eventually the Communist Chinese to stop supporting the North Vietnamese and their Communist allies in South Vietnam in return for American support of Soviet interests and a recognition of the mainland Chinese regime. To the North Vietnamese, he posed as a man willing and able to unleash more violence; he called it the "madman theory"—and he was to be portrayed to them, at his insistence, as a president ready to do anything reckless to end the war.[14]

Faced with a wary Congress and a strong antiwar movement, Nixon cloaked all these considerations in a policy of graduated withdrawal, a "Vietnamization" of the war, as it was called. Actually the last year of the Johnson term had witnessed a policy shift toward more use of South Vietnamese soldiers, and holding on to the urban areas rather than sweeping search and destroy missions in the rural regions. There was increasingly a tacit recognition that two governments were operating in South Vietnam—a pro-West government in the cities and a Communist one in many of the provinces, one visible in the daytime and one in control at night. But under Johnson, the U.S. troop strength reached over five hundred thousand and U.S. casualties continued to mount. Nixon tried to defuse the antiwar movement by buying time and hoping the Thieu government in the south would become stronger. What happened however was that the Thieu government became weaker, and the North Vietnamese, aided by other Communist governments, provided matériel and later men to increase the pressure on the South Vietnamese regime.

The Nixon-Kissinger foreign policy in Vietnam is often seen by its opponents as a long, drawn out failure. But within its own assumptions, it was successful on several counts. First, Nixon did somewhat split off North Vietnam from Russia and Communist China, athough he seriously misjudged their influence and ability to control their ally in Vietnam. Ho Chi Minh and his fellow partisans were dedicated revolutionaries and nationalists who knew that patience and time can be indispensable allies in Asia. Second, Nixon by withdrawing U.S. troops over a four-year period did convey a sense of "progress," such that the strength of the antiwar movement, still vigorous in 1969–71, dropped considerably in the country. Although critics of Nixon generally discount his real concern about the unsettled condition of the United States during the war, Raymond Price has noted that from January 1, 1969, to April 15, 1970, there were forty thousand bombings, attempted bombings, and bomb threats in the United States.[15]

At the beginning of the Nixon administration, the best estimates from the Pentagon were that it would take 8.3 to 13.4 years to pacify and control the Vietcong areas in the south. The Pentagon was also asked to present a highly confidential briefing on bombing options.

The president by mid-March 1969 began the secret bombing of Cambodia to cut the Vietcong supply lines and destroy North Vietnamese supply bases. Prince Norodom Sihanouk had looked the other way on North Vietnamese intrusions into his nation, and now he sanctioned American bombings as well. To keep this tacit understanding from leaking out to the press at home and contradicting the promise of U.S. withdrawals, the administration had the air force forge records of the flights to avoid having to report the incursions into Cambodia. This "dual reporting system," that is, false record keeping, was hidden even from the Strategic Air Command's normal control and monitoring. Nixon in his memoirs acknowledged that he supported the secret war because of Sihanouk's predicament and "the problem of domestic anti-war protest. My administration was only two months old, and I wanted to provoke as a little public outcry as possible at the outset." Kissinger later denied that he knew about the falsification of records, calling it "deplorable."[16]

In the first fourteen months of the bombings, the United States conducted more than 3,630 flights over Cambodia and dropped 110,000 tons of bombs. William Shawcross has chronicled the increased destruction of Cambodia during the Vietnamese war, calling it "a sideshow" to the main engagements. That sideshow ended up destroying the basic social fabric of that nation, turning it from a Switzerland into a war-divided Poland. In the process, the dynamics of war broke down the restraints of royalty and custom and led to the takeover of a Communist regime under Pol Pot, a government so brutal and genocidal that its role model can only have been Hitler's Third Reich. Years later, with Pot out of power, the Cambodian cities and countryside still did not know peace, prosperity, or even a decent calm.[17]

In the early months of the administration, the Nixon-Kissinger control was yet to be consolidated. In April 1969, a North Korean jet shot down a U.S. Navy EC 121, killing all thirty-one men aboard. Kissinger and the president pushed for immediate retaliation, but Secretary of State Rogers, Secretary of Defense Melvin Laird, and CIA Director Richard Helms disagreed. Later the press was to praise Nixon's restraint, but the episode only confirmed the president's and Kissinger's difficulties in attempting to ride roughshod over the bureaucracy. Having set the stage for circumventing Rogers, Nixon and Kissinger began to deal directly with the military, especially with the head of the Joint Chiefs, and often excluded the secretary of defense from the decision-making process.

For the president, the key problem remained Vietnam, and he pushed to gain influence with the Soviet Union to get that nation to exercise some restraint over the North Vietnamese Communists. In May, a military correspondent for the *New York Times* published an article describing the B-52 raids over Cambodia. Nixon, with Kissinger trying to prove his loyalty to his new boss, insisted on a series of wiretaps, including several on some members of the NSC staff and on important members of the media. The preoccupation with "leaks" became almost obsessive, and the president began to instigate and later countenance a special adjunct group to undertake surveillance and political intrigue that eventually led to the creation of the "plumbers" (a group to plug leaks) and the Watergate break-in. In part, the president's approval of this highly unorthodox and probably illegal operation grew out the CIA's general inability to operate legally domestically and FBI Director J. Edgar Hoover's unwillingness to become involved in such surveillance for Nixon. Hoover, a lifelong bureaucratic infighter, had learned that caution is sometimes the best ally of survival, especially in what was becoming an administration of purposeful deceit.[18]

Kissinger, however, was emerging as a master of intrigue as he expertly encouraged Nixon's animus toward Rogers and Laird. Privately he entertained aides with rumors of an alleged peculiar personal relationship between Nixon and Rogers, revelations about Nixon's intellectual shortcomings, the president's alleged evening drinking bouts, his personal hatreds of liberals, the press, the Jews, and other groups that had crossed the president in the past. This was the emotional glow of the Nixon honeymoon.

The early months also saw a major contradiction in the administration's policy toward North Vietnam. On the one hand, the president supported Laird's Vietnamization and a gradual unilateral withdrawal; on the other, he asked North Vietnam for a mutual withdrawal of forces from the south and a cessation of hostilities, which would guarantee that the Thieu government would stay in place. Obviously, the North Vietnamese had no real incentive to leave, and so Nixon and Kissinger planned an escalation of the bombing—an early dose of the madman theory.

While the president talked publicly of removing one hundred thousand U.S. troops by the end of the year, Kissinger and his aide, Alexander Haig, put together a policy study focusing on increasing the war effort. The plan called for the bombing of Hanoi, Haiphong, and other areas in North Vietnam, the destruction of the dike system, a ground invasion of North Vietnam, the closing of the north-south passes along the so-called Ho Chi Minh Trail (probably with nuclear weapons), and the bombing of North Vietnam's main railroad links with China. In addition, the administration sent a graphic message to the Soviets. For twenty-nine days, the Strategic Air Command was ordered to leave its nuclear-armed B-52 aircraft on combat ready status—a major jump in their state of readiness.[19]

As the antiwar sentiment mobilized for the October 15th peace moratorium marches across the United States, Kissinger continued to court the liberal press and skeptics in the Congress, asking them to give the new administration a chance to bring about peace. The president, sensitive to domestic opposition, had decided to give a more moderate speech to the American people than he planned and talked about a "just peace." He appealed for the support of the "silent majority" of Americans, and the polls showed later that 77 percent of those listening to him backed his policy.[20]

In the coming weeks, the administration moved to challenge the appeal of the antiwar movement by orchestrating the sending of letters to newspapers and placing advertisements attacking groups opposed to the president's policy. Vice President Spiro Agnew confronted the television networks, accusing them of biased reporting, and noting the concentration of power in the hands of a small, privileged elite operating out of New York City. The FBI and CIA were instructed to keep a close eye on radicals and dissidents, the draft was replaced by a lottery, and the president announced that two hundred thousand more men would be leaving Vietnam for home. Open, broad-based resistance began to decline as Nixon contemplated his next move.

But American concerns about an endless war continued. In November 1969, reports of a U.S. Army massacre of more than 350 South Vietnamese in the village of My Lai reached home. Horror, shame, guilt, patriotism, jingoism all mixed as Americans tried to sort out their feelings over the atrocity. An Indiana mother of one of the American soldiers involved lamented, "I gave them a good boy and they sent me back a murderer." Nixon, the commander in chief, privately attacked those who publicized the massacre; it was the work of "those dirty rotten Jews from New York," he concluded. Kissinger agreed that "all they want to do is make a scapegoat." At the end of the year, the president insisted on restoring a budget cut for the Provincial Reconnaissance Units, U.S.-led teams that targeted and killed Vietcong leaders in the south. He argued, "We got to have more of this. Assassinations. Killings. That's what they're doing [the other side]."[21]

Ironically by 1970, "Vietnamization" of the war meant an increase in bombing and brought the war further into Cambodia and into northern Laos. Only in this way could the Thieu regime be protected, and North Vietnam be made to understand that Nixon was a man to be reckoned with. By the end of 1969, the number of U.S. bombing missions over tiny Laos reached a total of 242,000. The president defended these raids as necessary to save the lives of American and South Vietnamese fighting forces and to curtail the infiltration of North Vietnamese troops and supplies along the Ho Chi Minh Trail. Kissinger added that the north had increased its troop strength in Laos, and was threatening Thailand. Strong opposition developed in the bureaucracy however as the State Department, CIA, and even Defense Department people balked at the risks.

In early 1970, Kissinger met with North Vietnamese representatives and pushed for an end to the hostilities. But the North Vietnamese delegation, headed by Le Duc Tho, insisted on a new government being formed in the south—a stipulation to which Nixon could not agree. Pointedly, Le Duc Tho asked Kissinger how the United States could expect to win while it was withdrawing troops, when it could not gain victory with a force of five hundred thousand soldiers helping Thieu's government. Obviously, the answer was massive bombing.[22]

Then to add to the administration's problems, the previously resilient regime of Prince Sihanouk was overthrown by a coup of anti-Communist Cambodians. The coup led to a civil war and eventually, as noted, to the establishment of a genocidal Communist government under Pol Pot. In April, United States and South Vietnamese forces had invaded Cambodia, a move the president insisted was meant to clean out the North Vietnamese sanctuaries in the "Parrot's Beak" or the eastern region. The invasion led to another wave of antiwar protests, campus demonstrations, and the killing of four students at Kent State University by the Ohio National Guard.[23]

In the United States Senate, the Cooper-Church amendment was introduced, which mandated the withdrawal of all U.S. forces from Cambodia after June 30, an extraordinary intrusion into presidential war-making powers and a clear sign to Nixon of growing public disapproval. The strategy and objectives of the president however were at times unclear. The president had excluded Laird and Rogers from having any major input in planning the invasion, and Nixon, egged on by Kissinger, was determined to show his toughness. Circumventing his own secretary of defense and the Joint Chiefs, he began to deal directly with General Creighton Abrams in Saigon and with other military leaders.

Nixon, in many ways one of the few presidents able enough to think about international politics in a global way, began to personalize the war in Southeast Asia. He told Kissinger on one occasion, "The liberals are waiting to see Nixon let Cambodia go down the drain the way Eisenhower let Cuba go down the drain." Angrily, he denounced some campus radicals as "bums," and soon the term became generalized by some of the press to indicate the president's alleged attitude toward youthful dissent overall. Then in a touching footnote, Nixon, weary and hyperactive after a news conference, visited, in the early morning, antiwar demonstrators near the Lincoln monument. There he genuinely attempted to reach out to them, beyond their hostility, to explain himself and his views in a sincere but at times clumsy way. Unfortunately, the press reported it as the president talking about football to the young and the sensitive.[24]

As opposition grew, Nixon became increasingly suspicious of those around him. Kissinger and Haig reflected those sentiments as well, and the FBI was asked to increase its wiretapping on two more members of the National Security Council staff after several members quit in protest over the Cambodian invasion. By June, the administration declared the Cambodian offensive a success, but consequently the South Vietnamese military was stretched into Cambodia as well. The North Vietnamese refused to meet Kissinger in Paris for more peace talks, the suspicious Khmer Rouge (Cambodian Communists) became more allied with Hanoi, and domestic opposition was intensified. The Cooper-Church amendment died in the House of Representatives, but as Kissinger concluded later, "the pattern was clear," the North Vietnamese could now see that even Congress was beginning to walk away from a seemingly endless war.

The Vietnam conflict and its divisive consequences took a considerable amount of Nixon's time and energy, but to his credit he retained an interest in global strategy and sought to reach some accommodation with the Soviet Union and more dramatically to restore relations with mainland China. Few Republican politicians had so vigorously attacked Truman over the fall of that ancient nation to the Communists, and Chiang's forces on Taiwan (Formosa) had a long-time friend and ally in Nixon. But he was determined to do what no Democratic president could have gotten away with—establish ties with Communist China. In the process he had to jettison U.S. commitments to Chiang in order to pursue his romantic diplomatic initiatives.

Amid all of this, the administration seemed to evince little concern with human rights and the panoply of difficulties associated with Third World nations. Even when severe problems erupted in Greece, the U.S.'s long-time ally, Nixon and Kissinger were rather detached. Appropriately enough, neither of them even mentions that nation in any major way in his memoirs. Quietly they supported the military junta in that country and overlooked human rights violations there. The same distance can be seen in the administration's policy in the Nigerian civil war between the federal government and the secessionist state of Biafra. For some reason, probably to spite his own State Department, Nixon wanted to recognize Biafra. Then Nixon decided he himself should mediate the dispute. Meanwhile the lives of a large number of Biafrans were being threatened by the war and the possibilities of starvation. Eventually the president and Kissinger decided not to take on the State Department and fell into line with its pro-federal government tilt. Curiously, Nixon on one occasion asked Kissinger, "They're going to let them starve, aren't they, Henry?"—referring to his own State Department. Kissinger's response was a clear "Yes," and then they moved on to other business.[25]

Throughout all of these ventures, Kissinger's role, first operational and then policy making in the broadest sense, became more pronounced. With the liberal elements of the press and his fellow academicians, Kissinger posed as a comrade sharing their concerns for a quick peace. With Nixon and his hard-line advisors, he was a frequent advocate of tougher action. He knew that in Washington knowledge is power, and his power reached into informal alliances with State Department people as he quieted contradictory intelligence findings from the CIA. Secretary of Defense Laird insisted that he was not being fully apprised of National Security Agency intelligence findings. To counter Nixon's and Kissinger's use of a backchannel to the Soviets, Laird tapped into the backchannel sources himself to find out what Kissinger and the president were doing!

After the wave of protests over the Cambodian invasion, Nixon insisted that the intelligence agencies prove that Communist agitators were behind the demonstrations. In addition, an aggressive domestic intelligence plan was presented by a low-level Nixon aide, Tom Clark Huston, which would later come to light during the Watergate hearings and be blown out of proportion. Huston proposed that the intelligence agencies be allowed to conduct searches and burglaries in violation of usual restraints and probably the letter of the law and the Constitution. Both Attorney General John Mitchell and FBI Director Hoover strongly opposed the proposal, and Nixon backed down. In fact, the CIA with President Johnson's approval had carried out a spying operation on American radicals in 1967 called "Project Chaos." Kissinger and Haig were aware of these reports and may also have asked the National Security Agency to eavesdrop on members of their own staff.[26]

The one strategic area of the world Nixon avoided letting Kissinger have jurisdiction over was the Middle East. Concerned about Kissinger's effectiveness because he was a Jew and anxious to give his secretary of state some role in foreign policy, the president let Rogers move into the vacuum. But Kissinger was quietly establishing backchannels with important Israeli leaders, undercutting the secretary's initiatives there as well. By 1969, the Arabs wanted the Israelis to give back the lands they conquered in 1967, and Israel demanded in turn that the Arab states recognize its right to exist. Especially difficult to deal with was the growing role of the Palestine Liberation Organization, which insisted on a separate state in the region.

By the end of 1969, the president and Kissinger feared that high-level talks between Israel and the Arabs would increase the power of the Soviet Union, and the president instead encouraged the Israelis to be more aggressive in their January 1970 raids into Egypt. The "Rogers Plan" put forth by the secretary of state had envisioned however that Israel would withdraw to its pre-1967 boundaries in the Sinai Desert in return for recognition from Egypt. He further proposed negotiations between Israel and Jordon over the West Bank, the future of a unified Jerusalem, and the fate of Palestine refugees. The Rogers Plan was abandoned by Nixon and Kissinger and vigorously opposed by Israeli politicians and the strong pro-Israeli lobby in the United States. Oddly enough, important parts of the plan would later become the keystone of President Carter's celebrated agreement.[27]

As Israel and Egypt seemed poised again for war, the Soviets were sending men and matériel into Egypt and warning of Israeli military power. Kissinger predicted a great power confrontation with the Soviets, but Nixon wanted a summit conference and was more restrained. Instead the president increased U.S. shipments to Israel and played a moderate role until the PLO threatened King Hussein of Jordan.

In September a Marxist faction of the Palestine guerrilla movement hijacked one Swiss, one British, and two American airplanes, and an angry Nixon ordered the navy to bomb guerrilla strongholds of the Palestine group. A more prudent Secretary of Defense Laird disobeyed the order, citing "bad weather" for his refusal to respond. The president also ordered a mobilization of naval power in the region as a show of force to the Soviets. When the Syrians began to undertake tank movements into Jordan, Nixon placed twenty thousand U.S. troops on alert and moved naval forces into the Mediterranean Sea. To the Israelis he pledged U.S. air strikes against Syrian tank forces if necessary, but the Syrians abruptly stopped their movements. Kissinger was to sing Nixon's praises, saying that he had "a great sense of timing; he knew instinctively when the moment for decision had arrived; and he would then act resolutely, especially if he could insulate himself from too much personal controversy." To Nixon and to Kissinger, the confrontation was a great power struggle, one involving the Soviet Union and its agents in the Middle East tinderbox.

In another part of the world closer to home, the president and Kissinger once again confronted the Soviet Union. After taking office, Nixon asked for an increase in operations by the CIA against Castro's regime in Cuba. News reached the administration that the Soviets were building a submarine base on that island near the harbor of Cienfuegos. The State Department, the CIA, and the Pentagon refused to climb on the panic bandwagon, and they viewed it as a recreational site for Soviet submarine crews. Kissinger, fearing that Nixon would not act decisively, leaked the submarine base report to the press, thus pushing the president closer to the brink. Soon, it became in Nixon's and Kissinger's eyes a replay of Kennedy's showdown in 1962, which they both admired. The Soviets seemed genuinely confused about the furor and officially denied that they were constructing a base there. Nixon and Kissinger praised each other's firmness as the Soviets supposedly abandoned Cienfuegos.[28]

By 1971, the situation in the Mideast worsened. The new president of Egypt, Anwar el-Sadat, made overtures to the United States, asking for help in a peace initiative in return for expelling the Russians from his nation. But Kissinger and Nixon for their own reasons did not pick up the signals and simply shelved Secretary Rogers's peace plan.

The Nixon-Kissinger mark was also left elsewhere, most controversially in the Latin American nation of Chile. Neither of them cared much about the Third World or underdeveloped countries unless they saw a Soviet threat there. Chile, however, filled the bill. In the 1960s, the CIA had established strong contacts with the ruling elites of that nation. Money was poured into favorable Christian Democrat party candidates' campaigns under the Kennedy and Johnson administrations. Nixon himself was less favorably inclined to the Chileans, especially as they became more demanding. Kissinger's view was that Latin America was not a significant region of the world. "Nothing important can come from the South. History has never been produced in the South. The axis of history starts in Moscow, goes to Bonn, crosses over to Washington, and then goes to Tokyo," the former professor explained.[29]

But in Chile, the political strength of Salvador Allende, a leftist figure of some stature, was growing. American investors, especially the ITT Corporation and its president, Harold Geneen, were concerned about an Allende victory in the presidential race and the probability that he would nationalize foreign industries. Geneen even offered to help bankroll the opposition in Chile and was willing to work with the CIA to further those objectives. Kissinger was generally unmoved by appeals from Nixon contributors, but the president was not. Nixon's old client, PepsiCo and its president, Donald Kendall, were also concerned, and Nixon ordered the CIA and other government agencies to move against Allende. According to journalist Seymour Hersh, CIA Director Richard Helms interpreted that directive as encompassing even the assassination of Allende if that were necessary. Later Helms was publicly to deny that extrapolation.[30]

The CIA acted on two tracks: anti-Allende propaganda and political programs, and a more secret strategy to use special CIA agents to work with right-wing Chileans who would overthrow the government if necessary. The latter approach was approved by the so-called "40 Committee," a high-level group of government leaders who were supposed to direct all covert CIA operations. The group was established by NSCM (National Security Council Memorandum) #40, thus its name. Money flowed quickly and surreptitiously, cover-up payments were sought for CIA agents, records were destroyed, congressional committees were later misled. Hersh has argued that the Chilean story was a precursor to Watergate. Nixon even withheld information from his own ambassador to Chile, and to further its programs the administration approved money going to those willing to stage a coup in Chile. The ambassador, Edward Korry, caught on to the doings, warned the White House about CIA activities, not realizing they were authorized at the highest levels of government, thus leaving a clear record that the president and Kissinger were fully aware of what was happening. Later in 1975, Kissinger and Haig would insist to the Senate that they had actually stopped the CIA's attempt at a coup in Chile. Nixon in 1976 would insist he did not know anything about the planning at all.[31]

When Allende was elected, the administration pushed for economic sanctions, and the CIA embraced a strong propaganda effort to discredit him. There were some serious concerns in the U.S. government that Allende, an avowed advocate of Fidel Castro, was a Communist or a front man for the Communists. Thus, Chile could be seen as a pawn in the great confrontation that had characterized the postwar world. Nixon surely shared some of those fears, but he seems to have been more influenced by his corporate benefactors and bent U.S. interests in part to satisfy their interests. In September 1973, a military coup overthrew Allende's government, and he was assassinated.

As Nixon and Kissinger shared their secrets, they became more closely intertwined even though neither one trusted or liked the other. Kissinger established interdepartmental committees, set their agenda, controlled the flow of information, and became in the process Nixon's closest advisor. Kissinger in 1971 insisted that the president "tended more and more to delegate the tactical management of foreign policy to me. . . . He did not believe that the conductor need be seen to play every instrument in the orchestra." But Kissinger was no second fiddle player; he began to move out of the president's shadow into his own celebrity status, soon eclipsing even Nixon in the area of the executive's choice, foreign policy.[32]

Later he argued that the president's deviousness was due to his distrust of his cabinet and his unwillingness to impose discipline on his administration. After the South Vietnamese invasion of Laos, Nixon decided to reinstall a taping system in the White House, probably because of his desire to have a permanent account of his conversations with Kissinger. Kissinger did not know of the existence of the system; the president on the other hand was not aware that Kissinger often taped his calls. Both were cognizant of the fact that the administration had approved wiretaps on newspaperpeople and government associates, taps that probably were at that time illegal and likely to cause problems if made public. Eventually, the tapes of those calls and conversations became a major Watergate issue, and led to Nixon's demise.[33]

One of the people recorded was Daniel Ellsberg, a former government analyst and later antiwar leader. Ellsberg leaked to several newspapers the *Pentagon Papers*, a series of studies ordered by Secretary of Defense Robert McNamara, which were highly critical of U.S. involvement in Vietnam. The papers did not cover the Nixon years, but the president was convinced, in large part by Kissinger, that the leaks represented a threat to national security and the government's ability to keep its allies' trust. When the Supreme Court upheld the right of the media to publicize the information, the administration's fears about leaks increased. As noted, the president and his advisors moved to set up a separate group of trusted agents to perform surveillance. Thus another piece of the Watergate story had fallen into place.

In September 1970, several months after the Senate considered the Cooper-Church amendment to pull U.S. troops out of Cambodia, that same body debated the McGovern-Hatfield amendment, which would force a withdrawal of all American troops from South Vietnam by December 31, 1971. It was defeated, but it showed the drift of sentiment. The administration, backed by some intelligence estimates, argued that the Thieu government was gaining in the war effort. In fact, Hanoi was preparing at that time for another major offensive after a respite from fighting. American confidence should have been more guarded, for after the South Vietnamese invasion of Laos in early 1971, Thieu's armies performed badly and they had retreated.

By mid-1971 Hanoi indicated it would accept a peace if an election were held in the south, a proposal that appealed to some American critics of the war and to some South Vietnamese foes of the Thieu regime. The South Vietnamese opposition was crystallizing around the nation's vice president, Nguyen Cao Ky, and military leader General Duong Van Minh. Nixon approved Kissinger's approaching the North Vietnamese about negotiations, and the administration abandoned its previous insistence on mutual withdrawals, and proposed that the North Vietnamese and the Vietcong be allowed to keep their troops in the south. Kissinger was willing to discuss a possible coalition government in Saigon, and he asked only for a "decent interval" between its establishment and its inevitable demise. Hanoi agreed to release American prisoners of war after the American withdrawal of troops and did not press the administration to oust Thieu. The election thus would provide the means to end Thieu's regime without the U.S. publicly abandoning an ally.[34] But in August, Ky was disqualified by the South Vietnamese Supreme Court and General Minh withdrew. The administration focused attention on its proposed breakthroughs with Russia and China, and the war in Vietnam continued.

In May 1971, the president, concerned about his chances for reelection and bogged down in the Southeast Asia regional war, announced a disarmament treaty with the Soviets. The main bait that caught the Soviets' attention though was not mentioned publicly—the promise of huge, cheap wheat sales. The Russians bought over $1 billion worth of wheat, which drove the prices up for U.S. consumers and others. The secrecy of the deal and the conditions of the treaty were initially kept from most of the U.S. bureaucracy, including American disarmament negotiators in Europe.[35]

The administration had pushed in 1969 for an antiballistic missile system and had proposed a limit on the number of nuclear launchers. Actually, the United States had already stopped deploying such launchers two years before; the restriction would only affect the Soviets anyhow. The president had Kissinger do most of the important negotiating himself as a way of maintaining secrecy and also denying to the U.S. delegation the credit that was important for his reelection campaign. Because he had frozen out most of the arms control bureaucracy, Kissinger concluded an agreement that did not control submarine-launched ballistic missiles, an obvious advantage to the Soviet Union, which was committed to a major buildup in that area. Such an omission would lead to serious military concerns and severe congressional criticism later. Thus, important components of Soviet strategic power were not covered by this slipshod approach, and the final agreement would be postponed so as to heighten the sense of achievement to be associated with the summit conference between Nixon and the Soviet leaders.[36]

The Nixon-Kissinger duo focused its attention also on overtures to Communist China. The idea of recognizing China was really Nixon's; in an article in *Foreign Affairs* in 1967, he argued that continued isolation of China made no sense any more. By late 1970, the president sent conciliatory messages quietly through a variety of diplomatic channels expressing to the Communist Chinese regime a desire for some reconciliation. After the poor Republican showing in the 1970 congressional elections, the defeat of two Supreme Court nominees, intense opposition to his Cambodian invasion, and campus riots against the war, Nixon needed a great foreign policy triumph, and China was now there for the taking and the traveling.[37]

The president let it be known that the future of Taiwan was not an international dispute, but an internal problem to be solved peacefully by the Chinese people. Nixon and Kissinger expected that the Chinese Communists would help the Americans reach a negotiated settlement in Vietnam, and they consequently supported China's ally, Pakistan, against the Soviet Union and India on the issue of the Bangladesh secessionist movement in East Pakistan.

Nixon played a high stakes game—one that only a noted anti-Communist warrior could sustain. He was selling out Taiwan and his old ally Chiang Kai-shek; he knew, however, that if the China approach failed, he would be highly vulnerable to attacks on the right from the China lobby. When the United States stood idly by and let the Communists replace the Taiwan regime in the UN Security Council, congressional conservatives were critical of the change, but the president himself said little beyond some mild words of nominal criticism of the United Nations.

Another respite in the Cold War came in Europe where the efforts of the socialist chancellor of West Germany, Willy Brandt, led to a diplomatic rapprochement that cooled down the chronic and dangerous disputes over the status of the city of Berlin. From the end of World War II and its uneasy alliance, the Russians and the West faced each other in that divided city. Truman, Eisenhower, and Kennedy had speculated about the chances of war in connection with Berlin. Brandt's "Ostpolitik" (Eastern policy) led to the Soviets granting the right of unimpeded access from West Germany to West Berlin and the right of West Berliners to visit East Germany and East Berlin. West Germany began negotiations over some persistent problems with Poland, the status of East Germany as a separate entity was somewhat acknowledged, and the Soviets were allowed to establish a consulate in that divided city.[38]

In their grand design, Nixon and Kissinger were allied in many secrets, the most pervasive being their own addiction to secrecy. One can sympathize somewhat with their concerns by looking at the disclosure of Kissinger's conversations at the highest levels about Nixon's desire to tilt toward Pakistan in its conflict with India over the secessionist movement in Bangladesh. Nixon had counted on Pakistani President Yahya Khan to approach China about his proposed dramatic visit, which would enhance his reelection chances in 1972. Despite Khan's brutal repression in Bangladesh, the president's decision was firm. He wrote, "To all hands. Don't squeeze Yahya at this time." Afterwards, Nixon was quoted as having threatened nuclear war with the Soviets during the India-Pakistan war if they intervened. Actually there is evidence that the Soviet Union was also urging restraint upon the Indians. But the conflict illustrated several lessons: how misjudgments can indeed lead to a threat of nuclear war, how desperate the president was to hold Pakistani favor, and how the administration had a right to suspect leaks and bureaucratic sabotage. The president and Kissinger would learn the last lesson all too well.[39]

Bureaucratic intrigue was vividly stripped bare when it was revealed that the Chairman of the Joint Chiefs of Staff, Admiral Thomas Moorer, and probably others high up in the Pentagon were employing a navy stenographer to spy on Kissinger in the NSC and to pass on secret documents to the military. Apparently, some of the Pentagon's top brass were concerned about Kissinger's clandestine diplomatic activities. The president and Kissinger had cut the secretary of defense out of the flow of information as they had the secretary of state. Now the military man they most trusted in the White House, Admiral Moorer, was betraying them.

The president was remarkably detached from the spying episode, and an angry Kissinger realized his own vulnerability. In fact in 1971, Nixon had also privately begun to question Kissinger's sanity. Nixon even went on to reappoint Moorer, a bad sign for Kissinger. In one sense, the president had the best of all worlds— a secretary of defense neutralized, a chairman of the JCS exposed and weakened, and an arrogant NSC assistant brought to heel.[40]

In early 1972, Nixon announced his candidacy for renomination, and a week later indicated his intention to withdraw seventy thousand more troops from Vietnam by May 1. Secretary Laird dutifully noted that all combat responsibilities now would be turned over the South Vietnamese. However, the peace talks were bogging down. To the public, the president reemphasized U.S. flexibility, bared some of the secrets of the previous futile negotiations with the North Vietnamese, and wrapped his policies in the American flag. His popularity in the polls began to increase, and the ratings of the Democratic front-runner for the presidency, Senator Edmund Muskie, of Maine began to drop.

And then in February the president and Kissinger left for Beijing; the secret diplomacy paid off handsomely as the Western press followed Nixon, picturing him as the Marco Polo of his time. A jealous Kissinger watched as the president emerged on center stage. Under administration pressure, the Communist Chinese quietly urged the North Vietnamese to negotiate a peace treaty. And the president chatting with an ailing Mao Tse-tung, toasting Chou En-lai, and strolling on the old wall captivated the viewing world.

But in March, the North Vietnamese answer was a major offensive to destroy Thieu. The president in response ordered a massive series of B-52 bombings, explored mining Haiphong harbor, and took the war more broadly into the north and against previously restricted targets. Apparently at this time, Kissinger made up his mind to devote his energies to a final ending of the war by a circuitous route that would alienate him from the president. As the administration withdrew U.S. forces and changed the draft law, the weakness of the South Vietnamese army became even more apparent. Kissinger sought some sort of face-saving settlement to allow an "honorable" withdrawal, and he hoped to keep Thieu in place for a while. Meanwhile, his assistant, Alexander Haig, was becoming privy to the president's thoughts and his reservations about Kissinger himself.[41]

The administration obviously feared that the new bombing would cause the Russians to cancel the summit. Kissinger had his reservations about the bombing, but the president directed retaliation, and Haig helped to support the commander in chief. But the Soviets for their own reasons were unwilling to abandon the summit after all; Nixon seemed to have understood the global dynamics better than his advisors. And consequently, the Hanoi offensive was curtailed. The lesson to the president was apparent: his geopolitical calculations were correct.

Thus, with U.S. troops leaving Vietnam, regardless of that poor country's plight, and his visit in China, the president went on to Moscow for his summit that would ratify the SALT I agreements. Seymour Hersh has summarized the agreement reached: the two nations would limit the number of antiballistic missile defense sites, they would freeze the number of land-based ICBM launchers, and they would restrict the number of submarine-based ballistic missile launchers. The interim agreement did not mandate a reduction in offensive weapons systems, but it placed a limit on missile launchers. As has been noted, no limit was placed on independently targeted warheads (MIRVs) on each missile. The last oversight would be especially unfortunate for future arms negotiations.[42]

In April, Kissinger tried to recover his earlier misstep by seeking to discuss SLBMs and advocating an agreement that granted the Soviets the right to build up to 62 submarines with 950 launchers. It is difficult to see how Kissinger's negotiating style effected any real constraint on Soviet rebuilding efforts. Back home, he tried to put a different face on the negotiations. Shrewdly, Secretary of Defense Laird pushed for increased military spending and support for the Trident nuclear submarine; in return, he would be quiet about Kissinger's negotiating errors. Surprisingly, Nixon was not much involved in the details or the difficult policy matters.

The interim agreement contained provisions to stop the conversion of lighter ICBMs into heavier ones, but no definition was given for either category. Although he did not explain the matter, Kissinger was aware that the Soviets were planning to install new Soviet weapons in old silos, which they did in May 1972. Later critics of SALT I were to argue that the Russians had violated the agreement. Meanwhile, the Pentagon and the U.S. SALT negotiators created a fire storm, fearing that Kissinger had given away too much. Nixon, however, stood firmly behind Kissinger this time, and later ordered firings in the Arms Control and Disarmament Agency, probably as a concession to the hawks in Congress.

By the summer of 1972, negotiations between Hanoi and the administration intensified. As has been noted, Kissinger in April had let it be known to the Russians that the United States would accept the presence of North Vietnamese troops in the south. One North Vietnamese official who served Le Duc Tho, Nguyen Co Thach, concluded that the most important factors in pursuing negotiations were the American withdrawal and the decision to allow North Vietnamese armies to stay in the south. The North Vietnamese, seeing their opportunity, pushed for the recognition of two "lawful" governments in the south.

Kissinger knew that his own shaky position in the administration would be propped up if he could pull off a peace treaty before the 1972 presidential election, and so he persevered. As Kissinger continued his search for a negotiated settlement, he faced increased resentment from Nixon over not being informed enough about the substance of negotiations in October. In addition, the president now was concerned about a negative response to the peace overtures at home, and he deliberately slowed down the pace of U.S. negotiations with Hanoi. Kissinger was to insist later that he shared with Nixon everything central to the negotiations, and that the president never countermanded his designs. But while he was involved in sensitive negotiations, Kissinger's own aide, Haig, was undermining his boss and warning the president and his inner circle of a possible "bloodbath" if Hanoi gained control of the south.[43]

The points of difference between Hanoi and the administration were the continual presence of North Vietnamese troops in the south, the idea of a coalition government in the south, and the implementation of the cease-fire. Kissinger had figured he would work on a compromise peace treaty with Hanoi, and that Nixon would bring Thieu into line. He went so far as to announce publicly that "peace is at hand," a statement that was to haunt Kissinger as the war escalated. On November 4, a strange interview with Kissinger was published in which he proclaimed himself basically a loner, and concluded that the American people admired the individual cowboy on horseback. The Harvard professor had become Gary Cooper, and Vietnam was his High Noon.[44] By the end of the year, a glum Kissinger was increasingly isolated from the White House and was left with the option of either resigning or going along with Nixon's decision to increase bombing during the Christmas season. He did the latter.

Thieu, opposing the proposed settlement, had increased his pressure on Nixon, and seemed to sense that he could prevail over Kissinger. Finally the president assured the South Vietnamese president of his continuing support, and pledged that despite the peace agreement's provisions for power-sharing, the administration would consider Thieu as the only proper authority in the area. If the North Vietnamese stepped up their attacks, the president would send U.S. air forces to bomb the Communists once again. Nixon's Christmas bombing was meant to convince Thieu of U.S. seriousness in that regard. As opposition grew in Congress, the administration realized that public patience was growing thin at least in the legislative branch. On January 5, 1973, Nixon pointedly assured Thieu, "Should you decide, as I trust you will, to go with us, you have my assurance of continued assistance in the post-settlement period and that we will respond with full force should the settlement be violated by the North Vietnamese."

In January, negotiations resumed between Kissinger and the

North Vietnamese delegation. A quick settlement was reached on terms similar to the October proposals. The war was quieted or so it seemed. Eventually the North Vietnamese would depose the government in the south, and the last of U.S. forces would leave ignominiously as Saigon fell. Later Kissinger would argue that the administration had done all it could to protect the Saigon regime. "We sought not an interval before collapse, but lasting peace with honor. But for the collapse of executive authority as a result of Watergate, I believe we would have succeeded," he insisted.[45]

The Nixon-Kissinger foreign policy is usually seen as the high point of that blighted presidency and a series of startling triumphs of American realpolitik. Supporters of the administration maintain the following: they ended the Vietnam War, reached arms control agreements with the Soviets, protected Western interests in the Middle East, and opened up the People's Republic of China. With Nixon's grasp of international politics and Kissinger's historical perspective and attention to detail, the United States displayed a surety of purpose and a vision rare in the post-World War II world.

Yet there are some serious qualifications or criticisms that can be laid alongside these views: the United States finally accepted peace terms in 1973 that were what North Vietnam generally offered in 1968. Was the death and destruction and domestic turmoil worth it? The agreements with the Soviet Union were real achievements, but Kissinger's intervention and the president's vague policies led to some questionable concessions. U.S. actions in Chile, Nigeria, Pakistan, and the Middle East were not, as has been seen, case studies in surety, morality, or hard calculations of national interest.

Critics of the Nixon administration see the same patterns of behavior in its foreign policy as in Watergate. The deception, the crude opportunism, the disrespect for law, custom, and tradition are precursors of the final act of the Nixon demise. More than any other administration, this one avoided consulting its own ambassadors, agency chiefs, Congress, and public. If foreign policy rests on consensus, then Nixon and Kissinger never laid the groundwork sufficiently for what they themselves saw as their greatest achievement, the reconstruction of American foreign policy.

Nixon and Kissinger though were somewhat correct in their assumption that much of the bureaucracy was hostile or passive in following new paths. Leaks, power plays, ridiculous jurisdictional disputes are crippling in delicate negotiations, but they are a part of democratic politics—the sloppy way we govern ourselves or let others govern us. Generally it may be said that Nixon and Kissinger were not wrong in some of their resentments, but innovative in their egotisms.

And yet, some of their propensity for secrecy and backchanneling information and decision making led to a fixation that brought forth a private intelligence unit being set up and funded outside of usual government safeguards. That unit, with its close ties to the president's inner circle and the executive himself, very easily became a tool to wreak havoc on enemies, real and imagined. Genuine concern for national security mixed with personal hurts and vendettas, just as it had in previous administrations and previous presidencies. But Nixon left a record of his thoughts, his hatreds, his half-cooked plans for paying back his foes. Nixon was not the only president whose mind and spirit were engaged in the desires to settle scores and take on the hostile world. Those thoughts are a part of the sad fantasies of many a leader and many an everyday workman. But Nixon had to share them with all of us.

WATERGATE: SYMBOL AND SYMPTOM

Watergate has become a symbol for malfeasance in office, for "high crimes and misdemeanors," for gross abuse of high governmental position. The short summary of the story is that members of the administration directed various individuals to break into the Democratic party headquarters in 1972. They were caught, and later confessed to having ties to the White House staff, which led to the inner circle of Nixon's White House. The president and others lied by denying such connections; taped conversations revealed that the president not only planned the cover-up of those ties, but may have actually instigated other illegal activities.

More supportive observers of the Nixon presidency insist that the Watergate affair is an aberration that came from a breakdown in the otherwise carefully crafted staff structure that sealed the mercurial and often resentful president from the consequences of his own musings and outbursts. Haldeman, Kissinger, and Ehrlichman took overall direction from the president, listened patiently to his stream of consciousness ravings, and oftentimes neglected to implement his petty vendettas. Only in the case of Nixon aide Charles Colson, it is argued, did a subordinate blindly follow the leader, and thus lay the groundwork for the extralegal group called the "plumbers." When speechwriter Ray Price asked Attorney General John Mitchell who Colson's constituency was, Mitchell responded, "The president's worst instincts." To his associates Nixon was a man of immense complexities, a many-sided personality who could not be totally understood. Price at one point concluded, "One part of Richard Nixon is exceptionally considerate, exceptionally caring, sentimental, generous of spirit. Another part is coldly calculating, devious, craftily manipulative. A third part is angry, vindictive, ill-tempered, mean-spirited."[46]

Some critics have also argued that the demise of the president was due in large part to an excess of Democratic partisanship and that party's control of both houses of Congress. After the election of 1972 Democratic Senator Sam Ervin of North Carolina is supposed to have predicted Nixon's impeachment even before any serious hearings on the matter were held; Jimmy Breslin has written of Majority Leader Thomas "Tip" O'Neill's careful leadership of the House Democrats toward that end early, right after Nixon's reelection. In coming to grips with Watergate, Haldeman in his memoirs speculates that Nixon was really set up by the CIA, which he was trying to control, and Ehrlichman in one of his novels has dramatized the same scenario.[47]

Liberals viewing the same events see them as a vindication of the Constitution, fair play, and the American way of politics. But some conservative commentators have chronicled the long history of abuses, similar in kind, but often not as varied or intense, by Democratic presidents, especially FDR and Lyndon Johnson. Usually forgotten are some important controversies, constitutional issues over executive privilege, the war powers, executive impoundment of funds, and the role of law and presidential discretion during times of national crisis and conflict.[48]

First, it must be acknowledged that Nixon entered the White House in a period of major turbulence, surely not of the magnitude of the Civil War or the Great Depression, but it was in a time when one president had been recently murdered, and a second president forced out of office as a consequence of the Vietnam War and passionate dissent at home. As noted, between January 1, 1969, and April 15, 1970, there were forty thousand bombings, attempted bombings and bomb threats recorded in the United States. When Nixon took office and continued to wage that war under the guise of a phased withdrawal, he too became a target of that hatred. Nixon was not paranoid in believing some people and organizations were out to get him from the start.[49] They were indeed. What he did not calculate correctly then was the rather broad support the American people gave him to continue to wage a costly and misdirected war for another four years. He also resented the tendency of old and new opponents to play rough. Play rough they did, as did Richard Nixon, from the very beginning of his career.

And it is correct that some Democratic presidents have violated the Constitution and committed some of the "dirty tricks" that Nixon and his circle later employed. But the leaders of his administration were involved on so many fronts in such noxious activities that it seemed at times a full-blown conspiracy could be etched out—which is exactly what Nixon's opponents, his panicked counsel John Dean, and rapacious newspaper reporters fleshed out.

Richard Nixon was guilty of high crimes and misdemeanors in the classic English sense of the expression—of abuse of his great office, not in any grand conspiracy against the republic or the liberties of its people, but in a reactive, petty, personalized resentment that struck out in an almost uncoordinated calculation of gestures and half-baked responses. Nixon was accused by the House Judiciary Committee of covering up a crime (the break-in), of attempting to use government agencies to obstruct justice and to harass people, and of general disrespect of the Congress.[50] In historical perspective, Lincoln and FDR respectively violated more people's rights in the Civil War suspension of the writ of habeas corpus and in the World War II internment of Japanese-Americans than Nixon ever reached. Necessity was seen at the time in both cases as providing sufficient vindication for those acts, although there were serious reservations later about FDR's order. Clearly, Richard Nixon abused his great office, instructed his closest aides to engage in illegal activities, and helped create the web that entangled his presidency. He began those abuses before Watergate.

In March 1969, the president's counsel, John Ehrlichman, called a New York City policeman and asked him to set up a private security unit in Washington for the purposes of providing investigative support for the White House.[51] Faced with legal restrictions on the CIA in domestic surveillance and Hoover's refusal to use the FBI, the administration was creating a special group of its own. Actually the CIA, through its branch called the Domestic Operations Division (DOD), had previously established a covert initiative involving the surveillance of domestic radicals. Johnson had put heavy pressure on the agency to increase that activity, and a new group began focusing on "Project Chaos." Nixon insisted on enlarging that program when he assumed office.[52]

As noted, the Huston Plan envisioned even more surveillance over the communications of U.S. citizens, surreptitious entries, and a wholesale oversight of suspected individuals. The FBI under Hoover had engaged in all of those activities in the past, but the director opposed the Huston Plan, probably seeing it as a threat to the bureau's autonomy, and also as political dynamite. At the same time, Nixon and Kissinger were disturbed by leaks about their foreign policy initiatives both in waging war and in conducting diplomacy.[53]

Nixon later argued that the president has the right to violate the law when national security is involved. His claim was vigorously attacked: the president is not above the law, and Nixon's extra-constitutional claim was just a subterfuge for his cover-up. Leaving aside the latter charge, Nixon is correct that presidents have at times, usually during extraordinary crises, acted outside the law and sometimes in violation of it and gotten away with those transgressions or been able to win Supreme Court decisions based on the necessity of the situation.[54]

However, the Court's oversight on some of these activities, for example wiretapping, has tightened up over the years. In the 1940s FDR ordered the FBI to use wiretaps on "fifth column" targets, mostly aliens, and may have wiretapped his own wife's friends, suspecting her of marital indiscretions. In 1946 Truman broadened the list to include alleged domestic subversives. The Kennedys wiretapped Dr. Martin Luther King, Jr., to see if his associates were Communist sympathizers, and Johnson used taps regularly. In 1967 though, the Supreme Court cracked down on such discretion and insisted on a court-ordered warrant. The next year, Congress passed a bill that required warrants in the much publicized fight on crime. However, neither body challenged the right of the executive to protect national security against foreign intelligence activities.

By 1969 the new attorney general, John Mitchell, argued that the executive could wiretap domestic groups or individuals who sought to attack or subvert the government illegally. But three years later the Supreme Court rejected that view, although again leaving out foreign intelligence agents. Whether the executive could use his discretionary powers to prevent indirectly foreign agents from benefiting from information the press or U.S. citizens uncover was not settled. In any case, Nixon began ordering wiretaps of prominent newsmen, his own associates in government, and even his brother, so his defense is usually written off. But still the principal issue is a complex one.[55]

As has been seen, the administration's preoccupation with leaks led early on to the creation of the "plumbers" to add to its intelligence gathering capabilities outside of normal government channels and legal restraints. Kissinger was especially concerned over the release by Daniel Ellsberg, an acquaintance of his at Harvard, of the *Pentagon Papers*. The attorney general labeled Ellsberg a person with Communist ties, and there was a fear he was in touch with the Soviets. There was also in the White House a different set of concerns—that conservatives might leak information on the Nixon-Kissinger intentions toward Moscow and Beijing in order to thwart administration foreign policy objectives.[56]

Later in 1971, Colson tried to bring into the administration's circle more sophisticated agents, most importantly a CIA operative, E. Howard Hunt, to deal with these problems. Hunt became involved not only in national security matters, but also in political "dirty tricks." Dirty tricks, or unethical political practices against the opposition, are not new in American politics. The Democrats had used such mixtures of silliness and malice against Nixon frequently. But Hunt and his hired colleagues ended up moving farther and farther away from the shores of political decency. Under Colson's guidance, Hunt cut and pasted a series of forged cables designed to implicate President Kennedy in the death of Diem. By midsummer 1971 Hunt was working with the "plumbers" group, mostly on narcotics control. The group then turned to the investigation of Ellsberg and broke into his psychiatrist's office to seek information on his patient. The "plumbers" also investigated Jack Anderson's alleged sources for a column on the administration's confidential policy toward the India-Pakistan war. Soon the Committee to Re-elect the President would hire Hunt and an associate, G. Gordon Liddy.[57]

Surveillance, espionage, and dirty tricks are expensive, especially when done outside of the funds available to a government agency. The Nixon people had access to millions of dollars of unreported money, which helped to fund these surreptitious activities, including the break-in and the attempted cover-up of Watergate. The chief fundraiser for Nixon's reelection, Herbert W. Kalmbach, had a secret fund of $1.6 million, mostly money unspent from the 1968 race. Nixon had strongly believed that his defeat in 1960 was due to

Kennedy's wealth, and that the Kennedys were known to have played loose and easy with campaign monies, as Hubert Humphrey learned in the West Virginia primary.

One of Nixon's major contributors was the shadowy millionaire Howard Hughes who gave extensive amounts to both parties, lived the life of a recluse in Las Vegas, and had had ties with Nixon's brother, Kennedy associate Lawrence O'Brien, and other major figures. Hughes and his company were also linked to the CIA, and the relationships between his agents and theirs were often extensive. The Nixon reelection effort also focused on the dairy industry, which critics charged had a quid pro quo arrangement to raise dairy prices nationally in return for a substantial contribution pledge of $2 million. Anthony Lukas has argued that Nixon's people focused in general on corporations that were having regulatory or rate problems with government agencies. The Nixon campaign staff also extensively solicited wealthy individuals such as investment brokers, Wall Street lawyers, and corporate presidents who wanted to be U.S. ambassadors. These sorts of targets and the sale of foreign posts were not Nixon innovations of course, but his administration did such fleecing with a thoroughness that antagonized even elements of corporate America.[58]

Kalmbach approved $400,000 going into the campaign of Albert Brewer, who was running against George Wallace for governor in Alabama. At the same time, the IRS began to investigate Wallace's brother's income tax returns. To Nixon critics and to the Wallaces, the strategy was clearly meant to force George Wallace out of the presidential race, and thus give the conservatives only one choice—Nixon. The White House also focused on the Democrats' probable nominee for president, Senator Muskie, and the senator and other Democrats were the object of all sorts of childish pranks as well as a real campaign of character assassination. While Nixon announced the mining of Haiphong harbor and the bombing of North Vietnam on May 8, bogus letters and telegrams of support sent out by Nixon's men flooded Congress.

But the most eventful dirty trick was the planned break-ins of Democratic national headquarters and the office of its chairman Lawrence O'Brien, at the Watergate apartments and office complex. A more extravagant plan against the Democrats had been outlined by Liddy to Mitchell, Jeb Magruder, and John Dean, which included wiretaps and electronic surveillance of the Democratic national convention and candidates, break-ins, kidnapping squads to capture radical leaders, mugging squads to deal with dissidents, call girls sent to compromise Democratic politicians, sabotaging of the air conditioning at the Democratic convention, and other such activities. Attorney General Mitchell apparently refused to go along with such proposals and told Liddy "to go back to the drawing boards and come up with a more realistic plan." Liddy did.[59]

Hunt and Liddy also attempted to retrieve information from a Las Vegas publisher, Hank Greenspun, who was supposed to have evidence that would compromise Muskie. The publisher was knowledgeable as well about some details of the Hughes empire—a preoccupation of Nixon for years. In addition, he had information on Hughes's $100,000 contribution to Nixon and thought the money was being used to furnish Nixon's personal residence at San Clemente. Nixon, who felt that he had suffered unfairly in the campaign in 1960 because of his brother's ties to Hughes, was especially sensitive to any new allegations and was also desirous of showing some unsavory relationship between Hughes and O'Brien.[60]

While the attorney general was reluctantly looking at a scaled-down Liddy plan, syndicated columnist Jack Anderson did it again—publishing an article linking an ITT's $400,000 contribution to the GOP convention to a settlement of an antitrust suit by the Justice Department. As for the "plumbers," Hunt and his associates broke into the Democratic headquarters, planted wiretapping bugs and left. The tap on O'Brien's phone did not work, although another tap yielded a string of conversations that led to speculations of a call girl service operating out of the headquarters. A second break-in resulted in the culprits being captured by the police, and soon they were traced back to Hunt and to the Committee to Re-elect the President, and eventually to the White House.

Haldeman in his memoirs speculates that the break-in may have been a more complicated event than assumed originally. He argues that O'Brien knew six weeks *before* the break-in that it would occur, and that James McCord was the source of that information. He also insists that CIA Director Helms had advance knowledge of the break-in, and that one of Hughes' agents in the Mullen Company was directing *Washington Post* reporter Bob Woodward to Colson as the villain and away from the CIA. Colson later informed Haldeman of his view that the CIA initiated the break-in, and he wanted to hire a private investigator to follow up the story. The motive under this scenario was to embarrass the president and prevent him from gaining control of the agency. Haldeman discounts his theory but as noted his associate, John Ehrlichman, in his novel *The Company*, lays out a plot similar to Haldeman's speculation.[61]

In 1984, investigative journalist Jim Hougan returned to the story and argued that the Democratic headquarters was never bugged until *after* the break-in when evidence was planted by the FBI. In his analysis, Hunt and McCord were still working for the CIA and were spying on a variety of people, including some in the administration. The real target of the bugging was not to learn more about the dealings of O'Brien, or to find political intelligence on the Democrats, but to gather information on the clients of prostitutes in the Columbia Plaza apartments. Caught in the act, the Watergate burglars protected "the Company" (the insider name for the CIA) and left the administration twisting in the wind. A sequel, written by two investigative reporters in 1991, argues that the break-in came at the initiative of John Dean, whose girlfriend (later his wife) was sharing an apartment with a call girl who in turn was tied to employees of the Democratic National Committee. Dean thus arranged the cover-up after "the plumbers" were discovered trying to get information on that operation, and Dean shrewdly got the frightened White House staff and the president maneuvered into pursuing a cover-up and obstructing justice.

Regardless of what Dean's role was, the CIA may have had some advance intimations of what was to come. Director of the CIA Helms, on hearing of the capture of the burglars, remarked, "Ah, well. They finally did it . . . A pity about the president, too, you know. They really blew it. The sad thing is, we all think, that's the end of it, and it may be just the beginning of something worse. If the White House tries to ring me through central, don't switch it out here, just tell them you reported McCord's arrest already and I was *very* surprised."[62]

The motive for Watergate will be a debated point for considerable time, but what seems most plausible is that Nixon pushed Colson hard for information on O'Brien and more political intelligence, and that Hunt and his associates received the go-ahead for a specific break-in, which the president and his closest aides did not know about in advance. It is highly possible that not only the CIA but also the FBI and some Pentagon officials may have known in advance of this plan and chose to do nothing to warn and protect the president out of disdain for his politicalization of their agencies or because, as in the case of the military, they resented his attempts to reach some accommodation with the Soviets and Communist

Chinese. They may have assumed Nixon would be cut down a peg or two; probably no one expected that it would lead to a constitutional crisis of the magnitude it did. But this, too, is speculation.

What is not speculation is that Nixon's handling of the Watergate affair blew his administration apart, led to his resignation, and the indictment and incarceration of his closest aides. Why did the president get involved in the cover-up at all? Why did his associates engage in a cover-up, obstruction of justice, so easily and so foolheartedly? One of those individuals, Jeb Magruder, when asked these questions, remarked lamely, "After all, *we* were the government."[63]

The immediate concern of the president and his men was that one of the burglars would admit to having ties with the White House. Hunt was demanding money to support the arrested men's families and to pay for defense fees. He also warned that "Watergate bugging is only one of a number of highly illegal conspiracies engaged in by one or more of the defendants at the behest of senior White House officials." The president and his counsel, John Dean, in a fateful interview discussed paying hush money to keep them quiet. The president insisted on short-circuiting the FBI's investigation by indicating the CIA was involved, and that therefore there had to be limits to the interrogations for national security reasons. Unlike in 1972, when the break-in was first reported, the media and Congress latched on to the controversy. During the election campaign, the major newspapers did not focus on the break-in, and of the 753 daily papers, all but 56 endorsed Nixon. Two congressional investigations in 1972 ended with nothing. At the *Washington Post*, two young reporters, Carl Bernstein and Bob Woodward, kept fishing for more information; indeed they claimed they were aided by a government informant, whom they labeled "Deep Throat" after the well-known pornographic film of the time.[64]

Meanwhile, Nixon questioned Colson about the initial break-in, and Colson supposedly denied any advanced knowledge about it. Soon documents were being destroyed; "national security" was proclaimed to cover up the trail of the loose cash that flowed, and the FBI was remarkably circumspect in its investigations.

On March 22, the president gave marching orders to John Mitchell, "I don't give a sh-t what happens, I want you all to stonewall it, let them plead the Fifth Amendment, cover-up or anything else, if it'll save it—save the plan [the cover-up plan]."[65] However, federal Judge John Sirica, who was trying the burglary case, refused to believe the burglars' pleas and sentenced them to harsh maximum sentences in order to get them to end their silence. A law and order Republican and former boxer, Sirica should have been Nixon's kind of judge, but now his unorthodox and at times questionable tactics led one of the former CIA agents, James McCord, to confess that higher-ups were involved in the break-in. The admission of McCord upset the cover-up strategy and had White House staff members scrambling to make their own best deal with the prosecutors to avoid being left taking the blame. Nixon tried to get Mitchell to assume responsibility, but the former attorney general refused.

By November 7, 1973 a year to the day after his monumental election victory, Nixon's popularity was seriously dropping, with only 27 percent of the sample in a Gallup poll thinking he was doing a good job. Congress had overridden his veto of the War Powers Act, which aimed at limiting the president's authority to wage undeclared war. Nixon lobbied Congress with his side of the story on the continuing Watergate controversy, and at one press conference he ineptly insisted, "People have the right to know whether or not their president is a crook. Well, I am not a crook."

Soon Nixon's counsel, John Dean, fearing he was now being maneuvered to take the full blame for the cover-up, gave to the prosecutors, the Senate committee, and finally the nation a full, integrated chronicle of the horrors of the Nixon administration. His testimony, rich in detail and devastating in implications and innuendo, linked together facts, documents, gossip, hostile Nixonian remarks into a coherent conspiracy that was supposedly aimed at destroying enemies and in denying Americans their basic civil liberties. Aided by a vigorously hostile media, especially in Washington and New York City, the administration had to fight endless brushfires over what was once called a "third-rate burglary."

In fairness to Nixon, one can claim that Dean's testimony painted a darker and more frightening picture in its comprehensiveness than the follies of the administration justified. Unfortunately though, each new disclosure fed the opposition, and Nixon tried to hold the line by reasserting executive privilege to protect his closest associates from testifying. Nixon argued that "under the doctrine of separation of powers, the manner in which the president personally exercises his assigned executive powers is not to submit to questioning by another branch of government. If the president is not subject to such questioning, it is equally appropriate that members of his staff not be so questioned, for their roles are in effect an extension of the presidency."[66]

He allowed a special prosecutor to be appointed, a Harvard professor and close Kennedy associate, Archibald Cox, and permitted his attorney general, Elliot Richardson, to give him a guarantee of autonomy. Of the thirty-seven lawyers Cox recruited, all but one were Ivy Leaguers, eighteen from Harvard, most of them were Democrats, and many had served under Robert Kennedy or his successor, Nicholas de B. Katzenbach. When Nixon later fired Cox, arguing that he was a subordinate in the executive branch, Richardson felt compelled to resign and the deputy attorney general, William Ruckelshaus, also left. The "Saturday Night Massacre," as the media quickly characterized it, led to increasing public outcry. Nixon then named a new attorney general, William Saxbe, and a new special prosecutor, Leon Jaworski, with whom the administration had similar problems in trying to withhold information. At the time of the firings, telegrams were running over one hundred to one against the administration, and the Quale poll showed Americans favored the impeachment of Nixon by a margin of 44 percent to 42 percent.[67]

While the Saturday Night Massacre was running its course, the Israeli Army on October 23 encircled the Egyptian twenty-thousand-man III Corps on the east bank of the Suez Canal. The United States and Russia came perilously close to a confrontation, and Kissinger and Defense Secretary James Schlesinger put American forces on Defense Condition 3 or stand-by alert. However, the next day, the two superpowers supported a UN resolution establishing an international peacekeeping force in the Mediterranean region. Two days later Nixon publicly called the situation "the most difficult crisis we've had since the Cuban confrontation of 1962." But the outrage over the Cox firings and the end of the special prosecutor's office continued, and suspicious detractors insisted that Nixon and Kissinger had overplayed the crisis in order to garner support from the public. To the enemies of Richard Nixon, nothing should divert attention from Watergate—the Russians and the Mideast to the contrary.[68]

While Nixon was fighting to uphold his claims of executive privilege, one of his low-level aides (also a former CIA agent), Alexander Butterfield, acknowledged that there existed a taping system that had been installed in the Oval Office and elsewhere to record the president's conversations. The battle shifted to getting those tapes to discover if Nixon did indeed have advance knowledge of Watergate, and if he were involved later in the cover-up.

Several Nixon associates have argued that the president reinstalled a taping system to protect his place in history. Butterfield believed that the president was "preoccupied with history and the place his presidency would have in history." Conservative columnist William Safire has maintained that Nixon was convinced "left-leaning historians would try to deny him his place in history." Nixon may also have thought the tapes would be helpful later in other controversies that might come up, that their incriminating evidence may have compromised others in such a way to get them to back off on attacking him, and that he may have indeed been convinced about the strength of his claim of executive privilege. It has also been suggested that Nixon may have taped his conversations to keep straight his understandings with Kissinger, whom he surmised was keeping a diary or was recording his conversations as well.[69]

In any case, the tapes existed and Nixon's enemies wanted them. The president refused at first to release the tapes, but offered to have a respected senator, John Stennis of Mississippi, listen to them and make summaries to answer the questions being raised. However, when the Supreme Court unanimously upheld the lower courts and asserted that Sirica had a right to hear the tapes as possible evidence in trials, Nixon politically had no choice but to comply. At that stage he could not withhold the tapes without arousing immense public opposition. Oddly enough the case did bring from the high court for the first time in history an acknowledgment that executive privilege was a legitimate claim that could indeed be made legally in American courts.

After Nixon decided to obey the Court and release the tapes, there was another firestorm of criticism of his tone, style, and language as exhibited in those recordings of his private conversations. Critics and some good friends of the president said they reflected poorly on the dignity of the great office he held. Unlike other presidents, who probably were as profane and even cruder than Nixon, this president had his idle remarks, his personal resentments, and his age-old animosities scattered before the citizenry. And sooner or later, the tapes revealed to most—including his Republican allies—that the president was involved in the cover-up after all. In the vocabulary of the times, they had found the "smoking gun," the proof of Nixon's guilt.

In late November, Judge Sirica sorted out the tapes the White

House turned over, and later in December he ruled that two of those tapes and part of a third were indeed properly covered by executive privilege. But Nixon was fighting a war on many fronts. His "Operation Candor" initiative, which opened up to public view many aspects of Nixon's personal life and finances, was backfiring. He released the most complete financial statement given by a president, but new questions were raised and his enemies used the information to good advantage. Nixon was also criticized for his purchase of two new expensive residences early in his tenure in office and for using government money to repair those residences and/or to upgrade their security and privacy. Some of those requirements were clearly due to Secret Service concerns, especially so soon after the murder of John F. Kennedy. A House subcommittee found that the San Clemente and Key Biscayne residences had cost the taxpayers $17.1 million—$10 million for fixed improvements and $7.1 million in personnel costs over five years. Then in the fall of 1973, newspapers carried the story that the president had paid almost no federal income taxes in 1970 and 1971. Indeed, Nixon paid the same amount of taxes that a family of three earning between $7,500 and $8,000 would have owed. More controversies swirled around the proper reasons for property improvements and the Secret Service's legitimate security concerns, and whether Nixon's deductions (especially for his donated public papers) were in order.[70]

The House Judiciary Committee began its hearings on impeachment, and the effect of the tapes was apparent as Republican moderates joined with Democratic liberals in presenting a statement of impeachment charges to the full House. Other Republicans insisted that impeachment had to rest on some evidence of "criminality," but House counsel John Doar maintained that impeachment was a "constitutional remedy addressed to serious offenses against the system of government." He further argued that while not every kind of presidential misconduct was sufficient to constitute grounds for impeachment of course, "the facts must be considered as a whole in the context of the office, not in terms of separate or isolated events. Because impeachment of a president is a grave step for the nation, it is to be predicated only upon conduct seriously incompatible with either the constitutional form and principles of our government or the proper performance of constitutional duties of the presidential office." The Judiciary Committee rejected some of the more divisive charges that had been presented, such as whether to cite Nixon's waging war in Cambodia, and settled on complicity in

the Watergate cover-up, abuse of power in the improper use of
governmental agencies, and refusing to comply with Judiciary Committee subpoenas. Some conservative Republicans had considered
proposing that Nixon be censured (as Andrew Jackson was) rather
than impeached, but support for that moderate step vanished with
the increasing revelations in the tapes that the president seemed to
have masterminded the cover-up himself.[71]

During the long and intense controversy over Watergate, the
prosecutors in the state of Maryland had allegedly received evidence
that Vice President Spiro Agnew while county commissioner and
then governor had received kickbacks from contractors. Agnew
asked the Speaker of the House, Carl Albert, to conduct a full investigation of the charges and cited a controversy involving Vice
President John C. Calhoun as a precedent. Speaker Albert refused
and decided to let the judicial process work its way. Under pressure from Attorney General Elliot Richardson, Agnew agreed to
plead no contest and resigned from the vice presidency. Nixon nominated and Congress approved Minority Leader Gerald Ford of Michigan to replace Agnew after getting an assurance from him that he
would support Texas politician John Connally for the presidency in
1976. Agnew's departure was a blow to the president. As he once
told John Ehrlichman, the vice president was his "insurance policy."
"No assassin in his right mind would kill me. They know that if
they did they would end up with Agnew," Nixon reasoned. The
president was probably thinking not just of potential assassins, but
also of the U.S. Congress.[72]

With the Judiciary Committee's vote and the release of more
taped conversations showing that the president was involved deeply
in the cover-up, impeachment in the House was a given fact. And,
after some discussions with Republican supporters in the Senate, the
president realized that conviction was also inevitable. He decided
to resign. Thus on August 9, 1974, after having won one of the
greatest victories in American politics less than two years before,
Richard Nixon was forced to resign and Gerald Ford succeeded him.
In his emotional farewell to his staff, Nixon admonished, "always
remember others may hate you, but those who hate you don't win
unless you hate them, and then you destroy yourself."

Any balanced history of those years must avoid the pitfalls of
attack and defense. Nixon did indeed abuse his office, but perhaps
not to the extent that his partisan critics worked up the populace to
believe at the time. Considering the disruptions in American politi-

cal life and in U.S. foreign policy, the little-discussed option of severe censure maybe should have been discussed more fully. It is true that his predecessors violated standards of constitutional probity and often personal morality. Nixon speechwriter Raymond Price recounts that James Roosevelt, son of the president, remarked, "Everything they're accusing him [Nixon] of my father did twice as much of." And FDR advisor,Thomas Corcoran told Price in the same vein, "The trouble with your people is that they're always writing memos. When we did that sort of thing, we never put it on paper." Price concludes with leftist journalist Nicholas Hoffman's prediction that historians would ask how a whole society lost its balanced judgment and behaved like a hysterical mob, taking special vengeance on a man "who conducted the office in much the same fashion as his predecessors." Perhaps there is some truth in those observations, but Nixon violated standards of political decency with an intensity and a flaunting that brought on most of his own troubles.[73]

At times the behavior of some segments of the media, the opposition party, and even the federal judiciary in the Watergate affair leaves one uneasy if not a bit queasy. If they could so easily destroy a sitting president, after a monumental popular victory, is any isolated citizen safe if he or she arouses their hostility under other circumstances? The response of those who drove Nixon from office was that he was guilty of impeachable acts and that such organized opposition was appropriate if not noble. Honest citizens involved in political disputes have nothing to fear. Yet the history of postwar America is full of instances on the right and left of the politics of character assassination, media misrepresentation, and congressional irresponsibility. Nixon was not above that style either when he was in active public life.

In the end, after all the charges and countercharges, Nixon gave us the best postscript on the sound and fury of this intense partisan battle: "I gave them the sword and they used it." The sword he gave them came not out of the rock of his own innocence, but from the web of illegal, illicit, and immoral acts he instigated, tolerated, and demanded from those around him. It is frequently argued that Nixon was an aberration, a fluke in the American political system. But in fact he was a sensitive barometer of the anxieties of the American people caught up in the postwar period, bearing alone the burdens of the Western democracies, deeply conservative and caring about what was happening to the old truths and the old values. Nixon spoke to those people and to the alliance of privilege and money that saw him as a break in the tradition of the expanding liberal welfare state. Oddly enough, he presided over one of the greatest expansions of that welfare state and despite the American right's fear of executive power, he was for better or worse in many ways one of most significant of the postwar presidents. He came to understand that the Democratic party's power base was eroding and that the real opposition party was an adversary media that was to undo him, Ford, and Carter. Only the ultimate media president, Ronald Reagan, would master it by substituting images for ideas, television for print, and even then he nearly ended up in serious trouble during the Iran-Contra controversy.

There are though real constitutional issues beyond all the blood and gore, genuine concerns about executive privilege, due process, and the president's war-making powers that can not be explained in good guy/bad guy terms. And the great triumphs of Nixon in opening up China, finally signing a peace treaty, reaching various accommodations with the Soviet Union, supporting some domestic reforms are really more complex and less sterling than meets the eye. The conduct of foreign affairs under Nixon and Kissinger exhibited some of the very same dark characteristics present in their domestic surveillance and in the Watergate cover-up—characteristics of leaders who do not feel comfortable in the messy, fluid, and usually directionless flux of democratic politics.

Nixon himself is the American dream come true: the poor boy with few early connections who aspires to greatness and becomes president of the United States. But it is the dream turned upside down—the recognition that ambition demands a price, that determination can lead to a narrowness of life and a denial of civilized restraint in search of the grail. Unlike Lincoln, another self-made man, Nixon nursed hurts and resentments, never really learning to enjoy his own considerable achievements. He once said that all of it, his downfall and demise, all of his resentments started early in the slights and heartaches the young so often feel and internalize in the cruel world of growing up. All but the most secure or the most oblivious know those hurts, but maturity is a rising out of those shadows and nightmares.

John Ehrlichman tells a tale of when Nixon and he had dinner at Nelson Rockefeller's Pocantico Hills estate in Westchester County, New York. After dinner the two of them were returning home, and Nixon remarked enviously, "Imagine living in a place like that."

Ehrlichman noted that Nixon was returning to the White House, retiring as president of the United States.[74]

THE FORD POSTSCRIPT

When Spiro Agnew resigned in scandal, Nixon needed a vice president who was respected by Congress and who would be easily ratified by that body. Although he had been a close acquaintance of Gerald Ford's for years, Nixon had reservations about his capacity to be president. On one occasion, he remarked to his old rival, Nelson Rockefeller, "can you imagine Jerry Ford sitting in this chair?" With Nixon's resignation, the amiable, easy-going former minority leader in the House of Representatives assumed that very office.[75]

Ford's greatest ambition was not to be president, but Speaker of the House, a post he realized he would probably never attain because of Democratic control of the lower house term after term. He had come to the House of Representatives in 1948 having compiled a record as a fine football player, a veteran of four years' service in war, and a rising politician with a strong local base in the Grand Rapids, Michigan area. Throughout his career, Ford conveyed a sense of personal openness and honesty, exactly the traits the successor to Nixon needed.

The initial popular response to Ford was universally positive and personal. When Nixon's helicopter flew off from the White House grounds that last time, Ford declared, "our long national nightmare is over." He reaffirmed his friendship with Congress, reached out to Democratic and liberal opinion makers, and let the press know that he started breakfast by toasting his own English muffins. Quite appropriately, he asked that Harry Truman's portrait be returned to the White House, an obvious attempt to replicate the kindred appeal of the common man from Independence, Missouri. During Watergate, Ford had defended Nixon nearly to the end, but once quietly remarked of the so-called administration's "enemies list," that anyone who needed a written list had too many enemies to begin with.

Ford, before and especially during his presidential term, was frequently portrayed as a clumsy and not terribly bright fellow. Actually Ford was in rather good shape for a middle-aged man, still full of energy and resilience from his more athletic days. As for

his intellectual capacity, he had compiled a good record of achievement at both the University of Michigan and Yale Law School. In
his discussions of economic policy during his presidency, he probably had a firmer grasp of that area than most of his contemporaries who sat in the White House. Ford's behavior during the seizure
of the boat *Mayaguez* off Cambodia showed that he had a good
understanding of military command problems as well.[76]

Ford's faults were however political. For a man who loved politics and was obviously successful at it, he was remarkably naive
about certain basic aspects. First, he lost considerable public support when he abruptly pardoned Richard Nixon a month after his
resignation. Congress and the media focused on the allegation that
Ford had made a deal with the disgraced president in order to inherit the office, and turned on Ford, reminding him of his simple
remark that "truth is the glue" of government. Ford dramatically
appeared before the House Judiciary Committee to deny any such
allegations, but the sense of disillusionment continued throughout
his term.[77]

In conversations with Ford, the issue of a pardon was indeed
raised by Nixon's chief of staff, Alexander Haig, in the last days of
Nixon's reign, and Ford had indicated at first that he was at least
willing to entertain the idea—a vague remark that Haig may have
used to encourage Nixon to resign. In a later discussion, Ford told
Haig that he did not want to be misunderstood; he would not play
any part in Nixon's ultimate decision. Haig at the time was trying
to get Nixon to see the inevitable and leave office. The extent to
which Haig kept the White House staff together then, consoled
Nixon, and did the public's business has never been fully told. In
any case, he may have used his conversation with Ford to mean
more than was intended at the time by the vice president.

Ford's reasoning for granting a pardon to Nixon was that he
wanted to put Watergate behind him and the nation, get out from
under the endless discussions and divisions about the tapes and their
custody, and reach beyond the Watergate break-in and congressional
animosity toward the executive branch. Ford was also apprised of
Nixon's deteriorating physical health and the alleged possibilities
of mental instability. In addition, he claimed that he was influenced
by an obscure 1915 legal case involving an editor named George
Burdick who was pardoned by President Wilson before an indictment was brought. The Supreme Court later ruled, "The president

had the power to pardon for a crime of which the individual has not been convicted and which he does not admit." Thus, instead of waiting for indictments and a conviction of Nixon before pardoning him, the new president acted abruptly with little advice from those around him.[78]

Unfortunately the pardon seemed like another chapter in the cover-up, a tying of "good old Jerry" to the dark king himself. His popularity plummeted overnight from 72 percent to 49 percent. Of the seventeen thousand telegrams and mailgrams received in the White House, some six to one were against the pardon. Some Ford associates saw his pardon as the leading cause of his defeat in 1976. His action probably played a role, but even more significant was the president's continued inability to fashion a cohesive White House staff. Truman's great advantage while he was in office was that he surrounded himself with some knowledgeable advisors who knew when to engage in bureaucratic infighting and when to cease such self-serving activity for the common interest. Ford's main circle— his own advisors and the holdovers from Nixon—engaged in endless pitched battles, intense even in a city known for such unbridled egotism. Ford was neither strong enough to end those conflicts, nor enough of a manager to run the executive branch in spite of such dissensions. Lacking any real managerial background and being a committed "nice guy," Ford was unable to leave his stamp on his own administration and on the troubled nation he found. The presidency is not just inspiration, it is also control. As the first unelected vice president in U.S. history and the first to attain the top office through the most novel constitutional path the nation had up to that time, Ford should have been more sensitive to the need to court public opinion and build a power base of his own, a power base built on his real assets—integrity and common sense.[79]

With the vice presidency open, Ford turned to the processes of the Twenty-Fifth Amendment again and chose for the second spot, the wealthy governor of New York, Nelson Rockefeller. The scion of one of the best-known philanthropic families in the world, Rockefeller had worked in Washington originally for FDR and compiled later a record of brilliant and expensive achievements in New York state. But since 1958, he had symbolized to many conservative Republicans everything they disliked about their own eastern cosmopolitan wing. Rockefeller then at age 66 accepted the honor of the nomination and consequently underwent incredible scrutiny, which focused on his personal and family wealth, and his remarkable generosity in giving and forgiving loans to friends and political associates. One wag noted that Rockefeller was a politician on the give and not on the take.

In order to ensure continuity and to send a signal of stability at home and abroad, Ford retained Henry Kissinger who in the closing months of the Nixon term had been given the position of secretary of state as well as retaining his national security advisor post. Rockefeller, Kissinger's sponsor in so many matters, wanted to see the same sort of coordination in domestic affairs as Kissinger imposed on foreign affairs. So he proposed to Ford that he be given carte blanche to establish a policy-making and implementation bureaucracy to oversee domestic governmental operations. Rockefeller observed that he intended to "make the Domestic Council a parallel operation to the National Security Council as a means of serving the president." Under his proposal the Domestic Council would coordinate both long-range planning and day-to-day decisions. It was Ford's advisors, especially his de facto chief of staff, Donald Rumsfeld, who struggled to cut the vice president back down to size by opposing such a grant of authority and power to Rockefeller. In 1991, however, Rumsfeld maintained that he in fact had not prevailed on this issue. He argued that Ford actually acquiesced originally in Rockefeller's plan to control domestic policy making, but that it soon became obvious to him that such an arrangement was unworkable, and it was abandoned by the president.

When he became president, Ford tried to avoid Nixon's administrative model with its strong chief of staff and hierarchical authority. Instead he wanted to be the center of the spokes of a wheel with eight or nine advisors bringing him information. Rumsfeld was initially introduced to the senior staff by Ford as "a coordinator" and not as a chief of staff, and his job was to devise and administer orderly decision-making processes. Ford's approach was similar to what Democrats Kennedy, Johnson, and even FDR preferred. Actually Nixon had a strong chief of staff, a tightly structured White House bureaucracy, but as his term was coming to an end, several of his cabinet secretaries, especially James Schlesinger at Defense and William Simon at Treasury, operated almost independently.[80]

Ford permitted Nixon's staff people to stay on, for an almost interminably long time in the eyes of some Ford partisans. Rumsfeld, who had served Nixon as well, observed,

The president was subject to two tugs. On the one hand, he recognized that these people [the Nixon appointees] were overwhelmingly fine, decent human beings . . . [but] the first thing the president had to do was to restore a sense of legitimacy to the executive branch. There was a need for continuity, but also there was a need for change—a sense of change. The solution, Ford decided, was to make the minimal number of changes that would be needed to allow the critical mass that remained to become once more legitimate. His aim was to create a Ford presidency, rather than a Nixon presidency over which Ford was simply presiding."[81]

After a while, however, Ford came to realize that his spokes in a wheel approach did not work, and he finally accepted a chief of staff without the official designation. The ascendancy of Rumsfeld, a former congressman from the Republican North Shore in Chicago, one-time head of the Office of Economic Opportunity, and ambassador to NATO, came about after a major reorganization of the Ford White House.[82] After Rumsfeld opposed Rockefeller's plan for control of domestic policy making, the two of them maintained very frosty relations. Rockefeller saw Rumsfeld as a major roadblock, intent on fostering his own personal ambitions, and devoid of any ideological or philosophical convictions.[83] Rumsfeld, on the other hand, argued that Rockefeller sometimes embraced schemes that Ford really disagreed with privately, and that the vice president's anger was misdirected at him.

By early 1975, Ford, who was seeking the Republican nomination, had also moved politically to the right. Concerned about the declining economy, influenced by conservative advisors, and recognizing that he had major problems with the right wing of the party, Ford was becoming reluctant to adopt Rockefeller's expensive governmental initiatives. In addition, Ford and surely Rumsfeld must have recognized that if Kissinger were controlling foreign policy, which he surely was, and Rockefeller were given carte blanche on domestic affairs, what would Ford do as president?[84] With Nixon's people still in second-echelon jobs, after the visible first-level appointees left, tensions increased, and Ford grew weary of the infighting. He later was to observe, "Throughout my political career, nothing upset me more than bickering among members of my staff. It was time-consuming, distracting, and unnecessary. I had told my aides that I wouldn't tolerate it. But it continued, even accelerated . . . and—given the ambitions and personalities involved—there didn't seem any way to put an immediate stop to it."[85] It was almost as if the president of the United States were an observer in his own administration.

Also, the new Ford White House had difficulty reaching closure on decisions. Trained in the passive ways of Congress with its emphasis on debate and consensus, Ford at times did not provide the type of tough leadership good presidents must exhibit. Ford was sensitive to the centralized Nixon system, but he was not as attuned to the problems of slippage in executive authority that his predecessor's demise induced in the government. Early in his presidency, Ford also chose to restore authority to cabinet secretaries, arguing that he was again abandoning his predecessor's predilections for relying on a strong White House staff.

Rumsfeld argued that the emphasis on consensus was exactly what the nation needed at that time, but it also accentuated the public perception of drift and the insiders' complaints of bureaucratic chaos. Years later after his defeat, Ford acknowledged that he was never fully successful in getting his staff to deal with long-range problems. He noted that he only had "thirty months" in office and that if he had been elected, many of the problems he faced with his staff would have been worked out.

Despite his love of Congress and the respect of many legislators for Ford personally, the president sought to maintain some check over the newly assertive legislative branch. The November 1974 congressional elections, held right after Nixon's resignation, led to a gain by the Democrats of forty-six seats in the House and four in the Senate. Thus, the new Congress had Democratic margins of 23 in the Senate and 147 in the House, one of the largest spread between the two parties since the election of 1936.

Ford generally abandoned Nixon's approach of impounding funds, a practice that Congress had voted to restrict severely. Instead the new president relied on the constitutional veto power to control expenditures. Ford vetoed more legislation per year in office than all but three other presidents, Cleveland, FDR, and Truman. While the others' vetoes included many private bills, Ford vetoed important pieces of legislation that he thought were "budget busters," as he put it. Still though, the president tried to keep channels of communication open. He retained his personal ties to congressmen and senators of both parties despite his conservative, limited government philosophy.[86]

It was Ford's fate also to preside over the final agonizing phase of American withdrawal in Vietnam and the fall of the south and surrounding areas to the Communists and their allies. Critics of the war had denigrated the domino theory, but in the Southeast Asian peninsula, the dominoes did indeed fall. American public opinion and Congress especially had turned away from pledging any more life and treasure to that cause, and in January 1975, the North Vietnamese won for the first time full control over a province in the south. The president asked a reluctant Congress for emergency military aid to assist South Vietnam and Cambodia, but opposition among House Democrats was intense.

By the end of March, the Communist forces swept through fourteen provinces in the south and were moving toward a rout of the Thieu government. In Cambodia, the last vestiges of independence were being extinguished by Communist forces there as well. Bitterly Thieu denounced the United States for failing to honor the pledges Nixon made to contain North Vietnamese aggression. He was correct—Nixon had indeed made pledges to resist any renewed Communist military initiatives. Later some historians have cited these as "secret" executive agreements, but as Kissinger has pointed out, the basic outlines of Nixon's assurances were widely publicized at the time.[87]

Unfortunately for Ford, he disregarded his aides' advice and left for a weekend vacation in Palm Springs, California, and another week at the home of a millionaire friend while South Vietnam and Cambodia were being crushed, and after Kissinger's Middle East overtures were also falling apart. Finally he announced simply that the war in Vietnam "is finished as far as America is concerned." By the time Congress approved a foreign aid bill, the North Vietnamese had taken even Saigon, and Americans were subject to watching on television their allies fleeing in humiliation, and U.S. troops being airlifted off the very roof of the American embassy. On May 1, Congress was unable even to agree on an assistance bill to care for Vietnamese refugees.[88]

To deal with some long-standing commitments and to bolster his image as president, Ford undertook in late 1974 a series of trips abroad. He visited Japan, South Korea, and the Soviet port city of Vladivostok. There he met with Russian leader Leonid Brezhnev to talk mainly about arms control, since the first SALT agreement was due to expire in October 1977. Nixon had tried to bring about a new agreement that would control MIRVs by establishing a limit on the number of warheads that could be fixed on a single missile and by capping the number of bombers. The SALT I agreement ended up freezing land- and sea-based ballistic missile levels, with the Soviet cap set at 2,360 and the U.S. cap at 1,710. There was no limitation on the number of heavy bombers, nor any limitation on the number of missiles each side could equip with multiple warheads. Ford concluded in his memoirs that this agreement would have worked to the United States' advantage when U.S. missiles were MIRVed. Nixon had proven to be unsuccessful in getting any additional agreements as his presidency came to an end, and Ford pushed in his talks for parity in terms of ballistic missiles at the levels of 2,400 and 1,320 MIRVs. The United States also wanted the Forward Base System of F-4s, F-111s, FB-111s, and nuclear weapons deployed in Western Europe not included in that number. Brezhnev countered with a demand that the United States stop production of the Trident submarine and cancel plans to build the B-1 bomber, which Ford rejected. Ford described his reaction later as "euphoric" after the Vladivostok meeting, and the tentative agreements for SALT II seemed ready to be signed and sealed after some refinements. Unfortunately, neither the president nor Kissinger had recognized ahead of time the extent of opposition that would come from the Pentagon.[89]

In another theater, the new president in spring 1975 faced his first real crisis when the American merchant ship SS *Mayaguez* was seized in international waters off the coast of Cambodia. Kissinger immediately raised the incident into a testing of U.S. will and Ford's leadership, portraying that isolated act as a serious blow to U.S. prestige and a consequence of the fall of Saigon. However, American destroyers and the aircraft carrier USS *Coral Sea* were too far away for an immediate response. The administration tried diplomacy, using the channels of the Communist Chinese, but these efforts were unsuccessful.

Ford not only heeded Kissinger's warning, but recalled the capture of the USS *Pueblo* by the North Koreans, which led to that crew being held in a prison camp for nearly a year before a settlement was reached. Ford and Kissinger decided to support a recovery of the *Mayaguez* and also a bombing of Cambodian shore points as well. Secretary of Defense Schlesinger disagreed with the bombing proposal, and the president later charged that the Defense Department bungled the operation by not following through on the bombing campaign as he directed. The U.S. Marines finally assaulted the island of Koh Tung near the immobilized ship, and the Cambodians released the crew to the delight of the administration. But the casualties involved in taking the island and the deaths from an unfortunate chopper crash reached forty-one, more than the number of crew members rescued.[90]

Despite some criticism from Congress, the public seemed to approve—as it usually does when a president takes strong action, and Ford's popularity in the opinion polls rose by eleven points. After the fall of Saigon, probably many people agreed with one Democratic congressman who concluded, "It's good to win one for a change."[91] The administration had also turned its attention to the Middle East and the possibilities of a negotiated peace between Israel and Egypt. Backed by seventy-six senators and the strong pro-Israeli lobby on Capitol Hill, the Israeli government refused Kissinger's peace initiatives. In meetings with Egyptian president Anwar el-Sadat, Ford and Kissinger supported however his idea of a buffer zone around the Gida and Metla passes, which the United States would monitor. They then presented the compromise to the Israeli government as an American proposal that would require Egyptian approval. But no settlement was concluded. Thus, the Ford administration was unsuccessful in trying to reach some accommodation in the troubled Middle East, but it did help to lay the groundwork for the major triumph of the Carter presidency—the Israeli-Egyptian peace treaty.

One of the most controversial aspects of Ford's foreign policy was his trip to the Helsinki Conference on security and cooperation in Europe. The thirty-five-nation pact drawn up there recognized the "legitimate" post-World War II boundaries, normalized the peculiar status of West Berlin, reaffirmed human rights, and lowered tensions between NATO and the Warsaw Pact nations. To some Americans of Eastern European backgrounds and those with families in nations forcibly attached to the Soviet Union, the pact amounted to the administration's approval of those occupations. The Soviets' acceptance of the "human rights" provisions was quickly criticized as a hollow affirmation never fully implemented at home. But Ford, following in Kissinger's footsteps and anxious to establish some stature on the international stage, went on to the conference and celebrated its dubious achievements. He claimed that the Russians gave important concessions, especially in abandoning the Brezhnev doctrine, their version of the Monroe Doctrine, which proclaimed that the Soviets would intervene to protect socialism in other countries than their own. Now under the Helsinki agreements they were supposed to have rejected the Brezhnev doctrine, even though the Russians reaffirmed that policy by overrunning Afghanistan several years later.

Ford's trip was opposed by influential newspapers and conservative politicians as well. The *Wall Street Journal* pleaded with the president, "Jerry, don't go." Even the liberal *New York Times* insisted that the trip was "misguided and empty." Governor Reagan, eyeing the presidency himself, criticized the trip, and hard-line Democratic Senator Henry Jackson also added his note of disapproval. Ford concluded, though, that the conference was important because it got the Soviets to renounce the Brezhnev doctrine and to move toward a final SALT II agreement.[92]

The main problems in the SALT II negotiations that remained were the status of the U.S. cruise missile and the Soviet's Backfire bomber. The Russians wanted the Americans to classify the Backfire as a nonstrategic weapon in return for approving U.S. long-range bombers in Western Europe. The United States also had developed a highly mobile subsonic missile that could be fired from manned aircraft, submarines, and surface missiles as well as from land-based launching pads. The Soviets obviously sought restraints on such a versatile weapon as well.

The two sides reached a tentative agreement on a limitation of 1,850 miles for the airborne cruise missiles and a range of 375 miles for its submarine-carried missiles. On MIRVs, the Soviets accepted the proposal that if they placed one MIRV in a certain location, the United States had a right to count every missile in that field as having a MIRV capability. On the Backfire bomber and on the complex issue of verification, the two sides were still not able to reach an agreement.

At the treaty signing in Helsinki, the president insisted that "peace is not a piece of paper. . . . To my country these principles are not clichés or empty phrases." The negotiations over SALT II were to continue after the Helsinki Conference, but at home Ford found that his new secretary of defense, Donald Rumsfeld, and the Joint Chiefs of Staff raised objections. After several discussions, the U.S. administration put forth a proposal to limit by 1981 the Soviets to 225 Backfire bombers and bar long-range cruise missiles from submarines. A further cut of 10 percent in the 2,400 ballistic missiles total was also put forth. The Soviets seemed interested, but Kissinger returned home to find renewed opposition from Rumsfeld and the Joint Chiefs, and the Soviets would not make any more concessions. SALT II slipped through Ford's fingers. Why he did not push harder and demand support from his new defense secretary and the chiefs remains a mystery. Even Rumsfeld posed that question to this author years later.[93]

On the domestic front, Ford faced some very difficult problems not of his own making. Partly as a result of Johnson's refusal to decide between guns and butter, war or reform, the economy was overheated, undertaxed, and laden with the seeds of inflation. Added to that problem was the growing strength of the Mideast cartel, OPEC, and the increasing dependence of the United States and the West on oil imports. For the industrialized nations, the results would be sharp inflationary pressures and trade deficits. For poor Third World countries, the price increases would be devastating. Ford, Nixon before him, and Carter afterwards, all tried to deal with the economic and energy nexus. None of them succeeded, and each paid a political price for his stewardship during bad times.

In December 1970, Nixon, faced with rising oil prices in the domestic market, laid aside the oil quota system and allowed more Canadian oil to enter. By August 1971, the president imposed wage and price controls to control inflation. But in the winter of 1972–73, fuel oil shortages were feared in many northern cities, and in October 1973, the president raised Arab animosity when he reequipped the Israelis in the Yom Kippur War. As an Arab embargo was implemented, Nixon pushed Congress to grant him emergency powers to control production and the uses of energy and to encourage the development of new energy technologies for national self-sufficiency.

When Ford became president in August 1974, imports had risen from 29 percent in 1972 to 38 percent of the U.S. oil total, making America more dependent on oil imports and more subject to Arab pressures. Ford's policy was to raise prices to check consumption and give domestic producers incentives to explore and uncap wells. Ford faced a Democratic-controlled Congress that was unwilling to accept a compulsory energy plan, and on December 1975, the legislative branch sent to the president a compromise energy bill that pushed back all domestic oil prices to an average of no more than $7.66 a barrel and gave the president the authority to decontrol oil over a forty-month period. Against the advice of some of his advisors, Ford signed the bill, figuring that half a loaf was better than none. Nixon and Ford had a similar problem in trying to deregulate natural gas prices as well, winning few concessions from Congress.

Vice President Rockefeller, in typical fashion, proposed a $100 billion corporation to encourage domestic energy sources, but Ford, seeing that the corporation was being attacked by conservatives as more big federal spending, abandoned the idea.[94]

In many ways Nixon, Ford, and Carter's policies were rather similar: energy conservation, exploration of alternative sources, and limitations on government spending. Nixon, however, was more willing to tamper with the economy to ensure his reelection, remembering in 1960 how the recession had hurt his candidacy. Carter, like Ford, proposed a major comprehensive energy initiative for Congress and both suffered defeat. Consensus on sacrifice in postwar America has been nearly impossible to achieve. Despite Kennedy's admonition to ask what one can do for one's country, his words have inspired but never become the basic prescription for our civic life. A politics organized around interest groups, with weak parties, and expensive political campaigns does not lend itself easily to discipline or coalitions. Ford's scrupulosity not to stimulate the economy, as Nixon and other presidents had done as elections approached, probably contributed in great measure to his failure to be elected.

When Ford took office, inflation had reached a level of 12 percent a year, wholesale prices had gone up over 20 percent, and the trade deficit had risen markedly. To show his desire to hold down inflation, Ford accepted the idea of a voluntary citizen program to be called Whip Inflation Now (WIN) and soon WIN buttons were established similar to the New Deal's Blue Eagle insignia. But the times and the generations were different, and WIN died stillborn, as the buttons became a joke and then collector's items.[95]

On October 8, 1974, Ford presented a major address to Congress on ending acreage limitations on several crops, reducing oil imports, examining restrictive trade practices, creating public service jobs, establishing a 10 percent tax investment credit and instituting a temporary tax surcharge of 5 percent. But by November, the administration predicted a major recession and shifted gears, fearing an increase in unemployment. Then the president advocated a tax cut, and WIN was soon scrapped.

The president also found himself making enemies because of several difficult domestic controversies. Ford had never been very interested in the environment and in ecological issues in general, but in the mid-1970s their advocates had become increasingly vocal and organized. The president vetoed the Surface Mining Control and Reclamation Act of 1974, arguing that it would cut coal production and hurt jobs. He also recommended that Congress repeal the requirement that the automobile industry adhere to substantially stronger emission standards. In addition, Ford alienated the president of the Seafarers International Union of North America, Paul Hall, by vetoing a "cargo preference" bill, aimed at ensuring that 20 percent of all foreign oil coming into the United States be on U.S. flagships. Later Ford further antagonized labor by refusing to grant final approval to a common situs picketing bill (which permitted secondary boycotts) supported by his own secretary of labor, John Dunlop, who then resigned in protest.[96]

In January, the president proposed a $16 billion tax cut, the imposition of high taxes on domestic and imported oil and natural gas, and a one-year moratorium on most new federal spending programs. Federal pay increases would be limited to 5 percent, and Social Security and government retirement cost of living adjustments would be also limited. Ford asked for a rebate of up to $1,000 per person to be credited on the 1974 tax returns and a $4 billion program for job creation. He pushed for government cuts and promised to follow his recommendations with more vetoes of budget-busting liberal programs. By February he issued a proclamation hiking import fees on petroleum products by $1 per barrel, by March it would be $2 per barrel, and then $3 one month after that. Ford clearly was pushing Congress into some action on the energy issue. In addition, he wanted early deregulation of oil and natural gas in order to cut consumption and encourage domestic productivity by increasing prices sharply.

Between two abortive assassination attempts on his life, the president continued on and decided to suspend U.S. grain sales to the Soviet Union because of the erratic nature of the market and a longshoremen's strike. The reaction in the Midwest, traditional Republican political territory, was ferocious. The administration finally concluded a more stable agreement, but Ford's decision did not endear him to farmers. To add to his difficulties, he also resisted pleas that the federal government help New York City, which was tottering on the brink of bankruptcy. The New York *Daily News* summarized the decision with a simple headline, "Ford to City: Drop Dead."

Ford continued to urge Congress to pass a permanent tax reduction of $28 billion, but only if it went along with cutting federal expenditures. The president, an old hand in the legislative branch, must have realized that a Democratic-controlled Congress coming toward election time would not approve curtailing the very domestic programs many of their senior members had created, which were important for liberal and urban constituencies.

Ford's political problems were compounded by increasing divisions and intrigue in his own house. Concerned about why his popularity had leveled off at only 47 percent despite what the president saw as some foreign policy successes and some improvements in the economy, Ford was told by one of his advisors that the public impression was that he was not clearly in charge. A shake-up was concocted that pushed Schlesinger out of Defense, put Rumsfeld in, deposed William Colby in CIA and substituted George Bush, and split the national security post away from Kissinger. Rumsfeld's detractors insisted that he was the architect of a Machiavellian scheme that eliminated Bush as a future contender for the vice-presidential slot on Ford's ticket and gave Rumsfeld one of the major cabinet secretaryships as a stepping stone to higher office.

But it is clear that Ford himself was the major initiator of this shake-up. He had a strong dislike for the perceived arrogance of James Schlesinger and recognized that William Colby was increasingly a liability after congressional investigations of the CIA. Ford was also a good enough politician to realize that Kissinger's dual role only added to his popular luster, and the president wanted some credit for the foreign policy objectives done in his name. Ford in his memoirs noted with disapproval Schlesinger's poor relations with Congress, his role in allegedly spreading the rumor that he had to reaffirm the chain of command in Nixon's final days to prevent a possible military coup, and his weariness over Schlesinger's battles with Kissinger. Schlesinger's dismissal though was soon transformed into a case of a strong secretary of defense who opposed the wishy-washy detente with the Soviets. Actually Schlesinger had in some cases been more of an advocate of military restraint than either Ford or Kissinger.[97]

In terms of the CIA, when Congress began its investigations of the agency, there was some criticism both of its intelligence operations and of Kissinger. Some congressmen felt that Kissinger had lied about the U.S. role in the overthrow of President Salvador Allende in Chile and about American activities toward Castro. With increasing challenges to his secretary of state, Ford evoked a claim of "executive privilege" to prevent the committees from extending their investigations further. As for the agency, Congressman Otis Pike argued in the House of Representatives that Ford and Kissinger had sought to block his committee's activities in order to cover up intelligence failures in Chile, Cypress, Vietnam, and the Middle East where Kissinger was involved and responsible for foreign policy. When another congressional subcommittee requested from the Commerce Department information on an Arab boycott against companies dealing with Israel or which were owned or operated by Jews, the secretary of commerce, Rogers Morton, refused to comply. Probably because Kissinger was involved in secret negotiations with Arab leaders in the Middle East, Ford invoked executive privilege again to block the release of information. The president himself had appointed a special commission headed by Rockefeller to examine charges of alleged misconduct of the CIA, but the CIA story grew and congressional committees ended up telling a tale of American-planned assassinations and dirty tricks with the strong implications that Presidents Eisenhower and Kennedy in particular were involved in the clandestine direction of murders and upheavals, although the evidence was often unconvincing to many observers.[98]

Several days after his shake-up of the cabinet, the president moved again, this time against Nelson Rockefeller. He candidly told the vice president that while he had contributed enormously to the administration, his presence on the ticket would be a liability in 1976. Rockefeller felt that Rumsfeld had used Ford's campaign chief, Bo Callaway, to increase opposition to his candidacy and to foster the dump movement. But again, it was probably Ford more than his chief of staff who calculated the president's best interest and moved into the breach. Having made his changes, Ford rested and waited for popular approval as he put his stamp on his own administration. But the news media began to label the changes "the Halloween Massacre," and the Gallup polls recorded a marked decline in the president's appeal vis-à-vis Governor Ronald Reagan of California.[99]

It was a phenomenon that Carter rediscovered in his administration. Firings, abrupt resignations, wholesale removals give the populace a sense of instability and generally tend to reflect poorly on the executive. Ford would have probably done better to clean house in the first several weeks, citing the need for a definite break with Nixon. Instead he got the worst of both worlds: criticism for the Nixon holdovers, even by his own inner circle, and then dismay at the later shake-ups.

The president's image became one of a man of limited intellectual gifts, a bumbler, and a boob who stumbled, literally, over his own feet. He became the subject of humor, and worst of all ridicule for these alleged faults, when he probably was the most physically fit and coordinated president in recent times. But image in politics pushes against reality, and Ford's achievements were being overwhelmed by real difficulties and some false barbs.

He found himself also challenged by an increasingly aggressive and well-financed right wing, which settled early on Governor Reagan as its candidate. With the demise of the New York Republican leadership and the movement of money and influence into the South and West, the political center of the GOP had shifted. The party had suffered a tremendous loss in 1964 when Goldwater was swamped by Johnson, not just in Congress but in the nurseries of political leadership, the governorships and statehouses. The conservatives took over control of the party apparatus and paid their dues by falling behind Nixon, that strange chameleon of conservative leanings and liberal departures. The end of Nixon meant the end of moderate Republicanism in an ironic way. Rockefeller's unceremonious dumping was the final curtain for liberal Republican strength.

By 1976 the great figures of East Coast Republicanism—Dewey, Eisenhower, Dulles, Clifford Case, Jacob Javits, and Nelson Rockefeller were gone. Ford with no real power base when he came to the presidency should have spent more time building the party and placing his own stamp on it. He did not. Reagan and the conservatives slowly, but effectively moved into control of many of the state organizations. Glumly, Ford later observed, "My supporters had been crisscrossing America lining up endorsements from prominent Republicans. We had most of the generals on our side. But Reagan had many of the troops."[100] In 1976, Ford woke up and appeared startled at the challenge. He apparently expected the nomination as a reward if he did a good job as president and assumed he would face Humphrey as his opponent. Instead he had to wage a closely fought battle against Reagan, and then had to take on the most conservative Democrat in recent memory who hailed from the South.

The conservatives had some specific gripes with the president as well. He had put forth a modest amnesty program for Vietnam War draft dodgers—a war many people felt should have been proudly waged and finally won. Ford had continued with Kissinger's policy of reaching some "detente" with the Soviets, signed the Helsinki pact, and pushed for more arms limitations. As the campaign approached, the foreign-sounding word "detente" itself was banned from the Ford administration lexicon. In the eyes of the conservatives, he had failed to appreciate the perfidious nature of the Soviets and been blind to the beginnings of the massive Russian military buildup taking place. Actually, Ford had pushed for an increase in the military budget and attempted in 1975 to stop the expansion of Soviet influence in southern Africa. The administration covertly gave arms to non-Marxist factions fighting in the civil war in Angola. However, fearing another Vietnam morass, the Senate by a vote of 54 to 22 passed an amendment to the defense bill prohibiting the use of U.S. government funds for such support. The following month the House concurred by 323 to 99.[101]

Ford's defense budget probably reflected his own wariness toward the Soviets and toward detente itself. He was aware of the Russian buildup after SALT I in 1972, and he was also sensitive to human rights violations before Carter's crusade, but heeded instead Kissinger's pleas for great power diplomacy. That approach prevailed when the press was told that Ford was reluctant to see novelist and Soviet émigré Aleksandr Solzhenitsyn, who had chronicled the Soviet gulags and the atrocities of the Stalinist era.

Ford had also allowed, in their eyes, both houses of Congress to investigate recklessly the CIA, leading to a series of damaging exposés about the agency. Lastly, Ford, the product of Midwest moderate Republicanism and a lifetime of consensus politics and compromise, was not an articulate spokesman for the new conservative philosophy. Reagan spoke their language; they loved his punch lines, his simple view of the world, his indictments of insider Washington. Ford was a pragmatist, an inside operator himself, a good guy who liked to solve problems and make the machine work. Reagan was a mythmaker, a communicator, a salesman with a shoeshine and a smile.

Ford barely beat Reagan at the convention, and while the Californian acknowledged the importance of party unity, he rarely campaigned for the president. Carter was a different foe than Ford expected. He was bright, calculating, and at times cutting. He could hit Ford from the left as a good Democrat and from the right as southern conservative, businessman, and engineer. His strength in the South was apparent and his appeal to fellow Christian fundamentalists and to blacks in urban and rural areas added a strange note of racial reconciliation to his appeal. Organized labor owed

little to Ford after the common situs picketing bill, and many farmers felt closer to the peanut farmer Carter than the man who stopped
grain sales for a while to the Soviets. Above all, Ford did not convey a strong sense of leadership that the American people wanted
to see in their president, even when he is wrong.

Ford grew considerably in the last year of his term. He took
stands that often were enlightened and far ahead of his time and
political counterparts. But the rivalries in his own house fostered a
sense of weakness and incompetence.[102] At times he seemed blasé
about the consequences of his political decisions and unconcerned
how they looked to the public and to those in the capital who love
to take the measure of a president, glorying in his problems and
difficulties. Candor, decency, trustworthiness should be enough in
life; but they are not sufficient or even necessary virtues in a prince.

At the end of his unelected term, Ford listened as Carter turned
to his departing predecessor and graciously began, "For myself and
for our nation I want to thank my predecessor for all he has done
to heal our land." It was a fitting summary to the Ford postscript.

CARTER'S UNCERTAIN TRUMPET

No president in this century had so little experience in government except Wilson, so little public visibility in the beginning of
his campaign, and so intense a personal ambition as Jimmy Carter.
He was the first candidate who lived in the Deep South of the Old
Confederacy to win the office since Zachary Taylor in 1850. Lyndon
Johnson had insisted that Texas was a western state and in many
ways he was correct. Carter accomplished that feat with substantial
black support both in the primaries and in the general election. He
was also the most conservative Democrat to enter the White House
since Grover Cleveland, yet he captured the presidency with a substantial number of liberal votes.

In the peculiar politics of national disintegration in the 1970s,
Carter turned normal debits into substantial assets. Upset with the
war and deeply disillusioned by the Watergate affair, the American
people responded warily at first to Carter's cry for a government
as good as its citizens, and a president running on his character
rather than on divisive ideological issues. Having gone through a
profound, searing religious crisis and reconversion in the fundamentalist Baptist tradition, Carter emerged in the mid-1960s with

a deep sense of assurance that bordered on arrogance. But that personal communion with God scored a sense of resonance with the rising religious right during that period and with millions of Protestant blacks to whom the church provided a haven in a hostile environment.

Carter's religious commitment was not a pose; it was a part of the man that animated his life and gave his ambition an almost messianic flavor. The American people may be at times jaded and cynical of politicians, but deep down they respect traditional values and the old moral admonitions—even if they do not live by them in their businesses, marriages, and neighborhoods. The war in Vietnam, the youthful rebellions of the 1960s, and the ethical lapses summarized as Watergate represented to many thoughtful and frightened people serious chasms that split them off from a simpler and more decent world of their youth. Carter caught the moment as Reagan was to do in a very different way four years later.

Carter also was not a professional politician as such, even though he briefly served on a local school board, had been a state senator, and finally was elected to one term as governor. He was a peanut farmer operating the family business, a man trained as an engineer when he was at the United States Naval Academy. As governor he had publicly abandoned the South's historic ties to segregation; yet his family's record was one of private racial toleration and timid public accommodation to traditional mores. He reaped the benefits of Dr. Martin Luther King Jr.'s courage and Lyndon Johnson's great achievements in civil rights without having been a part of the sacrifice or the suffering.[103]

As governor he had run a vaguely populist campaign and brought forth a term characterized by strained legislative relations and businesslike examination of government services in a state of modest proportions. He was invited to join David Rockefeller's Trilateral Commission, a group of influential and wealthy individuals interested in promoting ties among the United States, Western Europe, and Japan. Little known outside of Georgia in 1973, Carter began a determined and brilliant campaign to increase his visibility and sell his electability by running hard in the early Democratic primaries in 1976.

After George McGovern's surprise victory for the Democratic nomination in 1972, the news media was looking for a "dark horse" in 1976. When Carter finished strongly in the Iowa caucus, which involved a very small number of the party's voters in that state, some media pundits led by columnists in the *New York Times* "discovered" Carter. His victories in New Hampshire and his triumph over George Wallace in Florida suddenly began to create a bandwagon effect in the party, despite Carter's poor showing in several major eastern industrial states.[104]

Reporters covering any candidate like to be with a winner, and they were conscious or tacit allies of Carter's own political rise by making him a "viable candidate" where only months ago he was speaking to crowds of ten waking people in back rooms. The Democratic party's own demise was in part the reason for Carter's ascendancy. Major contenders such as Senators Edward Kennedy, McGovern, and Humphrey stayed out of the race. Wallace was a candidate of anger and not respectable; by 1976 he had to campaign from a wheel chair due to the effects of an earlier assassination attempt. Kennedy in-law Sargent Shriver, Senator Frank Church of Idaho, and the novice governor of California, Jerry Brown, all entered the race, but Carter still prevailed. Carter ran everywhere and when he lost in one place, he was celebrating a victory somewhere else the same night.

Projecting himself as a man of love and compassion, Carter played well the themes of national and sectional reconciliation, of populism and social conservatism. His nomination was a party love feast, and newspaper reporters marveled at his broad appeal to different segments, classes, races, and professions in a markedly fractured America. But while his appeal was wide, it was also rather thin—a mile wide, an inch thick as the political cliché went.

As Carter moved toward the general election, polls began to show that the American people were worried about his specific positions, his alleged fuzziness about the issues, the sense that they did not know this man after all. Carter's appeal plummeted as a battered Ford began to recover from the primary battles with Reagan. Carter advisors candidly wondered if the populace were turned off by the "weirdo factor" as they called it, that is Carter's mystical style of politics and his unfamiliar intensity.

In the campaign, Carter made some remarks that came back to haunt him. In an interview with *Playboy* magazine he confessed to having lusted in his heart after other women besides his wife and used some mild sexual slang. Why he felt it was necessary to expose his unfulfilled urges on the presidential stage was unclear; it was probably just a concomitant of his personal style of politics. But he lost the support of some of those who hate lust publicly and some of those who enjoy it privately. In another remark, he brought on himself black censure when he defended the "ethnic purity" of neighborhoods while still denouncing segregation. To some liberals and to blacks, Carter was sending a message to the racists that he was one of them.

In the debates with Ford, Carter was at first too deferential to the president of the United States. But in a later debate, Ford absurdly declared that Eastern Europe was not occupied by the Soviet Union—a mistake he stubbornly insisted on reiterating again and again. As he did so, it only confirmed the unfair stereotype of Ford as a mental dullard who left foreign policy to the able Kissinger. In the election Carter held on to enough of the traditional FDR coalition to squeak in, winning the electoral vote 297 to 240 and the popular vote 40.8 million to Ford's 39.1 million. Had Ford carried New York state with its forty-one electoral votes he would have prevailed.[105] The "outsider" Carter was in fact elected by the remnants of the old politics— especially union members, blacks, and his fellow southerners.

The usual verdict on the election is that Carter nearly lost because of his own outsider style, and that his weak organization whittled away nearly a twenty-plus point lead. In fact, when one considers that Carter was in many ways an unknown up to a year before the election, had little government experience, faced an incumbent president, and inherited a majority party in decline, his final victory can be appraised in a rather more positive light.

Washington, though, is a city of insiders, of easily kept corporate lawyers, lobbyists, and influence peddlers, of cocktail parties, capital gossip, and popular representatives who have only the vaguest ties to the people they allegedly govern. They take quick measure of the men and women who assume the commanding heights of power, and through the media influentials spread their prejudgments and suspensions of judgment across the land into the cities and into the provinces.[106]

Carter and his people claimed to owe little to those people, and probably they did owe less than most other candidates. When Speaker of the House of Representatives Thomas "Tip" O'Neill of Massachusetts met the president-elect, he offered his support, but warned that congressmen had their own political base and had run well ahead of Carter in their districts; Carter brushed off the advice, concluding that he would deal with Congress as he had with his state legislature.[107]

At his inauguration, he and his wife, Rosalyn, abandoned the presidential limousine and walked down Pennsylvania Avenue in a remarkably popular gesture of republican simplicity. Later he abandoned the tune "Hail to the Chief," which had been used to introduce previous presidents. His closest advisor, Hamilton Jordon, remarked that this was to be a government not beholden to the eastern circles of power and influence. If Zbigniew Brzezinski were to become national security advisor and Cyrus Vance secretary of state, then he would go back to Georgia, he insisted! In fact, Carter proceeded exactly along those lines and offered those two men those very same posts.[108]

Like FDR, Kennedy, and LBJ, he continued the practice of flooding the legislative branch with proposals, many of them on the difficult issues that had stymied Nixon and Ford—especially energy and the economy. He started off with a foreign policy that represented a sharp break with the postwar consensus on Soviet containment and the more nuanced realpolitik of Nixon and Kissinger. He returned to the inspiring rhetoric of Woodrow Wilson and reached deep into the well of idealism with which Americans feel so comfortable in many ways. Carter early on presented arms proposals so dramatic that the usually suspicious Russian leaders turned belligerent from the start. Upset with the new president's calls for "human rights," the Soviets felt less at home with this unknown quantity than with the more predictable Republican administrations.

Early historical judgments of the Carter presidency are nearly uniform in their conclusion that that term was a flat failure, due to the engineer president's love of detail, a personal naivete toward evil in the world, and a refusal to deal with official Washington. Actually the Carter presidency deserves a more mature judgment than that. The president's domestic record does not rival Lyndon Johnson's, but it is surely equal in some ways to those of Eisenhower, Truman, and even John F. Kennedy. His foreign policy successes at Camp David, in the Panama Canal treaty, and in reaching out to black Africa were substantial. And his much criticized initiatives in the SALT III negotiations form part of a continuum from the Nixon and Ford years to Reagan's treaty with the Soviets in 1987–88. Carter's greatest failure was his inability to match his policy objectives with the turbulent public mood of the 1970s—a gift he had in his extraordinary campaign in 1976, and which Reagan refined and really monopolized in the decade after.

What were Carter's programs and why did they run into so many reefs and shoals? In domestic affairs, Carter found the same economic problems that faced his Republican predecessors without the opportunity to strike a fully conservative pose to cut back on spending and eliminate social programs. The Democratic party that propelled him initially to the White House had lived off the legacy of FDR and the enhanced social vision of Lyndon Johnson. Its political appeal was as the party of compassion, and the great national social structures of Social Security, Medicare, government-sponsored housing, and student scholarship assistance had changed the very social fabric of the republic. As House Speaker O'Neill once observed, the Democratic party had created the American middle class, and he and his congressional colleagues in turn had no intention of cutting back on the very programs they had fought for and established. Ford could offer as an economic remedy cuts in social programs, Carter could not do so without attacking his political base.

Carter was, by his own description, a southern populist and that brand of politics has been historically concerned with government waste and debt as well as opposing elitism. The new president had promised to focus on government reorganization, tax reform, energy, deregulation of industries, job creation, and a balanced budget. It sounded very much like Ford's platform. On February 2, dressed in a sweater, the president presented his energy policy that emphasized voluntary cooperation and avoided mandatory controls. In his comprehensive energy speech of April, though, Carter called the complex issue "the moral equivalent of war" and asked for increased gasoline taxes, tax rebates to consumers, penalties for gas-guzzling cars, deregulation of newly discovered natural gas, more taxes on the use of natural gas to deter excessive use by industry and public utilities, tax credits for home insulation programs, decontrol of gas prices, and a postponement of "light water" nuclear breeder reactors.

Speaker O'Neill approved the creation of a select committee to coordinate energy legislation and facilitated its passage in the House. But in the Senate, jurisdictional committee battles slowed down consideration. By December, the House and the Senate were deadlocked, and the president refused to compromise with Senator Russell Long of Louisiana who headed the Finance Committee and represented throughout his career the oil and gas interests in Louisiana. Finally in November 1978, the president signed into law the National Energy Act, which was a major achievement but which did not incorporate some of his wide-ranging proposals. Oddly enough public comment focused on those differences, and Carter got little credit for his leadership. In 1979, OPEC price rises and the Iranian revolution against the shah made the energy problems even worse. The president in July called for a domestic summit conference on the issue, but the emphasis switched to a broad discussion of the supposed spiritual crisis in the country.[109]

In terms of welfare, the administration attacked the prevailing system as unfair and wasteful, and in its place Carter proposed a job creation plan and a greater federal takeover of those responsibilities—policies that came close to Nixon's Family Assistance Plan. The administration and its secretary of health, education and welfare, Joseph Califano, pushed for medical cost containment, which ran into intense lobbying from hospitals and others, and did not meet the desire of Senator Kennedy to pass a comprehensive and expensive medical health insurance plan. The president had also promised the National Education Association, one of the two largest teachers unions, to split Education off from HEW and create a separate department, a promise he fulfilled. To foster planning in the domestic areas, Carter abolished the Domestic Policy Council (which Nixon and Ford used) and substituted a Domestic Policy Staff responsible to him through his Domestic Policy Staff advisor, Stuart E. Eizenstat.[110]

Carter also insisted in pushing for a reorganization of the executive branch—one of the great preoccupations of presidents since Herbert Hoover, and one that probably has consumed executive efforts without having much of an impact on a president's control of the vast bureaucracy or its policy objectives. FDR had pressed for greater reorganization and control after the chaos of the New Deal; Herbert Hoover headed up a commission on reorganization for Truman; LBJ created, as FDR had, parallel structures for his new social programs; Nixon tried to revamp the bureaucracy and reorganize it in a rather bold way until Watergate; later, businessman W. R. Grace and his committee presented thousands of suggestions to Ronald Reagan on the same topic. But for Carter, reorganization was a campaign promise, and he harkened back to his record of success as governor where a reorganization more cosmetic than real was effected.

As for the economy, unemployment had fallen to about 8 percent a year later in 1976. Just before the election, the indicators showed an economic slowdown, one of the factors that probably cost Ford the election. The new president submitted proposals to trim taxes by $15 billion in a one-time cut in 1977 and another $15 billion in long-term job creation projects for 1978. After a pick-up in the economy, Carter abandoned the first part of his program, fearing inflation. In late 1978, inflation hit 9 percent and was rising, and the economy was reaching full employment. By early 1979 inflation in March topped 13 percent. Carter approved tight measures in order to drop the rate and allowed interest rates to rise, which would lead to a recession and disenchantment among traditional Democrats who had historically favored low rates and full employment.[111]

Carter tried to institute a voluntary approach to wage and price controls, but a mixture of inflation, high oil prices, rising interest rates, and uncertainty over U.S. economic policies furthered the impression that the administration did not know what it was doing, and may have worsened a bad situation. The party of FDR and its antidepression measures was now losing its popular trump card—economic prosperity.

The president was more successful in his commitments to women and minorities. His major achievement was a marked increase in the number of women and minorities given appointments, especially for federal district and appeals courts, where Congress had created 152 lower court judgeships in 1978. Carter appointed more people to lifetime posts in those courts than any other president, with 40 percent of those officeholders having been nominated in his one term. In the process, he appointed twenty-eight blacks, twenty-nine women, and fourteen Hispanics to the bench. He also was concerned about civil justice reform, privacy laws, fair housing, and a variety of other initiatives in domestic civil rights. Oddly enough, Carter in his memoirs speaks little about his record in these areas, except for his support for the Equal Rights Amendment and his nominations to the bench.[112]

His associate Griffin Bell has written that one of the problems of the Carter administration was the political liberalism of the middle levels of bureaucracy (many of them Carter appointees) who pushed their own liberal, feminist, racially activist agendas often at variance with administration policy.[113] If so, many Carter-labeled initiatives were probably the work and preoccupations of others, outstripping the Georgia circle of conservative Democrats around the president. Carter also neglected the party apparatus almost until it was too late in 1980 as he barely fended off Senator Kennedy's challenge in the early part of the primary season. In his campaign

for the White House and in his later rhetoric, he had been the outsider, one who went over the heads of the regulars and the party
leaders directly to the people. Thus after he was elected president,
Carter did not seize the party apparatus, he simply vanquished it.

At one point even Speaker O'Neill remarked, "We won the election, but you'd never know it." O'Neill's "we" was the Democratic
party; for Carter's advisors "we" meant themselves, the Georgia inner circle of friends and acquaintances. Carter later became more
sensitive to the importance of patronage and political liaison, appointing Tim Kraft to handle those matters and a veteran Democrat, Anne Wexler, to deal with traditional constituent groups that
were feeling abandoned. As Carter himself noted at the end of his
first year, "Horsetrading and compromising and so forth have always been very difficult for me to do."[114]

Carter's administration was set up like Ford's—with a spokes of
the wheel approach and not along the discredited centralized model
of the Nixon years. As the president insisted, "that's my way of
operating. That's the way I structured my warehouse, that's the way
I structured my governor's office and that's the way I structured
the White House." But after a year in office, even Carter's closest
advisors acknowledged that this approach was not working well. Too
much was falling between the cracks, and staff work was not getting done. After 1978, Hamilton Jordan acted as chief of staff and
by 1979, he assumed the title. As Carter's press secretary, Jody
Powell, concluded, "we found that we needed a greater degree of
centralization than we thought at the outset."[115]

Carter's effectiveness was hurt also by a series of controversies
involving his staff. Old friend and OMB Director Bert Lance was
forced to quit after criticism over some bank practices he engaged
in back in Georgia, and Jordan was accused of boorish behavior
toward an ambassador's wife, which he and others denied had happened, and of a drug charge, which was false. But Jordan himself
did not prove to be as effective a staff chief as he was a political
tactician. Powell bluntly concluded that it was partially Jordan's fault
that the White House was not as well run as it should have been.[116]

Criticism was also leveled, especially in the first year of his term,
at Carter's congressional liaison, Frank Moore, who seemed at times
insensitive or unknowledgable about congressional folkways. Carter
himself aggravated the situation by appointing Republicans to high-
paying jobs and by firing one of Speaker O'Neill's associates at

the Government Accounting Office. The president's veto of federal water projects almost led to a virtual revolt among his own party legislators and reinforced the view that he was an amateur in the White House. And Carter's problems were complicated further by the diffusion of congressional authority over a myriad of subcommittees in the 1970s and the dilution of party leadership in Congress, which impeded its ability to deliver even if Carter and his people had been more astute in their dealings. Also by this period, the spirit of legislative contention had grown since the Nixon years; as one Democratic senator in 1977 admitted, "We got such fun out of popping Nixon and Ford, we didn't want to give it up and be good boys any more." By 1979–80, many of those problems were being overcome, but as with Ford, first impressions stick.[117]

Still the aggregate record of support for Carter's proposals stacks up favorably with his Democratic predecessors. In 1977, Congress voted for 75.4 percent of his proposed legislation, compared to a first-year record of 88.0 percent for LBJ, 81.0 percent for Kennedy, 58.2 percent for Ford, 74.0 percent for Nixon and 89.0 percent for Eisenhower. The rate of support for Carter's legislative proposals went up to 78.3 percent in 1978, 76.8 percent in 1979 and 75.1 percent in 1980. Those overall figures, though, must be looked at within the framework of the types of legislation being proposed—whether they are controversial, have a long history of discussion behind them, and what the divisions of the House and Senate were by party, section, and ideology. What the rates of support do show is that the impression that Carter was a failure in legislative relations is incorrect. He did get authority to do some reorganization of the government, created a department of energy and a department of education, got modified energy legislation and a windfall profits tax, prevailed on the Panama Canal treaty, and halted the B-1 bomber—all very difficult issues. Rather than take on too little, Carter correctly acknowledged that in his first year, his biggest mistake was to "undertake too many things simultaneously." He did not prioritize for Congress his proposals, a mistake that he generally avoided in later years.[118]

It is in the area of foreign policy that Carter, a cautious and prudent man overall, attempted a profound redirection of American aims and strategy, especially in the first year of his presidency. After World War II, the United States accepted the basic assumptions of the policy of containment, the need to surround the Soviet Union with a string of military bases and oppose its alleged tendencies to expand its frontiers and spread Communism. As has been seen previously, Truman and his advisors were the architects of that foreign policy and created NATO, the Marshall Plan, the Truman Doctrine, and a host of efforts and agencies aimed at checking Stalinist Russia. Eisenhower agreed with those assumptions and his secretary of state, John Foster Dulles, added a Pacific Ocean anti-Communist alliance, SEATO. Kennedy raised the Cold War to a new fervor and intensity, and Johnson followed suit transforming Ho Chi Minh into Hitler and Vietnam into Czechoslovakia in 1938.

The Nixon-Kissinger foreign policy was cut from a different cloth with its emphasis on a global strategy that employed a balance of power, conceptualized five major power centers (the United States, USSR, Western Europe, Japan, and Communist China), and sought to link up U.S. responsiveness to Russian interests with Soviet restraint in the new international order being promoted. Carter's foreign policy in 1977 marked a distinct departure. The president and his major foreign policy makers saw the international system as increasingly pluralistic in which the threat from the Soviet Union was not a dominant concern. The new administration focused on human rights and democracy, arms control, the resolution of conflict in the Middle East and Africa, Third World economic development, and the promotion of a global economy. Whereas Kissinger had been preoccupied with East-West relations and showed a marked disdain for the problems of the Southern Hemisphere, the Carter administration was very much involved in seeking to improve North-South relations and the problems of the have-not nations.

The president's views were complimented by Secretary of State Cyrus Vance and to a more limited extent by his national security advisor, Zbigniew Brzezinski. Carter's basic approach owed some of its moral fervor and internationalism to the powerful Wilsonian idealism that had so captivated the United States and the world briefly during and right after World War I. Americans, so committed to democratic rhetoric and schoolyard notions of rules and fair play, have been especially prone to this tradition of international relations while at the same time increasing U.S. prominence and power in the world. The Atlantic Charter, the United Nations, Atoms for Peace, the Peace Corps all were animated by a simple people-to-people approach that proved congenial to many Americans despite the blemishes on their own democracy in those periods.

Carter and his advisors were knowledgeable about the swings

from idealism to power politics and back again over the decades. Their foreign policy showed an awareness of the cries for black freedom in southern Africa, the terrible poverty in the Third World, and the need for the first anticolonialist country, the United States, to reassert moral leadership after the military debacle in Vietnam. Even with these salutary concerns, though, the wisdom of the past forty years was not so easily proven wrong. The central challenge to American power and aspirations remained the Soviet Union, and in the 1970s its Communist leader, Leonid Brezhnev, had clearly embarked on a massive military buildup and an aggressive foreign policy. By 1978, the earlier consensus in the administration's upper echelon was beginning to wane as Brzezinski expressed public concerns about Soviet and Cuban intervention in Africa, especially in Ethiopia. By the end of the year, he spoke of an "arc of crisis"— that is, Soviet moves across the Persian Gulf and southern Africa coupled with problems in Iran.[119]

In addition, the administration early in the term had laid out at Carter's insistence a bold program for massive cuts in nuclear arms, far beyond what Ford and Kissinger were talking about in SALT II. The Soviets, rather than welcoming such overtures, recoiled sharply, seeing them as some trick and a departure from the basic framework already laid out in the talks they had with Ford and Kissinger. When the administration went public with its proposals, it was only adding to Soviet suspicions. The early failure of a Soviet-American nuclear arms pact was intensely discussed, and Carter was at first angry and then puzzled as he backtracked and laid out with Vance a more careful groundwork.[120]

As has been seen, one unresolved problem from the last meeting of Ford and Brezhnev at Vladivostok was the specification of restrictions on the versatile and mobile cruise missiles. That problem was matched by U.S. concern over the ambiguous status of the Backfire bomber. SALT I, signed by Nixon and Brezhnev in May 1972, was aimed at limiting defensive capabilities by agreeing to restrictions on both sides of antiballistic missile (ABM) defenses to two cities, one of which was to be the national capital. A second interim agreement froze for five years each side's launchers for intercontinental ballistic missiles (ICBMs) and submarine-launched ballistic missiles (SLBMs). The interim agreement did not specify the number of ICBMs to be limited since the Soviets refused to divulge that number. Critics of the agreement concluded that the freeze on offensive weapons left the Soviets with about 2,400 missile launchers compared to 1,700 for the U.S. As has been noted, Nixon administration officials had argued several points: that the agreement controlled future Russian developments, the United States had a major advantage with its bomber capacity, American ICBMs were more reliable, submarines and missiles were superior, and the U.S. had more far-flung bases and more sophisticated technology for MIRVs (multiple independently targetable reentry vehicles).

However, a year after SALT I was signed, the Soviets began testing a new generation of ICBMs with heavier payloads and some with multiple warheads. U.S. military planners feared a major Soviet advance in strategic power, and they warned that the Soviet SS-19 could carry six warheads—twice as many as the United States' Minuteman. As the Nixon administration negotiated SALT II, Congress and the Pentagon insisted on identical numerical limits for both sides. The proposed accord included a ceiling of 2,400 for total offensive strategic nuclear launch vehicles and a subceiling of 1,320 launchers for multiple warheads. The Soviets also did not insist on restricting U.S. nuclear weapons in Europe (the Forward Base System, in the parlance of the period). The United States had wanted the Soviet Backfire bomber limited by classifying it as a "heavy bomber," and the Soviets insisted on limiting the cruise missiles. Both weapons still remained in an ambiguous status after Ford and Brezhnev finished their deliberations. But with an election campaign going on and after considerable opposition from the Pentagon and increasing Soviet resistance to further concessions, the proposed accord was undone.[121]

The Soviets then insisted that Carter honor the major parameters of that proposal, while he wanted to put it behind him and move on a bolder SALT agreement. The president insisted (as Reagan was to do later in 1981) on a radical arms control proposal which only aroused suspicions of the normally suspicious Russian leadership. The Soviets were also concerned, or so they said, by Carter's campaign for human rights. The failure of the administration's first encounter with the Soviets led to public hand-wringing sessions about the causes of the alleged debacle and early charges of U.S. ineptitude. Consequently, the administration resorted to a slower and more piecemeal approach.

U.S. public opinion and congressional sentiment began to dwell on the charges that America was becoming a second-rate power, falling behind the Soviets. Concerns focused on parity and verification of any agreement, and Carter created more problems when he decided to cancel abruptly the B-1 bomber as an economy move. His decision, probably correct in the long run, denied the United States another bargaining chip with the Soviets and increased apprehensions at home. While Carter was having his agents negotiate with the Russians, he found himself subject to continuing criticism from Senator Henry Jackson, the powerful hawkish Democrat who was eyeing the White House, for having made too many concessions. Among some Western European allies there was also a fear of a growing imbalance in strategic forces that could have consequences for their own security. Carter's chief critic was the West German chancellor, Helmut Schmidt, who thought the president too naive to deal with the tough Russians. In the spring of 1978, Carter's problems grew as the Soviet- and Cuban-sponsored Ethiopian army was overwhelming a Somali secessionist movement in the Ogaden desert. And in April 1978, Carter announced that he would defer the deployment of the enhanced-radiation weapons, called the "neutron bomb," a step that also brought criticism and added to the impression that the president was not sensitive to the feelings of the Western allies and to the need to bargain from strength with the Soviets.

As negotiations proceeded, the Soviets pressed to prevent the United States from moving on with its MX (Missile Experimental) project, which the administration saw as an answer to the Russian SS-18 and SS-19. To decrease their vulnerability, the MX missiles were to be moved around in underground tunnels or on flatbed trucks in Wisconsin and Minnesota. After that absurd idea was dismissed, another plan was prepared to create a large number of holes in the earth and then randomly move the missiles around in a carnival-like shell game.

Talks also hit the brick wall of encryption of telemetry—or the scrambling of electronic data sent from rockets on warheads. The United States saw such interference as hindering its ability to judge if the Russians were cheating; the Soviet Union regarded such a curtailment as impinging on national sovereignty and security. Carter was growing concerned about the deadlock in negotiating, asserting, "I'm getting no credit for tough negotiating. I'm just getting beaten up on for failing to finish the thing." When the president triumphed at Camp David with the Egypt-Israeli agreement, the administration pushed hard to make it two major victories in a row. Carter abandoned his insistence on exempting conventionally armed

ALCMs (air-launched cruise missiles) from cruise restrictions and allowed the Russians to keep a vigorous research and development program going for a modernized ICBM.

But National Security Advisor Brzezinski's remarks on supporting Communist China upset the Russians, and once again relations soured. The overthrow of the shah in Iran brought renewed concern about verification because of the loss of critical U.S. intelligence bases on Iranian outposts. Faced with increased doubts about Senate ratification, the administration considered sending the treaty to both houses of Congress as an agreement rather than a treaty.

The SALT II proposal agreement was much more complex than its predecessor. The final package consisted of a treaty that was to run until 1985, an interim protocol to continue until 1981, and a statement of principles to be used in SALT III. The treaty proposed a ceiling of 2,400 missiles and bombers, which was to be reduced by the year 1982 to 2,250 missiles, and a protocol that prohibited the deployment of ground- and sea-launched cruise missiles with a range of over six hundred kilometers.

Despite the long, drawn-out, and eventually fruitless negotiations on SALT II, the Carter administration did garner some significant successes in 1978, and the Republicans proved to be important allies for the president in the Panama Canal treaties, Mideast plane sales, the lifting of the arms embargo against Turkey, and a moderate policy toward Rhodesia. Carter's triumph in getting a very recalcitrant Senate to accept the Panama Canal divestiture, and his later persistent negotiations with Egypt and Israel over the West Bank surely show the president in a very favorable light and represent two of the most skilled performances by any president.

By the start of his administration, the future of the Panama Canal was becoming a very difficult political and military problem. Many Americans feared that the loss of the Canal Zone would constitute a threat to the United States, and that the various unstable Panamanian governments would end up being unable to protect American passage through the canal. The history of Panamanian regimes before and since Carter clearly shows that such reservations were well founded. But Carter argued that continued American possession in the face of heavy opposition in that area would itself lead to a real security problem in the Canal Zone. Presidents before him had postponed the inevitable, and Carter paid a political price in some quarters by taking on the issue and not waiting until his second term. The final treaties returned most of the zone to the Panamanians and allowed them to join the United States in the operation and maintenance of the canal. The United States would have control of the canal as well as the right to protect it with its existing canal forces until 1999. After that, all American forces would be withdrawn. Under a separate treaty, the United States retained the permanent right to come back and defend the canal from any external threat. In time of emergency, warships of the United States would be guaranteed the right to expeditious passage.[122]

Carter noted that at this time 78 percent of the American people did not want to give up the canal. The president countered by inviting leaders from throughout the hemisphere to a signing ceremony, and he used the Panamanian head, General Omar Torrijos, directly in his ratification campaign. Torrijos proved to be rather effective with senators and aided the cause. The president sent State Department officials to over 1,500 appearances to defend the treaties and flew forty-five senators to Panama. Working closely with the bipartisan Senate leadership, the president plotted strategy and personally worked on wavering senators.

Carter's activities are almost a case study in effective presidential leadership. After his successes in the Senate, he faced serious difficulties in the House, which had to pass some implementing legislation. Several congressmen filed a lawsuit charging that any transfer of property had to be approved by both houses of Congress, although the Supreme Court eventually upheld the executive's actions. House committees though conducted hearings, and conservative politicians, led by Governor Reagan, used the issue to good effect. Like President Washington in the Jay Treaty controversy, Carter found the lower body insisting on intruding itself through the backdoor into the treaty-making process. The implementation legislation was needed to cover retirement benefits to employees and to transfer property and responsibilities for running the canal to the Panamanians. Again, Carter had to launch a massive lobbying effort in both houses of Congress to prevail. Later the president was to speculate that maybe he should have waited until his second term to tackle the issue. He concluded that eleven of the fourteen senators up for reelection who supported the treaty were defeated, plus one sitting president.[123]

Carter's second major triumph though was the Camp David Accords signed by Egyptian President Anwar el-Sadat and Israeli Prime Minister Menachem Begin. Those agreements, the fruits of eighteen months of laborious negotiations, led to a formal treaty signed on March 29, 1979. Since the establishment of a Jewish state after World War II and the increasing hostility of the Arab regimes, the Mideast had become a continuing tinderbox, which grew progressively worse. Carter did not face another immediate war between the Israelis and various Arab states, but he and his aides were aware of the bitter legacy of the October 1973 war, the threats of Soviet interest in the region, and skyrocketing oil price rises. In 1974–75, Secretary Kissinger had conducted shuttle diplomacy back and forth between the sides to reach a Mideast accord. He was not totally successful, but Carter building on his efforts undertook to conclude a peace treaty for that very difficult region, becoming in the process a true honest broker between Israel and Egypt.

To break the stalemate, Egyptian President Sadat in a brilliant political gesture appeared before the Knesset in Jerusalem, calling for a Geneva-type summit conference. When that dramatic venture yielded no real changes, Sadat realized that he needed American help to restore Egyptian lands captured in the last war with the Israelis. At first, President Carter advanced a vague formula that the Palestinians had a right to self-determination, a concession that brought on him the anger of the powerful pro-Israeli lobbyists and many influential Jewish Democrats. However, Israel's position was being hurt by the impression that its prime minister, Menachem Began, was inflexible and pushing for new settlements in the occupied lands.

To appease the so-called moderate Arab states, the administration put together an arms package for Israel and added to it jets for Egypt and Saudi Arabia. To facilitate some agreement, Carter took a difficult gamble and invited leaders to Camp David for personal negotiations. There Carter's incredible patience, love for detail, and profound knowledge of the Old Testament biblical sites proved to be invaluable ingredients in his eventual success. No president in recent memory has personally been as successful as Carter was in serving as a mediator in what is surely one of the most difficult international problems—the ancient and more contemporary hatreds of the nations, tribes, and religions of the Mideast.

With some help from Secretary Vance, the president actually wrote the proposed peace treaty. The parties approved a tentative set of accords, which restored Egyptian lands to that nation, had Egypt recognize Israel, and furthered normal diplomatic relations.

The accords, though, did not cover the more difficult issues of implementing Palestinian self-determination and what would be the fate of the West Bank and Gaza. Ten years later when those areas exploded with Palestinian discontent, the Reagan administration put forth proposals remarkably similar to those Carter had pressed for concerning the future of the Palestinians. And in 1993, the Israeli government and the Palestine Liberation Organization (PLO) recognized each other and began negotiations.

When in the late winter of 1979, it appeared that the impetus of the accords was being lost and implementation receding, Carter again gambled and went directly to the two nations. In a burst of shuttle diplomacy, he papered over the problems and ended the public acrimony. It was by any account an extraordinary exercise of diplomatic expertise, played for high stakes, not the least of which was the very effectiveness of the office that Carter held.[124]

Yet with these real achievements, the Carter administration hit several major crises that overshadowed its successes and cast into doubt the president's ability to lead. In dealing with a recalcitrant and demanding Congress, Carter found it as difficult as Nixon and Ford to get a comprehensive energy policy. As the prices set by the OPEC oil cartel rose dramatically, the United States experienced a frightening spiral of inflation and a deep sense of losing control over its destiny and its preeminent world role. Carter on one occasion decided to take up that problem and called together leaders from all walks of life to discuss the national malaise. He came back from Camp David with a speech that warned about the spiritual crisis affecting the American soul. Whether his prescription was correct or not is open to question; it was based on unverified opinion polls and some pop sociology floating around at the time, which focused on general anxieties and the loss of personal ethical standards. But the citizenry listened respectfully; then the president decided to bring order to his own house by firing three cabinet officers—Joseph Califano in HEW, W. Michael Blumenthal in Treasury, and Brock Adams in Transportation—and placing his political aide, Hamilton Jordon, in charge as chief of staff. Public confusion and media criticism followed, and the president lost much of the momentum he had generated.[125]

Meanwhile, the Soviet Union continued its massive arms buildup and struck a rather aggressive posture first in Africa and then invaded neighboring Afghanistan. In addition, charges were made in Congress and the media that the Russians had raised up a combat bridgade in Cuba. The administration joined in the overreaction, fearful of being seen as weak. The Soviets probably had not initiated any new force strength there, but the issue took on a life of its own.[126]

After the Afghan invasion, the chances of another SALT agreement being ratified by the Senate died a quick death. The president gave up his dream of dramatic cuts in nuclear arsenals and took a tough stand in the Persian Gulf, warning of the threat to U.S. interests, and creating a special mobile strike force to use there if necessary. The Soviets in Afghanistan, however, faced unexpected and intense opposition to this occupation, and years later ignominiously withdrew. In Iran, the sudden overthrow of the shah of Iran, Reza Pahlevi, toppled one of the United States' staunchest allies in that part of the world, thus adding to American anxieties. The shah had been placed and kept on the throne in large part through the efforts of the CIA in the 1940s and 1950s, and he became over the decades a cranky, but valuable pillar of American global politics. Domestic opposition grew in the ranks of liberal elements in Iran who resented his repression and from more powerful Islamic fundamentalists who distrusted his overtures to the West and its supposedly heathen ways. The "Shah of Shahs," as he called himself, emulated in opulent style the old Persian monarchs, launched a "White Revolution" to foster economic development, and established a secret police to crush dissent.

Most experts on Iranian politics expected that if the shah were overthrown it would be by the large Communist party in Iran, but instead the major focal point of dissent became militant Islamic elements. The shah, claiming later that American intentions were unclear, wavered between resistance and capitulation to those religious fundamentalists. He learned what many absolute monarchs have found: that moderation leads often not to pacification but to an acceleration of dissent and violence. Uncertain of the administration's backing and physically ill, the shah abdicated and fled.

The administration hoped for a moderate regime in its place and did not give the Iranian army any encouragement to intervene in a military coup d'état. Like so many revolutions, each wave of change brought more and more extreme elements to power; in Iran, Islamic followers under the spiritual and political leadership of Ayatollah Ruholla Khomeini began to prevail. The new rulers of Iran, who were originally less extreme, lost control of the state, and on one occasion the U.S. embassy was broken into, only to be restored later by the governing authorities. But then on November 4, 1980, a group of three thousand militants entered the U.S. embassy in Tehran, seized sixty-three people and encouraged by the Ayatollah Khomeini held on. Legitimate attempts by responsible Iranians and the administration to end the crisis were constantly thwarted in an incredible labyrinth of political intrigue in the theocracy being established in Iran.[127]

The president, weary of diplomacy, ordered a complex American rescue operation, which ended in failure. He took full responsibility, Secretary of State Vance resigned in protest over the use of armed forces, and the administration faced increasing public frustration and media magnification of the hostage crisis as it moved from weeks to months and into a year of prolonged captivity. In the last day of his presidency, the president was able to get the captives released without a single death, but they paid a year of their lives, and it helped cost Carter his office.[128]

All of these events weakened Carter's hold on the public and an emboldened Senator Edward Kennedy undertook a direct challenge to the president, charging that he had betrayed the liberal legacy of the Democratic party. Like Reagan taking on Ford four years before, the Kennedy confrontation undercut Carter's position even further and led to a real rift in the party. Actually Kennedy was a rather weak candidate with a checkered personal life that haunted his campaign. But the appeal of the Kennedy family to the memories of liberal Democrats was strong, and the desire for a restoration of Camelot and the vaguely recalled days of John F. Kennedy cut into Carter's more homespun appeal. Carter won the nomination, but a rapprochement was never reached with Kennedy in large part because of the senator's own personal recalcitrance. Reagan, fresh from devastating former Ambassador George Bush, sailed to an easy nomination victory and an incredibly strong electoral mandate over Carter.

The Carter presidency is usually portrayed as a failed one, a prime example of weak leadership and a basic inability to master political skills and the arts of communication. That consensus on failure is so strong that one is reluctant to depart from it, but such a judgment is incorrect. Carter in the very beginning did seem somewhat naive in foreign affairs and inept in domestic matters, especially in dealing with Congress. The people around him, those closest to him, were either not aware of the Washington folkways or just did not care to conquer the city that they sought to govern. They had run against the establishment and now were a part of it; they forgot that to change Rome one must first understand it. They made it chic to act like rubes—a kind of reverse snobbery that good old boys like to play on strangers.

The establishment figures that Carter brought in were often loyal not to him but their constituencies and Washington friends and clients. The middle echelons of government were filled with appointees whose orientations were often very different from Carter's conservatism and the moderate tones of the American people of the late 1970s. Too many players with too many agendas and too little loyalty undid the administration, Carter associate and Attorney General Griffin Bell concluded years later in his memoirs.

In dealing with Congress, Carter learned quickly, though, and his record in domestic affairs is surely as good as any postwar president except for Lyndon Johnson. The late 1970s was not a time for major social legislation or a radical expansion of the welfare state. An economy driven by inflation, plagued by oil shortages, beset by high interest rates is not fertile ground to plant the new. The economy was depressed enough to cause considerable suffering, but not depressed enough to stimulate reform. And as noted, it can be said fairly that Carter was the most conservative Democratic president in memory, a southern populist with that region's heritage of limited government and business efficiency. His model could be Cleveland not FDR.

Still, though, his record with Congress was not one of failure or neglect. In foreign affairs, Carter's position had been criticized as being shortsighted and unrealistic in terms of dealing with the U.S. rival, the Soviet Union. In part, the president contributed to that impression by his own remarks about how surprised he was at the invasion of Afghanistan. Yet Carter was correct that U.S. policy had under Nixon and Kissinger genuinely neglected human rights—the great moral issue that has animated American foreign affairs since Woodrow Wilson. No president has had a better sense of the powerful appeal that decency, racial progress, and liberty have, and he sought to position the United States on those grounds, although not totally successfully and not without considerable backsliding in his time in office.

But the conflict between American interests with its support of right-wing repressive regimes and this democratic rhetoric was increasingly apparent as the years went on. In Nicaragua, for example, the administration was pleased to see dictator Anastasio Somoza go, but found in its place the Marxist Sandinistas with their own dynamics of repression. That dilemma has haunted American foreign policy since World War II, and generally U.S. policy had supported abuses of the right out of fear of the extremes of the left. The problem is that such a Hobson's choice has often led to U.S. approval of right-wing repression or the penting up of frustrations that aid the appeal of Marxist alternatives. Kennedy proposed a democratic middle path, and it generally failed in Latin America and Africa. Carter continued to side with human rights struggles and faced the dilemmas in Iran, South Korea, Pakistan, Nicaragua, and elsewhere. Still he recognized that human rights and idealism have a place alongside realpolitik and the need to protect national interests.

His basic instincts on strategic arms limitations, Palestine self-determination, black rule in Africa, and the Panama Canal have proven to be correct, and became a part of the Reagan policies despite Reagan's own statements and instincts. One of Carter's speechwriters, James Fallows, wrote that Carter's was a passionless presidency that lacked a vision. But in foreign policy that is surely not the case. The president and his aides knew of the complexities and tensions in their choices and sought to move U.S. policy in specific directions.[129]

Like Truman, Carter left office with a sense of failure and public approbation. Surely his successor proved to be more adept in explaining his simple views of the world, views Americans enjoyed sharing in but which betrayed their promise as a great civilization. Carter sought to face and master difficult economic and global problems; Reagan to deny them. In honesty it must be admitted that people feel better with the latter than with the former kind of leadership. All societies want to kill the messenger rather than confront the message. Reagan sensed that; Carter could not accept that fact of political life. He was an engineer, a man trained to make facts lead to judgment and solutions. Reagan was an actor, skilled in a profession in which fact gives way to illusion, and illusion is the modern equivalent of social reality.

The Carter presidency is one of significant achievement and importance. Whether its true value remains hidden or will be eventually acknowledged by historians and then by the public remains to be seen. We Americans have a right to dissent, to be critical, to flail away at our leaders. But in that traditional cathartic process, we should at times step back from the fun of it all and recognize

that sometimes we get better leadership than we recognize . . . or
that we deserve. Perhaps, just perhaps, that was the case with Jimmy
Carter.

REAGAN AND THE
CONSERVATIVE CRUSADES

Politics is often a derivative profession, drawing men and women
who have been molded and succeeded or failed in other walks of
life. They bring with them the habits of a lifetime to politics and to
the leadership of an often fickle people. Washington and Eisenhower
remained military men in many ways long after their service was
done; Wilson lectured Congress and the nation as a good Calvinist
schoolmaster; Hoover and Carter analyzed public policy through the
rigid and exacting eyes of engineers. Ronald Reagan was, in one
sense, in a perfect profession for the late twentieth century presidency—he was an actor, a master of space and place and impressions.

Ronald Reagan led the charmed life of a handsome, personable,
small town boy who progressed from being a sports announcer to a
movie star to the leader of a visible labor union, and finally to a
citizen politician in the most populous state in the Union. He was
the son of a strong-willed mother and an alcoholic father who was
intensely committed to the Democratic party. For most of his early
years, Ronald Reagan was an admirer of the liberal New Deal and
the towering presence of Franklin D. Roosevelt. In fact, he insisted
on linking his conservative administration and his own attitudes to
the life and times of FDR. Characteristically, his use of television
and radio was patterned on Roosevelt's own immensely successful
radio addresses to the people.[130]

It has been fashionable to belittle Reagan's abilities as an actor,
but he was one of the most popular movie figures of that period.
With some pride, he has called himself the "Errol Flynn of the B-
movies." After World War II, however, his career began to floun-
der, and he headed up the Screen Actors Guild and defended
performers before Senator Joseph McCarthy's committee, uphold-
ing publicly their civil liberties, while secretly serving as an occasional informant for the FBI. He developed a deep fear of
Communists, whom he claimed had targeted him for elimination
during this period because of his opposition to their feeble attempts

to infiltrate the movie industry. Ironically, he had unknowingly flirted with Communist fellow traveler organizations and was seen by some as a rather extreme New Deal liberal. From his union presidency, he went on to host a television series and became a spokesman for General Electric. Reagan started giving uplifting quasi-political speeches for that company and gravitated toward the conservative orbit of his second wife and his new father-in-law. He also came to the attention of a small group of very wealthy Californians who supported him financially and calculated that he could become governor of their state and the president of the United States. They were correct, as Reagan in 1980 rode to a landslide victory, becoming the fortieth president.[131]

Unlike some other conservative politicians, Reagan was able to fuse traditional small town Republicans on Main Street with Wall Street operatives and religious fundamentalists—many of the last group once Democrats like himself. By 1980 large segments of the population felt threatened by the social movements of the 1960s and 1970s. The changing role of women, the new legal rights of racial minorities, the open advocacy in some quarters of easy sex and drugs, and the breakdown of middle-class family morality upset a good number of moderate voters. The backlash against the civil rights bills ended once and for all the Democratic hegemony over white voters in the South, as Lyndon Johnson predicted when he signed the Civil Rights Act in 1964. And as civil rights moved from the heady days of the 1960s toward affirmative action, protected categories of people, and goals for preferential hiring, white resistance began coalescing.[132] In addition, some of the large generational cohort born in the late 1940s challenged the mores of their parents and of postwar American society. That twenty-year span starting in the 1960s led to greater self-expression, creativity, and social reform, and it also led to hedonism, self-righteousness, and crude individualism.

It is ironic that the first television president and the first divorced president, whose own family life with his children was strained, should have become the bearer of the flag of the old values. It is odd that the strongest advocate of a war-centered patriotism should be a man whose military career involved only making training films in California while other men fought and died at Anzio, Omaha Beach, and Guadalcanal. But what was even more remarkable was that Ronald Reagan was never troubled by the gap between his life and his rhetorical descriptions of it. He could urge that the federal

government stamp out social welfare programs and let private philanthropy take its place, while he himself was at best a modest giver
to charities. He could describe in vivid detail the sacrifices of World
War II veterans at Normandy as if he were there himself, explaining once that he frequently visualized as real what were fictional
occurrences. But those blurrings between reality and make-believe
did not matter, for the American people had become a television
generation, and many of them lived for images and judged their
political leaders accordingly.

It was the show that mattered, and few could rival Reagan as
the master showman. His friends and his critics alike called him
"the Great Communicator," but nearly every one of his associates
who has shared his or her views of him publicly has reported that
Reagan was remarkably aloof and distinct from the very world about
which he was communicating. His foremost biographer, Lou Cannon, attributes that attitude to the fact that he was the child of an
alcoholic, and that it is not uncommon for such offspring to be lon-
ers who withdraw into their own world. The difference with Reagan was that his world was one of optimism and light, one in which
an aged man could still dream captivating dreams of youth. And in
the end, it was Reagan who gave the best definition of his time in
office when he said that politics was like acting—you start quickly,
coast along, and end up with a fast finish.

Reagan is a difficult act for historians to judge. He was able
brilliantly to mobilize people, to convey and motivate confidence
in the presidency and in the special mission of America.[133] Although
liberals hate to admit it, his sterling repetitions of the moral superiority of democracy and freedom helped to inspire the beleaguered
dissident elements especially in Communist Europe. One may scoff
at those flights of rhetorical fancies at home but, in the grim rooms
of Mother Russia and in the sullen parlors of Warsaw and Budapest,
Reagan's expressions were part of the explosives that by 1989 destroyed Communism as a philosophy and as a world order.

But the darker side of Reagan's terms became starker as the
nation paid the bills for an eight-year period of social neglect and
political paralysis. In 1981, his administration began with a major
tax cut that was meant to give people back more of their own money
and to slice the federal government down to size. But the president
was committed to a massive military buildup (actually begun under
Carter), which ended up costing nearly $1 trillion and which was

characterized by incredible waste, misallocation of resources, and a total lack of strategic priorities.

It is clear that the president had no real idea what his own economic policy was, and his budget director, former Congressman David Stockman, bluntly confessed that there were no philosophical underpinnings, except self-interest and greed.[134] The administration claimed that it was committed to supply-side economics that stressed tax cuts, limited government, and unbridled consumption. Some Reaganites argued that supply-side economics was not a new idea with this president, but that in fact it had been discussed in congressional committees as a way to encourage savings and higher productivity.[135] But the critics of such a cut saw the Reagan recisions as another version of the 1920s trickle-down theory: lower the taxes of the rich, and benefits will eventually drip down to the masses. What the Reagan tax cut of 1981 did was to slash the rates, especially for the wealthy, reduce the domestic welfare state, and use the savings to upgrade the military. The results were not just a shrinkage in the scope of the federal government's concerns, but also a major shift of money from domestic to military spending. The tax cuts helped lead to massive deficits in that period; the national debt jumped from $908 billion in 1980 to $2.68 trillion in 1989. Under Reagan, the debt accumulated was greater than the total from the administration of George Washington to that of Jimmy Carter.

The tax cut bill ran into initial rough sledding in Congress, especially in the Democratic-controlled House of Representatives. The Republicans had captured the Senate as a result of the 1980 election by a margin of 53 to 46, while the House remained Democratic, 242 to 189. Then on March 30, 1981, the president was seriously wounded in an assassination attempt outside the Washington Hilton hotel where he had made a speech. Reagan, in the first harrowing hours of his ordeal, was so heroic and good-natured that his courage and poise impressed the nation, and his popular stock rose markedly and probably aided his domestic proposals. The tax reduction package had several important effects besides cutting revenues and increasing the national debt. The cuts did help to stimulate the economy and played a role in what became a decade of good economic times, especially for the rich, and eliminated the financial base for new liberal spending programs from the Democrats.

The 1980s became a time of great accumulation of wealth for the upper classes as the average income of the top 1 percent of the nation doubled.[136] By 1990 even some conservative writers, such as Kevin Phillips, were aghast at the massive shift of wealth to the very rich, their often tasteless ostentations, the mindless mergers of corporations and financial institutions, and unregulated foreign investment.[137] By the late twentieth century, the United States led all other major industrial nations in the gap dividing the upper fifth of its population from the lower fifth. The number of millionaires increased from 574,000 in 1980 to 1.3 million by 1988, and America's top 420,000 households accounted for 26.9 percent of the nation's wealth. While the salaries and benefits of corporate CEOs and presidents increased astronomically, the number of middle-management jobs during the 1980s declined by as many as 1.5 million positions. Worse off were female-headed households, particularly those with children, where poverty levels especially among minority women reached frightening levels. The percentage of children living in poverty was double in 1986 what it was in 1967. For the first time in memory, commentators were talking about the next generation having a permanently lower standard of living than its parents.

The number of those under twenty-five years old who owned their own homes dropped from 21.3 percent in 1980 to 16.1 percent in 1987. And the same downward trend occurred among those in the various age brackets from twenty-five through thirty. As for Ronald Reagan's reactions, he simply offered the view that a rising tide lifts all boats, that is, that better breaks for the wealthy would benefit everyone—sooner or later. His personal philosophy was best spelled out in his declaration, "What I want to see above all is that this remains a country where someone can always get rich." But it would be a mistake to say that Reagan's appeal was simply to the top 10 percent of Americans. His constituency was not just the rich, but those who have an ambition to be rich; for them the American dream is predominantly circumscribed by wealth, the accumulation of goods, and the visceral pleasure of deal making. And in the first years of Reagan's initial term, the Democrats in Congress seemed disjointed, defensive, and distracted in their opposition to this new, and very old, public philosophy.

One unexpected occurrence was that as the federal government cut taxes, the states and localities had to assume more obligations so that the total tax receipts as a percentage of GNP by 1984 returned to where it was before Reagan took office. Still, about 27 percent of the gross national product, a relatively low level compared to other advanced industrial nations in the world, went to pay the total federal, state, and local tax bill. The 1980s witnessed a decline in the size and standard of living of the middle class—the traditional bastion of democracy. The adjusted wages of average workers by 1991 were below 1979 levels. Family incomes were maintained by wives going to work, with some social critics citing deleterious consequences for the upbringing of the nation's young. In 1960, 30 percent of wives with children under eighteen worked, by 1987 it was 65 percent. Some went to work because of their desire to continue or to begin a career in the work place, but many went to work to help to make ends meet.

Still the administration delivered on its agenda to cut taxes for the wealthy and to free business from many public restraints and government regulations. The tax bill slashed the top personal tax bracket from 70 percent to 28 percent (to be phased in over seven years), and by 1983, the percentage of federal tax receipts paid through corporate income taxes dropped to a mere 6.2 percent. The administration followed up those cuts with an almost total deregulation of American businesses in some sectors. Much of that deregulation policy was in place before Reagan took office, but his administration allowed massive mergers, corporate raidings, and redeployment of corporate assets, as twenty-five thousand deals worth over $2 billion took place. Most ominously, the administration and several key members of Congress allowed the savings and loan banks to expand their traditionally narrow range of operations, and at the same time, had the government guarantee personal accounts in those lending institutions up to $100,000. When many of the savings and loan associations ended up in trouble because of bad lending practices, the American taxpayers were left in the 1990s with an enormous and almost incalculable liability to fund irresponsible speculations, incompetent management, and rampantly deficient business practices in what was once one of the most conservative and responsible fields of American corporate life.

Equally ominous was the great transfer of economic power away from the United States to Western Europe and Japan. Obviously, the near monopoly of America in setting the world's economic directions had to end after the headiness of post–World War II experiences. But the United States because of its loose business practices, its speculative economy in the 1980s, and its rampant consumerism became the prime target for foreign investors and exporters. When Ronald Reagan became president, the United States was the largest creditor nation in the world, but by the time he left office it had become the largest debtor nation. Supporters of the Reagan administration have argued that the United States was simply a good investment with its stable government and its encouraging business climate, and they noted with approval how unemployment had fallen in the late 1980s and how in that period the United States had created more than 90 percent of the total new jobs recorded in the ten leading industrial democracies. Whereas inflation in the last year of Carter was 12.5 percent, the prime interest was 15.26 percent and civilian unemployment was 7.1 percent, Reagan's figures eventually were 4.4 percent, 9.32 percent, and 5.5 percent, respectively.

And in American society, the expressions of its way of life on television and in print revolved around the romances of the rich and the famous, as they were called. The president and his first lady, in the early years of the administration, played to that mythic dream, mining the parts for all they were indeed worth, emulating that upper sliver of the population. Ronald Reagan, the son of a politically liberal shoe salesman, had come half circle to a world he and so many of those who will never know riches loved—the mores and habits of the idle rich. The Reagan administration brought with it a legion of ideological conservatives, not of the Eisenhower or even of the Nixon variety, but men and women whose main themes were a distrust of government and a genuine disdain of liberal programs as the safety net of the losers in society. They began, under the president's benign gaze, a major attack on the liberal legacy, commencing with a challenge to the most popular liberal benefits program, Social Security, and suffered a major setback.

By midterm the economy had still not turned around sufficiently, and the Reagan revolution was in trouble. By 1982, however, Congress and the president teamed up to pass a "tax enhancement" bill—the largest single increase in U.S. history on top of a major increase in Social Security taxes, which was meant to guarantee the solvency of what is an actuarially unsound program. The result of this latter increase was a major shift or redistribution through a regressive levy of the total tax burden to lower- and middle-income households.[138]

Reagan's budget director, David Stockman, was later to criticize the president for failing to push his "revolution" to its (or Stockman's) logical consequences, and he portrayed Reagan as merely "a consensus politician," a figurehead unwilling to do battle to the death against the liberal welfare state. Reagan was indeed a consensus politician in some ways, but he was also unwilling to antagonize an American public that hates taxes but wants more governmental entitlements. The entitlements that go to the middle class—Social Security, veterans programs, aid to homeowners, Medicare—are firmly entrenched, but programs aimed at the poor lack a strong political base, and thus are vulnerable even though they are no less meritorious than the former category.

Reagan also was worried in his first term that after a year in office the American economy was still not stimulated enough by the tax cuts or by the president's own bold enthusiasms. The economic decline was one of the worst that the country had experienced since the Great Depression, as more than 11,500,000 people were out of work with another two to three million Americans still seeking employment, but not counted in the figures. Business shutdowns and farm foreclosures rose to startling levels, and advocates of the homeless created tent cities called "Reagan ranches"—a dark memory of "Hoovervilles" of the 1930s. As Democrats attacked him for his intentions to destroy the very programs they had worked a lifetime to create, the president criticized the basic tenets of the liberal welfare state and insisted that his administration "stay the course." Reagan did not know at that time that his own budget director did not believe in the economic figures he was promulgating, and that the president and his people had been deceived in accepting Stockman's calculations of revenues. That deception was revealed in an article in the *Atlantic* magazine in November 1981 in which William Grieder related that Stockman regarded "supply-side economics" of the Reagan administration as simply another form of the trickle-down theory so popularized in the 1920s.[139]

The chief reason for the end of inflation and the increase in unemployment in the first term, however, was the decision of the Federal Reserve Board, headed by Jimmy Carter appointee Paul Volcker, to have that body so tighten the money supply that the inflation rate had to tumble down. But the consequences for job creation and employment were dire, and the housing industry, automotive sales, farmers, and small business felt the effects of such an abrupt contraction. Reagan supported the stiff medicine, as inflation dropped to 5 percent by the end of his first year in office.[140] In the congressional elections in 1982, the GOP added a seat in the Senate and lost only twenty-seven seats in the House; there seemed to be popular support for harsh measures after all. As the economy began to pick up later, and as inflation was no longer a problem, other industrial societies began to look seriously at Reagan's tax cut strategy, and his personal discipline in staying the course became for some a model of tough leadership so different from Carter's ways. In 1986, the president changed gears and accepted the proposals from some in Congress to overhaul the tax code, which eliminated many special tax privileges and loopholes—an objective Democrats had talked about, but could not deliver even in progressive periods. The old president was proving to be a lithe moving target for liberals, and at times an unpredictable commodity for conservatives. To the chagrin of some of the GOP's right wing, this optimistic man could incorporate in his psychological makeup contradictions about his policy statements and simply reformulate them to prove that he was right all along.[141]

Even more mystifying at times to some of the faithful and some of his most dedicated foes was Reagan's foreign policy. In the beginning of his first term in office, the parody of Ronald Reagan was clear—he was a shoot-from-the-hip conservative cowboy who understood little of the complex world and rode only the traditional hobby of GOP, anti-Communism. He was especially attacked for his speech on January 29, 1981, when he asserted off-handedly that the Communists or "one-world Socialists" believed in a morality that allowed them to commit any crime in order to prevail over the Western democracies. Two years later, before a group of evangelical ministers in Florida, Reagan struck a similar theme by denouncing the Soviet Union as an aggressive "evil empire." Later in 1989–91 when the Eastern European countries threw off Russian control of their domestic affairs and when the Soviet Union itself came undone, Reagan's descriptions did not seem so far-fetched after all.[142]

Early in his first term then, Reagan easily filled the role of a staunch anti-Communist who showed little interest in arms control and was a foe of Gerald Ford's and Henry Kissinger's policies of detente. The Soviet leaders responded as might be expected—they were suspicious of Reagan and wary of his assertive animosities toward their way of life. Being traditional ideologues themselves they understood the dangers of Reagan the ideologue. Added to the Reagan calculation was his religious acceptance of the biblical notion of Armageddon, the fundamentalist view of the imminent end of the world. But Reagan, beyond those mixed considerations, had a strange dream—he hated the then-current American nuclear strategic doctrine of "mutual assured destruction," appropriately termed MAD.

That doctrine was based on the notion that the United States must pile up enough nuclear weapons so as never to be challenged in the first place at the brink. Many knew it was a dangerous doctrine, perhaps even an absurd and irresponsible doctrine, but it was the government orthodoxy in the United States, for NATO, and for the Soviet world in its planning as well. The justifications—moral and political—were based on the assumption that arming to the nuclear teeth created a balance of terror which protected the peace. Reagan had the simpleminded credulity to point to the terrible consequences of that view and challenge it with an absurd counterproposal—SDI, the Strategic Defense Initiative. The president advocated building the ultimate defense—a sort of protective bubble over the entire United States, a view he may have gotten from old science fiction films and/or from casual conversations with some scientists. The proposal was idiotic, but Reagan had undone the old balance of terror viewpoint by simply pointing to its inherent evil, a view shared by many thoughtful people over the years.

Initially, though, Reagan had denounced the SALT treaties with their intricate schemes for weighing nuclear advantages, throw weights, and verification. Friends and foes remarked how little the president knew about the basics of nuclear strategy, the difference between U.S. and Russian strategic assets, and what was happening at the negotiating tables engaged in disarmament's arcane language. The president started out with a belief that the United States could so outspend the Soviets that they would be forced to seek negotiations to reduce nuclear arms levels. Early in the administration, Reagan startled the Soviets by advocating the "zero-option" proposal, which would remove all Soviet SS-20s in Europe and Asia in return for the United States canceling deployment of cruise missiles and Pershing IIs. Thus the president was building up the military, proposing massive cuts in nuclear weapons, attacking Communism at its ideological source, and promoting a new world—all at once! His advisors divided among themselves, moved in and out of ascendancy, and the Soviets, faced with a series of changes in their own leadership, could not figure out how to respond to Reagan.[143]

In reviewing the fate of Eastern Europe, the president predicted that Poland would be the linchpin of opposition to Communism, and

that there would be "repeated explosions against repressions." In
the end, Reagan insisted Marxism-Leninism would join other tyrannies on the "ash-heap of history."[144] He was correct. Soviet leaders obviously did not concur in that pessimism, and they came to
regard the SDI not as a bold romantic innovation, but as a dangerous beginning of a new antimissile system that would disturb the
balance of power between the two superpowers. By Reagan's second term, Soviet leadership had passed to Mikhail Gorbachev whose
time in office would have profound effects on the total geopolitical
world. The U.S. president had not had a personal conference with
any previous Soviet leader, explaining whimsically, "The only reason I'd never met with General Secretary Gorbachev's predecessors was because they kept dying on me." Indeed from 1980 to
1985, the Kremlin's leadership went from the slow-moving neo-
Stalinist Leonid Brezhnev to KGB leader Yuri Andropov to party
operative Konstantin Chernenko to Gorbachev in 1985.[145]

Gorbachev was to begin a process of normalization that led to
the end of Communism in most of Eastern Europe and eventually
the toppling of that form of government in the Soviet Union and
that state's disintegration. Without the Red Army garrisoned in its
satellites, the Soviet Union could not keep its influence intact even
after forty years of Communist alliance politics. And in that nation,
the old security apparatus of party bureaucrats, secret police, and
army leaders began to crumble as strange expressions of democracy and traditional expressions of nationalism, Orthodox Christi-
anity, and Islam played havoc on the old empire.

As Gorbachev confronted Reagan in a series of summit conferences in the late 1980s, his strategy was to press for more extensive nuclear arms reductions similar to what had characterized
U.S.-Soviet relations for the last five American administrations. At
their various meetings, Reagan and Gorbachev worked on disarmament proposals and debated vigorously the president's dream of SDI,
the technology of which Reagan rather remarkably offered to share
with the evil empire's leaders! But by the beginnings of the Bush
administration, the scenario was to change, as Gorbachev and later
his successors in Russia and other former Communist states were
seriously talking about eliminating whole classes of nuclear weapons, an approach Reagan and Gorbachev started at the end of the
president's last term. Reagan was to move far beyond the traditional
arms control consensus in his own country and startled his conservative supporters as he simply waved aside their fears of the

Soviet Union by remarking blithely that he knew what was going on more than they did on the arms control issue. Going to Moscow in May 1988, Reagan pushed for democratic changes and quoted the great Russian poet Aleksandr Pushkin saying, "It's time, my friend, it's time."[146]

Reagan's excursions into Latin America and the Middle East were to prove to be less successful, and his serious policy choices had terrible costs at times. In Nicaragua, the president inherited Carter's hostility toward the new Marxist regime of the ruling Sandinistas. He praised the opposition armed forces in that nation, called the "Contras," identifying them with the American Founding Fathers and the leaders of the French Resistance in World War II. But Reagan was careful to avoid listening to the more hawkish conservative advisors, including his first secretary of state, Alexander Haig, who wanted to rid the hemisphere of Castro and the Nicaraguan Sandinistas in one fell swoop. The president went on to approve CIA covert activities and military aid to topple the Sandinistas, but he avoided any talk of using American troops. Referring to the demands of some American conservatives for more support, the president observed, "Those sons of bitches won't be happy until we have 25,000 troops in Managua, and I'm not going to do it." Although Reagan had often praised the American war effort in Vietnam, he did not wish to replicate that experience in his time in office.[147]

The president's main foreign policy advisors were also deeply divided about how to deal with the Nicaraguan situation and later El Salvador. Reagan, a poor manager and an inadequate policy maker, seemed to stay above the Nicaraguan fray, although he offered support to neighboring El Salvador and its president, Napoleon Duarte, to allow it to resist its own leftist guerrillas. Reagan began to accept a strategy of asking foreign governments to sponsor the Nicaraguan Contras in order to get around the increasingly tight restrictions being imposed by the Congress on American government support. He personally solicited the Saudi Arabian government and other nations to fund such arrangements. The director of the CIA, William Casey, and the National Security Council advisors in this period, Robert McFarlane and later Admiral John Poindexter, became advocates of covert activities to help the Contras. Secretary of State George Shultz and Secretary of Defense Caspar Weinberger both distanced themselves from the Contra support activities, fearing congressional and public criticism if those transactions became public, which eventually happened. Like Eisenhower, Reagan turned to the CIA to do what the U.S. armed forces could not do—to wage war without public notice through surrogates. Thus Reagan, the Great Communicator, gave up on communicating with the people over the heads of the liberals in Congress. And in the process, he was able to avoid having to confront the divisions in his own house on the issue.[148]

Under increasing criticism, the president appointed a blue ribbon committee to look at U.S. policy toward Central America. Headed by former Secretary of State Henry Kissinger, it proposed foreign aid to the region, economic development assistance, scholarships for Latin American students, and a literacy corps. But the administration's tone was being set by the more assertive CIA and two successive NSC directors who pushed for aid to the Contras and direct action against the Sandinistas. The final chapter was a bizarre scheme that came to be labeled the "Iran-Contra Affair" and that destroyed the president's ability to govern in his second term. Briefly, American agents led by CIA Director Casey and National Security Director John Poindexter permitted a marine colonel, Oliver North, to organize the sales of American arms to the Iranian government as a way to free U.S. hostages held in Lebanon. The holding of these hostages was deeply troubling to Reagan, and he was genuinely affected by the hostage families pleading with him to do something to bring their relatives home. Reagan was a man of sentiment, and their cause became his. He was not the disengaged executive when he persistently demanded action, and his aides responded accordingly.

The president and some of his advisors believed that they could buy the goodwill of the radical Iranian fundamentalists, who had just waged a costly war against the Iraqis. The United States quietly supplied advanced technical weapons, probably through the Israeli government, to the Iranians and received a very good price for those items. The profits could be used, it was explained to Colonel North by one of the Iranian middlemen, to assist American friends in Central America. North, who was deeply sympathetic to the anti-Communist cause, records that he received approval from National Security Council Director Poindexter to proceed along those very lines. Thus, the Iran-Contra connection was established.

At first, the public only learned of the arms for hostage deal with the Iranians, which was never completed; that exchange raised serious questions about dealing with terrorists, which the Reagan administration had promised not to do. The president denied that he ever approved any such swap, but his position was untenable as the logic of such a swap was apparent to nearly everyone else. The administration, seeking to avoid another Watergate type of public outcry, asked the attorney general and long-time Reagan loyalist, Ed Meese, to conduct a full investigation. During that review he found a document in North's files that laid out the second and more damaging link, the diversion of arms profits from Iran to the Contras. The issue now became a constitutional crisis—a direct attempt to circumvent Congress and assert covertly the executive's prescriptions to direct and fund foreign policy as he saw fit. Reagan swore he was unaware of the transfer of funds. The blame shifted from North to Poindexter to Casey to the president and his vice president and a former director of the CIA, George Bush. Congressional investigations, a special prosecutor, and several jury trials endeavored to find out who knew what when. At first, Poindexter took full responsibility, saying he made the decision to transfer funds from arms sales profits to assist the Contras, and that he did not talk to the president about the diversion; the chief executive must have the opportunity for deniability. North, in his memoirs, however, insists that the president was aware of the full transactions, but that he may not have remembered or paid attention at the time![149]

A presidential appointed committee, headed by former Senator John Tower of Texas, found no evidence that Reagan was aware of the transactions, but in a less than ringing endorsement, the panel concluded that his management style was woefully deficient. The president responded that he found good subordinates, appointed them to office, and let them run their agencies and departments uninhibited by him. Even friendly associates have concluded that Reagan had little curiosity about government and its workings, asked few questions even at cabinet meetings, was inattentive and often ill-prepared, and was more given to anecdotes than analysis. His was a committed administration with a disinterested executive nominally leading it. Ironically, it was this disinterestedness that made it difficult to link him to the Iran-Contra affair conclusively, thus probably saving his presidency. Actually though, the president was forceful in insisting on moving on Iran and the hostages, bypassing his own secretary of state and secretary of defense in the process. He was committed enough to solicit personally money for the Contras from outside the country, and he knew full well that if the public found out, the administration would be in serious trouble. When the matter was exposed, he praised Colonel North as a national hero and said his story would make someday a great movie—the finest kudos Ronald Reagan could lay on a mere mortal.

Reagan was also willing to show his commitment to the freedom fighters when he supported the Afghan mujahideen who were opposing the Soviet invasion of their homeland. Eventually Gorbachev saw Afghanistan as his Vietnam, and he pulled the Red Army out of that land, although a pro-Soviet regime proved to be viable until 1992, longer than the administration predicted. Also Reagan, under pressure from Congress and some of his own conservative supporters, eventually used his office to ease out the corrupt Ferdinand Marcos regime in the Philippines.[150]

In the Middle East, the president's ambivalent management style and his pronounced inability to resolve intergovernmental disputes led not just to institutional confrontations as in the Iran-Contra affair, but to the terrible tragedy of losing 241 marines in a terrorist attack on their temporary barracks in Lebanon. A nation once civil and prosperous, Lebanon by 1982 was a garrison state split by religious and ethnic factions and engaged in a bitter civil war in which nearly one hundred thousand people had died since 1975. The administration itself was deeply divided initially about the importance of Lebanon, although the president pronounced it a vital part of U.S. interests.

On July 17, 1981, Israel bombed the Palestine Liberation Organization headquarters in Beirut, and the United States pushed for a cease-fire in that nation between the warring factions, a settlement that lasted for nearly a year. Then on June 6, 1982, the Israelis launched a major invasion, aimed at crippling the strength of PLO's ally Syria by destroying Syrian surface-to-air missiles in the Bekaa Valley, shooting down more than twenty Syrian planes, and encircling the PLO inside Beirut. Once again the administration pushed for a cease-fire, but the Israelis bombed West Beirut again, intending to end once and for all the presence of their enemies so close to their border. The president's special envoy, Philip Habib, tried to get an American commitment to be a part of a proposed peacekeeping force that would guarantee the removal of the PLO from Lebanon to safe quarters elsewhere. The president unfortunately agreed to put U.S. troops into that morass without thinking about the consequences, American security objectives, and the true mission of

U.S. forces there. Throughout his administration, Secretary of State George Shultz and Secretary of Defense Caspar Weinberger had disagreed on the basic tenets of U.S. foreign policy, and once again this lack of consensus led the president to drift into a compromise.

At first, the Reagan policy in the Middle East seemed to work well, and on September 10, U.S. Marines were evacuated from Lebanon and went back to their ships. Then on September 15, the cease-fire ended after the president-elect of Lebanon, Bashier Gemayel, was murdered when a bomb at his party's office exploded. The Israelis entered West Beirut once again to protect their interests. Reagan, ignoring the advice of his Defense Department chiefs, reintroduced the marines into Lebanon to stabilize the situation. Instead as time progressed, the American presence entered into a more activist posture, one that seemed hostile to the Syrians and supportive of the Christian faction. Then on October 23, 1983, the marine headquarters was bombed by Muslim extremists and 241 servicemen were killed as the structure they were in totally collapsed. It was the worse disaster of the Reagan administration, and it brought forth a wave of public outcry and deep sorrow. A board of inquiry appointed by Reagan focused on the command problems in the operations and the unclear mission, but the clear culprit for putting the troops in harm's way was the lack of some sense of purpose from the commander in chief. One U.S. senator, Ernest Hollings of South Carolina, bluntly concluded, "They do not have a mission. If they were put there to fight, there are too few. If they were put there to die, there are too many."[151]

As the nation and the president mourned the deaths, the Reagan administration planned its own invasion of the island of Grenada in the Caribbean where the Marxist prime minister, Maurice Bishop, had been under house arrest and was murdered on October 19 by members of his own party. Fearful of anarchy in another part of the world and concerned about the fate of one thousand Americans there, many of them students at the St. George's School of Medicine, the president ordered American troops onto the island. His advisors were especially fearful of another hostage situation similar to what Carter had gone through for 444 days with Iran. The invasion force of five thousand men simply overwhelmed the island's opposition, despite terrible American intelligence and major logistical problems. It was a fine, short war and the American people responded positively to Reagan's display of leadership. Thirty hours after the invasion, U.S. medical students landed and some kissed American soil in Charleston, South Carolina. A fine media event was had by all.

In 1984, Reagan ran for reelection and won a huge electoral landslide victory, carrying forty-nine states against Democrat Walter F. Mondale who barely won his own home state of Minnesota and prevailed in the District of Columbia. The Roosevelt coalition was finally cracked, its great voting blocks split up as another president caught the American fancy. Reagan appeared as the confident, strong-willed leader with a deep sense of optimism and a real commitment to patriotism and national pride. Privately he was pleasant and disengaged, ill-informed and often passive. But some Americans lived on images not reality, and Reagan's handlers knew the new political realities.[152]

The president had agreed to a major shake-up of his staff, most importantly the swap of jobs for Chief of Staff James Baker, a Texas moderate and Bush associate, and Secretary of Treasury Donald Regan. The result was to be unsettling for the president and the administration. There had been some conversations about allowing Baker to go to the National Security Council, but conservatives intervened and Reagan, fearful of controversy as usual, demurred. Later, even the president was astute enough after the Iran-Contra affair to conclude, "My decision not to appoint Jim Baker as national security adviser, I suppose, was a turning point for my administration."[153] But in the glow of victory all seemed well. Reagan and his people cited his restoration of the nation's spirit; their slogan for reelection was "it was morning again in America."

A major anchor of reality for Reagan was his hard-headed wife, Nancy, who was subject to considerable criticism during his terms in office, but who at critical times provided some real practicality to his dreamy moods. She was pilloried for her pretentiousness, reliance on astrology, coldness, ruthless style, and conspicuous love of wealth and fashion, but the first lady occasionally intervened with Reagan and his staff to force him to make necessary and difficult decisions. Her advice did not always prevail, and at times it was petty instead of informed, but overall her views on the inadequacy of his staff, his ill-advised trip to a cemetery in West Germany whose graves included those of Nazis, and her plea for a more accommodationist foreign policy made more sense than his policies or inclinations at the time. In her memoirs, even she drops the adoring tone once in a while to comment that Ronnie was often just too kind.[154]

He was kind and rather uninterested, which made staff changes so very important. Unlike Eisenhower, Reagan had little high-level administrative experience to fall back on when staff members went awry. James Baker, his first chief of staff, was a man given to slow, methodical steps, the type of process that would have probably prevented Iran-Contra adventures. Secretary of Treasury Donald Regan, a brusque Wall Street executive, disliked compromise and political jockeying—the very stuff of White House life. He had worked hard on the Tax Reform Act of 1986, the most comprehensive reform and loophole closing package in American history. The president praised the bill, but once again was not involved in its passage except for signing the final proposal.[155] By the end of Reagan's first term, Baker and Regan had the president's approval to change jobs—with consequences no one could foretell.

The inadequacies of Donald Regan's White House staff was obvious early in his handling of a request for the president to visit a German military cemetery to symbolize the "end" of World War II animosities. It was a magnanimous act on the president's part, one aimed at placating German Chancellor Helmut Kohl's desire to show that the legacy of the war was indeed forgotten. But unfortunately, the cemetery located in Bitburg was also the resting place of some of the hated Waffen SS troops. The world Jewish community and numerous veterans groups, as well as others, expressed outrage; Reagan, a man of his word, stubbornly insisted on honoring his commitment to Kohl. One survivor of the Holocaust, Jewish writer Elie Wiesel, pleaded with the president, "That place, Mr. President, is not your place. Your place is with the victims of the SS."[156] It was a mistake compounded by insensitivity, one that showed early on the cracks in the edifice of the White House staff. The incident was to be a preface to the Iran-Contra affair in which the NSC and the CIA upstaged the major cabinet secretaries and set for the nation a clandestine policy of hostage-arms trading and a diversion of funds to the Contras. As has been noted, it threatened the integrity of the president and undercut his final years as chief executive.

The full measure of Ronald Reagan's presidency began to move from the passive buoyant optimism of the actor's repertoire to the harshness of controversy and personal vilification. Baker and his associates had kept the wolf away from Ronald Reagan's door. They directed and protected the aged president, often from himself, and filled America with images of easy hope and the vibrancy of its special destiny. After Reagan's first term, the stage directors changed, and the star stood at times naked and vulnerable in a hostile world.

Angry cries of impeachment once again filled the air—this time not over Watergate, but over the Iran-Contra affair. And then the president moved onto the world stage dealing directly with the Soviet leader, Gorbachev. Their meetings progressed from confrontation and ideological debates to a final positive accommodation that led to arms agreements that were startling in their size and scope. The Cold War was ending, and incredibly it was Reagan who had both helped encourage resistance to Soviet occupation and led the way to a reconciliation with their leaders while that very empire was collapsing. With self-confidence once again, Ronald Reagan concluded his time in office, saying, "We meant to change a nation, and instead we changed a world."[157]

The Reagan years provided an important reaffirmation of American self-confidence at home. But it was also a time of unmeasurable greed, corporate irresponsibility, and an unparalleled number of federal government officials accused of malfeasance and influence pedaling. To Reaganites, the American dream was simply individual economic success; there was no real concern about the family, the community, or the social fabric of the nation except as campaign slogans. There also was no recognition of the wisdom of the great British conservative Edmund Burke, who concluded that a nation is more than a holding company; it is a union of the past, the future, and the present generations.

Abroad, the Reagan administration did change the world—often not for the better. Its interventions in Nicaragua, Honduras, and El Salvador extracted heavier costs in terms of human life than were warranted. However, in the first instance, the Sandinistas were indeed a curse on their land and were voted out in an election that the United States—that is, the Reagan administration—was instrumental in holding. Overall, Reagan and his followers would credit the president with inspiring the forces of democracy all over the world, especially in the Soviet Union and its client states. America's old enemy and its empire ended up in disarray and crumbled by 1990–91; Reagan surely deserves some credit for that collapse along with the powerful tides of nationalism and ethnicity that swept over

Eastern Europe. Love him or hate him, Ronald Reagan did restore the notion of an activist presidency, despite his own passive temperament; he insisted that the presidency was capable of working changes in the nation. In the process, he vanquished the sense that the post-Roosevelt presidency was filled with tragedy, political humiliation, and popular despair.

Still, there was a void, an insensitivity to the plight of the most vulnerable in society that will be linked with the Reagan years and the president himself. For what differentiates a Reagan from a Roosevelt—Franklin or Theodore—is that sense of fellow feeling or sympathy with the suffering in society. It is the margin of hope that separates politics as mere intrigue from politics as moral leadership. Yet as far as Reagan was concerned, he was pleased as always with himself, recalling once again that, in his vocabulary, politics is like acting: you start quickly, coast a bit, and end with a fast finish.[158]

BUSH AND THE END OF THE COLD WAR

The Reagan terms brought with them the strengths of optimism and national self-assuredness and the weaknesses of fiscal irresponsibility and personal greed. For the aged entertainer—the California dreamer—reality seemed to impinge on the mix of images, feelings, and conservative ideology. Reagan's vice president and successor seemed deep down to know better, to have a vision of a "gentler and kinder America," as he put it. George Bush's sense of stewardship was honed in the finest eastern institutions, with a sense of noblesse oblige, tempered by the harsh context of domestic electoral politics.

It was frequently said that Bush had the best resumé in America—his span of posts and responsibilities was truly impressive. But one could very honestly pose disquieting questions: what has he done with those opportunities, what does he really believe in? When his presidency was over, the Reagan revolution spent, and the Bush ascendancy ended, those two questions were prominent in evaluations of his time in office.

George Bush was the son of a respected financier, investment banker, and United States senator, Prescott Bush. He went to the best prep schools and was ready to enter Yale University when he turned eighteen and joined, instead, the United States armed forces.

As a young seaman, and then as the youngest pilot in the navy, he compiled an extraordinary record of fifty-eight combat missions and received the Distinguished Flying Cross. He returned to the United States, completed Yale in two and a half years, and declined to join his father's investment firm, leaving to work his way eventually in the oil fields of Texas. With the money and influence of his high-reaching family and friends, he made his fortune and then turned to Republican politics.[159]

Bush was a congressman from Houston from 1967 through 1971 and was respected for his courage in supporting the Civil Rights Act of 1968. He ran for the Senate in Texas, lost, and was appointed the United States ambassador to the United Nations by President Nixon; later he was the chairman of the GOP during the difficult Watergate period, and chief U.S. liaison in China. He was chosen to be the director of the CIA by President Ford, served for a year, and in 1980 ran for the presidency. Reagan defeated him in a series of primaries, and later offered him the vice presidency after flirting with the absurd idea of being himself a "co-president" with Gerald Ford.[160]

Bush was a taciturn and extremely loyal vice president. In Reagan's terms and during Bush's presidency, there was a long debate as to whether George Bush supported or knew about the Iran-Contra affair—allegations that Bush persistently denied. After a brutal presidential campaign in 1988, Bush carried enough of the Reagan coalition of moderates, ideological conservatives, and religious fundamentalists to be elected in his own right.

George Bush was a decent, dedicated individual with a legion of friends and a host of acquaintances across the world. His presidency, though, was a strange and unstable mixture of measured strength in foreign affairs and general boredom or disinterest in domestic problems. Bush's philosophy of life was one that revolved around a conservative doubt that governmental activism or social tinkering, as it was called, with the current state of affairs could yield a better order of things. It was almost as if this contemporary figure reached back beyond the Roosevelts and Wilson to the Whig theory of the presidency once again.[161]

With his upper-class upbringing and his mild temperament, George Bush sought to avoid the intense partisanship and the general nastiness that so characterized American politics in that period of time. He recognized, however, that one had to slug it out occasionally in the domestic gutter, and he consented in his presidential campaign in 1988 to do just that. But it was almost as if he were genuinely uncomfortable with such lapses in breeding and etiquette. He started his presidency seeking to work with the barons of the Democratic party and Congress. It was a reasonable posture for a Republican chief executive, especially one who was not as emotionally involved in the right-wing ideologies as Ronald Reagan.

That decent readiness to compromise, especially on domestic matters, though, helped to split Bush off from the GOP right wing, both in Congress and across the nation. The major point of contention was the mounting public debt that had grown enormously under Ronald Reagan and Congress. Under pressure from his budget director, Richard Darman, and his chief of staff, John Sununu, and some major Republican leaders in the legislative branch, Bush agreed in 1990 to negotiate a deal with Democratic leaders that would involve both new taxes and major cuts in projected entitlement programs. In the 1988 campaign, however, Bush had pledged "no new taxes," in order to distance himself from the liberal Democratic nominee, Governor Michael Dukakis of Massachusetts, and to embrace the supply-side economics of his predecessor. Now he showed a willingness to walk away from the Reagan legacy and its most populist expressions—the traditional American hatred of taxes and big government.

The response among Republican members in the House of Representatives was at first belligerently negative, and the initial compromise was rejected. The second try, though, was successful, and George Bush became linked up in the popular mind with tax-and-spend liberals. Conservatives later charged that Democratic leaders had outwitted the president's aides and ended up taxing more and spending more after all. Bush's conscientious attempt to be responsible led to charges that he had betrayed his promises and lacked personal credibility. Rather than being seen as a man of courage, Bush was portrayed as a weak-kneed fellow who lacked Reagan's convictions.[162]

To add to the president's difficulties, he seemed to have no really strong moorings about some of the major domestic issues that troubled many Americans, and where he did express his views, his disengaged style seemed to belie any real sense of commitment. In many cases, Bush did not really care about the issues that caused public discontent. In other cases, he truly did not believe that the federal government could do more than exhort citizens to perform decent deeds. He stressed that American panacea—volunteerism— as the solution to the communal problems that so commanded public attention: education, race relations, housing, the homeless, crime, drug addiction, and a supposed undoing of the moral fabric of the republic. He highlighted those volunteer efforts as "points of light"—a welcome recognition of independent effort that ended up being seen as periodic bland celebrations of good works. The only domestic issue that the Bush administration dealt with quickly and decisively was the federal government's expensive bailout of the savings and loan banks, costing an estimated $300 billion or more over thirty years.

In the field of education, for example, George Bush for the first time since Roosevelt called the nation's governors together, using the occasion to discuss educational standards and the nation's deteriorating school systems. Held at Jefferson's academy, the historic University of Virginia, the president and the governors arrived at an informed agenda of reform, but years later, there was still no federal leadership, no real national resources put behind the efforts, and no follow-through by the White House.[163]

In the area of civil rights, Bush abandoned his personal commitment to blacks and became the first president in recent memory to veto a civil rights bill. Rhetorically feeding the conservative rank and file, the president attacked the bill as imposing "racial quotas" on the nation. Then after a public outcry, Bush accepted a compromise bill that incorporated most of the same provisions he objected to in the first place. Thus, he managed to alienate both the conservatives and the liberals in one fell swoop.[164]

The increasing costs of residential space, the loss of single-resident apartments and cheap rooming or boarding houses, the early and easy release programs for mentally impaired individuals, the more pervasive availability of cocaine, and some misguided federal welfare policies, all led to a marked and visible increase in the number of homeless in America. Bush showed little interest in those problems or in the complexities of urban life until a massive race riot rocked the city of Los Angeles after an incident of police brutality in 1992. Then he turned to his secretary of housing and urban development, former Congressman Jack Kemp, for some ideas on how to reform domestic affairs. Too little and too late, his critics were to charge.[165]

In these and in other areas of concern, Bush seemed genuinely

distant from the daily life of his fellow citizens. Attempts to hu-
manize him by showing him shopping or socializing with common
folk seemed to backfire, as if to underscore that the upper-class
president was just not used to associating with the aspirations and
aggravations of his fellow citizens. Obviously, by the very nature
of his high office, no modern chief executive is a regular worka-
day citizen. But the media played up the distance that we all know
exists, but do not wish to acknowledge, between the leader and the
led. And as the economy began to falter and unemployment rose,
especially among the white-collar middle class, Bush's disinterest
was magnified, even among his own party's right wing. In the end,
the alleged neglect of things domestic, especially in the area of the
economy, cost Bush the election in 1992 and the GOP the White
House. As he noted after the election, he was not able to convey to
the population that he truly cared about their problems.

Although Bush was a nonconfrontational and pragmatic politician, he was, as one observer has noted, the "zealous guardian of
executive prerogatives in the conduct of foreign policy." He stopped
effective congressional action to protest the massacre of dissenters
in China's Tiananmen Square, and he vetoed various foreign policy-
related bills including a resolution restricting the FS-X deal with
Japan, a foreign-aid appropriations bill that would infringe on the
executive's ability to conduct diplomacy, an intelligence authorization bill that would have tightened reporting requirements or contacts with foreign governments relating to possible "covert action,"
and a chemical weapons sanctions bill that he thought would hurt
U.S. exports. And it is usually forgotten that while Congress supported the deployment of U.S. forces in the Persian Gulf in early
October, Bush insisted on the authority as commander in chief to
send troops in when American strategy shifted and U.S. force
strength doubled after the election in November.[166]

Looking at Bush's successes in foreign policy, one would have
expected that his popularity would have carried him through those
difficulties and hesitations. But the president's approval ratings
proved to be merely a transitory expression of popular sentiment.
Bush's first dramatic foreign policy adventure was his authorization in December 1989 of American armed forces invading Panama
in order to capture the dictator, General Manuel Antonio Noriega,
who was being charged with links to international drug dealers and
profiteers. As former director of the CIA, Bush had relationships
with Noriega and his inner circle, who were associated over the

years with the intelligence agency. Critics of that agency had asserted that the CIA had across the world been relying on foreign contacts who were involved in drug dealings among the other unsavory activities. Noriega, so that critique went, was not a sudden convert to ill-gotten gains. After the invasion of Panama and the loss of life on both sides with twenty-three U.S. troops and five hundred Panamanians killed, the United States extradited Noriega to Florida for trial.[167]

While Panama was a quick sideshow, it was the demise of the Soviet Union that so preoccupied George Bush and tested his greatest assets: perseverance, patience, and quiet moderation. The policies of Mikhail Gorbachev in the Soviet Union led to a spirit of openness and reform and the unraveling of the socialist-militaristic state system. It is remarkable that no major expert in government or outside recognized the essential fragileness of that system. Indeed, while American decision makers were reasserting the need for more armaments and a more assertive foreign policy, the basic infrastructure of the Soviet state was becoming increasingly decadent, hollow, and unresponsive to popular demands. Once the Soviet military was not available for service in its Eastern European satellite system, Communist regimes crumbled overnight. It was extraordinary, not that this happened, but that it happened so quickly and so thoroughly. The basic assumptions of Marxist economics, the romantic dream of egalitarian socialism, the much vaunted organizational skills of the Leninist cadres were proven to be totally out of sync with the new realities of the modern technological industrial state, the international world of communications, ideas, and images, and the old realities of nationalism, religious fervor, and ethnicity.

Bush favored Gorbachev and until the very end, he supported his uncertain reform policies and his unstable leadership in the Soviet Union. After a preliminary review of American foreign policy in 1989, Bush and his secretary of state and long-time friend, James Baker, decided to push for increasing receptivity and dependability in the Soviet-American relationship. Faced with suspicion from their own Republican right wing, Bush and Baker waged a quiet program of support for the Soviet leader with an agenda revolving around nuclear disarmament, a relaxation of tensions in the Third World, and closer long-standing ties between the two remaining superpowers.[168]

Bush and Baker even tried to calm down the secessionist passions of the Baltic states, urging their leaders to give Gorbachev a chance to review their forced status in the Soviet empire. But they owed nothing to either the new Russian leadership or the timid and reserved American administration. Just as the satellite states of Eastern Europe fell away without the Soviet army's forced compliance, so too the Soviet Union began to come undone. First the Baltic nations and then some of the ethnic republics asserted their sense of nationhood, of language, and of unique heritage.

Within the Russian state, the population elected for the first time in its long history a president: Boris Yeltsin, a former Communist party boss, who campaigned as a democratic populist. Gorbachev insisted on preaching the importance of a united Soviet Union and the virtues of a humane Communist state, but he found that the middle way commanded fewer and fewer adherents. Then in an extraordinary turn of events, disgruntled right-wing politicians and army leaders planned a coup d'état and deposed the Communist leader, holding him captive in a resort area where he was vacationing. Yeltsin and thousands of Russians openly challenged the coup forces and prevailed. Gorbachev was rescued, restored to power, and then quickly discarded by the forces of reform simply as irrelevant. The Soviet empire and the Soviet Union were phased out.[169]

Bush had deliberately refused to do anything dramatic to celebrate the demise of the last great military superpower standing against the United States. He insisted on acting responsibly by not adding to the explosiveness of the situation, and by not celebrating the chaos as a necessary by-product of the triumph of liberty behind the old Iron Curtain. Thus it was that the Cold War ended—the great divide that separated the two nuclear states, the tense, danger-laden conflicts of ideology that had characterized the post-World War II period had seemingly concluded. Bush was to acknowledge that the United States had indeed prevailed in ways only previously dreamt of by the most optimistic of American decision makers.[170]

With the collapse of the Communist empires, the tight controls that submerged religious and ethnic expressions, hatreds, and manifestations of violence in those regions were eliminated. Just as the Hapsburg and Ottoman rulers had hindered the darker excesses of nationalism and religious rivalries, so too the centralized states of Stalin in the Soviet Union and Josef Tito in Yugoslavia had clamped down on much of the group violence that so troubled those areas in the past, substituting their own form of centralized terror instead.

It is an sad commentary on the twentieth century that police states should end up being praised for their sometimes salutary effects by preserving the peace in bizarre and brutal ways. But the Soviet state had curtailed nationalist animosities, and in Yugoslavia, the Serbian, Bosnian, and Croatian factions among others were forced to live in some semblance of civilized order. The demise of the Socialist states led to a breakdown of central authority, the rise of local autocrats and unchained nationalist militias, and increased ethnic-related violence in those regions. The West celebrated the end of the Soviet Union and the settling of the Cold War, while it seemed unable to mediate in meaningful ways the brutalities so historically characteristic of some of the Balkan peoples.[171]

The Bush administration tended to reformulate U.S. foreign policy away from the familiar pieties of containment to "a new world order" that focused on international trade, United Nations leadership, and a cautious use of force and persuasion in regional conflicts. The United States was the only superpower left in the world, and yet the administration could not admit that it was proposing by another name that American troops should become the policemen of the globe in the new world order.

The first significant test of this heady role took place in the Middle East, where the Baahist regime of Saddam Hussein in Iraq invaded the oil-rich emirate of Kuwait. Once again, the worldly George Bush had had dealings with Saddam, who had received extensive support from the Reagan administration. Iraq had waged a bloody, protracted conflict against the Muslim fundamentalist regime of Ayatollah Khomeini. After the seizure of the United States embassy in Tehran and the long 444-day captivity of American hostages during the Carter administration, the Iranian regime was clearly an anti-American government in everyone's eyes. The Iran-Iraq war led the Reagan administration to support Saddam by permitting the shipment to Iraq of U.S. arms and technology often through third parties such as Italy and Great Britain in order to avoid congressional prohibitions. Again, it was another Iran-Contra type of proceeding—to use guile to get around U.S. law in dealing with the uncertain Middle East. The administration even approved $1 billion in agricultural credits to Iraq, half of which was granted before the United States realized the true nature of Saddam's regime—even though it had years before systematically gassed his own Kurdish inhabitants.[172]

On August 2, 1990, Iraqi forces moved into Kuwait and totally occupied that nation. Prior to the invasion, Saddam had insisted that something had to be done to end the conflict between the two nations—a conflict he, himself, had instigated due to the shortage of cash for his government's operations, including its very large armed forces. The United States ambassador, April Gillespie, reiterated the Bush administration's position—the United States did not wish to intervene in border disputes, but it did not countenance the use of military force to settle such disputes. Later, her response would be seen as evidence that the State Department gave Saddam tacit approval for his actions.[173] At the time of the invasion, Bush and British Prime Minister Margaret Thatcher were in Aspen, Colorado, together for an awards ceremony. It has been argued that she put backbone in the president by demanding that he not be "wishy-washy," but instead respond as she had done when an Argentine military junta invaded the British-controlled Falkland Islands in 1982. In fact, Bush quickly made up his mind that the Iraqi invasion would not stand, and against the advice of some of his own military chiefs planned almost from the beginning to liberate Kuwait and to protect the more important sheikdom—Saudi Arabia.[174]

In contrast to his lackadaisical attitude toward domestic affairs and his restrained responses over the demise of the Soviet Union, Bush seemed to come alive as a true commander in chief. Even his severest critics acknowledged that his displays of diplomatic skill and military leadership were remarkable. Using his range of associates across the world, Bush built up a coalition of support unseen since Franklin Roosevelt. The usually uncertain Western democracies, the former Communist regimes, including Russia, the apprehensive Israelis, and the more moderate Arab states were all pressed into service. The United States insisted on United Nations approval, which it got more quickly than the ratification of war by the American Congress.

The president and Secretary of State Baker played out the diplomatic options with the inept Iraqi regime, leaving no choice but war or slow uncertain strangulation through an economic blockade. As the United States mobilized for a full-scale land war across the desert, it embraced other allied armies as well and insisted on getting other nations to fund the expense of the high-tech war. It was charged later that the Americans were in effect mercenaries for a decadent Arab regime, whose own sons were out of Kuwait when the war for their homeland was being waged.

Bush insisted that Saddam was like Hitler, and once again the

Churchillian rhetoric attacking appeasement at Munich was resurrected. He talked vaguely again of a new world order and argued
that Saddam, who was once a U.S. ally, was a madman who was
willing to use chemical and biological weapons on his own people
and was creating a nuclear weapons capability. Secretary Baker,
however, insisted that the war was being waged to protect oil interests and American jobs. While that analysis was probably correct,
Bush was more astute in realizing the need for Americans to have
a moral imperative to go to war—especially after the disillusionment of Vietnam. Also, the United States would only support wars
that were brief, and the military insisted on a quick massive buildup,
not the incrementalism used by Lyndon Johnson in Vietnam. Thus
it seemed that the political and military leadership had learned several lessons from that ill-fated conflict.[175]

By the time of the American liberation of Kuwait, the field commander in chief, General Norman Schwarzkopf, a Vietnam veteran,
had over five hundred thousand men and women under his command. More importantly, the air force saturated numerous targets
before the land troops moved in. The new generation of high-tech
weapons, many of them ironically developed under the Carter administration, were given full sway. The Americans were to praise
the air war and its new weaponry; only later were the partial deficiencies of those weapons admitted.

Still, American force was overwhelming, and the Iraqi forces,
the sixth largest army in the world, were defeated within several
days. Saddam called the conflict "the mother of all wars"; instead
it was a short campaign with little loss of U.S. life after one hundred hours of conflict. Kuwait was liberated, but the administration
decided not to allow the U.S. Army to move into Baghdad to rout
Saddam and his elite Republican Guard. In terms of casualties, 148
U.S. troops were killed, 467 wounded, and another 141 service personnel were killed in action. Iraq lost an estimated 100,000 dead
and 300,000 wounded. Later Bush would be criticized for not fin-
ishing the job, especially after Saddam refused to abide by the UN's
cease-fire requirements, and as he turned his forces in a campaign
of terror against the Kurds who had supported the allied cause.[176]

But Bush and his advisors had been correct. The declaration of
support for action taken by the Congress had barely passed the
Democratic-controlled Senate, and the road into Baghdad would
have been a perilous journey. To eliminate Saddam, the U.S. armed
forces would have had to leave the wide-open spaces of the desert

where airpower was so effective, and enter the streets, alleys, and byways of an ancient city honeycombed with terrorists, true patriots, and religious fundamentalists. It is doubtful if American public opinion or the pro-West Arab coalition would have held together for a long war of occupation in the Middle East. Besides, Bush had said it best, "No more Vietnams."

When the war ended so quickly, the president's popularity hit an incredible 89 percent approval—higher than any chief executive in polling history. The United States had a new generation of heroes, new chronicles of war stories, and a new victory against a frightened, if not overstated, foe. For the first time since 1945, the troops had won a real war, and it felt good, even to many of those who favored the more moderate course of economic sanctions, such as the chairman of the Joint Chiefs of Staff, General Colin Powell, another Vietnam veteran.[177]

For the first time in his adult life, Bush was the center of the limelight. Those critics who had previously attacked him over the years for his excessive flexibility, for being a "wimp" in the popular slang, were now quieted by the unique steadiness and resolve of their commander in chief. He had waited all his life for this triumph.[178]

And yet it came and went so quickly. As his mother told him in his youth, "Don't brag." And he didn't. He also did not or could not seem to follow up that triumph with leadership on the domestic front. A nation that could mobilize a force of half a million fighting people could not seem to deal with its homeside problems. That was not unusual, but Bush, unlike Wilson, FDR, Truman, and Johnson, did not even seem to try.[179]

The impressive demonstration of leadership in the Gulf War cast into even greater relief his disinterestness at home. Also, his caution with the Soviet Union was matched by genuine hauteur in responding to the crushing of the dissidents in Communist China. There the glasnost of Gorbachev had spread to the old Middle Kingdom as the aged heirs of Mao Tse-tung tried to seal off their unhappy nation from the winds of change. Unlike Gorbachev, they were willing to use the Red Army and spill blood to stop dissent from prevailing. In a brutal display of overwhelming force, the Chinese leadership ordered the military into Tiananmen Square in Beijing to suppress the new voices of reform and democracy. Bush's response was a perfunctory condemnation and a secret mission to reassure the Chinese leaders whom he claimed he knew best from his years as American representative to that nation.[180]

And as the regional conflicts of the world shifted, Bush tried an uncertain diplomacy in Bosnia against the brutal "ethnic cleansing" by the Serbs there. Faced with another civil war in Africa, the president, sickened by the sight of famine, especially among children, ordered U.S. troops into Somalia to keep the peace and bring the warring factions together. Again, he formed a Western coalition of conscience to serve as peacekeepers in a nation that basically lacked all the prerequisites of nationhood. That noble expedition would turn into a combat force as the U.S. Army supported one faction over another, and the cheers eventually turned to rage against the Western "imperialists" who only months before were heralded as peacekeepers.[181]

Thus, as the term of George Bush came to an end, he and his advisors seemed content to run for reelection based on the heady praise of the Persian Gulf War. But the fickle mood of the American people was being tempered by a sense of personal frustration and deep concern about domestic matters. First there grew up a genuine third party—or at least a third-person movement—rallying around an eccentric Texas billionaire, Ross Perot. Perot stressed economic themes, especially the mounting budget deficit, and he called for a more protectionist trade policy. At first he ran strongly in the polls. Then for personal, if not idiosyncratic reasons, he dropped out and then later reentered the race. In an era of weak parties and saturating television, he overcame many of the traditional liabilities of third-party candidates and won the largest percentage of the popular vote of any third-party candidate running for president since Theodore Roosevelt in 1912.

Bush found that he was also being attacked from the right by a conservative television commentator and newspaper columnist, Patrick Buchanan—an impish and quick-witted ideologue who had served faithfully in the Nixon and the Reagan White House. Although Bush defeated Buchanan in every primary, the latter's vote reached 37 percent in New Hampshire and over 30 percent in several other states, a showing that did not bode well for a sitting president.[182]

Almost too late did the president and his closest associates realize that his campaign was not well organized. His leadership came under severe scrutiny, and his messages seemed confused and disheartening to many. While the Democrats emphasized a new generation of leadership and party harmony, the Republican convention conveyed to the media interpreters a sense of right-wing stridency that accentuated the fault lines in the uneasy coalition within the GOP. Somehow in too many ways George Bush, the true hero of the Persian Gulf War, the steady hand who presided over the demise of the Soviet empire, the seasoned diplomat who quietly proclaimed the end of the Cold War, was being rendered obsolete. He was to be the last president of the World War II generation, the last to know the certainties of America's special mission in foreign affairs.

The election was a generational changing of the guard as in 1960. The Democrats nominated a career politician, Bill Clinton, who at the age of forty-six was the long-time governor of Arkansas. Clinton blended a record of skilled professionalism, technological awareness, and liberal public policy with an intense personal style that hallmarked sensitivity in an almost clinical sense. Although he generally ran behind the Democratic ticket across the nation, Governor Clinton carried 370 electoral votes from many of the larger states in the South, Northeast, and Great Lakes, including Illinois, Michigan, Massachusetts, Minnesota, New Jersey, New York, Ohio, Pennsylvania, Virginia, and California and a popular vote of 43 percent. President Bush got 38 percent and 168 votes—the lowest popular vote percentage since William Howard Taft in 1912. Ross Perot received 19 percent of the vote.

In one sense, Bush's defeat can be attributed to the concerns over a sluggish, but not depressed economy, and to a desire for change after twelve years of Republican control of the White House. But in a collective sense, the Bush record is remarkably similar to America's record in post-World War II politics. Since 1945, the United States has moved into being a superpower in almost all areas of endeavor. It has become an extraordinary colossus, a force that marks it as one of the most powerful states in the long annals of history. But in its domestic affairs it seems to be deadlocked by a self-indulgent legislative branch, a well-financed and intensely selfish interest group politics, and a real decline in concepts of sacrifice, commitment, and patriotism. Those two Americas parallel the two presidencies characterized by power and resolve in foreign policy and domestic deadlock and neglect. Thus it seems that as the presidency enters its third century of existence, it finds itself in the service of a republic that is given to fits of drift and spells of mastery.[183]

Epilogue

For two centuries the destiny of the American republic and the development of the presidency generally have gone hand in hand. The expansion of a modest nation resting on the Atlantic seaboard had been directly due to the Louisiana Purchase, the Mexican War, late nineteenth-century imperialism, and the growth of the United States into a global power since 1900. With each of these steps, we have witnessed the central role of the presidency.

Surely the chief executive position has changed extensively from its uncertain origins under George Washington. Some presidents such as Van Buren, Cleveland, and Carter have tried to moderate the more assertive aspects of American influence and manifest destiny broad. The accumulation of powers in the office of the presidency has not been a single trajectory—onward and upward. As we have seen, significant troughs in the 1850s, the late nineteenth century, and the 1920s belie that simplistic view.

But the presidency has been the linchpin in the American wheel of exceptionalism, and its incumbents have been the most immediate definers of that view. One can only compare the emphasis in foreign policy with the modest record of domestic reform that took place between Jefferson and Theodore Roosevelt. For many generations the limited role of the federal government and the position of the presidency in the public policy process curtailed the opportunity for the executive to champion an agenda of reform. When the presidents were involved in domestic controversies, they tended to focus on a single, persistent issue—the Bank of the United States, the tariff, civil service reform to cite three examples. Only the stark outbreak—and the fierce waging—of the Civil War is an exception.

Some presidents have had a sufficient number of similarities to be place together in discrete groups: the Federalists, the Jeffersonians, the Jacksonians, the Rooseveltian executives. And some of these presidents were quite skilled, some were inept, some visionary, some petty and vindictive, and many had at different times and even at the same times qualities that embraced all of those characteristics. One historian, J. Morgan Kousser, has defined the study of politics as "how institutions and elites refract society's desires."[1] Many of these presidents—especially the major ones—have done just that. They have reflected our desires, and they have also helped to create those desires, to legitimize them, and to spread them beyond our shores.

Now as the American constitutional political system advances into another century and into another millennium, the presidency remains, after the papacy, the second oldest major elective executive office in the world. And as the United States has moved into post-World War II primacy, the centerpiece of that ascendancy— the very engine of its movement—has been the presidency, the Rooseveltian model writ larger than even FDR could have imagined. Whether the president can be the hero of his own times, as Charles Dickens put it, is a continuing question. John Adams seemed to recognize the inherent possibilities in the modest office he assumed when he ordered a stonemason to chisel in the mantle of a White House fireplace the inscription: "may only wise men live here."

The republic would have been better served if Adams's prayer for wisdom extended far beyond that dwelling. For the essence of responsible democracy involves popular and informed consent resting on civility and justice. Only then can we demand that the presidency be worthy of the people it is supposed to serve.

Notes

CHAPTER 1:
THE PRESIDENT AS STEWARD OF THE PEOPLE

1. Edmund Morris, *The Rise of Theodore Roosevelt* (New York: Coward, McCann and Geoghegan, 1979); William Gatewood, *Theodore Roosevelt and the Art of Controversy* (Baton Rouge: LSU Press, 1970); William H. Harbaugh, *Power and Responsibility* (New York: Farrar, Straus and Giroux, 1961); Carleton Putnam, *Theodore Roosevelt*, vol. 1 (New York: Charles Scribner's Sons, 1958); *Letters of Theodore Roosevelt*, edited by Elting E. Morison and John Blum, 8 vols. (Cambridge: Harvard University Press, 1951–54); G. Wallace Chessman, *Governor Theodore Roosevelt* (Cambridge: Harvard University Press, 1965); George E. Mowry, *The Era of Theodore Roosevelt* (New York: Harper, 1958), p. 109; and Thomas Dyer, *Theodore Roosevelt and the Idea of Race* (Baton Rouge: LSU Press, 1980).

2. Mowry, *Era of Roosevelt*, p. 100.

3. Richard Hofstadter, *The American Political Tradition* (New York: Knopf, 1948), chapter 9.

4. Harbaugh, *Power and Responsibility*, chapter 9.

5. Mowry, *Era of Roosevelt*, p. 129.

6. Balthasar Meyer, *A History of the Northern Securities Case* (Madison: University of Wisconsin, 1906); Frederick L. Allen, *The Great Pierpont Morgan* (New York: Harper Bros., 1949); and Ron Chernow, *The House of Morgan* (New York: Atlantic Monthly Press, 1990).

7. Henry F. Pringle, *Theodore Roosevelt* (New York: Harcourt Brace and Co., 1931), pp. 253–54.

8. Mowry, *Era of Roosevelt*, p. 135.

9. Pringle, *Roosevelt*, p. 271.

10. Hofstadter, *American Political Tradition*, chapter 9, and Dyer, *Idea of Race*, passim.

11. Pringle, *Roosevelt*, pp. 279–300. Other studies of his Latin American diplomacy are: Howard Beale, *Theodore Roosevelt and the Rise of America to World Power* (Baltimore: Johns Hopkins University Press, 1956); William E. Leuchtenberg, "Progressivism and Imperialism: The Progressive Movement and American Foreign Policy, 1898–1916," *Mississippi Valley Historical Review* 39 (December 1952): 483–504; Dexter Perkins, *The United States and the Caribbean* (Cambridge: Harvard University Press, 1947); and his *The Monroe Doctrine, 1867–1907* (Baltimore: Johns Hopkins University Press, 1937); H. C. Hill, *Roosevelt and the Caribbean* (Chicago: University of Chicago Press, 1927); and S. W. Livermore, "Theodore Roosevelt, the American Navy and the Venezuelan Crisis," *American Historical Review* 51 (April 1946): 452–71.

12. Pringle, *Roosevelt*, p. 298.

13. Ibid., pp. 301–38; Harbaugh, *Power and Responsibility*, pp. 194–204; D. C. Miner, *The Fight for the Panama Route* (New York: Columbia University Press, 1940); and M. P. Duval, *And the Mountains Will Move* (Stanford: Stanford University Press, 1947).

14. Pringle, *Roosevelt*, pp. 339–58.

15. Beale, *Rise to World Power*, passim; Alfred W. Griswold, *The Far Eastern Policy of the United States* (New York: Harcourt, Brace and Co., 1938); Tyler Dennett, *Roosevelt and the Russo-Japanese War* (Gloucester: Peter Smith, 1959 reprint); Thomas A. Bailey, "The World Crisis of the American Battleship Fleet, 1907–1909," *Pacific Historical Review* 1 (December 1932): 389–423; Bailey, "The Root-Takahira Agreement of 1908," *Pacific Historical Review* 9 (March 1940): 19–40; Delbar McKee, *Chinese Exclusion Versus the Open Door* (Detroit: Wayne State University Press, 1977); and Eugene Trani, *The Treaty of Portsmouth* (Lexington: University of Kentucky Press, 1969).

16. Eugene N. Anderson, *The First Moroccan Crisis, 1904–1906* (Chicago: University of Chicago Press, 1930).

17. Thomas A. Bailey, *Theodore Roosevelt and the Japanese American Crisis* (Stanford: Stanford University Press, 1934), and Pringle, *Roosevelt*, p. 410.

18. Harbaugh, *Power and Responsibility*, part 4, and Pringle, *Roosevelt*, p. 414.

19. Pringle, *Roosevelt*, p. 428.

20. Ibid., p. 442 and passim, which includes Pringle's discussions of the deals.

21. Harbaugh, *Power and Responsibility*, pp. 290–93.

22. David H. Burton, *The Learned Presidency* (Rutherford, N.J.: Fairleigh Dickinson University Press, 1988).

23. John Morton Blum, *The Republican Roosevelt* (Cambridge: Harvard University Press, 1954), p. 2.

24. Ibid., p. 12.

25. Ibid., chapter 1.

26. William Manners, *TR and Will* (New York: Harcourt, Brace and World, 1969); Henry F. Pringle, *Life and Times of William Howard Taft*, 2

vols. (New York: Farrar and Rinehart, 1939); Herbert S. Dully, *William Howard Taft* (New York: Minto, Balch and Co., 1930); and Judith Icke Anderson, *William Howard Taft* (New York: W. W. Norton, 1981).

27. Paolo E. Coletta, *The Presidency of William Howard Taft* (Lawrence: University Press of Kansas, 1973), p. 58.

28. Ibid., p. 63.

29. Ibid., p. 89.

30. Alpheus T. Mason, *Bureaucracy Convicts Itself* (New York: Viking, 1941), and J. T. Ganoe, "Some Constitutional and Political Aspects of the Ballinger-Pinchot Controversy," *Pacific Historical Review* 3 (September 1934): 323–33.

31. Coletta, *Presidency*, p. 104.

32. Burton, *The Learned Presidency*, chapter 2.

33. Dully, *Taft*, chapters 26–28.

34. Walter V. Scholes and Marie V. Scholes, *The Foreign Policies of the Taft Administration* (Columbia: University of Missouri Press, 1970).

35. Coletta, *Presidency*, pp. 223–24.

36. Dully, *Taft*, chapter 29, and John Gable, *The Bull Moose Years* (Port Washington, New York: Kennikat Press, 1978).

CHAPTER 2:
PRIME MINISTER AND WORLD PROPHET

1. Any treatment of Woodrow Wilson is heavily indebted to the fine scholarship of Arthur S. Link, the editor of *The Papers of Woodrow Wilson* (Princeton: Princeton University Press, 1966–1993) and the author of a stream of biographies and monographs on this period, some cited below. Also of interest are: Ray S. Baker, *Woodrow Wilson: Life and Letters*, 8 vols. (Garden City: Doubleday, Page and Doubleday, Doran, 1927–39); Henry W. Bragdon, *Woodrow Wilson: The Academic Years* (Cambridge: Harvard University Press, 1967); John M. Cooper, *The Warrior and the Priest* (Cambridge: Harvard University Press, 1983); Sigmund Freud and William C. Bullett, *Thomas Woodrow Wilson* (London: Weidenfeld and Nicholson, 1966); John M. Mulder, *Woodrow Wilson, The Years of Preparation* (Princeton: Princeton University Press, 1978); George C. Osborn, *Woodrow Wilson: The Early Years* (Baton Rouge: LSU Press, 1968); Edwin A. Weinstein, *Woodrow Wilson* (Princeton: Princeton University Press, 1981); Neils Aage Thorsen, *The Political Thought of Woodrow Wilson, 1875–1910* (Princeton: Princeton University Press, 1988); and Arthur Walworth, *Woodrow Wilson* (Baltimore: Penguin, 1969 reprint).

2. Arthur S. Link, *Wilson: The Road to the White House* (Princeton: Princeton University Press, 1947).

3. Arthur S. Link, *Woodrow Wilson and the Progressive Era* (New York: Harper and Brothers, 1954), pp. 40–43.

4. Ibid., p. 47.

5. *Ibid*, p. 80.
6. Selig Adler, "Bryan and Wilsonian Caribbean Penetration," *Hispanic American Historical Review* 20 (May 1940): 198–226.
7. Link, *Woodrow Wilson and the Progressive Era*, pp. 84–85.
8. Issac J. Cox, *Nicaragua and the United States, 1909–1927* (Boston: World Peace Foundation, 1927).
9. Link, *Woodrow Wilson and the Progressive Era*, pp. 103–5, and his *Wilson the Diplomatist* (Chicago: Quadrangle Books, 1957), chapter 1.
10. Link, *Diplomatist*, pp. 17–24; Howard F. Cline, *The United States and Mexico* (Cambridge: Harvard University Press, 1953); Stuart A. MacCorkle, *American Policy of Recognition towards Mexico* (Baltimore: Johns Hopkins University Press, 1933); and Link, *Woodrow Wilson and the Progressive Era*, chapter 5.
11. Walworth, *Wilson*, book 2, pp. 1–12, and Arthur S. Link, *The Struggle for Neutrality 1914–1915* (Princeton: Princeton University Press, 1960).
12. Link, *Woodrow Wilson and the Progressive Era*, pp. 221–22.
13. Arthur S. Link, *Wilson: Confusions and Crises 1915–1916* (Princeton: Princeton University Press, 1964), and Ernest May, *The World War and American Isolation, 1914–1917* (Cambridge: Harvard University Press, 1959).
14. Link, *Woodrow Wilson and the Progressive Era*, pp. 253–55, and A. J. P. Taylor, *Illustrated History of the First World War* (New York: G. P. Putnam's Sons, 1964) for a quick summary aimed at the nonscholarly audience.
15. Link, *Woodrow Wilson and the Progressive Era*, chapter 10, and Richard Piper, *The Russian Revolution* (New York: Knopf, 1990).
16. Taylor, *World War I*, chapters 1–4; Keith Robbins, *The First World War* (New York: Oxford University Press, 1985); Winston S. Churchill, *The Unknown War: The Eastern Front* (New York: Charles Scribner's Sons, 1931); George F. Kennan, *The Fateful Alliance* (New York: Pantheon, 1984); Norman Stone, *The Eastern Front, 1914–1917* (New York: Charles Scribner's, 1978); D. F. Fleming, *The Origins and Legacies of World War I* (New York: Doubleday, 1968); Fritz Fischer, *Germany's Aims in the First World War* (New York: W. W. Norton, 1967); Graydon A. Tunstall, Jr., *Planning for War against Russia and Serbia* (New York: Columbia University Press, 1994); John M. Blum, *Woodrow Wilson and the Politics of Morality* (Boston: Little, Brown, 1956); Sidney B. Fay, *The Origins of the World War* (New York: Macmillan, 1949); and Patrick Devlin, *Too Proud to Fight* (New York: Oxford University Press, 1975).
17. F. Lee Burns, *Europe Since 1914* (New York: Appleton-Century-Crofts, 1949), chapter 1, and Correlli Barnett, *The Great War* (New York: G. P. Putnam, 1979).
18. Robert H. Ferrell, *Woodrow Wilson and World War I* (New York: Harper and Row, 1985), chapters 1–3.
19. Ferrell, *World War I*, pp. 36–63, and *Hoover-Wilson Wartime Correspondence*, edited by F. W. O'Brien (Ames: Iowa State University Press, 1974).
20. Josepheus Daniels, *The Wilson Era* (Chapel Hill: University of North

Carolina Press, 1946), pp. 160–71; Daniel R. Beaver, *Newton D. Baker and the American War Effort 1917–1919* (Lincoln: University of Nebraska Press, 1966); Edward M. Coifman, *The Hilt of the Sword* (Madison: University of Wisconsin, 1966); Peyton C. Marsh, *The Nation at War* (Garden City: Doubleday, Doran, 1932); and Christopher Ray, "Woodrow Wilson as Commander-in-Chief," *History* 43 (April 1993): 24–30.

21. Ferrell, *World War I*, chapter 5; Kenneth O. Morgan, "Lloyd George's Premiership," *The Historical Journal* 13 (1970) 130–57; David R. Woodward, *Lloyd George and the Generals* (Newark: University of Delaware Press, 1983); David R. Woodward, "Britain in a Continental War," *Albion* 12 (Spring 1980): 37–65; John Turner, *Lloyd George's Secretariat* (New York: Cambridge University Press, 1980); Peter E. Wright, *At the Supreme War Council* (New York: Putnam's, 1921); Tim Travese, *The Killing Ground* (London: Allen and Unwin, 1987); David R. Watson, *Georges Clemenceau* (New York: David McKay, 1976); Geoffrey Brunn, *Clemenceau* (Hamden, Conn.: Archon, 1968); Gregor Dallas, *At the Heart of a Tiger* (New York: Carroll & Gray, 1993); *Germany in the Age of Total War*, edited by Volker R. Berghahn and Martin Ketchen (Totowa: Barnes and Noble, 1981), especially chapter 3 on Rathenau; James Joll, *Intellectuals in Politics* (London: Weidenfeld and Nicholson, 1960), part 2; David Felix, "Walter Rathenau," *European Studies Review* 5 (1975): 69–79; and D. J. Goodspeed, *Ludendorff* (Boston: Houghton Mifflin, 1966), passim.

22. Clinton Rossiter, *Constitutional Democracy* (Princeton: Princeton University Press, 1948), p. 242.

23. Ibid, p. 242.

24. Ibid., pp. 250–53, and Harry N. Scheiber, *The Wilson Administration and Civil Liberties* (Ithaca: Cornell University Press, 1981).

25. Paul Fussell, *The Great War and Modern Memory* (New York: Oxford University Press, 1975), and Arno J. Mayer, *The Persistence of the Old Regime* (New York: Pantheon, 1981).

26. Arthur Walworth, *Wilson and His Peacemakers* (New York: W. W. Norton, 1986).

27. Ibid., part I.

28. Link, *Diplomatist*, p. 100; Watson, *Clemenceau*; passim; and Bruun, *Clemenceau*, passim.

29. Link, *Diplomatist*, p. 105.

30. Ibid., chapter 4; Arthur Walmouth, *Wilson and His Peacemakers*, parts 3 and 4; David Lloyd George, *The Truth about the Peace Treaties*, 2 vols. (London: V. Gollancz, 1938); Thomas A. Bailey, *Wilson and the Peacemakers* (New York: Macmillan, 1947); Roy W. Curry, *Woodrow Wilson and Far Eastern Policy* (New York: Bookman, 1957); Lloyd C. Gardner, *Wilson and Revolutions* (Philadelphia: Lippincott, 1976); and *Woodrow Wilson and a Revolutionary World*, edited by Arthur S. Link (Chapel Hill: University of North Carolina, 1982). The German treaty with Russia mandated that the Russians would lose 32 percent of its cultivable land, 27 percent of its railroads, 54 percent of its industry, and 89 percent of its coal mines. See Alan Bullock, *Hitler and Stalin* (New York: Knopf, 1992), p. 62.

31. Ferrell, *Wilson*, chapter 10; Lloyd E. Ambrosius, "Wilson, the Republicans, and French Security after World War I," *Journal of American History* 59 (September 1972): 341–52; Josepheus Daniels, *The Wilson Era*, part 11; and Jeffrey K. Tulis, *The Rhetorical Presidency* (Princeton: Princeton University Press, 1987), pp. 147–61.

CHAPTER 3:
THE REPUBLICAN ASCENDANCY, 1921–1933

1. Robert K. Murray, *The Politics of Normalcy* (New York: W. W. Norton, 1973), and Eugene P. Trani and David L. Wilson, *The Presidency of Warren G. Harding* (Lawrence: University Press of Kansas, 1977), chapter 1.

2. Randolph C. Downs, *The Rise of Warren Gamaliel Harding* (Columbus: Ohio State University Press, 1970); Andrew Sinclair, *The Available Man* (New York: Macmillan, 1965); Francis Russell, *The Shadow of Blooming Grove* (New York: McGraw-Hill, 1968); Robert K. Murray, *The Harding Era* (Minneapolis: University of Minnesota Press, 1969); Louis W. Potts, "Who Was Warren G. Harding," *Historian* 36 (1974); 621–45; and Charles L. Mee, Jr., *The Ohio Gang* (New York: M. Evans, 1982).

3. Tom Shachtman, *Edith and Woodrow* (New York: G. P. Putnam, 1981), chapters 13–17; Richard Hansen, *The Year We Had No President* (Lincoln: University of Nebraska Press, 1961); John D. Feerick, *From Falling Hands* (New York: Fallham Press, 1965); Kurt Winer, "Woodrow Wilson and a Third Nomination," *Pennsylvania History* 39 (April 1962): 193–211, and his "Woodrow Wilson's Plan for a Vote of Confidence," *Pennsylvania History* 38 (July 1961): 279–93; and Gene Smith, *When the Cheering Stopped* (New York: Bantam, 1965).

4. Murray, *The Politics of Normalcy*, pp. 42–46; James H. Shideler, *Farm Crisis* (Berkeley: University of California, 1957); John D. Hicks, *Republican Ascendancy, 1921–33* (New York: Harper and Row, 1960); Russell, *The Shadow of Blooming Grove*, chapter 10; and Trani and Wilson, *The Presidency of Warren G. Harding*, chapters 3 and 4.

5. Triani and Wilson, *The Presidency of Warren G. Harding*, chapters 5 and 6, with quote on FDR and Haiti on p. 133; Selig Adler, *The Uncertain Giant* (New York: Macmillan, 1965); L. Ethas Ellis, *Republican Foreign Policy* (New Brunswick: Rutgers University Press, 1968); Robert J. Maddox, *William E. Borah and American Foreign Policy* (Baton Rouge: LSU Press, 1969); Kenneth J. Crieb, *The Latin American Foreign Policy of William G. Harding* (Fort Worth: TCU Press, 1977); Melvyn Leffler, "The Origins of Republican War Debt Policy," *Journal of American History* 59 (December 1972): 585–601.

6. Triani and Wilson, *The Presidency of Warren G. Harding*, p. 172.

7. Ibid., chapter 7.

8. William Allen White, *A Puritan in Babylon* (New York: Macmillan, 1928); Donald R. McCoy, *Calvin Coolidge* (New York: Macmillan, 1967);

Claude M. Fuess, *Calvin Coolidge* (Boston: Little, Brown, 1940); and Jane Curtis, Will Curtis, and Frank Lieberman, *Return to These Hills* (Woodstock, Vt.: Curtis-Lieberman Books, 1985).

9. See: Thomas B. Silver, *Coolidge and the Historians* (Durham, N.C.: Carolina Academic Press, 1982) for a major revisionist review of Coolidge as a hardworking and cultivated individual.

10. Hicks, *Republican Ascendancy*, pp. 83–84, and Robert H. Zieger, *Republicans and Labor* (Lexington: University of Kentucky, 1969).

11. McCoy, *Coolidge*, chapter 18.

12. Ibid., p. 195.

13. Ibid., p. 200.

14. Fuess, *Calvin Coolidge*, pp. 339–40, and William J. Barber, *From New Era to New Deal* (New York: Cambridge University Press, 1985).

15. David Burner, *The Politics of Provincialism* (New York: Knopf, 1970), chapter 4; John Blasir, "Coolidge: The Image Maker: The President and the Press, 1923–29," *New England Quarterly* 46 (December 1973): 499–522; and Robert Maddox, "Keep Cool with Coolidge," *Journal of American History* 53 (March 1967): 772–80.

16. Burner, *Provincialism*, p. 288.

17. McCoy, *Coolidge*, pp. 368–81; Melvyn P. Leffler, *The Elusive Quest* (Chapel Hill: University of North Carolina, 1979); Joan Hoff Wilson, *American Business and Foreign Policy* (Lexington: University of Kentucky, 1971); Joseph S. Tulchin, *The Aftermath of War* (New York: New York University, 1971); and Bernard D. Cole, *The United States Navy in China* (Newark: University of Delaware, 1983).

18. McCoy, *Coolidge*, pp. 185–88, 359–63, and Merze Tte, *The United States and Armaments* (Cambridge: Harvard University Press, 1948).

19. McCoy, *Coolidge*, pp. 186, 365.

20. Ibid., p. 390.

21. The classic liberal critique of the Republican ascendancy is Arthur M. Schlesinger, Jr., *The Crisis of the Old Order, 1919–1933* (Boston: Houghton Mifflin, 1957). Similar themes are presented in John Kenneth Galbraith, *The Great Crash 1929* (Boston: Houghton Mifflin, 1961) which with Schlesinger's work have set for over a generation the general parameters of criticism of this period.

22. David Burner, *Herbert Hoover* (New York: Knopf, 1979); George Nash, *The Life of Herbert Hoover*, 2 vols. as of this date (New York: W. W. Norton, 1983 and 1988); Richard Hofstadter, *The American Political Tradition* (New York: Knopf, 1948), chapter 11; Herbert Hoover, *Memoirs of Herbert Hoover*, vols. 1–3 (New York: Macmillan, 1951–1952); Ray Lyman Wilbur and Arthur Mastick Hyde, *The Hoover Policies* (New York: Charles Scribner's, 1937); William Starr Myers and Walter H. Newton, *The Hoover Administration* (New York: Charles Scribner's, 1936); Joan Huff Wilson, *Herbert Hoover* (Boston: Little, Brown, 1975); Craig Lloyd, *Aggressive Introvert* (Columbus: Ohio State University Press, 1973); Harris G. Warren, *Herbert Hoover and the Great Depression* (New York: Oxford University Press, 1959); and Eugene Lyons, *Our Unknown ExPresident* (Garden City: Doubleday, 1940).

23. Burner, *Herbert Hoover*, chapter 8.

24. Donald R. McCoy, "To the White House: Herbert Hoover, August 1927–March 1929," pp. 29–49, and David B. Burner, "Before the Crash: Hoover's First Eight Months in the Presidency," both in *The Hoover Presidency*, edited by Martin L. Fausold (Albany: SUNY Press, 1974), pp. 50–68.

25. Burner, *Herbert Hoover*, chapter 9.

26. Hofstadter, *American Political Tradition*, chapters 11 and 12.

27. Martin L. Fausold, *The Presidency of Herbert Hoover* (Lawrence: University Press of Kansas, 1985), chapters 4 and 5.

28. Milton Friedman and Anna Jacobsen Schwartz, *The Great Contraction, 1929–33* (Princeton: Princeton University Press, 1965); Broadus Mitchell, *Depression Decade* (New York: Rinehart and Co., 1947); and Lester V. Chandler, *American Monetary Policies, 1928–1941* (New York: Harper and Row, 1971).

29. Fausold, *Presidency of Herbert Hoover*, pp. 80–81.

30. Kenneth Davis, *FDR: The New York Years, 1928–1933* (New York: Random House, 1988).

31. Fausold, *Presidency of Herbert Hoover*, chapters 7 and 8.

32. Ibid., chapter 9; Robert H. Ferrell, *American Diplomacy in the Great Depression* (New Haven: Yale University Press, 1957); William Starr Myers, *The Foreign Policies of Herbert Hoover* (New York: Charles Scribner's Sons, 1940); Selig Adler, "Hoover's Foreign Policy and the New Left," pp. 153–63, and Joan Hoff Wilson, "Reevaluation of Herbert Hoover's Foreign Policy," pp. 164–88 in Fausold, ed., *The Hoover Presidency*.

33. Fausold, *The Presidency of Herbert Hoover*, chapter 10, and Frank Freidel, *Franklin D. Roosevelt: A Rendezvous with Destiny* (Boston: Little, Brown, 1990), chapters 5 and 6.

CHAPTER 4:
THE ADVENT OF THE MODERN PRESIDENCY

1. The secondary literature on Franklin D. Roosevelt's life and administration is extensive and I have cited only those sources that I have specifically used in this narrative. A useful bibliographical tool is *Franklin D. Roosevelt: His Life and Times, An Encyclopedic View*, edited by Otis L. Graham and Meghan R. Wander (New York: G. K. Hall, 1985). The major studies are: Arthur M. Schlesinger, Jr., *The Age of Roosevelt*, 3 vols. to date (Boston: Houghton, Mifflin, 1957–); Kenneth S. Davis, *FDR*, 3 vols. to date (New York: Putnam, 1971 and Random House, 1985, 1986); Frank Freidel, *Roosevelt*, 4 vols. (Boston: Little, Brown, 1952–1973); Geoffrey C. Ward, *Before the Trumpet* (New York: Harper and Row, 1985) and his *First Class Temperament* (New York: Harper, 1989); Bernard Asbell, *The FDR Memoirs* (Garden City: Doubleday, 1973); Raymond Moley, *After Seven Years* (New York: Harper, 1939); Rexford G. Tugwell, *The Democratic Roosevelt* (Garden City: Doubleday, 1957); Frances Perkins, *The Roosevelt I Knew* (New

York: Viking, 1946); James MacGregor Burns, *Roosevelt: The Lion and the Fox* (New York: Harcourt, Brace and World, 1956); Samuel Rosenman, *Working with Roosevelt* (New York: Harper and Bros. 1952); Robert Sherwood, *Roosevelt and Hopkins* (New York: Harper and Bros., 1948); and Rexford G. Tugwell, *Roosevelt's Revolution* (New York: Macmillan, 1977).

2. Hugh Gregory Gallagher, *FDR's Splendid Deception* (New York: Dodd, Mead and Co., 1985).

3. For the view that administrative chaos was a sign of FDR's brilliance: see Richard Neustadt, *Presidential Power and the Modern Presidency* (New York: Wiley, 1990).

4. Richard Hofstadter, *The American Political Tradition* (New York: Knopf, 1948), chapter 12.

5. Arthur M. Schlesinger, Jr., *The Age of Roosevelt*, vol. 2,: *The Coming of the New Deal* (Boston: Houghton Mifflin, 1959); Burns, *Roosevelt: The Lion and the Fox*, passim; Elliot A. Rosen, *Hoover, Roosevelt and the Brains Trust* (New York: Columbia University Press, 1977); Frank Freidel, *Roosevelt: Launching the New Deal* (Boston: Little, Brown, 1973); James E. Sargent, *Roosevelt the Hundred Days* (New York: Garland, 1981); Ernest K. Lindley, *Roosevelt Revolution* (New York: Viking Press, 1933); Graham J. White, *FDR and the Press* (Chicago: University of Chicago, 1979); and Richard W. Steele, *Propaganda in an Open Society* (Westport, Conn.: Greenwood Press, 1985).

6. Burns, *Roosevelt: The Lion and the Fox*, p. 188.

7. Paul K. Conkin, *The New Deal* (New York: Thomas Y. Crowell, 1967).

8. Schlesinger, *The Age of Roosevelt*, vol. 2, chapters 26–31.

9. William Leuchtenberg, *Franklin D. Roosevelt and the New Deal* (New York: Harper and Row, 1963); Irving Betstein, *New Deal Collective Bargaining Policy* (Berkeley: University of California Press, 1950); and Andrew J. Badger, *The New Deal: The Depression, 1937–40* (New York: Noonday, 1989). See also: William Ivy Hair, *The Kingfish and His Realm* (Baton Rouge: LSU Press, 1991), p. 307.

10. Basil Rauch, *The History of the New Deal* (New York: Creative Age, 1944) is one of the earliest discussions of the distinctions between the first and the second New Deal.

11. Frank Freidel, *Franklin D. Roosevelt: A Rendezvous with Destiny* (Boston: Little, Brown, 1990), chapter 15.

12. Ibid., chapter 16; Burns, *Roosevelt: Lion and Fox*, chapter 14, p. 221, especially as FDR sees himself as the issue as noted in next paragraph. The "cat" analogy is on p. 285.

13. Burns, *Roosevelt: Lion and Fox*, pp. 230–34.

14. Ted Morgan, *FDR, A Biography* (New York: Simon and Schuster, 1985); Joseph Alsop and Turner Catledge, *The 168 Days* (Garden City: Doubleday and Doran, 1938); William E. Leuchtenburg, "Franklin D. Roosevelt's Supreme Court 'Packing' Plan," in *Essays on the New Deal*, edited by Harold Hollingsworth and William Holmes (Arlington: University of Texas Press, 1969); Paul L. Murphy, *The Constitution in Crisis Times* (New York: Harper and Row, 1972); Robert H. Jackson, *The Struggle for Judicial*

Supremacy (New York: Vintage, 1949); and Gregory A. Caldeira, "Public Opinion and the U.S. Supreme Court: FDR's Court Packing Plan," *American Political Science Review* 81 (December 1987): 1139–53; Arthur M. Schlesinger, Jr., is quoted (and reaffirmed to this author) as saying that FDR was reportedly willing to defy the Supreme Court to protect economic and political stability in the winter of 1935 when the Court was expected to overrule the government on gold redemption. FDR was prepared to issue a "dissent" of his own in the form of a set of proclamations and orders nullifying the expected decision. The Court upheld the government, however, by a vote of five to four. See Douglas Muzzlo, *Watergate Games* (New York: New York University Press, 1982).

15. Burns, *Roosevelt: Lion and Fox*, chapter 15.

16. Ibid., chapter 16.

17. Freidel, *Franklin D. Roosevelt: A Rendezvous with Destiny*, chapter 21. FDR feared a rollback of some of the New Deal. He insisted on personal Social Security "accounts" in order to stop Congress from repealing the system later. See Richard Neustadt and Ernest May, *Thinking of Time* (New York: Free Press, 1986).

18. Robert Dallek, *Franklin D. Roosevelt and American Foreign Policy, 1932–1945* (New York: Oxford University Press, 1979), prologue, and Donald C. Watt, *How War Came* (New York: Pantheon, 1989).

19. Frederick W. Marks II, *Wind over Sand* (Athens: The University of Georgia Press, 1988) makes a strong case that FDR was in the 1930s an appeaser of Hitler. The opposite view is expressed in Robert Edwin Herzstein, *Roosevelt and Hitler* (New York: Paragon House, 1989), which sees FDR as waging a calculated propaganda war against the Nazis before the attack on Pearl Harbor. See also: Arnold Offner, *American Appeasement* (Cambridge: Harvard University Press, 1969) and his *Origins of the Second World War* (New York: Praeger, 1975); Charles A. Beard, *American Foreign Policy in the Making, 1932–40* (New Haven: Yale University Press, 1946); Robert A. Divine, *Roosevelt and World War II* (Baltimore: Johns Hopkins University Press, 1969); and William Langer and S. Everett Gleason, *The Challenge to Isolation, 1937–1940* (New York: Harper, 1952).

20. Marks, *Wind over Sand*, chapter 1 and 6, and David G. Haglund, *Latin America and the Transformation of U.S. Strategic Thought 1936–1940* (New York: Harper, 1952).

21. Dallek, *American Foreign Policy*, chapters 1–4.

22. Burns, *Roosevelt: Lion and Fox*, p. 262.

23. Divine, *Roosevelt and World War II*, p. 8; on seeing war quote: Burns, *Roosevelt: Lion and Fox*, p. 277.

24. Marks, *Wind over Sand*, chapter 2; Henry L. Stimson and McGeorge Bundy, *On Active Service in Peace and War* (New York: Harper, 1947); Frederick C. Adams, "The Road to Pearl Harbor: A Re-examination of American Far Eastern Policy, July 1937–December 1938," *Journal of American History* 58 (June 1971): 73–92; and Dorothy Borg, *The United States and the Far Eastern Crisis of 1933–1938* (Cambridge: Harvard University Press, 1964).

25. Divine, *Roosevelt and World War II*, pp. 18–21; John McVickar Haight, "France, the United States, and the Munich Crisis," *Journal of Modern History* 32 (December 1960): 340–58; and William Langer and S. Everett Gleason, *The Challenge to Isolation*, passim.

26. Divine, *Roosevelt and World War II*, p. 21, and Burns, *Roosevelt: Lion and Fox*,pp. 384–90.

27. Burns, *Roosevelt: Lion and Fox*, pp. 390–97.

28. Ibid., pp. 420–21.

29. Divine, *Roosevelt and World War II*, p. 34, and Wayne S. Cole, *Roosevelt and the Isolationists 1932–1945* (Lincoln: University of Nebraska, 1983).

30. Herbert S. Parmet and Marie B. Hecht, *Never Again* (New York: Macmillan, 1968); Burns, *Roosevelt: Lion and Fox*, chapter 21; Joseph Barnes, *Willkie* (New York: Simon and Shuster, 1952); Samuel Rosenman, *Working with Roosevelt*, passim; James A. Farley, *Jim Farley's Story* (New York: Whittlesey House, 1948); and Edward J. Flynn, *You're the Boss* (New York: Viking, 1947).

31. Burns, *Roosevelt: Lion and Fox*, pp. 457–59; Walter Johnson, *The Battle against Isolation* (Chicago: University of Chicago, 1940); Herbert Feis, *The Road to Pearl Harbor* (Princeton: Princeton University Press, 1950); and William Langer and S. Everett Gleason, *The Undeclared War* (New York: Harper, 1953).

32. Divine, *Roosevelt and World War II*, chapter 2, and James MacGregor Burns, *Roosevelt: The Soldier of Freedom* (New York: Harcourt, Brace and Jovanovich, 1970), pp. 51–52.

33. Burns, *Roosevelt: The Soldier of Freedom*, chapter 2.

34. Ibid., p. 72.

35. Ibid., pp. 84–85; Waldo Heinrichs, *Threshold of War: Franklin D. Roosevelt and American Entry into World War II* (New York: Oxford University Press, 1988).

36. Morgan, *FDR*, p. 589.

37. Burns, *Roosevelt: The Soldier of Freedom*, p. 109.

38. Ibid., pp. 119–120.

39. Heinrichs, *American Entry*, pp. 166–79.

40. Dallek, *American Foreign Policy*, chapter 11; Heinrichs, *American Entry*, epilogue; Burns, *Roosevelt: Soldier of Freedom*, pp. 149–61; Sherwood, *Roosevelt and Hopkins*, p. 431; and Joseph P. Lash, *Roosevelt and Churchill 1939–41* (New York: W. W. Norton, 1976).

41. This narrative follows along with Burns, *Roosevelt: Soldier of Freedom*, part 1. See also John Colville, *The Fringes of Power* (New York: W. W. Norton, 1985); John Keegan, *The Second World War* (New York: Viking, 1989); and Forrest C. Pogue, *George C. Marshall: Ordeal and Hope, 1939–42* (New York: Viking, 1965).

42. Gordon A. Schwartz, *The Speculator: Bernard M. Baruch in Washington, 1917–1965* (Chapel Hill: University of North Carolina Press, 1981), chapter 7.

43. Ibid., p. 366.

44. Ibid., chapter 7 and John Blum, *V Was for Victory* (New York: Harcourt, Brace and Jovanovich, 1976); Scott Hart, *Washington at War* (Englewood Cliffs: Prentice Hall, 1970); and David Brinkley, *Washington Goes to War* (New York: Ballantine Books, 1988).

45. Morgan, *FDR*, chapters 22 and 23.

46. Burns, *Roosevelt: Soldier of Freedom*, chapter 19; Arthur D. Morse, *While Six Million Died* (New York: Random House, 1968); Martin S. Gilbert, *The Holocaust* (New York: H. Holt and Co., 1986); Arno J. Mayer, *Why Did the Heavens Not Darken* (New York: Pantheon, 1988); Sol Stern, "Roosevelt and the Jews: Bystander to Genocide," *New York Village Voice*, September 18, 1984, pp. 29–36; Henry R. Feingold, *The Politics of Rescue* (New Brunswick: Rutgers University Press, 1970); Patrick S. Washburn, *A Question of Sedition* (New York: Oxford University Press, 1986); Richard Drinnon, *Keeper of Concentration Camps* (Berkeley: University of California Press, 1986); Jacobus ten Broek, "Wartime Power of the Military over Citizen Civilians within the Country," *California Law Review* 41 (Summer 1953): 67–208; and Arthur M. Schlesinger, "Did FDR Betray the Jews," *Newsweek*, April 18, 1994, p. 14.

47. Victor Lasky, *It Didn't Start with Water*gate (New York: Dell, 1977), pp. 158–68.

48. Forrest C. Pogue, *George C. Marshall: Origins of Victory, 1943–45* (New York: Viking Press, 1973), chapter 2, and Burns, *Roosevelt: Soldier of Freedom*, chapter 10.

49. Burns, *Roosevelt: Soldier of Freedom*, chapters 10 and 12, and William Larsh, "W. Averell Harriman and the Polish Question, December 1943–August 1944," *Eastern European Politics and Societies* 7 (Fall 1993): 513–54.

50. Burns, *Roosevelt: Soldier of Freedom*, pp. 384, 390–91.

51. Marks, *Wind over Sand*, chapter 5; Dallek, *American Foreign Policy*, chapter 14; and Keith Eubsank, *Summit at Teheran* (New York: William Morrow, 1985).

52. The election is chronicled in Burns, *Roosevelt: Soldier of Freedom*, chapter 17 with chapters 11 and 12 on domestic affairs.

53. Freidel, *Franklin D. Roosevelt: A Rendezvous with Destiny*, chapters 37–38; In addition see Bruce Catton, *The War Lords* (New York: Harcourt, Brace and Co., 1948); Nathan D. Grudstein, *Presidential Delegation of Authority in Wartime* (Pittsburgh: University of Pittsburgh Press, 1961); Luther Gulick, "War Organizing of the Federal Government," *American Political Science Review* 38 (December 1944): 1166–79; and Jean Edward Smith, *Lucius D. Clay* (New York: Henry Holt, 1990), chapters 8–10.

54. Milton Viorst, *Hostile Allies: FDR and Charles DeGaulle* (New York: Macmillan, 1965), and Jean Lacoutrure, *DeGaulle: The Rebel, 1890–1944* (New York: W. W. Norton, 1990).

55. John P. Vloyantaes, "The Significance of Pre-Yalta Politics Regarding Liberated Countries in Europe," *Western Political Science Quarterly* 11 (June 1958): 209–28; Marks, *Wind over Sand*, chapter 5; and Stanislaw Mikolojczyk, *The Rape of Poland* (New York: Whittlesey House, 1948).

56. Ronald H. Spector, *Eagle against the Sun* (New York: Free Press, 1985). On alleged assassination plans, see Marks, *Wind over Sand*, p. 182.

57. A. J. P. Taylor et al., *Churchill Revised* (New York: Dial Press, 1969); Hart's article is in pp. 173–228; the early years of Churchill are examined in William Manchester, *The Last Lion*, 2 vols. to date (Boston: Little, Brown, 1983, 1988). His own history of the period is Churchill's *The Second World War*, 6 vols. (Boston: Houghton Mifflin, 1948–1953). Also of use are Maxwell P. Schoenfeld, *The War Ministry of Winston Churchill* (Ames: Iowa State University Press, 1972), chapters 3 and 4; *Churchill and Roosevelt: The Complete Correspondence*, edited by Warren F. Kimball, 3 vols. (Princeton: Princeton University Press, 1984); Colville, *The Fringes of Power*; passim; A. J. P. Taylor, *The War Lords* (New York: Penguin Books, 1978); Martin Gilbert, *Winston S. Churchill, vol. 6: 1939–1941, Finest Hour* (Boston: Houghton Mifflin, 1983) and *vol. 7: 1941–1945, Road to Victory* (1986): David Irving, *Churchill's War* (New York: Avon, 1990); Alistair Horne, *Harold Macmillan* (New York: Viking, 1989); and R. W. Thompson, *Generalissimo Churchill* (New York: Charles Scribner's, 1973).

58. Issac Deutscher, *Stalin* (New York: Viking, 1960); Adam Ulam, *Stalin* (New York: Viking, 1960); John Erickson, *The Road to Stalingrad* (Boulder: Westview Press, 1975) and his *Road to Berlin* (1983); and Albert Seaton, *Stalin As Military Commander* (New York: Praeger, 1976). The estimate of Stalin's attack on the generals comes from historian W. Bruce Lincoln.

59. Percy Ernst Schmann, *Hitler: The Man and the Military Leader* (Chicago: Quadrangle, 1971); Sebastian Heffner, *The Meaning of Hitler* (New York: Macmillan, 1979); and William Carr, *Hitler: A Study in Personality and Politics* (Baltimore: Edward Arnold, 1978). In 1937 Churchill called Hitler one of the "great figures whose lives have enriched the story of mankind" and an "indomitable champion," which is quoted in Robert R. James, *Anthony Eden* (London: Weidenfeld and Nelson, 1986), p. 136.

60. William Emerson, "Franklin Roosevelt as Commander in Chief in World War II," *Military Affairs* 22 (Winter 1958–59): 181–207; Eric Larrabee, *Commander in Chief* (New York: Harper and Row, 1987); Thomas Parrish, *Roosevelt and Marshall* (New York: W. Morrow, 1989); Pogue, *Marshall*, both volumes; Ed Craig, *General of the Army* (New York: W. W. Norton, 1990); and Richard W. Steele, *The First Offensive 1942: Roosevelt, Marshall and the Making of American Strategy* (Bloomington: Indiana University Press, 1973).

61. Theodore Draper, "Neoconservative History," *New York Review of Books* (January 16, 1986): 5–15 with rejoinder and reply in August 14, 1986.

62. John J. Sbrega, "The Anti Colonial Policies of FDR," *Political Science Quarterly* 101 (January 1986): 65–84.

63. Later assessments are in *The Roosevelt New Deal*, edited by Wilbur J. Cohen (Austin: University of Texas Press, 1981) and *The New Deal* (Austin: University of Texas Press, 1984); William Leuchtenberg, *In the Shadow of FDR* (Ithaca: Cornell University Press, 1985), and a more critical *The Rise and Fall of the New Deal Order*, edited by Steve Fraser and Gary Gerstle (Princeton: Princeton University Press, 1989).

CHAPTER 5:
THE COLD WAR AND AMERICAN LIBERALISM

1. William E. Leuchtenburg, *In the Shadow of FDR* (Ithaca: Cornell University Press, 1985), passim.

2. David McCullough, *Truman* (New York: Simon and Schuster, 1992); Richard Lawrence Miller, *Truman: The Rise to Power* (New York: McGraw-Hill, 1986); and Roy Jenkins, *Truman* (New York: Harper and Row, 1986).

3. The superb Donovan volumes are the best source for any study of the Truman years: Robert J. Donovan, *Conflict and Crisis* (New York: W. W. Norton, 1977), and *Tumultuous Years* (New York: Norton, 1980). The Rayburn quote is from his first volume, p. 13. Used here is *Conflict and Crisis*, pp. 11, 13, 24, 27; Donald R. McCoy, *The Presidency of Harry S Truman* (Lawrence: University Press of Kansas, 1984), p. 27; *Economics and the Truman Administration*, edited by Francis H. Heller (Lawrence: Regents Press of Kansas, 1981); Alonzo L. Hamby, *Beyond the New Deal* (New York: Columbia University Press, 1973); and Cabel Phillips, *The Truman Presidency* (New York: Macmillan, 1966).

4. Donovan, *Conflict and Crisis*, p. 76.

5. Ibid., pp. 81–86.

6. Henry L. Stimson and McGeorge Bundy, *On Active Duty in Peace and War* (New York: Harper and Row, 1948); Martin J. Sherwin, *A World Destroyed: The Atomic Bomb and the Grand Alliance* (New York: Knopf, 1975); Donovan, *Conflict and Crisis*, pp. 49, 96–98; Gar Alperovitz, *Cold War Essays* (New York: Anchor, 1970), chapter 4, and his "Did We Have to Drop the Bomb," *New York Times*, August 3, 1989, p. 23; and Thomas G. Paterson, "Potsdam, the Atomic Bomb and the Cold War," *Pacific Historical Review* 41 (May 1972): 225–38.

7. Robert A. Garson, *The Democratic Party and the Politics of Sectionalism, 1941–1948* (Baton Rouge: LSU Press, 1974).

8. Harry S Truman, *Years of Decision*, volume 1 of his *Memoirs* (New York: Doubleday, 1955), chapter 36.

9. Donovan, *Conflict and Crisis*, pp. 163–71, and Arthur M. Schlesinger, Jr., *The Imperial Presidency* (Boston: Houghton Mifflin, 1973), pp. 127–50.

10. Donovan, *Conflict and Crisis*, p. 215.

11. Forrest C. Pogue, *George C. Marshall: Statesman 1945–1959* (New York: Viking, 1987).

12. John Gimbel, *The Origins of the Marshall Plan* (Stanford: Stanford University Press, 1976); McCoy, *Presidency of Harry S Truman*, pp. 125–29; and Jean Edward Smith, *Lucius D. Clay* (New York: Holt, 1990), book 3.

13. Richard M. Freeland, *The Truman Doctrine and the Origins of McCarthyism* (New York: Knopf, 1972).

14. Harry S Truman, *Years of Trial and Hope, 1946–1952*, volume 2 of his *Memoirs* (New York: Doubleday, 1956); and Bert Cochran, *Harry Truman and the Crisis Presidency* (New York: Funk and Wagnalls, 1973), chapters 11 and 12.

15. John Sketsinger, *The Jewish Vote and the Creation of Israel* (Stanford: Hoover Institute Press, 1974); and Zvi Ganin, *Truman, American Jewry and Israel* (New York: Holmes and Meier, 1979). The quote on Jesus and the Jews is from Donovan, *Conflict and Crisis*, p. 319.

16. Barton J. Berstein, "The Ambiguous Legacy: The Truman Administration and Civil Rights," in his *Politics and Policies of the Truman Administration* (Chicago: Quadrangle Books, 1972), pp. 269–314; Donald R. McCoy and Richard T. Ruetten, *Quest and Response* (Lawrence: University Press of Kansas, 1973); and William C. Berman, *The Politics of Civil Rights in the Truman Administration* (Columbus: Ohio State University Press, 1970).

17. Donovan, *Conflict and Crisis*, chapters 40–43; Cochran, *Crisis Presidency*, chapter 26; Irwin Ross, *The Loneliest Campaign* (New York: New American Library, 1968); Allen Yarnell, *Democrats and Progressives* (Berkeley: University of California, 1974); and Richard Norton Smith, *Thomas E. Dewey and His Times* (New York: Simon and Schuster, 1982).

18. Thomas C. Reeves, *The Life and Times of Joe McCarthy* (New York: Stein and Day, 1982); David M. Oshinsky, *Conspiracy So Immense* (New York: Free Press, 1983); and Donovan, *Tumultuous Years*, p. 32.

19. Richard F. Haynes, *The Awesome Power: Harry S Truman as Commander in Chief* (Baton Rouge: LSU Press, 1973), pp. 126–27.

20. Herbert Feis, *The China Triangle* (Princeton: Princeton University Press, 1953); Robert M. Blum, *Drawing the Line* (New York: W. W. Norton, 1982); and June M. Grasso, *Truman's Two China Policy* (Armonk, N.Y.: M. E. Sharpe, 1987).

21. Donovan, *Tumultuous Years*, p. 160.

22. McCoy, *The Presidency of Harry S Truman*, chapter 8.

23. Donovan, *Tumultuous Years*, pp. 199–205.

24. Ibid., p. 212.

25. Robert J. Donovan, *Nemesis: Truman and Johnson in the Coils of War in Asia* (New York: St. Martin's Press, 1984), and Donovan, *Tumultuous Years*, pp. 220–22.

26. Lloyd C. Gardner, *Architects of Illusion* (Chicago: Quadrangle Books, 1970); *Cold War Critics*, edited by Thomas G. Paterson (Chicago: Quadrangle Books, 1971); Robert W. Tucker, *The Radical Left and American Foreign Policy* (Baltimore: Johns Hopkins University Press, 1971); and Donovan, *Tumultuous Years*, p. 255.

27. These expressions of support that gave MacArthur a sense of security are at variance with Truman's later actions and are cited in Donovan, *Tumultuous Years*, pp. 271–90. Also of importance are: Hayes, *Awesome Power*, chapters 11 and 12; Dean Acheson, *Present at Creation* (New York: W. W. Norton, 1969), pp. 452–511; and William Manchester, *American Caesar* (Boston: Little, Brown, 1978), chapter 9.

28. Donald R. McCoy, *The Presidency of Harry S Truman* (Lawrence: University Press of Kansas, 1984), and D. Clayton James, *The Years of MacArthur*, vol. 3 (Boston: Houghton Mifflin, 1985), chapters 17 and 18.

29. Donovan, *Tumultuous Years*, p. 348.

30. Ibid., p. 369.

31. McCoy, *Presidency of Harry S Truman*, pp. 274–77.

32. Andrew J. Dunar, *The Truman Scandals and the Politics of Morality* (Columbia: University of Missouri Press, 1984).

33. Maeva Marcus, *Truman and the Steel Seizure Case* (New York: Columbia University Press, 1977).

34. A popular volume that helped to set that positive view was Merle Miller, *Plain Speaking: An Oral Biography* (New York: Berkeley Books, 1973).

35. Francis H. Heller, *The Truman White House* (Lawrence: University Press of Kansas, 1980), and Alfred D. Sander, "Truman and the National Security Council 1945–1947," *Journal of American History* 59 (September 1972): 369–88.

36. The most comprehensive treatment of Eisenhower is the two-volume work of Stephen Ambrose, *Eisenhower* (New York: Simon and Schuster, 1983 and 1984). This quote is from vol. 2, p. 17. Also of use are: Piers Brendon, *Ike: His Life and Times* (New York: Harper and Row, 1986); Herbert S. Parmet, *Eisenhower and the American Crusades* (New York: Macmillan, 1972); and Peter Lyon, *Eisenhower: Portrait of the Hero* (Boston: Little, Brown, 1974).

37. Ambrose, *Eisenhower the President*, p. 35.

38. Lyon, *Eisenhower*, pp. 525–28.

39. Ambrose, *Eisenhower the President*, p. 54.

40. Elmo Richardson, *The Presidency of Dwight D. Eisenhower* (Lawrence: Regents Press of Kansas, 1979), chapter 4, and Ambrose, *Eisenhower the President*, p. 88.

41. Ambrose, *Eisenhower the President*, pp. 107, 111, on ending the Korean War and the quote on the death of soldiers in war.

42. Eisenhower's control is noted in John Ranelagh, *The Agency: The Rise and Decline of the CIA* (New York: Simon and Schuster, 1987), chapter 7. The quote on the dinner is in Ambrose, *Eisenhower the President*, p. 113.

43. John Newhouse, *War and Peace in the Nuclear Age* (New York: Knopf, 1989), pp. 107–16.

44. Fred I. Greenstein, *The Hidden Hand Presidency* (New York: Basic Books, 1982), chapter 5.

45. Arthur M. Schlesinger, Jr., *The Imperial Presidency* (Boston: Houghton, Mifflin, 1973), pp. 157–58; Dwight D. Eisenhower, *Mandate for Change*, volume 1 of his *Memoirs* (Garden City: Doubleday, 1963), pp. 311–31; and Raoul Berger, *Executive Privilege* (Cambridge: Harvard University Press, 1974), pp. 294–96.

46. Ambrose, *Eisenhower the President*, p. 190.

47. Greenstein, *The Hidden Hand Presidency*, p. 166.

48. Ambrose, *Eisenhower the President*, pp. 179–85; Brendon, *Ike*, chapter 14; Leslie H. Gelb and R. K. Betts, *The Irony of Vietnam* (Washington: Brookings Institution, 1979); G. C. Herring, *America's Longest War* (New York: Knopf, 1979); and *The Churchill-Eisenhower Correspondence 1953–55*, edited by Peter G. Boyle (Chapel Hill: University of North Carolina, 1991).

49. George Herring, "'In the Hands of the Blind': Eisenhower and Intervention in the Third World," in *Eisenhower and the Art of Leadership* (Gettysburg: Gettysburg College, 1990), pp 18–30.

50. Richardson, *Presidency of Dwight D. Eisenhower*, pp. 156–60.

51. Greenstein, *The Hidden Hand Presidency*, pp. 20–25; Lyon, *Eisenhower: Portrait of the Hero*, chapter 4; Eisenhower, *Mandate for Change*, chapter 19; and Ambrose, *Eisenhower the President*, p. 232.

52. Fred I. Greenstein, "Eisenhower as President: Finding and Defining the 'Hidden Hand,'" in *Eisenhower and the Art of Leadership*, pp. 6–15.

53. Ambrose, *Eisenhower the President*, pp. 257–67.

54. Dwight D. Eisenhower, *Waging Peace, 1956–1961* (Garden City: Doubleday, 1965), chapter 1.

55. Townsend Hooper, *The Devil and John Foster Dulles* (Boston: Little, Brown, 1973); Herman Finer, *Dulles over Suez* (Chicago: Quadrangle Books, 1964); Michael A. Guhin, *John Foster Dulles* (New York: Columbia University Press, 1972); Robert R. James, *Anthony Eden* (New York: McGraw-Hill, 1986), chapters 11–13; and Kennett Love, *Suez* (New York: McGraw-Hill, 1960.

56. Ambrose, *Eisenhower the President*, p. 381

57. Ibid., p. 471.

58. Emmett J. Hughes, *The Ordeal of Power* (New York: Atheneum, 1963) pp. 241–44, and Eisenhower, *Waging Peace*, pp. 162–76.

59. Richard Neustadt, *Presidential Power and the Modern Presidents* (New York: Wiley, 1990), chapter 4.

60. Eisenhower, *Waging Peace*, chapters 8 and 10, and Ambrose, *Eisenhower the President*, pp. 394, 397.

61. Maxwell Taylor, *An Uncertain Trumpet* (New York: Harper and Row, 1960); Walt Rostow, *The United States in the World Arena* (New York: Harper and Row, 1960); Roy E. Licklider, "The Missile Gap Controversy," *Political Science Quarterly* 58 (December 1970): 600–615; George B. Kistiakowsky, *A Scientist at the White House* (Cambridge: Harvard University Press, 1976); and Arthur M. Schlesinger, Jr., *A Thousand Days* (Boston: Houghton Mifflin, 1965), p. 499.

62. Ambrose, *Eisenhower the President*, p. 440.

63. Eisenhower, *Waging Peace*, chapters 13 and 15; Ambrose, *Eisenhower the President*, pp. 495–504. Eisenhower had contemplated creating a first secretary of government as a step to emulate the British system, cited by Bradley Patterson, Gettysburg College Conference on the Eisenhower Centennial, 1990.

64. Ambrose, *Eisenhower the President*, pp. 504–57.

65. Richardson, *Presidency of Dwight D. Eisenhower*, pp. 178–80; Ambrose, *Eisenhower the President*, p. 557; and Ranelagh, *The Agency*, chapter 10.

66. Ambrose, *Eisenhower the President*, chapter 22.

67. Ibid., p. 554.

68. Ibid., p. 565.

69. Michael R. Beschloss, *May Day* (New York: Harper, 1986).

70. Madeline G. Kalb, *The Congo Cables* (New York: Macmillan, 1982), part 1.

71. The Camelot analogy was made in a remark made to Theodore White by Jacqueline Kennedy. The legend is explored in William Manchester, *The Death of a President* (New York: Harper and Row, 1967), epilogue. Also of interest is his later account, *One Brief Shining Moment: Remembering Kennedy* (Boston: Little, Brown, 1983); Hugh Sidney, *John F. Kennedy, President* (New York: Atheneum, 1964); *J. F. Kennedy and Presidential Power*, edited by Earl Lathan (New York: D. C. Heath, 1972); Theodore Sorensen, *Kennedy* (New York: Harper and Row, 1965); Harris Wofford, *Of Kennedy and Kings* (New York: Farrar, Straus and Giroux, 1980); and Lewis J. Paper, *The Promise and the Performance* (New York: Crown Publishers, 1975). More critical treatments are: Bruce Miroff, *Pragmatic Illusions* (New York: David McKay, 1976); Henry Fairlie, *The Kennedy Promise* (Garden City: Doubleday, 1973); Gary Wills, *The Kennedy Imprisonment* (Boston: Little, Brown, 1981); Richard Walton, *Cold War and Counter Revolution* (New York: Viking Press, 1972); Nancy Clinch, *The Kennedy Neurosis* (New York: Grosset and Dunlap, 1973), and Richard Reeve, *President Kennedy* (New York: Simon and Schuster, 1993).

72. A more positive view than mine is presented in David Burner and Thomas R. West, *The Torch Is Passed: The Kennedy Brothers and American Liberalism* (New York: Atheneum, 1985).

73. Richard Whalen, *The Founding Fathers* (New York: New American Library, 1964); Peter Collier and David Horowitz, *The Kennedys* (New York: Warner Books, 1984); and Doris Kearns Goodwin, *The Fitzgeralds and the Kennedys* (New York: Simon and Schuster, 1987).

74. Michael P. Riccards, "Waging the Last War: Winston Churchill and the Presidential Imagination," *Presidential Studies Quarterly*, 16 (Spring 1986): 213–23.

75. Collier and Horowitz, *The Kennedys*, p. 258. The book was Cornelius Ryan, *Longest Day* (New York: Popular Library, 1959).

76. Walton, *Cold War and Counter Revolution*, passim.

77. The expression became used in a cruel indictment in David Halberstam, *The Best and the Brightest* (New York: Random House 1972), an examination of American involvement in Vietnam.

78. Arthur M. Schlesinger, Jr., *A Thousand Days* (Boston: Houghton Mifflin, 1965), pp. 162–63, and Larry Berman, *Planning a Tragedy* (New York: W.W. Norton, 1982), p. 16.

79. The Laos account is in Herbert S. Parmet, *JFK: The Presidency of John F. Kennedy* (New York: Penguin Books, 1983), chapter 6.

80. Schlesinger, *Thousand Days*, chapter 13.

81. Parmet, *JFK*, p. 159.

82. Peter Wyden, *Bay of Pigs* (New York: Simon and Schuster, 1979).

83. Thomas C. Reeves, *A Question of Character* (New York: Free Press, 1991), p. 272; Michael R. Beschloss, *The Crisis Years* (New York: Harper/Collins, 1991), pp. 144–45; and Parmet, *JFK*, p. 177.

84. Michael P. Riccards, "The Presidency in Sickness and in Health," *Presidential Studies Quarterly*, 7 (Summer 1977): 215–30, and Reeves, *Character*, p. 295.

85. Parmet, *JFK*, pp. 190–92.

86. Ibid., chapter 8; and Schlesinger, *Thousand Days*, chapter 15.

87. James MacGregor Burns, *The Deadlock of Democracy* (Englewood Cliffs: Prentice Hall, 1967).

88. Sorensen, *Kennedy*, Appendix A; *John F. Kennedy: The Promise Revisited*, edited by Paul Harper and Joann P. Krug (Westport, Conn: Greenwood Press, 1988), section 2; Paul C. Light, *The President's Agenda* (Baltimore: Johns Hopkins University Press, 1982); James L. Sundquist, *Politics and Policy* (Washington: Brookings Institution, 1968); and Seymour Harris, *Economics of the Kennedy Years* (New York: Harper and Row, 1964).

89. Grant McConnell, *Steel and the Presidency* (New York: W. W. Norton, 1963); Richard D. Mahoney, *JFK's Ordeal in Africa* (New York: Oxford University Press, 1983); and Thomas G. Paterson, *Kennedy's Quest for Victory* (New York: Oxford University Press, 1989).

90. Wofford, *Of Kennedy and Kings*, passim.

91. Reeves, *Character*, p. 214. This section follows closely my longer account in "The Dangerous Legacy: John F. Kennedy and the Cuban Missile Crisis," in Harper and Krug, eds., *John F. Kennedy*, pp. 81–104. Of special interest are David Detzer, *The Brink* (New York: T. Y. Crowell, 1979); Herbert S. Dinerstein, *The Making of a Missile Crisis* (Baltimore: Johns Hopkins University Press, 1976); Graham Allison, *Essence of Decision* (Boston: Little, Brown, 1971); Roger Hilsman, *To Move a Nation* (Garden City: Doubleday, 1967); Robert Kennedy, *Thirteen Days* (New York: W. W. Norton, 1969); Raymond L. Garthoff, *Reflections on the Cuban Missile Crisis* (Washington: Brookings Institution, 1987); Richard Berstein, "Soviets in Cuban Missile Crisis...," *New York Times*, October 14, 1987, p. 1; Walter Pincus, "Transcript Confirms Kennedy Link...," *Washington Post*, October 22, 1987, p. 18; David A. Welch and James G. Blight, "The Eleventh Hour of the Cuban Missile Crisis," *International Security,* Winter 1987/88, pp. 5–91; J. Anthony Lukas, "Class Reunion: Kennedy's Men Relive the Cuban Missile Crisis," *New York Times Magazine*, August 30, 1987, p. 22; Tad Szulc, *Fidel* (New York: Morrow, 1986); and Don Oberdorfer, "Cuban Missile Crisis More Volatile Than Thought," *Washington Post*, January 14, 1992, p. 1.

92. Parmet, *JFK*, p. 330. The early Vietnam policy is discussed in Henry Cabot Lodge, *The Storm Has Many Eyes* (New York: W. W. Norton, 1973); *The Pentagon Papers*, 4 vols. (Boston: Beacon Press, 1971); Halberstein, *The Best and the Brightest*, passim; Guenter Lewy, *America in Vietnam* (New York: Oxford University Press, 1978); Thomas J. Schoenbaum, *Waging Peace and War* (New York: Simon and Schuster, 1988), and the revisionist John M. Newman, *JFK and Vietnam* (New York: Warner, 1992).

93. Parmet, *JFK*, p. 335.

94. Ibid., pp. 333–36.

95. Doris Kearns, *Lyndon Johnson and the American Dream* (New York:

Harper and Row, 1976); Ronnie Dugger, *The Politician* (New York: W. W. Norton, 1982); George Reedy, *Lyndon B. Johnson* (New York: Andrews and McMeel, 1982); Merle Miller, *Lyndon: An Oral Biography* (New York: Putnam's, 1980); and the expansive Robert Caro, *The Years of Lyndon Johnson*, 2 vols. to date (New York: Knopf, 1982 and 1990).

96. Vaughn Davis Bornet, *The Presidency of Lyndon B. Johnson* (Lawrence: University Press of Kansas, 1983), pp. 114–16 and Kearns, *Johnson*, p. 170.

97. Kearns, *Johnson*, p. 191.

98. Daniel Patrick Moynihan, *Maximum Feasible Misunderstanding* (New York: Free Press, 1969); David Zarefsky, *President Johnson's War on Poverty* (University: University of Alabama Press, 1986); and Charles Murray, *Losing Ground: American Social Policy* (New York: Basic Books, 1984).

99. Hugh Davis Graham, *The Civil Rights Era* (New York: Oxford University Press, 1990); *The Great Society*, edited by Barbara C. Jordon and Elspeth D. Rostow (Austin: Lyndon B. Johnson School of Public Affairs, 1986).

100. Charles Whalen and Barbara Whalen, *The Longest Debate* (New York: New American Library, 1985).

101. Bornet, *The Presidency of Lyndon B. Johnson*, p. 114.

102. Ibid., p. 116; and Kearns, *Johnson*, p. 216.

103. Kearns, *Johnson*, pp. 222–26; and Miller, *Lyndon*, pp. 535–37.

104. Bornet, *Presidency of Lyndon B. Johnson*, pp. 133–34; and Kearns, *Johnson*, p. 232.

105. Kearns, *Johnson*, pp. 247–50. The next subchapter title is from an expression by historian Richard Hofstadter, *The Age of Reform* (New York: Knopf, 1955), p. 270.

106. Walter Le Feber, "Latin American Policy," in *Exploring the Johnson Years*, edited by Robert A. Divine (Austin: University of Texas Press, 1981), and Jerome Levinson and Juan de Onis, *The Alliance That Lost Its Way* (Chicago: University of Chicago Press, 1970).

107. Bornet, *Presidency of Lyndon B. Johnson*, pp. 173–77.

108. Ibid., p. 66.

109. Robert J. Donovan, *Nemesis* (New York: St. Martin's Press, 1984), pp. 27, 39, 40, 43; and Bornet, *Presidency of Lyndon B. Johnson*, p. 75.

110. Lyndon Johnson, *Vantage Point*, p. 116; Donovan, *Nemesis*, p. 57.

111. Bornet, *Presidency of Lyndon B. Johnson*, p. 79; and George C. Herring, "The War in Vietnam," in Devine, ed., *Exploring the Johnson Years*, pp. 27–82.

112. Donovan, *Nemesis*, pp. 191–205.

113. Bornet, *Presidency of Lyndon B. Johnson*, pp. 255–58; Norman Podhoretz, *Why We Were in Vietnam* (New York: Simon and Schuster, 1982); George C. Herring, *America's Longest War* (New York: Wiley, 1979); and Eric F. Goldman, *The Tragedy of Lyndon Johnson* (New York: Dell, 1969).

114. Henry F. Graff, *The Tuesday Cabinet* (Englewood Cliffs: Prentice Hall,

1970); Leslie Gelb and Richard Betts, *The Irony of Vietnam* (Washington: Brookings Institution, 1979); and Guenter Lewy, *America in Vietnam* (New York: Oxford University Press, 1978).

115. Bornet, *The Presidency of Lyndon B. Johnson*, p. 269.

116. *The Pentagon Papers*, chapters 4–8 (New York: Bantam Books, 1971).

117. Walter Issacson and Evan Thomas, *The Wise Men* (New York: Simon and Schuster, 1986).

118. Herbert Y. Schandler, *The Unmaking of a President* (Princeton: Princeton University Press, 1977); Harry McPherson, *A Political Education* (Boston: Little, Brown, 1972); and Marvin Kalb and Elie Abel, *Roots of Involvement* (New York: W. W. Norton, 1971).

119. Donovan, *Nemesis*, pp. 136–41; Bornet, *The Presidency of Lyndon B. Johnson*, pp. 273–74; Don Oberdorfer, *Tet!* (Garden City: Doubleday, 1971); Peter Braestrup, *Big Story*, 2 vols. (Boulder: Westview, 1977); and George Reedy, *Lyndon B. Johnson* (New York: Andrews and McMeel, 1982).

120. Thomas J. Schoenbaum, *Waging Peace and War* (New York: Simon and Schuster, 1988).

121. More sympathetic treatments of Robert Kennedy's career are: Arthur M. Schlesinger, Jr., *Robert Kennedy and His Times* (New York: Ballantine Books, 1978), and Jack Newfield, *Robert Kennedy* (New York: Dutton, 1969).

122. Theodore H. White, *The Making of the President 1968* (New York: Atheneum, 1969).

123. Donovan, *Nemesis*, p. 11.

124. I am more sympathetic to Johnson than the current historical and popular judgment in my "Failure of Nerve: How the Liberals Killed Liberalism," *Lyndon Baines Johnson and the Uses of Power*, edited by Bernard J. Firestone and Robert C. Vogt (Westport, Conn: Greenwood Publishers, 1988), pp. 77–88.

125. Kearns, *Johnson*, postscript.

CHAPTER 6:
THE COLD WAR AND AMERICAN CONSERVATISM

1. The Nixon tale is best told in Roger Morris, *Richard Milhous Nixon* (New York: Holt, 1990); Stephen Ambrose, *Nixon*, 3 vols. (New York: Simon and Schuster, 1987–91); Garry Wills, *Nixon Agonistes* (New York: Mentor, 1971); and the subject's own revealing *RN: The Memoirs of Richard Nixon* (New York: Grosset and Dunlap, 1978).

2. Raymond Price, *With Nixon* (New York: Viking, 1977), p. 30.

3. Conversation of author with John Ehrlichman, and Paul C. Light, *The President's Agenda* (Baltimore: Johns Hopkins University Press, 1982). On the new conservatism: William C. Brennan, *America's Right Turn* (Baltimore: Johns Hopkins University Press, 1994).

4. Moynihan was apparently influenced by the then popular biography

by Robert Blake, *Disraeli* (New York: St. Martin's Press, 1967), which Nixon notes in *RN*, pp. 681, 768.

5. Richard P. Nathan, *The Plot That Failed* (New York: Wiley, 1975), p. 7.

6. John Ehrlichman, *Witness to Power* (New York: Simon and Schuster, 1982), p. 223.

7. Daniel P. Moynihan, *The Politics of a Guaranteed Income* (New York: Vintage, 1973); Vincent J. and Vee Burke, *Nixon's Good Deed—Welfare Reform* (New York: Columbia University Press, 1974); and Jack D. Forbes, *Native Americans and Nixon* (Los Angeles: American Indian Studies Center of UCLA, 1984).

8. Nathan, *Plot*, pp. 48–49.

9. Ibid., pp. 78–79. Nixon in *RN*, p. 496, called Charles Colson his "political point man" and notes, "When I complained to Colson I felt confident that something would be done, and I was rarely disappointed."

10. H. R. Haldeman, *The Ends of Power* (New York: Times Books, 1978), p. 58. On p. 167 he argued that he had to build a wall around Nixon to protect Nixon from himself and his own vindictive tendencies.

11. Nathan, *Plot*, p. 69.

12. Tom Wicker, *One of Us* (New York: Random House, 1991) chapters 12 and 13 and John Ehrlichman's lecture at Shepherd College, February 14, 1991.

13. Kissinger's own memoirs are indispensable: *White House Years* and *Years of Upheaval* (Boston: Little, Brown, 1979 and 1982).

14. Seymour M. Hersh, *The Price of Power* (New York: Summit Books, 1983), p. 53.

15. Ray Price, *With Nixon* (New York: Viking, 1977), p. 153.

16. Hersh, *Price of Power*, pp. 50–60.

17. William Shawcross, *The Quality of Mercy* (New York: Simon and Schuster, 1984), and Kissinger, *Years of Upheaval*, chapter 8.

18. Wicker, *One of Us*, p. 645.

19. Hersh, *Price of Power*, p. 120.

20. Nixon, *RN*, pp. 401–14.

21. Hersh, *Price of Power*, pp. 134–35. Nixon's rather bland observations are in *RN*, pp. 499–500.

22. Kissinger, *White House Years*, pp. 441–48, on the first meeting with Le Duc Tho.

23. Herbert S. Parmet, *Richard Nixon and His America* (Boston: Little, Brown, 1990), pp. 589–90.

24. Hersh, *Price of Power*, p. 188, and Ambrose, *Nixon: The Triumph of a Politician* (volume 2 of his biography), pp. 355–58.

25. Richard J. Barnet, *Intervention and Revolution* (New York: World Publishing Co, 1968); Roger Morris, *Uncertain Greatness* (New York: Harper and Row, 1977); and Hersh, *Price of Power*, pp. 141–45.

26. Nixon's views are in *RN*, pp. 473–76.

27. Hersh, *Price of Power*, pp. 219–20.

28. Kissinger, *White House Years*, pp. 636–54.
29. Hersh, *Price of Power*, p. 263.
30. Ibid., p. 279.
31. Ibid., chapter 22, and R. R. Sandford, *The Murder of Allende* (New York: Harper and Row, 1975).
32. Hersh, *Price of Power*, p. 315.
33. Ehrlichman's lecture, and Haldeman, *The Ends of Power*, p. 195.
34. Frank Snepp, *Decent Interval* (New York: Random House, 1977).
35. Hersh, *Price of Power*, chapter 25, and Dan Morgan, *Merchants of Grain* (New York: Viking Press, 1979).
36. John Newhouse, *Cold Dawn* (New York: Holt, Rinehart and Winston, 1973), pp. 240–60.
37. Nixon, *RN*, pp. 545–46.
38. Kissinger, *Years of Upheaval*, p. 145.
39. Hersh, *Price of Power*, p. 449.
40. Ibid., p. 474.
41. Ibid., p. 508.
42. Ibid., p. 529.
43. Nguyen Tien Hung and Jerrold L. Schecter, *The Palace File* (New York: Harper and Row, 1986).
44. Kissinger's views of this difficult period for him are in his *White House Years*, pp. 1406–10. Haig's remark is in Hersh, *Price of Power*, p. 597.
45. Hersh, *Price of Power*, pp. 631–37.
46. Price, *With Nixon*, pp. 290–93.
47. J. Anthony Lucas, *Nightmare* (New York: Viking, 1976), pp. 235–86. I have followed closely his chronology. Haldeman's account in *The Ends of Power*, book 4, gives his views on the break in; Ehrlichman's novel traces a fictional cover-up and exposé to the CIA in *The Company* (New York: Pocket Books, 1977). See also: Jimmy Breslin, *How the Good Guys Finally Won* (New York: Viking, 1975), p. 12.
48. Victor Lasky, *It Didn't Start with Watergate*, passim.
49. Nixon's views are presented in *RN*, passim.
50. Howard Fields, *High Crimes and Misdemeanors* (New York: W. W. Norton, 1978).
51. Ehrlichman, *Witness to Power*, p. 59.
52. Hersh, *Price of Power*, pp. 209–11.
53. Nixon's view of the Huston Plan are in *RN*, pp. 473–74.
54. David Frost, *"I Gave Them a Sword"* (New York: Ballantine Books, 1978).
55. Nixon, *RN*, Presidency–1973 chapter; Lukas, *Nightmare*, passim.
56. Lukas, *Nightmare*, p. 71. At about that time, Nixon demanded from a recalcitrant CIA director, Richard Helms, the full file on the Diem assassination and also files on the Bay of Pigs, the Cuban Missile Crisis, and the 1958 landing of U.S. troops in Lebanon.
57. Wicker, *One of Us*, pp. 645–46.

58. Lukas, *Nightmare*, p. 134.

59. Ibid., p. 173.

60. Ambrose, *Nixon: The Triumph of a Politician*, pp. 501–2.

61. Haldeman, *Ends of Power*, p. 135; Ehrlichman, *The Company*, passim.

62. Jim Hougan, *Secret Agenda* (New York: Random House, 1984); Lukas, *Nightmare*, p. 211; Len Colodry and Robert Gettlin, *Silent Coup* (New York: St. Martin's Press, 1991).

63. Magruder's quote is in Lukas, *Nightmare*, p. 215.

64. Lukas, *Nightmare*, p. 258; John Dean, *Blind Ambition* (New York: Simon and Schuster, 1976); Carl Bernstein and Bob Woodward, *All the President's Men* (New York: Simon and Schuster, 1974), and Woodward and Bernstein, *The Final Days* (New York: Avon, 1976).

65. Lukas, *Nightmare*, p. 301.

66. *The Watergate Hearings: Break In and Cover Up* (New York: Bantam Books, 1973).

67. Douglas Muzzio, *Watergate Games* (New York: New York University Press, 1982), p. 96.

68. Lukas, *Nightmare*, p. 445; Nixon, *RN*, pp. 920–23.

69. Lukas, *Nightmare*, p. 374; Nixon, *RN*, pp. 500–502; Ehrlichman lecture; and *The Presidential Transcripts* (New York: Delacorte Press, 1974).

70. Lukas, *Nightmare*, p. 350; and *United States of America v. Richard M. Nixon* (New York: Law Reports, 1973) for the Supreme Court opinion and briefs.

71. *The End of a Presidency* (New York: Bantam Books, 1974); *The Impeachment Report* (New York: New American Library, 1974); and Leonard Lurie, *The Impeachment of Richard Nixon* (New York: Berkeley Publishing Co., 1973).

72. Ehrlichman, *Witness to Power*, p. 143, and Richard M. Cohen and Jules Witcover, *Heartbeat Away* (New York: Bantam, 1974).

73. Price, *With Nixon*, pp. 235, 291.

74. Conversation of Ehrlichman with author.

75. Robert T. Hartmann, *Palace Politics* (New York: McGraw-Hill, 1980).

76. Richard Reeves, *A Ford, Not a Lincoln* (New York: Harcourt, Brace Jovanovich, 1975), and James Cannon, *Time and Change* (New York: Harper/Collins, 1994).

77. Jerald F. ter Horst, *Gerald Ford and the Future of the Presidency* (New York: Third Press, 1974); I. F. Stone, "Mr. Ford's Deceptions," *New York Review of Books*, November 14, 1974, pp. 3–12; "Ford Decision Tied to View of Limits on Presidency," *New York Times*, October 2, 1974, p. 24; Clark R. Mollenhoff, *The Man Who Pardoned Him* (New York: St. Martin's Press, 1976). There is probably no precedent for a presidential appearance before a congressional committee although Carl Sandburg insisted in his biography of Lincoln that he did appear before a committee to deny the rumors that his wife was a Confederate spy. Sandburg gives no source for his statement.

78. Gerald R. Ford, *A Time to Heal* (New York: Harper and Row, 1979), pp. 164, 197.

79. Hartmann, *Palace Politics*, p. 290.

80. A. James Reichley, *Conservatives in an Age of Change* (Washington: Brookings Institution, 1981), p. 288. Rumsfeld's observation on Rockefeller and domestic policy making was made at the Center for the Study of the Presidency–Fortune Magazine Conference, Washington, D.C., June 26, 1991.

81. Hartmann, *Palace Politics*, p. 295.

82. Bradley H. Patterson, Jr., *The Ring of Power* (New York: Basic Books, 1988), pp. 295–306.

83. Reichley, *Conservatives*, p. 308.

84. Conversation of Rumsfeld with author, November 1987.

85. Ford, *A Time to Heal*, pp. 313, 184–85.

86. Hartmann, *Palace Politics*, p. 324.

87. Nguyen Tien Hung and Jerrold L. Schecter, *The Palace File* (New York: Harper and Row, 1986).

88. John Osborne, *White House Watch: The Ford Years* (Washington: New Republic Books, 1977), p. 102.

89. Ford, *A Time to Heal*, pp. 214–16.

90. Roy Rowan, *The Four Days of Mayaguez* (New York: W. W. Norton, 1975); Richard G. Head, Frisco W. Short, and Robert C. McFarlane, *Crisis Revolution* (Boulder: Westview Publishers, 1978)

91. Ford, *A Time to Heal*, p. 284.

92. Ibid., p. 300.

93. Ibid., p. 305. Rumsfeld has said in a perfunctory way to the author that he would have supported the treaty if directly asked to do so by the president. The fact that Ford did not demand such allegiance or that Rumsfeld did not simply give it says much about the president's staff problems.

94. Osborne, *White House Watch*, pp. 166, 266, and Ford, *A Time to Heal*, pp. 339–40.

95. Ford, *A Time to Heal*, pp. 194–204.

96. Ibid., pp. 226–27.

97. Hartmann, *Palace Politics*, chapter 15.

98. Ford, *A Time to Heal*, pp. 229–30, 356–57; Mollenhoff, *The Man Who Pardoned Him*, pp. 190–200; [Rockefeller] Commission on CIA Activities within the United States, *Report to the President*, June 1975.

99. Hartmann, *Palace Politics*, chapter 13.

100. Ford, *A Time to Heal*, p. 334.

101. Reichley, *Conservatives*, pp. 352–54.

102. John J. Casserly, *The Ford White House* (Boulder: Colorado Associated University Press, 1977).

103. Jimmy Carter, *Why Not the Best* (New York: Bantam Books, 1976); James Wooten, *Dasher* (New York: Summit Books, 1978); Betty Glad, *Jimmy Carter in Search of the Great White House* (New York: W. W. Norton, 1980); and Bruce Mazlich and Edwin Diamond, *Jimmy Carter* (New York: Simon and Schuster, 1979).

104. Glad, *White House*, p. 245.

105. Victor Lasky, *Jimmy Carter: The Man and the Myth* (New York: Rich-

ard Marek, 1979), pp. 308–9, and Kandy Stroud, *How Jimmy Won* (New York: William Morrow, 1977).

106. Hedrick Smith, *The Power Game* (New York: Ballatine Books, 1988).

107. Thomas P. (Tip) O'Neill, *Man of the House* (New York: Random House, 1987).

108. Lasky, *Jimmy Carter*, p. 161.

109. Jimmy Carter, *Keeping Faith* (New York: Bantam, 1982), pp. 93–114.

110. Ibid., pp. 84–90; Joseph Califano, *Governing America* (New York: Simon and Schuster, 1981); Stuart E. Eizenstat, "President Jimmy Carter, the Democratic Party, and Domestic Policy," delivered at the Hofstra University's Conference on the Carter Presidency, November 15, 1990.

111. Edwin C. Hargrove, *Jimmy Carter as President* (Baton Rouge: LSU Press, 1988), chapter 4.

112. M. Glenn Abernathy, Dilys M. Hill and Phil Williams, *The Carter Years* (London: Francis Pinter, 1984), and Laurence H. Shomp, *The Carter Presidency and Beyond* (Palo Alto: Ramparts Press, 1980).

113. Griffin B. Bell, *Taking Care of the Law* (Macon, Ga.: Mercer University Press, reprinted 1986), p. 22.

114. Glad, *White House*, pp. 133, 135, 151.

115. Ibid., p. 151; Bradley H. Patterson, *The Ring of Power* (New York: Basic Books, 1988); Jody Powell, *The Other Side of the Story* (New York: Morrow, 1984) and Robert J. Thompson, "The Spokes of the Wheel in Operation," delivered at Hofstra University Conference, November 15–17, 1990.

116. Glad, *White House*, p. 155.

117. Ibid., p. 185.

118. Ibid., p. 179; Eizenstat, "President Jimmy Carter"; Charles O. Jones, *The Trusteeship Presidency* (Baton Rouge: LSU Press, 1988); Barbara Kellerman, *The Political Presidency* (New York: Oxford University Press, 1984); Jon R. Bond and Richard Fleisher, "Carter and Congress: Presidential Style, Party Politics and Legislative Success," delivered at Hofstra Conference, November 15–17, 1990.

119. Jerel A. Rosati, *The Carter Administration's Quest for Global Community* (Columbia: University of South Carolina, 1987), and Gaddis Smith, *Morality, Reason and Power* (New York: Hill and Wang, 1986).

120. Carter, *Keeping Faith*, pp. 219–20.

121. Strobe Talbot, *Endgame: The Inside Story of Salt II* (New York: Harper and Row, 1979). My treatment of the SALT talks is taken from this informed account.

122. Carter, *Keeping Faith*, p. 158.

123. Glad, *White House*, pp. 183–84.

124. Carter, *Keeping Faith*, pp. 269–429; Cyrus Vance, *Hard Choices* (New York: Simon and Schuster, 1983).

125. Carter, *Keeping Faith*, pp. 121–22.

126. Zbigniew Brzezinski, *Power and Principle* (New York: Farrar, Straus and Giroux, 1983).

127. Gary Sick, *All Fall Down* (New York: Random House, 1985); Ken

Follett, *On Wings of Eagles* (New York: Morrow, 1983), Barry Rubin, *Paved with Good Intentions* (New York: Oxford University Press, 1980); Mohammed Reza Pahlavi, *Answer to History* (New York: Stein and Day, 1980); Hamilton Jordon, *Crisis* (New York: Putnam, 1982); and James A. Bill, *The Eagle and the Lion* (New Haven: Yale University Press, 1991). Sick charged in 1991 that Reagan agents made a deal with the Iranian government to hold the U.S. hostages until after the election in order to defeat Carter. It was an unsubstantiated claim.

128. Vance, *Hard Choices*, chapter 19.

129. James Fallows, "The Passionless Presidency," *Atlantic*, May 1979, pp. 33–46, 48.

130. Lou Cannon, *Reagan* (New York: G. P. Putnam's, 1982); Anne Edwards, *Early Reagan* (New York: William Morrow, 1987); Gary Wills, *Reagan's America* (Garden City: Doubleday, 1985); Ronald and Richard C. Hubler, *Where's the Rest of Me* (New York: Dell, 1965); Lawrence I. Barrett, *Gambling with History* (Garden City: Doubleday, 1983); Ronnie Dugger, *On Reagan* (New York: McGraw-Hill, 1983); and Michael P. Riccards, "Rendezvous with Destiny: The Influence of Franklin Delano Roosevelt on the Life and Presidency of Ronald Reagan," delivered at the Hofstra University Conference on the Reagan Presidency, April 23, 1993.

131. Edwards, *Early Reagan*, passim, and Michael Rogin, *Ronald Reagan, the Movie and Other Episodes in Political Demonology* (Berkeley: University of California Press, 1987).

132. Thomas Byrne Edsall with Mary D. Edsall, *Chain Reaction* (New York: Norton, 1991).

133. *The Reagan Legacy*, edited by Charles O. Jones (Chatham, N.J.: Chatham House, 1988); especially chapter 1 by Bert A. Rockman, and *The Reagan Revolution*, edited by B. B. Kymlicka and Jean V. Matthews (Chicago: Dorsey, 1988).

134. David A. Stockman, *The Triumph of Politics: How the Reagan Revolution Failed* (New York: Harper and Row, 1986); Robert Lekachman, *Greed Is Not Enough* (New York: Pantheon, 1982); and Fred Block, et al., *The Mean Season* (New York: Pantheon, 1987).

135. William Niskanen, *Reaganomics* (New York: Oxford University Press, 1988), Martin Anderson, *Revolution* (New York: Harcourt, Brace, Jovanovich, 1988); and *The Reagan Foreign Policy*, edited by William G. Hyland (New York: New American Library, 1987). For a more critical view see: Paul Kennedy, *The Rise and Fall of the Great Powers* (New York: Random House, 1987); Robert Kuttman, *The End of Laissez Faire* (New York: Knopf, 1991); Walter Russell Mead, *Mortal Splendor* (Boston: Houghton Mifflin, 1987); and Benjamin Friedman, *Day of Reckoning* (New York: Random House, 1988).

136. Robert Pear, "On Reaganomics' 10th Birthday Not all Celebrate," *New York Times*, August 11, 1991, pp. 1, 4; George F. Will, "Who's Better Off These Days," *Washington Post*, October 31, 1991; and Peter Passell, "Forces in Society and Reaganism Helped Dig Deeper Hole for Poor," *New York Times*, July 16, 1989, p. 1.

137. The following pages on the economic effects of the Reagan years follow closely Kevin Phillips, *The Politics of Rich and Poor* (New York: Random House, 1990), especially cited are pp. 11, 20, 21, 52, 78, 80, 122, 127,
205.

138. Quote is from Lou Cannon, *President Reagan: The Role of a Life Time*
(New York: Simon and Schuster, 1991), p. 109. This book is the major study
on Reagan's terms in office and is the background for much of this narrative.

139. Cannon, *President Reagan*, pp. 233, 240, 253, and William Greider,
The Education of David Stockman and Other Americans (New York: Signet,
1986).

140. William Greider, *Secrets of the Temple: How the Federal Reserve Runs
the Country* (New York: Touchstone Books, 1987).

141. Cannon, *President Reagan*, p. 271, and Jeffrey H. Birnbaum and Alan
S. Murray, *Showdown at Gucci Gulch* (New York: Random House, 1987).

142. Ronald Reagan, *An American Life* (New York: Simon and Schuster,
1990), pp. 569–70.

143. Cannon, *President Reagan*, pp. 297–303.

144. Ibid., p. 315.

145. Ibid., p. 740.

146. Dusko Duder and Louise Branson, *Gorbachev: Heretic in the Kremlin*
(New York: Viking, 1990); Cannon, *President Reagan*, pp. 782–86; and Strobe
Talbot, *The Master of the Game* (New York: Knopf, 1988).

147. Cannon, *President Reagan*, p. 337; Roy Guttman, *Banana Diplomacy*
(New York: Simon and Schuster, 1988); Alexander Haig, *Caveat: Realism,
Reagan and Foreign Policy* (New York: Macmillan, 1984); Mark Hertsgaard,
On Bended Knee (New York: Schocken Books, 1988); and Stephen Kinzer,
Blood of Brothers: Life and War in Nicaragua (New York: Putnam's, 1991).

148. Bob Woodward, *Veil: The Secret Wars of the CIA, 1981–87* (New York:
Simon and Schuster, 1987).

149. Theodore Draper, *A Very Thin Line* (New York: Hill and Wang, 1991);
Oliver North, *Under Fire* (New York: Harper/Collins, 1991); *Iran-Contra
Affair: Report of Congressional Committees*, H. Rep. #100–433 (Washington:
Government Printing Office, November 1987); and Constantine Menges, *In-
side the National Security Council* (New York: Simon and Schuster, 1988).

150. *The Tower Commission Report* (New York: New York Times Book,
1987); Cannon, *President Reagan*, p. 704, on his remark; Michael Ledeen,
Perilous Statecraft (New York: Charles Scribner's Sons, 1988); Jane Mayer
and Doyle McManus, *Landslide* (Boston: Houghton Mifflin, 1988); and Stanley
Karnow, *In Our Image, America's Empire in the Philippines* (New York:
Random House, 1989).

151. Cannon, *President Reagan*, chapter 15.

152. Peter Goldman and Tony Fuller, *The Quest for the Presidency 1984*
(New York: Bantam, 1985).

153. Reagan, *An American Life*, p. 448.

154. Nancy Reagan, *My Turn* (New York: Random House, 1989); Kitty
Kelly, *Nancy Reagan* (New York: Simon and Schuster, 1991); Don T. Regan,

For the Record (New York: Harcourt, Brace, and Jovanovich, 1988); and Michael K. Deaver, *Behind the Scenes* (New York: William Morrow, 1987).

155. Birnbaum and Murray, *Showdown*, pp. 286–87.

156. Cannon, *President Reagan*, p. 580.

157. Ibid., p. 792.

158. Some of the most critical views of Reagan's presidency and his disengagement come from his own inner circle: Stockman, *The Triumph of Politics*; Regan, *For the Record*; Deaver, *Behind the Scenes*; Haig, *Caveat*; Terrell Bell, *The Thirteen Men* (New York: Free Press, 1988); Peggy Noonan, *What I Saw at the Revolution* (New York: Random House, 1990); Larry Speakes, *Speaking Out* (New York: Charles Scribner's Sons, 1988); and Caspar Weinberger, *Fighting for Peace* (New York: Warner, 1990).

159. George Bush with Victor Gold, *Looking Forward* (New York: Doubleday, 1987); Joe Hyams, *Flight of the Avenger: George Bush at War* (New York: Harcourt, Brace, Jovanovich, 1991); Nicholas King, *George Bush A Biography* (New York: Dodd, Mead and Co., 1980); Webster Griffin Tarpley and Anton Chaitkin, *George Bush* (Washington, D.C.: Executive Intelligence Review, 1992); Garry Wills, "The Hostage," *New York Review of Books*, August 13, 1992, pp. 21–27; "The Leadership Thing," *Washington Post Magazine*, August 16, 1992; John P. Judis, *Grand Illusion* (New York: Farrar, Straus and Giroux, 1992); and Garry Wills, "Father Knows Best," *New York Review of Books*, November 5, 1992, pp. 36–40.

160. Richard Ben Cramer, *What It Takes* (New York: Vintage Press, 1993); Jack Germond, *Whose Broad Stripes and Bright Stars* (New York: Warner, 1989); and *Reagan and Public Discourse in America*, edited by Michael Weiler and W. Barnet Pearce (Tuscaloosa: University of Alabama Press, 1992), chapter 4.

161. Michael Duffy and Dan Goodgame, *Marching in Place* (New York: Simon and Schuster, 1992), and *Leadership and the Bush Presidency*, edited by Ryan J. Barilleaux and Mary E. Stuckey (Westport, Conn.: Praeger Books, 1992).

162. Lawrence J. Haas, *Running on Empty: Bush, Congress, and the Politics of a Bankrupt Government* (Homewood, Ill.: Business One Irwin, 1990); Kevin Phillips, *Boiling Point* (New York: Random House, 1993); Richard Fleisher and Jon R. Bond, "Assessing Presidential Support in the House II: Lessons for George Bush," *American Journal of Political Science* 36 (May 1992): 525–41; Terry Eastland, "Bush's Fatal Attraction," *Policy Review* 60 (Spring 1992): 20–24; and John Podhoretz, *Hell of a Ride* (New York: Simon and Schuster, 1993).

163. Charles Kolb, *White House Daze* (New York: Free Press, 1993), and Helmut Norpoth and Bruce Buchanan, "Wanted: The Education President," *Public Opinion Quarterly* 56 (1992): 87–99.

164. Kolb, *White House Daze*, pp. 249–58; *The Bush Presidency: First Appraisals*, edited by Colin Campbell, S.J., and Bert Rockman (Chatham, N.J.: Chatham House Publishers, 1991); Robert A. Shanley, *Presidential Influence and Environmental Policy* (Westport, Conn.: Greenwood Press, 1992); Jason

De Parle, "How Jack Kemp Lost the War on Poverty," *New York Times Magazine*, February 28, 1993, pp. 26ff; and Steven A. Shull, *A Kinder, Gentler Racism?* (Armonk, N.Y.: M. E. Sharpe, 1993).

165. Kolb, *White House Daze*, pp. 220–24, and Christopher Jencks, "The Homeless," *New York Review of Books*, April 24, 1994, pp. 20-27.

166. James Ceasar and Andrew Busch, *Upside Down, Inside Out* (Lanham, Md.: Littlefield Adams, 1993); Sam Howe Verhovek, "No More Mr. President, Just a Texan," *New York Times*, January 5, 1994, p. A6; and Larry Berman and Bruce W. Tentleson, "Bush and the Post-Cold War World: New Challenge for American Leadership," in Campbell and Rockman, eds., *The Bush Presidency*, p. 105.

167. Frederick, Kempe, *Divorcing the Dictator* (New York: G. P. Putnam, 1990), and Theodore Draper, "Did Noriega Declare War?" *New York Review of Books*, March 29, 1990, p. 13.

168. Michael R. Beschloss and Strobe Talbot, *At the Highest Levels* (Boston: Little, Brown, 1993).

169. Ibid., passim.

170. *Eagle in a New World*, edited by Kenneth A. Oye, Robert J. Lieber, and Donald Rothchild (New York: Harper/Collins, 1990); Kim R. Holmes, "In Search of a Strategy," *Policy Review* 58 (Winter 1991): 72–75; Terry L. Deibel, "Bush's Foreign Policy: Mastery and Inaction," *Foreign Policy* 84 (Fall 1991): 3–23; and Stanley Hoffman, "Bush Abroad," *New York Review of Books*, November 5, 1992, pp. 54–59.

171. Roy Gutman, *A Witness to Genocide* (New York: Macmillan, 1993).

172. Alan Friedman, *Spider's Web* (New York: Bantam Books, 1993) pp. 282–83, and Kenneth R. Timmerman, *The Death Lobby* (Boston: Houghton Mifflin, 1992).

173. Rick Atkinson, *Crusade* (Boston: Houghton Mifflin, 1993), and Lawrence Freedman and Efraim Karsh, *The Gulf Conflict, 1990–91* (Princeton: Princeton University Press, 1992).

174. Jean Edward Smith, *George Bush's War* (New York: Henry Holt and Co., 1992); Stephen R. Graubard, *Mr. Bush's War* (New York: Hill and Wang, 1992); and Theodore Draper, "The True History of the Gulf War," *New York Review of Books*, January 16, 1992, pp. 46–53, and January 30, 1992, pp. 38–45.

175. Bob Woodward, *The Commanders* (New York: Simon and Schuster, 1991).

176. Atkinson, *Crusade*, pp. 488–500, and Seymour M. Hersh, "Missile Crisis," *New Yorker* 80 (September 26, 1994), pp. 86-99.

177. Woodward, *Commanders*, chapter 16.

178. U.S. News and World Report, *Triumph Without Victory* (New York: Random House, 1992).

179. Harrison E. Salisbury, *The New Emperors* (New York: Avon Books, 1992), and Oye, Lieber, and Rothchild, *Eagle in a New World*, chapter 10.

180. Don Oberdorfer, "The Path to Intervention," *Washington Post*, Decem-

ber 6, 1992, pp. 1ff, and Keith B. Richburg, "American Casualties in Somalia," *Washington Post*, August 12, 1993, p. 1.

181. Ceasar and Busch, *Upside Down*, chapter 2; Grover G. Norquist, "The Unmaking of the President," *Policy Review* 63 (Winter 1993): 10–17; Robin Toner, "How Bush Lost Five Chances to Seize the Day," *New York Times*, October 11, 1992, section 4, p. 1; William Safire, "Bush's Gamble," *New York Times Magazine*, October 18, 1992, pp. 30ff; Tom Rosenstiel, *Strange Bedfellows* (New York: Hyperion, 1993); and Jack W. Germond and Jules Witcover, *Mad as Hell* (New York: Warner, 1992).

182. Ceasar and Busch, *Upside Down*, chapter 2.

183. Aaron Wildavsky, "The Two Presidencies," in his edited *Perspectives on the Presidency* (Boston: Little, Brown, 1975), and Richard Rose, *The Post Modern Presidency*, 2nd ed. (Chatham, N.J.: Chatham House Publishers, 1991), chapter 15.

EPILOGUE

1. J. Morgan Kousser, "Toward Total Political History: A Rational Choice Research Program," *Journal of Interdisciplinary History* 20 (Spring 1990): 521–60.

Index

451

About the Author

MICHAEL P. RICCARDS is the president of Shepherd College in Shepherdstown, West Virginia. He has been president of St. John's College in Santa Fe, provost of Hunter College in New York City, Dean of Arts and Sciences at the University of Massachusetts-Boston, a faculty member at SUNY College at Buffalo, and Special Assistant to the Chancellor of Higher Education in New Jersey. He has been a Fulbright Fellow to Japan, a National Endowment for the Humanities Fellow at Princeton University, a Henry Huntington Library Fellow, and a member of the National Advisory Committee of the Center for the Study of the Presidency in New York City. Dr. Riccards has also been the chair of the New Mexico Endowment for the Humanities and a member of the West Virginia Council for the Humanities. He is the author of several books, numerous articles, and a dozen verse plays. He is married and has three children.